Managing Diversity

Managing Diversity

Human Resource Strategies for Transforming the Workplace

Edited by
Ellen Ernst Kossek and Sharon A. Lobel

BLACKWELL
Business

Copyright © Blackwell Publishers Ltd, 1996

Editorial organization © Ellen Ernst Kossek and Sharon A. Lobel, 1996

First published 1996
2 4 6 8 10 9 7 5 3 1

Blackwell Publishers Inc.
238 Main Street
Cambridge, Massachusetts 02142
USA

Blackwell Publishers Ltd
108 Cowley Road
Oxford OX4 1JF
UK

British Library Cataloguing in Publication Data

A CIP catalogue record for this book is available from the British Library.

Library of Congress Cataloging-in-Publication Data

Managing diversity: human resource strategies for transforming the
  workplace / edited by Ellen Ernst Kossek and Sharon A. Lobel.
      p.   cm. — (Human resource management in action series)
    ISBN 1–55786–597–3 (alk. paper)
    1. Diversity in the workplace. 2. Multiculturalism.
  3. Minorities—Employment. 4. Personnel management. I. Kossek,
  Ellen Ernst. II. Lobel, Sharon Alisa. III. Series: Human resource
  management in action.
  HF5549.5.M5M36   1996
  658.3′041—dc20   96–6456
                                                             CIP

Typeset in 10 on 12 pt Melior
by Graphicraft Typesetters Ltd, Hong Kong
Printed in the USA

This book is printed on acid-free paper

Dedication

This book is dedicated to our families: our parents, children and husbands for their enduring support of our efforts to balance our work with our personal lives

Ellen Ernst Kossek and Sharon A. Lobel

Contents

Contents

Series Preface

Human resource management policies and practices require organizations to strike a balance between opposing forces or influences. For example, equity competes with efficiency, merit challenges egalitarianism, and control confronts empowerment. One of the more challenging of these dualities today is the reality of diversity and the need for commonality.

On the one hand, the diversity of the workforce has been increasing, for several well-known reasons. Shifts in demographics and labor force participation have changed the composition of employment in favor of women, nonwhites, and older workers. New patterns of international immigration have brought more cultural and ethnic heterogeneity to the workplace. Rising levels of education have made workers more aware of their uniqueness and fueled the expectation that companies should tolerate – and even accommodate – differences among individuals and groups.

But on the other hand, this is just the time when organizations need to emphasize greater purposefulness, commonality, and commitment to organizational goals. One reason is that these are changing and unpredictable times; another is that, in order to deal with change, firms are seeking greater teamwork and cooperation among employees and units of the company.

How, then, do you strike the proper balance between diversity and commonality? Does the organization favor one over the other? Or, as it has been said, does the organization strive to make diversity an asset, that is, to glorify differences in pursuit of common interests?

The initial response of companies to the challenges of diversity has been to offer employees cultural awareness and sensitivity training. While this type of instruction can be helpful, firms have come to recognize that the challenges of diversity require more than training. Diversity impacts the organization not just in the attitudes of employees but at multiple points in the conduct of human resource management and the achievement of organizational goals.

Professors Kossek and Lobel, who have been active researchers on diversity, have produced a book of commissioned papers that recognize the broad implications of diversity in organizations. By commissioning papers, the editors have been able to bring together the insights of researchers and practicing experts in a timely fashion.

This book is part of the Blackwell Series on Human Resource Management in Action, which is devoted to the publication of works on the important and current human resource issues affecting organization performance. Managing diversity is – and is likely to remain – one of those issues.

Myron Roomkin

Acknowledgements

We would like to thank the authors of the chapters in this volume for their willingness to participate in this project and for their responsiveness to our editorial suggestions. Rachel Oh, a research assistant from Michigan State University, was very helpful in reviewing some of the chapters and providing a graduate student's perspective on readability. Kathy Witte, a secretary at Michigan State University, provided invaluable administrative assistance. We thank Richard Burton and Rolf Janke from Blackwell, and Myron Roomkin, editor of this series of volumes, for their enthusiasm and support. We also thank the School of Labor and Industrial Relations at Michigan State University and the Albers School of Business and Economics at Seattle University for their administrative support of this project.

Ellen Ernst Kossek
Sharon A. Lobel

A Note on the *Field Guide*

A *Field Guide* containing cases is available to educators and managers who are using this book for course use and training. Available in the *Field Guide* are the following cases:

"Crossing Borders: The Experience of a Mexican American Human Resource Manager in a Maquiladora"
  * *Bernardo M. Ferdman and Placida I. Gallegos*

"Adapting Human Resource Systems to Manage Global Diversity: The Case of Amoco Production Company"
  * *Ellen Ernst Kossek*

"A Tale of Four Doctorates: Managing within Group Differences in Learning Styles"
  * *Keith James*

"Managing Diversity as a Vehicle for Culture Change: Confronting Monocultural Dominance at IBM"
  * *Ellen Ernst Kossek*

"Functional Diversity at Work: A Client-Driven Case for Managing Diversity"
  * *Toni A. Gregory and Ronald P. Lewis*

"To Do or Not to Do: Initiating Diversity Programs"
  * *Everette J. Freeman*

"Understanding Linkages Between Organizational Development and Diversity Management"
- *Roosevelt Thomas*

For a copy of the *Field Guide*, please contact:

Blackwell Publishers Inc.
238 Main Street
Cambridge, Mass. 02142
USA

or call Dana Silliman at 00–1–617–577–3452.

1

Introduction: Transforming Human Resource Systems to Manage Diversity – an Introduction and Orienting Framework

Ellen Ernst Kossek and Sharon A. Lobel

Many employers have acknowledged the importance of the increasing diversity in the labor force. They have begun to question the effectiveness of human resource (HR) systems that were largely designed for a more homogeneous workforce (Jackson, 1992b). Although researchers have made suggestions about how to adapt existing HR systems, these suggestions are often in general terms, such as the need to change culture (Cox, 1991). Scholarly and practical knowledge is still evolving regarding the design and integration of specific HR policy areas, such as compensation or selection, in support of a strategy for managing diversity.

The purpose of this book is to consider the implications of diversity for the development and synthesis of specific HR policy areas. The contributed chapters provide a range of perspectives on the significance of workforce diversity for the HR domain and the workplace in general. Scholars who are experts on HR issues review the degree to which current theory and practice have incorporated issues of diversity management. The authors provide examples of some specific sources of diversity among employees, scrutinize the effectiveness of current HR practices, and suggest approaches for modifying HR systems to support a managing diversity strategy. The implications of employee diversity for future theory and practice are offered. We asked authors to be speculative in making suggestions for future initiatives, even if the published literature they had to draw on was limited.

Before giving an overview of the chapters, we first provide a definition of diversity. Then we discuss the organizational rationale for adapting HR systems to manage diversity. We provide a framework to help decision-makers and scholars understand the linkages among factors in the organization's environment, the managing diversity strategy and other strategic choices, HR policy areas, and individual, group, and organizational outcomes.

Definition of Diversity

It is a well publicized fact that 45 percent of all net new additions to the workforce in the 1990s will be nonwhite (half of whom will be immigrants mainly from Latin-American and Asian countries) and that two-thirds of these will be women (Johnston and Packer, 1987; Cox, 1993). While race/ethnicity and gender are the most recognized forms of diversity, there are other types with important implications for HR systems. They include disability, family structure, sexual orientation, and ethnic culture. Each of these potentially overlapping identity group memberships can affect an employee's attitudes and behaviors in the workplace, as well as influence his or her ability to work well with other organizational members. New sources of diversity from within the organization are likely to emerge as well, such as employees from nontraditional lines of business, functions that have historically had a subordinate role, or a newly acquired subsidiary with a distinctive culture (Thomas, forthcoming). Thus, we consider diversity to be not only derived from differences in ethnicity and gender, but also based on differences in function, nationality, language, ability, religion, lifestyle, or tenure.

Why Adapt Human Resource Systems to Manage Diversity?

Organizations and their cultures are a function of the kind of people in them, who are a result of an A–S–A (attraction–selection–attrition) cycle (Schneider, 1985; 1987). HR policies enable firms to attract, select, and retain different kinds of people, which is why various organizations act and feel as if they have different cultures. In effect, the people make the place (Schneider, 1985), and the design and administration of HR systems make the people. Individuals are generally attracted to and selected by organizations that appear to have members with values similar to their own; over time, employees who do not fit in well with the dominant culture eventually turnover from the firm (Schneider, 1985; 1987). In the long run, a workforce historically can be characterized by more homogeneity than heterogeneity in social characteristics.

Organizations have traditionally had HR systems based on models of homogeneity; they promote similarity not diversity (Schneider and Rentsch,

1988; Ferris et al., 1994). Jackson (1992b) provides a number of examples illustrating how traditional HR management models foster workforce homogenization: recruiting practices emphasize hiring people from sources that have historically been reliable; selection practices stress choosing candidates similar to those who have been successful; training programs foster uniform ways of thinking; and policies are often designed to limit supervisor latitude in addressing employees' unique needs. Similarly, decision-makers have tended to hire, promote, and evaluate people in terms of the degree to which they are like their own image (Ferris et al., 1994). Such an approach has been coined "homosocial reproduction" by Kanter (1977), referring to the tendency of selection and promotion systems to allow only those employees to pass through who fit with the characteristics of the dominant coalition.

Unfortunately, too much similarity in the organization can be detrimental to long-term growth, renewal, and the ability to respond to important environmental changes such as dynamic market conditions, new technologies and ideas, societal shifts, or the changing expectations of the workforce. HR policies supporting diversity can help the culture continually adapt in response to new environmental demands. Such systems are critical for attracting, selecting, motivating, developing, and retaining a highly skilled, diverse group of employees who possess the key success factors needed to compete in today's changing marketplace.

Limitations of Prevailing Approaches to Managing Diversity

Many employer benefits of managing diversity have been noted in the literature (for a discussion of the value of diversity, see Cox and Blake, 1991). At the individual level, for example, performance can be enhanced when negative diversity-related barriers to productivity are removed (Cox, 1993). When workgroup diversity is managed effectively, groups will develop processes that can enhance creativity, problem-solving, workgroup cohesiveness, and communication. At the organizational level, performance may improve: marketing may be enhanced, since firms are hopefully able to better mirror and adapt to diverse markets; flexibility can be heightened; and improved recruitment of the best new labor force entrants can result (Cox, 1993).

Despite these reported benefits, their realization has remained elusive for most firms. This is because traditional HR strategies to manage diversity have largely been introduced piecemeal, lacking integration with other systems. Consequently, they do not change the culture to support the management heterogeneity; and they end up failing. The three predominant traditional HR approaches for managing diversity are diversity enlargement, diversity sensitivity and cultural audits.

Diversity enlargement approaches increase the representation of individuals of different ethnic and cultural backgrounds in an organization (Kossek et al., 1995). The newly hired employees are expected to assimilate into the existing corporate culture. The goal of this strategy is to create diversity by changing an organization's demographic composition and increasing the numbers of people of color in the firm. Employers seem to assume that increasing diversity and exposure to minority employees will result in improved individual and organizational performance. It is also assumed that little or no change needs to be made in organizational systems in order for minority employees to perform up to their potential. In addition, diversity enlargement hiring strategies are viewed by some employers as being coerced by labor market demands and popular, "politically correct" state of the art management sentiment, instead of being initiated voluntarily. Such faulty assumptions and resistance to what is perceived as forced change undermine the effectiveness of this approach.

Diversity sensitivity approaches acknowledge the existence of cultural distance and attempt to teach individual members about cultural differences via training (Ferdman, 1989). Often training sessions are held to help sensitize employees to stereotyped differences of various employee racioethnic and gender groups. The goal is to promote communication and understanding, and to build relationships among members of different backgrounds.

Yet accentuating dissimilarity will not necessarily enhance performance; and, when conducted in isolation, may even promote stereotyping and tokenism. Diversity training efforts have often failed by trying to raise consciousness without making any concomitant changes in the culture or relevant HR systems such as reward and performance practices. Consequently, many employees are likely to be cynical when they attend training sessions that have no clear link to business objectives and are neither supported by other HR system changes, nor by the new behavioral expectations of colleagues and managers (Morrison et al., 1993).

A third strategy, the *cultural audit*, generally tries to determine what is blocking the progress of nontraditional employees. A consultant collects data via focus groups or surveys. These data are analyzed to assess various demographic groups' identification of the major obstacles they face in the current culture (Morrison et al., 1993). Members of diverse group backgrounds may be asked to talk about how the current culture, which generally is viewed as favoring white males, hurts the performance of white women and racioethnic minorities. For example, an increasing cadre of employees is no longer willing to suppress important cultural differences and those that do risk the potential costs of added stress and lower performance (Cox, 1993).

While we concur that it is appropriate to assess the current culture's effectiveness in allowing all employees to contribute to their fullest potential, we believe that conducting cultural assessments as an isolated strategy is likely to fail. They rarely focus on the redesign of HR systems and practice, such as pay and promotion systems, which give clear messages about what behaviors in the culture are valued. The audits may leave the impression that the white male culture in the organization is the problem; therefore, the change must predominantly come from white men (MacDonald, 1993). Clearly, managing diversity is a mutual process and the new culture must be designed to be inclusive to allow all members to contribute to their fullest potential. Cultural audits not only need to focus on the differences between groups, but should also identify the similarities between groups that the culture and supportive HR systems can reinforce to achieve organizational objectives. Finally, cultural audits tend to largely rely on cross-sectional data. Even when longitudinal data are collected, rarely are pre- and post-data able to be matched to a specific respondent, and therefore it is impossible to know whether change has truly occurred, although HR system modifications may have been made.

To summarize, there are several factors common to the three traditional diversity approaches – diversity enlargement, diversity sensitivity, and cultural audits – which prevent firms from realizing the potential benefits to be gained from increased diversity in the workplace. First, these methods do not reinforce culture change. Second, they have the limitation of often being introduced as isolated strategies without being linked to other relevant HR subsystems. Third, they all assume in-group homogeneity. That is, it is presumed that all members of a minority group, be it women, racio-ethnic minorities or the differentially abled, have the same HR needs. We will now describe the kind of analytic process we believe is required to develop more effective diversity approaches and, consequently, to reap the benefits of enhanced workplace diversity.

Orienting Framework of HR Strategies for Managing Diversity

In figure 1.1, we provide a framework for integrating a managing diversity strategy with HR policy areas and other strategic choices. This framework is designed to help decision-makers and scholars understand the linkages between environmental drivers, managing diversity and other organizational strategic choices, HR policy areas, and individual, group, and organizational outcomes. *This orientation is offered to encourage managers and scholars to view managing diversity as a means to achieving organizational ends, not as an end in itself.* It is based on the assumption that HR policies shape employee attitudes and behaviors and reinforce the organizational culture, thereby affecting the success of strategy implementation and the organization's ability to adapt to environmental change.

Environmental drivers shape the *strategic choices* organizations have in designing their firms, including a strategy for managing diversity. Managers must identify the objectives of a managing diversity strategy and clarify their relevance to other strategic choices. These choices determine the design of *HR policy areas*. Yet before an organization can redesign HR policy areas, it must first identify desired *individual* and *organizational* outcomes.

Figure 1.1 Human resource strategies for managing diversity: an orienting framework

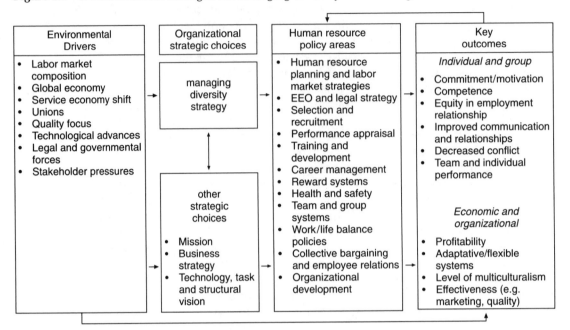

This analysis will then inform the ways in which these areas should be reshaped, since they drive key individual, group, and organizational outcomes. In effect, a firm must look ahead to the last box of the figure: *desired outcomes*, before it can take a step back and identify how existing HR systems need to be reshaped, designed, and re-integrated. Unfortunately, all too often companies identify HR strategies and policy actions – ranging from diversity training to a mentoring program – without first clearly determining the strategic linkages or the desired results.

The first box of figure 1.1 shows some of the key environmental drivers of a managing diversity strategy and other organizational strategic choices. Drivers include the well publicized labor-market demographic shifts, as well as the global economy, service industry shift, rising unionization in industries with the most diverse labor force, enhanced quality focus, increasing technological complexity, legal and governmental forces, and pressures from more vocal organizational stakeholders, such as communities and shareholders.

It has been well documented that the new entrants to the *labor market* are more ethnically and racially diverse (Johnston and Packer, 1987). In addition, the family has changed dramatically. Increasingly, families consist of single parents or dual-career couples who are less likely to have the ability or desire to work the long hours that the organization man did in the past. The workforce also includes more long-term single persons who have needs that are not likely to be met by traditional company reward systems.

As Jim Preston, the CEO of Avon Products (cited in Thomas, 1991), comments: "by 1995, three out of four people coming into the workplace will be women and minorities ... if you are going to attract the best of those people, into your organization, you'd better have a culture ... an environment in which those people feel they can prosper and flourish. If you don't, they'll go elsewhere and you will be at a competitive disadvantage."

Economic *globalization* is another important driver of organizational strategic choices. The passage of the North American Free Trade Agreement that governs trade relations between the US, Canada, and Mexico, and opens Mexico's markets, will mean a likely increase in maquiladora plants and the transfer of some jobs to Mexico. The European Union, which began in 1992, makes Europe the largest free market in the world (Noe et al., 1994). The disintegration of the Soviet Union and the conversion of its former Communist countries to capitalistic systems provide significant opportunities for massive new foreign investment. Countries in the Pacific Asian Basin and China have also become major economic players. Foreign sourcing is on the rise and companies are increasingly dealing with these and other global partners (Jackson and Alvarez, 1992). HR management in this global economy is clearly more complex. Not surprisingly, the chief causes of failure in multinational ventures often stem from a lack of understanding of basic differences in managing human resources at all levels in foreign surroundings.

The major shift toward a *service economy* means that employees need to be able to "read" customers who are likely to be increasingly diverse (Bell, 1973; Jackson and Alvarez, 1992). In addition, employees in service roles are likely to be self-monitors of their own behavior, often taking on responsibilities that might be handled by a supervisor. The increasing diversity of the workforce means that there will be more variability regarding the notions of what constitutes "good service" and effective self-management. Clearly, managing diversity and other strategies must support the needed changes in socialization, training, job design, compensation, performance and appraisal systems for this new work context (Jackson and Schuler, 1992).

The service economy shift also has implications for *unionization*. Currently, about 17 percent of the US workforce is unionized, a figure that has remained stable for the past six years (Brickner, 1995). The only reason for this steady percentage, despite massive loss of jobs in the manufacturing sector, is that the greatest job growth and growth in new union members have been in service sectors such as health care, technical and office jobs, and the government. Employees in these industries are much more likely to be female or minority than those in manufacturing. Clearly, unions and their increasingly diverse membership may be key factors to consider in developing a managing diversity strategy.

The widespread focus on improving *total quality* is another environmental driver of organizational strategy. Total quality management is a process of constant evaluation of systems to empower groups of employees to meet customer needs to the greatest extent possible at the lowest cost (Fernandez,

1993). Since customers are becoming more demanding, and reflect a wider range of preferences than in the past, an organization must design HR systems to support customization for an increasingly diverse customer base. For example, systems need to be developed to reward flexibility in thinking and action in order to make readjustments to meet a range of changing consumer demands.

Technology has made it possible for a more diverse group of people to work than in the past. Increasingly the disabled and other individuals are able to have their talents tapped due to opportunities from telecommuting, teleconferencing, and computer technology advances. Technology also leads to an expanded base of sources of customer information. Increasingly diverse employees with more varied capabilities will have greater access to more information more rapidly than ever before. Consequently, business and information management has become more complex. These trends, coupled with growing labor shortages of critical skills, will increase an organization's need to consider the impact of technological changes on different segments of the workforce.

Competitive advantage will come not from mere investment in new technologies, but from a firm's ability to apply new technologies more rapidly and more effectively than others. This ability depends on the skill and motivation of the workforce (Pfeffer, 1994). Unfortunately, as the pace of technological change increases, it is likely that HR systems increasingly will be out of sync with technological demands (Hesketh and Bochner, 1994). More and more there may be a lack of joint optimization between organizations' social/HR systems and production/technological systems (Pava, 1986).

Legal and government forces also have an impact on managing diversity and other organizational strategic choices. The Civil Rights Act of 1964 and the Executive Order which created affirmative action have been at the root of the managing diversity approach in many organizations. In recent years, a host of new legislation, relevant to diversity, has been enacted. For example, the Family and Medical Leave Act requires employers of over 50 employees to provide 12 weeks of unpaid leave for family and medical emergencies. The Age Discrimination in Employment Act prohibits age discrimination against employees over 40. The Americans with Disabilities Act requires employers to remove barriers to employment of qualified individuals with disabilities. Finally, the Immigration Reform and Control Act of 1986 requires that employers verify that employees are either US citizens or aliens authorized to work in the US. The law also states that foreign status cannot be used as a reason to reject applicants as long as they can prove their employment eligibility.

Despite these mandates, many employers either openly flout the laws or are ignorant regarding their implementation (Shellenbarger, 1994). For example, age discrimination cases make up a large portion of those filed with the Equal Employment Opportunity Commission (EEOC), and the number of complaints continues to rise (Noe et al., 1994). Similarly, the passage of the Americans with Disabilities Act has resulted in a dramatic rise in the number of complaints related to disability reported to the EEOC. In the US, resistance to legislative mandates has been expressed in backlashes against affirmative action (Kaufman, 1995). The 1994 passage of Proposition 187 in California, limiting the provision of government services to illegal immigrants, also reflects growing anti-immigration sentiment.

A final environmental force pertains to the increased pressure from organizational *stakeholders*, who perceive they have a major role to play in the management of an organization. For example, shareholders are becoming increasingly vocal and involved in actual management of the business. The expectations for profitability have intensified and a number of CEOS in firms ranging from Kmart to General Motors have been fired or downgraded at the prompting of their boards of directors. Ineffective management of diversity will have a negative impact on organizational performance as a result of lowered productivity and morale, lawsuits, and poor reputation. Therefore, we anticipate diversity to be of increasing interest to shareholders. There has also been a rise in shareholder interest in the social responsibility of the organization which has affected how and where (e.g. South Africa) a company can do business.

Local communities are an example of another stakeholder group that is becoming more powerful. Communities are increasingly vocal regarding their expectations that firms be good corporate citizens and provide jobs to the individuals who live in the neighborhood. As communities become more diverse, it necessarily follows that firms will face increasing pressures to try to hire and mirror the market that surrounds them.

Organizational strategic choices

Strategy is a logic for how to achieve movement in some direction (Kotter and Heskett, 1992). Strategy determines how tasks, technology, and people should be organized to enable the organization to meet desired global objectives.

Articulating a managing diversity strategy   The analysis of environmental drivers (see figure 1.1) will help an organization determine its objectives for a managing diversity strategy. Unfortunately, most organizations have not been clear about the specific benefits they seek to gain. None the less, it is critical for organizations to delineate the goals of such a strategy.

For some firms, increasing diversity is viewed as an end in itself, that is, as a way to respond to environmental drivers, such as legal mandates or changing demographics. Managers are not completely sure of the organizational objectives they hope to achieve by enhancing diversity; they just know that they should, or by virtue of what is available in the labor market have to, have a more diverse workforce. If this is the view, then a managing diversity strategy needs to focus on how the firm can increase diversity without losing benefits of organizational homogeneity, such as consistency in organizational values, current productivity and quality levels (Thomas, 1990). For other firms, such as Corning, diversity may be seen as a means to increase productivity and quality (Morrison et al., 1993). When managing diversity is seen as a means to attain organizational objectives, it is especially important to engage in the kind of systems thinking we present in figure 1.1.

Other strategic choices A managing diversity strategy must fit with the mission and values of the firm. An organization's mission pertains to its basic reason for being and its identity. Defining a mission involves such questions as: "Who are we?" "What do we want to be?" and "How will we survive and grow in our environment?" (Schein, 1985). A firm's mission and values help develop a shared mindset and a common understanding about how the work is done (Ulrich and Lake, 1990). Robert Haas of Levi Strauss comments (Howard, 1990, p. 134): "In a more volatile and dynamic business environment, the controls have to be conceptual . . . It's the ideas of a business that are controlling, not some manager with authority. Values provide a common language for aligning a company's leadership and its people." Accordingly, Levi Strauss has integrated aspects of its managing diversity strategy into its aspirations statement. For example, the leadership that Levi Strauss feels is necessary:

> values a diverse work force (age, sex, ethnic group, etc.) at all levels of the organization, diversity in experience, and diversity in perspectives. We have committed to taking full advantage of the rich backgrounds and abilities of all our people and to promoting a greater diversity in positions of influence. Differing points of view will be sought; diversity will be valued and honestly rewarded, not suppressed. (Howard, 1990, p. 135)

As another example, at Digital Equipment Company, members are encouraged to respond to, acknowledge and reward different opinions. Management believes that a common acceptance of diversity will enable the firm to be more effective globally and respond to many varied customer demands.

Shared mindsets and mission statements are increasingly likely to reflect an acceptance of diversity and the need to honor varied interests of organizational constituents (Kotter and Heskett, 1992; Ulrich and Lake, 1990). More and more, it is likely that higher-performing organizations will have value systems that emphasize caring about all constituents; they will strive for fairness to everyone, and ignore no one (Kotter and Heskett, 1992). Mission statements that incorporate diversity and articulate the desire for shared values explicitly recognize the link between the HR strategy and the bottom line.

Jackson and Alvarez (1992) argue that diversity strategy should be integrated with *business strategies*, such as globalization, cost, innovation, speed, quality, and customer service. Effective HR management is increasingly becoming recognized as a major source of competitive advantage in *globalization* (Pucik, 1993). For example, rather than limit training to cross-cultural knowledge, as has traditionally been done, current emphasis is on developing multicultural teams and networks (Pucik, 1993). In selection, instead of merely ascertaining managers' abilities for cross-cultural adaptation, now the emphasis is on selecting managers capable of designing supportive HR systems for a multicultural workforce (Pucik, 1993).

Some companies seek to gain competitive advantage with a business strategy that emphasizes being a *low-cost producer*. From an HR perspective, this means that labor costs should be kept low relative to one's competitors. If a firm has much higher turnover than its competitors or is unable to differentiate itself from other employers in order to attract the top talent, it will face increased costs. Policies, such as flexible work hours to accommodate school and personal scheduling needs, good health benefits, child care assistance, and tuition reimbursement, might help a firm gain a competitive edge in attracting and retaining employees from nontraditional groups.

Innovation is another business strategy some firms pursue. For example, the need for constant innovation is stressed by John Sculley, a former CEO of Apple Computers: ". . . we are moving from a mass-production orientation to mass customization. As we gain the ability to customize products for people, localities and regions, markets are splitting. . . . Consumers are not middle class or upper class; they're hybrids. These days someone might buy a cheap digital watch, yet drive a Mercedes." Thus, today's markets are demanding the organizational capability to simultaneously meet many tastes and manage diversity. It is imperative that a labor force maintain a cadre of talent that can develop the newest and latest advances for each market. Creativity and responsiveness to new markets are increasingly likely to be related to effective management of a diverse labor force.

As new markets open up, the *speed* with which a firm is able to get to a market may be another source of competitive advantage. Successful implementation of this business strategy will be dependent on the ability to buy talent with unique skills. For example, a company that wishes to enter markets such as Mexico or countries of the former Soviet Union must be able to attract new members who may come from these cultures and/or have knowledge of these foreign markets. The inability to attract and retain individuals with foreign know-how may mean that a firm will be unable to get to a market quickly enough and may miss critical opportunities.

Similarly, given that the customer mix is changing, it may be beneficial for firms to hire talent that mirrors the market and that will be sensitive to the needs of new customer groups. This will enable the organization to implement a business strategy of providing excellent *customer service*. For example, Avon was able to turn around its inner city markets and make them one of their most successful endeavors by re-assigning them to Hispanic and African-American marketing managers (Dreyfus, 1990). Understanding the mores of doing business in many cultures may be another aspect of serving customers effectively. For example, Americans tend to be impatient and expect to be trusted on the basis of their credentials, while in other cultures, careful cultivation of trust and friendship must be completed before one will become a business client (Thiederman, 1991).

11

Thiederman provides examples of sayings from the Chinese ("Friendship first, business second") and Puerto Ricans ("One must take time to become a 'buena gente,'" i.e. a nice person), to illustrate the importance of understanding many cultures as a critical customer service capability.

Many firms pursuing a *quality* enhancement strategy rely on teams to a greater extent than in the past. Since this strategy holds that all parts of the organization must collaborate to enhance a product, interventions that improve collaboration across and within diverse groups are relevant here (Jackson, 1992a). Quality has been linked to morale indices of cooperation, communication and interpersonal relationships (Ulrich et al., 1991), which are all likely to be enhanced by diversity interventions. To successfully produce world class products of the highest quality, a firm must create an atmosphere where all employees, regardless of their sources of diversity, are involved to the fullest of their abilities, feel they are treated fairly, and believe that their ideas will be listened to when they speak candidly (Fernandez, 1993).

The *technology, task, and structural vision* is another area in which the organization makes strategic choices. Current technologies, tasks, and structures are antiquated in many organizations. Traditional assembly lines will increasingly be abandoned as the workplace (which may include the home as an alternative workplace) is redesigned to support teams, greater worker control, and multitasking.

Although many companies are choosing to make teams a fundamental organizing tool, few have effectively used their HR strategies and policy areas to support the team concept. In order for teams to be successful, member empowerment and risk-taking must be sanctioned. HR policies must manage intergroup dynamics related to workgroup diversity in: (1) personal demographics; (2) performance competencies; (3) values, beliefs, and attitudes; (4) personality, cognitive, and behavioral styles; and (5) organizational demographics (McGrath et al., 1994). Diversity in each of these areas may influence team outcomes. Diversity in values, which may be linked to functional membership, may affect the degree to which one can get consensus on group goals. As another example, research has shown that differences in age, education and industry tenure predict turnover in top management teams (Jackson et al., 1991). In yet another study, heterogeneous groups were found to be more cooperative in a task than all-white groups, in part due to a higher propensity to value a group orientation among Asian-, African-, and Hispanic-Americans (Cox et al., 1991). Without managing the various sources of diversity in a particular team, groups will have lower morale, longer decision times, and more communication problems (Cox, 1993). Mechanisms for fast upward/downward and lateral communication and processes to support collaboration and cross-fertilization need to be developed for these new organizational designs.

As mentioned earlier, technology heightens disparities in needed skills – increasingly the best-paying jobs will require greater knowledge of math and computer literacy than even before (Johnston and Packer, 1987); and jobs that traditionally demanded manual, clerical, or repetitive skills now will require more cognitive, intellectual, and self-initiating abilities. Workers need to be increasingly multiskilled as there will be few single-skill jobs (Hesketh and Bochner, 1994). Constant, rapid technological change necessitates ongoing training to help workers adapt to the new technology (Ulrich and Lake, 1991). HR systems, such as those related to training or career development, will have to be adapted to be more individualized and flexible in assessment (Hesketh and Bochner, 1994).

To summarize, in figure 1.1, the arrows indicate that the managing diversity strategy is linked with other strategic choices; and all of these strategies are linked with HR policy areas. In other words, an HR strategy, such as managing diversity, is assumed to be an integral part of the process of achieving business objectives. The framework helps make this assumption explicit and puts HR strategies on the organizational agenda as a legitimate business issue for discussion.

HR policy areas

Having scanned the environment and developed an organization's strategy, it is now critical to see whether the existing mix of HR practices reinforces the skills, attitudes, and behaviors necessary to implement the strategy. Figure 1.1 lists the key HR policy areas that will be influenced by the organization's strategic choices. This book includes chapters by invited contributors for each of the HR policy areas depicted. We will give below a preview of a main theme suggested by each of our contributing authors. The selected topics are not presented as all-inclusive, as new issues are likely to emerge in the future.

Individual, group, and organizational outcomes Before a firm can determine how to redesign HR systems, it must identify preferred performance outcomes. The main outcomes achievable by HR policies relate, at the first level, to attitudes and behaviors of employees and groups of employees, and at a second level, to economic and organizational issues. We will first examine outcomes at the individual and group level which include: (1) commitment; (2) competence; (3) perceived equity; (4) communication; and (5) performance.

When determining whether an HR policy is effective, a key question involves *commitment*: "To what extent does the policy motivate employees to work together toward the achievement of common organizational goals" (Beer et al., 1984). Beer and his co-authors maintain that HR policies promote commitment if they are designed not only to enhance performance, but also to promote individual identity, psychological involvement and self-worth. Commitment as an outcome of managing diversity effectively means that all individuals will be committed to organizational goals and will be motivated to perform to the best of their abilities.

Competence pertains to this question: "Do our human resource practices enable us to attract, develop and retain the right mix of skills, talents, and capabilities needed at the right place and the right time?" (Beer et al., 1984). Competence as an outcome of managing diversity effectively means that a firm will have representatives from diverse groups throughout the organization. In other words, hiring and promotion patterns should be examined not just in terms of numerical representation, but also across functions and levels. In support of this approach, research shows that lacking diversity at the top levels of a firm can negate the positive potential aspects of diversity at the lower levels (Ely, 1994).

A perception of *equity* is an important individual and group-level outcome of HR policies. An equity challenge in managing diversity relates to the assumption that what is provided to one employee must be offered to all. Managers need HR systems that will allow them to feel comfortable saying yes to one employee and no to another and will still enable their decisions to be viewed as fair. The paramount standard to be used might be the application of what researchers refer to as the performance effectiveness goal (Sheppard et al., 1992). By this standard, individuals and groups will receive outcomes consistent with the quantity and quality of the results they produce. Since implementing this standard will be difficult, we suggest that firms have procedures for handling disagreements over fairness of outcomes. For example, HR outcomes are more likely to be viewed as fair if there is: (1) representative member diversity at all decision-making levels; (2) an opportunity for appeal to a principal actor regarding HR decisions; and (3) a limited right of review for groups who may want to challenge a decision (Sheppard et al., 1992).

Improved *communication* among members of different cultures is another important HR-related outcome. As an executive from Xerox noted at a recent conference on diversity (see Morrison et al., 1993, p. 66): "If there is a hostile work environment, employees who are members of minority cultural groups will feel more threatened and more likely to have a need to 'cling on more tenaciously to what they consider to be important.'" He argues that people are more likely to reach out to others if they feel that their own needs are not being ignored.

The most critical goal of HR policies is to enhance *performance* of individuals and teams. At Avon, managing diversity is viewed as a necessary condition for enhancing performance. According to one of their videos on diversity: "This is not some benevolent activity on our part. There is self-interest here. We have to have a culture and environment in which these people can flourish." The performance of managers can also be assessed in terms of how well they manage diversity. Accountability should go beyond current practices, such as holding managers responsible for the statistical representation of different groups across levels or functions, turnover and promotion rates, and representation in high-potential programs and key positions (Morrison et al., 1993, p. 50). Managers should also be held accountable for using individual and group capabilities to their fullest potential to enhance performance.

Economic and organizational outcomes Some key organizational and economic outcomes from designing HR systems to manage diversity are profitability, adaptive/flexible systems, multicultural balance, and increased effectiveness.

Enhanced *profitability* is likely to accrue from cost savings and increased productivity. Reduced turnover is the saving most easily calculated from managing diversity. When turnover occurs, the firm is likely to incur the costs of recruiting and selecting a new individual and of lowered productivity from having the position empty or filled by a less experienced employee. In addition, the firm will lose the company dollars invested for training and development of the employee who left. For example, Ortho Pharmaceutical reported a saving of $500,000 largely from lowering minority turnover (Bailey, 1989). At Corning, the company estimated it was losing between $2 and $4 million a year from its significantly higher turnover of women and minorities compared with white men (Morrison, 1992). Cost savings are also likely to stem from reducing legal fees and company time spent on managing grievances. For example, AT&T was ordered by the US government to pay approximately $66 million to women who were denied benefits during pregnancy and after childbirth (Keller, 1991).

Although less easily calculated than turnover, the positive financial benefits of having more favorable employee attitudes can also be estimated via behavioral costing (Cascio, 1991). For example, employees will be less likely to be absent if they have high satisfaction and they will be more likely to exert higher effort and choose more effective performance strategies. Although not yet applied to improved attitudes from managing diversity, behavioral costing has been used to calculate the effects of attitudinal improvement on absences and illnesses, voluntary turnover, and mistakes that cost the firm money (Macy and Mirvis, 1976). Behavioral costing represents a potentially fruitful approach for calculating the benefits of enhancing diversity climate.

Profitability can also result from increased productivity due to innovation and enhancing access to new markets. For example, Gannett Media Corporation credits team diversity as a key factor in the great success of the launching of *USA Today*; Avon views its vastly improved sales in inner-city markets as being due to minority leadership; and Maybelline Corporation was able to greatly exceed the industry standard for new product success by developing a cosmetic focused on an ethnic segment (Cox, 1993).

A key benefit from managing diversity relates to the fostering of *adaptive* and *flexible* organizational systems, which can be a source of competitive advantage in an environment of changing market conditions. In addition, firms that possess healthy *multicultural environments* will be much more likely to be able to respond to new pressures. Such firms will also be more likely to avoid the view that there is only one best way to achieve success. Multicultural balance, by definition, means that one group's needs are not being met at the expense of others'.

Another organizational benefit of managing diversity is increased *effectiveness* in organizational processes. For example, Thomas (1991) argues that since total quality demands that employees be empowered and committed, and managing diversity leads to these outcomes, then effective managing of diversity is a prerequisite for total quality management. Quality is but one example of the potential for enhanced effectiveness. Increased effectiveness in marketing and recruitment have also been argued (Cox, 1993; Morrison, 1992).

Conclusion

We have argued that organizations need to delineate the objectives of a managing diversity strategy, *before* making decisions regarding the design and implementation of specific HR policy areas and activities. In this way, HR activities can be tailored and shaped with the desired consequences in mind. More importantly, different objectives imply that different policy areas be emphasized and utilized. If the desired consequence, for example, is greater teamwork among diverse group members, then perhaps reward systems need to be fashioned to promote collaboration and sharing of information. Jobs would need to be restructured to encourage members to see the achievement of their own tasks as tightly coupled with those of their co-workers. Employees could be selected who have collectivistic values and enjoy working in teams.

Alternatively, if the desired objectives were to manage diversity to improve marketing to nontraditional markets, HR practices would be redesigned to recruit and retain an employee population that mirrors the market. Under this situation, employees might be selected for key jobs based on their expertise in growing nontraditional markets. Rewards would emphasize performance supporting high growth in market share in new markets. Tasks and work systems would be designed to allow employees to be rewarded for tailoring products to the needs of distinct market niches.

The importance of first articulating the desired consequences of a managing diversity strategy and then tailoring HR practices accordingly should be kept in mind as a touchstone throughout this book, which is organized into four parts discussing the implications of a managing diversity strategy for HR policy areas. These include: recruiting and selection, development and motivation, special employee groups, and strategic linkages. Part One focuses on strategies regarding recruiting and selecting a diverse workforce in light of current developments in EEO, HR and labor market planning, and selection. Part Two includes chapters on adapting mentoring, training and development, performance appraisal, and compensation and benefits systems to better fit with the complexities of changing demographics. Part Three contains chapters on special topics – work/life, unions, health and safety, and disability – and their relationship to diversity. The fourth part includes HR policy areas pertaining to general business strategy and the use of teams.

The need for HR systems to adapt to dramatic labor force changes is arising just as many firms are undergoing long-term changes in the nature of the employment relationship, intense competition, and restructuring into global firms (Bridges, 1994). Organizations and scholars have a unique opportunity to redesign HR systems to better manage and motivate a heterogeneous workforce. We hope that this book is an important vehicle for beginning the important task of workplace redesign and renewal.

REFERENCES

Bailey, J. (1989). How to be different but equal. *Savvy Woman*, November, 47.

Bartlett, C., and Ghoshal, S. (1987). Managing across borders: New organizational responses. *Sloan Management Review*, Fall, 43–53.

Bartlett, C., and Ghoshal, S. (1991). What is a global manager? *Harvard Business Review*, September–October, 124–32.

Beer, M., Spector, B., Lawrence, P. R., Mills, D. Q., and Walton, R. (1984). *Managing Human Assets*. New York: Free Press.

Bell, D. (1973). *The Coming of Post-industrial Society: A Venture in Social Forecasting*. New York: Basic Books.

Bowen, D., and Schneider, D. (1988). Services marketing and management: Implications for organizational behavior. *Research in Organizational Behavior,* 10(43–80). Greenwich, CT: JAI Press.

Brickner, D. (1995). Personal communication. Director, Labor Program Service, School of Labor and Industrial Relations. Michigan State University, East Lansing, Michigan.

Bridges, W. (1994). The end of the job. *Fortune*, 130, September 19, 6274.

Business Week (1994). Special Report: Rethinking work, October 17, 74–85.

Cascio, W. (1991). *Costing Human Resources: The Financial Impact of Behavior in Organizations*. Boston: PWS Kent.

Cox, T. (1991). The multicultural organization. *Academy of Management Executive*, 5(2), 34–47.

Cox, T., and Blake, S. (1991). Managing Cultural Diversity: Implications for Organizational Competitiveness. *Academy of Management Executive*, 5, 45–56.

Cox. T. (1993). *Cultural Diversity in Organizations: Theory, Research, and Practice*. San Francisco: Berrett-Koehler.

Cox, T., Lobel, S., and McLeod, P. (1991). Effects of ethnic group cultural difference on cooperative versus competitive behavior on a group task. *Academy of Management Journal*, 34, 827–47.

Dreyfus, J. (1990). Get ready for the new work force. *Fortune*, April 23, 165–81.

Ely, R. (1994). The effects of organizational demographics and social identity on relationships among professional women. *Administrative Science Quarterly,* 39, 203–38.

Ferdman, B. (1989). Affirmative action and the challenge of the color-blind perspective. In F. A. Blanchard and F. Crosby (eds), *Affirmative Action in Perspective* (169–76). New York: Springer-Verlag.

Fernandez, J. P. (1993). *The Diversity Advantage*. New York: Lexington Books.

Ferris, G. R., Fink, D. D., and Galang, M. C. (1994). Diversity in the workplace: The human resources management challenges. *Human Resource Planning*, 16, 41–51.

Gardenswartz, L., and Rowe, A. (1993). *Managing Diversity: A Complete Desk Reference and Planning Guide*. Homewood, IL: Business One Irwin.

Hesketh, B., and Bochner, S. (1994). Technological change in a multicultural context: Implications for training and career planning. In H. Triandis, M. Dunnette, and L. Hough (eds), *Handbook of Industrial and Organizational Psychology*, 2nd ed., vol. 4 (191–240). Palo Alto, CA: Consulting Psychologists Press.

Howard, R. (1990). Values make the company: An interview with Robert Haas. *Harvard Business Review*, September–October, 133–44.

Jackson, S. E. (1992a). Preview of the road to be traveled. In S. Jackson and Associates (eds), *Diversity in the Workplace: Human Resource Initiatives*. New York: Guilford Press.

Jackson, S. E. (1992b). Stepping into the future: Guidelines for action. In S. Jackson and Associates (eds), *Diversity in the Workplace: Human Resource Initiatives*. New York: Guilford Press.

Jackson, S. E., and Alvarez, E. (1992). Working through diversity as a strategic imperative. In S. Jackson and Associates (eds), *Diversity in the Workplace: Human Resource Initiatives* (13–36). New York: Guilford Press.

Jackson, S. E., Brett, J. F., Sessa, V., Cooper, D. M., Julin, J. A., and Peyronnin, K. (1991). Some differences make a difference: Individual dissimilarity and group heterogeneity as correlates of recruitment, promotion, and turnover. *Journal of Applied Psychology*, 76, 675–89.

Jackson, S. E., and Schuler, R. S. (1992). *HRM Practices in Servicebased Organizations: A Role Theory Perspective. Advances in Services Marketing and Management*, vol. 1 (123–57). Greenwich, CT: JAI Press.

Johnston, W. B., and Packer, A. E. (1987). *Workforce 2000: Work and Workers for the 21st Century*. Indianapolis: Hudson Institute.

Kanter, R. M. (1977). *Men and Women of the Corporation*. New York: Basic Books.

Kaufman, J. (1995). How workplaces may look without affirmative action. *Wall Street Journal*, March 20, B1.

Keller, J. J. (1991). AT&T will settle EEOC lawsuit for $66 million. *Wall Street Journal*, July 18, B2.

Kossek, E., and Zonia, S. (1994). The effects of race and ethnicity on perceptions of policies and climate regarding diversity. *Journal of Business and Technical Communication*, 8(3), 319–34.

Kossek, E., Zonia, S., and Young, W. (1995). The limitations of organizational demography. *Proceedings of the October 1994 Conference "Work Team Dynamics and Productivity in the Context of Diversity."* Center for Creative Leadership and The American Psychological Association. Greensboro, NC: Center for Creative Leadership.

Kotter, J. P., and Heskett, J. (1992). *Corporate Culture and Performance*. New York: Free Press.

MacDonald, H. (1993). The diversity industry. *New Republic*, July 5, 22–5.

McGrath, J. E., Berdahl, J., and Arrow, H. (1994). No one has it but all groups do: Diversity as a collective, complex, dynamic property of groups. Paper presented at Conference Productivity and Interpersonal Relations in Work Teams. Greensboro, NC: Center for Creative Leadership, October 7–9.

Macy, B., and Mirvis, P. (1976). A methodology for assessment of quality of work life and organizational effectiveness in behavioral economic terms. *Administrative Science Quarterly*, 21, 212–26.

Morrison, A. (1992). *The New Leaders*. San Francisco: Jossey-Bass.

Morrison, A., Ruderman, M., and Hughes-James, M. (1993). *Making Diversity Happen: Controversies and Solutions*, Greensboro, NC: Center for Creative Leadership.

Noe, R., Hollenbeck, J., Gerhart, B., and Wright, P. (1994). *Human Resource Management: Gaining a Competitive Advantage*. Burr Ridge, II: Irwin.

Pava, C. (1986). Redesigning sociotechnical systems design: Concepts and methods for the 1990s. *Journal of Applied Behavioral Science*, 22, 201–22.

Pfeffer, J. (1994). *Competitive Advantage Through People*. Boston: Harvard Business School Press.

Pucik, V. (1988). Strategic alliances, organizational learning and competitive advantage: The HRM agenda. *Human Resource Management*, 27(1), 77–93.

Pucik, V. (1993). Globalization and human resource management. In V. Pucik, N. Tichy, and C. Barnett (1993), *Globalizing Management: Creating and Leading the Competitive Organization*. New York: John Wiley.

Schein, E. H. (1985). *Organizational Culture and Leadership*. San Francisco: Jossey-Bass.

Schneider, B. (1985). The people make the place. Presidential Address. Society for Industrial and Organizational Psychology, American Psychological Association Annual Convention, Los Angeles, August.

Schneider, B. (1987). The people make the place. *Personnel Psychology*, 40, 437–53.

Schneider, B., and Rentsch, J. (1988). Managing climates and cultures: A futures perspective. In J. Hage (ed.), *Futures of Organizations* (181–203). Lexington, MA: Lexington Press.

Sculley, J. (1988). *Odyssey: From Pepsi to Apple*. New York: Harper and Row.

Shellenbarger, S. (1994). Many employers flout Family and Medical Leave Act, *Wall Street Journal*, July 26.

Sheppard, B., Lewicki, R., and Minton, J. (1992). *Organizational Justice*. New York: Lexington Books.

Tajfel, H. (1978). *Differentiation Between Social Groups: Studies in the Social Psychology of Intergroup Relations*. New York: Academic Press.

Thiederman, S. (1991). *Profiting in America's Multicultural Marketplace: How to Do Business Across Cultural Lines*. New York: Lexington Books.

Thomas, R. (1990). From affirmative action to affirming diversity. *Harvard Business Review*, 68, 107–17.

Thomas, R. (1991). *Total Quality, Managing Diversity: Keys to Competitive Advantage in the 1990's*. Atlanta, GA: American Institute for Managing Diversity.

Thomas, R. (forthcoming). Redefining Diversity. New York: AMACOM.

Triandis, H. C., Kurowski, L. K., and Gelfand, M. J. (1994). Workplace Diversity. In H. Triandis, M. Dunnette, and L. Hough (eds), *Handbook of Industrial and Organizational Psychology*, vol. 4, 2nd ed. (769–827). Palo Alto, CA: Consulting Psychologists Press.

Ulrich, D., Halbrook, R., Meder, R., Struchlik, M., and Thorpe, S. (1991). Employee and customer attachment: Synergies for competitive advantage. *Human Resource Planning*, 14(2), 89–103.

Ulrich, D., and Lake, D. (1991). *Organizational Capability: Competing from the Inside Out*. New York: John Wiley.

Walton, R. (1985). Work innovations in the United States. In M. Beer and B. Spector (eds), *Readings in Human Resource Management*. New York: Free Press.

Weick, K. E. (1985). The significance of corporate culture. In P. Frost et al. (eds). *Organizational Culture* (381–9). Beverly Hills, CA: Sage.

Part One
Recruiting and Selecting a Diverse Workforce

Introduction to Part One

Many employers have identified the objective of recruiting and selecting a diverse workforce as an important organizational goal. Being perceived as an "employer of choice" by the most talented individuals in today's labor force is a critical capability needed to compete successfully in an increasingly competitive marketplace. In Part One, the reader will find three important chapters on integrating a managing diversity strategy with EEO, human resource and labor market planning and staffing.

Elaine Yakura helps us begin our journey by providing a broad framework for thinking about managing diversity. Chapter 2 will highlight the incongruities she sees in the abilities of organizations to manage diversity within employee groups based on the current approach of merging diversity programs with the EEO and affirmative action systems already in place. At the time of writing, the Clinton Administration began an official review of affirmative action policy in the US. This timely chapter is helpful in pushing policy-makers, employers, and students to delineate the basic assumptions of a managing diversity strategy, and contrast these with those underlying EEO and affirmative action. She adeptly notes that each of these terms comes from different sources and is grounded in differing basic assumptions. For example, EEO is consistent with the principles of equality and meritocracy; affirmative action emphasizes preferential treatment and race and gender consciousness; and managing diversity promotes the inclusion of all groups whether or not they are legally protected. Furthermore, managing diversity, unlike the other approaches, has been more readily linked to organizational competitiveness and profitability. Yakura's chapter bridges legal, organizational behavior and HR scholarship in her analyses of these differences and her suggestions about the organizational conditions needed to support a managing diversity strategy.

In chapter 3, Richard Arvey, Ross Azevedo, Daniel Ostgaard, and Sumita Raghuram discuss the implications of a diverse labor market for HR planning.

Like Yakura, they argue that organizations must identify the basic assumptions underlying their approach to managing diversity. A firm's posture on this will determine the types of HR planning activities used to match the available supply of labor with an organization's demand. The authors identify four types of organizational postures regarding HR planning to manage diversity. Under the moral diversification strategy, firms seek to incorporate heterogeneity into the organization because of the belief that having a more diverse workforce is inherently "good" on moral or ethical grounds. The business diversification strategy focuses on the notion that profitability is enhanced by reducing legal costs and increasing productivity. A passive nondiscrimination approach is reflected in the reactive diversification strategy, where firms do little proactively to manage diversity, but become more heterogeneous simply as a byproduct of the increasing diversity in the labor pool. The last posture is an anti-diversification strategy, or innovation-resistance approach. Here the organization resists seeking diversity since it values a highly homogeneous organizational population in order to minimize conflict and differences within the firm.

Once labor market strategies have been identified, employers need to implement recruitment and staffing policies to successfully attract diverse talent. In chapter 4, Robert Heneman, Nancy Waldeck, and Michele Cushnie review the literatures on recruitment, selection, and employment to examine how diversity considerations affect staffing decisions. They note the existence of many barriers to the entry of diverse segments of the labor force into organizations and contend that legally mandated affirmative action programs are unlikely to eliminate these barriers. For this reason, employers should take steps to use recruitment tools in a way that minimizes their potential bias in selection. The chapter largely focuses on racial and gender issues related to staffing, since most of the published literature has been done in relation to African-American and white men and women. The chapter makes a number of practical suggestions as to how traditional recruitment and selection systems need to be redesigned to ensure that they are not implemented in ways that exclude individuals who are diverse in comparison with the current organization's mix.

2

EEO Law and Managing Diversity

Elaine K. Yakura

Managing diversity is currently enjoying a great deal of support from the business community and has been prominently featured in *Business Week*, *Fortune*, and the *Wall Street Journal*. Proponents of diversity in organizations have emphasized its benefits (Cox, 1993; Thomas, 1991; Fernandez, 1993); managing diversity is portrayed as a product of enlightened corporate self-interest. This honeymoon of managing diversity and business stands in stark contrast to the current debates on affirmative action: Greene (1989, p. 1) has noted, "affirmative action is, in no uncertain terms, a controversial policy." In 1995, the controversial nature of affirmative action manifested in several key events, including an official review of affirmative action policy by the Clinton Administration (*Wall Street Journal*, July 20, 1995), the abolition of affirmative action in student admissions and faculty hiring by the University of California (*Los Angeles Times*, July 21, 1995), and a US Supreme Court decision that significantly narrowed the scope of minority set-aside programs in government contracting (*Adarand v. Pena*). Part of the controversy surrounding affirmative action stems, I believe, from a lack of clear understanding of the assumptions underlying equal employment opportunity law. The ideals of equality and justice run deep in American society, yet these ideals unravel all too easily when applied to particular situations. My contention is that we need to unpack the assumptions underlying equal employment opportunity policies in order to understand why affirmative action "seems to excite extreme opinion" (Crosby, 1994, p. 13). Otherwise, the notion of managing diversity has the potential to become just as problematic over time.

Why do I say this? Because I believe that "managing diversity" simply adds another layer of meaning on to an already confused set of assumptions underlying the concepts of equal employment and affirmative action. Although they are not well articulated, assumptions such as meritocracy and colorblindness go to the core values of self, identity and worth in our society. These concepts are easy to endorse as abstractions, but they become much more difficult to endorse when applied in a specific situation. As Karst (1993, p. 109) has noted, "Sometimes the light bulb goes on when we hear ourselves saying things we have never before articulated – and in the field of race relations most of what we feel lies in that shadowy zone." The existence of this "shadowy zone" explains why the assumptions underlying these concepts are so difficult to articulate. Yet, at the same time, the implications of these assumptions can be enormously volatile. Because managing diversity builds on this same foundation of unarticulated yet volatile assumptions, it is subject to the same difficulties as earlier policies intended to foster equal employment opportunity (EEO).

My goal in this chapter is to begin untangling the meanings of the terms equal employment, affirmative action, and managing diversity, as well as to articulate the assumptions that underlie each of them. These concepts are generally not well understood (cf. Crosby, 1994; Clayton and Crosby, 1992; Kravitz and Platania, 1993; Turner, 1990), so I will begin the chapter with a capsule discussion of the law on EEO and affirmative action. Because this enormously complex area of the law (which also touches on disciplines such as ethics, philosophy, psychology) cannot realistically be summarized in a chapter, the treatment here will be cursory at best and readers will be referred to more detailed treatments wherever possible. Given this backdrop, I will then discuss the assumptions underlying these concepts and demonstrate how they are often poorly articulated as well as contradictory. Interestingly, most of the writing (legal or otherwise) on both EEO and affirmative action is directed at justification of a pro or con position, rather than an exploration of the underlying assumptions. The chapter ends with a brief summary of suggestions for organizational implementation that flow from the literature and the arguments made here. Many of the recommendations are straightforward, or even self-evident (such as enhancing communication). But because of the ambiguous and emotionally charged nature of the problems, they are hard to accomplish in practice.

But first, some caveats. The context of the US and the EEO law which it spawned is unique, and I must confine my remarks to this context. An international comparison would be extremely illuminating, but is beyond the scope of this chapter. Also, I have had to ignore the burgeoning area of state employment law, since this is different for each jurisdiction. All I can do is mention that it exists. Finally, I have chosen to adopt a proactive rather than a reactive stance. I am assuming that HR professionals reading this chapter want to do the best they can given resource constraints, and not just the minimum possible to avoid litigation. To make an analogy: it is illegal to commit murder, but this is hardly an appropriate guideline for managing interpersonal relationships. Likewise, discriminatory employment practices are illegal, but employers who are serious about equal employment opportunity must go well beyond legal requirements.

Legal Background

Historical backdrop

Employment relationships in the United States at common law have been considered "at will" relationships since the late 1800s (Player, 1992). This meant that, broadly speaking, employers were free to hire or terminate employees and to set workplace rules of their own choosing. Segregation was the prevailing norm for institutions in the US into the 20th century (Epstein, 1992). Women had "separate spheres," influenced by the onset of industrial capitalism:

> The early stages of industrial capitalism involved increasing specialization and the movement of production out of the home, which resulted in heightened sex segregation. . . . [Women] came to occupy women's "separate sphere," a qualitatively different world centered on home and family. Women's role was by definition incompatible with full participation in society. (Taub and Schneider, 1982, p. 125)

An even more severe form of segregation existed for race relations, where "separate but equal" was the constitutional standard set by the Supreme Court in *Plessy v. Ferguson* (163 U.S. 537) in 1896. *Plessy* held that a Louisiana law mandating racially separate passenger accommodations on trains was constitutional despite the Fourteenth Amendment's provision for equal protection under the law for all citizens. The Supreme Court in *Plessy* (163 U.S. at 549) found that an African-American was "not lawfully entitled to the reputation of being a white man." Thus, the institutions in the US were allowed to treat nonwhites not only separately but with inferiority.

This precedent generally obtained until 1954, when the Court struck down "separate but equal" as unconstitutional in the landmark case, *Brown v. Board of Education* (347 U.S. 483). This case dealt with segregation in the public schools, and the Court expressly rejected the standard set in *Plessy*. Emphasizing the significance of education in our society, the Court found that

> [s]egregation of white and colored children in public schools has a detrimental effect upon the colored children. The impact is greater when it has the sanction of the law; for the policy of separating the races is usually interpreted as denoting the inferiority of the Negro group. (347 U.S. at 494)

Thus, with respect to access to educational and other institutions, the US had begun to move toward a different standard for equality.

Equal opportunity

As Blumrosen (1993, p. 41) has noted, "[e]vents in the late 1950s and early 1960s, including peaceful sit-ins, freedom rides, and other demonstration gained increasing public sympathy for the principle of equality [footnote omitted]." The Civil Rights Act was enacted in 1964 and prohibits discrimination in voting, public accommodations, public education, and employment. Title VII of the Civil Rights Act (42 U.S.C.A. § 2000e, et seq.) sits at the core of federal employment discrimination law and prohibits discrimination by employers (with 15 or more employees) on the basis of "race, color, religion, sex, or national origin." Other laws that regulate employment discrimination include the Age Discrimination in Employment Act of 1967, the Americans with Disabilities Act of 1990, the Rehabilitation Act of 1973, the Immigration Reform and Control Act of 1986, and the Equal Pay Act of 1963 (Curry-Swan, 1990; Sedmak and Levin-Epstein, 1991). The proliferation of statutory regulation of the employment relationship is but one indication of the distancing from employment "at will."

Affirmative action

Title VII of the Civil Rights Act contains broad prohibitions against certain acts of employment discrimination. The more specific and measurable requirements pertaining to equal employment are found in the Executive Order 11246 (29 C.F.R. 2477, as amended), signed by President Lyndon Johnson in 1965. This order applies generally to federal contractors and subcontractors and requires that these employers "take affirmative action to ensure that applicants . . . and employees are treated . . . without regard to their race, color, religion, sex, or national origin" (Gamble, 1992, p. 244). Affirmative action plans created pursuant to this executive order are overseen by the Office of Federal Contract Compliance Programs of the Department of Labor. Such plans are defined as "a set of specific and result-oriented procedures to which a contractor commits itself to apply every good faith effort" (Holloway, 1989, p. 10). A plan typically includes a review of an organization's employment practices, a statistical comparison of the current workforce to the available labor pool to see if there is "underutilization," and the establishment of goals and timetables (Curry-Swan, 1990). Goals and timetables speak to increasing the number of members of protected classes in an organization's workforce within a given period of time. The company must document its efforts and provide evidence as to the progress toward these goals. As Jones (1993, p. 350) has noted, "failure to reach the goal does not require [sanctions], but may result in an investigation to determine what good-faith efforts he made to achieve the objectives." The term quota has sometimes been used to characterize these goals. But fixed quotas usually result from court-ordered affirmative action plans where a company has been found guilty of discrimination; typical affirmative action goals are quite flexible.

There is a great deal of uncertainty and confusion as to the effects of affirmative action programs. Thomas (1994, p. 27), for example, asserts that their achievements have been "stupendous." On the other hand, Blumrosen (1993, p. 305) argues that "neither the supporters nor the opponents of equal employment laws give the laws much credit for effectiveness." A variety of researchers have attempted to measure the economic impact of affirmative action programs, and the measurable results are not overwhelming. For example, O'Neill and O'Neill (1992, pp. 102–3) assert that there is "no good evidence that the federal program of affirmative action with numerical hiring goals, which reached its peak between 1974 and 1980, had a significant and lasting effect on the relative economic status of black men." Uri and Mixon (1992, p. 124), on the other hand, using time series data covering the period 1947–88, found that women in the 20–54 age group benefited in terms of greater stability of employment (i.e. less sensitivity to short-run variations in employment) over the period 1965–80 while they lost some gains over the period 1981–8 (corresponding to the tenure of the Reagan Administration).

During the Reagan Administration, Clarence Thomas was appointed chair of the Equal Employment Opportunity Commission, which administers and enforces Title VII and other equal employment laws. Thomas changed the enforcement policy of the EEOC, and Greene (1989, p. 174) noted that "EEOC staff have reported that goals and timetables are no longer encouraged or permitted as a remedy." It is interesting to note that executive orders (and the regulations promulgated thereunder) may be revoked or amended by the President with the stroke of a pen. As Player (1992, p. 22) has noted, "[n]otwithstanding the rhetoric of the Reagan–Bush administrations condemning quotas, neither President has exercised his power to revoke or amend the [affirmative action] program." At this time, affirmative action appears to be under increasing attack, so it is important to realize that it can change at any time.

Related developments

Case law has developed much of the statutory and regulatory framework which makes up employment discrimination law. This has been the ground for development of several other important concepts: disparate treatment, disparate impact, the lack of interest defense, reverse discrimination, and sexual harassment.

Disparate treatment versus disparate impact   Under Title VII, to prove disparate treatment, an employee must show that the employer's discriminatory conduct "was actuated by some illegal motive" (Epstein, 1992, p. 160). For proving disparate impact, however, an employee need not give evidence of intent to discriminate. Rather, it suffices to show that the employment practices are discriminatory "in impact." *Griggs v. Duke Power Co.* (401 U.S. 424, 1971) was the first of the disparate impact cases, and prohibited the employer, Duke Power Company, from requiring intelligence tests or high school diplomas for low level jobs, since the employer could not demonstrate that these requirements were a "business necessity" and closely related to the particular job. The Griggs case was the first to use statistical tests to show that employment practices disproportionately excluded protected classes. With the advent of disparate impact, where discriminatory intent is inferred from the race or gender make-up of the workforce, plaintiffs in Title VII actions began to use statistics to uncover these more subtle forms of discrimination which would manifest themselves in underrepresentation.

In 1989, the Supreme Court decided five cases related to employment discrimination that were interpreted as "sympathetic to employers' interests" (Blumrosen, 1989, p. 175). *Wards Cove Packing Co. v. Antonio* (490 U.S. 642, 1989), the best known of these cases, realigned the defendants' burden of proof. In *Wards Cove*, the employer's unskilled cannery workers were nearly all Filipinos or Alaska Natives; workers in unskilled non-cannery jobs, almost all of whom were better paid than cannery workers, were predominantly white. The two groups of workers were housed in separate dormitories and ate in separate dining halls (Karst, 1993, p. 83). The employer claimed that cannery workers "lacked interest" in the higher-paying jobs. This case affirmed the employer's use of the "lack of interest" defense when charged with discriminatory employment practices under Title VII.

With the lack of interest defense, organizations would seek to "justify patterns of sex and race segregation in their workforces by arguing that these patterns resulted not from any actions they had taken, but rather from women's and minorities' own lack of interest in higher-paying nontraditional jobs" (Schultz, 1990, p. 1759). But employees do not form their job preferences in a vacuum; they form them in response to cultural norms and workplace practices (i.e. their preferences are socially constructed). These norms and practices include lack of support, intimidation and harassment of members of protected classes who seek to cross into jobs which have not traditionally been held by these individuals. For instance, in *EEOC v. Sears, Roebuck & Co.* (628 F.Supp. 1264, N.D.Ill. 1986; affirmed, 829 F.2d 302; 7th Cir. 1988), the EEOC presented statistical evidence that women with similar qualifications to men were significantly less likely to get commissioned, higher-paying sales jobs than men. The court concluded that the women lacked interest in these positions, since "they disliked the perceived 'dog-eat-dog' competition," preferring instead the "more enjoyable and friendly" non-commissioned sales jobs (628 F.Supp. at 1324–5). Efforts to prove disparate impact in these cases are not always successful, but job barriers have sometimes been broken (Holcombe and Wellington, 1992).

Partially in response to the 1989 Supreme Court cases, the 1991 Civil Rights Act was enacted. Overturning *Wards Cove*, the Act, among other things, shifts the burden of proof back to the employer and codified the "disparate impact" theory (Paul, 1992). The passage of this 1991 Civil Rights Act was at the center of a storm of public controversy about quotas, but, according to Nager (1993, p. 1057), "the debate about its passage is almost deafeningly silent on the subject of affirmative action in employment." It is beyond the scope of this chapter to summarize the provisions of this Act or to speculate about its eventual impact, but see Paul (1992) and Nager (1993) for more in-depth analyses of the 1991 Act.

Reverse discrimination   Reverse discrimination is a concept most closely associated with the Supreme Court decision *Regents of the University of California v. Bakke* (438 U.S. 265, 1987). In 1971, the faculty at the UC Davis Medical School voted to set aside 16 seats in the entering class of 100 for qualified minority candidates. Since they were operating at the time a "nearly all white" medical school (Blumrosen, 1993, p. 226), the faculty gave scores on standardized tests less weight than other factors, such as background or experience. Bakke was one of the rejected white candidates who had higher scores than some of the black candidates who were admitted to the class. In a narrow vote (5–4), the Supreme Court held that the minority admissions program was unlawful and that Bakke had to be admitted to the class, while noting that the university could give consideration (of a lawful sort) to race in future admissions procedures. *Bakke* is an enormously complex case that created a river of commentary, legal and otherwise, in its wake (Greene, 1989). This case stands firmly in the center of the debate between those who argue that affirmative action represents reverse discrimination and those who argue that it does not.[1]

Because education is viewed as a scarce resource, as well as a key to social and economic advancement, admissions has continued to be an arena where fairness is contested. From elementary schools through high schools and universities, claimants have alleged unfairness in selection and admissions procedures. For example, one parent of a 4-year-old child has claimed that the UCLA on-campus, elementary "laboratory school" is "reserving slots for the rich and famous" (*Los Angeles Times*, July 13, 1995). Chinese-American students have challenged the San Francisco school district's desegregation plan for limiting the enrollment of Chinese-Americans in "alternative" schools such as Lowell High School, where academic achievement would ordinarily be the main criterion for admissions. The San Francisco school district desegregation plan limits the enrollment of any one group to 40 percent, so that Chinese-American students must attain higher scores than those of other groups to gain admission. Lowell High School is seen as a pipeline to prestigious UC Berkeley (*Los Angeles Times*, July 13, 1995), and slots are highly sought after. But Berkeley, as well as other elite institutions across the United States, has also come under fire for discriminating against Asian-American applicants (Takagi, 1992). Berkeley officials have defended their admissions policies by arguing that "the real problem is that Asian overrepresentation was undermining diversity" (Takagi, 1992, p. 74). These examples illustrate that the definitions of "privileged" groups shift with politics and context.

The use of affirmative action in university admissions may soon be put to a more conclusive test. In *Hopwood v. State of Texas*, the plaintiff is appealing an opinion by the US Court of Appeals. Hopwood was denied admission to the University of Texas law school although she alleges she was better qualified than several African-American and Mexican-American students who were admitted. The US Court of Appeals ruled that the admissions procedure was unconstitutional because there were three separate admissions committees – one each for Mexican-Americans, African-Americans, and other applicants. The law school changed its admissions procedures so that all applicants are reviewed by a single committee, although the law school still uses race as a factor to enhance minority admissions (*Legal Times*, October 17, 1994). It is not clear yet whether the US Supreme Court will hear this case, but if it does, it would create an opportunity for the Court to revisit the legality of any kind of affirmative action in university admissions.

Sexual harassment   The furor over the testimony of Professor Anita Hill at the appointment hearings of Supreme Court Justice Clarence Thomas appears to have had an impact on sensitivity to issues of sexual harassment (Aaron, 1993, pp. 24–7). Successful sexual harassment court cases are a relatively recent development. The first time that the Supreme Court considered such a case was in 1986, in *Meritor Sav. Bank, FSB v. Vinson* (447 U.S. 57, 1986). In this case, the Court held that an employee had the right to be free from a hostile working environment which is tolerated or created by an employer under the sex discrimination prohibition in Title VII. Under federal regulations, a "hostile environment" is one created by "unwelcome sexual advances, requests for sexual favors, and other verbal or physical conduct of a sexual nature" (29 CFR § 1604.11(a)(3)). In any given case, the determination of what constitutes a "hostile environment" is subject to interpretation; at least one jurisdiction has adopted a "reasonable victim" standard, which analyzes harassment from the victim's point of view (*Ellison v. Brady*, 924 F.2d 872, 9th Cir. 1991). The Court noted: "we believe that a sex-blind reasonable person standard tends to be male biased and tends to systematically ignore the experiences of women."

In addition to sexual harassment claims based on a hostile environment, there are also "quid pro quo" discrimination claims where a person with supervisory responsibility conditions work-related benefits upon the receipt of sexual favors. Hauck and Pearce (1992, p. 33) have noted that there are several possible sources of harassment that can create liability for employers, including supervisors, co-workers, and people outside the organization: "[i]n general, the law assumes that the more discretionary influence a person has over the job benefits of an employee, the greater the opportunity to impose odious sexual conditions of employment. . . . harassment initiated by co-workers is considerably less than the liability for supervisors, because co-workers are not in a position to impose adverse conditions of employment." In some cases, even clients may be a source of harassment, although since clients are also a source of revenue, this can create a particularly difficult situation (*Wall Street Journal*, November 4, 1994).

There is some evidence that successful sexual harassment claims are increasing. A recent *Los Angeles Times* article (September 2, 1994) noted that the amount of Equal Opportunity Commission sexual harassment case awards for 1993 ($25.2 million) was double that of 1992. And what is thought to be the largest award for punitive damages in a sexual harassment case was recently granted by a jury in a case before the San Francisco Superior Court. The suit was brought by a former legal secretary against a then-partner at Baker and McKenzie, one of the world's largest law firms headquartered in Chicago:

> She alleged that Greenstein dumped candies into a breast pocket of her blouse, groped her breast, pressed against her from behind and pulled her arms back to "see which (breast) is bigger.' . . . During the trial, more than half a dozen other women testified that Greenstein had grabbed them, propositioned them or made lewd remarks in incidents dating back to 1988. . . . Greenstein, 49, admitted offensive behavior toward two secretaries, but denied Weeks'

accusations. His lawyer said Weeks made up her complaints to save her job, and that they were "the product of an overactive imagination" and motivated by reading an office handbook on sexual harassment. (*Los Angeles Times*, September 2, 1994)

According to several jurors, the award for $7.1 million was based on tithing 10 percent of the capital of the firm. The magnitude of this award (plaintiff had only requested $3.7 million) serves as a warning for employers who fail to take steps to correct any harassment. In other cases, such as *Intlekofer v. Turnage* (973 F.2d 773, 9th Cir. 1992), courts have held that an employer is required to take immediate action to end the harassment once the employer knows *or should have known* of the action. Note that the employer need not have actual knowledge of the harassment to be held liable.

In their defense, employers have recently taken to citing prompt disciplinary action against the alleged harasser (such as denial of bonuses or termination), or the use of training programs to avoid findings of liability. But training programs alone will not protect employers; the jury in the Baker and McKenzie case did not find the firm's training programs to be an adequate defense. Worse yet, some training programs can cause problems, as in the case of the complaint filed by Douglas Hartman against the Federal Aviation Administration (FAA). Hartman, an air traffic controller, complained that in June 1992, he attended a mandatory diversity workshop in which "he sat quietly while minority employees vented their outrage and anger at white males like him," and "was subjected to a 'gauntlet,' in which female employees taunted him and other male employees with sexually explicit words and phrases and . . . groped him sexually" (*Investor's Business Daily*, May 17, 1995).

The FAA example reminds us that complaints of harassment can be filed by members of any group, a point that is reinforced in a recent suit against Jenny Craig. A group of men, who called themselves the "Boston Eight," complained that they "were denied promotions or fired from Jenny Craig because of their sex" (*Wall Street Journal*, November 29, 1994). The treatment they complained of included, "unfavorable sales assignments, orders to perform demeaning tasks, and a constant barrage of humiliating remarks." Furthermore, the men complained that they were excluded from social activities that were common among the women, such as conversations or gift-giving. Regardless of whether the treatment they received meets the legal standard for harassment, one can speculate that these men found it difficult to assimilate to the culture of an organization founded and dominated by women.

Recent developments

As of this writing, the legal basis for affirmative action has been undergoing change on several fronts. Given the increasingly heated political climate, such changes are likely to continue or even accelerate. For example, the Clinton Administration recently completed its review of affirmative action policy. Their objective was to "mend, not end" affirmative action by providing additional guidelines for implementation (*Los Angeles Times*, July 20, 1995). In California, however, the University of California Board of Regents voted to eliminate the use of "race, religion, gender, color, ethnicity, or national origin as criteria in its admissions decision beginning January 1, 1997, and in hiring and contracting decisions beginning January 1, 1996" (*Los Angeles Times*, July 21, 1995). At the same time, the Regents ordered University officials to develop a policy that would "ensure that the student body remains diverse." University officials expressed skepticism at how such a policy could be formulated, but the University may still use social or economic disadvantage as an admissions criterion (*Los Angeles Times*, July 21, 1995).

The legal foundation for affirmative action is also undergoing significant changes. On June 12, 1995, the US Supreme Court handed down *Adarand v. Pena*. In this case, Adarand Construction submitted the low bid for highway guard rail work, but lost the bid to Gonzalez Construction Co. Gonzalez Construction had been certified as a small disadvantaged business, so the prime contractor selected Gonzalez in order to receive the monetary compensation provided by federal statute for hiring a small disadvantaged business. Adarand claimed that the presumption that certain races, such as Hispanic-Americans, are socially and economically disadvantaged set forth in the federal statute and regulations discriminates on the basis of race. The Supreme Court found that the standard of "strict scrutiny" (rather than the previously applied "intermediate scrutiny") must be applied to all race-based actions by any federal government entity. These actions must serve a "compelling government interest" and be "narrowly tailored" to further that interest.

Given its controversial history, the reactions to the attacks on affirmative action have been both positive and negative. Some believe that the group preferences have served to divide groups, so that abolition of affirmative action will have a positive effect. Other express fears that doing away with affirmative action will mean commitments to diverse workforces will fade (*Wall Street Journal*, April 19, 1995). It is hoped that programs for managing diversity will avoid the negative connotations that become associated with affirmative action.

Managing diversity

Managing diversity is a term that has been in vogue for several years, and probably has as many definitions as there are people who practice it. One definition is provided by Thomas (1994, pp. 33–4): "enabling every member of your work force to perform to his or her potential." Cox (1993, p. 11) offers a more detailed definition:

> ... planning and implementing organizational systems and practices to manage people so that the potential advantages of diversity are maximized while its potential disadvantages are minimized ... the goal of managing diversity as maximizing the ability of all employees to contribute to organizational goals and to achieve their full potential unhindered by group identities such as gender, race, nationality, age, and departmental affiliation.

Part of the motivation for managing diversity can be found in the changing demographics in the US workforce. As Johnson and Packer's (1987) *Workforce 2000* has pointed out, the growth rates of many so-called minority groups in the US have surpassed that of the majority, and members of these groups will make up a substantial part of the workforce by the 21st century. Given this impetus, managing diversity has been espoused by the business community. The belief that it can increase profits prevails in some organizations. For example, targeting minority entrepreneurs (the fastest growing segment of the small business market) allows some organizations to compete more effectively (*Wall Street Journal*, August 23, 1994). Understanding differences can only make companies more effective in this market. In addition, US businesses have become more accepting of the need to work in teams and to work with individuals who come from different cultures (Fernandez, 1993). One such example is Voice Processing Corp., a speech recognition software developer which predicts that "overseas customers will account for half" of the company's revenue (*Wall Street Journal*, October 12, 1994). There are 11 nationalities represented and 30 languages spoken by the 40 employees at the company's headquarters.

From the above discussion, it is evident that equal employment, affirmative action, and managing diversity are quite distinct concepts, not only in content, but in derivation. Affirmative action could be said to have been derived from equal employment opportunity in that Executive Order 11246 was signed and federal regulations were promulgated under Title VII of the 1964 Civil Rights Act. But equal employment opportunity broadly prohibits discrimination in employment while affirmative action is a remedial program for implementing that standard in particular organizations. Managing diversity, on the other hand, is a business initiative that refers to the goal of having every individual within an organization achieve their potential. So far, managing diversity is more an ideal than a reality, although a number of illustrations of managing diversity as implemented in organizations have been provided in the literature (Cox, 1993; Fernandez, 1993; Thomas, 1994; Gentile, 1994; Jackson et al., 1992).

Assumptions Underlying EEO, Affirmative Action, and Managing Diversity

The assumptions that underlie each of these concepts are nearly as important as their legal foundations because these assumptions shape the ways in which we think and act around issues of EEO and diversity. The relationships between these assumptions are rather subtle and complex; they connect to some of our most deeply held values, such as equality, yet they challenge us to reconsider what these values mean in specific instances.

Table 2.1 shows three major concepts that bear on employment practices. It indicates the source of each concept and its underlying assumptions. As we shall see, the assumptions underlying each of these concepts are fraught with difficulties and conflicts. EEO embodies widely held ideals: equality,

Table 2.1 Source and assumptions underlying concepts

Term	Source	Underlying assumption	
Equal employment	Statute	1	Equality/egalitarianism
		2	Meritocracy
		3	Race and gender neutrality
Affirmative action	Executive order and federal regulations	1	Preferential treatment
		2	Race and gender consciousness
Managing diversity	Academics and practitioners	1	Diversity/uniqueness of individuals
		2	Competition/profitability of organizations
		3	Inclusion of all groups, legally protected or not

meritocracy, and neutrality with respect to race and gender. Affirmative action, on the other hand, is intended to implement the ideals of EEO. The rationale for affirmative action may be EEO, but it is experienced by many as interfering with those very ideals by unfairly redistributing a fixed pie. In a sense, managing diversity is a return to the idealism of EEO, although the specific assumptions differ in important ways.

Before delving into the specifics, it is important to realize that the *level* of analysis for each of these concepts is very important. At an individual level, affirmative action may look very different than it does at an organizational or even at a global level. Clayton and Tangri (1989) note that at the level of "microjustice," an individual might receive preferential treatment under affirmative action. But individual decisions aggregate to an outcome at a macro level that may appear very different: past practices may have resulted in a situation in a particular industry where women or other protected classes are vastly underrepresented. There are three levels of possible interpretation: (1) the individual level (e.g. comparing the qualifications of two competing candidates for a particular job); (2) the organizational level (e.g. representing the percentage of members of a protected class in an organization); and (3) the societal level (e.g. comparing employment statistics aggregated across organizations). The level of analysis is quite salient for the assumptions underlying each of our three main approaches, because what may appear unfair at one level may appear quite reasonable at another.

Equal employment

The concept of EEO meets with general approval because it matches a set of values that are closely held by many people: equality or egalitarianism (Dovidio et al., 1989; Hill, 1991), meritocracy (Young, 1990; Haney and Hurtado, 1994), and race and gender neutrality (Aleinikoff, 1991). At first blush, these concepts are so general as to be unobjectionable. But upon closer scrutiny, one finds that these ideals tend to mask a great deal of disagreement about what is meant in particular situations. As a result, they are not so easily translated into practice.

When people agree that equality is an important criterion for employment decisions, it is not evident that they are referring to the same underlying assumptions. It is important to note that there are different *kinds* of equality: equality of creation, equality of opportunity, equality of treatment, and equality of result. The Declaration of Independence asserts that "all men are created equal." Aside from the gender bias inherent in this statement, it is clear that all men share the quality of being human. This type of equality is quite fundamental, but other than this basic commonalty, equality of creation cannot be reconciled with reality: race and gender top a long list of obvious differences. Of course, one could argue that the authors of this statement were focused more on the rights which adhere equally to each individual. But it is certain aspects of these rights that are in question in the context of this discussion. Ironically, when the Declaration of Independence was signed, the institution of slavery denied even equality of creation to people of African descent.

Equality of opportunity can be distinguished from equality of creation. One can imagine a set of students who are all granted admission to a prestigious university. Some members of the new class, however, may be unable to attend for a variety of reasons, such as cost. One could further imagine that in certain circumstances, society would wish to bear the costs of "evening things up" by providing these individuals with the same opportunity as the others. They might provide scholarships to those students so that the opportunity for education was equalized. While this accommodation adds cost, many organizations have deemed that this cost is worthwhile to somewhat mitigate otherwise restricted opportunities. In other cases, this accommodation is deemed too costly.

Equality of treatment is another kind of equality which enters into the discussion, but which may or may not be desirable in a given circumstance. There are occasions when differential treatment is desired by individuals. For example, an employee might desire more or less demanding assignments depending upon whether he or she was finishing up a degree, caring for a parent with Alzheimer's or nearing retirement.

Equality of result is another category that may seem to conjure up images of radical communism, where everyone gets the same share of the collective pie. But it is easy to think of situations in our own culture where this standard of equality clearly applies. In the event of an earthquake or some other workplace disaster, for example, one would hope that the result would be the same for each employee and that everyone would emerge unharmed, whether otherwise equal or not.

Thus, the interpretation given to the generic category "equal" changes with the meaning assigned to the term and the context of the discussion. Gaining consensus on equality as a general criterion is very straightforward. But upon further reflection, equality is a highly problematic concept. In any given situation, it is unlikely that we all share the same interpretation of what equal means.

Meritocracy, another value which permeates the US culture, assumes that superior individual performance should be commensurately rewarded.

> The merit principle holds that positions should be awarded to the most qualified individuals, that is, to those who have the greatest aptitude and skill for performing the tasks those positions require. The principle is central to legitimating a hierarchical division of labor in a liberal democratic society which assumes the equal moral and political worth of all persons. Assuming as given a structural division between scarce highly rewarded positions and more plentiful less rewarded positions, the merit principle asserts that this division of labor is just when no group receives privileged positions by birth or right, or by virtue of arbitrary characteristics such as race, ethnicity, or sex. The unjust hierarchy of caste is to be replaced by a "natural" hierarchy of intellect and skill. (Young, 1990, p. 200)

Thus, meritocracy reflects something like equality of treatment, but it is not necessarily consistent with equality of creation, for instance. People, if created equal, would presumably perform equally well. Meritocracy is also inconsistent with equality of result, since variable reward for variable performance is the norm for meritocracy; sales representatives working on commission earn widely disparate salaries, but this is perceived as fair because they have "earned" it. And as Young and others have pointed out, our organizations do not always function as meritocracies. It is difficult to measure merit; we are forced to rely on imperfect proxies such as test scores and recommendations. And, people have been known to make mistakes.

Given the American ideal of equality, another appealing aspect of EEO is the notion of neutrality with respect to race, gender or other protected classes, which most often appears in the literature as "colorblindness." A principle of neutrality would mean that decisions and behavior would not be influenced by, for example, race or gender (Strauss, 1986; Aleinikoff, 1991). The underlying assumption of affirmative action, however, is preferential treatment in recognition of differences between groups. Eberhardt and Fiske (1994, p. 216) note that the very acknowledgement of different groups is at odds with our espoused ideal of neutrality:

> To ignore race and gender bolsters people's sense of themselves as not thinking in a prejudiced manner. Affirmative action policies, however, require that employers explicitly take group-based characteristics (such as race and gender) into account. This requirement, then, is squarely at odds with the demands of maintaining a non-prejudiced self-image.

Some would prefer to ignore the egregious acts of our past and start all over; the historical slate would be wiped clean, and categories such as race and gender would be erased when it comes to questions of employment law. In this view, preferential treatment of any kind is an unnecessary reminder of times gone by:

> Racial preferences reflect an unhealthy obsession with past wrongs – terrible wrongs, to be sure, but wrongs which racial preferences will not undo, and wrongs which should now be put behind us. (Carvin et al., 1993, p. xiii)

While enforced amnesia may be an attractive alternative to some, there is a problem with this approach: all the categories in question are socially constructed (Berger and Luckmann, 1967; Conley and O'Barr; 1990; Scheff, 1968). They are woven into the fabric of our consciousness, our language, and our daily lives. Unless we could wipe our brains the way we format computer disks, this approach cannot work. We would continue to carry with us these "neutral" concepts imbued with old values.

The social construction of the ideals underlying equal opportunity is not just a theoretical point; it is extremely important for organizational practice. The meanings of terms like equality or meritocracy are influenced by the dominant culture. What appears meritorious, for example, is a culturally-bound category, based on the expectations and interests of the dominant group. Haney and Hurtado (1994, p. 239) make the argument very nicely:

> The very concept of "merit" and the associated notions of "ability" and "qualification" are socially constructed categories. How we define, measure, and value these concepts, as well as the specific manner in which they are applied in any given setting, are social conventions rooted in a dominant culture view of reality. This is not to say that some people do not "perform differently" from others. Of course they do. But "performance" – its measurement and meaning – is not a category of nature.

The culturally-bound definition of merit is illustrated in the case of *Price Waterhouse v. Hopkins* (109 S. Ct. 1775, 1989). Hopkins, a woman, played a key role in securing business for the firm and was highly regarded by clients, but she was denied partnership in Price Waterhouse and filed suit for sex discrimination. The lower court found that Price Waterhouse had based part of the partnership decision on sex stereotyping, based in part on evidence such as the following: "One partner described her as 'macho'; another suggested that she 'overcompensated for being a woman'; a third advised her to 'take a course in charm school'" (109 S. Ct. 1778, 1989). A trait such as "macho" may not have disqualified a male candidate, but this trait was apparently intolerable in a female. Although Hopkins performed well, socially constructed traits other than "performance" or "merit" determined the partnership decision.

Personal grooming, including clothing and hair style, is another arena in which cultural assumptions hold sway. Courts generally protect grooming codes that treat males and females differently if the code "conforms to societal standards for grooming" such as requiring a jacket and tie for men or a dress for women. However, if the grooming rule poses a greater burden on one than the other, they are considered a form of discrimination. One example of this is in *Carroll v. Talman Fed. Sav. and Loan Ass'n* (604 F.2d 1028, 7th Cir. 1979), where the Court struck down a requirement that female employees wear a uniform while the men wore business attire of their own choice. But, as Caldwell (1991, p. 393) has noted, "Judgments about aesthetics do not exist apart from judgments about the social, political, and economic order of a society." Caldwell writes about *Rogers v. American Airlines* (527 F.Supp. 229; S.D.N.Y. 1981), which upheld American's policy of not allowing braided hairstyles. In doing this, the Court noted American's assertion that the plaintiff, a black female, had adopted the prohibited hairstyle shortly after it had been popularized by a white actress, Bo Derek, in the film *10*. Caldwell (1991, p. 391) in writing eloquently about the opinion, states:

> [t]he very use of the term "popularized" to describe Bo Derek's wearing of braids – in the sense of rendering suitable to the majority – specifically subordinates and makes invisible all of the black women who for centuries have worn braids in places where they and their hair were not overt threats to the American aesthetic.

Of her own reaction (Caldwell also wears her hair braided, in a pageboy style) to "being the unwitting object of one in thousands of law school hypotheticals," she says: "[m]ostly, I marveled with sadness that something as simple as a black woman's hair continues to threaten the social, political, and economic fabric of American life" (Caldwell, 1991, pp. 367–8).

Employers have sometimes used "customer preference" as justification for grooming rules as well as non-English rules. In *Garcia v. Gloor* (618 F.2d 264; 5th Cir. 1980), the employer's customers, who were from a community which was 75 percent Hispanic, preferred to be addressed in Spanish. Of the 39 employees, 31 were Hispanic, and most were bilingual. The employer prohibited employees from speaking Spanish on the job unless they were speaking to Spanish-speaking customers. The plaintiff had been fired because he had answered a question from another employee in Spanish about an item requested by a customer. These kinds of cultural norms are quite salient when used to justify workplace rules. The opportunity to speak one's own language in the workplace or wear one's hair as one chooses is contingent on socially constructed norms.

Thus, we find that the core value underlying EEO is unclear, because "equality" is not something that can be measured with a ruler. The dimensions along which equality might be measured are culturally and contextually specific, the level of analysis (individual, organizational, or societal) is often ambiguous, and the very notion of "equal" shifts depending on whether one is concerned with creation, opportunity, treatment, or results. What appears to be a clear articulation of a core American value turns out to be fraught with difficulties.

Affirmative action

In spite of its internal contradictions, EEO is the ideal which affirmative action is intended to help implement. It is not surprising, therefore, that affirmative action has been the subject of enormous confusion and controversy:

> There is much confusion concerning the meaning of affirmative action resulting, in significant part, from the vast array of often inconsistent practices and policies that fall under the rubric.   (Rosenfeld, 1991, p. 42; footnotes omitted)

> . . . [S]trong reactions often appear to occur despite – or perhaps because of – a general lack of familiarity with what affirmative action entails. Both at the

level of specific practices and at the level of social philosophy, there seem to be many different ways to conceptualize affirmative action, and not all of them are widely applauded. (Crosby, 1994, p. 13)

Affirmative action has developed several negative and inappropriate connotations. It has sometimes served to stigmatize minorities, who may be treated as though they obtained employment just because of their minority status (Major et al., 1994; Delgado, 1991). Gray (1992, p. 24) notes that "in the abstract, affirmative action does not require or mean the hiring or promotion of the unqualified or the less qualified. It means making race, gender, disability, or Vietnam veteran's status a determining factor in an employment decision." Many have argued that affirmative action places an unfair burden on its beneficiaries (Arthur et al., 1992; Rodriguez, 1982; Steele, 1990) but others have argued that these negative effects are avoidable (Clayton and Crosby, 1992).

Another negative connotation for affirmative action closely related to stigma is that of quotas. This is closely related to the perception that employment opportunities are a zero-sum game, where one group's gains necessarily imply another group's losses. Many affirmative action plans do not require that fixed quotas be met: "While quotas *may* be used in affirmative action programs, they are by no means a required feature and many contemporary programs do not use them" (Cox, 1993, p. 248). None the less, affirmative action is often equated with the imposition of quotas that lead to the hiring of unqualified people "just to make the numbers."

There is also the connotation that affirmative action is equivalent to reverse discrimination. This belief is perhaps best illustrated by the Reagan Administration's simple view of affirmative action: "affirmative action is reverse discrimination and any form of discrimination is unconstitutional" (Greene, 1989, p. 4). There are, of course, less extreme views which nevertheless equate affirmative action with a form of preference which should not be condoned. Carter (1991, p. 228) describes a position which is much more subtle, in which there is not a colorblind society, but one in which "we can at once take account of it and not punish it."

Delgado (1991) has argued that affirmative action may be viewed differently if placed in a broader perspective.

> For more than 200 years, white males benefited from their own program of affirmative action, through unjustified preferences in jobs and education resulting from old-boy networks and official laws that lessened the competition. Well, if you were a member of the majority group and invented something that cut down the competition, made you feel good and virtuous, made minorities grateful and humble, and framed the "minority problem" in this wondrous way, I think you would be pretty pleased with yourself. (Delgado 1991, pp. 1224–5)

By truncating history at a particular point and wiping the slate clean, we gain a very different perspective on the issue of just who is a beneficiary of affirmative action. As Delgado points out, some members of our society have enjoyed over 200 years of affirmative action of an unlabeled sort, which can hardly be undone in the decades since Title VII was enacted. We would also gain a very different perspective from an individual, organizational, or societal view. One's beliefs about affirmative action can fluctuate depending on what has recently happened in one's career. But as Carter and others have pointed out, it seems inevitable that some type of differentiation be made or standards be set. What is fascinating is that some seem, on their face, much more invidious than others. Here is one example of what seems, on its face, a benign distinction:

> As Justice Blackmun pointed out in his spirited dissent in Bakke, academic institutions have traditionally awarded preferences to children of alumni, wealthy applicants, and those connected with the famous and the powerful. Those preferences which maintain the established order have gone unquestioned, while preferences given to the disadvantaged have become subject to increasingly stricter scrutiny. (Klein, 1989, p. 63)

The social construction of these norms is what makes the difference, and much will rest on our ability to tease out and understand these cultural distinctions.

Although affirmative action is the chief means of implementing EEO under US law, the assumptions underlying these concepts are directly contradictory. EEO has come to represent equality and neutrality, while affirmative action has come to represent preference and stigma. The polarization of EEO and affirmative action lies at the heart of a vast and often acrimonious debate. The tensions that have arisen do not ease the path towards a harmonious workplace. Rather, they tend to create more tensions and misunderstandings within organizations as they attempt to deal with issues of employing a diverse workforce.

Managing diversity

Managing diversity brings a new set of assumptions that lie uncomfortably on top of the EEO/affirmative action debates. The key assumption underlying managing diversity is that all individuals are unique, which contrasts starkly with EEO's assumptions of a homogenized equality and neutrality. Proponents of diversity link this uniqueness of individuals with the firm's potential for enhanced performance and the promise of greater creativity and responsiveness to changing markets. Competition and profit then become the impetus for investing in increasing the potential for every individual, whether they are a member of a protected class or not. Each individual's uniqueness is to be valued (as opposed to being a matter of stigma with affirmative action), and even members of dominant groups (whites or males) are part of this effort. Thus, managing diversity is safe from charges of reverse discrimination, since every individual is included. Everyone, black or white, male or female, physically challenged or not, is given the chance to live up to his or her potential. Another part of the appeal of managing diversity is that responsibility rests with individuals; how hard they work determines how well they will be rewarded. Thus, managing diversity does manage to avoid the more pejorative aspects of affirmative action. At the same time, it retains the popular ideals which underpin the notions of equality without moving completely to the neutrality pole, which Carter (1991, p. 227) describes as a "world made dull and (literally) colorless."

Note that managing diversity is quite defensible at the individual level, because every individual (ideally) gets the opportunity to live up to his/her potential. Visions of the zero-sum game where the white male is edged out by others (whether qualified or not) fade, and are replaced by visions of organizations where everyone is attempting to be all they can be, thus boosting the competitiveness and profitability of the organization. Presumably, at the societal level, there is a gigantic trickle-up effect, and managing diversity programs result in the advancement of those who have best actualized their potential regardless of their group membership.

There has been no conclusive evidence that managing diversity has a salutary effect on an organization's bottom line or the hiring and promotion of organizational members. But this has not stopped organizations like Levi Strauss, which is committed to its vision of diversity in spite of a recent slowdown in sales. According to Levi Strauss's chairman and chief executive Robert D. Haas, "in the long run, the cultivation of a culture devoted to such values as diversity and empowerment will make Levi's all the more responsive to the marketplace" (*Business Week*, August 1, 1994).

One somewhat cynical view holds that managing diversity has been devised to co-opt white males. Given that affirmative action has been at the center of a storm of controversy, it has been abandoned in favor of managing diversity. By focusing on managing diversity and its inclusion of all individuals, the tensions created by the affirmative action debates can be ignored. In this view, managing diversity could be seen as "lip service" to the interests of white males, while "actually" serving to promote minority interests. Another cynical perspective views managing diversity as the focus of so much hype that it runs the risk of becoming a "flavor of the month." So much rhetoric surrounds this ideal that, in the organizational vernacular, people often "talk the talk" but don't "walk the walk." Jackall (1988) has described the symbolic dexterity with which managers in organizations sometimes jockey concepts and couch organizational behaviors. To the extent that organizations use managing diversity as a shield for claims of harassment and discrimination rather than a genuine means of promoting equal opportunity, its effectiveness will be diluted.

At this point in time, managing diversity is largely at the stage of idealism. It holds out the promise of a workplace where each individual, including members of historically privileged groups, realizes his or her potential. As in the case of EEO, however, the precise nature of that realization remains ambiguous. By focusing on individual differences (and ways to accommodate or exploit those differences for the greater good), the rhetoric of diversity tends to mask group differences along dimensions of power or status that have grown up over hundreds of years (Lubiano, 1992). As Minow (1990) has noted, each difference drawn between people has an implicit comparison, with an unstated point of reference. This point of reference contains implicit assumptions about what is deviant and what is normal. Whether we like it or not, members of dominant groups tend to create and maintain a dominant norm or culture, and it is within that cultural context that abstract ideals like equality get defined and played out. What remains to be seen is whether the ideals of managing diversity can be implemented in a way that overcomes the structural tendency for dominant groups to remain dominant.

Remedies and Recommendations

Affirmative action plans have been part of organizational life in the US since the mid-1960s. Yet perceptions of affirmative action are often characterized by confusion and/or ignorance; few organizational members know much about their employer's affirmative action program (unless, of course, they are responsible for it). But what does this have to do with managing diversity? Historically, intergroup relations (whether the group is based on race, gender, disabilities, or professional identities) in our society have been fraught with tensions. Attempts at legal intervention have been equally problematic. Cox (1993) and Thomas (1991) have provided detailed description and guidelines for the design of diversity change programs. These sources provide a wealth of valuable suggestions, but until we gain more experience and conduct more research specifically on the topic of managing diversity (e.g. Kossek and Zonia, 1994), the best source of guidance that we have concerning the implementation of these programs comes from our many years of research and experience with affirmative action programs.

Whether implementing an affirmative action program or a managing diversity program, there are some basic lessons which emerge. First, most researchers agree that commitment from the senior management in the organization is key to the success of an affirmative action program (Hitt and Keats, 1984; Jones, 1991; Taylor, 1991). The same is true for programs on the management of diversity. However, I would argue that a critical precondition to the commitment of senior management is their own understanding of these issues. As noted above, this arena is fraught with discord and ignorance. Unless top managers have grappled with these concepts and acquired a deeper, personal knowledge of at least the central concepts, the commitment on their part will only be a shallow thing. To follow through on managing diversity, top management and key members of the organization need to have thought through the contradictions of the kind raised here so that they can present them to members of the organization clearly and consistently. It is very easy to fall into contradictions when dealing with this subject and to send the wrong or mixed messages. Such messages undermine the credibility of management commitment, leaving the impression that the policies in question are in fact just window dressing. In such a situation, no plan could succeed.

Commitment is a necessary but not sufficient condition for success of

Figure 2.1 Factors needed to support managing diversity

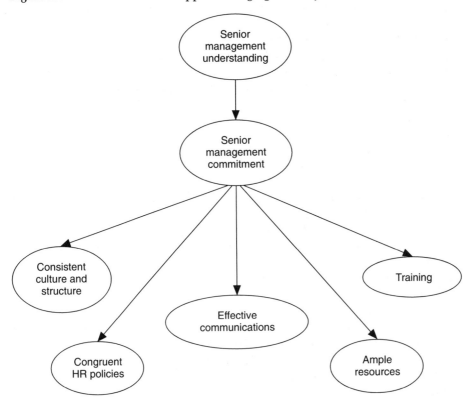

affirmative action plans (Blanchard, 1989). Other researchers have identified several factors which flow from high-level commitment, including effective communications, allocation of adequate resources for the program, training, congruent HR policies and practices (such as recruiting, promotion, retention and reward systems), and the cultivation of a supportive organizational structure and culture (see figure 2.1).

These factors are largely commonsense, of course; it would be unrealistic to expect hundreds of years of history to dissolve without considerable, focused effort. Clearly, top management commitment is critical to marshaling the kinds of resources and attention that are necessary. One major factor that makes for a successful affirmative action plan is to develop an effective means of communicating the affirmative action program to everyone in the organization. As we have seen, affirmative action has many different connotations, many of which are negative. Only by clearly and repeatedly communicating the specifics of the organization's program can these negative connotations be mitigated. In addition, in the case of either affirmative action or managing diversity, there must be more than a surface level of commitment which is communicated. Taylor (1991) has termed this a "consistent and authentic approach" which he argues is essential in an effective communications strategy.

The HR policies and practices should be well integrated with the goals of any program, as well as the strategic goals of the organization, as Kossek and Lobel argue in chapter 9. This is particularly critical for those organizations implementing managing diversity programs. Organizational members will be quick to judge the system for evidence of preferences of one sort or the other. Some affirmative action programs have been undermined by the perception that promotion systems did not reinforce the same values as the affirmative action plan. Others have hit roadblocks because the culture of the organization has been hostile to the advancement of all members of the organization. Again, the leadership of top management is key in shaping organizational culture (Schein, 1992). All of these changes require the persistent scrutiny of organizational members for the constant fine-tuning that is required for continuous improvement.

Training, obviously, would be quite useful for acquiring this understanding, not only at top management levels, but also throughout the organization. Part of the issue with affirmative action plans had to do with the lack of information with respect to the plans in one's own organization. By clearly and repeatedly offering information through a variety of sources, including regular, updated training courses, the lack of information would become less of an issue in the disputes surrounding preference. In addition, some researchers have argued that, by conveying specific information about particular individual hiring or promotion decisions, any adverse impact of affirmative action plans can be greatly reduced (Dovidio et al., 1989). Given that managing diversity initiatives will follow on affirmative action plans, heeding this advice can only enhance their likelihood of success.

Conclusion

Over the years, legal intervention in employment practices has had an ambiguous impact on workplace relations. Title VII of the 1964 Civil Rights Act established EEO, and Executive Order 11246 (29 C.F.R. 2477, as amended), signed by President Lyndon Johnson in 1965, established affirmative action. These laws and regulations appear to embody deeply held American values, but they have proved controversial and sometimes difficult to implement effectively. Managing diversity is a recent arrival on the scene, and although it has no statutory basis, we have to be careful in translating it into practice lest it become tainted as well. Evidence indicates that in at least some cases, managing diversity programs are viewed with suspicion (Kossek and Zonia, 1994). The key to progress lies in understanding the difficulties that earlier policies and programs have faced, because these difficulties remain formidable.

Justice Blackmun, in his concurring and dissenting opinion in *Bakke* (at 403), penned the following line: "the time will come when an 'affirmative action' program is unnecessary . . . we could reach this stage within a decade at the most." Alas, his prediction has not yet come to pass. This should not be surprising, since the debates around EEO and affirmative action issues have sometimes been virulent and always divisive. These issues rock our very foundations, and go to the heart of our identity, merit, and self-worth. But we can take away lessons from these debates, and perhaps forge a deeper understanding of these disturbing issues. By learning from the experiences of successful affirmative action programs, perhaps we can avoid their pitfalls. This may seem obvious, or even simple-minded, but in these solutions lie the answers to many of the other problems plaguing organizations today. The proof, as they say, will be in the pudding.

NOTE

1 A recent article in *New York Times Magazine* (June 11, 1995) juxtaposed the current activities of Dr Allan Bakke, an anesthesiologist in Rochester, MN, who "has no private practice and works on an interim basis" at a community hospital, and Dr Patrick Chavis, an obstetrician-gynecologist who has "an enormous practice comprising entirely poor people on medicaid" in south central Los Angeles. Dr Chavis was one of the last students admitted under the affirmative action program successfully challenged by Dr Bakke.

REFERENCES

Aaron, T. E. (1993). *Sexual Harassment in the Workplace: A Guide to the Law and Research Overview for Employers and Employees.* Jefferson, NC: McFarland & Co.

Aleinikoff, T. A. (1991). A case for race-consciousness. *Columbia Law Review*, 91, 1060–125.

Arthur, Jr, Winfred, Doverspike, D., and Fuentes, R. (1992). Recipients' affective responses to affirmative action interventions: A cross-cultural perspective. *Behavioral Sciences and the Law*, 10, 229–43.

Berger, P., and Luckmann, T. (1967). *The Social Construction of Reality* (1966 ed.). Garden City, NY: Doubleday.

Blanchard, Fletcher, A. (1989). Effective affirmative action programs. In F. A. Blanchard and F. J. Crosby (eds), *Affirmative Action in Perspective* (193–208). New York: Springer-Verlag.

Blumrosen, A. W. (1989). The 1989 Supreme Court Rulings concerning employment discrimination and affirmative action. *Employee Relations Law Journal*, 15: 175–86.

Blumrosen, A. W. (1993). *Modern Law: The Law Transmission System and Equal Employment Opportunity.* Madison, WI: University of Wisconsin Press.

Caldwell, P. M. (1991). A hair piece: Perspectives on the intersection of race and gender. *Duke Law Journal*, 1991, 365–96.

Carter, S. L. (1991). *Reflections of an Affirmative Action Baby.* New York: Basic Books.

Carvin, M. A., La Noue, G. R., Lunn, J., Ryland, W. H., and Clegg, R. (1993). *Racial Preferences in Government Contracting.* Washington, DC: National Legal Center for the Public Interest.

Clayton, S. D. (1992). Remedies for discrimination: Race, sex and affirmative action. *Behavioral Sciences and the Law*, 10, 245–57.

Clayton, S. D., and Crosby, F. J. (1992). *Justice, Gender, and Affirmative Action.* Ann Arbor, MI: University of Michigan Press.

Clayton, S. D., and Tangri, S. S. (1989). The justice of affirmative action. In F. A. Blanchard and F. J. Crosby (eds), *Affirmative Action in Perspective* (177–92). New York: Springer-Verlag.

Clegg, R. (1993). Introduction. In M. A. Carvin, G. R. La Nove, J. Lunn, W. H. Ryland, and R. Clegg (eds), *Racial Preferences in Government Contracting* (pp. v–xii). Washington, DC: National Legal Center for the Public Interest.

Conley, J. M., and O'Barr, W. M. (1990). *Rules versus Relationships: The Ethnography of Legal Discourse*. Chicago: University of Chicago Press.

Cox, T. (1993). *Cultural Diversity in Organizations*. San Francisco: Berrett-Koehler.

Cox, T., and Blake, S. (1991). Managing cultural diversity: Implications for organizational competitiveness. *The Executive*, 3, 45–56.

Crosby, F. J. (1994). Understanding affirmative action. *Basic & Applied Social Psychology*, 15, 13–41.

Crosby, F. J., and Blanchard, F. A. (1989). Introduction: Affirmative action and the question of standards. In F. A. Blanchard and F. J. Crosby (eds), *Affirmative Action in Perspective* (3–7). New York: Springer-Verlag.

Curry-Swan, L. (1990). *Managing Equally and Legally*. Jefferson, NC: McFarland & Co.

Delgado, R. (1991). Affirmative action as a majoritarian device: Or, do you really want to be a role model? *Michigan Law Review*, 89, 1222–31.

Dovidio, J. F., Mann, J., and Gaertner, S. L. (1989). Resistance to affirmative action: The implications of aversive racism. In F. A. Blanchard and F. J. Crosby (eds), *Affirmative Action in Perspective* (83–102). New York: Springer-Verlag.

Eberhardt, J. L., and Fiske, S. T. (1994). Affirmative action in theory and practice: Issues of power, ambiguity, and gender versus race. *Basic and Applied Social Psychology*, 15, 201–20.

Epstein, R. A. (1992). *Forbidden Grounds: The Case Against Employment Discrimination Laws*. Cambridge, MA: Harvard University Press.

Fernandez, J. P. (1981). *Racism and Sexism in Corporate Life*. Lexington, MA: Lexington Books.

Fernandez, J. P. (1993). *The Diversity Advantage: How American Business Can Outperform Japanese and European Companies in the Global Marketplace*. New York: Lexington Books.

Gamble, Barbara S. (ed.) (1992). *Sex Discrimination Handbook*. Washington, DC: BNA.

Gentile, M. C. (ed.) (1994). *Differences that Work: Organizational Excellence through Diversity*. Cambridge, MA: Harvard Business Review.

Gray, J. A. (1992). Preferential affirmative action in employment. *Labor Law Journal*, 43: 23–30.

Greene, K. W. (1989). *Affirmative Action and Principles of Justice*. New York: Greenwood Press.

Haney, C., and Hurtado, A. (1994). The jurisprudence of race and meritocracy: Standardized testing and "race-neutral" racism in the workplace. *Law and Human Behavior*, 18, 223–48.

Hauck, V. E., and Pearce, T. G. (1992). Sexual harassment and arbitration. *Labor Law Journal*, 1992, 31–9.

Hill, T. E., Jr (1991). The message of affirmative action. *Social Philosophy and Policy*, 8, 108–29.

Hitt, M. A., and Keats, B. W. (1984). Empirical identification of the criteria for effective affirmative action programs. *Journal of Applied Behavioral Science*, 20(3), 203–22.

Holcombe, B. J., and Wellington, C. (1992). *A Search for Justice*. Walpole, NY: Stillpint Publishing.

Holloway, F. A. (1989). What is affirmative action? In F. A. Blanchard and F. J. Crosby (eds), *Affirmative Action in Perspective* (9–19). New York: Springer-Verlag.

Jackall, R. (1988). *Moral Mazes: The World of Corporate Managers*. New York: Oxford University Press.

Jackson, Susan E., and Associates (eds) (1992). *Diversity in the Workplace*. New York: Guilford Press.

Johnson, W. B., and Packer, A. E. (1987). *Workforce 2000: Work and Workers for the 21st Century*. Indianapolis, IN: Hudson Institute.

Jones, Jr, Augustus J. (1991). *Affirmative Talk, Affirmative Action*. New York: Praeger.

Jones, J. E. (1993). The rise and fall of affirmative action. In H. Hill and J. E. Jones (eds), *Race in America: The Struggle for Equality* (345–69). Madison, WI: University of Wisconsin Press.

Karst, K. L. (1993). *Law's Promise, Law's Expression: Visions of Power in the Politics of Race, Gender, and Religion*. New Haven, CT: Yale University Press.

Klein, Hilary B. (1989). Cutting the mustard: Affirmative action and the native of excellence. *Women's Rights Law Reporter*, 11: 61–6.

Kossek, E. E., and Zonia, S. C. (1994). The effects of race and ethnicity on perceptions of human resource policies and climate regarding diversity. *Journal of Business and Technical Communication*, 8(3), 319–34.

Kravitz, D., and Platania, J. (1993). Attitudes and beliefs about affirmative action: Effects of target and of respondent sex and ethnicity. *Journal of Applied Psychology*, 78, 928–38.

Lubiano, W. (1992). Black ladies, welfare queens, and state minstrels: Ideological war by narrative means. In T. Morrison (ed.), *Race-ing Justice, En-gendering Power* (323–61). New York: Pantheon.

Major, B., Feinstein, J., and Crocker, J. (1994). Attributional ambiguity of affirmative action. *Basic and Applied Social Psychology*, 15, 113–41.

Minow, M. (1990). *Making all the Difference*, Ithaca, NY: Cornell University Press.

Morrison, T. (ed.) (1992). *Race-ing Justice, En-gendering Power*. New York: Pantheon.

Nager, G. D. (1993). Affirmative action after the Civil Rights Act of 1991: The effects of "neutral" statute. *Notre Dame Law Review*, 68, 1057–94.

O'Neill, D. M., and O'Neill, J. (1992). Affirmative action in the labor market. *Annals of the American Academy of Political Science and Society*, 523, 88–103.

Paul, N. A. (1992). The Civil Rights Act of 1991: What does it really accomplish? *Employee Relations Law Journal*, 71(567–91).

Player, M. A. (1992). *Federal Law of Employment Discrimination*. St Paul, MN: West Publishing Co.

Robinson, R. K., Allen, B. M., and Abraham, Y. T. (1992). Affirmative action plans in the 1990s: A double-edged sword? *Public Personnel Management*, 21, 260–72.

Rodriguez, R. (1982). *Hunger of Memory: The Education of Richard Rodriguez*. New York: Bantam.

Rosenfeld, M. (1991). *Affirmative Action and Justice: A Philosophical and Constitutional Inquiry*. New Haven, CT: Yale University Press.

Scheff, T. J. (1968). Negotiating reality: Notes on power in the assessment of responsibility. *Social Problems*, 16, 3–17.

Schein, E. H. (1992). *Organizational Culture and Leadership* (2nd ed.). San Francisco: Jossey-Bass.

Schultz, V. (1990). Telling stories about women and work: Judicial interpretations of sex segregation in the workplace in Title VII cases raising the lack of interest argument. *Harvard Law Review*, 103, 1750–843.

Sedmak, N. J., and Levin-Epstein, M. D. (1991). *Primer on Equal Employment Opportunity* (5th ed.). Washington, DC: Bureau of National Affairs.

Steele, Shelby (1990). *The Consent of Our Character: A New Vision of Race in America.* NY: Harper Collins.

Strauss, D. A. (1986). The myth of colorblindness. In P. B. Kurland, G. Casper, and D. J. Hutchinson (eds), *The Supreme Court Review* (99–134). Chicago: University of Chicago Press.

Takagi, D. Y. (1992). *The Retreat from Race: Asian-American Admissions and Racial Politics*, New Brunswick, NJ: Rutgers University Press.

Taub, N., and Schneider, E. M. (1982). Perspectives on women's subordination and the law. In D. Kairys (ed.), *The Politics of the Law* (125–6). New York: Pantheon.

Taylor, Bron R. (1991). *Affirmative Action at Work.* Pittsburgh: University of Pittsburgh Press.

Thomas, R. Roosevelt (1991). *Beyond Race and Gender: Unleashing the Power of Your Total Work Force by Managing Diversity.* New York: AMACOM.

Thomas, R. Roosevelt (1994). From affirmative action to managing diversity. In M. C. Gentile (ed.), *Differences that Work: Organizational Excellence through Diversity* (27–46). Cambridge, MA: Harvard Business Review.

Thompson, D. E., and DiTomaso, N. (1988). *Ensuring Minority Success in Corporate Management.* New York: Plenum.

Thompson, D. E., DiTomaso, N., and Blake, D. H. (1988). An overview of corporate policies and practices. In D. E. Thompson and N. DiTomaso (eds), *Ensuring Minority Success in Corporate Management* (303–19). New York: Plenum.

Turner, M. E., and Pratkanis, A. R. (1994). Affirmative action as help: A review of recipient reactions to preferential selection and affirmative action. *Basic and Applied Social Psychology*, 15, 43–69.

Turner, R. (1990). *The Past and Future of Affirmative Action.* New York: Quorum Books.

Uri, N. D., and Mixon, W. Jr (1992). Effects of U.S. equal employment opportunity and affirmative action programs on women's employment stability. *Quality and Quantity*, 26, 113–26.

Young, I. M. (1990). *Justice and the Politics of Difference.* Princeton, NJ: Princeton University Press.

3
The Implications of a Diverse Labor Market on Human Resource Planning

Richard D. Arvey, Ross E. Azevedo,
Daniel J. Ostgaard, and Sumita Raghuram

Organizations engage in strategic planning as a way of managing the future, as a tool to attempt to reduce the turbulence in the world around them. While many definitions of strategic planning can be set forth (see, for example, Ansoff, 1984; Galbraith and Nathanson, 1978; and Hamermesh, 1986), we view the process as one of four major steps. The first is for the organization to decide what and where it is! This means that the organization must specify what it is and where it is going among the variety of input and output markets within which it operates, so that it can move to the next step; identifying organizational goals and objectives. This leads to the third step. determining how these goals and objectives will be met.

The third step involves planning, including the additional determination of objectives and how they will be accomplished, in the various functional areas of the organization; financial planning, market planning, production/sales/service planning, and human resource planning (HRP). The last step involves combining the outputs of the individual functional areas into a formal plan together with a mechanism for assessing the success of the strategic plan and for making course corrections to assure ultimate achievement of the organization's targets.

Given these steps/distinctions, this chapter deals with but part of one of them: the impact of a diverse labor market on the variety of HRP activities engaged in by firms and employers within the context of strategic planning. We suggest that there are a number of HRP activities directly affected by diverse labor markets as well as a number of indirect effects and we will explore these themes. Our objective is to develop what we believe are some of the major implications of diverse labor markets on HRP mechanisms and activities, and to outline some ideas concerning possible methods for dealing with these implications. We note at the outset that our chapter will *not* be empirically based, nor will it reflect the entire depth and spectrum of discussion in this area. Instead, we intend to be speculative and thematic in our approach to provide some focus to both practitioners and behavioral scientists.

What Is a Diverse Labor Market?

It may be helpful to first consider what we mean by a "diverse labor market." Many definitions would develop diversity along the lines of clearly identifiable features of people which represent targets of bias or discriminatory action (e.g. race, gender, age, and handicapped status). Other definitions expand the concept to include social and cultural characteristics such as religion, language patterns, ethnicity and so forth. Even broader conceptualizations (e.g. Triandis et al., 1990) embrace the notion that diversity means anything which sets individuals apart from one another (e.g. sexual orientation, value differences, political affiliation). For our purposes, we develop our ideas using a broader view of diversity, where it is conceptualized around both visible and invisible attributes of individuals (e.g. Jackson et al., forthcoming). Our reasons for adopting this broad perspective towards diversity are: (1) managing diversity is a complex issue and adopting a definition that stresses demographics (race, gender, age, and disability status) alone may provide myopic and overly simplistic solutions; and (2) a broader perspective makes our arguments and discussions more inclusive of the issues that emerge from diversity. We run the risk of not being able to provide a precise way by which diversity can be measured. But the risk is worthwhile because by focusing on features in addition to demographics we believe the approach will provide a more accurate depiction of diversity. Moreover, this approach emphasizes that managing diversity necessarily implies managing certain invisible characteristics of people which may or may not stem from the visible features of individuals traditionally considered.

What Do We Mean by Human Resource Planning?

We assume that the audience is well aware of the variety of HRP techniques. These include the following kinds of processes and activities: (1) the assessment of future human resource (HR) needs (or the demand for labor) for short-, intermediate-, and long-term horizons (Jackson and Schuler, 1990); (2) the assessment of the relative supply of labor in the short, intermediate, and long run; (3) a comparison of the predicted needs versus the predicted supply of labor and an assessment of what kinds of talent will be necessary in the future or where labor should be reduced; (4) the deployment of various HR activities to meet these objectives (e.g. recruitment, downsizing); and (5) the assessment of how well these objectives have been met or realized. The focus of this chapter, then, is how a diverse labor force impacts these various processes in organizational settings. It may be worth while to point out some different positions or postures organizations might take in terms of dealing with diversity and the implications such postures might have with regard to their HRP efforts. These include the following.

Moral diversification strategy (MDS)

Incorporating heterogeneity into the organization and creating a more diverse workforce is desirable for at least two reasons. First, having a diverse pool of employees is inherently "good" on moral and ethical grounds. Cascio (1992) has identified a similar posture which he labels "pure affirmative action" (p. 149) and indicates that organizations in this posture will make a "concerted" effort to search out diversity class individuals to expand their applicant pool.

Second, businesses are finding that diversity improves their competitive advantage. A diverse culture has varied tastes and can make diverse contributions. From a marketing and customer service point of view, employees with a breadth of background similar to those of consumers can help a company to understand and provide better services to the marketplace. In Canada and the US, many organizations are tapping the ethnocultural expertise in their workforce to gain access to lucrative markets, both local and abroad (Taylor, 1995). Companies such as IBM and Avon realize that their market is made up of all races, religions, and sexual orientations and, therefore, a diverse workforce is deemed vital to their companies' success (Rice, 1994).

Business diversification strategy (BDS)

Creating a diverse workforce is consistent with the business objectives of the firm because it leads to diminished legal costs (e.g. Title VII lawsuits) and increased productivity (Cox and Blake, 1991).

Reactive diversification strategy (RDS)

Creating a diverse workforce is simply a byproduct of the labor market. There are more diverse individuals in the market and the firm's labor supply will reflect this diversity. Organizations following this approach would discourage discrimination and bias against diverse labor pools and individuals but not affirmatively attempt to utilize the talents of these pools and/or individuals. Again, Cascio (1992, p. 149) identifies a similar posture which he labels "passive nondiscrimination" in which there is no active effort to include all individuals but where all classes of individuals are treated equally.

Anti-diversification strategy (ADS)

Creating a diverse workforce is not an important value for these organizations; in fact, it might even be considered a negative because of philosophical assumptions that the organization works more smoothly, has less conflict, and has a greater array of basic talent under conditions where the workforce is relatively homogeneous (Lott and Lott, 1965).

We believe that firms which adopt these different postures will approach and pursue HRP activities quite differently. Those adopting an MDS posture will aggressively seek out a diverse workforce, those adopting a BDS will be proactive in their HRP activities, but not as aggressive as those in an MDS, and those adopting an RDS will be somewhat laissez-faire in their HRP activities. Organizations adopting an ADS might actively discourage activities that could promote the recruitment and hiring of individuals who are diverse.

Moreover, these postures could be associated with very different approaches to sourcing and utilizing labor. For example, at a macro level, firms may locate facilities close to or far away from diverse labor pools. In Minneapolis/St Paul there are examples of firms that strategically elected to build and staff plants close to or within the boundaries of predominantly black and low socioeconomic neighborhoods to explicitly provide employment to disadvantaged minorities. In other instances, organizations have been known to strategically locate their plants in cities or regions, usually the suburbs, which have relatively homogeneous labor pools (i.e. predominantly white, well educated) in order to capitalize on these labor pools and avoid diversity issues.

As will become apparent, the latter approach will become progressively more difficult to take. The increasingly diverse demographic composition and geographic dispersion of the population and, in turn, the labor force, will make it ever less likely a firm can ignore the labor market when conducting its HRP activities. For some jobs, the relevant labor pool is national, so relocation won't help avoid diversity.

Traditional HRP focuses on the labor market and labor market issues. Later in this chapter we will deal with diversity implications for HRP on the supply of labor in the external labor market, supply in the internal labor market, and the organization's demand for labor.

Impact of Diversity on the Assessment of External Labor Supply

One of the recent "facts" facing organizations is that the labor force does and will continue to reflect diverse labor pools. We will not repeat all of the statistical evidences regarding the labor market, but a few of the major trends which have been noted are as follows:

Table 3.1 Demographic composition of the workforce, 1988 and 2000

	1988	*2000*
Total in thousands	121,669	141,134
Sex (%)		
Male	55	53
Female	45	47
Race (%)		
White[a]	86	84
Black[a]	11	12
Asian and Other	3	4
Hispanic[b]	7	10

[a] Includes Hispanics.
[b] Hispanics can be of any race.
Source: Barnum (1991)

- The average age of the workforce will rise and the pool of young workers entering the labor market will shrink. According to Johnston and Packer (1987), between 1986 and the year 2000, the number of people in the population between the ages of 35 and 47 will jump by 38 percent, and the numbers aged 48–53 will increase by 67 percent, compared with an overall population growth of 15 percent. A recent *Business Week* cover story (September 12, 1994) makes these same forecasts.
- More females will enter the workforce. According to Johnston and Packer (1987), by the year 2000, approximately 47 percent of the workforce will be women and 61 percent of women will be at work.
- Minorities will make up a larger share of new entrants into the labor force.
- White males will no longer be the dominant demographic group entering the labor market.

Table 3.1 depicts the demographic composition of the workforce in 1988 and the projections for the year 2000. These data indicate that different groups are clearly represented in the labor force now and that their representation will grow in the future.

Barnum (1991) makes a second point; these data also show that the basic composition of the workforce has been diverse and that the changes cited and developed by authors such as Johnston and Packer have to do with new *entrants* to the workforce, not necessarily the composition of the entire workforce. The issue is one of stocks versus flows. Thus, while we see demographic changes in the supply of labor, the majority of workers are and will continue to be white males for several decades into the next century.

It is worth nothing that some disagree with the picture presented by Barnum (1991), based on different approaches and different questions being asked. For example, Atwater and Niehaus (1994) show (using demand

Table 3.2 National demographic composition of whites and blacks in selected occupations (%)

	Executive/ managerial	*Professional*	*Service*	*Machine operator*	*Laborer*
White (%)	90.2	88.6	78.7	80.6	9.5
Black (%)	6.2	6.9	17.3	14.8	15.9

Source: Bureau of Labor Statistics, US Department of Labor (1994), *Employment and Earnings*, 41(1), p. 204

models) that there will be fewer changes in the diversity of the workforce in the year 2000, no shortage of technical skills in a declining market, (using a supply model) that there will be a serious decline in employment of black males, and a shortage of opportunities for white males across occupational classifications. Obviously, whether the generally accepted approach or that of Atwater and Niehaus prevails remains to be seen. The issue is that there is more than one perspective on what will happen in the labor market by the year 2000. HR planners must be ready to recognize the diversity therein whatever the future brings.

While precise figures concerning the numbers and types of disabled workers are not available, there are some estimates of the proportion of the population who exhibit some disability. According to the Minnesota State Council on disability, on average, 17 percent of the population is disabled and among the disabled, 60 percent are mobility impaired.

We also know that there are fairly dramatic differences in terms of diversity representation across jobs and occupations. For example, using data collected based on a random sample of over 800 individuals representing the North Carolina workforce in 1989, Tomaskovic-Devey (1993) finds that while females comprise 52.6 percent of the workforce, they are more typically represented in clerical jobs where they comprise 81.8 percent. Females also represent 41.3 percent of managers, which is not particularly high compared to their representation in the labor force and suggests a "glass ceiling" effect. Similarly, while 21.6 percent of the workforce is made up of black workers, they are more heavily represented in laborer (30.9 percent) and operative (31.9 percent) occupational groups, a finding which is not at all surprising. Nor is black representation among managerial jobs particularly high (10.7 percent) compared to their participation in the labor force.

Local labor markets also show differential representation of diverse groups across different jobs and occupations. Organizations typically consult Census data to determine the degree of minority representation in local communities to determine the degree to which their organization's demographics match those of the relevant local labor market. For example, Table 3.2 details data concerning the representation of whites and African-Americans in the national labor market for certain job types as of 1993.

What is the impact of these supply type data for HRP activities? Such

Table 3.3 Pool size: 1993 doctorate recipients

	White	Foreign	Native American	Asian	Black	Hispanic
Life sciences	4,301	2,407	14	219	122	126
Physical sciences	3,109	2,818	11	182	41	89
Social sciences	4,396	1,397	19	104	205	182
Engineering	1,888	3,249	2	218	41	56
Humanities	3,171	835	13	60	95	130

Source: Summary Report, 1993 Doctorate Recipients, US Universities. Washington, DC: National Academy of Sciences, National Research Council, Doctorate Records Project, 1995

data permit HR planners a glimpse of what the existing labor market looks like in terms of diversity activities. Perhaps those firms with an MDS will review such market data more carefully in attempting to locate talent from diverse populations. It certainly appears that there is a relative shortage of diverse workers with professional skills and knowledge. In addition, there appear to be future skill and ability shortages across the entire job spectrum. As was pointed out in Johnston and Packer (1987), the labor force of the next several decades will have severe skill shortages relative to the demands of the labor market. Future entrants to the world of work will be lacking in many of the necessary basic job skills which employers will be seeking.

Such information also helps HR planners understand that the education and training pipeline for minorities is relatively small and extended. For example, a recent *Science* magazine article details the relative shortage of minorities with PhDs. Table 3.3 presents the pool size for 1993 doctoral recipients. It is obvious that there is a dearth of US minority group individuals receiving higher-level degrees; thus the labor market for members of these groups with higher educational levels may be characterized by more difficulty in recruiting in the future. The pipeline is and will continue to be very narrow for minorities and diverse labor pools in certain occupations; organizations with different postures may take different measures in their attempt to recruit from this pipeline of individuals. While all organizations may need to pay wage premiums, those organizations incorporating either an MDS or a BDS may go beyond this in their efforts to attract and retain diverse individuals. Such organizations may sponsor education and training for individuals not yet in the organization (e.g. high school work/ study programs), provide even more training for lower-level employees, etc., with the efforts of organizations in an MDS being more progressive and rigorous than those of BDS organizations. For example, Pacific Bell (an organization we would place in an MDS or a BDS) attempts to broaden and deepen its applicant pool to include more diverse external labor pools (primarily Hispanic) through summer internships and scholarships (Gottfredson, 1992). Similarly, Xerox has been known to develop relationships with schools and black community organizations which allow them recruiting access to top black graduates. Organizations in an RDS may be content with merely offering the wage premium and hoping that this alone will be enough to attract these diversity class individuals. Finally, organizations in an ADS may make attempts to avoid the recruitment of these individuals.

Part of the increased difficulty involved in HRP stems from the fact that diversity considerations require planners to recognize and deal with more than just the types and numbers of workers who are needed. With diversity, HRP considerations have to be given to fulfilling associated needs and aspirations of the diverse workforce. Some of the more obvious examples include considerations given to the work site modifications necessary to accommodate the disabled, the extra space and facilities required to deal with such issues as day care for employees' children, and the more diverse menus in the cafeteria necessary to accommodate eating needs and styles of different workers. Other less obvious examples include the ability to provide evaluation systems and upward mobility opportunities perceived as fair and acceptable by the diverse workers. This means the job of the planner is far more encompassing and holistic than it ever has been. Forecasting will still be an essential part of HRP but planning will also need to encompass managing and programming for diverse employees once they have been recruited and hired.

Impact of Diversity on the Assessment of Internal Labor Supply

While the presentation here is nontechnical, it should be recognized that various quantitative and non-quantitative HRP models have been developed over the years. These are used to describe and estimate the occupational movement of workers within the organization, help establish HR objectives, and assess the success of the organization in meeting those objectives.

One obvious planning technique is simply to descriptively assess the numbers and percentages of diversity classifications represented in the various jobs and classification levels within the organization. Such data are often used to determine if particular jobs have relative under- or over-representation of certain groups. Tomaskovic-Devey (1993) states that men and women rarely work in the same jobs in the same organizations and goes on to state that *token* integration of diversity class individuals is much more common than is demographic balance (emphasis added). Thus, in states like Minnesota, New York, and Washington and cities like Colorado Springs, Colorado, and San Jose, California public organizations are required to review their compensation programs *vis à vis* female and male "dominated" jobs to determine if female dominated jobs are under-compensated compared to comparably valued male dominated jobs; in Wisconsin public entities are required to make the comparison on a race-based basis as well (Roth and Azevedo, 1995). An obvious method to avoid pay equity compensation claims allowed by comparable worth legislation is for

Box 3.1   Diversity and international HRP: the case of the European Union

One of the most challenging tasks is mixing diversity and has occurred in the European Union. Following the Treaty of Rome in 1957, the Single European Act of 1986, the adoption of a "Social Charter" in 1989, and the Treaty of Maastricht in 1992, Europe has evolved toward a single labor market where workers are free to move from country to country to obtain employment (Addison and Siebert, 1991; Thompson, 1994). This diversity of workers has provided both promise and challenge for the European HR planner.

The task of opening up the European Union to free movement of workers was accomplished by providing broad citizenship rights which were to be honored by all countries. This means employers planning to meet HR needs in any given country must face the potential of filling a job opening with a foreign worker by providing for that worker's integration into the workforce as well as dealing with merging that worker's family into the larger economic and social environment of the host country. In perhaps no other situation in the world have the problems of mixing diversity and HRP been as large.

It remains to be seen how the movement of diverse workers throughout Europe will affect the planning of organizations there where, in general, HRP has been practiced more widely than in the United States (Bryant, 1965). The geographically constrained labor markets in these countries and the corresponding limits on available HR have required organizations to work more effectively to ensure full utilization of available workers. Some European countries – including France, Germany, and Switzerland – have planned for the importation of diverse groups of foreign workers as part of their national HRP (Aubert, 1989; Piore, 1979). This has not always worked in the long run because of nationalism and feelings of job deprivation toward "foreigners" on the part of domestic workers (Martin, 1980). Just as recent attacks on "affirmative action" have occurred in the United States because white males believe they are deprived of jobs which have been given to minorities and women, so too have there been attacks (including violence) on foreign workers in European countries by host country workers who feel that their work is being given to "outsiders" (ECC, 1993).

organizations to identity jobs which have differential rates of participation and to hire or move individuals into these underrepresented jobs.

Obtaining a descriptive "fix" on the age distribution of an organization may also serve as useful information to HR planners and executives. For example, such a data base may permit the inference that a large portion of the current labor force is nearing retirement and replacements will need to be found, benefit programs may need to be examined, and so forth.

More complex procedures can be used to assess the mobility of diverse labor pools within the organization across jobs and time. Markov models allow the identification of the transition probabilities among individuals across jobs (Heneman and Sandver, 1977); career path models allow examination of chains of movement through the organization; and transition models look at hierarchical movements within the firm (Hooper and Catalanello, 1981). In the case of each of these models, it is possible to assess the traditional or historical movement of workers among the organization's jobs. They allow the identification of jobs with good opportunities for advancement, jobs where advancement rates may be acceptable, those jobs which are dead-end and permit no or limited mobility, and jobs which experience greater or less turnover or exit routes to outside the organization. By so doing, the planner obtains a visual understanding of occupational movement within the organization which serves several useful purposes in a world of diversity.

These tools allow the organization to identify the promotion and transfer paths that currently (and historically) exist in the organization. Also, by implementing and assessing such models on the basis of the diversity classifications, it is possible to determine the lines of job opportunity available and those closed to particular groups of workers. Finally, these models allow the organization to benchmark the diversity status of all of its jobs such that it is possible to assess the organization's success in attaining its objectives. Obviously, there is circularity here as these models/tools affect both the establishment of HR objectives and the measurement of success in fully achieving them.

It is these models which can identify analytically the "glass ceiling," which has been defined as "those artificial barriers based on attitudinal or organizational bias that prevent qualified individuals from advancing upward in their organizations into management-level positions" (US Department of Labor, 1991). From an HRP perspective, the designation glass ceiling may be attached to *any* barriers within the organization which limit the promotional and growth opportunities of employees in an artificial way. One of the reasons behind the existence of a glass ceiling is attributed to the inability of the minority to meld with the majority culture. As an example, a high percentage of male managers is likely to create a culture that is mostly male and indifferent or hostile to women's advancement. Women report they are ignored, not taken seriously, and shunted into support jobs far from their organization's core business where there is little chance of breaking through the glass ceiling. Even those companies that make extraordinary efforts to recruit and promote women often fail to make the culture hospitable to them (Sharpe, 1994). According to a New York women's research and advocacy group, women in sales have had a hard time advancing because they find it difficult to entertain customers in traditional ways such as fishing and golf outings (Shellenbarger, 1995).

This identification process has implications for many of the HRP activities in the organization. Indeed, the recognition of problem situations through the use of specific quantitative models sets the stage for the full array of

HRP activities which can help the organization achieve the diversity balance it seeks.

A potential limitation imposed on HRP efforts to assess the current internal labor supply is that such efforts might actually expose the organization to litigation. One of the authors (Arvey) has given expert testimony in a court case involving an organization being charged with age discrimination. Part of the evidence used by the plaintiffs to demonstrate age bias are the HRP documents where the executive management attempted to learn of retirement plans for employees over 60 years of age. The use of age data in identifying potential retirees is claimed to be evidence of age discrimination. Thus, one of the potential problems of using diversity classification data in HRP efforts is legal exposure.

Organizations can attempt to expand their internal supply of individuals representing diverse characteristics in a number of different ways. Such employees may be "fast tracked," given special training and development opportunities, provided mentors, assigned to pivotal jobs that provide critical experience, and so forth in order to develop and enlarge internal talent. Such an approach has been used by Xerox, where it focused on what it termed "pivotal jobs." To create upward mobility among women and minorities, the company examined the backgrounds of top executives and identified the so-called pivotal jobs these managers had once held. Xerox then set goals for getting minorities and women assigned to these jobs and helped develop their talent pools through on-the-job training.

The other significant problem associated with maintaining a constant supply of employees is the fact that companies find it difficult to retain a diverse workforce. While it is relatively easy to hire women and employees from different racial backgrounds, many of them face a plateau, lose their drive and quit or get terminated (Thomas, 1990). However, with well-implemented diversity programs, some firms in fact have been able to reduce their minority turnover. Ortho Pharmaceutical, a division of Johnson and Johnson, has tracked its minority turnover as a result of its managing diversity program started in 1986. They experienced a reduction in their turnover from twice the minority representation to one equal to the minority representation. The USDA Forest Services also boasts of one of the highest minority retention rates in the nation.

Managing disparate talents to achieve common goals is the challenge behind diversity. For this, it is important to develop a corporate culture that encourages employees to examine their assumptions, values, and differences. It also requires appraisal systems to be developed that are perceived as fair by all employees. Stereotyping and other biases of supervisors may lead to the use of differential evaluation standards for the same level of performance.

Moreover, the special efforts necessary to keep the diverse talent that exists in the organization, and to avoid loss due to dissatisfaction and/or being lured away by other organizations, may have large payoffs. The advantages to the employer of expanding and developing a supply of internal talent of diverse employees are obvious, including recruitment costs being reduced, training time cut, and specific human capital development being sustained.

Implications of Diversity on Assessment of Demand for Labor

There are a number of methods by which organizations have traditionally attempted to forecast the kinds of labor as well as the number of employees needed to meet organizational objectives. These range from ground-up estimates where individual managers estimate their needs over a fixed time horizon (say one year) to elaborate Delphi studies which look at the entire framework of goods and/or services to be provided by the organization over an extended period of time (three to five years) to determine the necessary future occupational composition of the workforce.

Organizations may fear that planning for diversity will require substantial work above and beyond what is currently done; this is not necessarily the case. The process of job analysis, for example, reviews jobs without explicit or implicit consideration of the race, ethnic background, or gender of the incumbent. Similarly, the design of new jobs in response to changing directions of the organization generally does not require designing or configuring tasks and duties as a function of race, gender, and so forth. In fact, to do so might expose the organization to Title VII lawsuits. In developing estimates of an organization's labor requirements, the idea is to precisely define job requirements in terms of the tasks, duties, and responsibilities of the positions as well as the corresponding incumbent knowledge, skills, abilities, and other characteristics (KSAOs) which are necessary to perform the job. From these processes the organization can subsequently develop the machinery necessary to acquire in the external and internal labor markets the people to meet its HR needs. There are two elements to these processes which we believe are more central to diversity considerations when developing the demand specifications of jobs.

The first involves possible additional effort required when dealing with questions of physically handicapped or otherwise impaired workers. Partly in response to the requirements imposed by the Americans with Disabilities Act (1990), organizations are developing greater specificity concerning the physical demands of jobs. That is, more sophisticated methods are being used to learn about the physical demands imposed by the execution of the various tasks, duties, and responsibilities associated with jobs/positions. For example, figure 3.1 presents a form used by one organization to analyze the physical requirements of positions within the firm.

Arvey et al. (1992) used a variety of job analytic techniques (i.e. critical incidents, task inventory, literature reviews) to develop an understanding of the physical requirements for the performance of police officer jobs. The use of such techniques may permit organizations to determine more precisely

Figure 3.1 Employer job description

Identifying Information	Employee's Name		Job Title	Location

Note: In terms of a workday, "Occasionally" equals 1% to 33%; "Frequently," 34% to 66%; Continuously," 67% to 100%.

In a work day, employee must: (Check full capacity for each activity)

Sit	☐ No	☐ 1	☐ 2	☐ 3	☐ 4	☐ 5	☐ 6	☐ 7	☐ 8	☐ 9	☐ 10	☐ 11	☐ 12 (hrs)
Stand	☐ No	☐ 1	☐ 2	☐ 3	☐ 4	☐ 5	☐ 6	☐ 7	☐ 8	☐ 9	☐ 10	☐ 11	☐ 12 (hrs)
Walk	☐ No	☐ 1	☐ 2	☐ 3	☐ 4	☐ 5	☐ 6	☐ 7	☐ 8	☐ 9	☐ 10	☐ 11	☐ 12 (hrs)

Employee's job requires:	Not at all	Occasionally	Frequently	Continuously	Comments
Bend/Stoop					
Squat					
Crawl					
Climb height					
Reach above shoulder level					
Crouch					
Kneel					
Balance					
Push/Pull					

Employee's job requires he/she carry:	Never	Occasionally	Frequently	Continuously	Comments
Up to 10 lbs.					
11–24 lbs.					
25–34 lbs.					
35–50 lbs.					
51–74 lbs.					
75–100 lbs.					

Employee's job requires he/she lift:	Never	Occasionally	Frequently	Continuously	Comments
Up to 10 lbs.					
11–24 lbs.					
25–50 lbs.					
51–74 lbs.					
75–100 lbs.					

Job requires employee use feet for repetitive movements as in operating foot controls:

Right	☐ Yes ☐ No	Left	☐ Yes ☐ No	Both	☐ Yes ☐ No			
Left	☐ Yes ☐ No	Left	☐ Yes ☐ No	Both	☐ Yes ☐ No			

Job requires employee use hands for repetitive action such as:

	Simple grasping	Firm grasping	Fine manipulating
Right	☐ Yes ☐ No	☐ Yes ☐ No	☐ Yes ☐ No

Employee's job requires: Comments

Working on unprotected heights	☐ Yes ☐ No	_____
Being around moving machinery	☐ Yes ☐ No	_____
Exposure to marked changes in temp. and humidity	☐ Yes ☐ No	_____
Driving automotive equipment	☐ Yes ☐ No	_____
Exposure to dust, fumes and gases	☐ Yes ☐ No	_____

Job requires employee to use head and neck in:

Static position ☐ Yes ☐ No   Frequent flexing ☐ Yes ☐ No   Frequent rotating ☐ Yes ☐ No

Comments (if appropriate, not frequency per hour or day)

Job can be modified: (if yes, specify)

	Title	Date
Employer Representative Signature ▶		

the physical demands of jobs and therefore allow the recruitment and selection of disabled individuals into jobs when they can perform the essential functions. The development of such data would permit an organization to proactively recruit disabled individuals, identify disabled applicants who could perform such jobs, discourage discriminatory activities, and so forth.

The second element is that certain jobs and positions might be identified where the KSAOs of diverse applicants would be necessary, such as foreign language skills, knowledge of local neighborhoods, and similar qualifications. These KSAOs could be very useful in terms of helping the organization meet specific labor needs. For example, a police department might find through their job analysis efforts that the job effectiveness will be enhanced for officers who have specific neighborhood knowledge, who understand certain dialects, who are familiar with the problems of inner city children, and so forth. Prudential Global Advisors have found their diverse workforce to be a distinct advantage because of their ability to deal with minority clients. The workforce composition allows the clients to feel more comfortable than in dealing with other stereotypical Wall Street firms. Another interesting example where KSAOs of a diverse workforce may be necessary is that of Voice Processing Corporation, a small business manufacturing software that allows machines to process voice commands. A diverse workforce has been central to the successful foreign expansion of this company (Selz, 1994).

For these firms, the identification of such specific KSAOs might lead to the recruitment and selection of a more diverse workforce than if such KSAOs were not identified. The point we are developing here is that while these characteristics are not *inherently* involved in tasks, duties, and responsibilities associated with jobs, the KSAOs required might be more characteristic of applicants from more diverse labor pools than a traditional white male labor market.

A final trend related to the assessment of the demand for labor concerns complexity changes among modern jobs. Data suggest that more complex knowledge, skills, and abilities are needed to perform most jobs being created in our industrial economy, and that the complexity level of jobs is increasing for even traditional relatively lower-skill jobs. Johnston and Packer (1987) indicate that among the fastest-growing jobs, the trend toward higher educational requirements is striking. "Of all the new jobs that will be created over the 1984–2000 period, more than half will require education beyond high school, and almost a third will be filled by college graduates. Today, only 22 percent of all occupations require a college degree" (p. 97). From the perspective of hiring a more diverse workforce, these data are somewhat disturbing; the picture for unskilled African-American and Hispanic males in terms of their future job opportunities is somewhat dim because of their relatively low educational and skill achievements compared to the higher and more complex skills required for future jobs (1987, pp. 101–3).

How Diversity Impacts the Human Resource Objectives Set by the Organization

It is the imbalance between demand for and supply of – internal and external – workers that poses the most challenging questions for the HR planner. Organizations must now set goals and objectives targeting the kinds of talent and numbers of people needed or, conversely, decide what kinds of talent is least needed and where to reduce workers. Additionally, organizations must decide what the appropriate mix of diverse workers should be across the organization and in what jobs.

Earlier it was noted that organizations may plan for diversity by: (1) making explicit efforts to hire specifically targeted diverse labor pools (aggressive affirmative action); (2) setting targets in terms of specific talents needed (e.g. language skills, etc.) which tend to be associated with diverse labor pools; or (3) ignoring diversity in setting objectives.

A typical response of organizations to any shortfall in the utilization of diverse work groups is to engage in the development of affirmative action plans. Such a plan is intended to establish goals and timetables for the achieving of equal employment opportunity in the organization (Cherrington, 1991). And one must not be misled into thinking that affirmative action plans are a practice of the past, especially in a planning context.

A careful reading of the recent Supreme Court decision, *Adarand Constructors, Inc. v. Federico Pena, et al.* {115 S.Ct. 2097, 132 L.Ed. 2d 158, 16 FEP 1828 (1995)}, shows that the Court did not rule out affirmative action plans as some have contended. What it really did was to argue that all such plans must meet what is termed the "strict judicial scrutiny" standard in determining whether they are valid HRP activities. This is a stronger standard than either an "intermediate judicial scrutiny" (which was created as new law in this case) or a standard of "rational relationship to a legitimate government interest." What the Court has done is remand back to the lower courts the process of determining precisely what "strict scrutiny" means in these affirmative action programs so that, in a real sense the *legal* status of such programs awaits judicial determination and is likely to be a long time in the determination.

It should be evident, therefore, that the *practical* status of well designed affirmative action plans is such as to provide the advantage of focusing attention on the HR needs of the organization, identifying potential answers to those needs, and establishing the strategies for making those answers operational regardless of how they are implemented. In this context, the employer is required to analyze thoroughly both the organization's workforce and the local (or otherwise relevant) labor market to identify possible underutilization of protected class workers and establish goals and timetables to ensure that these diverse workers are brought into the fold. Obviously, the affirmative action plan is an important component of HRP.

But there are limitations associated with these plans as well. Available

Table 3.4 Comparison of rates of change in size: major demographic groups in Minneapolis, Minnesota, 1980 and 1990

Racial group	1980	1990	Annual rate of change (%)
White	323,831	288,967	−1.3
Black	28,433	47,948	5.9
Asian/Pacific	4,104	15,723	16.1
Native American	8,933	12,335	3.7
Hispanic[a]	4,684	7,900	5.9

[a] Individuals of Hispanic origin may be of any race.
Source: *Minneapolis Population and Racial Change, 1950–1990.* Minneapolis, MN: Minneapolis City Planning Department, 1991

labor market data often are not of sufficient quality to make the types of determinations an organization needs in deciding on future HR utilization. Employers seeking certain occupational groups may find that the numbers detailed in relevant labor markets are unobtainable or aggregated in a fashion which makes them useless. Moreover, as most labor market data that provide occupation, race, and ethnic background information come from the decennial Census of Population, there is typically a substantial time lag between collection and ultimate use of the data by an employer; the entire characteristics of the labor market may have changed during that period.

This can be a particularly important problem when the demographic changes in the labor market are dramatic. Consider table 3.4 which reports the changes in the size of demographic groups in Minneapolis, Minnesota, between 1989 and 1990. The *annual* rates of increase of the minority groups were all above 3 percent and the rate was over 16 percent for Asians and Pacific Islanders. Such rates of change can play havoc with any affirmative action plan and its implementation.

A second major problem with affirmative action is that in hiring or in promotions it provides, at best, opportunity for job entry but little else. Thus, managers typically institute an affirmative action program and then "await" results (Thomas, 1990). The reason that such initiatives come undone, according to Thomas, is that affirmative action programs are artificial, whereas challenges from diversity require continuous attention and effort to reality. Because of inadequate upward mobility opportunities or a hostile culture subsequent to the recruitment effort, minorities show a higher propensity to leave a given employer and can turn promising results around.

A third issue associated with the traditional efforts to expand diversity is that, in their current form, interventions such as affirmative action programs may lead to a perception of reverse discrimination by the majority group. On the other hand, minority and other diverse employee groups (as well as non-minority employees) find these programs offensive because there is often a stigmatization associated with them which suggests that such diverse workers are less qualified than white male counterparts (Heilman et al., 1992). Kravitz and Platania (1993) found that employees preferred other forms of recruitment and selection in terms of bringing in diverse employees but disapproved of quota and/or preferential treatment strategies.

In setting objectives, the diversity-cognizant planner must realize that planning for broad-based HR utilization requires a profound awareness of the differences, indeed sometimes conflict, among different cultures. The arrivals from South East Asia are examples of the phenomenon; the Cambodians, the Vietnamese, and the Japanese have a variety of longstanding cultural conflicts. Setting diversity goals without taking these potential conflicts into account could lead to organizational dysfunctions. From the planning perspective, the American organization which establishes a diversity program and then, in quite good faith, places a Japanese in charge of implementation may find that there could be immediate conflicts between the various ethnic groups and the diversity director. We need to work to achieve our business goals while recognizing and valuing the differences among individuals (Gordon, 1992). HRP must become part of the organizational culture; all the HRP in the world will do no good if the organization's culture will not accept it. Cries of "It won't work here," "We've never done it that way," and "We don't want *them* working with us!" can torpedo the best developed diversity planning efforts.

Impact of Diversity on the Use of HR Practices in Achieving Objectives

There are several issues and problems associated with achieving objectives in terms of hiring and promoting diverse employees. One problem that emerges is the issue of "critical mass." Organizations planning for diversity often find themselves "spinning their wheels" because of the inability to bring enough diverse workers into the organization. The problem here is that it may take a critical mass of diverse workers in order for such employees to feel welcome and accepted. A sincere effort at planning for and implementing the entrance of one or two diverse workers into the organization may fall flat because of the sense of isolation and/or overexposure in the role as "token" (Kanter, 1977). To illustrate the contrast, during the 1980s, Stanford University became a mecca for black physics students; one graduate student commented that the number of black graduate students in the program had reached "critical mass" (Culotta, 1993).

Another problem with achieving diversity objectives is simply that it may take considerable time. Investigation of the workings of job promotion and transfer mechanisms in organizations show that the processes are slow, almost cumbersome, in that it takes long periods of time before organizations with the best of intentions begin to show a complete demographic profile which reflects their objectives and efforts. Turnover is often relatively slow in organizations and attempts to change the HR characteristics of an organization can be impeded by the workforce already in place even in the organization with the best of intentions (Steffy and Ledvinka, 1986). Things may be further slowed by increased turnover among those diverse individuals one wants to keep, a point to be expanded below, because it is generally more difficult to keep minority and female workers if good job opportunities also are available elsewhere.

Finally, the nature of underlying business conditions may limit achieving diversity objectives. Xerox found it much easier to reshape the demographic composition of workers when the organization was growing. When expanding, organizations are hiring and promoting with greater frequency; this allows faster achievement of diversity goals. Conversely, under conditions where expansion is slow or nonexistent, or during cutbacks or downsizing, the organization is not hiring or promoting with such frequency. Therefore, changing the demographic composition will require a significantly longer time frame.

It is the purpose of other chapters in this book to discuss the impact of diversity on recruitment and selection. However, we mention a few themes which we believe are relevant here. First, organizations might need to pursue special recruitment methods to attract qualified diverse labor pools. For example, different recruitment methods might provide greater "yields" of qualified diversity group members than somewhat traditional methods. For example, it might be that the use of current employees as a source for recruitment might be a more effective method of identifying top-quality diverse candidates than newspaper advertising (Neckerman and Kirschenman, 1991).

Another aspect of recruitment methods of diverse labor pools has to do with the relative time lags involved during the recruitment process. A study by Arvey et al. (1975) showed that organizations having substantial delays between the various selection hurdles (e.g. time between testing and an interview) tend to lose a greater proportion of minority group members. The implication of this study is that to keep diverse applicants in the recruitment pipeline, greater efforts should be made to streamline the recruitment and selection process.

Second, we believe that organizations might want to showcase their diversity efforts in their recruitment methods. One of us (Arvey) conducted a small study examining college student reactions to a random sample of college recruitment videotapes used to help attract candidates. The tapes which enjoyed the most positive reactions were those that featured aspects of a diverse workforce prominently. That is, tapes that included actors with ranges of age and race and that included females and disabled employees were rated much more favorably than videos featuring only white males.

Similarly, consider the marketing strategies of Wal-Mart. One sees television and newspaper advertising which includes sales associates of both genders and a variety of ethnic groups. While these are intended to draw a diversity of customers into Wal-Mart stores, they also can serve the purpose of publicizing the diversity of the workforce at Wal-Mart and indicate that those who are seeking employment could find a home there. By combining diversity in advertising with diversity in employment, the culture of this organization appears to display a welcome air to all.

There are also several issues related to the selection of diverse workers. It is well known that certain racial minorities perform less well on cognitive tests often used in screening applicants (Arvey and Faley, 1988). While these tests demonstrate relatively high validities across almost all jobs, organizations might consider trading off productivity yields associated with using such tests and adopt alternative selection procedures with the objective of hiring greater numbers of diverse workers. The employment interview, for example, appears to have higher validity than once believed (McDaniel et al., 1994), but does not appear to have as much adverse impact as cognitive tests when screening minorities (Arvey and Faley, 1988). Greater reliance might be given to this particular subjective decision-making tool when selecting employees compared to cognitive testing procedures in order to increase the yield of diverse candidates in the screening processes.

But perhaps of greatest significance for the HR planner coping with a diverse world is the need to change the orientation of the HR function in the organization which often reflects a conflict between traditional HRP and planning for diversity. As Ferris et al. (1993) point out, the basic nature of the HR function in the organization is intended to reinforce homogeneity rather than diversity. HR practitioners work to select, hire, promote, and transfer those who have the same ideologies, work values, and cultures as those who already inhabit the organization. Kanter (1977) talks of the selection and promotion processes in the organization as "homosocial reproduction systems," reflecting their role of maintaining the status quo rather than accepting a world of diversity.

Another component of this issue has been raised in studies of the "fit" of workers for the organization. Judge and Ferris (1992) talk of a model in which "fit" is the primary consideration in the selection and promotion processes in an organization. Based on this model, the overall fit of the worker often is more important than specific skills and abilities for the job. Thus, organizations may function suboptimally by selecting people who seem to fit but do not have the requisite skills (Ferris and King, 1991).

In light of these issues, Miron et al. (1993) point to the need for reengineering the entire range of HR processes, and the role of the HR planners in helping to design and build the systems which move forward from the present to the future. This means, for many organizations, the redesign of the hiring, promotion, and compensation practices which are at present intended to reward those who "fit" – those who replicate what already exists in the organization – and to punish those who are "outsiders" in any sense of the word.

All of this need for change is especially crucial when one considers that many diverse workers are bicultural and, while they strive to "fit in" to their organizations, they still maintain the norms and value systems of their native culture. What organizations should do is strive for mutual accommodation as cultures meet rather than attempt to force minorities to assimilate to a dominant culture (Cox et al., 1991). The changing demographics in the US speak to a world quite different from the one organizations are used to and an environment which must be fully recognized in order to be successful.

Summary and Conclusions

It has been the premise of this chapter that there are a number of implications of a diverse workforce on HRP activities in the firm. We argued above that diverse workers will be a growing segment of the supply of labor for firms. We also argued that while there are not explicit components of jobs which attach directly to diverse workers, firms could develop more specific information about jobs and positions which would permit the recruitment and selection of more diverse workers, such as the disabled, etc. We outlined some of the postures firms might take when engaging in setting HR goals and objectives *vis à vis* their position on whether to attract and promote diverse workers. Some firms will engage in aggressive activities to acquire and deploy diverse talent; other firms will be much less aggressive. We also developed specific issues associated with the mechanisms by which diverse talent may be recruited and selected. Finally, we pointed out the role of the HR planner in moving the HR management function away from a traditional view toward an orientation where diversity becomes an accepted and integrated part of the operation.

This chapter has been relatively void of research citations and contributions, reflecting the status of the literature. We believe much more research effort could be devoted to understanding some of the issues developed here. In fact, the chapter was frustrating to write because of the paucity of research literature associated with diversity and HRP efforts. With the exception of research detailing the labor supply demographics, we uncovered very little on diversity and HRP directly. Such research questions as the following need to be pursued:

- Are "pipelines" for diversity class individuals truly constricted for certain occupations? If so, for what occupations, and what are the impacts of these narrower "pipelines" on firm efforts to recruit, select, and retain diverse job candidates?
- What happens when the different firms all compete for the same talent among diverse job candidates?
- Where should recruitment efforts be best targeted to attract diverse job candidates?
- How should firms decide what particular posture they will take with regard to attracting, selecting, and promoting diverse applicants and employees? Are there such postures and what are their determinants, if they exist?
- How do firms develop a "culture" which permits the encouragement of recruiting and selecting employees as well as the promotion of diverse workers?

- How does the HR planner design a system which emphasizes the importance of diversity to the organizations?
- What are the resistance points in moving from a traditional form of HR management to a form which encourages diversity?

It is the answers to these questions which will provide the foundation for the HRP function in the coming century. It is here that HRP will make its full contribution to the strategic planning of the organization (Ansoff, 1984).

REFERENCES

Addison, J. T., and Siebert, W. S. (1991). The Social Charter of the European Community: Evolution and controversies. *Industrial and Labor Relations Review*, 44(4), July, 597–625.

Ansoff, H. I. (1984). *Implanting Strategic Management*. Englewood Cliffs, NJ: Prentice-Hall.

Arvey, R. D., and Faley, R. A. (1988). *Fairness in Selecting Employees*, 2nd ed. New York: Addison-Wesley.

Arvey, R. D., Gordon, M. E., Massengill, D. P., and Mussio, S. J. (1975). Differential dropout rates of minority and majority job candidates due to "time lags" between selection procedures. *Personnel Psychology*, 28, 175–80.

Arvey, R. D., Landon, T. E., Nutting, S. M., and Maxwell, S. E. (1992). Development of physical abilities tests for police officers: A construct validation approach. *Journal of Applied Psychology Monograph*, 77(6), 996–1013.

Atwater, D. M., and Niehaus, R. J. (1994). Diversity implications from an occupational human resource forecast for the year 2000. *Human Resource Planning*, 16(4), April, 29–50.

Aubert, G. (1989). Collective agreements and industrial peace in Switzerland. *International Labor Review*, 128(1), 373–88.

Barnum, P. (1991). Misconceptions about the future US work force: Implications for strategic planning. *Human Resource Planning*, 14(3), 209–19.

Bryant, D. T. (1965). A survey of the development of manpower planning policies. *British Journal of Industrial Relations*, 3(3): 279–90.

Bureau of Labor Statistics, US Dept. of Labor (1994). *Employment and Earnings*, January, 41(1).

Cascio, W. F. (1992). *Managing Human Resources: Productivity, Quality of Work Life, Profits*, 3rd ed. New York: McGraw-Hill.

Cherrington, D. J. (1991). *The Management of Human Resources*. Boston: Allyn and Bacon.

Cox, T., Jr, and Blake, S. (1991). Managing cultural diversity: Implications for organizational competitiveness. *The Executive*, 5, 45–56.

Cox, T. H., Lobel, S. A., and McLeod, P. L. (1991). Effects of ethnic group cultural differences on cooperative and competitive behavior on a group task. *Academy of Management Journal*, 34(4), 827–47.

Culotta, E. (1993). Trying to change the face of science. *Science*, 262(12), 1089–96.

ECC (European Community – Commission) (1993). *Legal Instruments to Combat Racism and Xenophobia*. Luxembourg: Office for Official Publications of the European Community.

Ferris, G. R., Fink, D. D., and Galang, M. C. (1993). Diversity in the workplace. *Human Resource Planning*, 16(1), 41–51.

Ferris, G. R., and King T. R. (1991). Politics in human resource decisions: A walk on the dark side. *Organizational Dynamics*, 20(2), 59–71.

Galbraith, J. R., and Nathanson, D. A. (1978). *Strategy Implementation: The Role of Structure and Process.* St Paul, MN: West Publishing.

Glass Ceiling Commission, US Dept. of Labor (1991). *A Report on the Glass Ceiling Initiative.* Washington, DC: US Dept. of Labor.

Gordon, J. (1992). Rethinking diversity. *Training*, January, 23–30.

Gottfredson, L. S. (1992). Dilemmas in developing diversity programs. In S. Jackson (ed.), *Diversity in the Workplace: Human Resource Initiatives.* New York: Guilford Press.

Hamermesh, Richard G. (1986). *Making Strategy Work.* New York: John Wiley.

Heilman, M. E., Block, C. J., and Lucas, J. A. (1992). Presumed incompetent? Stigmatization and affirmative action efforts. *Journal of Applied Psychology*, 77(4), 536–44.

Heneman, H. G., and Sandver, M. G. (1977). Markov analysis in human resource administration: Applications and limitations. *Academy of Management Review*, 2(4), 535–42.

Hooper, J. A., and Catalanello, R. T. (1981). Markov analysis applied to forecasting technical personnel. *Human Resource Planning*, 4(2), 41–54.

Jackson, S. E., and Schuler, R. S. (1990). Human resource planning: Challenges for industrial/organizational psychologists. *American Psychologist*, 45(2), 223–39.

Jackson, S. E., May, K. E., and Whitney K. (forthcoming). Understanding the dynamics of diversity in decision making teams. In R. A. Guzzo and E. Salas (eds), *Team Decision Making Effectiveness in Organizations.* San Francisco: Jossey-Bass.

Johnston, W. B., and Packer, A. H. (1987). Workforce 2000: *Work and Workers in the 21st Century.* Indianapolis: Hudson Institute.

Judge, T., and Ferris, G. R. (1992). The elusive criterion of fit in human resource staffing decisions. *Human Resource Planning*, 15(4), 47–68.

Kanter, R. M. (1977). *Men and Women of the Organization.* New York: Basic Books.

Kravitz, D. A., and Platania, J. (1993). Attitudes and beliefs about affirmative action: Effects of target and of respondent sex and ethnicity. *Journal of Applied Psychology*, 78(6), 928–38.

Lott, A. J., and Lott, B. E. (1965). Group cohesiveness and interpersonal attraction: A review of relationships with antecedent and consequent variables. *Psychological Bulletin*, 64, 259–302.

Martin, P. L. (1980). *Guestworker Programs: Lessons from Europe.* Washington, D.C.: US Department of Labor, Bureau of International Labor Affairs, Foreign Publications Group, Monograph no. 5, US Government Printing Office.

McDaniel, M. A., Whetzel, D. L., Schmidt, F. L., and Maurer, S. D. (1994). The validity of employment interviews: A comprehensive review and meta analysis. *Journal of Applied Psychology*, 79(4), 599–616.

Metropolitan Council (1991). *1990 Census Cross-Tabulations of Age, Race, and Hispanic Origin Data for Twin Cities Metropolitan Area Communities.* St Paul, MN: Metropolitan Council.

Miron, D., Leichtman, S., and Atkins, A. (1993). Reengineering human resource processes. *Human Resource Professional*, 6(1), 19–23.

Neckerman, K. M., and Kirschenman, J. (1991). Hiring strategies, racial bias, and intercity workers. *Social Problems*, 38(4), 433–47.

Piore, M. J. (1979). *Birds of Passage: Long-Distance Migrants in Industrialized Society.* Cambridge: Cambridge University Press.

Rice, F. (1994). How to make diversity pay. *Fortune*, August 8.

Richards, E. L. (1994). *Law for Global Business*. Burr Ridge, IL: Richard D. Irwin.

Roth, L., and Azevedo, R. E. (1995). *Implementing Comparable Worth in Minnesota Local Government*. Report to the Center for Urban and Regional Affairs, University of Minnesota.

Selz, M. (1994). Enterprise: Small company goes global with diverse workforce. *Wall Street Journal*, October 12.

Sharpe, R. (1994). The waiting game: Women make strides but men stay firmly in top company jobs. *Wall Street Journal*, March 29.

Shellenbarger, S. (1995). Workplace: Sales offer women fairer pay, but bias lingers. *Wall Street Journal*, January 24.

Steffy, B. D., and Ledvinka, J. (1986). The impact of five definitions of "fair" employee selection on long-run minority employment and employee utility. Unpublished manuscript. University of Minnesota.

Taylor, C. (1995). Building a case for diversity: Workforce diversity, managing diversity. *Canadian Business Review*, March, 12.

Thomas, R. R. (1990). From affirmative action to affirming diversity. *Harvard Business Review*, March–April, 107–17.

Thompson, M. (1994). Industrial relations and free trade. Paper presented at the Joint Session of the Industrial Relations Research Association and the North American Economics and Finance Association, Boston, January 4.

Tomaskovic-Devey, D. (1993). *Gender and Racial Inequality at Work: The Sources and Consequences of Job Segregation*. Ithaca, NY: ILR Press.

Triandis, H. C., Kurowski, L. L., and Gelfand, M. J. (1990). Workplace diversity. In M. D. Dunnette and L. M. Hough (eds), *Handbook of Industrial and Organizational Psychology*, 2nd ed., vol. 4. Palo Alto, CA: Consulting Psychologists Press.

4

Diversity Considerations in Staffing Decision-making

Robert L. Heneman, Nancy E. Waldeck, and
Michele Cushnie

The need for organizations and those who study organizations to incorporate diversity considerations into staffing decision-making has never been greater. This is because of the changing nature of the labor market, jobs, and laws and regulations detailed throughout this book. Organizations must consider diversity issues in making staffing decisions in order to be competitive in the changing business environment (Cox and Blake, 1991). The goals of this chapter are to show how diversity considerations impact staffing decisions, and how organizations can use staffing procedures to meet the goals of having a multicultural workforce.

In order to achieve these goals, we begin with some background on the concepts of staffing and diversity. Next, we review the literature as it relates to the three major sets of staffing decisions: recruitment, selection, and employment. Finally, we conclude each section with the major implications of the literature review for theory development and practice.

Background

Staffing decision-making

Staffing decision-making refers to three sets of decisions made by employers to match people with jobs as they flow into and through the organization.[1] These three sets of decisions are recruitment, selection, and employment (Heneman and Heneman, 1994). Recruitment refers to the identification of job applicants in the labor market and the attraction of these applicants to the organization. Selection refers to the assessment and evaluation of applicants to see to what extent their qualifications match up with the requirements of the job. Employment refers to deciding which applicants are eventually extended an offer of hire by the organization.

Diversity

Diversity refers to segments of the labor market which have traditionally been excluded by organizations when making staffing decisions. These segments have often been overlooked when deciding where and who to recruit, who to pursue further in the selection process, and who to extend an employment offer to. Segments of the labor market that we are referring to can be categorized by age, race, sex, color, religion, national origin, disability, sexual orientation, regional orientation, culture, and long-term unemployment.

A risk we run in defining diversity in such a broad manner is that the concept becomes meaningless (Schmidt, 1993). In spite of this risk, we have chosen to use a broad definition for two reasons. First, it is consistent with the definition currently used by organizations (Carrell and Mann, 1993). In order to improve present organizational practices, we must build upon existing organizational beliefs. Second, from a theoretical perspective of staffing planning (Begin, 1991), organizations do segment labor markets by many characteristics including diversity categories. It is important to use all of the categories for our theories of staffing planning to be comprehensive.[2]

Importance of diversity to staffing

There are many reasons why organizations and those who study them need to integrate diversity considerations into staffing decision-making. From a research perspective, much of the diversity and staffing research has relied a great deal upon "shotgun empiricism." Diversity characteristics have been mechanically correlated with staffing decisions with little regard given to theories about why we might expect certain relationships. This is especially true in the study of diversity characteristics other than age, gender, and race. As a result, while we know that diversity characteristics are related to staffing decisions, we know little about "why" this is the case.

More effective staffing decisions can be made if more theoretical precision is used to integrate diversity and staffing. For example, while it is important to know that an organization does not have any women managers, it is even more important to know why this is the case. The correct response by the organization may be quite different if the lack of women managers is due to gender stereotypes or if it is due to a poorly developed selection device which inadvertently discriminates against women. In the former case training may be needed while in the latter case, a new selection device may be needed.

Using staffing practices to build a diverse workforce is also important from a business perspective. Such a workforce may help organizations to be more effective. Several studies highlight this possibility. Cox et al. (1991) found that ethnically diverse groups were more likely to act cooperatively than non-ethnically diverse groups especially when the work situation favored cooperation. Research reviewed by Triandis et al., (1990) indicates that diverse groups do well on other dimensions of effectiveness including creative and high-quality decisions.

Current practice in some companies is also consistent with the belief that diverse groups promote organizational effectiveness. As reported in Mitchell and Oneal (1994), both MCI and Levi Strauss have taken steps to emphasize diversity. This is because of the belief that diversity will decrease conformity and increase creativity in the workforce. It is also in recognition that a growing part of their customer base is diverse, and if they want to be in touch with their customer needs, they need to be represented by a diverse workforce.

Some business executives are now being held accountable for their diversity activities. For example, US West Corporation has developed a "Pluralism Performance" measure that is used to appraise the top 125 officers on how well they meet a pluralism (diversity) related criterion (Caudron, 1992). At Hoechst Celanese they have gone one step further. Not only are their performance appraisals based on diversity considerations, but so too are their subsequent pay increases (Rice, 1994).

Diversity can also create problems for the majority group in the organizations, which need to be addressed when staffing for diversity. Solomon (1991) reported that white males are feeling "left out" as diversity programs are implemented. In a review of the literature, Triandis et al. (1990) reported findings that stress and turnover may be increased with diverse work teams.

In conclusion, the integration of diversity issues into staffing decision-making is a critical step for organizations to undertake in developing a staffing strategy consistent with organizational effectiveness. They are increasingly coming to this conclusion, evidenced by the heavy emphasis placed on staffing activities in meeting diversity goals (Carrell and Mann, 1993). Care must be exercised to ensure that staffing practices are indeed contributing to the goals of diversity in organizations.

Staffing and diversity philosophy

An important component of deciding how to staff the organization is the staffing philosophy (Heneman and Heneman, 1994). One element of this is how much attention to devote to diversity considerations in making staffing decisions. Operationally, this philosophy can be spelled out in a "values" or "aspiration" statement regarding the importance of diversity activities to the organization. This statement outlines the organization's commitment to diversity, but is not frequently used currently in organizations. Only about one-third of US employers have any sort of diversity policy (Carrell and

Mann, 1993) let alone values or aspiration statement. Some organizations such as Levi Strauss, however, do have an aspiration statement which can be used as a model to follow. These statements are expected to be used more frequently in the future (Mitchell and Oneal, 1994). As will be shown throughout this chapter, the values or aspiration statement is used as a philosophical guide in making recruitment, selection, and employment decisions.

There are two major philosophical approaches to take with staffing and diversity (Carrell and Mann, 1993). Under a legalistic approach, staffing for a diverse workforce will only be done up to the point of considering those people for jobs who are legally protected. This approach is reactive as steps to staff a diverse workplace are only taken in order to be in compliance with equal employment opportunity (EEO) and affirmative action (AA) laws and regulations. It also excludes some diversity categories such as the long-term unemployed who are not afforded EEO/AA legal protection. The goal of a legalistic philosophy (the most frequently used one) is to simply do only those things required by law.

A second approach is a business-oriented one. This is a proactive philosophy where the staffing of a diverse workplace is voluntarily initiated. As a result, it quite often reaches out to diverse groups not protected by laws and regulations. The goal is to increase organizational effectiveness by having a diverse workforce, which may be a source of competitive advantage for organizations. Arguments for diversity as a source of competitive advantage are shown in box 4.1.

Depending upon which philosophy is adapted, different staffing activities are likely to take place. For example, an organization with a legalistic philosophy would probably not hire the homeless because they are not required by law to do so. On the other hand, Days Inn, an organization that adopted a business-oriented approach has recruited and hired the homeless since 1988, because many of those hired have proven to be successful performers (*EMA Reporter*, 1992).

All organizations are required to take the legal view. It is voluntary whether organizations take the business view of diversity. Not all are ready to take a business perspective because some do not have the necessary preconditions needed to develop certain elements of a diverse workplace. For example, not all organizations would be able to deal with the special needs of the homeless. Other organizations can and should adapt a business orientation to diversity.

Van de Grift et al. (1994) have developed a list of conditions external and internal to the organization which are likely to motivate a business-oriented philosophy. External conditions include the lack of a court-ordered consent decree, customer preferences for the hiring of a diverse workforce, and lobbying groups placing pressure on the organization to hire a diverse workforce. Internal conditions include diversity training in the organization, top management support, a current diverse workforce, and the hiring of people for lower level jobs.

Box 4.1 Managing cultural diversity can provide competitive advantage

1	Cost argument	As organizations become more diverse, the cost of a poor job in integrating workers will increase. Those who handle this well will thus create cost advantages over those who don't.
2	Resource-acquisition argument	Companies develop reputations on favorability as prospective employers for women and ethnic minorities. Those with the best reputations for managing diversity will win the competition for the best personnel. As the labor pool shrinks and changes composition, this edge will become increasingly important.
3	Marketing argument	For multinational organizations, this insight and cultural sensitivity that members with roots in other countries bring to the marketing effort should improve these efforts in important ways. The same rationale applies to marketing to subpopulations within domestic operations.
4	Creativity argument	Diversity of perspectives and less emphasis on conformity to norms of the past (which characterize the modern approach to management of diversity) should improve the level of creativity.
5	Problem-solving argument	Heterogeneity in decision and problem-solving groups potentially produces better decisions through a wider range of perspectives and more thorough critical analysis of issues.
6	System flexibility argument	An implication of the multicultural model for managing diversity is that the system will become less determinant, less standardized, and therefore more fluid. The increased fluidity should create greater flexibility to react to environmental changes (i.e. reactions should be faster and at less cost).

Source: Cox, T. J., and Blake, S. (1991). Managing cultural diversity: Implications for organizational competitiveness. *Academy of Management Executive*, 5(3), 45–56

Staffing and diversity literature

In reviewing the scientific and practitioner-oriented literature on staffing and diversity, two important findings stand out concerning the issues that have been considered. First, theory, research, and practice regarding diversity and staffing have been focused on women, older people, and African-Americans. Very little consideration has been given to other attributes. Second, almost all of the attention has been directed toward selection rather than recruitment and employment decisions. These findings suggest needed areas of study in the future and boundaries to the conclusions reached here. If further progress is to be made in promoting a multicultural workforce, then organizations and researchers must take a broader view of diversity and staffing than has so far been the case.

Recruitment

One major area of staffing decision-making is recruitment and includes decisions made about who, when, and how to recruit. These decisions and others are influenced by the following diversity considerations.

Barriers to entry

Individuals with diverse backgrounds are sometimes not targeted or pursued by organizations. There are a number of reasons for this exclusion, and some practical solutions which will now be reviewed. Several explanations have been developed for the systematic exclusion of women and minorities in recruitment efforts (Reskin and Hartmann, 1986; Powell, 1987; Braddock and McPartland, 1987). At the risk of oversimplification, these explanations can also be used as a starting-point to explain why other diverse segments of the labor market are overlooked in recruitment efforts. Drawing heavily upon the reviews, there are five major explanations or theories.

The first explanation is stereotyping where recruiters may target and pursue individuals for jobs on the basis of stereotypes they hold about the job, the person, and the interaction between the person and the job. For example, some jobs are characterized as being for men (e.g. firefighter) while others are characterized as for women (e.g. nurse). Also, men are seen as having masculine characteristics (e.g. strength) and women are seen as having feminine characteristics (e.g. nurturance). In turn, it is sometimes believed that only men should be sought for firefighter positions and women sought for nursing positions. Although this example may seem overly simplistic and dated, unfortunately it is not. Women continue to be systematically discriminated against for the firefighter position.

The second explanation is the conflict between work and personal life. The belief is that lifestyle choices outside of work will have a negative impact on performance at work. Individuals with diverse backgrounds are excluded, for example, because they have personal obligations such as child-rearing, caring for the elderly, or assisting a partner with AIDS. These personal life circumstances are seen as hindrances to good job performance.

A third explanation is legal barriers where individuals with some diversity characteristics are excluded from recruitment efforts because the law does not protect them. For example, there are very few laws and regulations which prevent employers from not hiring those with a certain sexual orientation. As previously discussed, this is a reactive approach to diversity followed by many if not most employers, but it poses a barrier to non-protected individuals.

The fourth explanation is self-selection where it is argued that individuals with diverse backgrounds take themselves out of consideration for recruitment efforts by organizations. An employer may assume, for example, that persons with physical disabilities may not want to be considered for a news anchor position. This argument is that persons with certain attributes do not want to hold certain jobs.

The fifth explanation is segregated social networks. It is often said that in getting hired it is more important "who you know" than "what you know." Individuals with diversity characteristics may not be as well situated in terms of having a network of social relationships which lead to information about job openings. The "good ole boy" network, for example, often serves to inform only white males of the job openings available.

Affirmative action

In response to these barriers to entry, many organizations have voluntarily or legally been mandated to take affirmative action (AA). That is, they have taken steps in the recruitment process to target and attract individuals with diverse backgrounds. Historically, for legal reasons, affirmative steps have been taken usually only for minorities and women. With increasing emphasis on a business philosophy in staffing decision-making, many organizations have taken steps to recruit other diverse groups as well.

Recently, there have been a few empirical studies looking at AA. Kravitz and Platania (1993) looked at the beliefs held by undergraduates towards AA plans. Those plans targeting women and the disabled were seen more favorably than those targeting minorities. Women rated AA plans more favorably than did men. African-Americans and Hispanics rated them more favorably than did whites. The recruiting and training of minorities and women were viewed more favorably than was providing compensation for previous discrimination or requiring that organizations hire unqualified minorities and women.

Heilman and her colleagues (Heilman et al., 1992; Heilman et al., 1987) found that AA to recruit minorities may actually hurt those people it was intended to serve. Having the label of being an "affirmative action hire" led to a belief that the person was less competent and less likely to make headway in his or her career. Moreover, those who were provided with preferential hiring treatment characterized their own performance as being less than those who were hired on the basis of their qualifications.

The result of these AA studies should be used cautiously as they are based primarily on the study of undergraduate students. Nevertheless, they are still relevant as many of these students had at least some work experience and some are likely to be the managers of tomorrow. The results show that diversity efforts should not end simply with recruitment efforts. Additional effort must be taken to overcome the stigma of being an AA or diversity hire. Diversity efforts to simply "improve our numbers" are not likely to be successful. In fact, efforts to improve numbers may work against the goals of a multicultural workforce. Simply hiring a diverse workforce may perpetuate barriers by reinforcing beliefs that certain individuals are given preferential treatment (Crosby and Clayton, 1990). Care must be taken to fully integrate all new hires into the workforce.

Practical steps

Even though there is a small amount of research on recruitment and staffing, there is a large amount of prescriptive advice presented in the literature based upon company practice. Practical steps in the recruitment process to insure a diverse work force will now be reviewed.

The recruitment process typically involves four steps: planning, strategy development, search, and evaluation (Heneman and Heneman, 1994). Each of these steps will be described, followed by steps to emphasize diversity considerations at each juncture.

The recruitment process begins with planning. Attention is paid to both organizational and administrative matters. The connection between the business plan of the organization and staffing for diversity can be made by the use of an aspiration or values statement discussed previously. A diversity council can also be created to serve as a link between senior executives and those with diverse backgrounds, as has been done at Levi Strauss (Mitchell and O'Neal, 1994). In order to gather top management support for diversity, top executives can be required to join organizations in which they are a minority member. This practice is followed at Hoechst Celanese (Rice, 1994) and would seem to be an excellent way for executives to become more aware of the needs and talents of diverse individuals. Organizations may employ a diversity coordinator to ensure that diversity programs are actually carried out. An example of an actual coordinator's job description is shown in box 4.2. The roles of managers and employees in various diversity activities can be clarified through job descriptions. Finally, community volunteers from targeted diversity groups can be enlisted to help the organization create successful recruitment programs.

The next step in the recruitment process is to develop a recruitment strategy. To do so requires an examination of when, where, and how to look. Qualified applicants with diverse backgrounds are in strong demand in the labor market. As a result, recruitment efforts in this arena may need to start much sooner than in traditional recruitment. For example, possible candidates can be given early exposure to the organization through internships, co-ops, and summer programs. This was one of the steps taken by Pacific Bell and one of the reasons they were awarded an Exemplary

Box 4.2 Job description for a diversity coordinator

Description of Duties

General Statement of Duties: Develops and implements a diversity affairs program, including evaluating a targeted selection program, developing a network of resources and promoting CompuServe's commitment to diversity affairs. Leads and coordinates a volunteer diversity recruitment program for associates.

Supervision Received: Works independently with direction from Manager, Employment

Supervision Exercised: No supervisory duties required.

Examples of Duties: (Any one position may not include all of the duties listed, nor do the listed examples include all that may be found in this job.)

Develops diversity affairs program, including assisting in developing recruitment strategies, developing, implementing and evaluating a targeted selection program, identifying and resolving minority recruitment issues and ensuring compliance to federal employment laws.

Develops a network of resources to attract qualified targeted applicants for various position levels by attending career fairs, open houses and large-scale recruitment functions.

Interacts with managers and employment representatives to discuss minority applicant pool, available resources, compensation and recruiting and selection practices.

Interacts with communities, schools, businesses and professional organizations to promote CompuServe's commitment to diversity affairs. Participates in programs sponsored by external minority affairs groups.

Recruits, interviews and screens targeted applicants. Evaluates applicants' qualifications and recommends job placement to managers and employment representatives. May extend offers of employment.

Leads and coordinates a volunteer diversity recruitment program for CompuServe's associates to attract prospective applicants and to inform participants of recruitment opportunities and related employment information.

Assists in developing recruiting materials, including brochures and classified advertisements for targeted groups.

Participates in training associates on diversity programs and issues. Compiles and prepares recruitment related reports.

Knowledge, Skills and Abilities

Knowledge of interviewing and recruitment practices. Thorough knowledge of employment laws and regulations. General knowledge of CompuServe's products, services, divisions and departments. Excellent written and verbal communication skills. Personal computer skills. Ability to diplomatically deal with a variety of individuals on all levels. Ability to identify and resolve issues. Ability to conduct group presentations. Ability to travel. Ability to work non-standard hours.

Minimum Qualifications

Education: BA/BS degree in business administration, human resources or related field or equivalent education and experience.

Experience: Two years experience in exempt level recruiting, including experience dealing with mid-level management and/or senior technical and professional positions.

Desirable: Minority recruitment experience. Public and community relations experience. Information service/telecommunications experience.

Source: Reprinted by permission of CompuServe International

Voluntary Effort Award from the US Department of Labor in 1990 for their diversity efforts. Inducements such as relocation allowances and day care may also need to be provided to be competitive in the labor market. Sourcing candidates requires casting a wide net and looking at many sources of candidates not traditionally considered. Examples of nontraditional recruitment sources are shown in box 4.3. Job posting systems should be used internally so that qualified internal candidates with diverse backgrounds can identify themselves. Internal searches should also be coupled with searches external to the organization. This is especially important when the organization currently does not have a diverse workforce.

After developing a strategy, the next step is to conduct the search. Brochures can be developed which emphasize diversity in order to attract diverse applicants. For example, Pacific Gas and Electric has a brochure entitled *PG&E's Commitment to Meeting the Needs of Multicultural Californians* in several languages (Whalen, 1991). Advertisements can be used which target the needs of diverse groups. For example, ads for a fast food chain target the needs of older workers which are met by working at the fast food chain (e.g. supplement social security, retraining, and social interaction with other people) (Fyock, 1990).

In searching for applicants, too much attention is often focused on advertisements. Research has shown that job applicants report finding jobs more often through family and friends (Schwab et al., 1987; Bostnick and Ports, 1992). In order to make contact with family and friends, organizations must

---

Box 4.3   Selected diversity recruitment sources

- Urban League
- Professional associations
- State employment agencies
- Churches
- Community agencies
- Military
- State fair employment agencies
- Regional equal employment opportunity offices
- State Department of Rehabilitation
- Private industry councils
- Historically black universities and colleges
- Temporary agencies
- Displaced homemakers network
- Hispanic Association of Colleges and Universities
- National Organization for Women
- National Association of Negro Business and Women's Clubs
- National Federation of Business and Professional Women's Clubs
- League of United Latin American Citizens
- National Black MBA Association
- American Business Women's Association
- National Indian Education Association
- American Council for Career Women
- Association of Retarded Citizens

---

be proactive in the community. McDonald's, for example, has hired over 9,000 disabled individuals since 1981 with its McJobs Program (Laabs, 1991). To do so, they have partnered with local school systems, vocational rehabilitation agencies, and parents.

The final stage of recruitment is evaluation. Attention not only must be paid to the number of diverse candidates hired, but also to the success of the placements. Attention should be devoted to monitoring the experiences of those hired over time to be sure that they are properly assimilated into the organization and placed in meaningful jobs which match their talents. At this stage of the recruitment process it becomes clear that the aspiration statement guiding diversity efforts must include an operational statement of which categories of the workforce are considered "diverse." Only by clearly defining these categories can be seen the extent to which organizations are successful in recruiting within each category.

Selection

A second major area of staffing decision-making is selection. Selection refers to the assessment and evaluation of job applicants. An assessment and evaluation is made of the extent to which the applicant's qualifications meet the requirements of the job. In order to make these decisions, selection devices known as predictors are used. Predictors which have received attention in the diversity literature, and will be covered in this section, include paper and pencil tests and interviews. Selection decisions are also influenced by diversity considerations. Ones that have been covered in literature and will be reviewed in this section include barriers to favorable assessments, age, race, sex and gender, sexual orientation, and disabilities.

Barriers to favorable assessments

Selection is an assessment and evaluation process rather than a one-time hire/no hire decision. Job applicants progress through three stages as they go from applicant to being extended an offer of employment (Heneman and Heneman, 1994). First, they become candidates when the assessment and evaluation shows that they have the minimum qualifications for the job. Second, candidates become finalists when the organization is willing to consider them further based on additional assessments which have been conducted. Third, finalists become offer receivers after yet another round of assessments take place.

At each stage of the selection process there may be barriers to favorable assessment due to diversity characteristics. These barriers may vary by stage of selection process, predictor used, and diversity characteristics. Unfortunately, the current state of theory development is not yet specific enough to detail all these variations. There are, however, some general theories about barriers and some theories about specific barriers due to diversity characteristics which will be reviewed next in this section. Whenever possible practical steps to eliminate these barriers will be addressed, although there is not a large amount of practitioner-oriented literature in this area of staffing and diversity. Organizations need to pay more attention to selection processes as a means to enhance diversity efforts. Too much emphasis has been placed on recruitment in hopes that jobs alone will meet the goals of diversity. Sound selection is also clearly needed to ensure a good "fit" between the applicant and the job.

One theory of why individuals with diversity characteristics are not selected is information bias (Braddock and McPartland, 1987). Information bias occurs when selection decisions are made on the basis of information that individuals with diverse backgrounds have difficulty providing. One source of difficulty is the amount of information. For example, because of high youth unemployment in minority communities, it may be difficult for young minorities to provide much information when job experience is used as a predictor. Another source is the credibility of the information provided. Selection decision-makers may have unfamiliarity with or stereotypes about, for example, all church affiliated schools when education is a predictor.

A second theory is statistical discrimination theory (Braddock and McPartland, 1987). The reason that applicants do not move through the selection process to being hired is because their diversity characteristics are used as predictors or "signals" about the likelihood of successful job performance without consideration given to variation within each diversity characteristic. For example, women may be excluded from the job of firefighter because sex and gender is used as a "signal" for low strength, and strength is a requirement of the job. Simply using the signal "female" ignores the fact that there are individual differences in strength among women. Some women are stronger than others and some women make excellent firefighters.

A third general theory is "similar to me." This theory refers to selection decision-makers who only select those applicants with similar non-job-related backgrounds. People with diverse backgrounds are unlikely to be selected unless the evaluator has a diverse background. "Similar to me" can take place in three forms: perceived similarity which refers to perceptions about how similar the applicant and evaluator are; perceptual congruence which refers to how similar perceptions about the job are between evaluator and applicant; and actual similarity which refers to the similarity between actual characteristics of the applicant and evaluator (Turban and Jones, 1988). Turban and Jones suggest that perceived similarity is likely to have the largest exclusionary bias against those with diverse backgrounds.

Additional theory development is needed with "similar to me" theory. Most of the research has been done at a macro level looking at broad similarities like gender or race. It would also seem important to consider selection biases in terms of differential ethnic attributes as well. Skin color, the shape of eyes, stature, and hair type are all readily observable characteristics which may inhibit the selection of diverse applicants. Verbal accents and nonverbal mannerisms may also need to be included especially when culture and regional orientation are considered as diversity characteristics. For example, Lindsay et al. (1991) found that recognition memory is greater for faces of one's own race than of others' races. To the extent that memory of one person among many applicants is a determinant of who is hired, facial characteristics may have an influence.

Age stereotypes

There are many stereotypes about older workers. Chief among them is the belief that as people age, their performance declines. However, research has failed to reveal a relationship between performance and age (McEvoy and Cascio, 1989; Warr, 1990). This appears to be true regardless of measure of performance or type of job.

There are two interesting implications regarding the lack of a relationship between age and performance. First, the lack indicates that laws need to be updated to eliminate the mandatory retirement ages specified for professors, firefighters, and police. Warr (1990) reviews evidence suggesting that there may be significant differences in the validity of tests between various age groups. Hence, the validity coefficients of predictors need to be calculated by age groups.

Second, while there is no relationship between actual age and performance, certainly perceptions of these relationships exist (Rosen and Jerdee,

1976; Bird and Fisher, 1986). It is often assumed, for example, that being too young is detrimental to performance because one does not have the necessary knowledge and experience. On the other hand, it is often assumed that being too old is also detrimental as ageing is believed to be associated with becoming slow and forgetful. These negative stereotypes about ageing limit the ability of organizations to develop a more heterogeneous workforce with respect to age. Studies indicate that older workers are viewed as being less promotable than younger workers due to stereotypes about age (Rosen and Jerdee, 1976; Siegel, 1993).

Race stereotypes

Research on race as it relates to staffing, like age, is conducted quite frequently, but with very little theoretical rationale. Typically, race is treated as a side issue rather than an explanatory variable of theoretical interest. Another limitation is that often African-Americans are studied with little consideration given to Hispanics and Asian-Americans. Clearly, more theory and research is needed as the US continues to diversify along racial lines. Moreover, discriminatory pressures against members of certain races may intensify in the future. Temple (1990) reviews evidence showing that AIDS is more prevalent among certain ethnic groups which may provide additional reason to discriminate against workers.

Theories have been developed outside of human resources to explain why racial discrimination takes place. It may be helpful to draw upon these theories to understand the exclusion of certain races from advancement in the selection process. One such area to draw upon is social psychology. Three different theories of stereotypes may explain why whites may be treated as in-group members and given preferential treatment in hiring decisions while individuals with diversity characteristics are treated as out-group members and are rejected in the selection process. These three theories are complexity-extremity theory, assumed characteristics theory, and expectancy-violation theory (Jussim et al., 1987).

Complexity-extremity theory suggest that in-group members have more contact with other in-group members than with out-group members. As a result of the richness of the experience, in-group members are evaluated along a greater number of dimensions than are out-group members (the complexity component). Also, because fewer dimensions are used for out-group members, this makes it easier to make extreme assessments (the extremity component). Under this theory, minorities do not receive the same consideration in selection decisions as the majority because less information is sought out about their qualifications.

Assumed characteristics theory suggests that in-group members are assumed to have more positive values, traits, and socioeconomic status than out-group members. As a result, in a selection setting, in-group members may be assumed to be good hires unless or until disconfirming evidence is brought up. On the other hand, out-group members may be rejected before they even have a chance to present their positive features because of the initial assumption serving as a strong signal to reject the out-group member. This theory suggests that majority applicants are assumed to have good qualifications while minorities are assumed to have poor qualifications on the basis of other factors, such as economic status.

Expectancy-violation theory indicates that when a person's expectations regarding another person are violated, the person who violated the expectations will receive stronger ratings in the direction of the violation. For example, one stereotype held by recruiters might be that people in the north are more intelligent than people in the south. If a recruiter is recruiting at a northern and a southern school, an average student from the south would receive below average ratings if that person attended a northern rather than a southern school. Had that person from the south attended a southern school he or she would have received an average rating.

Sex and gender stereotypes

Based on the work of Uger (1979), Powell (1987) defined sex as actual differences between men and women and gender as beliefs about how men and women differ. Using this distinction, Powell conducted a major review of the empirical literature on sex and gender as it relates to recruitment and selection decisions. Several important findings were reported. First, the sex of the applicant and the sex of the evaluator were shown to have little impact upon selection decisions. A more recent study by Graves and Powell (1988) again shows the absence of an effect for applicant sex. Second, the applicant's gender sometimes biased selection decisions and other times it did not. The greater the amount and relevance of information about the job and applicant received by the evaluator, the less that gender biased the decision. This finding was confirmed in a meta-analysis of empirical studies by Tosi and Einbender (1985).

Research also suggests that attributions of success and failure may explain the relationship between sex and personnel decisions (Heilman and Guzzo, 1978; Deaux, 1976). Applied to selection decisions, attribution theory suggests that positive information (e.g. good sales record) will be attributed to luck or an easy assignment for women, but the same record for men will be attributed to their ability or effort. On the other hand, negative information about a woman will be attributed to a lack of effort or ability while negative information about a man will be attributed to a difficult assignment or bad luck.

Another theory relating to sex and gender is sex-role spillover (Gutek and Cohen, 1987). This theory suggests that gender-based roles are carried over to work. This is especially true when there is a large number of one sex at work in relation to the other sex. Traditional gender roles for the majority sex are imposed upon the minority sex. In a study of working adults in Los Angeles, it was found that sex-role spillover resulted in women being considered sexual objects and harassed (Gutek and Cohen, 1987). Based on the findings, one might expect that women in the minority role would be selected less frequently and when selected, be placed in traditionally female occupations such as secretary.

Sexual orientation

Very little research has been conducted on sexual orientation as it relates to selection decisions. In two studies homosexuals were rated as having less positive personality characteristics than heterosexuals (Krulewitz and Nash, 1980; Gurwitz and Marcus, 1978). This may be problematic to diversity efforts given the recent resurgence in personality tests as predictors (Bernardin and Bownas, 1985). Lance (1987) reported more positive attitudes towards homosexuals, the more exposure and interaction people have with them. Only one study looked directly at sexual orientation as it relates to selection decisions. O'Brien and Vest (1988) constructed a measure of beliefs about employing homosexuals. It was administered to 250 managers in a manufacturing plant. The results showed a strong negative correlation between beliefs about homosexuality and the likelihood of rejecting a homosexual applicant for a job. More negative beliefs about the consequences of employing homosexuals at work were correlated with beliefs that homosexuals will be rejected from further consideration in the selection process. Although not many studies have been conducted, these results seem to indicate that homosexuals may face strong resistance to being hired. This appears to be especially true when negative personality traits are assigned to homosexuals and when the evaluator has little interaction with homosexuals.

Disabilities stereotypes

With the exception of much prescriptive advice on how to comply with the Americans with Disabilities Act, there is very little literature on disability considerations as they relate to staffing decision-making. This is an area in critical need of additional study. Two earlier studies suggest that there are many negative attitudes towards people with disabilities (Tringo, 1970; Yuker, 1987). Certainly, these negative attitudes would be expected to influence selection decisions. Additional study is needed to explain why a negative effect is likely to occur.

Interview

Some research attention has been devoted to diversity as it relates to the interview as a predictor in selection decisions. In terms of the interviewer, a field study by Phillips and Dipboye (1989) found that preinterview impressions of the applicant held by the interviewer influenced the interviewer's evaluation after the interview. This finding suggests that prejudicial beliefs about individuals with diverse backgrounds may spill over into the interview itself. Furthermore, Binning et al., (1988) found that interviewers seek negative information about same-sex interviewees, but seek out positive information about opposite-sex interviewees. One explanation for this result is that interviewers are sensitive to possible sex and gender bias in the interview and may even overcompensate for it.

Recent research indicates that the type of interview shows promise as a mechanism for promoting diversity. Motowidlo et al. (1992) conducted five studies using the structured behavioral interview. This bases questions on a job analysis, organizes information around behavioral situations, requires the interviewer to take notes, requires the interviewer to make ratings on scales with behavioral illustrations, and combines ratings mechanically to form a selection decision. Differences in scores between blacks and whites were low for all of the studies using the structured behavioral interview. In addition, men and women were found to have small differences in interview scores in four of the five studies.

Another interesting aspect of the Motowidlo et al. (1992) study was the use of doctoral student raters who were provided audio portions or transcripts of the taped interviews. It was concluded that valid judgements could be made about interviewees even when interviewers did not have access to information about interviewee appearance, behavior, or vocal characteristics in the face-to-face context of an interview. This finding raises the interesting possibility that interviews not requiring face-to-face interaction (e.g. computer-based) may allow for valid judgements without preferential treatment given to the majority group.

Linn et al. (1992) reviewed evidence which suggests that interviewers give higher ratings to those applicants who are similar to themselves. One aspect of similarity is race. Hence, it is expected that interviewees who are of the same race as the interviewer will receive higher interview ratings than those of a different race. Linn et al., found in their study of selection procedures for custodians in a school system that structured behavioral interviews resulted in less same-race bias than did structured interviews. They also found that same-race bias could be lessened when a panel of interviewers was used with mixed-race backgrounds.

Testing

The use of paper and pencil tests (especially cognitive ability tests) as predictors in selection decisions continues to be studied in relation to diversity. One issue which has received considerable attention over the years is how fair tests are to individuals with diverse backgrounds. Typically, this issue has been explained in the context of the selection of women and African-Americans. Arvey and Sackett (1993) summarized the research regarding test bias and found that racial differences in scores do exist for cognitive ability tests. It has also been shown that these tests are valid for majority and minority groups. That is, the tests predict job performance for minority and majority members equally well.

The use of cognitive ability tests is also likely to have adverse impact on the minority group.

The use of cognitive ability tests remains a political, social, and economic decision (Gottfredson and Sharf, 1988). Organizations must pay careful attention to the existing laws and regulations. Attention must also be paid to the procedures that are used to make selection decisions. Perceptions of fairness by applicants not only relate to the outcomes they received (e.g. invited in for second interview), but also the procedures that were used to make the decision. Tests which are seen as being job-related, consistently administered, a source of timely feedback, and of economic necessity are more likely to be seen as fair by test takers (Gilliland, 1993). Finally, consideration may need to be given to predictors other than cognitive ability tests, such as training and experience requirements, which seem to have less adverse impact (Heneman and Heneman, 1994).

Practical implications

As has been shown throughout this section many sources of bias against people with diverse backgrounds enter into selection decision-making. Fortunately, this same body of research points to ways to minimize these sources of bias which may stand in the way of diversity. Recommended actions follow.

1   More theory and research is needed to understand the processes which lead to or detract from a diverse workforce. The answer does not appear to reside solely in the type of predictor used, but in the process by which the predictor is used. A good example is the problem of same-race bias. Reasons for same-race bias are found in complexity-extremity theory, assumed characteristics theory, and expectancy-violation theory (Jussim et al., 1987). By understanding the underlying process involved in same-race bias, creative solutions can be uncovered. Linn et al. (1992) found that not only is the type (structured behavioral) of interview important, but so too is the process (mixed-race panels) used. Biases are minimized when interviews are job-related and rely upon the judgements of both nonminority and minority interviewers.

2   Not only should multiple evaluators with diverse backgrounds be used in selection decision-making, but so too should multiple sources of information about the applicant be solicited. A structured format should be used in presenting and evaluating this background information about the candidate (Motowidlo et al., 1992; Tosi and Einbender, 1985). For example, an application blank is structured to gather consistent data across applicants whereas a résumé is not structured as the data presented are idiosyncratic to the applicant.

3   Decisions about applicants should not be made solely on the basis of global ratings such as "hire/don't hire" the applicant. Instead, multiple dimensions and items should be used regardless of the predictor. This should be done in order to make it more difficult for employers to utilize only extreme scores in applicant selection (Jussim et al., 1987). With multiple dimensions and items, decision-makers must justify their extreme scores.

4   The content of predictors should always be job-related. To do so, predictors should be developed on the basis of a thorough job analysis. This process not only results in less opportunity for bias, but can also

improve applicants' reactions to the system (Gilliland, 1993). By having job-related criteria, applicants can see that they are being judged on the basis of their qualifications rather than their diversity.

5　Training is needed for interviewers which relates specifically to diversity issues. Cultural diversity may require an examination of traditional considerations of what constitutes a "good" applicant. For example, quiet mannerisms and reluctance to take the initiative to speak during an interview may be interpreted as a sign of lack of interest in the job by the applicant. This interpretation may be incorrect, however, as in some cultures quiet mannerisms and reluctance to take the initiative are signs of respect for the interviewer.

6　The research on interviewing continues to be concentrated on examining attributes of race and gender. This area should be broadened to examine the issues which arise when interviewing other diverse groups. Practitioners have little information as to what techniques are advisable or inadvisable to utilize when interviewing a person of another culture or ethnic group. There needs to be assessment of how issues of language barriers, differences in work experiences, resume styles and content as well as nonverbal cues are to be considered when conducting an interview with a person of a nontraditional group.

Employment

A third major area of staffing decision-making is employment. In this area, decisions are made about which finalists will be offered the jobs and what the starting salary should be. Diversity concerns identified in the literature which need to be considered in this area of staffing include closed internal labor markets, the glass ceiling, veterans' preferences, and starting wage differentials.

Closed internal labor markets

Members of diverse groups may not make it to the employment stage of staffing due to closed internal labor markets (Braddock and McPartland, 1987). Groups of employees available for promotions inside the organization form the internal labor market. Movement into and within this market is often restricted to employees in the majority group. Hence, labor markets are sometimes "closed" to employees with diverse backgrounds. This restriction usually arises from rules which govern movement in and through internal labor markets. These rules consist of specific policies and procedures, three of which are troublesome to diversity efforts (Heneman and Heneman, 1994).

The first occurs when organizations follow a policy of "promotion from within." Under this policy, only current employees are promoted to higher-level jobs in the organization. If the current workforce is not diverse, then it will continue to remain this way because diverse candidates are not brought in from the outside. This problem will be further compounded if the organization follows a policy of using employee referrals to select entry-level employees. Chances are that nondiverse employees will refer other nondiverse people to the organization.

The second troublesome rule is when organizations use a closed internal recruitment system. Under this type of policy, current employees are not made aware of job vacancies. Promotion and transfer opportunities are only made known to the human resource (HR) department, line managers with vacancies, and contacted employees. Employees who become finalists are decided behind the scenes. The HR group identifies candidates and managers select the best ones. While this approach is efficient, it does not allow candidates with diverse backgrounds to identify themselves as such. As a result, qualified candidates with diverse backgrounds may be overlooked.

A final policy which may be troublesome is the heavy weight placed on seniority in deciding who the eventual job offer receivers will be. This is especially true in unionized settings where there are seniority provisions in the labor agreement. However, even in nonunion firms, seniority is often a deciding factor (Foulkes, 1980). Because individuals with diverse backgrounds are less likely to have high levels of seniority, they are less likely to be selected as job offer receivers in the employment process.

Veterans' preferences

When there are many finalists for a position, employers may rely upon discretionary methods to make a decision as to which will receive job offers (Heneman and Heneman, 1994). At the margin, employers may give preferential treatment to those with diverse backgrounds. While this may help the goal of diversity for some, it may hurt this goal for others. Employment for one group of diverse finalists may be at the cost of a loss of employment for another group.

One documented example of this tradeoff is preferences for veterans which may impede the progress of women (Kennedy, 1990). Under the Veteran's Preference Act and Veterans Readjustment Program, employers need to take affirmative action to hire veterans. Because there were many more men than women in Vietnam, preferential treatment for Vietnam veterans may exclude women. This appeared to be the case in a study of a large government facility by Kennedy (1990). Whether this issue is problematic elsewhere remains to be seen. But it is suggestive of tradeoffs which may need to be made between diversity categories.

The glass ceiling

The phrase "glass ceiling" refers to barriers which prevent both women and minorities from advancing to higher levels in the organization. It also refers to the crowding of women and minorities into staff positions. Employees with other diversity characteristics may suffer from these same barriers, but not have been studied under the banner of the "glass ceiling" to date. Barriers refer to closed internal labor market characteristics and stereotyping covered in this chapter.

Only a few studies have been conducted on the glass ceiling and the results have been decidedly mixed in terms of its prevalence (US Department of Labor, 1991; Powell and Butterfield, 1994; Shenhav, 1992). The mixed findings from these studies suggest that although the glass ceiling may not be as widespread as initially thought, it is something that needs to be monitored in many organizations. Even in those not found guilty of discrimination in court, the costs of a glass ceiling can be quite high. For example, it was estimated that the cost was $15.3 million for a Fortune 500 utility company with 27,000 employees (Stuart, 1992). These costs included coaching and mentoring, underutilized potential, and turnover.

There appear to be three major causes of the glass ceiling (US Department of Labor, 1991). First, organizations do not hold managers and executives accountable for equal employment opportunity and affirmative action. Hence, even though the laws exist to protect women and minorities, they are not always adhered to. Second, closed internal labor markets operate in organizations. Women and minorities are sometimes not made aware of job openings at higher levels. Third, there is a lack of training and developmental opportunities for women in organizations so that they can improve their qualifications and chances for promotion.

In order to encourage organizations to take the steps necessary to shatter the glass ceiling, the Department of Labor has initiated the Exemplary Voluntary Efforts (EVE) Awards program for federal contractors. Winners so far include well-known organizations such as Saturn and Motorola and less well-known organizations such as Wisconsin Gas Company (US Department of Labor, 1992).

Starting pay differentials

One outcome of a glass ceiling is lower wage rates for minorities and women. This is usually discussed in the context of comparable worth. While total compensation is beyond the scope of this chapter, starting salaries are a part of the employment process, are sometimes less for individuals with diverse backgrounds, and are reviewed here.

It is well documented that women's salaries are less than men's (Gerhart, 1990). One of the reasons for this differential appears to be the starting salaries of men and women. When job offer receivers are men they tend to be granted larger starting salaries than when they are women (Buttner and Rosen, 1987; Cox and Harquail, 1991; Gerhart, 1990). This starting pay differential is reflected in two different forms. First, the actual salary is less (Cox and Harquail, 1991; Gerhart, 1990). Second, rather than offering women comparable salaries to men during a period of a labor shortage, employers may automate jobs, offer a signing bonus rather than a comparable salary, or hire women from foreign labor markets with lower salary expectations (Buttner and Rosen, 1987).

Although it is difficult to say exactly why this differential in starting pay for the same jobs with people of the same qualifications exists, Gerhart (1990) provides evidence from one large organization which suggests that the difference may be due to a lack of information by employers. That is, employers have a great deal of information, including actual performance, about current employees with which to make pay decisions. For new employees, however, this information, especially regarding performance, is difficult to come by. As a result, employers may draw upon rough "signals" of potential performance including sex and gender. As shown throughout this chapter, this signal is subject to any number of stereotypes which may downgrade the starting salaries of women.

Although pay differentials for other diversity characteristics have been studied, most notably race, the study of differences in starting pay needs to be extended to other diversity characteristics. For example, a study by Baldwin and Johnson (1994) suggests that salaries for the disabled are low. This study suggests that employers may also rely on disability as a signal to set lower starting pay in the absence of information about work experience.

It was also shown in the Baldwin and Johnson (1994) study that the wages offered to the handicapped were less than the wages offered to the disabled. As studied using a classification scheme by Tringo (1970), the handicapped have more noticeable impairments (e.g. missing limbs, blindness, retardation) than do the disabled (e.g. diabetes, heart disease, arthritis). This result clearly points to the need to study differences within diversity categories as well as between diverse individuals and the majority group.

Implications for theory and practice

Very little is known about employment decisions relative to recruitment and selection decisions. This is especially true with regard to diversity as shown by the brevity of this section. According to Gerhart (1990), however, it is an area of major importance, as part of the wage disparity between men and women appears to be directly linked to employment decisions.

In terms of practice, the limited information available suggests several steps that employers can take to insure that diversity efforts are not thwarted by closed internal labor markets, the glass ceiling, and low initial salaries. In general, the recommendation here is that employment decision-makers gather as much information about the job, and background data about people to receive offers, as is possible. In the absence of detailed information about the duties and requirements of the job, decision-makers may mistakenly assume that diverse finalists should not receive offers or should receive low pay on the basis of broad generalizations about what requirements are needed to perform the job. Inferences about requirements based on broad job titles can be very misleading. Hence, a thorough job analysis is required.

In the absence of detailed information about the finalists, employment decision-makers rely upon stereotypes. Some predictors provide more detailed information than do others. For example, an accomplishment record (Hough et al., 1983) provides much more data than does an application blank. An application simply lists the title of the positions held by the person. An accomplishment record details in behavioral and results-oriented terms what it is the person accomplished in these positions.

In closed internal labor markets, seniority is often a deciding factor in extending employment offers. Number of years as a measure of seniority, like job title as a measure of experience, is a very general signal which may not match up with the specific requirements of the job. Better predictors which are more difficult to administer, but may give more opportunity to individuals with diverse backgrounds and limited years of seniority, are training and work experience evaluation methods. These methods look at the types of experiences one gains through seniority rather than simply looking at number of years experience (Ash and Levine, 1985; McDaniel et al., 1988).

Two final recommendations can also be made to start to eliminate the glass ceiling. First, executives need to be held accountable for diversity issues. As mentioned above, performance ratings and pay increase can be in part determined on the basis of progress in diversity efforts. Second, developmental opportunities need to be provided for finalists. Rather than simply rejecting diverse finalists from a job offer and telling them "better luck next time," they instead need to be given feedback and guidance on how to improve their chances of receiving a job offer in the future.

Summary of Major Issues

The review of the literature and suggestions presented in this chapter identified a number of major issues which need to be addressed in theory development, research, and practice if the goal of having a diverse workforce is to be achieved. A brief summary of these issues by area of staffing decision-making follows.

The literature on recruitment suggests that there are many barriers to the entry of diverse components of our labor force into organizations. Explanations which address this issue include stereotyping, work and personal life conflicts, legal barriers, self-selection, and segregated social networks. Research has shown that legally mandated affirmative action programs are unlikely to eliminate these barriers. In fact, such programs may even hurt those they were intended to serve. In order to address these barriers, a business-oriented philosophy to staffing planning may need to be adopted. This philosophy includes the use of aspiration statements, diversity councils, rewards for diversity efforts, open posting systems, nontraditional recruitment sources, and the evaluation of recruitment efforts. Issues which will require additional investigation include an understanding of the dynamics involved in each theory and strategies for dealing with the negative reactions towards affirmative action efforts.

The literature on selection has begun to identify barriers to favorable assessments of applicants with diverse characteristics. These barriers are captured in several theories including information bias, statistical discrimination, and "similar to me." An issue that remains to be addressed is how these general theories may vary by stage of the selection process, predictors used, and diversity characteristics. Specific research streams have started for the diversity characteristics of age, race, sex and gender, and sexual orientation. Other issues that remain to be explored in the selection arena are diversity in religion, national origin, disability, regional orientation, culture, and long-term unemployment. Specific research on diversity as it relates to the interview and testing has been conducted, but additional research needs to be addressed to other commonly used predictors (e.g. application blanks). Additional research is also needed on the processes used to make decisions with these predictors. Practice issues which appear promising to the promotion of diversity efforts include using multiple sources of information, multiple ratings of qualifications, trained evaluators, and predictors developed on the basis of a thorough job analysis.

The literature on recruitment has identified closed internal labor markets, the glass ceiling, and starting pay differentials as barriers to extending employment offers to finalists. An important issue which needs further investigation is conflicts that occur, as in the case with veterans and women, when members of two different diversity characteristics are competing for the same job. A number of ideas for practice in the employment area have been advanced. Foremost among these ideas, as it is based upon research, is the idea that more information about candidates and jobs is needed rather than less in order to combat a closed decision-making system which may exclude those with diversity characteristics and which may send false signals about the qualifications of the applicant.

NOTES

1 Due to space limitations, the flow of applicants out of the organization, and issues regarding orientation and socialization will not be covered here. It should be noted that there are many other staffing activities which support recruitment, selection, and employment decisions in organizations. These include job analysis, labor market analysis, laws and regulations, and performance appraisal. These staffing support activities are covered in other chapters and will not be reviewed further here.

2 It is also our belief, however, that for theory development to be further advanced, diversity needs to be studied on a category-by-category basis as well as on an overall basis. The current state of theory development only allows us to use a category-by-category approach in a few places. Just because a theory works well in explaining one category of diversity, this does not necessarily mean that it will work in explaining another category as it relates to staffing decision-making.

REFERENCES

Arvey, R. D., and Sackett, P. R. (1993). Fairness in selection: Current developments and perspectives. In N. Schmitt, W. Borman, and Associates (eds), *Personnel Selection in Organizations* (171–202). San Francisco: Jossey-Bass.

Ash, R. A., and Levine, E. L. (1985). Job applicant training and work experience evaluation: An empirical comparison of four methods. *Journal of Applied Psychology*, 70, 572–6.

Baldwin, M., and Johnson, W. G. (1994). Labor market discrimination against men with disabilities. *Journal of Human Resources*, 24, 1–19.

Begin, J. P. (1991). *Strategic Employment Policy*. Englewood Cliffs, NJ: Prentice-Hall.

Bernardin, H. J., and Bownas, D. A. (1985). *Personality Assessments in Organizations*. New York: Praeger.

Binning, J. F., Goldstein, M. A., Garcia, M. F., and Scattaregia, J. H. (1988). Effects of preinterview impressions on questioning strategies in same- and opposite-sex employment interviews. *Journal of Applied Psychology*, 73, 30–7.

Bird, C. P., and Fisher, T. D. (1986). Thirty years later: Attitudes toward the employment of older workers. *Journal of Applied Psychology*, 71, 515–17.

Bostnick, S. M., and Ports, M. H. (1992). Job search methods and results: Tracking the unemployed, 1991. *Monthly Labor Review*, December, 29–35.

Braddock, J. H., II, and McPartland, J. M. (1987). How minorities continue to be excluded from equal employment opportunities: Research on labor market and institutional barriers. *Journal of Social Issues*, 1, 5–39.

Buttner, E. H., and Rosen, B. (1987). The effects of labor shortages on starting salaries for sex-typed jobs. *Sex Roles*, 17, 59–71.

Carrell, M. R., and Mann, E. E. (1993). Defining workforce diversity programs and practices in organizations. *Labor Law Journal*, 44, 755–64.

Caudron, S. (1992). US West finds strength in diversity. *Personnel Journal*, 71, 40–4.

Commerce Clearing House (1993). *1993 SHRM/CCH Survey: Human Resources Management*, May 26. Chicago Commerce Clearing House.

Cox, T. H., and Blake, S. (1991). Managing cultural diversity: Implications for organizational competitiveness. *The Executive*, 3(45), 56.

Cox, T. H., and Harquail, C. V. (1991). Career paths and career success in the early career stages of male and female MBAs. *Journal of Vocational Behavior*, 39, 54–74.

Cox, T. H., Lobel, S. A., and McLeod, P. L. (1991). Effects of ethnic group cultural differences on comparative and competitive behavior on a group task. *Academy of Management Journal*, 34, 827–47.

Crosby, F., and Clayton, S. (1990). Affirmative action and the issue of expectancies. *Journal of Social Issues*, 46, 61–79.

Deaux, K. (1976). Sex: A perspective on the attribution process. *New Directions in Attribution Research*. Hillsdale, NJ: Lawrence Erlbaum.

Deutsch, Shea and Evans, Inc. (1992). *Human Resources Manual*. Atlanta, GA: Deutsch, Shea and Evans, Inc.

EMA Reporter (1992). Alternative recruitment methods to take center stage at Fall conference. *EMA Reporter*, 18, 3–5.

Foulkes, F. K. (1980). *Personnel Policies in Large Nonunion Companies*. Englewood Cliffs, NJ: Prentice-Hall.

Fyock, C. D. (1990). *America's Workforce is Coming of Age*. Lexington, MA: DC Heath.

Gerhart, B. (1990). Gender differences in current and starting salaries: The role of performance. *Industrial and Labor Relations Review*, 43, 418–33.

Gilliland, S. W. (1993). The perceived fairness of selection systems: An organizational justice perspective. *Academy of Management Review*, 18, 694–734.

Gottfredson, L., and Sharf, J. C. (eds) (1988). Fairness in employment testing: foreword. *A Special Issue of the Journal of Vocational Behavior*, 33, 255–490.

Graves, L. M., and Powell, G. N. (1988). An investigation of sex discrimination in recruiters' evaluations of actual applicants. *Journal of Applied Psychology*, 73, 20–9.

Gurwitz, S. R., and Marcus, M. (1978). Effects of anticipated interaction, sex and homosexual stereotypes on first impressions. *Journal of Applied Psychology*, 8, 47–56.

Gutek, B. A., and Cohen, A. G. (1987). Sex role spillover, and sex at work: A comparison of men's and women's experiences. *Human Relations*, 40, 97–115.

Heilman, M. E., Block, C. J., and Lucas, J. A. (1992). Presumed incompetent? Stigmatization and affirmative action efforts. *Journal of Applied Psychology*, 77, 536–44.

Heilman, M. E., and Guzzo, R. A. (1978). The perceived causes of work success as a mediator of sex discrimination in organizations. *Organizational Behavior and Human Performance*, 21, 346–57.

Heilman, M. E., Simon, M. E., and Pepper, D. P. (1987). Intentionally favored, unintentionally harmed? Impact of sex-based preferential selection on self perceptions and self-evaluations. *Journal of Applied Psychology*, 72, 62–8.

Heneman, H. G., III, and Heneman, R. L. (1994). *Staffing Organizations*. Burr Ridge, IL: Irwin, Mendota House, and Austen Press.

Hough, L. M., Keynes, M. A., and Dunnette, M. D. (1983). An evaluation of three "alternative" selection procedures. *Personnel Psychology*, 36, 260–70.

Jussim, L., Coleman, L. M., and Lerch, L. (1987). The nature of stereotypes: A comparison and integration of three theories. *Journal of Personality and Social Psychology*, 52, 536–46.

Kennedy, R. B. (1990). Preference for veterans may impede women. *Personnel Journal*, 69, 124–6.

Kravitz, D. A., and Platania, J. (1993). Attributes and beliefs about affirmative action: Effects of target and of respondent sex and ethnicity. *Journal of Applied Psychology*, 78, 928–38.

Krulewitz, J. E., and Nash, J. E. (1980). Effects of sex role attitudes and similarity on men's rejection of male homosexuals. *Journal of Personality and Social Psychology*, 38, 67–74.

Laabs, J. L. (1991). The golden arches provides golden opportunities. *Personnel Journal*, 70, 52.

Lance, L. M. (1987). The effects of interaction with gay persons and attitudes toward homosexuality. *Human Relations*, 40, 329–36.

Lindsay, D. S., Jack, P. C., and Christian, M. A. (1991). Other-race face perception. *Journal of Applied Psychology*, 76, 587–9.

Linn, T. R., Dobbins, G. H., and Farh, J. L. (1992). A field study of race and age similarity effects on interview ratings in conventional and situational interviews. *Journal of Applied Psychology*, 77, 363–71.

McDaniel, M. A., Schmidt, F. L., and Hunter, J. E. (1988). A meta-analysis of the validity of methods for rating training and experience in personnel selection. *Personnel Psychology*, 44, 283–309.

McEvoy, G. M., and Cascio, W. F. (1989). Cumulative evidence of relationship between employee age and job performance. *Journal of Applied Psychology*, 74, 11–17.

Mitchell, R., and Oneal, M. (1994). Managing by values. *Business Week*, August 1, 46–52.

Motowidlo, S. J., Carter, G. W., Dunnette, M. D., Tippins, N., Werner, S., Burnett, J. R., and Vaughan, M. J. (1992). Studies of the structured behavioral interview. *Journal of Applied Psychology*, 77, 571–87.

O'Brien, F. P., and Vest, M. J. (1988). A proposed scale to measure beliefs about the consequences of employing homosexuals. *Psychological Reports*, 63, 547–51.

Phillips, A. P., and Dipboye, R. L. (1989). Correlational tests of predictions from a process model of the interview. *Journal of Applied Psychology*, 74, 41–52.

Powell, G. N. (1987). The effects of sex and gender on recruitment. *Academy of Management Review*, 12, 731–43.

Powell, G. N., and Butterfield, D. A. (1994). Investigating the "glass ceiling" phenomenon: An empirical study of actual promotions to top management. *Academy of Management Journal*, 37, 68–86.

Reskin, B. F., and Hartmann, H. I. (eds) (1986). *Women's Work, Men's Work: Sex Segregation on the Job*. Washington, DC: National Academy Press.

Rice, F. (1994). How to make diversity pay. *Fortune*, August 8, 79–86.

Roberson, L., and Gutierrez, N. C. (1992). Beyond good faith: Commitment to recruiting management diversity at Pacific Bell. In S. E. Jackson and Associates (eds), *Diversity in the Workplace: Human Resource Initiatives* (65–88). New York: Guilford Press.

Rosen, B., and Jerdee, T. H. (1976). The nature of job-related age stereotypes. *Journal of Applied Psychology*, 61, 180–3.

Schmidt, F. L. (1993). Personnel psychology at the cutting edge. In N. Schmitt, W. Borman, and Associates (eds), *Personnel Selection in Organizations* (497–516). San Francisco: Jossey-Bass.

Schwab, D. P., Rynes, S. L., and Aldag, R. J. (1987). Theories and research on job search and choice. In K. M. Rowland and G. R. Ferris (eds), *Research in Personnel and Human Resource Management*, vol. 5 (129–66). Greenwich, CT: JAI Press.

Shenhav, Y. (1992). Entrances of blacks and women into managerial positions in scientific and engineering occupations: A longitudinal analysis. *Academy of Management Journal*, 35, 889–901.

Siegel, S. R. (1993). Relationship between current performance and likelihood of promotion for old versus young workers. *Human Resource Development Quarterly*, 4, 39–50.

Solomon, C. M. (1991). Are white males being left out? *Personnel Journal*, 70, 88–94.

Stuart, P. (1992). What does the glass ceiling cost you? *Personnel Journal*, 71, 70–80.

Temple, T. E., III (1990). Employers prepare: Hope for AIDS victims means conflict in your workplace. *Labor Law Journal*, October, 694–9.

Tosi, H. L., and Einbender, S. W. (1985). The effects of the type and amount of information in sex discrimination research. *Academy of Management Journal*, 28, 712–23.

Triandis, H. C., Kurowski, L. L., and Gelfand, M. L. (1990). Workplace diversity. In H. C. Triandis, M. D. Dunnette, and L. M. Hough (eds), *Handbook of Industrial and Organizational Psychology*, vol. 4 (485–558). Palo Alto, CA: Consulting Psychologists Press.

Tringo, J. L. (1970). The hierarchy of preference toward disability groups. *Journal of Specialized Education*, 4, 295–306.

Turban, D. B., and Jones, A. P. (1988). Supervisor–subordinate similarity: Types, effects and mechanisms. *Journal of Applied Psychology*, 73, 228–34.

Uger, R. E. (1979). Toward a redefinition of sex and gender. *American Psychologist*, 34, 1085–95.

US Department of Labor (1991). *Labor Department Report on the Glass Ceiling Initiative*. Washington, DC: US Department of Labor.

US Department of Labor (1992). *News*, September 17.

Van de Grift, C., Greenberger, D., and Heneman, R. L. (1994). *External and Internal Forces Impacting the Use of Diversity in Staffing Decisions*. Unpublished manuscript. Ohio State University.

Warr, P. (1990). Age and employment. In H. C. Triandis, M. D. Dunnette, and L. M. Hough (eds), *Handbook of Industrial and Organizational Psychology* (485–558). Palo Alto, CA: Consulting Psychologists Press.

Whalen, J. J. (1991). Workplace diversity and cracking the ceiling. *Public Utilities Fortnightly*, 128, 12–13.

Yuker, H. D. (1987). *The Disability Hierarchies: Comparative Reactions to Various Types of Physical and Mental Disabilities*. Hofstra University. Unpublished manuscript as cited in Baldwin and Johnson (1993).

Part Two
Developing and Motivating a Changing Workforce

Introduction to Part Two

Developing a context where employees are able to engage in continuous learning and to align personal and organizational goals is a critical organizational capability. In Part Two, human resource experts discuss how mentoring, performance appraisal, training and reward systems can be used as strategic levers for creating employee–employer partnerships. Kathy Kram and Douglas T. Hall are two renowned scholars in the areas of mentoring and career development. Their chapter considers the implications of growing complexities of the mentoring process: those that stem from environmental turbulence and those that stem from the increasingly diverse workforce. They argue that the nature of mentoring has been fundamentally transformed by this new context. Formal mentoring programs are likely to be less effective since mentors may be insecure about their own futures and their career experiences may be less relevant to the environment faced by organizational newcomers. They argue that learning will become more relationship-based and informal. Employees at all levels of the firm must now begin to build relationships with people who may differ in terms of gender, race, and/or cultural background. Kram and Hall contend that organizations must redesign systems to better support diversity in individuals. In particular, they consider the challenges associated with the mentoring needs and experiences of young white males, senior white males, senior women and/or minority pioneers, young and mid-level women, and young and mid-level people of color.

Development of employees occurs not only via mentoring systems, but also through formal performance feedback and goal-setting. Chao Chen and Nancy DiTomaso have a very thought-provoking and practical chapter on how demographic diversity influences the performance appraisal process. They consider the implicit cultural norms currently underlying most appraisal systems. In other words, performance standards are determined by the cultural beliefs, values and norms of those designing the performance appraisal system, who largely come from an Anglo-American background. Because definitions of performance effectiveness may differ across cultural and/or demographic subgroups, Chen and DiTomaso point out the mismatch likely to occur when the standards of performance chosen by one subgroup are used to evaluate the performance of other subgroups who do not share the same assumptions. For example, behaviors and attitudes considered to make a "good employee' can differ greatly between subgroups favoring individualistic values (often white) and subgroups predisposed toward collectivism (often people of color). Regarding gender, the research reviewed by the authors indicates that at managerial levels, the relationship between having a high appraisal rating and receiving greater merit increases is much stronger for men than for women, suggesting that bias is most prevalent in jobs where women have historically been underrepresented. Research on bias in rating and rating formats indicates that there may be a preference for minority members to favor objective measures of outcomes (the end result or what is actually produced) rather than subjective measures of the process (the how) of performance. Yet outcome- and objective-based measures are not a panacea for eliminating bias. It is increasingly difficult to link individual performance to organizational outcomes, given the growing interdependence of work processes.

Training has been identified as one of the most prevalent human resource strategies used to adapt the workplace toward greater integration of diverse cultural groups. J. Kevin Ford and Sandra Fisher consider the implications of growing diversity for the redesign of the widely used general training systems model. Needs assessment and delivery systems should take into account differences in motivation, trainability, and skill gaps of employee subgroups. Ford and Fisher also share a conceptually based framework to define the "diversity" of diversity training programs. Training systems vary in the extent to which they are based on assumptions of assimilation (where minorities are mainstreamed into the dominant culture), accommodation (where the dominant culture changes to accommodate the minority), and pluralism (where many cultures coexist). They discuss the conditions under which training initiatives are likely to be successful and examine the implications of varying assumptions for the design, delivery, and evaluation of diversity training programs.

In chapter 8, Alison Barber and Christina Daly consider the relationship between compensation and diversity from two perspectives. First, they consider whether and how compensation can be used to provide incentives for managers to engage in good diversity management practices. They argue that what constitutes good diversity management is hard to define and measure. Consequently, organizations claiming to reward diversity management may be relying implicitly on affirmative action-based views. Second, they consider whether and how compensation can contribute to an atmosphere in which diverse organizational members can perform to their highest abilities. Systematic differences in reward preferences could indicate that a compensation system that is effective and efficient for one group of employees may be less effective for another group of employees. Given that race- and gender-based differences in reward preferences are diminishing over time, they argue that tailoring systems to meet differences in unique individual preferences (rather than stereotyped group-based preferences) may be the best approach. They also discuss the implications of implementing new compensation strategies, such as group-based pay, with the increasingly diverse labor force.

5

Mentoring in a Context of Diversity and Turbulence*

Kathy E. Kram and Douglas T. Hall

It has now been over a decade since organizational leaders, scholars, and human resource (HR) specialists recognized the critical role of mentoring and other types of relationships in development at every career stage (McCauley and Young, 1993; Kram and Bragar, 1992; McCall et al., 1988). Indeed, formal mentoring programs, networking groups and core groups began to proliferate in the 1980s to promote effective developmental relationships for newcomers, high-potential candidates, and individuals from diverse backgrounds (Keele et al., 1987; Walker and Hansen, 1992; Kram and Bragar, 1992). These have generally served to make mentoring more available, particularly when the organizational context has recognized, rewarded, and supported those who embrace the mentoring role.

The purpose of this chapter is to draw attention to several emergent complexities of the mentoring process: those that stem from increasing turbulence within and surrounding organizations (e.g. downsizing, restructuring, rapid changes in technology, mergers and acquisitions, business failures), and those that stem from the fact of an increasingly diverse workforce. *Our view is that the nature of mentoring and other developmental relationships has been fundamentally transformed by this new turbulent context.* If HR strategy, systems, and programs are to effectively foster developmental alliances that promote individual and organizational learning,

* Support for this chapter was provided by the Executive Development Roundtable at the Boston University School of Management. The authors gratefully acknowledge the technical support of Karen Kralios, Cindy L. Newson, and Stefanie Pryor, as well as the helpful comments of Gene Andrews, Marcy Crary, Ellen Kossek, Sharon Lobel, Meryl Louis, and David Thomas.

these new complexities – and the ways in which relationships have been transformed by them – must be better understood.

These twin forces of turbulence and diversity require us to rethink what mentoring – and other developmental relationships – look like and *could* look like in the contemporary work environment. To re-view mentoring, we will begin by redefining the nature of developmental alliances in the new context, and delineating the new competencies now required. Then, we will consider the unique developmental challenges that individuals from varied backgrounds face and how these can be addressed. Finally, we will consider various approaches to enhancing the range of developmental alliances available to a diverse workforce, and define several avenues for creative action and research.

Developmental Alliances in the New Context

Environmental turbulence and increasing workforce diversity require everyone to be a learner. Career paths are no longer clearly defined, and career advancement no longer necessarily means movement up the organizational hierarchy. Instead, lateral movement or redefinition of one's current job may be needed to grow new skills and competencies. And, individuals can no longer expect to have lifelong careers in one organization. Since the rules of the game and career opportunities are in such flux, it is difficult for mentors to offer advice to their junior colleagues. In addition, all employees must now build relationships with people who differ in terms of gender, race, and/or cultural background.

The major mentoring-related development concerns of diverse segments of today's workforce can be summarized in several identity group categories, as follows.

Young white males: worried about their own development

The current cohort of young white males may be the first of their identity group to have a strong sense of identity group awareness. For older white men, there was little sense of group identity here; it was like the fish's (un)awareness of water. Our research indicates that while white men in the early stage of their careers may know cognitively that the career contract has changed, they still, at an emotional level, want to enjoy the traditional fast-track, high-security organizational career of their fathers (Hall and Kram, 1994). And they fear that senior management's first priority for those scarce advancement opportunities might be to promote women, people of color, and other underrepresented groups. Indeed, as one faculty colleague has commented, "I know from my own experience [that] some of the young white male master's candidates I teach silently scapegoat white women and minorities for dominating on-campus job placement and career opportunities."

There is a sense of discontinuity here – the young white men, who grew up in a state of privilege, now feel at a disadvantage, perhaps for the first time in their lives. While the values of their generation – and (for some of them) their own experiences with mothers who have careers – may make them sensitive to and supportive of diversity work, their feelings of competition or inequity may hinder their ability to form developmental relationships with people whom they see as different.

As one indication of the depth of this feeling, consider the 1994 US elections, in which the major issues were diversity-related (e.g. welfare and crime, two issues often considered to be code words for race; Proposition 187 in California, stopping social service benefits to undocumented immigrants). The demographic group that voted most heavily Republican in congressional races (and showed the greatest shift in voting from 1992) was white men (*New York Times*, 1994). And the age group with the highest percentage Republican vote was young men, 30–44 years old, the years of strongest concerns for career advancement (Hall, 1976). One interpretation of these voting results is that young white men, feeling alienated from their restructured corporations, insecure in their jobs, or underemployed or unemployed, were scapegoating other groups by voting for candidates who professed to be "tough" on criminals, welfare, undocumented immigrants, and government spending to aid these groups.

Senior white males: besieged, yet responsible

Another identity group with increasing concerns that affect their willingness to mentor are white men in midcareer and midlife. This is the leading edge of the baby boom cohort (Hall and Richter, 1990). After a lifetime of competition with a large cohort of peers, just when they had "made it" to a senior management level, the era of downsizing and restructuring was upon them. And since these fortysomething senior people represent large salaries, their jobs have been the prime candidates for elimination. To compound the situation, the ax falls when they are entering a period of peak financial need, with college tuitions, big mortgages, perhaps responsibilities for ageing parents, along with other accoutrements of an upper middle class lifestyle. This demographic group has suffered greater losses in income level over the last few years than any other group. (And just to rub salt in the wounds, at the same time CEO pay and company profits have been booming (Dumaine, 1994).

To make matters more complex for this group of midcareer white males, however, as long as they are still in their positions of corporate power, they are the ones responsible for implementing corporate diversity programs. So, at a time when they are feeling very insecure about their own careers, they are charged with providing more favorable career conditions for nontraditional younger employees. Yet no one is providing comparable attention and support to their careers. In fact, they are generally seen as the oppressors of the underrepresented groups they are charged with helping. The result is a mix of feeling not understood, pressured, and besieged with threats from all directions, very much aware of their friend next door in the suburbs who has been out of work for 14 months (Smith, 1994). This complex mix of feelings does not contribute to effective developmental relationships with these underrepresented groups.

The senior pioneers: stuck in midlevel and midlife

Another group consists of white women, women of color, men of color and foreign nationals who are getting stuck in their careers, blocked by the glass ceiling. While senior white women and people of color face distinctive concerns and challenges posed by their gender and race, they are all – as Morrison (1992) defines them – nontraditionals and pioneers. That is to say, they are among the first in their respective identity groups to achieve middle and senior management positions in white male dominated settings. While they are seen by their younger identity group colleagues as "successes" in the system, they still feel they have not arrived at the top level.

They feel pressured by these younger group members, as well as by senior white men, to provide more mentoring to their own group. At the same time, the top group is telling them to "be more like us" and put in 70 hours a week to earn that final move upward. And, of course, there are strong pressures from family and others in their personal lives to be more available to them. They certainly have the capacity to provide mentoring to subordinates in their identity groups, and they often do, but their resentment of feeling pressured to do more may affect the emotional quality of the developmental relationships they establish. There is a real need to understand better the career and psychosocial needs of these pioneers as they work through the next steps in their own personal lives and careers.

Women and people of color: bailing out!

Perhaps related to the concerns of the senior pioneers, we continue to see high levels of turnover in many corporations among junior level women and people of color. In addition to glass ceiling and personal life issues, high turnover may also be due to inadequate socialization and mentoring during the early years. With downsizing and slower growth, opportunities for women and people of color are more limited (as they are for everyone). Also, these nontraditionals have few successful role models who can show them how to make it in this new career context. Organizational pressures and the difficulty of attaining or maintaining top level jobs are often intertwined with personal issues related to the costs of "fitting in" and feed into nontraditionals' calculations about leaving versus staying.

It appears to us that many nontraditionals look at the difficult quality of work life of many top level jobs today and simply decide that it is not worth the work and sacrifice necessary for people who look like them to win and then maintain those positions. For example, women may not want to emulate senior women pioneers who are perceived as successful, but

111

Table 5.1 Developmental relationships

In a traditional context: Career and psychosocial assistance from seniors is highly valued	*In a transformed context: Career assistance from seniors is less valued*
Mentor as coach and counselor	Mentor as co-learner
Homogeneous relationships	Heterogeneous relationships
One-to-one hierarchical relationships	Hierarchical, peer, and team relationships
Long-term, single mentorship	
Some coaching and counseling available	Shorter-term and multiple relationships (e.g. core groups, mentoring circles)
	Greater availability of coaching, counseling, and mutual learning through dialogue

with considerable costs to their personal lives. Similarly, people of color may not want to adapt to the homogeneous career culture, viewing senior minority pioneers as having given up too much of their own identities in order to be accepted and successful. Perhaps one of the most effective ways to improve the mentoring and career development environment for non-traditional employees would be to reengineer top jobs to make them more people-friendly (i.e. with the flexibility and autonomy to decide how one's role is enacted).

This, then, completes our listing of the "cast of characters" in the "developmental drama" unfolding in today's turbulent organizations. Now it is time to look more at the drama itself. We will now re-view mentoring, as it exists in the new environment.

Re-viewing Mentoring in the New Context

Mentoring theory and research are rooted in a world which no longer exists, a world of more stable and homogeneous organizational environments. (A summary of this changed context is shown in table 5.1). From early studies we learned that significant relationships between juniors and seniors had the potential to serve career functions and psychosocial functions; the former were aimed primarily at advancing the junior's career, and the latter were aimed primarily at enhancing self-esteem, identity and self-worth (Kram, 1983; Levinson et al., 1978; Dalton and Thompson, 1986).

Lower value of seniors' career advice

Over time, other researchers began to observe that developmental relationships could take a variety of forms. The most enduring and intimate are those commonly labeled as mentoring relationships – those that provide the widest range of psychosocial and career functions and are experienced as quite special. It is now clear that a continuum of relationships exist from short-term instrumental types on one end, to the more enduring and intimate on the other (Thomas, 1990; Thomas and Kram, 1988), and that relationships with peers can also serve learning and development in critical ways (Kram and Isabella, 1985).

We now know that challenging assignments combined with a variety of developmental relationships are essential for learning and development (McCall et al., 1988; McCauley et al., 1989). Given the realities of turbulence and workforce diversity, what are the current and future possibilities for developmental alliances, and how will they look different from those in more traditional contexts?

These changes in environmental conditions may have had more impact on the career, or task-oriented, functions of mentoring than on the psychosocial functions (support, identity growth, etc.) (Kram, 1988). Indeed, the pervasive instability of careers – and the associated uncertainty about what opportunities the future holds – can render certain advice and coaching obsolete and misleading. In contrast, it seems clear that regardless of specific environmental conditions, simply being in a mentoring relationship and receiving emotional support (for both junior and senior party) may be the most important form of career assistance in today's uncertain, high-stress work environment (Kram and Hall, 1991).

Mentors as co-learners

The mentor role has traditionally been conceptualized as one in which the mentor is the expert and the protégé is the learner (although we also know that seniors can also receive important benefits (e.g. self-esteem, satisfaction) from the relationship, (Kram, 1988; Phillips-Jones, 1982; Zey, 1984)).

With the transformation of context, it seems clear that seniors are necessarily becoming learners as well. First, they are no longer experts on career strategy; what worked for seniors in more stable periods will not work for those that seek their guidance on how to navigate to the top of organizations where the "rules" have changed. While seniors may have some insight on the question of survival (given their wisdom of experience and their proximity to decision-makers), they are novices under the new rules, new products, new services, and new technologies. Thus, they are most likely to find themselves co-inquirers in the search for work meaning and career growth in the midst of turbulence. There is some evidence that plateaued managers in a downsizing environment may find some of the personal meaning they are seeking in new relationships with protégés who seek and value their attention and guidance (Kram and Hall, 1991).

Heterogeneous relationships

In this new environment, seniors have the opportunity in their relationships with juniors to learn about the values, needs and perspectives of the younger generation – especially with a diverse workforce. Those who are effective in enabling and empowering a diverse group of employees to work towards a shared vision and set of objectives have discovered the ability to be flexible and attentive to the variety of needs that employees bring to work (Hall and Parker, 1993; Cox, 1993).

Indeed, many organizations have implemented formal mentoring programs to support diversity objectives. Usually senior white men are matched as mentors with junior women and people of color who are viewed as having high potential. Objectives for the program explicitly include the opportunity for senior white men to learn how to coach and counsel those of different backgrounds, to understand better the unique challenges faced by women and people of color, and/or to define policies and practices which best promote diversity in management. For example, companies with such activities include General Electric, NYNEX, Corning, Xerox, Imperial Oil, Dupont, and Northern Telecom.

Working as a co-learner, however, requires a personal stance which may be unfamiliar and/or discomforting for some senior people, Whereas in more stable times coaching and counseling skills were sufficient for the mentoring role, now mentors must also be willing to ask questions, listen and be open about what they don't know and about what they need to learn.[1]

Alternatives to one-on-one hierarchical mentoring

It has become increasingly clear that the one-on-one hierarchical dyad is not the only vehicle for mentoring in the new workplace. Over a decade ago, *peer relationships* were found to be equally valuable in providing both instrumental and psychosocial support to individuals at every career stage (Kram and Isabella, 1985). And they offer unique advantages to individuals, being both more accessible and enduring than most mentoring alliances. At the same time, as organizations have downsized and become flatter and structured around teams, there is a growing recognition that individuals can mentor and learn from various members of their work teams, in addition to the boss (Handy, 1990; 1994). Finally, as the pace of change continues to increase, and resources continue to be constrained, managers and executives are turning toward internal or external coaching as a vehicle for focused and immediate learning (Smith, 1993).

While peer relationships occur naturally through daily work contact and the discovery of common concerns, a number of strategies have emerged to foster peer mentoring, particularly for organizational newcomers. For example, as part of socialization practices, newcomers are matched with "big buddies" who have only a few more years of experience than the newcomer. These pairs are intended to help the newcomer learn the ropes and get established. In assuming the role of "big buddy," the more experienced peer has the opportunity to develop his or her coaching skills and to feel empowered by the act of helping a less experienced colleague.

This type of initiative is based on the assumption that newcomers benefit from multiple relationships with seniors and peers. While the immediate supervisor and other seniors may provide good assignments, coaching and exposure, peers can most readily empathize with the challenges of organizational sense-making, and thus provide a unique kind of support (Louis, 1980; Louis et al., 1983). The very basics – including finding an apartment, figuring out the logistics of banking one's paycheck, learning all the players' names and responsibilities, building a relationship with one's boss, and figuring out the job itself – are more discussable with a "close in age and status" peer.

Peer relationships are also important at other career stages. Most notably, as the workforce becomes increasingly diverse, women and people of color find great value in sharing the challenges posed by being different from the dominant group with peers who share common group memberships (Thomas, 1990; Ibarra, 1993). It is quite common in most organizations to find established networks that exist for the purpose of peer mentoring around common challenges posed to particular identity groups. In essence, gatherings of these groups provide a forum where peer mentoring begins and flourishes.[2]

Shorter-term and multiple relationships

In the context of *teams* (project teams, task forces, committees), task-related peer mentoring can flourish, particularly if the team leader or manager creates expectations and recognition to support such mutual learning. Regardless of the particular task at hand – whether it be product development, installation of a new system, manufacturing of a product, or something else – if a team is necessary, then members have complementary knowledge and skills to share with each other. When coaching, supporting, and learning become part of the work to be done and part of the regular performance review process, members will find many opportunities to learn from each other. And, to the extent that teams bring together individuals at different career stages, both hierarchical and peer mentoring, as well as task and personal learning can occur.

In recent years, another kind of group has emerged that exists for the primary purpose of personal learning, rather than for the purpose of accomplishing task-related work. Deriving from the challenges of increased workforce diversity, these groups have taken two primary forms: *core groups* (also called dialogue groups) (e.g. at DEC (Walker and Hansen, 1992)) and *mentoring circles* (e.g. NYNEX). Core groups bring together individuals of diverse backgrounds who want to learn how to more effectively build supportive relationships with those who come from different gender, racial, and/or cultural backgrounds. Mentoring circles bring together one or several senior managers with junior or midlevel professionals/managers for the purpose of supporting the latters' development. In both instances, participation is voluntary, and trained facilitators help the groups to develop an effective process for mutual learning.

Greater availability of coaching

Finally, internal and external coaches are increasingly viewed as key resources in helping managers and executives learn, particularly when time is very limited and developing new competencies and perspectives is essential (Smith, 1993; Pryor, 1994). Often used in conjunction with a management development program or a 360-degree feedback process, a coach will help an individual to reflect on his or her own experience, interpret data about his or her impact on the organization, and develop strategies for building a wider repertoire of effective behavioral responses to current challenges. While not labeled as such, these alliances are a form of peer mentoring; the coach provides a sounding board, support, active listening and advice in much the same way that a trusted and informed peer might. The value of external coaches is now becoming more recognized as a unique forum for bringing new perspective into the organization, and insuring confidentiality and a safe environment in which to maximize personal learning (Kinlaw, 1993; Mink et al., 1993).

Now that we have considered how mentoring has changed in the new workplace, let us consider how the nature of development for various employee groups has been altered. Not surprisingly, progress has been mixed.

Diversity and Development in a Turbulent Context

A central concept in current work on diversity is identity (Alderfer, 1983), and identity is also a major component of development in the career (Hall, 1976). Of the four facets of career development (performance, attitudes, adaptability, and identity), Hall (1976) has described identity as probably the most important:

> It is the person's sense of identity which, by definition, helps [one] evaluate [oneself]. It tells [a person] how [he or she] fits into the social environment. And it tells [one] about [one's] uniqueness as a human being. . . . In Western society the development of one's personal sense of identity is closely tied to the establishment of one's occupational identity. . . . (Hall, 1976, p. 134)

Thus, career development is a synthesizing process, increasing the fit over time between personal identity and career role, integrating the person and the work environment. And, as we have already seen, people in different identity groups have quite different experiences in their careers, particularly in their mentoring relationships.

Socioeconomic status and mentoring

Mullen (1994) reports from her review that younger people, men, those from higher socioeconomic backgrounds, nonwhite individuals, and shorter-tenured employees were more likely to be mentored than were women, white individuals, people from lower socioeconomic backgrounds, and longer-tenured employees.

One intriguing study found that for people from upper-middle and upper-class backgrounds, those who had the most career mentoring also received the most promotions. This relationship was not found for lower socioeconomic groups (Whitely et al., 1991). The authors predicted these findings, based on the positive effects of perceived similarity between mentor and protégé, resulting in strong interpersonal bonds and commitment from the mentor. Protégés from higher social classes "may also share social values, skills and networks with senior managers, thus forging strong bonds" (p. 334), which would contribute to their career progress.

Thus, these results suggest that social class diversity in the mentoring relationship may *impede* the junior member's career progress. There may be a "rich get richer" phenomenon, in which employees who are already privileged by their demographic background receive unequal developmental benefits from mentoring in their work settings. (The "good news" in the Whitely et al. (1991) study was that this class-moderated effect was not found for total compensation; mentoring was positively related to compensation across class groups.)

Racioethnic identity and development

Let us consider more specifically racioethnic identity, and how it affects the nature of development through mentoring. Almost thirty years ago, Erikson (1966) pointed out that members of minority groups, such as African-Americans, have to do double identity work, resolving both what it means to be a mature human being and what it means to be a member of their identity group in a predominantly white society. More recently, research on black professional women has illustrated the range of complicated issues that they face as they develop careers in white male-dominated settings (Bell, 1990).

Cross-race relationship are similarly complex. We can expect, however, that relationships across racial boundaries present an even greater challenge to those white individuals who have had little experience in their communities with people of different races (in contrast to white men mentoring white women, where at least they have had relationships with wives, daughters and co-workers beforehand). The lack of familiarity and awkwardness individuals are likely to experience in building relationships across racial boundaries probably accounts for why it happens so infrequently in organizations (Thomas and Alderfer, 1989; Kram and Bragar, 1992).

Mentoring availability and race Concerning the availability of mentoring to different racial groups, the literature contains mixed findings. Koberg et al. (1992) reported that nonwhite minority members were more likely to be mentored than were white individuals. However, Cox and Nkomo (1991), in a study of 729 black and white MBAs, found that blacks reported significantly less mentoring assistance than whites. These findings are in line with Whitely et al.'s (1992) finding that people from higher socioeconomic status (SES) backgrounds, which is often correlated with being white, received *more* mentoring than lower SES members.

Mentoring process and race   Thomas (1990) demonstrates how the history of race relations in the US infuses relationships in organizations; and in particular, how negative archetypes derived from slavery make it very difficult for whites and blacks to form positive developmental alliances with each other. Because these irrational dynamics occur largely at an unconscious level, they are very difficult to understand, much less alter.

Thus, racial stereotypes and "taboos" make it very difficult for even well-intentioned individuals of both races to develop effective alliances with each other. As Thomas (1989) argues, cross-race and cross-gender relationships may be the most difficult, given historical dynamics in which "white men dominated because black men could not adequately protect their families, especially black women, from white men's whimsical and most often violent intrusion" (1989, p. 282). For example, senior white men's attempts to mentor black women can be experienced as follows: "White men appropriate black women, black women can rise up by going along with this, and black men are angry and suspicious" (p. 282).

As an example of the impact of stereotypes and taboos, we have observed in one large professional services firm that senior white managers have concerns about the competence of associates who are not white males. These concerns lead them to be more cautious about initiating mentoring relationships and working closely with people in these other groups, particularly African-Americans and women. Certainly, this can be a problem in a demanding, fast-moving, high-stakes environment where people need to be able to depend upon their co-workers' output and to have trust in the quality of their work. This may also explain phenomena such as health problems (James et al., 1994) and low representation (Ibarra, 1993) of people of color and women in higher-level positions and in informal networks in predominantly white male organizations.

What seems most to influence the ability of blacks and whites to build meaningful developmental alliances is how both parties handle racial complexities. Identifying two main strategies – denial and suppression or direct engagement – Thomas (1993) found that when both individuals used the same strategy for managing racial complexities, they were able to form deep mentoring relationships. When one party preferred to deny race issues and the other wanted to make them discussable, the relationship was likely to remain more distant and instrumental. It these instances, seniors could provide career functions such as sponsorship and challenging assignments, but interpersonal intimacy would be quite limited.

Thomas (1990; 1993) suggests that black managers benefit from what he calls "dual support" – relationships with both black and white seniors. From their white mentors they are most likely to get the sponsorship, coaching, and exposure that positions them for advancement; and from their black mentors they derive the psychosocial support, including role modeling, counseling and friendship. The latter could empathize with and model strategies for handling challenges posed by being black in a white organization.

The dynamics of cross-cultural relationships parallel those observed in cross-race relationships (Adler, 1991). As organizations compete in the global marketplace it becomes that much more essential that individuals are able to mentor across cultural boundaries so that individuals of different cultural backgrounds can grow in their careers and organizational performance can be supported – rather than hindered – be work relationships that necessarily cross cultural boundaries. This requires better understanding of the cultural stereotypes that infuse such alliances, and a willingness to develop the competencies to build authentic communication with those of different backgrounds.

Gender and development

Like individuals of racial minority group backgrounds, women face unique identity issues as they move through their careers. Most often, these manifest themselves as difficult choices to be made in effectively managing work and family roles. Indeed, a review of adult development literature on women clearly suggests that identity development is quite different from that of men (Gallos, 1989; Baker-Miller, 1991; Bell, 1990).

Cross-gender mentoring relationships may be limited in value since male mentors are unlikely to provide adequate role models or empathy for the complexities that women face. Here lies the value of having multiple relationships with both men and woman who can provide an array of career and psychosocial functions (Kram and Bragar, 1992). None the less, cross-gender relationships are critical, particularly for the career functions that they provide (e.g. sponsorship, coaching, challenging assignments).

Mentoring availability and gender   As was true with race, there are differing results on gender and availability of mentoring. Cox and Nkomo (1991) and Dreher and Ash (1990) found no significant gender differences in reported receipt of mentoring over the span of the career. Similar results were reported by Raggins and McFarlin (1990). Thomas (1990), and Turban and Dougherty (1994). Koberg et al. (1992), however, did find men more likely to be mentored than women.

Mentoring process and gender   We have learned from earlier studies of cross-gender mentoring that subtle – and not so subtle – dynamics can prevent developmental alliances between men and women from getting beyond the initiation phase (Kram, 1988; Bowen, 1984; Burke, 1984). First sexual tension and fears of intimacy make both men and women cautious about spending informal time together, occasions when coaching and counseling often flourish. And while, with experience, men and women learn how to manage these tensions, we have found in our own research, currently in process, that the threat of litigation can perpetuate a cautious

119

attitude about initiating interaction with someone of the opposite sex. As one executive told us, "Just once, I'd like to have an open dialogue with a female subordinate without feeling that I needed to have a lawyer present!" (Hall and Kram, 1994).

More subtle, perhaps, are the stereotypes that men and women bring to relationships about appropriate sex role behavior (Owen and Todor, 1993). From intergroup theory we know that such stereotyping of the other group can lead to self-fulfilling prophecies, reinforcing original perceptions (Alderfer, 1983). Consequently, as women and men build developmental alliances they may unknowingly collude in familiar and stereotypical roles. For example, junior women may find themselves acting as if they need protection, while senior men willingly provide more protection than they might to their male protégés. While in the short run such protection might be warranted and useful particularly in hostile environments, in the longer run such behavior undermines junior women's capacity to establish independence, authority and a credible track record.

These subtle gender expectations are less well understood as they relate to women in more senior roles in organizations. It is becoming increasingly clear that both men and women experience discomfort with women in positions of authority, in part because, historically, expectations of appropriate behavior for managers and for women are in conflict (O'Leary and Ickovics, 1992; Kram and McCollom, forthcoming. Thus as women gain status and experience in organizations, their increasingly assertive behavior may collide with tacit yet powerful expectations of how women should behave. Male executives will not be as willing to mentor, sponsor and coach them, and/or potential protégés will experience them as unnurturing and/or unavailable to support their development (Parker and Kram, 1993).

These complexities help to explain the phenomenon of the glass ceiling to some extent (Morrison et al., 1987). The reluctance of senior male executives to promote women into executive roles is rooted in deeply held gender stereotypes and expectations (Ruderman et al., 1995). Morrison et al. (1987) suggest, based on their study of successful female executives, that corporate cultures maintain a "narrow band" of acceptable behavior for women. Thus, for example, as they get promoted, their assertive behavior (necessary to do the job) will often be labeled as "too aggressive." While increasing numbers of managers have been successful in challenging the stereotypes that interfere with helping young women to launch new careers, the personal learning and change required to transcend the potent effects of assumptions related to who should hold and exercise power at the top of organizations is far more difficult.

Indeed, we found in our diversity word with one organization that executive males saw senior women as "too aggressive" and junior women as "too passive" or "lacking in confidence" (Hall and Kram, 1994). While these women had been identified as high performers and high-potentials, these criticisms of their styles were holding them back from further advancement. Our hypothesis is that these views reflect deeply held and unarticulated stereotypes and expectations that vary systematically by organizational level. We further hypothesize that it is generally easier to move beyond the negative views of junior women than it is to move beyond the negative views of senior women, reflecting a fundamental discomfort with women holding positions of power.

Another important consequence of these gender stereotypes is that the value of opposite-sex role models is limited. While senior men can coach, sponsor, and protect junior women, their style and approach to handling some challenging situations at work may not be appropriate or acceptable to these protégés. For example, the female protégé who emulates her male mentor's behavior in conflict situations may be labeled as too pushy or aggressive; these negative attributions may then prevent her from attaining the next promotion or challenging assignment. Similarly, the experience of work/family conflicts is quite different for women and men, given powerful expectations held of appropriate behavior for mothers and fathers (Hall, 1991; 1993).

There does appear to be one gender-related difference in mentoring which is emerging from the literature: women seem to be more effective in learning from mentoring and other relationships than are men. Noe (1988), in studying formal mentoring programs in nine educational institutions, found that women were seen as utilizing their mentors more effectively than were male protégés. In a similar vein, Van Velsor and Hughes (1990) found that women leaders were significantly more likely than men to use learnings from other people as key development events. While part of his difference may be women's restricted access to other developmental experiences, such as challenging assignments, Van Velsor and Hughes also report that women learned more from reflection and self-assessment than did their male counterparts. Thus, it appears that women are more aware of their identity in the workplace and better able to utilize help from relationships for development than are men.

Strategies to Enhance Mentoring

During the last few years, considerable progress has been made in clarifying the range of strategies available for enhancing the availability and quality of mentoring in organizations (Murray and Owen, 1991; Kram and Bragar 1992). While formal programs were once thought to be the most direct and effective way to establish and encourage mentoring, it is becoming clear that these have limitations which render them appropriate in some, but not all, situations (Kram and Bragar, 1992). Now, it is more commonly recognized that a variety of human resources programs and practices can be designed (or modified) to directly encourage, reward and support mentoring and other developmental alliances (see table 5.2).

Formal mentoring programs

One of the best reasons to consider a formal mentoring program is to legitimize and facilitate relationships between individuals who might otherwise not easily build rapport with one another. In an increasingly diverse

Table 5.2 Strategies to enhance mentoring

Strategy	Outcomes
Create a formal program to benefit *all* groups (white males included)	• Relationships between individuals from different identity groups • Mentoring for a small group of high-potentials • Good learning for white males
Include mentoring in the performance management and compensation systems	• Accountability for developing others • Feedback to individuals on their relationship skills • Reduced tension caused by compensation inequities
Provide education and training – for everyone	• Opportunities to learn core relationship competencies • Deeper understanding of mentoring alternatives • Learning for white males
Build mentoring into succession planning and development practices: a "hook" for senior white males	• Greater top management attention to assessment and development of nontraditionals • Effective assignment management process • Mentoring for high potential candidates • Active development of nontraditionals
Encourage dialogue groups, networks, and mentoring circles – for everyone	• Enhanced relationship-based learning opportunities • Mentoring between individuals from different identity groups • Good learning (safe, yet challenging) for senior white males)
Encourage work teams to provide mentoring	• Enhanced mentoring for real-time, business-driven learning

workforce, then, it may be necessary to create such mechanisms for men and women and/or majority and minority individuals to build developmental alliances. Indeed, many of the formal mentoring programs initiated in recent years were for this purpose (Kram and Bragar, 1992; Murray and Owen, 1991).

Most formal mentoring programs are designed to facilitate developmental relationships for high-potential candidates, and/or women and people of color, but they aid the learning of privileged groups (e.g. senior white males) as well. With a particular target population in mind, program objectives and design can be tailored to the needs of the participants. Educational components will often include segments on coaching, counseling and competencies required to work with people of different backgrounds. Formal programs that support diversity initiatives usually involve cross-gender and cross-race alliances; in one telecommunications company, "diversity partnerships" were created to bring together minority men and women to address common challenges posed to them in a white-male-dominated company.

It appears that these initiatives can promote the learning, development and advancement of both protégés and mentors (Noe, 1988; Burke, 1984; Chao et al., 1992). For example, at a large oil company, senior male mentors were matched with high-potential female protégés for the purpose of enhancing the women's development opportunities. Because careful attention was given to selecting and matching the pairs, the educational component of the program, and the ongoing follow-up process, these paired relationships became mutually beneficial for most who participated. Even as the company went through a period of downsizing, most of the pairs remained intact and continued to provide support and learning opportunities for both parties.

However, many such programs are not as successful. The reasons for this are now fairly clear. When participation is not entirely voluntary, mentors or protégés may come to resent their involvement and therefore negatively relate to their mentoring partner. In addition, if participants do not attain adequate educational preparation to initiate and build relationships with people of diverse backgrounds, it is all too likely that the relationships will remain superficial and become a source of frustration and/or disillusionment. Finally, if the program is implemented in a cultural context that does not reward managers for taking the time to develop junior colleagues, or trust between juniors and seniors is generally eroded, then formally arranged relationships will not thrive, but rather mirror these unsupportive dynamics (Kram and Bragar, 1992).

Attention to these design issues can maximize the potential benefits of such alliances. Indeed, there is now sufficient empirical evidence to suggest that formal mentoring relationships are associated with positive career outcomes including organizational socialization, satisfaction, and salary (Chao et al., 1992), and that these arranged relationships can provide both career and psychosocial support (Noe, 1988). As long as the contest supports a well-designed program, positive results for most who participate can be expected.

Even if conditions are optimal, there are at least two major limitations of formal programs that should not be overlooked. First, they can accommodate only a small number of people, because of the resource-intensive nature of working with matched pairs, over time, with education and training provided. (This is a problem if there is a large population that needs help.) Second, such formal programs communicate the message that one mentor relationship – rather than a network of developmental relationships – is key to enhancing individuals' development (Kram and Bragar, 1992).

Thus, under certain conditions, establishing a formal program can be a good strategy for enhancing mentoring. These conditions include: voluntary participation; adequate education, training and follow-up; a relatively small target population who otherwise are not likely to attain adequate mentoring from senior white males; an explicit intention that the program is a springboard for developing multiple developmental alliances beyond those formally created; and a cultural context that generally supports attention to development.

Performance management and compensation systems (especially for senior white males)

Systems that appraise and manage performance can substantially affect the extent to which individuals take the time to develop relationships that support others' (as well as their own) development. Whether or not a formal mentoring program exists, mechanisms that *acknowledge* the importance of coaching and counseling, *monitor* whether individuals are attending to the development of their subordinates' and peers' learning, *provide feedback* and *reward* managers on how well this relational work is done, contribute to a culture that supports development and developmental relationships.

In practice, such systems include appraisal processes that assess how well individuals are contributing to others' learning, and also include discussions with superiors about actions that are taken to support learning and development of one's subordinates and peers. This combination of assessment and dialogue is especially important in an increasingly diverse workforce. Too often, managers will avoid the difficult work of giving critical feedback (particularly to someone of a different race, gender, or cultural background). Rather than experience the anxiety and incompetence associated with discussing sensitive issues which might evoke anger and disappointment – if not threats of discrimination – individuals will instead focus on what they know how to do well (i.e. giving positive feedback, working with subordinates they already know). As a result, people of different backgrounds do not get needed developmental feedback, and relationships that cross gender, racial and cultural boundaries do not evolve.

A 360-degree feedback process is especially useful for helping individuals to understand how they are perceived by others, and areas in which they can improve their performance and relationships (Hollenbeck, 1992). Through anonymous feedback from subordinates, peers, customers, as well as superiors, individuals have the opportunity to attain a realistic view of how well they contribute to others' learning as well as how they might alter their style to become more of a mentor and coach to others. Short of this comprehensive process, many organizations are conducting upward appraisals and/or soliciting peer feedback as input to the formal appraisal process.

It is becoming increasingly common to include diversity objectives in the annual review process as a means to hold individuals accountable for developing people of different backgrounds (Morrison, 1992; Rice, 1994). Companies such as Xerox, Burger King, and Hoechst Celanese all have policies establishing diversity as a business objective, for which managers are held accountable. This creates expectations that individuals will identify women and people of color in their business units that have potential, and then actively develop them through challenging assignments, coaching, and exposure.

As a next step, managers who are appraised as excellent developers of underrepresented employees should be *rewarded* for this work. At Hoechst Celanese, after Ernest Drew became CEO, workforce diversity became one of four performance criteria (equally weighted) which affected executives' pay and bonuses. As Clarence C. Kegler, manager of a Hoechst Celanese textile plant in Shelby, North Carolina, observed, "When Ernie started hitting people in the pocketbook, they began to value diversity" (Rice, 1994, p. 80). (Drew describes himself as the company's diversity "steward".)

Education and training – for everyone

Most employees can benefit from the opportunity to better understand how to initiate and nurture relationships that enable mutual learning. There are a variety of workshop and seminar designs available to provide vehicles for learning the coaching and counseling skills so fundamental to the mentoring process (cf. Phillips-Jones, 1982, 1993a and b; Murray and Owen, 1991; Shea, 1992; Kram, 1988). These structured opportunities to learn about mentoring, to reflect on one's own experience in relationships, to practice fundamental listening, feedback and self-disclosure skills, and to clarify expectations for new mentoring alliances are essential to the success of formal mentoring programs. Ray Hood-Phillips, a management consultant and former vice president of diversity affairs at Burger King, works to insure that the content of a program is "not combative, guilt-driven, or contemptuous of white males, which some programs are" (Rice, 1994, p. 84). Creating safe-yet-challenging learning opportunities for white males is an important ingredient of a well-designed program.

These same designs are equally valuable where formal mentoring programs would not fit with the organization's culture but where there is none the less a desire to enhance individuals' mentoring capabilities. Indeed, many organizations have defined this as their primary strategy for enhancing the mentoring process: offer education to individuals at every career stage, and encourage them to build alliances that support their development as well as others' development. In combination with such educational alternatives, some organizations distribute lists of workshop participants to facilitate individuals connecting with others who have a special interest in mentoring.

Dialogue groups, networks, and mentoring circles – for everyone

We know from the systems theory concept of "requisite variety" that a diverse and turbulent environment demands an equally diverse set of relationship competencies, as well as social support in developing them. New development technologies enable individuals to reflect on and learn from their own experience, and in particular, to learn in relationships with others. Schon (1990), Senge (1990), and Isaacs (1993) have focused on the competencies required for learning through dialogue – including listening, articulating one's assumptions, setting aside one's own position, reflecting on one's own knowledge, and the willingness to assume a tentative stance.

Barbara Walker was the first practitioner to apply the dialogue method to diversity in her work at Digital Equipment Corporation (Walker and Hansen, 1992), and in our own work we have found it to be a powerful method for opening up communication. This learning technology is an important way to "Keep it safe" and to provide challenge at the same time (an especially important set of conditions for the learning of senior white males). Thus, "learning how to learn" and "valuing differences" have become core competencies for managing in a turbulent and diverse environment.

While homogeneous networks have been around since the mid-1970s, it is only in recent years that these have been viewed more formally as mentoring circles, which can support organizational objectives. Whereas in the early years, networks that brought particular identity groups together were experienced as threatening and subversive, they are now more often seen as vehicles for reducing the isolation that many from diverse backgrounds experience upon entry into white and male-dominated settings. Those who participate in such networks build developmental alliances with peers and seniors who share common experiences and concerns; they also find access to information and job opportunities that can enhance their career development. Such groups also help to focus executives' attention on specific issues of concern that otherwise might go unnoticed (e.g. work/family concerns, lack of mentorship for women or people of color, etc.).

Succession planning and development practices: a "hook" for senior white males

Hall (1994) has argued that building diversity into management and executive development programs (as a way of strengthening the talent pool) is one of the most basic current needs in the improvement of such programs. And, in fact, leadership development processes serve as an important "hook" to interest senior management (who are usually white males) in fostering mentoring alliances, particularly for women, people of color and foreign nationals who would otherwise find it difficult to connect with senior white males in their organizations.

Many well-managed organizations, large and small, have found that decisions about key assignments are best deliberated in a group context, in order to benefit from the multiple perspectives available on particular candidates (Hall and Foulkes, 1991). Indeed, when assignment and succession planning decisions are made by individuals, rather than a group, a variety of biases often will govern such decisions, and go unnoticed (Hall, 1986). For example, in settings where there is an increasingly diverse pool of candidates to draw upon, there is mounting evidence that without careful (group) deliberation, executives will tend to choose candidates who they feel most comfortable with and who are most similar to them (Ruderman et al., 1994). This "similar to me" phenomenon can lead to a process of "executive cloning" (Hall, 1986; 1994).

There are several mechanisms that can facilitate effective succession planning, and in turn, effective developmental alliances for high-potential candidates. First, it is critical that the group responsible for identifying candidates clarify the requirements of specific positions (linking to the business strategy) as well as the development needs of particular candidates. Second, in order to insure that candidates of diverse backgrounds are adequately considered for key positions, it is quite useful to make diversity an explicit objective in the succession planning process (Morrison, 1992), in the same way that it is made an objective in a manager's business plan.

Identification of candidates is only one part of the process. Thus, an important third step is development plans that support candidates in moving into key positions. Leadership development research clearly suggests that the assignments and relationships candidates experience are the most critical factors in their development (McCall et al., 1988; Hall, 1994).

Finally, when development plans call for participation of diverse groups of junior and senior people in management and/or leadership development programs on site or off site, this can be an excellent opportunity to foster developmental alliances that strengthen the impact of such experiences (McCauley and Young, 1993).

Mentoring in natural work settings: diverse work teams

There are undoubtedly other innovative ways yet to be discovered to promote developmental relationships among individuals of diverse background. For example, when project teams or task forces are being formed, many organizations make a conscious attempt to create diversity in their membership. This consideration of diverse staffing should be a regular part of assignment decisions to increase the likelihood that team members will form developmental alliances with each other. The increased use of teams for responding to the turbulence of the business environment, coupled with the increasing diversity of the workforce, offer untapped opportunities for mutual learning and support. Looking for such natural learning opportunities in regular work activities is as essential as the formal programs and practices already outlined.

Conclusions: Implications for Human Resource Research and Strategy

Our central thesis here has been that the new chaotic corporate environment demands (*and contributes to*) continuous and real-time learning for survival (Waterman et al., 1994). This is true both for individuals and for organizations. And there is no way that this learning can be limited to traditional methods of organization and individual development – through assessment of learning needs, diagnosis of the current level of competency, development of new learning programs, delivery of these programs, evaluation, and revision. With this traditional organizational development approach, by the time the program is up and running, the learning needs have shifted.

What is needed is a learning technology that contains intelligence – that is self-learning, and that is right there on the spot where the business tasks that require learning are being addressed (Hall, 1994). One technology that is uniquely suited to provide rapid-response, real-time, and business-driven learning is mentoring. Historically, however, mentoring has been seen as a way of helping individuals develop their careers, not as an element of business strategy. Not only has mentoring been seen as aimed at the individual, but more recently it has become associated with diversity programs and with disadvantaged individuals.

Thus, mentoring – as a developmental tool – has been two steps away from the organizational mainstream: (1) it has focused on individuals, not strategy; and (2) those individuals are low-power, often marginal employees. As a result, it is often not taken too seriously by top management. Let us consider some of the implications of this situation for research and strategy.

Implications for research on mentoring and learning

The primary need is for more research on the issue raised at the beginning of this chapter: how do mentoring processes relate to the process of organizational adaptation to a dynamic environment? Little of the literature covered in this chapter addresses this issue of organization-level learning. Yet when we look seriously at organizational learning processes, a major way they occur is through *social networks* and the opening up of previously blocked information channels and the releasing of human energy and commitment (Wheatley, 1992; Handy, 1994).

We need careful research on how learning occurs in networks. Sproull and Kiesler (1992) have identified ways that electronic communication can produce what they call second-order effects, beyond productivity and cost improvements, and these effects entail more complex patterns of learning and the formation of community. What we do not know is the process by which this learning occurs, although it does appear to lower barriers to participation often found in face-to-face meetings, such as race, gender, nationality, and age. Viewed through the lens of mentoring, it would be possible to examine the detailed dynamics of electronic communication patterns to see what it is in the process of the relationships that produces organizational learning.

The same benefits of a mentoring lens would result in more careful studies of the processes of effective teams. Like networks, teams are increasingly becoming the "stuff" of which organizations are made (Hirschhorn, 1991; Ketchum and Trist, 1992). We know teams are effective as organizational agents of learning, but we need more detailed process research to know why. In particular, in-depth studies of teams would illuminate the conditions and processes that facilitate both task and personal learning among members.

And finally, there is a need for careful research to study the links between dyadic learning from mentoring and any resulting organization-level learning. Organization learning is not simply the aggregate of individual and dyadic learning. There is a transformative process which fundamentally alters the nature of the system as a result of learning processes at the individual and group levels (Isaacs, 1993; Weisbord et al., 1993). People have described this transformative process with words like "mystery" and "magic." Our view is that much of the current interest in spirituality (e.g. Moore, 1992; Peck, 1993; Redfield, 1993; Conger et al., 1994) in organizations is in part a seeking for the meaning of this system transformation process. Our view is that a careful empirical tracking of learning effects at successively higher levels of systems would be another useful tool in the search for this meaning.

Research is also needed to revisit the concept of career stages (Hall, 1976) and the new ways in which career stages manifest themselves and relate to mentoring relationships in contemporary, more permeably-bounded organizations (Mirvis and Hall, 1994). Are stages such as exploration, establishment, advancement, maintenance, and disengagement still relevant today? Do they happen in sorter *learning cycles*, such that individuals go through several series of these cycles over the total work life (1994)?

Earlier, Kram (1988) and Baird and Kram (1983) had described the different career-related needs of mentor partners in various career stages, all of which were based upon, the assumption that the mentor had more career-related experience and knowledge than the protégé. It is increasingly difficult to identify the modal developmental needs of individuals in the establishment stage, the advancement, or the maintenance stage in the contemporary environment. Moreover, how do those varying needs impact the development of a mentoring relationship?

And what is the current status of the general stages or phases of the mentoring relationship (Kram, 1988)? Do we still find a cycle of initiation, cultivation, separation, and redefinition in a complete mentoring relationship? Does the overall span of the relationship tend to be shorter now, along with shorter cycle times in most other organizational endeavors? Is the process of initiation more complex now, with more managed mentoring relationships? It would be useful to study formal mentoring programs with an eye to examining what interventions facilitate smooth movement from one phase to the next. And, with greater mobility, does redefinition take place as often, or are such relationships more likely to end completely now?

Finally, while considerable progress has been made in understanding the complexities of developmental relationships that cross gender and racial boundaries (Thomas, 1993; Cox, 1993; Kram, 1988; Ibarra, 1993) more study of the evolution of these alliances will further clarify the challenges posed by diversity and the competencies required to develop productive alliances.

This kind of inquiry is essential if individuals of diverse backgrounds are to have the opportunities to learn and to address central developmental concerns through mentoring.

Relational learning and organizational strategy

There is much untapped potential in developmental relationships as a vehicle for developing and implementing organizational strategy. With all of the focus in recent years on corporate strategy, we have lost sight of the fact that strategy is pursued by *strategists* – executives working individually and collectively. Little attention has been paid to the process by which executives learn as they pursue strategic objectives and intent. Strategy has been viewed as something "out there," beyond the experience of the executives involved. We need to think more about the *purpose of the organization in terms that have a very personal, human meaning for employees* (Bartlett and Ghosal, 1994).

Recent research (Quinn, 1992) has shown that executive learning is a key part of the strategy process. And we know from the work of Argyris and Schon (see, e.g. Argyris, 1994) that unexamined and overlearned programs of behavior often trap executives in loops of dysfunctional decision-making.

What is needed is a clear, simple process for executives to engage in self-learning as a means to improving strategic decisions. We would argue that this kind of "meta-learning" should contain the following elements:

- a clear time frame (for ongoing long-term personal change process, as well as very focused, short-term skill development);
- guided self-reflection;
- 360-degree feedback (from peers, boss, subordinates, customers, and others);
- a personal coach;
- use of the above elements to produce a careful self-assessment; with clear learning objectives.

A recent survey of corporate practices in the area of executive coaching has found that these elements are essential to make the learning relevant to the personal development needs of the individual and to the needs of the business (Pryor, 1994). This sort of learning can take place in a formal executive education program, but it happens more often on the job, simply as part of helping the executive improve her or his effectiveness at work.

When this process works well, the executive discovers a *self-directed process of personal learning*, in addition to improving the specific competencies which were targeted for development (Hall, 1994). The more powerful meta-skills of self-reflection, obtaining feedback, and collaborative learning through relationships result in a higher level of adaptability, which is what the contemporary rapidly-changing environment demands in an executive (Seibert et al., forthcoming).

The role of the HR executive is to design and champion a process that will promote this kind of relationship-based learning. *The critical task for the HR professional is to make the learning elements user-friendly and work-enhancing.* For example, to promote a diversity strategy in a professional services firm, a group of senior male executives were asked to conduct a "dialogue"-type (Isaacs, 1993) conversation with junior women, the objective being to understand as much as they could the experience of being a woman professional in that organization. Since the objective was *understanding*, not problem-solving or action, the executives were encouraged to put their own perspectives aside and simply try to hear what the women were saying about their personal experiences.

The senior male executives had originally been resisting the diversity initiative as "nice to do, but a diversion from real work." After having these dialogue sessions they were able to experience for themselves how undiscussable gender issues had been sapping productivity in their own business units. And from one simple conversation, each senior executive was able to develop an action plan for improving the effectiveness of his unit. Each plan was submitted in writing to the head of the division, who later met with each executive to discuss and possibly modify the plan. The group of executives serve as developmental resources to one another. Outside consultants are also being utilized as coaches to the executives. Each action plan has a six-month time frame.

Concluding thoughts

In sum, then, it appears that relationship-based learning represents an important missing link in organizational transformation. No matter how much an organization is reengineered, restructured, or realigned, if the structures and tasks are changed but the people are not, then the new structure is doomed. We need to stop thinking of individual development and organization development as two separate tasks. In fact, one of the best forms of action learning for executives is to consciously design learning experiences around ongoing organizational transformation activities.

To make this link between relational learning and business strategy, we need to understand more about the basic processes of developmental relationships. As we saw from our review of the literature on mentoring and career development, much of the research here has had an "input-output" quality to it: e.g. studies of availability of mentoring versus career outcomes. As Taylor Cox described the research on group identity outcomes, "Unfortunately, nearly all of the empirical work on group identity effects of mentoring have addressed quantitative measures of mentor help more than the quality of the relationships" (Cox, 1993, p. 204). We need more "thick description" (i.e. data with rich detail) of the dynamics of various kinds of mentoring relationships (e.g. Kram, 1988; Thomas, 1993; Cox, 1993).

And we also need more research and practice (and research-in-practice) dealing with the links between diversity work, developmental relationships, and corporate strategic success. Ten years ago the concept of linking HR practices to corporate strategy was only a lofty goal (albeit a much-discussed one). We are just now beginning to develop some very concrete ways to make these linkages happen (Seibert et al., forthcoming; Hall, 1994). This is an ideal time for creative action research on these real-time learning processes. And, given the sensitivity of the issues involved – a potent brew involving power, sex, and race – this is an ideal time for conviction and courage on the part of HR researchers and practitioners.

NOTES

1 These "relational" competencies required of mentors in today's context are more aligned with those that women tend to enact more easily than men as a result of sex role socialization (Fletcher, 1994; Belenky et al., 1986; Jordan et al., 1991). This suggests that male executives who want to build developmental alliances with high-potentials of diverse backgrounds face the challenge and excitement of considerable personal learning about relational skills such as nurturing and open-ness. It also helps to understand why – without focused attention on developing these new competencies – mentoring across gender and racial boundaries doesn't happen.

2 It is quite common, for example, to find various associations within a given organization that cater to particular groups such as black managers, women managers and executives, Hispanic employees, Asian employees, etc. Each of these are likely to have regular meetings in which special topics of common concern are addressed, with or without guest speakers. While these vary in terms of the extent to which they are funded and sanctioned by the organization, they generally provide a very important source of peer mentoring for those who attend.

REFERENCES

Adler, N. J. (1991). *International Dimensions of Organizational Behavior*, 2nd ed. Boston: PWS-Kent.

Alderfer, C. P. (1983). An intergroup perspective on group dynamics. In J. Lorsch (ed.), *Handbook of Organizational Behavior*. Englewood Cliffs, NJ: Prentice-Hall.

Argyris, C. (1985). *Strategy, Change and Defensive Routines*. Boston: Pitman.

Argyris, C. (1994). Good communication that blocks learning. *Harvard Business Review*, July–August, 77–85.

Baird, L., and Kram, K. E. (1983). Career dynamics: Managing the superior–subordinate relationship. *Organizational Dynamics*, Summer, 46–64.

Baker-Miller, J. (1991). The development of women's sense of self. In J. V. Jordan, A. G. Kaplan, J. Baker-Miller, I. P. Stiver, and J. L. Surrey (eds), *Women's Growth in Connection* (11–27). New York: Guilford Press.

Bartlett, C. A., and Ghosal, S. (1994). Changing the role of top management: Beyond strategy to purpose. *Harvard Business Review*, November–December, 79–88.

Belenky, M. F., Clinchy, B. M., Goldberger, N. R., and Tarule, J. M. (1986). *Women's Ways of Knowing*. New York: Basic Books.

Bell, E. L. (1990). The bicultural life experiences of career-oriented black women. *Journal of Organizational Behavior*, 11(6), 459–77.

Bowen, D. D. (1984). The role of identification in mentoring female proteges. *Group and Organizational Studies*, 11, 61–74.

Burke, R. (1984). Mentors in organizations. *Group and Organization Studies*, 9(3), 353–72.

Chao, G. T., Walz, P. M., and Gardner, P. D. (1992). Formal and informal mentorships: A comparison on mentoring functions and contrast with nonmentored counterparts. *Personnel Psychology*, 45, 1–16.

Conger, J., and Associates (1994). *Spirit at Work: Discovering the Spirituality in Leadership*. San Francisco: Jossey-Bass.

Cox, T., Jr (1993). *Cultural Diversity in Organizations*. San Francisco: Berrett-Koehler.

Cox, T. H., and Nkomo, S. M. (1991). A race and gender group analysis of the early career experiences of MBAs. *Work and Occupations*, 18, 431–46.

Dalton, G., and Thompson, P. (1986). *Novations: Strategies for Career Management*. Glenview, IL: Scott, Foresman.

Dreher, G. F., and Ash, R. A. (1990). A comparative study of mentoring among men and women in managerial, professional, and technical positions. *Journal of Applied Psychology*, 75, 539–46.

Dumaine, B. (1994). A knockout year for CEO pay. *Fortune*, July 25, 94–103.

Erikson, E. H. (1966). The concept of identity in race relations: Notes and queries. *Daedalus*, 95, 145–71.

Fagenson, E. A. (1989). The mentor advantage: Perceived career/job experiences of protégés versus non-protégés. *Journal of Organizational Behavior*, 10, 309–20.

Fletcher, J. (1994). *Toward a Theory of Relational Practice in Organizations: Feminist Reconstruction of Real Work*. Unpublished doctoral dissertation. Boston: Boston University School of Management.

Gallos, J. V. (1989). Exploring women's development: Implications for career theory, practice and research. In M. B. Arthur, B. S. Lawrence, and D. T. Hall (eds), *Handbook of Career Theory* (110–32). New York: Cambridge University Press.

Hall, D. T. (1976). *Careers in Organizations*. Glenview, IL: Scott, Foresman.

Hall, D. T. (1986). Dilemmas in linking succession planning to individual executive learning. *Human Resource Management*, 25(1), 235–65.

Hall, D. T. (1991). Promoting work/family balance: An organization change approach. *Organizational Dynamics*, 18, 5–18.

Hall, D. T. (1993). The invisible daddy track. *Newfacts*, Spring, 3–4.

Hall, D. T. (1994). Executive careers and learning: Aligning strategy, selection, and development. Technical report. Executive Development Roundtable, School of Management, Boston University.

Hall, D. T., and Foulkes, F. K. (1991). Senior executive development as a competitive advantage. *Advances in Applied Business Strategy*, 2, 183–203.

Hall, D. T., and Kram, K. E. (1994). White men and diversity: Questions about the meaning of privilege. Working paper. Boston University.

Hall, D. T., and Parker, V. A. (1993). The role of workplace flexibility in managing diversity. *Organizational Dynamics,* 22(1), 5–18.

Hall, D. T., and Richter, J. (1990). Career gridlock: Baby boomers hit the wall. *Academy of Management Executive*, 4, 7–22.

Handy, C. (1990). *The Age of Unreason*, Cambridge, MA: Harvard Business School Press.

Handy, C. (1994). *The Age of Paradox*. Boston: Harvard Business School Press.

Hirshhorn, L. (1991). *Managing in the New Team Environment*. Reading, MA: Addison-Wesley.

Hollenbeck, G. (1992). 360 *Degree Feedback and Development Plans*. Boston, Mass.: Executive Development Roundtable, Boston Univesity School of Management.

Ibarra, H. (1993). Personal networks of women and minorities in management: A conceptual framework. *Academy of Management Review*, 18(1), 56–87.

Isaacs, W. N. (1993). Taking flight: Dialogue, collective thinking, and organizational learning. *Organizational Dynamics*, Autumn, 24–39.

James, K., Lovato, C., and Khoo, G. (1994). Social identity correlates of minority workers' health. *Academy of Management Journal*, 37, 383–96.

Johnston, W. B., and Packer, A. H. (1987). *Workforce 2000: Work and Workers for the 21st Century*. Indianapolis: Hudson Institute.

Jordan, J. V., Kaplan, A. G., Baker-Miller, J., Stiver, I. P., and Surrey, J. L. (1991). *Women's Growth in Connection*. New York: Guilford Press.

Keele, R. L., Buckner, K., and Bushnell, S. J. (1987). Formal mentoring programs are no panacea. *Management Review*, 76, February, 67–8.

Ketchum, L. D., and Trist, E. (1992). *All Teams Are Not Created Equal: How Employee Empowerment Really Works*. Newbury Park, CA: Sage.

Kinlaw, D. C. (1993). *Coaching for Commitment*. San Diego, CA: Pfeiffer.

Koberg, C. S., Boss, W., Chappell, D., and Ringer, R. C. (1992). An investigation of the antecedents and outcomes of mentoring. Paper presented at the Annual Meeting of the Academy of Management, Las Vegas.

Kram, K. E. (1983). Phases of the mentor relationship. *Academy of Management Journal*, 26(4), 608–25.

Kram, K. E. (1988). *Mentoring at Work: Developmental Relationships in Organizational Life*. Lanham, MD: University Press of America.

Kram, K. E., and Bragar, M. C. (1992). Development through mentoring: A strategic approach. In D. Montross and C. Shinkman, *Career Development: Theory and Practice* (221–54). Chicago: Charles C. Thomas Press.

Kram, K. E., and Hall, D. T. (1991). Mentoring as an antidote to stress during corporate trauma. *Human Resources Management*, 28(4), 493–510.

Kram, K, E., and Isabella, L. A. (1985). Mentoring alternatives: The role of peer relationships in career development. *Academy of Management Journal*, 28(1), 110–32.

Kram, K. E., and McCollom, M. E. (forthcoming). When women lead: The visibility–vulnerability spiral. In E. Klein and F. Gabelnick (eds), *New Paradigms for Leadership in the Twenty-First Century*. New Haven, CT: Yale University Press.

Levinson, D. J., Darrow, D., Levinson, M., and McKee, B. (1978). *Seasons of a Man's Life*. New York: Alfred Knopf.

Louis, M. R. (1980). Surprise and sense-making: What newcomers experience in entering unfamiliar organizational settings. *Administrative Sciences Quarterly*, 25, 226–51.

Louis, M. R., Posner, B., and Powell, G. (1983). The availability and helpfulness of socialization practices. *Personnel Psychology*, 36, 857–66.

McCall, M. W., Jr, Lombardo, M. M., and Morrison, A. M. (1988). *The Lessons of Experience*. Lexington, MA: Lexington Press.

McCauley, C. D., Ohlott, P. J., and Ruderman, M. N. (1989). On-the-job development: A conceptual model and preliminary investigation. *Journal of Managerial Issues*, 1, 142–58.

McCauley, C. D., and Young, D. P. (1993). Creating developmental relationships: Roles and strategies. *Human Resources Management Review*, 3(3), 219–30.

McKenna, G. F. (1988). Analysis of the benefits of being a mentor in a formal induction program. Unpublished doctoral dissertation. Chicago: Loyola University of Chicago.

Mink, O. G., Owen, K. Q., and Mink, B. P. (1993). *Developing High-Performance People: The Art of Coaching*. Reading, MA: Addison-Wesley.

Mirvis, P. H., and Hall, D. T. (1994). Psychological success and the boundaryless career. *Journal of Organizational Behavior*, 15, 365–80.

Moore, T. (1992). *Care of the Soul*. New York: HarperCollins.

Morrison, A. M. (1992). *The New Leaders: Guidelines for Leadership Diversity in America*. San Francisco: Jossey-Bass.

Morrison, A., White, R., and Van Velsor, E. (1987). *Breaking the Glass Ceiling*. Reading, MA: Addison-Wesley.

Mullen, E. J. (1994). Framing the mentoring relationship as an information exchange. Technical report. Ames, IA: Iowa State University.

Murray, M., and Owen, M. A. (1991). *Beyond the Myths and Magic of Mentoring: How to Facilitate an Effective Mentoring Program*. San Francisco: Jossey-Bass.

New York Times (1994). Portrait of the electorate: Who voted for whom in the House. November 13, 24.

Noe, R. A. (1988). An investigation of the determinants of successful assigned mentoring relationships. *Personnel Psychology*, 41, 457–79.

Noe, R. A. (1991). Mentoring relationships for employee development. In J. W. Jones, B. D. Sterffy, and D. W. Bray (eds), *Applying Business in Psychology*. Lexington, MA: Lexington Press.

Ohlott, P. J., Ruderman, M. N., and McCauley, C. D. (1994). Gender differences in managers' developmental job experiences. *Academy of Management Journal*, 37(1), 46–67.

O'Leary, V. E., and Ickovics, J. R. (1992). Cracking the glass ceiling: Overcoming isolation and alienation. In U. Sekaran and F. Leong (eds), *Womanpower: Managing in Times of Demographic Turbulence* (7–31). Newbury Park, CA: Sage.

Owen, C. L., and Todor, W. D. (1993). Attitudes toward women as managers: Still the same. *Business Horizons*, 36, 12–16.

Parker, V. A., and Hall, D. T. (1993). The role of workplace flexibility in managing diversity. *Organizational Dynamics*, 22(1), 4–18.

Parker, V. A., and Kram, K. E. (1993). Women mentoring women: Creating conditions for connection. *Business Horizons*, 36(2), 42–51.

Peck, M. S. (1993). *A World Waiting to be Born: Civility Rediscovered*. New York: Bantam Books.

Phillips-Jones, L. L. (1982). *Mentors and Proteges*. New York: Arbor House.

Phillips-Jones, L. L. (1993a). *The Mentoring Program Design Package*, 2nd ed. Grass Valley, CA: Coalition of Counseling Centers.

Phillips-Jones, L. L. (1993b). *The New Mentors and Proteges*. Grass Valley, CA: Coalition of Counseling Centers.

Pryor, S. E. (1994). Executive coaching: Sign of stigma or success? Technical report. Executive Development Roundtable, School of Management, Boston University.

Quinn, J. B. (1992). *Intelligent Enterprise*. New York: Free Press.

Raggins, B. R., and McFarlin, D. B. (1990). Perceptions of mentor roles in cross-gender mentoring relationships. *Journal of Vocational Behavior*, 37, 321–39.

Redfield, J. (1993). *The Celestine Prophecy*. New York: Warner Books.

Rice, F. (1994). How to make diversity pay. *Fortune*, August 8, 78–86.

Ruderman, M. N., Ohlott, P. J., and McCauley, C. D. (1990). Assessing opportunities for leadership development. In K. E. Clark and M. B. Clark, *Measures of Leadership*. West Orange, NJ: Leadership Library of America.

Ruderman, M. N., Ohlott, P. J., and Kram, K. E. (1995). Promotion decisions as a diversity practice. Working paper. *Journal of Management Development*, 14, 6–23.

Schein, E. H. (1993). On dialogue, culture, and organizational learning. *Organizational Dynamics*, Autumn, 40–51.

Schon, D. A. (1990). *Educating the Reflective Practitioner.* San Francisco: Jossey-Bass.

Seibert, K. W., Hall, D. T., and Kram, K. E. (forthcoming). Strengthening the weak link in strategic executive development: Integrating individual development and global business strategy. *Human Resource Management,*

Senge, P. M. (1990). *The Fifth Discipline: The Art and Practice of the Learning Organization.* New York: Doubleday.

Shea, G. F. (1992). *Mentoring: How to Develop Successful Mentor Behaviors.* Los Altos, CA: Crips Publications.

Smith, L. (1993). The Executive's New Coach. *Fortune*, December, 126–34.

Smith, L. (1994). Burned-out bosses, *Fortune*, July 25, 44–52.

Sproull, L., and Kiesler, S. (1992). *Connections: New Ways of Working in the Networked Organization.* Cambridge, MA: MIT Press.

Thomas, D. A. (1989). Mentoring and irrationality: The role of racial taboos. *Human Resources Management*, 28(2), 279–90.

Thomas, D. A. (1990). The impact of race on managers' experience of developmental relationships: An intraorganizational study. *Journal of Organizational Behavior*, 2, 479–92.

Thomas, D. A. (1993). Racial dynamics in cross-race developmental relationships. *Administrative Sciences Quarterly*, 38(3), 169–94.

Thomas, D. A., and Alderfer, C. P. (1989). The influence of race on career dynamics: Theory and research on minority career experiences. In M. Arthur, D. T. Hall, and B. S. Lawrence (eds), *Handbook of Career Theory* (133–58). New York: Cambridge University Press.

Thomas, D. A., and Kram, K. G. (1988). Promoting career-enhancing relationships in organizations: the role of the human resource professional. In M. London and E. M. Mone (eds), *Career Growth and Human Resource Strategies: The Role of the Human Resource Professional in Employee Development* (49–66). New York: Quorum Books.

Turban, D. B., and Dougherty, T. W. (1994). Role of protégé personality in receipt of mentoring and career success. *Academy of Management Journal*, 37, 688–702.

van Velsor, E., and Hugles, M. W. (1990). *Gender Differences in the Development of Managers: How Women Managers Learn from Experience*, report no. 145. Greensboro, NC: Center for Creative Leadership.

Walker, B. A., and Hansen, W. C. (1992). Valuing differences at Digital Equipment Corporation. In S. Jackson and Associates (eds), *Diversity in the Workplace: Human Resource Initiatives.* New York: Guilford Press.

Waterman, R. H., Jr, Waterman, J. A., and Collard, B. A. (1994). Toward a career-resilient workforce. *Harvard Business Review*, July–August, 87–95.

Weisbord, M., and 35 International Co-authors (1993). *Discovering Common Ground.* San Francisco: Berrett-Koehler.

Wheatley, M. J. (1992). *Leadership and the New Science: Learning about Organization from an Orderly Universe.* San Francisco: Berrett-Koehler.

Whitely, W., Dougherty, T. W., and Dreher, G. F. (1991). Relationship of career mentoring and socioeconomic origin to managers' and professionals' early career progress. *Academy of Management Journal*, 34, 331–51.

Zey, M. (1984). *The Mentor Connection.* Homewood, IL: Dow Jones-Irwin.

6
Performance Appraisal and Demographic Diversity: Issues Regarding Appraisals, Appraisers, and Appraising

Chao C. Chen and Nancy DiTomaso

A recent survey by the American Productivity and Quality Center found that only 62 percent of surveyed employees thought that their performance was evaluated fairly (*Wall Street Journal*, 1990). Commentators on the survey said they expected an even higher proportion of employees dissatisfied with their reviews. Another recent study found that black managers "often shrug off negative performance reviews from white supervisors," presumably on the assumption that they are biased (Wynter, 1994). And, research on "brown-nosing" found that employees who try to gain the favor of the boss gain a 4–5 percent advantage over those who rely on performance alone (Conner, 1993). These headlines signal that performance appraisal continues to be a very complex and tricky management task. Like decisions about raises and promotions, performance appraisal often makes no one happy.

Past research on performance appraisal processes has found extensive evidence of bias, error, and favoritism (Binning, 1986; Cooper, 1981b; Holzbach, 1978; Huber, 1989; Murphy et al., 1982; Oppler, 1992; Schoorman, 1988; Smither et al., 1989; Tsui and Barry, 1986). As the workforce becomes more diverse culturally and demographically and as business activities become more global, it is likely that there will be even more opportunity in performance appraisal systems for misunderstandings, hard feelings, and lawsuits (see Markiewicz (1993) on law suit against Ford Motor Company;

and Moskowitz (1992) on suit against AT&T). At the same time, there are major changes under way across most large companies in the way that appraisals are being done. Among other new techniques, the use of 360-degree feedback, i.e. adding appraisals by both peers and subordinates to supervisor evaluations, has been gaining popularity among many large firms, such as AT&T, Baxter International, Dow Chemical, Eastman Chemical, and Honeywell (Lublin, 1994; Shellenbarger, 1994; Maynard, 1994). Motorola has been experimenting with letting peers contribute to decisions about annual pay (Swoboda, 1994). Given their continued use, the continued challenge to doing them right, and the growing complexity of company and arrangements, it is important for human resource (HR) mangers to understand how cultural and demographic diversity impacts performance appraisal systems.

In this chapter, we discuss how cultural differences shape the norms which underlie performance systems; research on bias in appraisals (both against those who are different and for those who are similar); and fairness as a criterion for evaluating the effectiveness of systems. In addition, we discuss the choice of rating formats to meet the needs of a diverse workforce. Finally, we discuss the changing nature of work and organizations and the effects of these changes on performance appraisals with a diverse workforce.

The Performance Appraisal Process

Performance appraisal is a very complex process. It involves an analysis of what employees are supposed to do (e.g. by means of a job analysis or the setting of standards expected by the employer); the gathering of information about the employee on the job (often compared in some way to an evaluation of the employee's capabilities); an evaluation or judgement of an employee with respect to what was expected; and a decision about how to use such information in other management decisions (see definitions by Bernardin and Beatty, 1984, p. 13; Cascio, 1986, p. 73; and Milkovich and Newman, 1987, p. 301). Performance appraisal, thus, involves both pre- and post-appraisal activities, because choices have to be made about how the appraisal is structured and how the information is to be used, in addition to whatever choices are made about the appraisal itself. The process is made more complicated, as well, because the measurement standard is often not of behavior, but rather of traits or characteristics, such as loyalty or enthusiasm. In addition, individual employees are often evaluated, formally and informally, in comparison to other employees. In some cases, forced distributions require managers to rank each employee in reference to others so that a fixed proportion are placed within each part of the distribution. In other cases, companies allow mangers to rate each employee individually, but then, they often find that evaluations across employees are highly skewed toward the most favorable evaluations.

How one gets evaluated, then, depends on many factors. For example, the social, organizational, and personal relations between the appraiser and the appraisee; the measuring format; the particular performance dimensions appraised; and the criteria of effectiveness all may have effects on performance appraisal outcomes. It is no wonder, therefore, that there are many who feel that performance appraisal systems are primarily *demotivators*. Consider the very serious description of typical problems with performance appraisal offered by a recent book on quality management:

> The performance review, no matter how well the format is designed is a one-way street. Someone the individual didn't select gets to perform a very personal internal examination. There are no certificates on the wall stating the qualifications of the reviewer. Yet the effect on the individual's present and future is as real as if everyone knew what he or she were doing.
>
> Now this might lead one to think that the reviews are therefore very negative and have the effect of doing bad things to people. Once in a while that happens, but the overwhelming bundle of performance reviews are kind and gentle. They provide raises, recommend promotions, and in general exude goodwill. . . .
>
> The result of all this is to make the reviews counterproductive. They not only don't weed out the bad; they don't bring the good to the surface. And that is what drives people nuts. (Crosby, 1984, p. 16)

In order to capture some of this complexity, and therefore deal with the issue of diversity and performance appraisal seriously, we want to make clear that we view performance appraisal in its most general form. We feel strongly that one has to understand performance appraisal, not only in terms of the appraisal itself, but also with reference to the pre-appraisal and post-appraisal processes and with reference to the context in which the appraisal takes place. This broader view is also more descriptive of what performance appraisal is in real organizations, and it focuses attention on the taken-for-granted assumptions that underlie the appraisal process.

Performance Appraisal and Diversity

The embeddedness of cultural assumptions in performance appraisal systems

A great deal of the research on performance appraisal has addressed the cognitive processes which are required to undertake evaluations (Cooper, 1981a; Wexley and Klimoski, 1984; DeNisi and Williams, 1988). Two topics, in particular, have been addressed in this research: "how prior expectations or knowledge of prior performance levels affect the way information is processed," and "the role of memory in the rating process" (Bretz et al., 1992, p. 323). The research tends to show that in order to undertake the complex cognitive tasks necessary to do performance appraisals, the appraisers typically construct or adopt some kind of cognitive framework to facilitate selecting, organizing, recalling from memory, and analyzing information. Researchers label such frameworks categories, prototypes, schemata, scripts, or implicit theories, by which they mean that there is an unspoken and often unconscious understanding on the part of the evaluator about what constitutes good or appropriate performance (Abelson, 1981; Feldman, 1981; Lord et al., 1984; Nathan and Lord, 1983).

We prefer the term implicit theory, because it captures the automatic and tacit nature of these frameworks, that is, that they are neither conscious, nor carefully examined. Indeed, in a very precise sense they are often "mindless" (Langer, 1978), in that we do not think about them. Instead, we react out of habit, as if on "automatic pilot" (Gudykunst, 1994, p. 11). Mindless behavior in this sense is an efficient way to communicate with people who are like ourselves, but when dealing with those we think of as different – whom Gudykunst calls "strangers" – it can often lead to misunderstanding, misjudgement, and ineffectiveness (1994, p. 4).

Cultural assumptions, or implicit theories, are part of the symbolic systems which we learned in childhood socialization as the right – or moral – way to be (1994). Langer's research (1989) indicates that unless we make an effort to bring such assumptions to the surface, then we are likely to automatically act in reference to them in our relationships with others. Certainly, in a process like performance appraisal where we are explicitly engaged in the evaluation of other people, such unexamined cultural assumptions are likely to be taken into consideration in our judgements. Research on performance appraisal has focused on how implicit theories can cause errors in judgement regarding the match between an employee's performance and the standards set by the organization. In most of this literature, there seems to be an assumption that to eliminate errors in evaluation one need only conform to the accepted technical procedures for doing appraisals (Cascio, 1986). We want to expand this focus to include a consideration of how the performance criteria and standards used by organizations may themselves be implicit theories. That is, there may be cultural assumptions implicit in the choice of the performance standards themselves.

We argue that in most organizations, such standards are largely determined by the cultural beliefs, values, and norms of those designing the performance appraisal system. Because cultural frames of meaning differ across cultural or demographic subgroups, there is likely to be a mismatch between the standards of performance chosen by one subgroup if it is used to evaluate the performance of subgroups which do not share the same assumptions. If a company has the option to work and do business with a homogeneous population, then there may not be much concern about how cultural values affect performance appraisal standards and processes. Such an option is not likely, however, because of the diversity of the available workforce, the laws which require employers to give equal opportunity to people from different subgroups, and the growing importance of globalization for both domestic and international firms. Thus, the workforce, markets, and competitors are increasingly diverse, and successful companies must understand cultural and subcultural differences in many respects, including in the performance appraisal process.

To illustrate the connection between cultural values and implicit theories of performance, consider the well-known cultural dimension of individualism versus collectivism, which has been found in extensive research to be a primary dimension of cultural difference across nations (Hofstede, 1980a, Triandis, 1989). Individualism is "the degree to which people in a country prefer to act as individuals rather than as members of groups" (Hofstede, 1993, p. 89). Collectivism is the opposite, i.e. the preference to act as members of a group rather than as an individual. Hofstede (1980a; 1980b; 1984; 1993) found that Asian, Latin-American, and most East and West African countries are more collectivistic, whereas Western and Northern European and Anglo-Saxon countries are more individualistic. In addition to these cross-country differences, some research on race and ethnic groups within the US has found that US-born, minority ethnic groups retain cultural heritages from their region or country of origin. Thus, Asian-, black- and Hispanic-Americans tend to be more collectivistic than white Americans (e.g. Marin and Triandis, 1985; Triandis et al., 1984; 1990; Cox et al., 1991).

Individualism and collectivism have also been conceptualized as differences in "self construal" (Marcus and Kitayama, 1990), that is, a conception of the self as an independent actor versus the self defined only in reference to group membership. These differences in orientation toward the self in relation to others will have an effect on how managers perceive employees and vice versa. Consequently, someone from a more individualist culture, for example, is likely to evaluate employees from more collectivist cultures more negatively than would someone who shared collectivist cultural values. The same, of course, would be true in reverse. These differences are quite likely to be evident in global business interactions. For example, Hofstede (1993, p. 91) argues that US management culture is idiosyncratic compared to much of the rest of the world. He gives examples of differences between the US and Germany, Japan, France, Holland, and the "overseas Chinese" (those from Taiwan, Hong Kong, and Singapore). Increasingly these distinctions are relevant within the US workforce as well, because of the increased presence of immigrants in the workforce and the increased presence of foreign investment in the US.

To continue the example of individualism and collectivism, consider the image from each perspective of what constitutes a good employee. Workers from collectivist cultures are more likely than those from individualist cultures to place value on maintaining the social harmony of the group and being a "good citizen" by following collective group norms. Collectivists are likely to express their values by being self-effacing, hesitant to complain, accommodating to external demands, and less likely than would individualists be to take credit for accomplishments. To a collectivist, these behaviors are ways of demonstrating loyalty and commitment to the group, and thus, ways to increase effectiveness. An individualist, however, might view such behaviors as submissiveness (a negative characteristic in an individualist context), lack of confidence, lack of initiative, and even lack of competence. From an individualistic perspective, an effective worker is one who is explicit and aggressive about individual goals; broadcasts achievement; seeks recognition and visibility; stands up for his or her rights, and is quick to protest unfair treatment. To a collectivist, such behaviors would be viewed as selfish, inconsiderate, crude, shallow, and uncooperative. Because in many ways, the behaviors of a "good employee" from an individualist perspective are contradictory to those from a collectivist perspective, there would likely be a great deal of misunderstanding in a performance appraisal done by an evaluator who held views opposite of the evaluatee.

Individualism versus collectivism is only one of five dimensions which Hofstede (1993) argues are major cultural distinctions across countries. The other four include power distance (the degree of inequality considered normal among people in a country); masculinity and femininity (the degree "to which tough values like assertiveness, performance, success, and competition . . . prevail over tender values like the quality of life, maintaining warm personal relationships, service, care for the weak, and solidarity"); uncertainty avoidance ("the degree to which people in a country prefer structured over unstructured situations"); and long-term versus short-term orientation (values oriented toward the future versus toward the present and the past) (Hofstede, 1993, pp. 89–90). Each of these distinctions would lead to conflict and misunderstanding if they were not shared by evaluator and evaluatee.

To give one more salient example in the US context, consider how a difference in assumptions about power distance would affect how one thinks of being a good leader or a good subordinate. To value small power distance means a preference for equality of status, while to value high power distance means an assumption that status distinctions should be maintained between those in different positions of authority. A subordinate who assumes that power distance should be small will most likely be very open about trying to influence the boss, will not hesitate to challenge the supervisor's views, will assume that it is correct to negotiate for the best deal, will not think it unusual to demand special consideration, and will protest unfair – or even non-privileged – treatment. In contrast, subordinates who presume large power distance will most likely demonstrate good performance by obeying instructions, accepting job assignments without asking questions, making accommodations without complaint, and sacrificing to meet a supervisor's demands. Supervisors who expect small power distance will see the role of the leader as that of a coordinator, a facilitator, or an advisor. Supervisors who expect large power distance will see the role of the leader as that of a commander, an authority, or an expert.

In these examples, the culturally determined implicit theories about what it means to be a good and effective employee, a subordinate, or a leader will have substantive effects on performance appraisal outcomes. That is, each participant in the process may have very different criteria and standards for evaluating performance. Most important in this discussion is that such cultural values will usually be thought of as natural and universal, and unless consciously addressed, will be taken for granted as the framework for evaluating the performance of employees. Even if made explicit, cultural values are not easily changed or modified. Thus, one needs to do more than to choose to act otherwise, if one is to be effective with a diverse workforce. As these examples should make clear, performance criteria and standards that have been established by a homogeneous group for a homogeneous workforce may be inappropriate for a diverse workforce. If those determining the performance criteria hold individualistic values – as is true in most US work settings – one would expect a misinterpretation at best, and most likely, an undervaluing, of the performance of employees from more collectivist cultures or subcultures.

It is important to note that there are some similarities between the differences described as individualism and collectivism across countries and differences that have been described as existing, both within the US and across countries, between genders. Work done primarily on the US has suggested that there is a difference between men and women in a preference for "connectedness" versus "autonomy" in relationships with others, with women wanting to be more connected and men wanting to be more autonomous. This distinction has been used in reference to a range of behaviors and values, including moral development, conversational styles, and preferences for learning environments (Belenky et al., 1986; Tannen, 1993; Gilligan, 1982). Cross-cultural research on child-rearing practices is consistent with the US research on gender, in the finding that girls across nations and societies are generally socialized for nurturance, responsibility, and obedience, whereas boys are socialized for self-reliance and achievement (Barry et al., 1957). The difference in this regard has been labeled a "love" versus a "duty" ethos (Bernard, 1971). These traditional values may be reinforced by sex-segregated workplaces, to the extent that women are concentrated in jobs which require nurturing or serving, while men are concentrated in jobs which allow them to exercise authority and responsibility (Trice and Beyer, 1993, p. 242).

There are major disagreements in the literature on gender about whether such differences are due to biological differences, social circumstances, or socialization (e.g. Bem, 1993). Whatever the source, however, if such differences in perspective exist between men and women, then one would expect that men and women would have different implicit theories about effective performance, which would likely parallel the differences we discussed among individualists and collectivists. Such differences may be evident in terms of norms regarding competition versus cooperation and equality (treating people alike) versus equity (treating people according to what they contribute) (Powell, 1988, p. 154), especially as these are relevant to interactions with co-workers and subordinates. There is a distinction, however, which is not consistent between the literature on gender and that on cross-cultural management. US women appear to value low power distance as much as do US men. Thus, if women are generally more collectivist in their orientations than are men, this is not, in the US case, necessarily associated with a preference for high power distance in the sense of submissiveness to authority.

The evidence for bias in performance ratings: race, gender, and age differences

Social categorization, stereotypes, and attribution   Human perception relies heavily on categories and categorization. As Gudykunst explains:

> When we select information from the environment we need to organize it in some way. We try to find meaningful patterns. We do this by putting things or people into categories. Categorization is a fundamental aspect of thought. . . . Our categorizations are based on only selected aspects of the things or person. . . . Once we have created the category, we assume that things within the category are similar and that things in different categories are different. . . . Once the categories are formed, we tend to take them for granted and assume there are gaps between them.   (Gudykunst, 1994, pp. 112–13)

Understanding the processes by which we categorize people is important because the existence of categories often leads to other psychological processes which are extremely relevant in the performance appraisal process. Although there is an extensive literature on these issues, we can provide only a very brief overview here (see, e.g. Taylor, 1981; Taylor and Falcone, 1982; Tajfel, 1978; 1982; Brewer, 1981; Brewer and Miller, 1988; Gudykunst, 1994; Ross, 1977; Kelley, 1967; Pettigrew, 1979). The research has tended to show that there are very predictable outcomes to social categorization (psychologically dividing people into separate groups).

The existence of categories is also associated with the designation of "in-groups" (those we think of as like ourselves and who are favored) and "out-groups" (those who are thought of as not like ourselves and who are not favored). The selectivity of information used to make these distinctions also leads to stereotyping, in which negative pre-judgements are made about out-group members, and an attribution process in which we tend to think the worst of others and the best of ourselves. The typical structure of such attributions is that we credit the successes of ourselves and our in-group members to positive character (e.g. skill or ability) and our failures to circumstances (e.g. bad luck or unfavorable situations). At the same time, we tend to attribute the success of out-groups to circumstances (e.g. good luck or easy tasks) and the failures to personal qualities (e.g. lack of skill or ability). When these sorts of processes emerge in performance appraisal, they can lead to favoritism and bias (Beauvais and Spence, 1987; Binning, 1986; Cooper, 1981b; Deaux and Emswiller, 1974; Feather and Simon, 1975; Heilman, 1983).

There are some very important aspects of categorization that need to be addressed (Feldman, 1981; 1986; DeNisi and Williams, 1988; Wexley and Klimoski, 1984). First, categorization is not a passive, but an active cognitive activity. That is, people not only cognitively record what is happening in the world; they also construct it through categorization. Second, categories become expectations through which confirming information is actively searched (Green and Mitchell, 1979) or inferred (McElroy and Downey, 1982). As noted, once the categories are formed, we tend to take them for granted. Research has shown that information which would disconfirm our existing categories tends to be discounted (Cooper, 1981a; 1981b). Third, categories are often further abstracted into general impressions that are easy to store, recall and use (Cooper, 1981a; 1981b; Nathan and Lord, 1983). Cognitive processes such as these can lead to what is known in performance evaluations as a halo effect, the tendency to generalize a favorable evaluation of one dimension to all dimensions (e.g. to assume that neatness also means cooperativeness and loyalty). Furthermore, such cognitive processes tend to be automatic. We are usually not consciously aware of how we form evaluations of others – we mindlessly apply implicit frameworks – and we do not easily change our minds once judgements are formed (Feldman, 1981; Schoorman, 1988).

The research on performance appraisal has shown that these processes of categorization, differentiation and evaluation of people according to race, gender, and age categories can have important effects on performance appraisal outcomes. To summarize: individuals are first categorized on the bases of social grouping (e.g. gender, race, and/or age). These categorizations carry with them stereotypical characteristics (such as, females are emotional; blacks are aggressive; and older people are slower workers). The categories and associated stereotypes then become expectations and frameworks, which orient those people who are conscious of gender, race, or age role expectations to attend to, or even actively seek for, confirming information and to ignore disconfirming information about women, racial and age groups. The use of implicit frameworks about group differences would then be used automatically – and unconsciously, unless the evaluator made a conscious effort to modify or change them. In this scenario, the final appraisal made by a rater for whom gender, race, or age differences are especially salient will be a function of the stereotypes that rater has about various groups. (See research, e.g. by Heilman, 1983; Isaacs, 1981; Pazy, 1986; Rosen and Jerdee, 1973; 1976; Schein, 1978; Schwab and Heneman, 1978.)

Negative stereotyping, such as described is even more likely in groups with unbalanced representation of subgroups, i.e. where there is a minority (Kanter, 1977; Sackett et al., 1991). Sackett et al. found in a study of 486 work groups across a wide variety of jobs and organizations that women received lower ratings when they were less than half of the work group, and especially when they were 20 percent or less. Only when women were more than 50 percent were the ratings likely to be more positive than those of men, but the effects were not symmetrical. When women were in the majority, their ratings tended to be only moderately better than those of men (.03 to .26 of a standard deviation better), whereas when women are a small minority, their ratings tend to be as much as half a standard deviation lower than men's, even after controlling for differences in cognitive ability, psychomotor ability, education, and experience. Sackett et al. did not find the same results for blacks. The ratings of blacks continued to be more negative than those of whites except in groups where blacks were 90 percent or more of the work group.

The research on bias in performance appraisal – especially given that discrimination is illegal and subject to legal damages – is, to say the least, complex and controversial. For the same reasons, it also may be subject to political influences, and thus difficult to take at face value. In other words, it needs to be interpreted and understood in its context. It provides evidence; it does not provide proof about whether bias does or does not exist in any given context or toward any given group. If bias exists, it can take place in several different ways. First, bias can be either for or against a given group. Second, bias can be detected with reference to who is being evaluated (the ratee), who is doing the evaluating (the rater), and the interaction between the two (the rater–ratee interaction). Third, there are contextual factors (moderators) which may change the relationships that otherwise would be found. Some of the moderators which have been found in the research on performance appraisal bias, in addition to the composition of the work group, include: the level of performance of the person being rated (whether high or low, for example); the congruence between the role expectations of the person and the job; the time the research was conducted (e.g. either before or after the civil rights and women's movements made evidence of bias consequential for managers and organizations); and the type of study (e.g. whether laboratory research, with limited information and artificial work settings, or field research, in real organizations, with real evaluators and evaluatees). How these moderators work will be discussed with reference to the research on specific subgroups.

Race effects in performance ratings　The research on race effects in the US has been on blacks and whites. Very little research has been on other ethnic group differences. A meta-analysis and a commentary on the meta-analysis have been published on this research, but additional research continues to appear (see Kraiger and Ford, 1985; and Sackett and DuBois, 1991). To summarize this research indicates some of the complexity of the subject matter. Although individual studies have found different results, early research (e.g. pre-1970) generally found that blacks are rated lower than whites. Later research (after 1970) continues to find that blacks are rated lower on average, but in most cases, the size of the effects are more moderated. Some research has found that blacks are rated higher than whites (Bigoness, 1976), but only because black evaluators rated blacks higher. Some research had found that both blacks and whites rated members of their own race higher (Kraiger and Ford, 1985), but some other analyses found that both black and white supervisors rate whites higher (deJung and Kaplan, 1962; Schmitt and Lappin, 1980; Sackett and DuBois, 1991). The earlier error in interpretation was attributed to studies that used data on peer evaluations of blacks by blacks. The magnitude of the effect in favor of whites in studies of supervisory ratings is greater for white than for black supervisors. Further, the evidence tends to show that whites are especially favored on ratings of technical skill and task-related behaviors (Sackett and DuBois, 1991; Cox and Nkomo, 1986).

Although there is some discrepancy in the literature, it appears that race effects are more likely to be found in field studies than in laboratory studies (Dipboye, 1985; Kraiger and Ford, 1985). The reasons for differential effects across types of studies vary. Field studies, for example, cannot control for differences in true performance, and therefore, it is difficult to separate out bias, error, and true difference in performance. When studies have had a measure of actual performance, they have found that the performance level accounted for 50–70 percent of any differences found between groups. Laboratory studies, while controlling for performance level, tend to provide very little information on the ratee. That is, laboratory studies almost always use either paper or video depictions of the ratees, and such information is devoid of the behavioral, affective, and social dimensions that would be available to real managers in organizations (Dipboye, 1985).

The studies of race, as well as gender and age, also have found other complex processes under way. For example, there is some evidence to suggest that in laboratory studies, with inexperienced student subjects, one is more likely to get "socially desirable" responses (i.e. the answers that the subjects think are most acceptable to the researcher). There is also evidence of "ambivalent" responses (Katz and Glass, 1979), in which subjects view themselves as fair and unprejudiced, but at the same time they have negative evaluations of minorities or women, for example. In order to deal with their unsettledness about their conflicting views, they end up overrating or underrating, depending on the signals they get (Mullins, 1982; Dipboye, 1985; Heilman et al., 1988). For example, Mullins found that those subjects who scored highest on prejudice were those who gave the highest ratings to black subjects. In a series of recent studies consistent evidence has been found for a more modern form of bias which was labeled by Dovidio et al. (1992) as aversive racism. They found that given the social and political egalitarian ideal in the US, whites now find it difficult to acknowledge to themselves or to others that they hold biased views. Consequently, in situations where there are strong norms against bias, whites are less likely to show bias against out-groups, but may show favor toward other whites. In a study of 2,445 scientists and engineers from 24 US companies (Smith et al., 1995), performance evaluations showed a generalized favoritism toward whites but no antagonism against nonwhite or female employees.

Some researchers argue that lack of confidence in rating those who are different would lead to a restriction of range (Schmitt and Lappin, 1980), but the evidence for this is not clear. For example, some studies have found that among low performers, blacks receive higher ratings than do whites, but this same effect is not necessarily found among high performers (Schmitt and Lappin, 1980; Bigoness, 1976; Hamner et al., 1974). There has also been some presumption that bias is less likely to be found when performance measures are objective, but the research on the format of ratings does not find that format is a major factor in the results.

Across this research, the race of the ratee accounts for only a small proportion of the variance in ratings. In most cases, it accounts for no more than 1–4 percent of the variance, and usually no more than 2 percent. As will be pointed out in the following section, research also found the gender effect rather small. One wishes that the remaining large variance could be accounted for by true performance, suggesting limited racial and sex biases. We, however, caution such optimistic attribution because other factors related to biases rather than true performance may also explain the small effect of race and gender. As discussed above, the legal concerns about evidence of discrimination, the effect of social desirability, which few studies have controlled for, and the effect of ambivalent beliefs and attitudes may mask biases but do not in any way increase rating accuracy.

Gender effects in performance ratings   The research on gender and performance ratings has been more mixed in results than has the research on race (Nieva and Gutek, 1980). Some research has found that women are rated higher or no differently than men (Mobley, 1982; Pulakos and Wexley, 1983; Bigoness, 1976), while other research has found that women are rated lower than men (Schmitt and Lappin, 1980; Pazy, 1986). Some of this research has the same complexity of interpretation as the research on race effects: laboratory studies which tend to find that women are rated higher in very restricted circumstances; larger samples which find that when in a minority women are rated lower; and interactions with performance, such that high-performing women are rated favorably when evidence is provided of their qualifications.

One of the issues in this research which is not necessarily consistent with the research on race, however, is the discrepancy in the nature of these studies with the structure of the labor market. Because studies which attempt to examine potential bias try to compare similarly-situated men and women, by definition, they must consider women and men in the same types of jobs, doing the same type of work. The largest proportion of the variance in income differences between men and women, however, is because they are not often found in the same jobs doing the same work (Reskin and Padavic, 1994; Auster, 1989). In fact, "fewer than 10 percent of Americans have a coworker of the other sex who does the same job, for the same employer, in the same location, and on the same shift" (Bielby and Baron, 1986). While there is also a great deal of race segregation in jobs, it is not as extensive as sex segregation. There are more instances of black and white men working alongside each other, as well as of black and white women, but much less mixing across genders. Thus, one of the main modifiers of gender effects in performance ratings is the "sex congruity" of the job and the extent to which women's performance is contrary to expected gender roles. In sex-typed "women's" jobs, women do as well as men. In "men's jobs," women are evaluated lower than men, unless evidence is provided that they are especially competent. There also appear to be time and social desirability effects, with more evidence of bias against women in earlier studies than in later ones and less in settings where there are legal concerns about evidence of discrimination. When the issue of sex differences is made especially salient for the subjects, the researchers are less likely to find sex effects (Heilman, 1984).

One of the persistent concerns in many of the studies on gender bias in performance ratings is that the evidence on bias in ratings is so mixed, while the evidence on income inequality clearly favors men (Reskin and Padavic, 1994). This suggests that there is either a weak relationship between the outcomes of performance ratings and job success or that there is something very unusual about the studies being done. There may be evidence for both. As suggested, it is still an unusual situation for women to be working in the same jobs and at the same level as men. Further, a recent study suggests that favorable performance appraisals "pay off" better for men than for women:

> ... at managerial levels, the relationship between appraisal ratings and salary was much stronger for men than women. The wage gap favored men by only $342 at lower levels, while it was $2,340 greater for men at higher levels. These findings suggest that the salary allocation process, not the performance appraisal process, may be the source of bias in large organizations. (Drazin, 1987, p. 157)

In summary, the research on gender effects tends to show that women in the same kinds of jobs doing work of the same quality are evaluated as well as or better than men, but that women are not often given access to these kinds of jobs. Evaluations of women are, however, affected by sex role stereotypes, and women receive better ratings when they are evaluated in "women's jobs," unless clear evidence is provided independent of the evaluation of exceptional performance. In all such studies, gender accounts for very little of the variation in ratings.

Age effects in performance appraisal   Most of the research on age bias in performance ratings have tended to find a negative correlation between age and supervisory ratings, while finding little evidence of a negative correlation between age and objective measures of performance (Avolio et al., 1990; Avolio and Waldman, 1990; Ferris et al., 1985; 1991; Halverson, 1991; McEvoy and Cascio, 1989; Rosen and Jerdee, 1976; Schmidt et al., 1986; Schwab and Heneman, 1978; Shore and Bleicken, 1991; Waldman, 1993; Wladman and Avolio, 1986). Studies specifically of technical workers have found a curvilinear relationship, with lower ratings of both the youngest and the oldest employees, and a peak rating in the mid-30s (Dalton and Thompson, 1971). While in most cases, the studies have not been able to separate out true performance from the evaluations, it is generally accepted that most subjective performance ratings include an element of "potential," which leads to discounted ratings for older workers who have fewer years left to work (McEvoy and Cascio, 1989).

Some general tendencies   The evidence for or against bias in performance ratings by gender, race, and age is similar in many respects to evaluations based on other types of categorizations, e.g. disability, ethnicity, and sexual orientation. While it is not possible for us to review all aspects of how diversity relates to performance appraisals, we can summarize some of the general themes. To the extent that there is more homogeneity among the raters than there is among the ratees, then there is likely to be a potential for bias in ratings, unless there are very clear and enforceable safeguards against it. To the extent that group differences are salient, biases are likely to come into play if there are signals that they are acceptable, but they are likely to be suppressed – even reversed – if it is clear that bias is not an acceptable outcome. This does not mean that ratings will be done in the latter situation according to "true" performance. Rather, it is likely that raters will try to outwit the system to cover any biases that they may feel. It appears from the study of group composition that white women have been more successful in gaining favor when they are well represented in the labor force, but black workers have not been able to do the same. There is a substantial amount of evidence that older workers still are at a disadvantage compared to younger workers in most work situations where they are subordinate.

Perhaps as troubling as any evidence of bias is that performance appraisals appear to have a more symbolic than substantive meaning in many work situations. That is, there is much less variance in ratings than would be expected. The general tendency for ratings to be "kind and gentle" has been attributed to several factors: that employers who continue to need the cooperation of employees do not like to give them bad news; that there is a minimally acceptable level of performance that will be tolerated before an employee is terminated, thus leading to ratings mostly on the high side; and that fear of law suits, among other negative consequences, give supervisors strong incentives to restrict the range of their evaluations. Using performance appraisals only for symbolic purposes, however, can mask the workings of privilege by making it harder to trace how some groups end up disproportionately represented in the best jobs and at the highest incomes.

Fairness as a criterion for evaluating performance appraisal

The same factors which contribute to restriction of range in performance evaluations overall contribute to a divergence in the way performance evaluations are viewed by researchers versus practitioners. While researchers are mostly concerned with finding better methods for avoiding error (Bernardin and Beatty, 1984; Bretz et al., 1992), managers are more concerned with fairness and acceptance of performance appraisal systems by employees. It is not, of course, that researchers are not concerned with fairness, but rather that they seem to believe that if appraisals are accurate they will also be thought of as fair. Fairness is, thus, thought of as an outcome of accurate performance appraisal in the view of most researchers.

There may be good justification, however, for considering fairness as an independent and primary criterion for performance appraisal (Jackson and Alvarez, 1993). By giving attention to fairness as a criterion, it removes performance appraisal from a strictly interpersonal concern to one that addresses, intergroup and institutional issues as well. It also avoids the restricted emphasis on technical and psychometrical issues, by addressing social and political ones as well.

Concern with fairness is a major theme in the organizational behavior research on "justice." Sheppard et al. (1992) identified three types of justice in organizations: distributive, procedural, and system. Distributive justice refers to fairness in the distribution of outcomes; procedural justice refers to fairness in the processes and procedures by which outcome decisions are made; and system justice refers to fairness in the authority system (i.e. in the way the system is run). These concepts can help us understand some of the issues regarding fairness in performance appraisal systems.

If ratings are correlated with group membership, such that one group consistently receives higher (or lower) ratings than another, then there is an issue of distributive justice. Even if a person thinks that his or her own evaluation has been fair, he or she may still think that the system is unjust if the group to which he or she belongs is consistently rated less favorably than others (Assiz, 1992). A concern for procedural justice may be evident if a group feel that they are disadvantaged, for example, by the definition of performance criteria (e.g. only those with college degrees are accepted for management training), by how information is gathered (e.g. only by the supervisor's judgement), and by whether they are given sufficient feedback or have access to a grievance system. To feel that the system is just, one may look beyond the specifics of the performance appraisal itself. For instance, if minority group members are not able to perform as well as the members of the majority because of cumulative disadvantages in past history, there may be a feeling that the system itself contributed to their lower performance. Lack of access to development opportunities, good job assignments, and other resources that make it possible to do a good job lead to a feeling of disadvantage, even if evaluations are based on "true" performance (Kanter, 1977; Greenhaus et al., 1990).

Thus, organizations must give attention to what happens before and after the appraisal, as well as to what happens in the evaluation procedure itself. It is not enough to hire by the numbers, but not to develop people. Nor is it enough to send people to training, but then to never give them access to better jobs. These kinds of issues are frequently raised in discussions regarding discrimination in organizations. There is extensive evidence that many groups feel unfairly treated, even when the "objective" situation would suggest otherwise (Fernandez, 1991, p. 192).

Appraisal methods and formats

Some of the research on potential bias has suggested that some rating formats are less likely to be biased than are others, but the evidence tends to show that bias can occur no matter what the format of the evaluation (Cascio, 1986, p. 96; Kraiger and Ford, 1985). Different kinds of formats can be used, and each has advantages and disadvantages. There are three major types of formats: trait, behavioral, and outcome-based. Traits evaluate the characteristics of the ratee (e.g. loyalty or dependability). Behavioral measures evaluate what the ratee does (e.g. takes initiative). Outcome-based measures quantify results (e.g. sales volume or units produced). Outcome-based measures are supposedly more objective, because they are quantifiable. Trait and behavioral measures have more of a subjective component, because they rely on the judgements of the evaluator.

Although behavior-based scales seem to be more favored by researchers, trait- and outcome-based methods are more popular with practitioners. According to Bernardin and Villanova's survey (1986), having "raters evaluate ratee traits" is one of the most common conditions in performance appraisal. A more recent survey of performance appraisal practices (Bretz et al., 1992) found that trait-based scales are the norm with non-exempt employees, whereas Management by Objectives (MBO), which uses outcomes as the major evaluation component, is the preferred format for executives, managers, and professional employees.

There appears to be a preference among those in the minority for objective measures of outcomes, rather than of subjective measures of the process of performance (Thompson and DiTomaso, 1988). The reasoning is that if those who otherwise may be subject to biased evaluations are able to be evaluated on what they do rather than on what they are, then bias will be minimized. This argument, however, does not take into consideration the issue just raised, namely the access to resources, information, and support to get the job done. The preference for evaluating outcomes rather than processes has the same kind of underlying rationale. Because cultures and subcultures may have different styles of interactions and different constraints, those in the minority are likely to be disadvantaged if they are evaluated on how they get the job done rather than on what they actually accomplish. A good example of this distinction is the concern with "face time," namely, the amount of hours one is present in the office where the boss can see. Women, especially, may be disadvantaged if they are judged by how many hours they spend at the office rather than by how well they do the job (Reskin and Padavic, 1994).

Outcome-based and objective measures, however, are not panaceas for eliminating bias. As noted already, the research evidence suggests that each format may be equally prone to bias. Even outcome measures are subject to possible perceptual distortions and attribution errors. Further, it is increasingly difficult to determine the link between individual performance and organizational outcomes. The growing interdependence of work processes will increasingly make it difficult to determine who has contributed what. Outcomes in a knowledge-based economy may be far less tangible than they were in an industrial economy, and therefore, also much more difficult to measure and evaluate.

The changing nature of work and organization and the impact on performance appraisal

The potential for cultural bias to be incorporated into appraisals is easy to understand, once one recognizes that cultural frameworks or implicit theories shape conceptions of effective and ineffective performance. Bias can be incorporated into appraisals in the pre-appraisal stage as well, as previously noted. The topic which has received the most attention in this regard is in reference to job analyses. The growing literature on "comparable worth" has been precisely about the extent to which job analysis frameworks were "gendered," such that jobs held mostly by women are always evaluated as less worthy than jobs held primarily by men (McNally and Shimmin, 1984; Jaussaud, 1984; Buono and Rosen, 1993; Steinberg, 1992).

Furthermore, the natures of jobs are themselves said to be changing. Indeed, the very concept of job has been challenged (Bridges, 1994). If these trends are being accurately predicted, then the bases on which performance appraisal systems are built are likely to be even more fragile. As work becomes more complex and dependent on the special expertise of employees from multiple fields, supervisors will find it increasingly hard to claim that they know the content of jobs better than the occupants. In any case, as job occupants become more diverse and as job content becomes more difficult to characterize, the ability to measure performance against an understanding of what the job requires will likely become more subjective (Auster, 1989).

Techniques, such as 360-degree feedback (Nowack, 1993), add new layers to the evaluation process, and may thereby add, as well, new sources of bias. With the advent of such systems, then, one cannot address potential bias by restricting training only to supervisors, or even to one's own employees. Extra-organizational actors, like customers, clients, and suppliers, are also increasingly having a say in performance appraisal outcomes. So far little research has been done on the diversity implications of 360-degree feedback. Some questions that might be addressed include: Should the feedback from peers and subordinates be used only for the purposes of employee development, or should they also have weight in decisions regarding promotion? What are the advantages and disadvantages of having anonymous 360-degree feedback? Who should have access to the evaluation from a 360-degree appraisal system (e.g. only the employee, the employee and the supervisor, or more broadly, all who participated)? Finally, more research should be done to examine the effects of broader participation in evaluations on the perceived fairness and acceptance of the performance appraisal system.

Despite the preferences in previous discussions of diversity and performance appraisal for outcome-based evaluations, there is a potentially important role as well for including subjective dimensions in the appraisal process. For managers, including a subjective component may focus the manager's attention on both the process and the outcomes of their management activities. That is, it is not enough to get the work tasks done today, if in the process one alienates, offends, or demotivates employees who need to do the work tomorrow. Thus, an evaluation of process should be an integral part of the manager's own evaluation. In many companies with specific policies regarding diversity, managers are being held accountable in both performance and reward systems for how effectively they manage and develop employees from different cultures and subcultures (see discussion, for example, in Thompson and DiTomaso, 1988; and in Cox, 1993).

Although the objective outcomes of a unit under a given manager may be laudatory, adding a subjective appraisal could on the one hand validate the objective outcomes and on the other identify process problems that may not otherwise be evident. Adding such a component can motivate managers to attend to the process variables that lead to outcomes, as well as the outcomes themselves. For organizations in highly competitive and fast-paced environments, this additional area of knowledge may make the difference between surviving for the long term and being only a short-term player. Good process skills are essential for the effective management of diversity.

The kind of training that most companies have used with reference to their performance appraisal systems are rater training programs, and such training programs do seem to help reduce errors in appraisals (Bretz et al., 1992). Two other topics that have not usually been a part of such training, however, should be added. First, such training should include cultural and/or diversity training. Second, training should be done for both peers and subordinates, as well as for managers. If culture affects one's interpretation of and attributions about others, then appraisal training should deal with issues concerning the accuracy of interpretations and attributions of employees from different cultural or subcultural backgrounds. In addition, it should be sensitive to differences in cultural norms about behaviors and effective feedback tactics. For example, many insights are likely from the intercultural and attribution training programs proposed by Triandis et al. (1994). In all such training, recognition of cultural ethnocentrism in human perception and evaluation is a first step towards addressing potential biases. If 360-degree feedback continues to be widely used, then such training should not be confined to managers only.

Summary and Conclusion

Changes are necessary in the way we think about and structure performance appraisal systems due to: (1) the increasing diversity of workforce composition; (2) the increasing interdependence in the way jobs are structured; and (3) the transformation of both organizations and jobs in an increasingly global economy. To the extent that performance appraisal has served important purposes for organizations, from determining who is contributing what to the organizational bottom line to determining what needs to be done to facilitate better performance, it has been one of the important tools of management. At the same time, it is well known that there are virtually no performance evaluation systems that satisfy the needs of all involved, including the organization as a whole, the managers, the employees, and other stakeholders. There are always questions regarding any performance appraisal system about accuracy, fairness, and the likely impact on future motivation and contribution. To the extent that existing systems have failed to address the embeddedness of dominant cultures, then they are not likely to be effective with a diverse workforce. Understanding how and when implicit theories, which are culturally based, come into play in how performance appraisals are structured, conducted, and interpreted by those affected by them adds an important element to creating more effective systems of evaluating performance.

Additionally, it is important to acknowledge and find ways to address potential biases that come from intergroup conflict, derived from categorizations and stereotypes. If some groups are systematically disadvantaged by existing performance appraisal structures, then it is increasingly likely the performance appraisal systems themselves may become the subject of future debate around issues of inequality, as they have been in the recent past. In this regard, how to maintain a sense of fairness regarding a system that makes consequential decisions about people's lives is a continuing and essential challenge for management researchers and practitioners.

Finally, the changes under way in the nature of jobs and the structure of network relationships across organizations – whether as spider webs or spider plants (Reich, 1991; Morgan, 1993) – are creating an environment where performance appraisals which are designed for individual assessment and based on assumptions regarding commonly agreed-upon values are likely to be increasingly out of kilter with the populations most affected by them. As organizations are becoming de-bureaucratized, employees are becoming more empowered, and rewards are becoming more unequal, there is a growing challenge to revise the procedures on which performance appraisals have always been based and to re-examine the taken-for-granted assumptions about who should have input and how it should be used. Like many aspects of management these days, knowledge of how to do performance appraisals is facing continuous and dramatic change. It is important to know where we have been in order to know how to get from here to where we want to be. Taking diversity into consideration in the design, implementation, and consumption of performance appraisal systems is essential for management effectiveness and organizational survival.

REFERENCES

Abelson, R. P. (1981). Psychological status of the script concept. *American Psychologist*, 36, 715–29.

Assiz, A. E. (1992). Procedural justice and the allocation of power in intergroup relations: Studies in the United States and South Africa. *Personality and Social Psychology Bulletin*, 736–47.

Auster, E. R. (1989). Task characteristics as a bridge between macro- and micro-level research on salary inequality between men and women. *Academy of Management Review*, 14(2), 173–93.

Avolio, B. J., and Waldman, D. A. (1990). An examination of age and cognitive test performance across job complexity and occupational types. *Journal of Applied Psychology*, 75, 43–50.

Avolio, B. J., Waldman, D. A., and McDaniel, M. A. (1990). Age and work performance in non-management jobs: The effects of experience and occupation type. *Academy of Management Journal*, 33, 407–22.

Barry, H., Bacon, M., and Child, I. (1957). A cross-cultural survey of some sex differences in socialization. *Journal of Abnormal and Social Psychology*, 55, 327–32.

Beauvais, C., and Spence, J. T. (1987). Gender, prejudice, and categorization, *Sex Roles*, 16, 89–100.

Belenky, M. F., Clinchy, B. M., Goldberger, N. R., and Tarule, J. M. (1986). *Women's Ways of Knowing: The Development of Self, Voice, and Mind*. New York: Basic Books.

Bem, S. L. (1993). *The Lenses of Gender: Transforming the Debate on Sexual Inequality*. New Haven, CT: Yale University Press.

Bernard, J. (1971). *Women and the Public Interest*. Chicago: Aldine.

Bernardin, H. J., and Beatty, R. W. (1984). *Performance Appraisal: Assessing Human Behavior at Work*. Boston: Kent.

Bernardin, H. J., and Villanova, P. (1986). Performance appraisal. In E. A. Locke (ed.), *Generalizing from Laboratory to Field Settings* (43–62). Lexington, MA: Lexington Books.

Bielby, W. T., and Baron, J. N. (1986). Men and women at work: Sex segregation and statistical discrimination. *American Journal of Sociology*, 91, 759–99.

Bigoness, W. J. (1976). Effect of applicant's sex, race, and performance on employers' performance ratings: Some additional findings. *Journal of Applied Psychology*, 61(1), 80–4.

Binning, J. F. (1986). Explaining the biasing effects of performance cues in terms of cognitive categorization. *Academy of Management Journal*, 29(3), 521–35.

Bretz, R. D., Milkovich, G. T., and Read, W. (1992). The current state of performance appraisal research and practice: Concerns, directions, and implication. *Journal of Management*, 18(2), 321–52.

Brewer, M. B. (1981). Ethnocentrism and its role in interpersonal trust. In M. Brewer and B. Collins (eds), *Scientific Inquiry and the Social Sciences*. San Francisco: Jossey-Bass.

Brewer, M. B., and Miller, N. (1988). Contact and cooperation: When do they work? In P. Katz and D. Taylor (eds), *Eliminating Racism*. New York: Plenum.

Bridges, W. (1994). The end of the job. *Fortune*, September 19, 62–74.

Buono, A. F., and Rosen, M. (1993). Comparable worth: Theories and evidence. *Personnel Psychology*, 46(4), 869–73.

Cascio, W. F. (1986). *Applied Psychology in Personnel Management*. Englewood Cliffs, NJ: Prentice-Hall.

Conner, C. (1993). Brown-nosers cross finish line first. *Denver Post*, October 17, G, 1, 2.

Cooper, W. H. (1981a). Ubiquitous halo. *Psychological Bulletin*, 90, 218–44.

Cooper, W. H. (1981b). Conceptual similarity as a source of illusory halo in job performance ratings. *Journal of Applied Psychology*, 66, 302–7.

Cox, T. H. (1993). *Cultural Diversity in Organizations*. San Francisco: Berrett-Koehler.

Cox, T. H., Lobel, S. A., and McLeod, P. L. (1991). Effects of ethnic group cultural differences on cooperative and competitive behavior on a group task. *Academy of Management Journal*, 34, 827–47.

Cox, T. H., and Nkomo, S. M. (1986). Differential appraisal criteria based on race of the ratee. *Group and Organizational Studies*, 11, 101–19.

Crosby, P. B. (1984). *Quality without Tears: The Art of Hassle-free Management*. New York: Plume.

Dalton, G., and Thompson, P. (1971). Accelerating obsolescence of older engineers. *Harvard Business Review*, September–October, 57–67.

Deaux, K., and Emswiller, T. (1974). Explanations of successful performance on sex-linked tasks: What is skill for the male is luck for the female. *Journal of Personality and Social Psychology*, 29, 80–5.

deJung, J. E., and Kaplan, H. (1962). Some differential effects of race of rater and ratee on early peer ratings of combat attitude. *Journal of Applied Psychology*, 46(5), 370–4.

DeNisi, A. S., and Williams, K. J. (1988). Cognitive approaches to performance appraisal. In K. M. Rowland and G. R. Ferris (eds), *Research in Personnel and Human Resources Management*, vol. 6 (109–55). Greenwich, CT: JAI Press.

Dipboye, R. L. (1985). Some neglected variables in research on discrimination in appraisals. *Academy of Management Review*, 10, 116–27.

Dovidio, J. F., Gaertner, S. L., Anastasio, P. A., and Sanitioso, R. (1992). Cognitive and motivational bases of bias: Implications of aversive racism for attitudes towards Hispanics. In S. B. Knouse, P. Rosenfeld, and A. L. Culbertson (eds), *Hispanics in the Workplace* (75–108). Newbury Park, CA: Sage.

Drazin, R. (1987). Wage differences between men and women: Performance appraisal ratings vs. salary allocation as the locus of bias. *Human Resource Management*, 26(2), 157–68.

Feather, N. T., and Simon, J. G. (1975). Reactions to male and female success and failure in sex-linked occupations: Impressions of personality, causal attribution, and perceived likelihood of difference consequences. *Journal of Personality and Social Psychology*, 31, 20–31.

Feldman, J. M. (1981). Beyond attribution theory: Cognitive processes in performance appraisal. *Journal of Applied Psychology*, 66, 127–48.

Feldman, J. M. (1986). Instrumentation and training for performance appraisal: A perceptual-cognitive viewpoint. In K. M. Rowland and G. R. Ferris (eds), *Research in Personnel and Human Resources Management*, vol. 4 (45–99). Greenwich, CT: JAI Press.

Fernandez, J. P. (1991). *Managing a Diverse Work Force: Regaining the Competitive Edge*. Lexington, MA: D.C. Heath.

Ferris, G. R., Judge, T. A., Chachere, J. G., and Liden, R. C. (1991). The age context of performance evaluation decisions. *Psychology and Aging*, 6, 616–22.

Ferris, G. R., Yates, V. L., Gilmore, D. C., and Rowland, K. M. (1985). The influence of subordinate age on performance ratings and causal attributions. *Personnel Psychology*, 38, 545–57.

Gilligan, C. (1982). *In a Different Voice*. Cambridge, MA: Harvard University Press.

Giniger, S., Dispenzieri, A., and Eisenberg, J. (1983). Age, experience, and performance on speed and skill jobs in an applied setting. *Journal of Applied Psychology*, 68, 469–75.

Green, S. G., and Mitchell, T. R. (1979). Attributional processes of leaders in leader–member interactions. *Organizational Behavior and Human Performance*, 23, 429–58.

Greenhaus, J. H., Parasuraman, S., and Wormley, W. M. (1990). Effects of race on organizational experiences, job performance evaluations, and career outcomes. *Academy of Management Journal*, 33, 64–86.

Gudykunst, W. B. (1994). *Bridging Differences: Effective Intergroup Communication*, 2nd ed. Thousand Oaks, CA: Sage.

Halverson, G. (1991). Older workers shine in study of performance. *Christian Science Monitor*, May 24, 9, 1.

Hamner, W. C., Kim, J. S., Baird, L., and Bigoness, W. J. (1974). Race and sex as determinants of ratings by potential employers in a simulated work-sampling task. *Journal of Applied Psychology*, 59, 705–11.

Heilman, M. E. (1983). Sex bias in work settings: The lack of fit model. In B. Staw and L. Cummings (eds), *Research in Organizational Behavior*, vol. 5 (269–98). Greenwich, CT: JAI Press.

Heilman, M. E. (1984). Information as a deterrent against sex discrimination: The effects of applicant sex and information type on preliminary employment decisions. *Organizational Behavior and Human Performance*, 33, 174–86.

Heilman, M. E., Martell, R. F., and Simon, M. (1988). The vagaries of sex bias: Conditions regulating the undervaluation, equivaluation, and overvaluation of female job applicants. *Organization Behavior and Human Decision Processes*, 41, 98–110.

Hofstede, G. (1980a). *Culture's Consequences*. Beverly Hills, CA: Sage.

Hofstede, G. (1980b). Motivation, leadership, and organization: Do American theories apply abroad? *Organizational Dynamics*, 9 (Summer), 42–63.

Hofstede, G. (1984). The cultural relativity of the quality of life concept. *Academy of Management Review*, 9, 389–98.

Hofstede, G. (1993). Cultural constraints in management theories. *Academy of Management Executive*, 7, 81–94.

Holzbach, R. I. (1978). Rater bias in performance ratings: Superior, self-, and peer ratings. *Journal of Applied Psychology*, 59, 638–42.

Huber, V. L. (1989). Comparison of the effects of specific and general performance standards on performance appraisal decisions. *Decision Sciences*, 20(3), 545–57.

Isaacs, M. B. (1981). Sex role stereotyping and the evaluation of the performance of women: Changing trends. *Psychology of Women Quarterly*, 6, 187–95.

Jackson, S. E., and Alvarez, E. B. (1993). Working through diversity as a strategic imperative. In S. E. Jackson and Associates (eds), *Diversity in the Workplace* (13–29). New York: Arrow Press.

Jaussaud, D. P. (1984). Can job evaluation systems help determine the comparable worth of male and female occupations? *Journal of Economic Issues*, 18(2), 473–82.

Kanter, R. (1977). *Men and Women of the Corporation*. New York: Basic Books.

Katz, I., and Glass, D. C. (1979). An ambivalence-amplification theory of behavior toward the stigmatized. In W. G. Austin and S. Worchel (eds), *The Social Psychology of Intergroup Relations* (55–70). Monterey, CA: Brooks/Cole.

Kelley, H. H. (1967). Attribution theory in social psychology. *Nebraska Symposium on Motivation*, 15, 192–238.

Kraiger, K., and Ford, J. K. (1985). A meta-analysis of ratee race effects in performance ratings. *Journal of Applied Psychology*, 70(1), 56–65.

Landy, F. S., and Farr, J. L. (1980). Performance rating. *Psychological Bulletin*, 87, 72–107.

Langer, E. (1978). Rethinking the role of thought in social interaction. In J. Harvey, W. Ickes, and R. Kidd (eds), *New Direction in Attribution Research*, vol. 2. Hillsdale, NJ: Erlbaum.

Langer, E. (1989). *Mindfulness*. Reading, MA: Addison-Wesley.

Lord. R. G., Foti, R. J., and DeVader, C. (1984). A test of leadership categories, information processing, and leadership perception. *Organizational Behavior and Human Performance*, 34, 343–78.

Lublin, J. S. (1994). Turning the tables: Underlings evaluate bosses. *Wall Street Journal*, October 4, B, 1, 3.

Marcus, H. R., and Kitayama, S. (1990). Culture and the self: Implications for cognition, emotion, and motivation, *Psychological Review*, 98(2), 224–53.

Marin, G., and Triandis, H. C. (1985). Allocentrism as an important characteristic of the behavior of Latin Americans and Hispanics. In R. Diaz-Guerrero (ed.), *Cross-cultural and National Studies in Social Psychology* (69–80). Amsterdam: North Holland.

Markiewicz, D. A. (1993). Suit alleges bias in Ford evaluations. *Detroit News*, June 10, E, 1, 5.

Maynard, M. (1994). Evaluations evolve from bottom up. *USA Today*, August 3, B. 6:3.

McElroy, J. C., and Downey, H. H. (1982). Observation in organizational research: Panacea to the performance attribution effect? *Academy of Management Journal*, 25, 822–35.

McEvoy, G. M., and Cascio, W. F. (1989). Cumulative evidence of the relationship between employee age and job performance. *Journal of Applied Psychology*, 74, 11–17.

McNally, J., and Shimmin, S. (1984). Job evaluation and equal pay for work of equal value. *Personnel Review*, 13(1), 27–31.

Milkovich, R., and Newman, J. (1987). *Compensation*. Plano, TX: Business Publications.

Mobley, W. H. (1982). Supervisor and employee race and sex effects on performance appraisals: A field study of adverse impact and generalizability. *Academy of Management Journal*, 25(3), 598–606.

Morgan, G. (1993). *Imaginization: The Art of Creative Management*. Newbury Park, CA: Sage.

Moskowitz, D. B. (1992). Poor job performance rating may cost company dearly. *Washington Post*, January 27, WBIZ, 15:1.

Mullins, T. W. (1982). Interviewer decisions as a function of applicant race, applicant quality, and interviewer prejudice. *Personnel Psychology*, 35, 163–74.

Murphy, K. R., Garcia, M., Kerkar, S., Martin, C., and Balzer, W. (1982). Relationship between observational accuracy and accuracy in evaluating performance. *Journal of Applied Psychology*, 67, 320–5.

Nathan, B. R., and Lord, R. G. (1983). Cognitive categorization and dimensional schemata: A process approach to the study of halo in performance rating. *Journal of Applied Psychology*, 68, 102–14.

Nieva, V. F., and Gutek, B. A. (1980). Sex effects on evaluation. *Academy of Management Review*, 5(2), 267–76.

Nowack, K. M. (1993). 360-degree feedback: The whole story. *Training and Development*, 47, 69–72.

Oppler, S. H. (1992). Three approaches to the investigation of subgroup bias in performance measurement: Review, results, and conclusions. *Journal of Applied Psychology*, 77(2), 201–17.

Pazy, A. (1986). The persistence of pro-male bias despite identical information regarding causes of success. *Organizational Behavior and Human Decision Processes*, 38, 366–77.

Pettigrew, T. F. (1979). The ultimate attribution error. *Personality and Social Psychology Bulletin*, 5, 461–76.

Powell, G. N. (1988). *Women and Men in Management*. Newbury Park, CA: Sage.

Pulakos, E. D., and Wexley, K. N. (1983). The relationship among perceptual similarity, sex, and performance ratings in manager–subordinate dyads. *Academy of Management Journal*, 26, 129–39.

Reich, R. B. (1991). *The Work of Nations*. New York: Vintage.

Reskin, B., and Padavic, I. (1994). *Women and Men at Work*. Thousand Oaks, CA: Pine Forge.

Rosen, B., and Jerdee, T. H. (1973). The influence of sex-role stereotypes on evaluations of male and female supervisory behavior. *Journal of Applied Psychology*, 57, 44–8.

Rosen, B., and Jerdee, T. H. (1976). The influence of age stereotypes on managerial decisions. *Journal of Applied Psychology*, 61(4), 428–32.

Ross, L. (1977). The intuitive psychologist and his shortcomings. *Advances in Experimental and Social Psychology*, 10, 174–220.

Sackett, P. R., and DuBois, C. L. Z. (1991). Rater–ratee race effects on performance evaluation: Challenging meta-analytic conclusions. *Journal of Applied Psychology*, 76(6), 873–7.

Sackett, P. R., DuBois, C. L. Z., and Noe, A. W. (1991). Tokenism in performance evaluation: The effect of work group representation on male–female and white–black differences in performance ratings. *Journal of Applied Psychology*, 2, 263–7.

Schein, V. E. (1978). Sex role stereotyping, ability, and performance: Prior research and new directions. *Personnel Psychology*, 31, 259–68.

Schmidt, F. L., Hunter, J. E., and Outerbridge, A. N. (1986). Impact of job experience and ability on job knowledge, work sample performance, and supervisory ratings of job performance. *Journal of Applied Psychology*, 71, 432–9.

Schmitt, N., and Lappin, M. (1980). Race and sex as determinants of the mean and variance of performance ratings. *Journal of Applied Psychology*, 65, 428–35.

Schoorman, F. D. (1988). Escalation bias in performance appraisals: An unintended consequence of supervisor participation in hiring decisions. *Journal of Applied Psychology*, 73(1), 58–62.

Schwab, D. P., and Heneman, H. G. (1978). Age stereotyping in performance appraisal. *Journal of Applied Psychology*, 63, 573–8.

Shellenbarger, S. (1994). Reviews from peers instruct – and sting. *Wall Street Journal*, October 4, B, 1:4.

Shellhardt, T. D. (1991). Business buzzwords: Managing: New R&R doesn't give executives any rest. *Wall Street Journal*, December 13, B, 1:1.

Sheppard, B. H., Lewicki, R. J., and Minton, J. W. (1992). *Organizational Justice: The Search for Fairness in the Workplace*. New York: Lexington Books.

Shore, L. M., and Bleicken, L. M. (1991). Effects of supervisor age and subordinate age on rating congruence. *Human Relations*, 44, 1093–105.

Smith, D. R., DiTomaso, N., Farris, G. G., and Gordero, R. (1995). Correlated error and bias in performance ratings of scientists and engineers. Working paper. Department of Sociology, Rutgers, NJ.

Smither, J. W., Collins, H., and Buda, R. (1989). When ratee satisfaction influences performance evaluations: A case of illusory correlation. *Journal of Applied Psychology*, 74(4), 599–605.

Steinberg, R. J. (1992). Gendered instructions: Cultural lag and gender bias in the Hay system of job evaluation. *Work & Occupations*, 19(4), 387–423.

Swoboda, F. (1994). Motorola experiments with letting workers' peers weigh their pay. *Washington Post*, May 22, H, 8:1.

Tajfel, H. (ed.) (1978). *Differentiation Between Social Groups*. London: Academic Press.

Tajfel, H. (ed.) (1982). *Social Identity and Intergroup Relations*. Cambridge: Cambridge University Press.

Tannen, D. (ed.) (1993). *Gender and Conversational Interaction.* New York: Oxford University Press.

Taylor, S. E. (1981). A categorization approach to stereotyping. In D. L. Hamilton (ed.), *Cognitive Processes in Stereotyping and Intergroup Behavior* (83–114). Hillsdale, NJ: Erlbaum.

Taylor, S. E., and Falcone, H. (1982). Cognitive bases of stereotyping: The relationship between categorizatior nd prejudice. *Personality and Social Psychology Bulletin,* 8, 426–32.

Thompson, D. E., and DiTomaso, N. (eds) (1988). *Ensuring Minority Success in Corporate Management.* New York: Plenum.

Triandis, H. C. (1989). Cross-cultural studies of individualism and collectivism. In J. Berman (ed.), *The Nebraska Symposium on Motivation* (41–133). Lincoln: University of Nebraska Press.

Triandis, H. C., Kurowski, L. L., and Gelfand, M. J. (1994). Workplace diversity. In H. C. Triandis, M. Dunnette, and L. Hough (eds), *Handbook of Industrial-Organizational Psychology* (768–827). 2nd ed., vol. 4. Palo Alto, CA: Consulting Psychologists Press.

Triandis, H. C., Marin, G., Hui, C. H., Lisansky, J., and Ottati, V. (1984). Role perceptions of Hispanic young adults. *Journal of Cross-Cultural Psychology,* 15, 297–320.

Triandis, H. C., McCusker, C., and Hui, C. H. (1990). Multi-method probes of individualism–collectivism. *Journal of Personality and Social Psychology,* 59, 1006–20.

Trice, H. M., and Beyer, J. M. (1993). *The Cultures of Work Organizations.* Englewood Cliffs, NJ: Prentice-Hall.

Tsui, A. S., and Barry, B. (1986). Interpersonal affect and rating errors. *Academy of Management Journal,* 26, 586–99.

Waldman, D. A. (1993). Aging and work performance in perspective: Contextual and developmental considerations. *Research in Personnel and Human Resource Management,* 11, 113–62.

Waldman, D. A., and Avolio, G. J. (1986). A meta-analysis of age differences in job performance. *Journal of Applied Psychology,* 71, 33–8.

Wall Street Journal (1990). Labor letter: Employee evaluation. October 16, A, 1:5.

Wexley, K. N., and Klimoski, R. (1984). Performance appraisal: An update. In K. M. Rowland and G. R. Ferris (eds), *Research in Personnel and Human Resources Management,* vol. 2 (35–79). Greenwich, CT: JAI Press.

Wynter, L. E. (1994). Black managers reject white bosses' criticism. *Wall Street Journal,* February, 2, B, 1:1.

FURTHER READING

Barnes-Farrell, J. L., L'Heureux-Barrett, T. J., and Conway, J. M. (1991). Impact of gender-related job features on the accurate evaluation of performance information. *Organizational Behavior & Human Decision Processes,* 48(1), 23–35.

Bass, A. R., and Turner, J. N. (1973). Ethnic group differences in relationships among criteria of job performance. *Journal of Applied Psychology,* 57, 101–9.

Cafferty, T. P., DeNisi, A. S., and Williams, K. J. (1986). Search and retrieval patterns for performance information: Effects on evaluation of multiple targets. *Journal of Personality and Social Psychology,* 50, 676–83.

Cleveland, J. N., and Shore, L. M. (1992). Self- and supervisory perspectives on age and work attitudes and performance. *Journal of Applied Psychology*, 77, 469–84.

Cline, M. E., Holmes, D. S., and Werner, J. C. (1977). Evaluations of the work of men and women as a function of the sex of the judge and type of work. *Journal of Applied Psychology*, 7, 89–93.

Czajka, J. M., and DeNisi, A. S. (1988). Effects of emotional disability and clear performance standards on performance ratings. *Academy of Management Journal*, 31(2), 394–404.

Deaux, K., and Taynor, J. (1973). Evaluation of male and female ability: Bias works two ways. *Psychology Reports*, 31, 20–31.

DeCotiis, T., and Petit, A. (1978). The performance appraisal process: A model and some testable propositions. *Academy of Management Review*, 3, 635–46.

DeNisi, A. S., Robbins, T. L., and Cafferty, T. P. (1989). Organization of information used for performance appraisals: Role of diary-keeping. *Journal of Applied Psychology*, 74, 124–9.

Edwards, M. R. (1991). Accurate performance measurement tools. *HR Magazine*, 36(6), 95–8.

Faley, R. H., Kleinman, L. S., and Lengnick-Hall. M. L. (1984). Age discrimination and personnel psychology: A review and synthesis of the legal literature with implications for future research. *Personnel Psychology*, 37, 327–50.

Fossum, J. A., Arvey, R. D., Paradise, C. A., and Robbins, N. E. (1986). Modeling the skills obsolescence process: A psychological/economic integration. *Academy of Management Review*, 11, 362–74.

Fox, H., and Lefkowitz, J. (1974). Differential validity: Ethnic group as a moderator in predicting job performance. *Personnel Psychology*, 27, 209–33.

Gabor, A. (1992). Take this job and love it. *New York Times*, January 26, 3, 1:2.

Ha, W. C., Kim, K. S., Baird, L., and Bigoness, W. J. (1974). Race and sex as determinants of ratings by potential employers in a simulated work-sampling task. *Journal of Applied Psychology*, 59, 705–11.

Hall, F. S., and Hall, D. T. (1976). Effects of job incumbents' race and sex on evaluations of managerial performance. *Academy of Management Journal*, 19, 476–81.

Heneman, H. G., III (1977). Impact of test information and applicant sex. *Journal of Applied Psychology*, 62, 524–6.

Ilgen, D. R., and Youtz, M. A. (1986). Factors affecting the evaluation and development of minorities in organizations. In K. Rowland and G. Ferris (eds), *Research in Personnel and Human Resource Management: A Research Annual* (307–37). Greenwich, CT: JAI Press.

Lee, D. M., and Alvares, K. M. (1977). Effects of sex on descriptions and evaluations of supervisory behavior in a simulated industrial setting. *Journal of Applied Psychology*, 62, 405–10.

Martin, J. (1992). *Cultures in Organizations*. New York: Oxford University Press.

Maurer, T. J., and Taylor, M. A. (1994). Is sex itself enough? An exploration of gender bias issues in performance appraisal. *Organizational Behavior & Human Decision Processes*, 60(2), 231–51.

McConkie, M. L. (1979). A clarification of the goal-setting and appraisal processes in MBO. *Academy of Management Review*, 4, 29–40.

McDaniel, M. A., Schmidt, F. L., and Hunter, J. E. (1988). Job experience correlates of job performance. *Journal of Applied Psychology*, 73, 327–30.

Palmer, A. T. (1993). Workers add grades to bosses' report cards. *Chicago Tribune*, July 18, 7, 4:1.

Peters, L. H., O'Conners, E. J., Weekely, J., Pooyan, A., Frank, B., and Erenkrantz, B. (1984). Sex bias and managerial evaluations: A replication and extension. *Journal of Applied Psychology*, 69, 349–620.

Pheterson, G. T., Kiesler, S. B., and Goldberg, P. A. (1971). Evaluation of the performance of women as a function of their sex, achievement, and personal history. *Journal of Personality and Social Psychology*, 19, 110–14.

Pulakos, E. D., White, L. A., Oppler, S. H., and Borman, W. C. (1989). Examination of race and sex effects on performance ratings. *Journal of Applied Psychology*, 74, 770–80.

Rice, B. (1985). Performance review: Examining the eye of the beholder. *Across the Board*, 22(12), 24–32.

Robbins, T. L., and DeNisi, A. S. (1993). Moderators of sex bias in the performance appraisal process: A cognitive analysis. *Journal of Management*, 19(1), 113–26.

Roberts, G. E. (1992). Linkages between performance appraisal system effectiveness and rater and ratee acceptance. *Review of Public Personnel Administration*, 12(3), 19–41.

Schmidt, F. L., and Johnson, R. H. (1973). Effect of race on peer ratings in an industrial setting. *Journal of Applied Psychology*, 57, 237–41.

Shore, L. M., and Thornton G. C. (1986). Effects of gender on self- and supervisory ratings. *Academy of Management Journal*, 29(1), 115–29.

Terborg, J. R., and Ilgen, D. R. (1975). A theoretical approach to sex discrimination in traditionally masculine occupations. *Organizational Behavior and Human Performance*, 13, 352–76.

Tsui, A. S., and O'Reilly, C. A. (1989). Beyond simple demographic effects: The importance of relational demography in superior–subordinate dyads. *Academy of Management Journal*, 32, 402–23.

Waldman, D. A., and Avolio, B. J. (1991). Race effects in performance evaluations: Controlling for ability, education, and experience. *Journal of Applied Psychology*, 76(6), 897–901.

Wall Street Journal (1993). Labor letter: Work teams. September 7, A, 1:5.

Wall Street Journal (1993). Labor letter: Reliable references. February 23, A, 1:5.

Wexley, K. N., and Pulakos, E. D. (1982). Sex effects on performance ratings in manager–subordinate dyad: A field study. *Journal of Applied Psychology*, 67, 433–9.

White, M. C., Crino, M. D., and DeSanctis, G. L. (1981). A critical review of female performance, performance training and organizational initiative designed to aid women in the work-role environment. *Personnel Psychology*, 34, 227–47.

7

The Role of Training in a Changing Workplace and Workforce: New Perspectives and Approaches

J. Kevin Ford and Sandra Fisher

Businesses today are spending an ever increasing amount of money on training their own workforce. One estimate suggests that over $210 billion is spent every year in the United States alone on workplace training (Carnevalle et al., 1990). The demand for more training has mainly arisen because of the view that people represent the primary source of enduring competitive advantage (e.g. Pfeffer, 1994). While profits are still being achieved through strategies such as the import of new technologies and corporate downsizing, many organizations recognize that their core productive capacity and long-term viability must be based on quality of the human resources in the organization.

The focus on training as a key lever for organizational effectiveness will likely continue into the next century. The increasing scope and complexity of the changes occurring in the workplace such as team-based work systems, the focus on quality, and the movement towards reengineering all require a highly trained workforce. Progressive organizations have devoted considerable resources to training workers to be better prepared to deal with the changing realities of the workplace.

The changing workplace is taking place at a time when organizations are also undergoing major changes in their workforce. For example, evidence suggests that there is an increasing percentage of minorities joining the workforce as well as large increases in the number of women, especially women with children (Offerman and Gowing, 1990). These changes can have an important impact on the dominant culture of the organization. The workforce is also ageing – between 1986 and 2000, the number of persons aged 48 to 53 will increase by 67 percent (Johnston and Packer, 1987). The ageing workforce coupled with downsizing poses challenges for career progression issues as well as for issues of retraining. In addition, there is an increasing percentage of dual career families with multiple responsibilities and shifting needs. There is a widening monetary gap between the highly educated, highly skilled and the less educated, lower skilled workers in our society. This gap has heightened efforts to deal with workplace illiteracy and training for the hard-core unemployed. Laws such as the Americans with Disabilities Act have emphasized the need for organizations to be proactive in assimilating disadvantaged individuals into the workforce.

As the diversification of the workforce continues, organizations must confront changing expectations and needs. The dominant culture and its system of beliefs, values, and norms that has developed within a relatively homogeneous workforce is challenged by its increasing diversity. In addition, problems with the educational system for our youth along with the need for more complex cognitive skills in the workplace have led many to conclude that a skills shortage is imminent. The diversification of the workforce calls for an even greater emphasis on how to effectively utilize the human resources (HR) of the organization. Training is often seen as an avenue for developing a more effective workforce.

There are at least five explanations for why training has become a popular approach for dealing with the complex issues relevant to the changing workforce. First, future projections have created a new awareness of the changing demographics of the workforce. As the pool of available employees becomes less white and less male, organizations are driven to find ways to integrate this new mix of employees into the organizational culture. Such thinking has also led to a reevaluation of the effectiveness of the existing dominant organizational culture for the continued viability of the firm.

Second, there are legal issues surrounding training and development opportunities in the workplace (Noe, 1988; Hartel, 1994). From this perspective, all employees must be given equal access to training, mentoring, and other development activities to avoid disparate treatment in the workplace. The Americans with Disabilities Act, for example, requires that training be accessible to employees with disabilities.

Third, the business necessity perspective claims that productivity and profits depend on full utilization of the workforce. Training is seen as a key method for eliminating artificial barriers to individual development and capabilities. Workforce diversity can become an asset rather than a liability if the workforce is properly trained (Johnson, 1994).

The fourth explanation revolves around ethical or fairness reasons for considering training programs. For example, a procedural justice approach suggests that perceptions of fairness are critical for organizational viability. Training is viewed as one way to potentially improve perceptions of fairness if all employees are given equal opportunities to gain the knowledge and skills necessary to be effective in the organization.

The final perspective is that individual workers themselves are recognizing that their knowledge and skills may be inadequate for their current jobs as well as for future career goals. In some cases, the shortfall is in basic reading and math literacy skills. In other cases, improvements in skills relevant to advanced technical issues such as blueprint reading, statistical process control, and computer word processing are required. The training challenge for individual workers begins at the transition from school to work, but is applicable to people of all ages and in all sectors of the economy. As managers and employees confront issues of downsizing and corporate restructuring, training emerges as a key to survival as well as to professional development.

The purpose of this chapter is to focus on the role of training and development relevant to the changing workforce and workplace. It highlights new approaches to training that are focused on meeting the needs and challenges of a more diverse workforce. The first section briefly describes the instructional systems model and the key issues in the assessment, design, and evaluation of training. The section concludes with a description of the limitations of existing training research and practice. Three perspectives emerging in the training field to better deal with the challenges posed by a more diverse and changing workforce are then presented. The second section discusses each of the three new perspectives and the methods and approaches that can be used to improve the effectiveness of a training system given the changing nature of workforce and workplace. The final section reflects upon the challenges and potential for training systems in helping organizations move forward into the 21st century.

The Instructional System Design Model

A well-established framework for organizing the important steps of training is the instructional systems design (ISD) model (see, e.g. Dick and Carey, 1985; Goldstein, 1991). The instructional systems model describes the systematic development and interrelated components of training programs, emphasizing three key components: (1) training needs assessment; (2) training design, methods and delivery; and (3) training evaluation and transfer. This section briefly describes these key components of the ISD model and introduces three training system perspectives that are emerging, in part, to respond to the changing workforce.

Components of the ISD model

Training needs assessment is the first step in the systematic development of a training program. Training needs analysis consists of three interrelated components: organizational analysis, operations analysis, and person analysis (Ostroff and Ford, 1989). Organizational analysis involves examining the entire organization to determine where training is needed. This system-wide analysis typically examines whether the existing goals of the organization might be better met by increasing employee knowledge and skills or by changing attitudes. Once it is determined where training is needed, an operations analysis is conducted to determine: (1) the tasks performed on the job; (2) the knowledge, skills, and abilities (KSAs) needed to perform those tasks; and (3) the performance standards or competencies required to perform each task. The identification of tasks, underlying knowledge and skills, and performance standards provide a comprehensive analysis of the job. Person analysis assesses whether individuals are performing at expected levels. If not, the next step is to determine whether any performance gaps found might be a result of inadequate knowledge, skills or attitudes that are alterable through training and developmental activities.

Needs assessment provides information on what, where, when, and who needs to be trained. Program design is the process of developing a plan of instruction for each training program to be offered. Traditionally, developing a plan of instruction begins with the specification of instructional objectives which provide statements of the desired end states for trainees. Once instructional objectives are written, the focus of the training design process shifts to the sequencing of training events and the incorporation of learning principles (e.g. practice, feedback) to maximize learning. The second primary step in the training design phase is to create a learning environment that enhances trainee motivation and optimizes learning. The third step is to select or develop an appropriate instructional method. In organizational settings, the most popular methods are on-the-job training (show and tell) and classroom instruction (lecture, discussion, and demonstrations). It is critical that the training method selected is appropriate for meeting the instructional objectives and the training context. Training evaluation involves the development of an information gathering methodology to help decision-makers make judgements. Training evaluation information is critical for determining the success of the program in meeting its stated objectives, and what refinements in the training are needed to improve its quality.

A key focus of evaluation efforts should be on the transfer of training or the extent to which trainees effectively apply the knowledge, skills, and attitudes gained in a training context to the job context. Expected outcomes of the transfer process include both the generalization of trained skills to the job and the maintenance or long-term retention of trained knowledge and skills (Baldwin and Ford, 1988). Generalization involves more than mimicking trained responses to particular events that occurred during training. It requires trainees to exhibit behaviors identical or of similar type to those learned in training in response to similar but not identical settings, people, or situations to those presented in training. Maintenance is the length of time that trained skills and behaviors continue to be used effectively on the job.

The changing nature of training: three new perspectives

Applications of the ISD model have resulted in advances in training needs methodologies, training methods, and evaluation techniques. However, training practice and research have often taken an overly simplistic approach to assessing, designing, and delivering training given the changing realities of the workplace and workforce (Ford and Kraiger, 1995). In fact, the type of training research and practice that has been typically spawned by the ISD model has become, in at least three ways, incompatible with the needs of a changing workplace and workforce. New perspectives are emerging in the training field to more effectively develop the HR within the organization.

Reductionist versus a holistic perspective   The first issue concerns the basic building blocks of a training system. It has been noted that training research and practice have become quite reductionist in nature (Ford and Kraiger, 1995). Training systems have almost exclusively relied on breaking tasks down to their individual elements – tasks, knowledge, skills. These discrete entities (individual tasks and KSA statements) are then used to develop a training plan of instruction that is viewed in isolation from other training initiatives. For example, tasks or KSAs that are rated as important, frequently performed, and difficult to learn are typically given high priority for inclusion in a training program (e.g. Goldstein, 1993). An underlying assumption of this reductionist approach is that tasks, jobs, and even training programs are best viewed as separable or independent from one another.

The challenges posed by the changing nature of the workforce call for a more holistic approach to training needs assessment, design, and evaluation. For example, the necessity to blend diverse needs and expectations with the organization's desire for greater cooperation and teamwork across individuals and job functions has highlighted limitations in the reductionist approach to training. As work becomes more multifaceted and team-oriented with its emphasis on cooperation and tolerance for others, training systems must begin to understand the need to take more of a holistic or systems perspective to jobs and learning within the organizational system.

Massed training versus customized training   The second issue concerns the level at which the training intervention is focused. Training systems have typically emphasized efficiency of effort through "training for the masses." An underlying assumption of this approach is that similarities across people and groups within the organization are more important or salient than differences. Therefore, trainees can be treated equally (e.g. given the same training method) with the expectation that similar learning outcomes will occur across individuals. Training large groups of trainees at one time or using the same training program across a number of groups of trainees is certainly an economical approach. In addition, such an approach was quite appropriate when the workforce was relatively homogeneous in composition (i.e. white, male) and where the basic goal of training was blending individuals to be more alike in terms of goals, knowledge, skills, and attitudes.

The increasing diversity of the workforce has led trainers to question more carefully the "costs" involved in the massed training approach. Individuals are not interchangeable, but have different goals, expectations, needs, skills, and their own criteria of success. While business necessity dictates a certain level of job performance, the changing workforce questions whether there is one best way to reach those outcome goals. Instead, the growing diversity of people requires a greater diversity in the methods used to train and develop individuals in the organization. This customization approach in which training is tailored to meet individual needs is consistent with a more holistic perspective to people and their work.

Reinforcing the status quo versus leading cultural change   A third issue concerns the use of training as a driver of change in the organization. Traditionally, training initiatives have focused on reinforcing the values, norms, and belief structures of the dominant culture. This is vividly seen in the socialization techniques used on newcomers to assimilate them not only to their job but also to "how things really work around here." From this traditional perspective, the training system is like a maintenance sub-system (Katz and Kahn, 1978) that is supportive of other subsystems such as production. In this supportive role, training is a system that emphasizes the need to maintain the status quo within the organization.

With workforce changes, organizations are more aware of the need for questioning the dominant culture and for considering how best to integrate and fully utilize a diverse HR population within the organization. Given how important training and development can be in inculcating organizational norms and values, it is not surprising that organizations are now turning towards training to propel desired cultural change. A key issue today, then, is use of training for not only enhancing the value of diversity in the workplace but also as a driver for cultural change. At one level, diversity training can provide individuals with the knowledge and skills necessary to embrace diversity in their workplace. At another level, it can be a potent signal to employees that a change in the status quo is not only desirable and possible, but necessary.

Summary

The changing workforce emphasizes the need for training that is holistic rather than reductionist, customized rather than mass-produced, and that emphasizes cultural change rather than simply reinforcing the status quo. The movement to match the complexity of the workforce with the training systems requires a more dynamic and flexible approach to training needs assessment, design, and evaluation. Each new perspective to training and how it deals with the changing realities of the workforce is discussed below.

A Holistic Approach to Training

The changing workforce highlights the need for an expanded role for training and development in meeting organizational and individual needs. This role suggests that the needs assessment strategies must emphasize not only individual jobs and tasks but also the interactions and teamwork patterns among employees. Similarly, training design has tended to view each training program as an individual, isolated event. A more holistic approach to design requires that attention be devoted to understanding the appropriate sequencing of learning experiences across a career. A holistic approach also views training evaluation from a systems perspective. From this perspective, whether trained knowledge and skills are being used on the job is more a function of the work context and subsystem rather than the individual accomplishment or failing of trainees. A description of these issues is provided below.

Training needs assessment

Needs assessment approaches have clearly advanced the systematic development of training programs. Nevertheless, one limitation of the traditional approaches to needs assessment has been its focus on individual jobs and the elements of those jobs. As noted by Morgan et al. (1986), most organizations today must not only develop employee knowledge and skills relevant for task accomplishment ("taskwork") but also must develop "teamwork" or interpersonal skills. The need to develop interpersonal skills is compounded by the increasing diversity in organizations (Offerman and Gowing, 1990), as employees must interact with dissimilar others. The combination of identifying taskwork and teamwork dimensions relevant to training needs assessment provides a more comprehensive or holistic perspective towards the people in the organization. Employees do not just perform tasks but must interact and coordinate efforts.

The emphasis on teamwork leads to different methods and approaches for training needs assessment. Operations analysis must focus not only on identifying tasks, KSAs and performance standards for individual jobs, but must also identify the communication and coordination linkages across individuals with different jobs. Person analysis can focus on the performance "gaps" between employees rather than only examining performance gaps within each individual. Levine and Baker (1991), for example, have coined the phrase "team task analysis," and have developed a methodology to analyze deficiencies in team level interactions. The gaps identified involve the differences between the expectations regarding the level and quality of teamwork against the reality of the workplace. Training efforts can then be considered to best fill that performance gap.

For example, as part of the development of an overall training plan for a small manufacturing company that the first author has worked with, the social network of relations within the plant's employees was identified. This network analysis helped to quantify the levels of cooperation and coordination required across the organization. A person analysis that prioritized the groups and individuals that were most in need of improvement relevant to cooperation and coordination of efforts was then conducted. Social network analyses such as completed in this case often show that women and minorities are in greatest need of improving their integration into the organizational network (Ibarra, 1993; Morrison and Von Glinow,

1990). Thus, in addition to prioritizing needs around technical training, the training plan also included training on team-building which focused on the development of more cooperative relationships across shifts and functions.

Training design

The reductionist approach to training directs attention to the development of training programs to meet a specified need. Such an approach to design and delivery ignores the fact that a training event is not an isolated activity. Newly developed training programs may complement or hinder previous training and development activities. For example, with an ageing workforce, retraining is viewed as critical to the more effective utilization of these human resources. A key issue, though, is whether the training design relevant to these new programs helps individuals link previous knowledge and skills to the new knowledge and skill requirements. Without such a linkage, the training is likely to be viewed with suspicion and fear, thus leading to lowered levels of learning and transfer.

This notion of linkages with past experiences suggests that training is best thought of as an organizational episode, i.e. a series of cumulative experiences and the cognition and feelings associated with those experiences (Baldwin and Magjuka, forthcoming) rather than as a detached event. Thus, training design cannot focus simply on training needs assessment data concerning what knowledge and skills should be the focus of training (or retraining), but must also include additional information on what experiences individuals are bringing to the training program. In this way, advance organizers can be incorporated into the training design to ensure that the linkage between existing and new knowledge and skills is made (see Ausubel, 1968). In addition, a sequence of learning can be developed that builds upon previous experience. As noted by Knowles (1978), to reject adult experiences and background is to reject the adult.

A holistic approach to training design views employees as whole individuals, not just workers. For example, Weyerhauser Structurwood includes spouses and families of employees in initial training efforts (Cutcher-Gershenfeld et al., 1991). The training program is intended to explain the effects of shift work on employees and their families. Organizations are offering other types of training programs to help families deal with the pressures of balancing work and family, such as parenting classes (Zedeck and Mosier, 1990). In addition, the multiple responsibilities and time pressures felt by dual-career families have led organizations to consider innovative training and education opportunities such as the use of distance learning for those individuals willing to work towards an advanced degree.

This more holistic perspective to training design emphasizes the need to better understand how knowledge and skills develop over time within individuals and groups of individuals as well as how training may bridge gaps between work and nonwork life. An example of this more holistic approach to organizational learning is the recent work by the Center for Creative Leadership (CCL). CCL has conducted a series of studies focusing on how managers learn, change, and grow over the course of their careers (McCall et al., 1988). The research found that the lessons or fundamental skills discovered by successful managers included the importance of having compassion and sensitivity towards others, developing the resourcefulness to cope with the demands of the managerial job and make decisions, and creating a work environment that is conducive to subordinate productivity, satisfaction, and development. These are all skills that are becoming more relevant in a workplace characterized by a diverse population. A greater understanding of the learning process over time (in this case high level executives) can guide the development of training experiences to build needed knowledge and skills over the course of a career.

In addition to the life experience of trainees, training design must include consideration of the broad range of basic skills brought to training by diverse employee groups. Organizations can no longer assume new hires have the requisite knowledge needed to learn job-related skills, as many new entrants to the workforce will be undereducated youth (Goldstein and Gilliam, 1990). A more holistic approach to training design could combine the teaching of basic skills with more job-related content areas. For example, Domino's Pizza teaches the reading and math skills needed at the same time it teaches employees how to make dough (Goldstein and Gilliam, 1990). It has been suggested that combining basic skills training with job skills training is more cost effective, as well as providing a relevant context in which to learn the basics.

Training evaluation

Research on training evaluation and transfer has typically focused on the reactions of trainees to the training program and the amount of learning that occurred during the training. At times, attempts have been made to examine the transfer of knowledge, skills, and attitudes from an individual training program to the workplace (Baldwin and Ford, 1988). While such an individual level focus is obviously warranted, it is also limiting. It implicitly assumes that each training program is independent from others and from other events and activities occurring within the organization. Any training program, though, is nested within a larger training system which includes a variety of training programs, methods, instructors, and evaluation techniques. Similarly, the training department and its training programs are embedded within a larger organizational system. The larger organizational system conveys information regarding the importance of the training programs through strategic decisions, the reward and promotion system within the organization, and through the operationalization of policies and procedures at the production level.

A more holistic approach to evaluation takes a systems perspective to change as the focal point for evaluation. A systems perspective highlights the interrelatedness of the various subsystems in the organization and how those subsystems may help or hinder efforts to apply training to the job. For example, Ford et al. (1992) found that newcomers who had been trained on a variety of skills were often denied the opportunity to perform the skills on the jobs by their supervisor. The opportunity to perform is quite relevant given attempts by organizations to enhance opportunities for women and minorities to move into jobs in which they have not historically been well represented. In a recent case study, Cutcher-Gershenfeld et al. (1991) found that workers retrained to become proficient in a skilled trade were often not used effectively by supervisors who preferred to wait for the more experienced skilled tradesperson especially for the complex and demanding jobs. Thus, the training may be adequate, but the managerial subsystem is not prepared to best utilize the new human resources in the organization.

In addition, a systems perspective forces one to evaluate the unintended as well as the intended consequences of training on the other subsystems within the organization. For example, Klein and Ralls (forthcoming) reported that unintended consequences arose when employees were given training on computer-aided design and drafting. The researchers noted that the computer-based training altered the relative distribution of technical expertise between the supervisors and their subordinates as subordinates acquired specialized skills that the supervisors lacked. This led to the supervisors feeling less confident in their own ability to provide meaningful guidance and feedback and lowered their credibility in the eyes of the employees. Training relevant to diversity issues may also have potentially negative unintended consequences, and should be evaluated with a systems perspective.

This new holistic perspective to training evaluation suggests that there is value in moving from an individual level to the organization level. Evaluation efforts should identify the organizational subsystems that may be the root cause for the lack of transfer to the job as well as to identify the unintended consequences of training effects on daily operations across the different organizational subsystems.

Customization of Training

The need to customize training to meet individual needs has a relatively long history in the training and educational fields. In the educational field, studies have been completed on tracking students (i.e. placing high-ability students together and placing lower-ability students together in a class). With such tracking, the instructional content, method and delivery can be developed to more closely match group needs based on ability levels.

In the training field, a similar philosophy has led to work on aptitude-treatment interactions (ATI) in which the instructional method is matched with the ability levels of the participants. It has been suggested that the training of low-ability individuals should focus on more concrete issues while training for high-ability individuals can include more abstract or conceptual issues. For example, more concrete examples and demonstrations might be given to low-ability trainees who are being trained on complex troubleshooting skills while the high-ability group may begin, instead, with an extensive discussion of the theoretical underpinnings of electric currents. While a number of efforts have been conducted to examine ATI, research evidence is inconclusive as to the effectiveness of this approach to learning. Nevertheless, the notion of "customizing" training to better fit individual needs remains appealing.

Training technologies are improving to such a degree that the potential for customizing training for individuals (rather than groups of individuals matched on ability or some other dimension) is becoming more of a reality. The customization of training needs assessment, design and evaluation has direct implications for meeting the needs of the increasing diversity of backgrounds and experiences embedded in the workforce.

Training needs assessment

The traditional perspective to training needs assessment has assumed that individuals come into the organization with basic literacy skills such as reading, writing, arithmetical computation, speaking English, and oral communication (Business Council for Effective Literacy, 1987). Consequently, most efforts at needs assessment have focused on training newcomers for specific technical skills so that job duties can be performed. Organizations have begun to recognize that this underlying assumption is quite problematic given the growing problems with basic educational issues in the United States.

The research that has examined issues of literacy indicates that the problems are fairly substantial in the workplace. It has been estimated that one-third of the US population is functionally or marginally illiterate (Kozol, 1985). The decline in basic skills is occurring at a time when jobs are requiring more complex cognitive skills (Goldstein and Gilliam, 1990). The gap between expectations and the quality of the applicant pool has prompted many organizations to identify the level of basic skills for newcomers and for incumbents (Workinger and Ruch, 1991). As one example, the Educational Testing Service found that of those tested between age 21 and 25, only 25 percent of whites, 7 percent of Hispanics, and 3 percent of blacks could follow directions to travel from one location to another using a complex bus schedule (Offerman and Gowing, 1990).

Consequently, a growing number of businesses are taking on the role of educators, allocating money into basic literacy, high school equivalency, and other basic skills courses so that all employees can read, write, and do basic calculations. As one example, Polaroid has created a comprehensive literacy program that assesses basic skills and analyzes the basic skill levels needed to complete a specific job successfully. The "literacy gaps" identified through this approach often lead to the customization of training activities to bring individual employees to an expected level (e.g. 12th grade reading level). This emphasis on remedial training has led to a tighter association between organizations and local high schools and community colleges.

Literacy issues are also becoming more important as organizations utilize sophisticated equipment and move to team-oriented systems that require the extensive use of basic reading, writing, and math skills. Learning the basics is often a prerequisite for learning more complex technical skills. In addition, learning the basics allows for greater involvement and empowerment of the employees in process improvement projects such as gathering and interpreting statistical process control data.

As an example of this approach to needs assessment, a small parts-manufacturing company has over the last four years moved from a functional to a cellular work design. The functionally-based system placed few demands on individual employees, as they worked on only one machine and interacted rarely with other functional areas. With the restructuring, employees are now working in teams and are cross-trained so that each cell can take raw stock steel and transform it into finished products such as sprockets and gears. Employees have also been empowered to solve quality problems at the source and to work together to make improvements in the system. The organizational restructuring, therefore, requires individuals to have more skills than were previously demanded of them. Early in the change process, management became aware that a number of current employees did not have the basic skills needed to match the increasing complexity of the changing workplace. In addition, a new selection system began to uncover gaps in basic skills of many job applicants. These basic skills included such things as reading blueprints, translating fractions into decimals, and interpreting gages properly to set tolerances. Individual needs for basic skills training were determined. The company then hired high school English and math teachers to develop individualized instruction programs to best meet those needs.

Training design

Traditionally, training design has focused on the trainer being in control of the learning content, sequencing, design, and delivery of training. In addition, the training program is typically delivered in group settings where the trainee is often a passive recipient of training material. However, greater heterogeneity in organizations has led to increased interest in issues of the customization of training programs to better meet individual needs. There are two key approaches for redesigning training to meet changing requirements. One approach is technological, in which computer programming allows for variability in the learning process across trainees. A second concerns explicit attempts to ensure that the process of learning is put more in the control of the learner.

Technological approaches   The behaviorist traditions of the 1950s gave rise to programmed instruction as a training methodology. With greater availability of microcomputers, programmed instruction has given way first to computer-assisted instruction (CAI) – computer-based training grounded in the programmed instruction methodology – and, more recently, to intelligent tutoring systems (ITS). The latter methodology consists of computer-based instructional programs which adapt to the needs and abilities of the learner (e.g. Acker et al., 1991). In general, with ITS, responses by trainees can be continually analyzed by the computer to determine the appropriate pace for effective instruction. ITS also automatically adjusts the types of problems and tasks presented to the trainees in response to previous training performance.

An obvious advantage of the ITS is that the system helps to individualize the learning process. Given the increasing diversity within organizations, this represents a major step forward. A not so obvious advance of intelligent tutoring type systems concerns the use of training instructors. As with other techniques, ITS should not be seen as a standalone system. Most learners prefer human interaction as well. With ITS, the instructors can focus their energies on analyzing the data on trainee progress, determine problem areas, and help individual trainees who may require additional practice. In this way, instructor time is used more efficiently and effectively.

Adult learning and learner control   The changing workforce has also highlighted the need for training to be designed differently to increase the adult learner's receptiveness to new learning and to increase the likelihood that learning actually takes place. This is especially apparent with older workers who must be retrained or provided with advanced training programs to remain competent in their jobs. These individuals have rich, varied work and life experiences that must be incorporated into training through structured experiential or hands-on exercises rather than relying on lecture-oriented training methods. Experienced workers have a more problem-centered time perspective which requires a problem-solving rather than a theoretical orientation to training.

From an adult learning perspective, trainees are seen as self-directed individuals who enjoy planning and carrying out their own learning experiences, as well as evaluating their own progress. Learner "control" is a construct now being actively investigated in the training field. Learner control refers to the extent that trainees have the opportunity to select the method, timing, and style of the training, practice, and/or feedback portions of training.

Several hypothesized advantages of learner control are enhanced motivation to learn and the development of internal attributions for success (Milheim and Martin, 1991). However, learner control also can result in more opportunities to develop and test personal strategies, or to recognize the relationships between one's actions and subsequent outcomes. There are a variety of ways of building learner control into learning environments including the use of interactive software, allowing trainees to select an instructional strategy appropriate to their preferred learning styles, or encouraging trainees to decide when they have had sufficient time to practice or rehearse new skills. Giving learners *complete* control over instruction is less effective than conventional instructional methods (Milheim and Martin, 1991). The most effective method for learning is to allow learners control over the pace and sequence of instruction, but to provide advice or suggestions for next steps (Tennyson and Rasch, 1988). In addition, instructional methods in which the group of trainees serve as a support system for each trainee's individual learning, and the instructor gradually turns over control to the trainees are effective ways to achieve learner control (Brown and Palinscar, 1989).

Additional considerations in the customization of training programs include flexibility in the scheduling of programs and composition of trainee groups. Given the increased frequency of flex-time, telecommuting, and job sharing (Offerman and Gowing, 1990), not all employees who would like to attend a training program will be able to attend during the usual business hours. Employees may also use scheduling flexibility to arrange trainee groups to fit a particular need. Some women in organizations may prefer to attend women-only training sessions (Morrison and Von Glinow, 1990). A customization approach to training design would allow for the flexibility to meet these needs.

The recent Americans with Disabilities Act has profound implications for customization of both needs analysis and training design. Training must be accessible to all employees, regardless of physical abilities (Hartel, 1994). In needs analysis, one must question whether the skills taught in training are essential functions. If not, a person with a disability may not be required to perform those skills on the job, and the training should be adapted accordingly. In training design, reasonable accommodation must be made for all disabled employees. Disabilities could include visual or hearing impairments or learning disabilities. Could braille training manuals or a reader be provided? Could an interpreter be provided if a lecture is planned? Individual customization of the plan of instruction is particularly relevant, as individuals within a particular class of disabilities vary enormously in their capabilities (Brannick et al., 1992). It has been suggested that trainers allow the individual trainee with a disability to suggest how he or she might best be accommodated in the learning process (Fischer, 1994).

Training evaluation

Training researchers have called for the use of experimental designs to determine if the training is successful (e.g. Goldstein, 1993). Experimental designs help determine if a group of trainees, as a whole, seem to have gained something from training over and above a control group that did not undergo the training program. This normative approach to training evaluation provides an overall evaluation of success. Organizations can then estimate if the costs of training are outweighed by the average performance improvement for the group as a whole.

Such a normative approach to evaluation does not provide an indication of whether all individuals have mastered the necessary material. In addition, this traditional perspective makes an assumption that everyone must learn at the same rate or build and transfer skills in the same way through a particular training program or sequence of programs. This approach ignores individual differences in learning and how individuals build upon learning experiences on the job to become proficient and effective workers.

A more customized approach to evaluation focuses on the question "what is to be learned" (Campbell, 1988) and how best to obtain the expected outcomes. From this perspective, evaluation should emphasize mastery of the training objectives, i.e. did the training lead to the desired level of proficiency for each individual. This requires the clear identification of what knowledge and skills are expected as a function of training and the development of an evaluation system to determine individual competencies. In addition, such an approach must recognize that there are many paths by which individuals can obtain mastery skills and that individuals can proceed at a rate that fits their needs. In this way, regardless of the diversity of the workforce, each individual knows what is expected of him/her to obtain valued rewards such as pay increases and promotions – yet there is flexibility in the system to allow individuals to develop their own approach to learning and development.

For example, at Weyerhauser Structurwood, employees are actively involved in making decisions regarding training assessment, design, and evaluation (Cutcher-Gershenfeld et al., 1991). The plant is organized around production teams that have a team leader rather than supervisory personnel. The teams work on different processes in the transition of wood to value-added products such as floor paneling. Each team is responsible for many personnel-related activities including the determination of training needs within the team and finding ways of meeting those needs. The participative process of the company is driven by a pay-for-knowledge system in which employees receive salary increases based on the number of production processes they master through training and experience. Thus, employees can determine individually the skills they wish to learn, and the rate at which they advance.

To become a master at a skill, the employee must first pass a written exam regarding the production process and safety. Each employee creates an individual development plan in conjunction with the team to specify the knowledge and skills needed, how they will be learned, and the time frame for acquisition. The individual is then trained on the job by masters of that function, as it is the team's responsibility to prepare employees for mastery. A mastery board consisting of two managers, a team leader, and three peers is then convened to administer an oral examination that places equal emphasis on interpersonal skills, technical skills, and safety skills. Once mastery is obtained, it is up to the team to make sure that this mastery is transferred to the job and retained over time. This employee-oriented participatory training and reward system has led to an effective, manageable training system in which the development and retention of mastery level skills is the critical objective of the individually focused program of learning activities. Their approach is aptly summarized by the acronym of LUTI – first you *learn* a skill, second you *utilize* the skills to build to a mastery level of proficiency, third you *teach* other, more novice workers to build their initial skills, and then you *inspect* whether the trainees are applying what they know to the job.

Leading Cultural Change

A key mechanism organizations have traditionally used to socialize or assimilate individuals into the norms and values of the organization is initial orientation and training and developmental activities (Feldman, 1989). The purpose of training for newcomers is often not only to provide the knowledge and skills necessary to complete job assignments but also to mold individuals into the existing organizational culture. A good example of this molding process is the police system in which training is extensive and conveys a sense of what individuals should do on the job as well as what attitudes are or are not acceptable to be considered part of the mainstream. In this way, training is viewed as an organizational subsystem that serves to reinforce and maintain the status quo.

Given how important training and development can be in inculcating organizational norms and values, it is not surprising that organizations are now turning towards training as a tool for leading cultural change. This new perspective to training contends that training may be the most direct way to approach the issues and concerns that arise with a changing workforce. This has led to a large increase in the number and scope of training efforts that address workforce diversity issues. At one level, diversity training can provide individuals with the knowledge and skills necessary to embrace diversity in their workplace. At another level, diversity training can be a potent signal to employees that a change in the status quo is not only desirable but possible. This alternative perspective contends that training systems can develop and implement proactive, framebreaking interventions as well as the more typical interventions that meet specific training needs in the organization.

Training needs assessment

The key training needs assessment issues regarding diversity training are concerned with organizational analysis. Typically an organizational analysis is the study of the entire system in terms of its goals, resources, and performance with an emphasis on the extent to which organizational goals are being achieved. For this analysis, measures such as efficiency and productivity indices, quality records, retention rates, customer complaints, and supervisory performance appraisal ratings might be gathered as input. Thus, an organizational analysis tends to emphasize products and services with the intent to determine if training can be helpful in better meeting tangible goals.

The changing workforce has led many organizations to reevaluate the dominant culture in the organization and its underlying values and belief system. This reevaluation requires that an organizational analysis address not only tangible products and services, but also identify the deeply held values within the organization. In this way, the readiness of the organization for a cultural change can be examined and the role of training in that change process explored.

179

More specifically, an organizational analysis can focus on the identification and clear articulation of the vision and values regarding workforce diversity in the organization. Vision and values refer to the core guiding principles and associated strategies that frame organizational decisions. In developing that vision, it is critical that an organizational analysis examines the extent to which diversity is viewed as integral to organizational effectiveness rather than separate from the key business needs of the firm. More specifically, prior to initiating training for cultural change, an organizational analysis should be completed that explicitly addresses what diversity means, what the overall goals are relevant to workforce diversity and cultural change, and how the movement towards valuing diversity will be supported. An organization that has broadly defined workforce diversity, clearly articulated its goals, and constructed support systems across levels around key diversity issues, is ready to implement training to further the change process. This issue of readiness of the organization to benefit from training is critical to the ultimate success of any training effort aimed at facilitating diversity.

Defining diversity   Vision and values represent the long-term strategy of the firm towards enhancing diversity and the values that are to become the way of the future in the organization. Prior to enhancing diversity, a key first step is for top management to clearly define what diversity means within an organizational setting. Diversity can mean many things to different people.

Diversity has traditionally been defined in terms of race, ethnicity, and culture. There are calls to extend the definition of diversity beyond racial or minority group status (e.g. Armitage, 1993; Morrison, 1992; Jackson, 1992). Loden and Rosener (1990) categorized diversity-related variables into two dimensions. Race and ethnicity fall in the primary dimension, along with age, gender, physical abilities/qualities, and sexual orientation. The secondary dimension of diversity characteristics contains education, geographic location, income, marital status, military experience, parental status, religious beliefs, and work experience. DeLuca and McDowell (1992) indexed the various types of people diversity into race and gender, cultural diversity, situational diversity (e.g. age, marital status, and education), and behavioral diversity (e.g. different work styles and problem-solving approaches). Diversity can also be characterized as issues of conflict, power and dominance. From this perspective, the minority is defined as the condition of being repressed (Pedersen, 1988). Morrison (1992) contends that sharing control with people who are different is a primary issue in diversity.

The treatment of diversity in many organizations creates a mismatch between easily measurable, identifiable markers of diversity, and the complex issues which can be dealt with on a training agenda. Many organizations look toward the traditional, visual aspects of diversity, not the second-tier diversity classifications or the internal differences such as perspective, control issues, or communication style. Yet, these second-tier issues are at the heart of defining how the day-in-the-life within the organization will be different as a function of the move towards enhancing diversity.

Organizations that narrowly define diversity issues are likely to develop training interventions that are quite different from those that view diversity from a larger perspective. For example, a narrow definition may lead to short-term training that focuses on differences across "cultures" while a broader definition may lead to greater attention to the building of interpersonal and communication skills that are generalizable across a variety of situations faced in the work environment.

Organizational goals for acculturation   Once diversity has been clearly defined, the second step is for top leadership to identify and articulate the goals of the diversity initiative. At the most general level, goals must be developed around the issues of acculturation. Acculturation occurs when two or more distinct cultures come into contact, and is the process through which the resulting conflicts are resolved (Berry, 1980).

Several researchers have drawn parallels between international cross-cultural and intra-national diversity issues (Tung, 1993; Triandis et al., 1993). Both situations involve a minority culture member attempting to adjust to and work in the majority culture. There are several alternatives to the acculturation process by which the dominant culture and any minority culture treat cultural differences. The literature has identified three major approaches that organizations may take relevant to workforce diversity: (1) assimilation; (2) accommodation; and (3) pluralism/multiculturalism.

An assimilation goal occurs when the dominant culture in an organization remains intact (Tung, 1993) as members of the non-dominant group are expected to adapt to the norms, values, and behaviors of the majority group. Minority groups fit into the organization by giving up some of their cultural identity and by taking on aspects of the dominant culture. This is the most common type of acculturation (Cox, 1991) and forms the basis for most training and socialization interventions. This view is often discussed in terms of an emphasis on organizational efficiency, which requires a "one best way" attitude, less tolerance of differences, and a focus on helping members of the non-dominant culture to assimilate into the existing culture.

Accommodation is defined as an adjustment to differences which occurs when members of the majority culture make some changes to allow minority members into the culture. Minority members will also have to adapt to their new surroundings, yet with accommodation, the focus is on changing the majority members. Accommodation involves a recognition that workforce changes require some changes in the organization (Goldstein and Gilliam, 1990). Yet the focus of the change is on minimizing disruptive influences that can occur from culture clashes (Ferdman, 1992; DeLuca and McDowell, 1992).

The goal of pluralism/multiculturalism involves an integration of two or more cultures that is characterized by members of each culture retaining significant aspects of their own culture, while viewing other cultures as having qualities that are attractive (Tung, 1993). All individuals involved retain valuable elements of their own culture, while combining other elements with those of other cultures. Thus, pluralism is a bilateral process where all members make efforts to change as well as to appreciate differences.

Of course, organizations will often have a complex set of activities that focus on some combination of assimilation, accommodation, and multiculturalism. The critical issue for training needs assessment is to determine what the vision for the cultural change effort is and how that vision can be operationalized in the work setting. In other words, a key question for organizational analysis is how committed the organization is to moving towards a more pluralistic orientation and how to best use training as a way of reaching its diversity goals. For example, a key question to ask is how an organization that is supportive of multiculturalism will operate differently in the future. This includes considering how the norms and values of the organization will change as a function of interventions to change the existing culture.

Training design

Most training design issues revolve around what is the appropriate mix of learning activities for a particular type of training program. With diversity training, the goal is often not only to build knowledge and skills, but also to change attitudes and ultimately the culture of the organization to embrace diversity. Thus, training design must go beyond individual programs to consider what is the appropriate mix of training and developmental experiences that will best move the organization forward. This mix could include efforts at assimilation and accommodation as well as pluralism.

Training methods and assimilation Many training programs emphasize assimilation. Such programs reinforce the norms, values, and perspectives of the dominant culture in an organization (Tung, 1993). The focus of training is on helping members of the non-dominant group to adapt to the norms, values, and behaviors of the majority group.

Support has been provided by several researchers to include pre-hire individuals in assimilative training efforts (Pettigrew and Martin, 1987; Sessa, 1992; Roberson and Guiterrez, 1992). Efforts in this area have included Xerox's Step Up program, through which African-Americans are trained and then hired for permanent positions in the organization (Sessa, 1992). Pacific Bell offers internships and education assistance to minorities, particularly Hispanics, prior to making hiring decisions (Roberson and Guiterrez, 1992). Similar programs are advocated by Pettigrew and Martin (1987) as a method of addressing a possible root cause issue – the relatively smaller number of qualified minority applicants given the increasing demand.

Training can also focus on giving information to minorities who have entered the organization which eases the transition into the workplace. Roberson and Guiterrez (1992) and Fernandez (1981) have reported the use of training to expose nontraditional employees to the inevitable discrimination within the organization, and to help prepare them to deal with it.

An example is Proctor and Gamble's "On Boarding" orientation program, designed specifically for women entering the organization and designed to develop an awareness of the issues of working within the dominant culture (see Cox, 1991).

Another training method noted in the diversity literature is to improve the skills of nontraditional employees to allow them to function more effectively in the organization. Recommended skills to be improved include technical skills, assertiveness, and informal networking (Sessa, 1992; Fernandez, 1981). Language training may also be useful, whether the trainee is an immigrant to the US learning English, or an American expatriate learning German or Japanese before going overseas (Cox, 1993).

Training methods for accommodation   Diversity training can also focus on accommodation. An accommodation goal emphasizes the adjustment to the changing workforce by members of the majority culture. The focus of the training is to minimize disruptive influences that can occur from culture clashes (Ferdman, 1992; DeLuca and McDowell, 1992) through changing majority members. Examples include training programs that outline legislation concerned with minority issues, such as Equal Employment Opportunity guidelines, the Americans with Disabilities Act, Age Discrimination Act or other civil rights legislation, as well as detailing the implications of these laws for the particular organization (Morrison, 1992). Making the majority aware of how their actions are perceived by minority members is another training method as some majority members may be unaware that certain actions are offensive. For example, many men do not realize the range of behaviors which women might find offensive or threatening, and which thus would be considered sexual harassment (Pettigrew and Martin, 1987).

With an accommodation strategy, training is oriented to change existing attitudes and to minimize biases that could adversely affect nontraditional organizational members (Ilgen and Youtz, 1986; Ferdman, 1992; Pettigrew and Martin, 1987). Alderfer's (1992) Race Relations Competence Workshop is an example of this emphasis. There workshops focus on educating managers and increasing their understanding of race relations within the organization. Results suggest that the workshops lead to a deeper appreciation for how an individual's perceptions of events can impact important managerial decisions such as promotions and career progressions of minority groups members.

Other programs concentrate on training majority employees on new skills or behaviors which help to reduce the operation of biases in the organization. It has been hypothesized that cognitive distortions may be present in the performance ratings and evaluations of minority members. For example, if a male supervisor holds the belief that women are too emotional, he may pay more attention to the rare emotional outburst of a female employee, while ignoring her day-to-day rational behavior. From this perspective, managers need to be taught to avoid such biases through the use of techniques such as behavior sampling strategies (Ilgen and Youtz, 1986). Pettigrew and Martin (1987) advocate the use of behavior modeling techniques in training efforts, citing an example of the use of videotapes to teach white interviewers how to respond appropriately to black interviewees. Before the training, white interviewers interacted with black interviewees in a manner which discouraged good performance by the black interviewees, thus reducing their chances of being hired.

Training methods to build pluralism   The goal of pluralism and multiculturalism involves a complex integration of two or more cultures. Training programs can directly attempt to ensure that all organizational members involved retain valuable elements of their own culture, while combining other elements with those of other cultures. Thus, training oriented towards pluralism emphasizes the bilateral process where all members make efforts to change as well as to appreciate differences.

   To aid the movement towards pluralism/multiculturalism, training efforts can be directed towards presenting factual information to all employees concerning differences between employees. For example, special ethnic days can be celebrated in the workplace, allowing employees to learn about the cultural background of others (Morrison, 1992; Gottfredson, 1992). Triandis et al. (1993) suggest other types of training to highlight and explain workplace differences including self/cultural insight, experiential training, and exposure to the strengths of each group. These three methods encourage trainees to interact with members of the other culture, and become acquainted with another point of view.

   One method of encouraging such understanding is through appreciating differences (Ferdman, 1992; Tung, 1993). Many researchers assert that highlighting the differences between people and the reasons behind their actions will help alleviate intergroup tensions. Tung recommends that organizations "reduce prejudice by increasing discrimination" (1993). In other words, teaching employees about individual and group differences in behaviors, attitudes, and values across employees allows for greater acceptance of these differences with a subsequent reduction in conflict.

   A second method concerns the breaking down of intergroup barriers. People tend to treat individuals whom they perceive as members of the in-group differently than out-group members. Organizations can reduce conflicts by encouraging employees to define the in-group on the basis of workgroups rather than race, gender, or other diversity variables. Ferdman (1992) and Gottfredson (1992) have suggested that training needs to emphasize cooperation and shared goals, and de-emphasize traditional intergroup differences. Triandis et al. (1993) also emphasize perceived similarity between people. They suggest that an individual who perceives him- or herself as highly similar to others in the organization will experience more positive social interactions, while perceived differences can cause negative outcomes. Therefore, training methods which decrease the cultural distance and increase the perceived similarity between people should increase positive outcomes.

   Finally, others have suggested an individual-based method of understanding intergroup differences. Every person, regardless of his/her background, is a member of at least one identifiable group (Ely, 1993; Ferdman, 1992). Ely (1993) suggests that each individual should explore what these various group memberships mean to them, and how they have affected their lives. For example, a white, Catholic woman belongs to both a majority group (white) and a minority group (woman), and may also identify with a religious group (Catholic). Through exploration of these group memberships, individuals can attempt to understand others' differences.

Training programs have also been developed to build the skills of all organizational members such that all members feel accepted in the organization. Tung (1993) suggested that all employees could be trained to communicate better with one another. She has proposed a hierarchy of communication competencies through which organizational members become progressively more sensitive to the way in which their messages are received by various people, and they learn to communicate in a way which is appropriate to the situation. Sorcher and Spence (1982) investigated a training program in a South African organization in which *both* white supervisors and black production workers were taught appropriate interaction behaviors for use with one another. Research results suggest that the program reduced tensions and increased comfort in the work environment.

Training evaluation

Prior to evaluating any training program, a key question to be answered is "what is to be learned" (Campbell, 1988). Kraiger et al. (1993) contend that learning must be viewed as a multidimensional construct. In the diversity literature, Pedersen (1988) proposes three stages of diversity training which progressively increase the involvement required of the trainees.

The first stage, knowledge/awareness, focuses on raising employee awareness of diversity issues. Pedersen (1988) viewed awareness training as a self-needs assessment process. Training at this level consists primarily of the dissemination of factual information, the examination of the concept of diversity, and the identification of general factors that can influence attitudes and behaviors towards others. Many diversity programs involve self-assessment of perceived similarities and differences between different groups of employees, typical communication styles, attitudes towards affirmative action and attributions of success and failures of minority group members. It is assumed that this heightened awareness will lead eventually to a deeper level of attitude and behavioral change.

In the second stage, increasing understanding, training efforts are directed towards actual attitude change through a fuller understanding of diversity issues and their impact on others. For example, Morrison (1992) discussed a program in which traditional managers were told how racial and gender differences can affect the organizational experience and career of a nontraditional manager. The goal was to break down stereotypes. Many of these programs use videotapes and role plays to go beyond simple awareness to a greater understanding of the negative emotional and performance effects of stereotypes, values, and behaviors on minority group members.

In the third stage, skill/behavior, employees gain skills that can lead to new behaviors in the work setting. Such training can focus on building or developing employee skills such as coaching, providing performance feedback, and conflict resolution in order to create a work situation that supports diversity. These interpersonal and communication skills which have often been discussed as key managerial skills are now seen as critical for all types of jobs in the organization.

Training evaluation studies have typically examined increases in knowledge or skills as a function of training. In addition, reactions from trainees as to the quality and usefulness of the training experience are also often collected. As noted above, a large number of diversity training efforts are directed towards increased understanding, sensitivity, and tolerance of others. This increased understanding is expected to lead to a change in the climate or culture of the organization relevant to the valuing of diversity in the workforce.

Thus, while the immediate objectives of a diversity training program are increases in awareness, understanding or skills, the more distal objective is often to improve the climate or culture of the organization relevant to people. Climate refers to employee perceptions regarding, in this case, the value of diversity in the workplace. Climate perceptions are usually thought of in the training field as part of the initial needs analysis phase of the ISD model. They are viewed as potential barriers to the success of future training endeavors. With diversity training, the emphasis is not on climate perceptions prior to developing training, but on the *change* in climate perceptions as a function of diversity training efforts.

Thus, from this new perspective to training, changes in the perceptions of how much the organization and its members value diversity are an important source of evaluative information about the success of the training interventions (Cox, 1993). Climate measures can be taken from employees prior to and at multiple times after training initiatives relevant to diversity have been introduced. A number of dimensions of climate can be examined, but one basic dimension of overall climate is the quality and style of interpersonal relations (supportive, warm, open, non-stressful) among workgroup members (Schneider, 1985). Such perceptions, because they may have major impacts on people's reactions to events in an organization, can have important effects on behavior and performance on the job.

The interpretation of changes in attitudes, including climate perceptions, is complex and potentially problematic. Many consultants begin a diversity change effort with an organizational "diversity audit," or a survey of current attitudes (Geber, 1990; MacDonald, 1993). An existing measure of pre-intervention attitudes makes it convenient to measure post-intervention attitudes to look for changes. Nevertheless, interpretations of change scores from attitude surveys must be made with caution. Attitudinal outcomes such as increasing tolerance for diversity can best be evaluated by following the principles of attitude measurements (Chaiken and Stanger, 1987).

Measures of attitudes must take into account both the direction of feelings and the strength of the reaction. The first focus of measurement is whether the direction of attraction toward an attitude object is consistent with learning objectives (e.g. valuing diversity). With this traditional measurement focus, attitude items relevant to valuing diversity are listed with a scale that allows the respondent to indicate a preference or rejection of the object (e.g. an agree/disagree scale). The second, less traditional, focus of measurement concerns attitude strength, or how deeply an individual holds an attitude. Abelson (1988) suggests a number of ways of using self-report measures to operationalize attitude strength. These include how strongly individuals hold to their views, how important their views are to self-perception, how concerned they are about the issue in question, and how often they think about the issue.

In addition to considerations of attitude strength and direction, three types of attitude change are possible as a result of diversity change efforts; alpha, beta, and gamma change (e.g. Golembiewski et al., 1976; Terborg et al., 1980). Alpha change represents changes in self-reports from a pre- to a post-training attitude survey. The assumption is that any mean level changes noted from the pre- and post-attitude survey are real and they have occurred within the relatively stable mindset of the individual and a fixed system of measurement. Beta change involves the recalibration of the measurement tool used. In particular, the psychological distance between the response intervals used to measure the attitudes towards diversity may change as a function of an intervention. Gamma change involves a redefinition of one's conception of a phenomenon like diversity. It involves a major change in perspective or frame of reference. Questions on the survey are reinterpreted within the new framework or perspective, and thus the very meaning of each attitude item has changed as a result of the training intervention. With diversity programs focused on understanding, the expected learning outcome could be a gamma change in the trainees. Paradoxically, while such changes may be desirable, there is little attempt in the diversity literature to measure such change.

To supplement attitude and climate measures, suggestions for observable, measurable signs of cultural change due to diversity training have been made. Possible indicators of success include turnover and retention data, reasons for turnover as indicated in exit interviews, the composition of the applicant pool, employee morale and satisfaction, productivity, organizational reputation, the number of grievances and Equal Opportunity Employment complaints, movement of women and minorities in the organization, salary equity, product innovation, and increased market share of diverse customers (Johnson, 1994; Jamieson and O'Mara, 1991; Geber, 1990). However, these measures are also susceptible to measurement problems, including criterion contamination and deficiencies. For example, an increase in complaints concerning racist behavior might reflect a greater awareness of racial issues, and a greater willingness to report such incidents, rather than an increased rate of such behaviors.

In conclusion, cultural changes toward valuing diversity cannot be expected to happen in a short period of time. Organizations must view diversity training as part of a larger change process which may take several years to occur, rather than an isolated program with immediate results (Gottfredson, 1992; Johnson, 1994). Evaluation of these programs must similarly take a longer-term perspective, and may include measures ranging from culture and attitude change to job performance data. Johnson (1994) stresses the importance of tying diversity training to performance outcomes. Linking diversity training with performance or productivity improvement would provide substantial support for the contention that diversity training is a matter of business necessity (Thomas, 1992).

Implications and Final Remarks

Organizations are subcultures of the American way of life. What is happening in American culture is reflected in the norms, values, and cultures of its organizations. A key issue today is how organizations can effectively adapt to the increasing diversity of the workforce. The United States has tended to minimize the issue of diversity and tolerance of differences throughout its history by proclaiming America to be "the great Melting Pot." It has been assumed that everyone should assimilate into the American culture, and be like everyone else.

This chapter has highlighted the complexity of issues involved in the use of training as a tool for addressing the changing workplace and workforce. New perspectives and approaches are emerging within the training field that have direct implications for how organizations can better adapt and utilize their diverse human resources. The new perspectives emphasize the need for training to (1) take a more holistic approach toward people and how they interact in work settings; (2) customize training to better fit individual needs as well as to meet organizational expectations; and (3) become a proactive force in changing the existing norms, climate, and culture of the organization.

Based on these three new perspectives, training systems are developing more innovative approaches to meeting the many challenges of the workplace and workforce. Nevertheless, there are a number of limitations that have direct influence on how effective training can be in meeting these challenges. First, success at meeting organizational goals for diversity requires an integrated approach across organizational levels that includes other interventions besides training. While training can be a key leverage point in change processes, other structural interventions may also have a critical impact on changing norms, values, and behaviors. Cox (1991) and others have discussed various ways to increase the value of diversity in organizations through interventions such as developing advisory boards, revamping reward systems, changing work schedules, and developing formal mentoring systems. As one example relevant to cultural change, Cox cites the creation of special minority advisory boards that have direct access to senior executives to discuss diversity issues and to make recommendations as to how the climate of the organization can become more supportive of diversity. Thus, other organizational change initiatives must be enacted that complement training interventions. If not, training will be viewed as isolated from the everyday workings of the organization and the knowledge and skills gained will not transfer to the job.

Second, organizations are not isolated from society and its problems and issues. Thus, while organizations may be pushing hard for greater tolerance for diversity through training initiatives, society as a whole has been slow to react to the need for greater tolerance and understanding. For example, literacy remains a major problem in society. While organizations are taking on more of the role of educator, there are still limits to what organizations can do to redress a large, ongoing societal problem. Societal differences in educational opportunities and background and abilities cannot be totally overcome by organizational efforts. This calls for greater linkages between educational institutions and organizations.

Third, the prognostications of what the workforce will be like in the future (e.g. Goldstein and Gilliam, 1990) have fed a frenzy of activities within organizations to address diversity issues prior to their becoming bigger issues in the future. While organizations should be applauded for taking some positive, forward looking steps, it must also be realized that they should not expect change to occur too quickly. Organizations, like society in general, are often slow to change. Thus, regardless of the training methods used, a key issue for overall success is the staying power of the overall push for diversity issues in organizations. Today's hot topic can soon become a passing fad. Given the realities of the changing workforce and workplace, the diversity issues will not go away. For example, the large number of baby boomers in the workplace will be slowly moving towards retirement over the next 10–15 years. How to best utilize these talents while not frustrating the goals and aspirations of the younger generation will remain a key human resource issue.

Fourth, the possibility that diversity programs may create additional conflict in the workplace, or do more harm than good, increases the urgency to learn strategies to evaluate the effectiveness of diversity training. Individuals may feel threatened by programs which highlight biases and discrimination, and that focus on promoting women and minorities in the organization (Galen and Palmer, 1994). Other programs may have the effect of making individuals feel guilty and focus on atonement for sins of the past (Karp and Sutton, 1993). Conflict between other ethnic groups may also increase, as subgroup divisions can be reinforced in diversity awareness seminars. Thus, what "awareness" has been awakened by diversity training must be systematically studied and related to valued organizational outcomes.

In conclusion, the movement towards a more holistic approach to training that is customized to better meet individual needs and is proactive rather than reactive to problems is certainly an encouraging sign. While the changing workplace and workforce have been key drivers of these new perspectives and approaches to training, they are not the only drivers. There are most likely as many differences within groups (e.g. older workers) in terms of knowledge, skills, and abilities as there are between groups (e.g. older versus younger workers). In addition, given the increasing complexity of the workplace, organizations are viewing these new approaches as desirable and cost effective. Thus, these new perspectives and approaches to training should continue to be important elements in the training systems of the future.

REFERENCES

Abelson, R. P. (1988). Conviction. *American Psychologist*, 43, 267–75.

Acker, L., Lester, J., Souther, A., and Porter, B. (1991). Generating coherent explanations to answer students' questions. In H. Burns, J. Parlett, and C. Redfield (eds), *Intelligent Tutoring Systems: Evolutions in Designs* (151–76). Hillsdale, NJ: Erlbaum.

Alderfer, C. (1992). Changing race relations embedded in organizations: Report on a long-term project with the XYZ corporation. In S. E. Jackson (ed.), *Diversity in the Workplace: Human Resource Initiatives*. New York: Guilford Press.

Armitage, M. (1993). Managing cultural diversity globally and domestically: A federal model for examining programs and competencies for leader effectiveness. Paper presented at the seventh annual meeting of the Society for Industrial and Organizational Psychology, San Francisco.

Ausubel, D. P. (1968). *Educational Psychology: A Cognitive View*. New York: Holt, Rinehart, and Winston.

Baldwin, T. P., and Ford, J. K. (1988). Transfer of training: A review and directions for future research. *Personnel Psychology*, 41, 63–105.

Baldwin, T. P., and Magjuka, P. (forthcoming). Training as an organizational episode: Pre-training influences on trainee motivation. In K. Ford and Associates (eds), *Training Effectiveness in Work Organizations*, Hillsdale, NJ: Erlbaum.

Berry, J. W. (1980). Acculturation as varieties of adaptation. In A. M. Padilla (ed.), *Acculturation: Theory, Models, and Some New Findings* (9–26). Boulder, CO: Westview Press.

Brannick, M. T., Brannick, J. P., and Levine, E. L. (1992). Job analysis, personnel selection, and the ADA. *Human Resource Management Review*, 2(3), 171–82.

Brown, A., and Palinscar, A. S. (1989). Guided, cooperative learning and individual knowledge acquisition. In L. B. Resnick (ed.), *Knowing, Learning, and Instruction: Essays in Honor of Robert Glaser* (393–452). Hillsdale, NJ: Erlbaum.

Business Council for Effective Literacy (1987). *Job-related Basic Skills: A Guide for Planners of Employee Programs*. New York: Business Council for Effective Literacy.

Campbell, J. P. (1988). Training design for performance improvement. In J. P. Campbell, R. J. Campbell, and Associates (eds), *Productivity in Organizations* (177–216). San Francisco: Jossey-Bass.

Carnevalle, A., Gainer, L., and Villet, J. (1990). *Training in America*. San Francisco: Jossey-Bass.

Chaiken, S., and Stangor, C. (1987). Attitudes and attitude change. *Annual Review of Psychology*, 38, 575–630.

Cox, T. (1991). The multicultural organization. *Academy of Management Executive*, 5(2), 34–47.

Cox, T. (1993). *Cultural Diversity in Organizations: Theory, Research, and Practice*. San Francisco: Berrett-Koehler.

Cutcher-Gershenfeld, J., Ford, J. K., Speer, J., McHugh, P., and Guililand, S. (1991).

The Scope and Implications of Private Employer-specific Training Initiatives in Michigan: A Case Study Analysis. East Lansing, MI: Social Science Research Bureau, Michigan State University.

DeLuca, J. M., and McDowell, R. N. (1992). Managing diversity: A strategic "grassroots" approach. In S. E. Jackson (ed.), *Diversity in the Workplace: Human Resource Initiatives* (37–64). New York: Guilford Press.

Dick, W., and Carey, L. (1985). *The Systematic Design of Instruction*. Glenview, IL: Scott Foresman.

Ely, R. (1993). Realizing a multicultural workforce. Paper presented at the Annual Meeting of the Academy of Management, Atlanta, GA.

Feldman, D. C. (1989). Socialization, resocialization, and training: Reframing the research agenda. In I. Goldstein and Associates, *Training and Development in Organizations* (376–416). San Francisco: Jossey-Bass.

Ferdman, B. M. (1992). The dynamics of ethnic diversity in organizations: Toward integrative models. In K. Kelley (ed.), *Issues, Theory, and Research in Industrial/ Organization Psychology*. New York: Elsevier Science.

Fernandez, J. P. (1981). *Racism and Sexism in Corporate Life: Changing Values in American Business*. Lexington, MA: Lexington Books.

Fischer, R. J. (1994). The Americans with Disabilities Act: Implications for measurement. *Educational Measurement: Issues and Practice*, Fall, 17–37.

Ford, J. K., and Kraiger, K. (1995). The application of cognitive constructs and principles to the instructional systems model of training. In C. Cooper and I. Robertson (eds), *The International Review of Industrial and Organizational Psychology*, vol. 10. New York: John Wiley.

Ford, J. K., Quinones, M., Sego, D., and Sorra, J. (1992). Factors affecting the opportunity to perform trained tasks on the job. *Personnel Psychology*, 45, 511–27.

Galen, M., and Palmer (1994). White, male and worried. *Business Week*, January 31, 50–5.

Geber, B. (1990). Managing diversity. *Training*, July, 23–30.

Goldstein, I. (1991). Training in work organizations. In M. D. Dunnette and L. M. Hough (eds), *Handbook of Industrial and Organizational Psychology*, 2nd ed., vol. 2 (507–602). Palo Alto, CA: Consulting Psychologists Press.

Goldstein, I. (1993). *Training in Work Organizations*, 3rd ed. Pacific Grove: Brooks/ Cole.

Goldstein, I., and Gilliam, P. (1990). Training systems in the year 2000. *American Psychologist*, 45, 134–45.

Golembiewski, R. T., Billingsley, K., and Yeager, S. (1976). Measuring change and persistence in human affairs: Types of change generated by OD designs. *Journal of Applied Behavioral Science*, 12, 133–57.

Gottfredson, L. S. (1992). Dilemmas in developing diversity programs. In S. E. Jackson (ed.), *Diversity in the Workplace: Human Resource Initiatives* (37–64). New York: Guilford Press.

Hartel, C. E. J. (1994). Vantage 2000: Diversity mentoring, uplifting downsizing, technocommuting and other vantage points. *The Industrial–Organizational Psychologist*, 31(3), 87–9.

Ibarra, H. (1993). Personal networks of women and minorities in management: A conceptual framework. *Academy of Management Review*, 18(1), 56–87.

Ilgen, D. R., and Youtz, M. A. (1986). Factors affecting the evaluation and development of minorities in organizations. In K. M. Rowland and G. R. Ferris (eds), *Research in Personnel and Human Resources Management*, vol. 4(307–37). Greenwich, CT: JAI Press.

Jackson, S. E. (1992). *Diversity in the Workplace: Human Resource Initiatives*. New York: Guilford Press.

Jamieson, D., and O'Mara, J. (1991). *Managing Workforce 2000: Gaining the Diversity Advantage*. San Francisco: Jossey-Bass.

Johnson, S. J. (1994). Connecting diversity efforts in the workplace with business mission, goals and objectives. *Performance Improvement Quarterly*, 7(1), 31–9.

Johnston, W. B., and Packer, A. H. (1987). *Workforce 2000: Work and Workers for the Twenty-first Century*. Indianapolis: Hudson Institute.

Karp, H. B., and Sutton, N. (1993). Where diversity training goes wrong. *Training*, July: 30–4.

Katz, R., and Kahn, R. (1978). *The Social Psychology of Organizations*, 2nd ed. New York: Wiley.

Klein, K. J., and Ralls, R. S. (forthcoming). The unintended organizational consequences of technology training: Implications for training theory, research, and practice. In K. Ford and Associates (eds), *Training Effectiveness in Work Organizations*. Hillsdale, NJ: Erlbaum.

Knowles, M. S. (1978). *The Adult Learner: A Neglected Species*, 2nd ed. Houston, TX: Gulf.

Kozol, J. (1985). *Illiterate America*. New York: Anchor Press/Doubleday.

Kraiger, K., and Ford, J. K. (1985). A meta-analysis of ratee race effects in performance ratings. *Journal of Applied Psychology*, 70(1), 56–65.

Kraiger, K., Ford, J. K., and Salas, E. (1993). Application of cognitive, skill-based, and affective theories of learning outcomes to new methods of training evaluation. *Journal of Applied Psychology*, 78, 311–28.

Levine, E. L., and Baker, C. V. (1991). Team task analysis: A procedural guide and test of the methodology. Presented at the sixth annual conference of the Society of Industrial and Organizational Psychology, April, St Louis, MO.

Loden, M., and Rosener, J. B. (1990). *Workforce America! Managing Employee Diversity as a Vital Resource*. Homewood, IL: Business One Irwin.

McCall, M. W., Lombardo, M. M., and Morrison, A. M. (1988). *The Lessons of Experience*. Lexington, MA: Lexington Books.

MacDonald, H. (1993). The diversity industry. *The New Republic*, July, 22–5.

Milheim, W. D., and Martin, B. L. (1991). Theoretical bases for the use of learner control: Three different perspectives. *Journal of Computer Based Instruction*, 18, 99–105.

Morgan, B. B., Glickman, A. S., Woodard, E. A., Blaise, A. S., and Salas, E. (1986). Measurement of team behaviors in a Navy environment. NTSC-TR-86-014. Orlando, FL: Naval Training Systems Center.

Morrison, A. M. (1992). *The New Leaders: Guidelines on Leadership Diversity in America*. San Francisco: Jossey-Bass.

Morrison, A. M., and Von Glinow, M. A. (1990). Women and minorities in management. *American Psychologist*, February, 200–8.

Noe, R. A. (1988). Women and mentoring: A review and research agenda. *Academy of Management Review*, 13(1), 65–78.

Offerman, L. R., and Gowing, M. K. (1990). Organizations of the future. *American Psychologist*, 45, 95–108.

Ostroff, C., and Ford, J. K. (1989). Assessing training needs: Critical levels of analysis. In I. Goldstein and Associates (eds), *Training and Development in Organizations* (25–63). San Francisco: Jossey-Bass.

Pedersen, P. (1988). *A Handbook for Developing Multicultural Awareness*. Alexandria, VA: American Association for Counseling and Development.

Pettigrew, T. F., and Martin, J. (1987). Shaping the organizational context for Black American inclusion. *Journal of Social Issues*, 43(1), 41–78.

Pfeffer, J. (1994). *Competitive Advantage Through People: Unleashing the Power of the Work Force*. Boston: Harvard Business School Press.

Roberson, L., and Guiterrez, N. C. (1992). Beyond good faith: Commitment to recruiting management diversity at Pacific Bell. In S. E. Jackson (ed.), *Diversity in the Workplace: Human Resource Initiatives*, pp. 65–88. New York: Guilford Press.

Schneider, B. (1985). Organizational behavior. *Annual Review of Psychology*, 36, 573–611.

Sessa, V. I. (1992). Managing diversity at the Xerox Corporation: Balanced workforce goals and caucus groups. In S. E. Jackson (ed.), *Diversity in the Workplace: Human Resource Initiatives*, pp. 37–64. New York: Guilford Press.

Sorcher, M., and Spence, R. (1982). The interface project: Behavior modeling as social technology in South Africa. *Personnel Psychology*, 35, 557–81.

Tennyson, R. D., and Rasch, A. (1988). Linking cognitive learning theory to instructional prescriptions. *Instructional Science*, 17, 369–85.

Terborg, J. R., Howard, G. S., and Maxwell, S. E. (1980). Evaluating planned organizational change: A method for assessing alpha, beta and gamma change. *Academy of Management Review*, 5, 109–21.

Thomas, R. R., Jr (1992). Managing diversity: A conceptual framework. In S. E. Jackson (ed.), *Diversity in the Workplace: Human Resource Initiatives*, pp. 306–18. New York: Guilford Press.

Triandis, H. C., Kurowski, L. L., and Gelfand, M. J. (1993). Workplace diversity. In H. C. Triandis, M. D. Dunnette, and L. M. Hough (eds), *The Handbook of Industrial and Organizational Psychology*, vol. 4 (769–827). Palo Alto, CA: Consulting Psychologists Press.

Tung, R. L. (1993). Managing cross-national and intra-national diversity. *Human Resource Management*, 32(4), Winter, 461–77.

Workinger, R. K., and Ruch, K. E. (1991). Workforce literacy: Problems and solutions. *Human Resource Development Quarterly*, 2, 251–62.

Zedeck, S., and Mosier, K. (1990). Work in the family and employing organization. *American Psychologist*, 45(2), 240–51.

8
Compensation and Diversity: New Pay for a New Workforce?

Alison E. Barber and Christina L. Daly

Introduction

The management of diversity is a critical issue for today's businesses. Projections of an increasingly heterogeneous workforce and extensive competition in diverse global marketplaces have caused some to call diversity management "a strategic imperative" (Jackson and Alvarez, 1992). As a result of these concerns many companies are implementing what have come to be known as diversity initiatives: a collection of programs, including training, career development, and incentives, that are aimed at improving management of a diverse workforce. Also, what MacDonald (1993) refers to as the "diversity industry" has been spawned: a growing pool of consultants is available to help companies manage diversity.

Effectively managing diversity requires sweeping changes in organizational culture (Geber, 1990; Offerman and Gowing, 1993; Triandis et al., 1994). Lawler (1980) and Kerr and Slocum (1987) argued that compensation systems can be particularly useful in initiating such broad-based organizational change. The importance and visibility of pay and benefits to employees guarantees that changes in these variables will capture their attention. Furthermore, the systemic and institutional nature of compensation programs guarantees that changes in pay and benefits will become deeply embedded in the organization's culture. In short, changes in compensation systems can provide a strong and clear signal of the organization's values (Kerr and Slocum, 1987) as well as its commitment to change (Lawler, 1980).

Our focus is on how reward systems can be used to create environments in which people of diverse backgrounds can all contribute effectively. We note that compensation can be used to facilitate diversity management in two ways: first, to enable all employees to achieve higher levels of productivity and satisfaction in the corporate environment, and, second, to encourage managers to work effectively with a diverse group of employees (Haight, 1990). Our emphasis is on two specific dimensions of diversity: racioethnic and gender. Although we recognize that there are many other aspects of diversity (e.g. age, physical disability status, occupational level), adequate treatment of each of these issues would take us well beyond the space limitations of this chapter. We focus on race and sex as core characteristics because they are highly visible, and because significant changes have occurred along these dimensions recently within the US workforce (Geber, 1990). However, we note that social and historical forces have resulted in relationships between these characteristics and others. For example, both minorities and women tend to hold lower-level jobs than white males (Powell, 1988; Tuch and Martin, 1991), and women are more likely than men to be responsible for dependent care (Wiersma, 1990). Thus it is sometimes difficult to disentangle race or gender from other characteristics.

In addition, we recognize that diversity in the workplace is a question of the *mixture* of demographic and other characteristics that exists, rather than the specific characteristics of individual employees. However, to date there is little information about how the composition of an employee group might influence the appropriateness or effectiveness of compensation practices. Therefore we rely on existing evidence regarding demographic differences at the individual level as a starting-point.

Finally, we do not directly address the issue of pay discrimination. Earnings gaps between races and genders are well documented, and there is substantial literature devoted to explaining and reducing these gaps (e.g. Blau and Kahn, 1994; Groshen, 1991; Sorenson, 1994). While we do not mean to understate the importance of discrimination in pay level, a discussion of these issues is beyond our scope.

The structure of the chapter is as follows. In the first section, we provide a theoretical perspective on reward systems. We address differences in preferences for monetary versus nonmonetary rewards across genders and racioethnic groups, and also discuss intergroup differences in values and beliefs regarding the fair allocation of rewards. In the second section, we evaluate how well current compensation practices support diversity. We discuss the effectiveness of traditional pay programs and evaluate "new pay" programs within a diversity-oriented environment. Finally, we make recommendations for compensating the increasingly diverse workforce.

Rewards and Diversity – A Theoretical Perspective

The use of rewards

A theme common to many theories of employee motivation is that rewards are necessary to induce and sustain certain desired actions from employees.

Rewards, if they are to be effective, must be valued by employees; rewards that are not valued will not be sought. Thus managers in general, and compensation managers in particular, need to be concerned about employee preferences for a variety of potential rewards. The fact that different forms of rewards – for example, monetary or nonmonetary – may be more or less valuable to different individuals can influence how effective compensation programs are. For example, if employees value monetary more than nonmonetary rewards, then a compensation system which provides monetary incentives should be relatively successful in motivating and satisfying the employees. Furthermore, within a compensation program, decisions regarding the amount of resources to devote to different types of monetary rewards (i.e. direct pay versus benefits) should be based on how highly valued those rewards are.

One concern that organizations must deal with is the possibility of substantial variation in reward preferences among individuals within a single organization. Generally, reward programs have been designed on a "one size fits all" basis: all employees are offered the same forms of reward. However, if employee reward preferences are themselves diverse, then compensation systems that assume homogeneous preferences may be flawed. Therefore, in this section we explore the possible relationships between workforce diversity and reward preferences.

Before moving on, it is important to note that there is some disagreement as to whether organizational compensation systems based on monetary rewards are, or can be, effective *for anyone*. Kohn (1993) criticized the ability of *any* type of financial incentive plan to achieve the kind of changes in employees that managers typically desire. Reward systems, according to Kohn, succeed only at securing temporary compliance: they do not and can not result in lasting, deeply held changes in employee values, attitudes, or behaviors. Instead, they merely motivate employees to engage in specific behaviors that they know will be rewarded, and to engage in those behaviors only as long as rewards are forthcoming. So while rewards may temporarily change what people do, Kohn argued that they do not create any enduring commitment to the desired behaviors.

Kohn's arguments, however, focus primarily on the direct, individual effects of rewards. They do not address the possibility that compensation and reward systems can be useful in changing or reinforcing organizational culture (Kerr and Slocum, 1987; Lawler, 1980), which in turn may have substantial impact on values, attitudes, and long-term behaviors, either through shaping the values of existing employees or through changing the type of employee who joins and remains with the organization. While empirical evidence regarding the impact of pay systems on organizational culture is currently lacking (Gomez-Mejia and Balkin, 1992), there is evidence that organizations that achieve high degrees of "fit" between compensation elements and organizational strategy do perform better than other organizations (e.g. Balkin and Gomez-Mejia, 1990; Gomez-Mejia, 1992). Thus, research at the organizational level suggests that compensation practices, broadly defined, do make a difference.

Reward preferences

The debate over the relative value of monetary and nonmonetary rewards is an important and pervasive part of the management literature (Brief and Aldag, 1989). It is relevant to the context of diversity management in that systematic differences in reward preferences across demographic subgroups could imply that a reward system that is effective and efficient for one group of employees might be less effective for another group. What appears to be equal treatment might, under such a scenario, result in unequal motivation. In the following sections, we discuss whether such systematic differences exist.

Racioethnic differences Research on racioethnic differences in reward preferences has focused almost entirely on comparisons between blacks and whites. As Berger (1986) notes, research on other racioethnic groups such as Hispanics remains "in a state of infancy" (p. 205). Therefore the following discussion applies primarily to differences among blacks and whites. However, we note that research including a broader array of racioethnic groups is badly needed.

In general, existing evidence has indicated that blacks tend to value monetary rewards, such as pay and benefits, over nonmonetary rewards such as personal growth or status, while the reverse is true for whites (Bloom and Barry, 1967; Moch, 1980; Shapiro, 1977; Shiflett, 1988; Tuch and Martin, 1991; Weaver, 1975). Two explanations for this pattern of results are frequently offered: the effects of past experiences, and different underlying value systems.

Historically, racial discrimination has led minority and nonminority employees to experience dissimilar events throughout their working lives. Traditional paths for promotion and achievement often have not been available to minority group members because of job discrimination (Bloom and Barry, 1967). This situation may have caused a lack of confidence on the part of the minority group members as to their ability to obtain rewards related to advancement and growth (Berger, 1986). Frustration with the lack of opportunity to satisfy such intrinsic needs may have created a greater emphasis on lower-order, extrinsic needs (Alderfer, 1969) and thus a heightened preference for monetary rewards.

A second explanation for observed differences in reward preferences between minority and nonminority employees is based on differences in cultural values. There is evidence to suggest that minority group members tend to have more communal values than whites, including stronger ties to family (Cox, 1991; Cox et al., 1991). To individuals with these value structures, monetary rewards – either pay-based or benefit packages – can be particularly valuable in that they can be shared with other members of one's family. In contrast, most intrinsic rewards are of value primarily to the individual, and therefore may be less interesting to a person with strong communal values.

Before concluding that differences in reward preferences are linked to racioethnic identity *per se*, an alternative explanation must be considered. In recent US history, racioethnic minorities have often been confined to lower-level jobs and occupations (US Department of Labor, 1994). It may be that reward preferences are primarily a function of social class and occupational level, which may be partially determined by racioethnic status (Harry, 1975; Tuch and Martin, 1991). Tuch and Martin found substantial support for this structural explanation. Shapiro (1977) also found a reduction in the observed differences in reward preferences when holding socioeconomic status constant. However, in his study race continued to account for about half of the original amount of variance explained. Moch (1980) similarly found that race continued to influence satisfaction with rewards after structural variables were taken into account. Thus it appears that observed differences in reward preferences between blacks and whites can be partially, but not entirely, attributed to socioeconomic factors.

Gender-based differences   While some recent studies have found few significant differences in reward preferences between men and women (e.g. Lefkowitz, 1994), other research has shown that women tend to place a higher value on nonmonetary job attributes, particularly those associated with interpersonal relations (e.g. type of supervision and relationships with co-workers), than on monetary concerns (e.g. Bartol and Manhardt, 1979; Beutell and Brenner, 1986; Bigoness, 1988; Harris and Earle, 1986; Jurgensen, 1978; Manhardt, 1972; Schuler, 1975; Subich et al., 1986). On the other hand, men, more than women, have focused on the importance of monetary rewards in relation to work (e.g. Bigoness, 1988; Haberfeld, 1992; Hollenbeck et al., 1987; Major and Konar, 1984; Manhardt, 1972; Schuler, 1975). Explanations for these findings tend to focus on gender-role socialization or on past job experiences.

Traditionally, men and women have held different roles in US society. Men have been seen as breadwinners who financially support the family, and women as caregivers and nurturers who focus on maintaining the family relationships (Schwartz, 1989). To the extent that these family roles carry over into the workplace, one might expect men to place higher value on monetary rewards, as high earnings facilitate their primary role of providing economic support for the family. In contrast, women may feel less pressure to provide economic support. Instead, they might place higher value on the social and interpersonal aspects of work. Such a focus would be consistent with the role of nurturer, and therefore might help reduce feelings of work–family role conflict (Wiersma, 1990).

Past job experiences, such as gender-based pay discrimination, may also affect the way in which women assign importance to rewards. Gender-based pay differentials have been well documented, even between men and women of comparable qualifications (e.g. Rigdon, 1993). Research evidence suggests that women have lower expectations for the amount of pay that they will earn than do men in comparable work roles or positions (Jackson et al., 1992; Major and Konar, 1984). Frustration with their inability to obtain high pay may cause women to undervalue this particular reward (Festinger, 1957; Haberfeld, 1992). In other words, women may adjust their reward values based on what they believe they can realistically obtain.

Finally, some have argued that apparent gender differences in reward preferences are actually a function of differences in occupational level. Differences across hierarchical levels are well documented, with extrinsic rewards typically more salient to lower-level employees (Harry, 1975). Some studies concluded that controlling for occupational level virtually eliminated gender differences in preferences (e.g. Wiersma, 1990). However, others found gender differences even after factors such as occupational level and socioeconomic status were taken into account (e.g. Lacy et al., 1983; Mottaz, 1986).

Again, before concluding that these observed differences between men and women in reward preferences are stable, one should note that to the extent that societal role differences, gender-based pay discrimination, and occupational segregation are diminishing, differences in reward preferences should also diminish. The fact that several recent studies (Jackson et al., 1992; Lefkowitz, 1994) have failed to find significant differences between men and women in preferences for high pay may be evidence of this trend.

Benefit preferences Aside from the possible variation among individuals in preferences for monetary versus nonmonetary rewards, there is a common assumption that employees of different genders and racioethnic backgrounds may differ in their preferences for employee benefits, an indirect form of monetary reward. Historically, benefits plans were often geared toward traditional employees (i.e. employees with children and a nonworking spouse; Barber et al., 1992; Stelluto and Klein, 1990). The possibility that such plans would fail to meet the needs of an increasingly diverse workforce was a significant factor in the implementation of flexible benefits plans (*Employee Benefit Plan Review*, 1989).

Some evidence does support the argument that benefit preferences are demographically determined. For example, researchers have found differences in preferences for pension plans between older and younger workers (Chapman and Otterman, 1975); also, there are variations in preferences for health and medical coverage for employees who have dependents versus those who do not (Nealy, 1963). More recently, investigators have found women use sick leave more often than men, perhaps because of greater dependent care responsibilities (Kroesser, 1991; Rogers, 1993); and that men are more likely than women to receive medical benefits from their employers (Seccombe, 1993). While these studies do not deal with preferences directly, they may imply different preferences for these benefits on the part of women and men.

In contrast to these findings, Milkovich and Newman (1993) concluded upon reviewing the literature that in general demographic groupings fail to predict benefit preferences. In addition, Barber et al. (1992) failed to find significant relationships between demographic characteristics and actual benefits choices made under a flexible benefits plan. Miceli and Lane (1991) suggested that benefit preferences may be determined by individual differences other than demographic characteristics, such as preference for leisure or desire for security.

Summary The research evidence discussed above indicates systematic mean differences in reward preferences by gender and by racioethnic group. Racioethnic minorities tend to place *more* value on monetary rewards than nonminorities, and women tend to place *less* value on monetary rewards than men. This suggests that financial incentives may be particularly effective motivators for racioethnic minorities, and particularly *in*effective motivators for women. Therefore organizations interested in optimal diversity management would be wise to investigate the tastes and preferences of their workforce to ensure that an appropriate blend of monetary and nonmonetary rewards is available to all employees. Attention should also be paid to variations in preferences for different forms of monetary rewards (e.g. pay versus benefits).

However, certain caveats are in order. First, while significant mean differences in reward preferences do exist, substantial variation also exists *within* gender and racioethnic groups. Second, there is reason to anticipate that group differences will diminish over time. Third, empirical research has provided only weak evidence regarding anticipated demographic differences in benefit preferences. Therefore, attempting to design an appropriate compensation package on the basis of demographic factors alone is unlikely to optimize individual motivation.

The allocation of rewards

The importance of monetary and nonmonetary rewards is one significant predictor of the impact compensation systems can have on employee motivation. A second major determinant is the basis for allocating pay. The approach used to allocate pay or other rewards within a group can influence individual attitudes, workgroup relations, and both individual and group productivity (Deutsch, 1985).

Historically, US management has focused almost entirely on one specific allocation rule: the equity norm (Adams, 1965; Meindl, 1989). According to this rule, rewards should be distributed in accordance with each individual's contribution. Those who contribute more to an endeavor deserve a greater share of the profits of that endeavor.

While the equity norm is pervasive in the organizational and management literature (Deutsch, 1985), social psychologists have identified and studied alternative views on what is considered fair in the distribution of rewards. The most commonly studied alternative is the equality or parity rule, where rewards are distributed equally across recipients, regardless of relative contribution. An extensive literature on when and where these different rules apply has been developed. For the purposes of this chapter, however, we focus on those differences related to racioethnic status and gender.

Racioethnic differences   It has been argued that to some extent distributive justice norms are culturally determined (Meindl, 1989). This perspective suggests that the preferred means of allocating rewards is not an inherent part of human nature; rather, it is the outgrowth of specific cultural values and socialization (Sampson, 1975). For example, evidence documents fairly consistent differences in allocation preferences between individuals in Western cultures (e.g. the US, Australia), who tend to favor equity-based distributions, and individuals in Eastern cultures (e.g. China and Japan), who tend to favor more equal distributions (e.g. Bond et al., 1982; Kashima et al., 1988; Leung and Park, 1986).

Explanations for these patterns generally are based on fundamental value differences between cultures, often focusing on differences in individualism and collectivism. Individualism and collectivism are opposing points on a single cultural dimension (Hofstede, 1984). In individualistic societies, the self is defined as an autonomous individual, and individual goals take precedence over group goals. In contrast, collectivist societies define the self as a member of a group (e.g. family or workgroup), and the goals of the group take precedence over personal interests (Hofstede, 1984; Triandis et al., 1994).

In individualistic societies, individual excellence and competitive behavior are valued. These behaviors are encouraged and reinforced by equity-based distributions. In contrast, collectivist societies emphasize the importance of group harmony and cohesiveness, a value reinforced by equal distributions of rewards. Therefore, we would expect a preference for equitable distributions in primarily individualist societies (e.g. North American and northern and western Europe), and a preference for equal distributions in primarily collectivist societies (e.g. Asia, Latin America, and much of Africa) (Hofstede, 1980). This prediction is consistent with existing cross-cultural research.

However, there is a great deal of risk associated with drawing broad conclusions about the reward allocation preferences of an entire national culture. Recent research suggests that such preferences are in fact rather complicated. For example, to some extent the expressed preference for equal distributions in either collectivist or individualist societies appears to be influenced by group cohesiveness: individuals are more likely to prefer equal distributions among closely knit group members than among members of a less cohesive group (e.g. Bagarozzi, 1982; Chiu, 1990).

In addition, there are dangers in extrapolating cross-cultural research findings to the context of racioethnic diversity within the US. One primary concern is whether the values and behaviors of US minority group members reflect the values of the society in which they have their cultural roots or the predominant Anglo culture. Cox et al. (1991) reviewed evidence that suggests that Hispanic, black, and Far Eastern minorities in the US do in fact hold values consistent with collectivist traditions. Therefore, one could infer that racioethnic minorities in the US are likely to be more oriented toward equal distributions, and less oriented toward equitable distributions, than their nonminority counterparts.

However, Cox et al. also noted that many minority group members are in fact "bicultural," being inherently oriented to one value set while being conscious of, and on occasion behaving in a manner consistent with, the predominant Anglo value set. In addition, there is substantial variation in values within demographic groups. Thus, while there is some reason to believe that distributive justice preferences differ across racioethnic subgroups, there is still much to be learned about the circumstances under which these differences are likely to emerge and what their implications for effectively managing a diverse workforce might be. In particular, we know little about how these differences might shape attitudinal or behavioral reactions to organizational reward systems.

Gender differences   Research has frequently indicated that men and women differ in what they perceive as fair in the allocation of rewards (Kahn et al., 1980; Major and Deaux, 1982). It has been argued that males are more likely to divide resources based on equity – that is, in accordance with relative contributions – while women are more likely to divide them equally. These differences may be linked to differences in gender-role socialization. Deutsch (1985) and Sampson (1975) suggested that the equity norm is compatible with competitive, individualistic, status-oriented concerns (characteristic of male socialization), while the equality norm is compatible with interpersonal and relationship concerns (characteristic of female socialization) (Jackson, 1987). Watts et al. (1982) provided evidence supporting this reasoning, finding that sex-linked personality characteristics were related to reward allocation practices.

More recent research has refined the circumstances under which gender differences in allocation norms emerge and has found them to be somewhat less consistent than initial arguments implied. For example, Major et al. (1989) found that distribution preferences varied by gender in work relationships but not in personal relationships. Jackson (1987) found that men were likely to rely on equity when allocating rewards to other men, and women were more likely to rely on equality when allocating rewards to other women, but that no gender differences existed when allocations were being made to someone of the opposite sex.

Certainly, many questions remain regarding when and why gender differences in perceptions of distributive justice exist. However, there is sufficient evidence that differences *do* exist, particularly in the workplace (Major et al., 1989), and those differences appear to depend on the demographic homogeneity of the workgroup (Jackson, 1987). Thus, workgroup diversity *per se* may have implications for the appropriate distribution of financial rewards.

Summary   The literature reviewed above, while not extensive, suggests that there may be differences between diverse types of individuals in preferred methods for allocating rewards. The composition of workgroups (whether demographically homogeneous or heterogeneous) may have additional influences on allocation norms. Therefore, a compensation system that is ideal for one type of employee in one context (e.g. a white male

Table 8.1 Traditional versus new pay – selected characteristics

	Traditional (algorithmic)	*New (experiential)*
Basis for pay		
Criteria for pay increases	Tenure	Performance
Level of performance measurement	Individual	Individual and aggregate
Time orientation	Short-term	Long-term
Risk sharing	Low	High
Type of control	Monitor of behaviors	Monitor of outcomes
Reward distribution	Hierarchical	Egalitarian
Administrative framework		
Decision-making	Centralized	Decentralized
Governance structure	Authoritarian	Participative
Nature of pay policies	Bureaucratic	Flexible

Source: Abridged from Gomez-Mejia and Balkin, 1992

working with other white males) may be less than ideal for employees of other backgrounds or in other work environments. Discrepancies between actual reward allocation practices and employees' preferred allocation practices could lead to lower satisfaction and lower commitment to the organization among those employees whose values differ from the values reflected by the compensation system (Meglino et al., 1989).

Current Practices in Compensation: Implications for Diversity

Compensation practices in US organizations are in a state of flux. As companies vie to become or remain competitive in the new global economy, the effectiveness of compensation policies in enhancing productivity is repeatedly being questioned. Dissatisfaction with traditional pay practices, such as merit-based pay, is on the rise. A plethora of books and articles about "the new pay" provides suggestions for modifying and updating pay practices (e.g. Caudron, 1993; Feldman, 1991; Giblin et al., 1990; Kanter, 1987; Stelluto and Klein, 1990). We will now evaluate the effectiveness of both traditional and new pay systems in attracting, retaining, and motivating a diverse workforce.

In contrasting "traditional" with "new" pay arrangements, we rely primarily on the work of Gomez-Mejia and Balkin (1992). In general, these authors characterize traditional pay systems as relying primarily on standardized, automated procedures. Such systems tend to create universal approaches to pay, with little consideration given to extenuating circumstances or individual exceptions. In contrast new pay is characterized by flexibility, and is highly responsive to special circumstances and changing environments. Table 8.1 presents a comparison of some of the distinguishing characteristics of these two models. We focus on two subsets of differentiating characteristics: criteria for the allocation of rewards, and administrative flexibility.

The criteria used to distribute rewards are an important distinction between these models. In the traditional pay system, rewards are often based on how long one has been part of the organization rather than on performance. When performance is rewarded, it tends to be at the individual level, often evaluating an individual's behaviors rather than the outcomes that are achieved. The primary elements of pay in the traditional model are base wages or salaries and benefits, which do not fluctuate greatly over time. A compensation approach typical of the traditional model is merit pay. Under merit pay systems, individual performance ratings, often based on subjective criteria, are used to determine pay raises. These increments become a permanent part of the employee's base pay. Because they are generally small, in recent years barely exceeding the inflation rate (Giblin et al., 1990; Kanter, 1987), there is in effect little performance-based variation in pay from year to year.

In contrast, there is a great deal of variability in rewards under the new pay. Performance-contingent bonuses, which can fluctuate dramatically from year to year, represent a large proportion of an individual's total compensation. The size of one's bonus is generally based on quantitative measures of group or organization outcomes, rather than on assessments of individual behaviors or traits. A representative approach to reward allocation under the new pay is profit sharing. Under profit sharing, a sometimes sizable portion of an employee's annual pay is based on the organization's financial performance (i.e. its profitability). This payment is in the form of a one-time bonus (as opposed to a permanent increment to base pay) and provides no guarantee of comparable future bonuses. Thus, there is room for substantial fluctuations in pay over time based on the performance of the organization.

A second important distinction between traditional and new compensation plans occurs in plan administration. Traditional plans tend to be highly bureaucratic: decisions regarding pay outcomes are made centrally, with little room for flexibility, exceptions, or employee input. In contrast, flexibility is one of the hallmarks of new pay systems. These plans are decentralized, and substantial discretion is allowed. Accommodation of idiosyncratic pay programs is encouraged.

This distinction can be highlighted by contrasting traditional versus flexible benefits plans. Traditional plans provide identical benefit packages to all employees. While the package may be designed to meet the needs of the majority of employees, there is no mechanism by which individuals whose needs are different can make adjustments to their plan. In contrast, an organization taking a flexible approach to compensation might implement flexible or cafeteria benefits. Under such systems, employees choose among a variety of benefits or among varying levels of benefits that are subject to certain constraints (e.g. limits on total benefits expenditures). This procedure allows individual employees to tailor their benefits to their own preferences.

In the following sections, we evaluate the effectiveness of both traditional and new pay plans in facilitating diversity management. We organize this discussion around two questions: first, what impact do these practices have on the productivity and comfort of a diverse mix of employees? And second, how effective are these compensation approaches in encouraging managers to create an atmosphere conducive to diversity?

Traditional pay versus new pay in the accommodation of diverse interests

We turn first to the question of whether traditional pay systems are likely to be effective in maximizing the contribution and satisfaction of a diverse workforce, and whether new pay systems represent an improvement. Many of the characteristics that distinguish traditional from new pay are relevant to this discussion. Given space limitations, however, we focus on three factors: individual versus group level, subjectivity versus objectivity, and flexibility.

Individual level versus group level rewards and the accommodation of diversity Traditional pay systems focus primarily on individual performance. As the importance of team-based management increases, however, this individual approach becomes increasingly problematic. Individual contributions are hard to identity when employees work interdependently, and differentiating among individuals in terms of rewards may introduce unwanted internal competition (Sisco, 1992). Therefore, there is a distinct trend in US organizations to move away from individual-level rewards and toward rewards aggregated at the group, division, or even organizational level.

While these changes have not been initiated specifically to accommodate a more diverse workforce, they do have implications for diversity management. Traditional individual-level systems are compatible with the equity norm of distributive justice: those who contribute the most receive the greatest reward. However, the individual equity norm is not universally applicable. Those who are interested in protecting social relationships and preserving group harmony (e.g. women and minorities from collectivist traditions) may find it difficult to function well under individual equity-based systems for several reasons. First, individuals may be rewarded for acting in their own self-interest (i.e. behaving in ways that will enhance their own individual performance even if such behavior is inconsistent with the goals of the group). Those whose values contradict such behavior will either have to violate their values or face the possibility of lower rewards. Second, the administration of individual rewards may be uncomfortable for those who identify primarily with the group (Copeland, 1988). Being "singled out" for any purpose may be embarrassing to such individuals, and what was intended as reward may be experienced as punishment.

For those whose values orientation places stronger emphasis on the group, the new pay – with its emphasis on group achievement and group rewards

– may be preferable. However, such systems may be *less* desirable for those whose values are more individualistic. In fact, conflict between individualistic employees and group-oriented management systems can lead to a "free-rider" effect, where individuals reduce or withhold their own individual efforts while still expecting to share in group rewards (Wagner, 1992).

Subjectivity versus objectivity: political influence in pay systems It is increasingly recognized that few management systems are completely rational; politics are an unavoidable part of organizational functioning (Ferris and Judge, 1991). Traditional pay systems are no exception. Employees have at least two opportunities to use political influence tactics under such systems: in the determination of initial starting salary and in the determination of later pay raises.

Initial salary level is especially critical in traditional pay systems. Base pay is a substantial component of an individual's total compensation, and future rewards, in the form of percentage increments or raises, compound the original base. Therefore, the success with which one negotiates an initial salary can have a substantial impact on career earnings (Gerhart, 1990). The use of subjective performance appraisals allows employees two avenues of political influence in obtaining later raises: directly, through negotiating for higher raises, and indirectly, through influencing performance ratings on which raises are based. Research evidence indicates that employees can improve their performance ratings by engaging in ingratiating political behaviors (e.g. Wayne and Ferris, 1990; Wayne and Kacmar, 1991). Under traditional pay systems, such inflation of performance ratings will generally translate into larger pay raises. There is also evidence that employees can use political influence tactics in negotiating higher merit increases directly (Bartol and Martin, 1990; Freedman, 1978). This suggests that in order to fare equally well under a traditional compensation system, employees of diverse demographic backgrounds must have equal political influence skills.

However, evidence suggests that such skills may not be equal across groups. For example, a series of studies has indicated that men negotiate higher starting salaries than women (Gerhart and Rynes, 1991; Stevens et al., 1993). While these findings may reflect pay discrimination on the part of employers, they may also indicate that men are more familiar with the appropriate use of influence tactics than are women, due to differences in organizational socialization and mentoring (Dreher et al., 1989; Stevens et al., 1993). Another potential explanation is that men have higher pay expectations than women (Jackson et al., 1992), and higher expectations are related to higher pay outcomes (Freedman, 1978; Major et al., 1984).

While we did not find any specific evidence regarding the negotiating skills of racioethnic minorities, we anticipate that their results would be similar to those found for women, and for the same reasons: lower expectations, combined with less familiarity with "the rules of the game," will likely lead to lower outcome in the salary negotiation process.

Would new approaches to pay alleviate the disadvantages faced by minorities and women due to the role of politics in compensation? It is naive to expect any compensation system to fully eliminate political influence. However, several characteristics of the new pay might reduce the role of politics. First, the quantitative measures of group, division, or organization performance typical of the new pay are less susceptible to manipulation, either by employees or managers, than subjective performance ratings. Second, the fact that rewards are often allocated to groups rather than to individuals should reduce any particular individual's ability to manipulate his or her own compensation. Third, the fact that base salary plays a smaller role in the overall compensation package under the new pay suggests that starting salary negotiations will be less influential in determining one's career compensation.

Flexibility   As noted earlier, traditional pay systems tend to be centralized, bureaucratic, and inflexible. In general, they are designed to accommodate the interests of the "typical" employee, which in many cases means the employee who was typical in the mid-20th century (Stelluto and Klein, 1990). This approach is particularly apparent in the design of employee benefit packages. Many organizations offer a single package that is intended to meet the needs of all employees, regardless of their tastes, preferences, or situation. However, from the theoretical arguments stated above, we know that preferences may differ across gender and racioethnic backgrounds.

In contrast, the new pay provides flexibility for both employer and employee. For the employer it comes in the form of variable pay: when total compensation is tied to organizational performance, payroll expenses rise when the company is doing well and fall when the company is struggling. For the purposes of this chapter, we are more interested in flexibility for the individual employee, which is typically found with respect to employee benefits. For example, flexible (or cafeteria style) benefit plans provide employees with a sum of money to allocate among different benefits as they choose. Paid time off (PTO) programs allow employees to determine whether time off is to be used for vacation or for illnesses (HR Focus, 1994). Reimbursement accounts permit individual employees to shift a portion of their pre-tax salary into accounts which are used to pay for medical or child-care expenses (Stelluto and Klein, 1990).

At present, there have been few initiatives in allowing individual choice in aspects of compensation other than benefits. One ambitious attempt to provide flexibility in cash compensation was explored by DuPont. They proposed to allow individual employees to choose what portion of their pay would be based on company performance. However, this initiative was abandoned because of conflicts with Securities and Exchange Commission requirements (McNutt, 1990).

The advantages of flexibility in designing compensation programs that suit a variety of diverse needs and interests are obvious. As long as there are differences in preferences for types of rewards or reward allocation methods, no single program will accommodate all workers. Flexibility permits the individualization of compensation and therefore facilitates the fine-tuning of reward systems to maximize the motivation of a diverse group of employees.

Does flexibility in compensation introduce any problems from a diversity management perspective? As long as equal amounts of flexibility are provided to all employees (e.g. through formal, centralized flexibility options such as cafeteria benefits), problems are unlikely. However, if flexibility in practice means that exceptions are made for some employees but not for others, then politics, favoritism, and even discrimination become significant issues. It is important to recall that some of the compensation practices now viewed as rigid and bureaucratic (e.g. job analysis and job evaluation; Mahoney, 1991) have been accepted by the courts as appropriate techniques for avoiding bias in compensation (Cooper and Barrett, 1984).

Summary: pros and cons of new pay versus old pay   Traditional pay practices in some ways constrain efforts to effectively manage a diverse workforce. Equity orientations, individual-level rewards and inherent subjectivity lead to systems that are more efficient and effective in motivating some employees than others. To some extent, new pay practices ameliorate these difficulties, in the sense that group-oriented pay practices based on objective measures are likely to be preferred over traditional pay practices *by some members of the workforce*. It is important, however, to note that there are employees for whom the traditional pay may be quite appropriate. Substituting one approach for the other may simply change *which* workers are being properly motivated.

One approach that avoids the problem of motivating only part of the workforce is flexibility. If pay systems can be designed to incorporate employee needs and interests on an *individual* basis, then all employees can be equally motivated. However, beyond experience with flexible benefits plans, US corporations have little experience with such individualization, and it is unclear how or whether such programs would work.

An alternative approach would be to offer a combination of approaches in administering compensation. For example, organizations can provide both individual-level and group-level rewards. Such a strategy would meet the needs of those who are more individualistic in orientation, while not abandoning the interests of those who are more group-oriented. However, it also would result in an elaborate and complicated reward system, which may be difficult for employees to understand. In addition, such a hybrid system might be perceived as sending mixed messages to employees regarding the kinds of behaviors valued by the organization.

Traditional pay versus new pay in providing incentives for diversity management

We focused above on how the increasingly diverse workforce likely will respond to a variety of compensation practices. Compensation and diversity are also related in another, perhaps more direct, way: financial incentives can be used to encourage managers to practice effective diversity management.

Existing uses of incentives in diversity management Many practitioners and researchers believe that one of the keys to effective diversity management is holding individual managers accountable for their actions (e.g. Copeland, 1988; Morrison, 1992). Two of the more important techniques identified by Morrison for enhancing accountability are the inclusion of diversity in individual managers' performance evaluations and in the determination of their compensation. For example, Amtrak and Hughes Aircraft Company base compensation in part on affirmative action achievements (Cox, 1991; Haight, 1990). Honeywell and AT&T use employee surveys to assess how well managers handle diversity, and tie results of these surveys to compensation (Geber, 1990; Graddick, 1994).

A primary strength of this approach lies in its ability to clearly communicate organizational values with respect to diversity management. As noted earlier, explicit linkages between an individual's pay and a specific organizational objective can draw attention to that objective and increase employee awareness of its importance to the organization (Lawler, 1980; Kerr and Slocum, 1987).

On the other hand, perhaps the most troublesome aspect of traditional merit pay in the context of diversity management is identifying and measuring exactly which attitudes or behaviors associated with diversity management will be rewarded. Even Kohn (1993) agreed that incentive plans can be very powerful determinants of short-term behavior in that employees are likely to exhibit exactly those behaviors that are rewarded. However, if the "wrong" behaviors are rewarded, employee behaviors will be inappropriate (Kerr, 1975). Therefore, the task of defining and measuring the appropriate behaviors is critical.

Unfortunately, there is a great deal of uncertainty, even among diversity advocates, as to what constitutes good diversity management. Managing diversity means creating an environment where all individuals can contribute effectively. But the exact steps required to create this environment are at present unclear (Copeland, 1988; Geber, 1990; MacDonald, 1993). Thus identifying those attitudes, behaviors, and outcomes that should be rewarded is a daunting task.

One apparent solution is to reward those elements of diversity management behaviors that *can* be identified and measured. Rather than rewarding success at guiding a diverse set of employees to achieve their maximum potential, many organizations are in fact using incentives to reward changes in the statistical demographic profile of the organization or its subunits (Morrison, 1992). In such cases, managers would be rewarded for hiring or promoting nontraditional (typically, female and minority) employees. Such reward systems probably encourage managers to increase the diversity of their workforce. However, it is not clear that they encourage managers to create climates in which those diverse workers can be productive. As Cox (1991) and Morrison (1992) argued, there is a need to go beyond mere statistics in assessing effective diversity management.

An alternative is to use employee feedback to assess how well diversity is being managed. This approach is consistent with the trend toward 360-

209

degree feedback, where managers are assessed not only by their superiors but also by their subordinates and peers. Such an approach can provide valuable insights to managers, and can contribute greatly to their development in managing diversity. However, organizations currently using 360-degree feedback have been reluctant to use results of this process as the basis for formal performance appraisals or for compensation, promotion, or other tangible rewards. Their primary concern is that using employee feedback for purposes other than development will introduce biases and political gamesmanship into the system (Lublin, 1994; O'Reilly, 1994). In fact, some organizations that initially tied 360-degree feedback to managers' pay have either eliminated or weakened that tie (Lublin, 1994; Shellenbarger, 1994).

Thus both numerical profiles and employee feedback have weaknesses as measures of effective diversity management. The challenge, of course, is to identify measures that are both comprehensive and valid. One option would be to develop assessment techniques based on managerial behaviors. However, many concede that we do not yet know what behaviors constitute good diversity management. Until a clearer picture emerges of what good diversity managers *are* or *do*, the appraisal task will remain formidable.

"New pay" and diversity initiatives The drawbacks of merit pay have resulted in many organizations looking for alternative compensation systems. These newer approaches to compensation typically avoid subjective assessments of individual performance in favor of aggregate, objective measures of organizational performance. These systems may or may not be helpful in motivating managers to effectively manage a diverse workforce.

One of the intended advantages of these new pay systems is that they do not require the specification and measurement of individual attitudes and behaviors. Instead, the focus is on higher-level (organization or group) outcomes. Individual actions are rewarded to the extent that they contribute to overall group or organization success. It is expected that this focus will encourage employees to engage in any and all behaviors that might be of value to the organization, rather than focusing on some smaller and perhaps inappropriate subset of behaviors that are directly rewarded by an individual-level system (Cummings, 1994; Sisco, 1992).

A consequence of this approach from the diversity management standpoint is that it eliminates the need to define specific behaviors that constitute good diversity management. Instead these new pay systems often rely on inadequate measures such as affirmative action progress. Rather than being explicitly defined and assessed, diversity management is rewarded indirectly as one of many elements that might contribute to organizational performance. In other words, it is rewarded to the extent that it enhances organizational productivity or profitability.

However, a number of factors limit the effectiveness of organization-level rewards in motivating good diversity management. Perhaps most important is whether managers accept that better diversity management will result in improved group or organizational performance. In fact there may be room for doubt regarding the advantages of diversity. Evidence reviewed by Triandis et al. (1994) suggests that the relationship between workforce diversity and group or organizational performance is mixed: diversity can lead to higher creativity and better decision-making under certain circumstances, but under other circumstances can lead to lower levels of group cohesion, more stress, and higher turnover. If managers question the connection between diversity and productivity, they will have little incentive to attend to diversity issues under productivity-based incentive plans. This is particularly likely to be a problem where incentive plans take a relatively short-term focus (as many do); payoffs to effectively managing diversity may be far more visible in the long run. Therefore companies with a genuine interest in diversity management and with short-term, results-based compensation systems would be wise to find other ways to communicate and reinforce the importance of diversity to managers (for example, through training programs).

Conclusion

Can reward systems contribute to effective diversity management? As argued above, there is widespread agreement that rewards can change behaviors in the short term. However, whether they can have broader impact on long-term attitudes and values remains an open question. This distinction between short-run behaviors and long-run values returns us to a fundamental issue in defining diversity management. Does managing diversity simply imply changes in behaviors (e.g. persuading managers to hire more women and minorities – an affirmative action approach)? Or does it require changes in attitudes (e.g. encouraging employees to value different perspectives as well – a valuing diversity approach)? Reward systems should be able to achieve the former objective. Their ability to achieve the latter is more controversial. We propose that the more ambitious or extensive an organization's diversity objectives, the more likely it is that it will need to go beyond the compensation system to achieve the scope of change that it desires. However, this does not detract from the importance of including the compensation system as a factor for organizational change.

How can reward systems contribute to effective diversity management? Clearly, more research and practical experimentation are required before the best methods can be identified. Evidence does suggest that gender and racioethnic differences are likely to influence the effectiveness of reward systems. But we know little about how the gender and racioethnic *composition* of groups influences reactions to compensation. Furthermore, to this point few creative compensation initiatives have been employed. Managerial incentive plans tend to reward little more than statistical progress (i.e. affirmative action), and systematic attempts to maximize the motivating power of rewards for diverse workers are lacking. We hope that the issues raised in this chapter will stimulate additional work in this area.

We note in closing that while there are apparent differences across demographic groups in reactions to reward systems, reactions are also influenced by a host of other individual and contextual factors. In other words, demographic status is hardly the only determinant of the effectiveness and acceptability of specific reward systems. The argument that reward systems should be designed with the needs and preferences of the workforce in mind has relevance well beyond gender and racioethnic status. Paying attention to these issues may be more than good diversity management; it may simply be good management.

REFERENCES

Adams, S. J. (1965). Inequity in social exchange. In L. Berkowitz (ed.), *Advances in Experimental Social Psychology*, vol. 2 (267–96). New York: Academic Press.

Alderfer, C. P. (1969). An empirical test of a new theory of human needs. *Organizational Behavior and Human Performance*, 4, 142–75.

Bagarozzi, D. A. (1982). The effects of cohesiveness on distributive justice. *Journal of Psychology*, 110, 267–73.

Balkin, D. B., and Gomez-Mejia, L. R. (1990). Matching compensation and organizational strategies. *Strategic Management Journal*, 11, 153–69.

Barber, A. E., Dunham, R. B., and Formisano, R. A. (1992). The impact of flexible benefits on employee satisfaction: A field study. *Personnel Psychology*, 45, 55–75.

Bartol, K. M., and Manhardt, P. J. (1979). Sex differences in job outcome preferences: Trends among newly hired college graduates. *Journal of Applied Psychology*, 64, 477–82.

Bartol, K. M., and Martin, D. C. (1990). When politics pays: Factors influencing managerial compensation decisions. *Personnel Psychology*, 4, 599–614.

Berger, P. S. (1986). Difference in importance of and satisfaction from job characteristics by sex and occupational type among Mexican-American employees. *Journal of Vocational Behavior*, 28, 203–13.

Beutell, N. J., and Brenner, O. C. (1986). Sex differences in work values. *Journal of Vocational Behavior*, 28, 29–41.

Bigoness, W. J. (1988). Sex differences in job attribute preferences. *Journal of Organizational Behavior*, 9, 139–47.

Blau, F., and Kahn, L. (1994). Rising wage inequality and the U.S. gender gap. *American Economic Review*, 84, 23–8.

Bloom, R., and Barry, J. R. (1967). Determinants of work attitudes among negroes. *Journal of Applied Psychology*, 51, 291–4.

Bond, M. H., Leung, K., and Wan, K. C. (1982). How does cultural collectivism operate? The impact of task and maintenance contributions on reward allocation. *Journal of Cross-Cultural Psychology*, 13, 186–200.

Brief, A. P., and Aldag, R. J. (1989). The economic functions of work. In G. R. Ferris and K. M. Rowland (eds), *Research in Personnel and Human Resource Management*, rd. 7 (1–23). Greenwich, CT: JAI Press.

Caudron, S. (1993). Mastering the compensation maze. *Personnel Journal*, 72, June, 64A-64O.

Chapman, B., and Otterman, R. (1975). Employee preference for various compensation and benefits options. *Personnel Administrator*, 25, 31–6.

Chiu, C. (1990). Distributive justice among Hong Kong Chinese students. *Journal of Social Psychology*, 130, 649–56.

Cooper, E. A., and Barrett, G. V. (1984). Equal pay and gender: Implications of court cases for personnel practices. *Academy of Management Review*, 9, 84–94.

Copeland, L. (1988). Valuing diversity, part 2: Pioneers and champions of change. *Personnel*, 65, July, 44–9.

Cox, T., Jr (1991). The multicultural organization. *Academy of Management Executive*, May, 34–47.

Cox, T. H., Lobel, S. A., and McLeod, P. L. (1991). Effects of ethnic group cultural differences on cooperative and competitive behavior on a group task. *Academy of Management Journal*, 34, 827–47.

Cummings, C. M. (1994). Incentives that really do motivate. *Compensation and Benefits Review*, 24, May–June, 38–40.

Deutsch, M. (1985). *Distributive Justice*. New Haven, CT: Yale University Press.

Dreher, G. F., Dougherty, T. W., and Whitely, W. (1989). Influence tactics and salary attainment: A gender-specific analysis. *Sex Roles*, 20, 535–50.

Employee Benefit Plan Review (1989). Demographics: Driving force behind flexible plans. 10, April, 14–16.

Feldman, S. (1991). Another day, another dollar needs a new look. *Personnel*, 68, January, 9–13.

Ferris, G. R., and Judge, T. A. (1991). Personnel/human resource management: A political perspective. *Journal of Management*, 17, 447–88.

Festinger, L. (1957). *A Theory of Cognitive Dissonance*. Evanston, IL: Row, Peterson.

Freedman, S. M. (1978). Some determinants of compensation decisions. *Academy of Management Journal*, 21, 379–409.

Geber, B. (1990). Managing diversity. *Training*, 27, July, 23–30.

Gerhart, B. (1990). Gender differences in current and starting salaries: The role of performance, college major, and job title. *Industrial and Labor Relations Review*, 43, 418–33.

Gerhart, B., and Rynes, S. L. (1991). Determinants and consequences of salary negotiations by graduating male and female MBAs. *Journal of Applied Psychology*, 76, 256–62.

Giblin, E. J., Wiegman, G. A., and Sanfilippo, F. (1990). Bringing pay up to date. *Personnel*, 67, November, 17–18.

Gomez-Mejia, L. R. (1992). Structure and process of diversification, compensation strategy, and firm performance. *Strategic Management Journal*, 13, 381–98.

Gomez-Mejia, L. R., and Balkin, D. B. (1992). *Compensation, Organizational Strategy, and Firm Performance*. Cincinnati, Ohio: South-western Publishing.

Graddick, M. (1994). Personal communication. Executive Vice President, Corporate Human Resources, AT&T.

Groshen, E. (1991). The structure of the female/male wage differential. *Journal of Human Resources*, 26, 457–71.

Haberfeld, Y. (1992). Pay, valence of pay and gender: A simultaneous equation model. *Journal of Economic Psychology*, 13, 93–109.

Haight, G. (1990). Managing diversity. *Across the Board*, 27, March, 22–9.

Harris, C. T., and Earle, J. R. (1986). Gender and work values: Survey findings from a working-class sample. *Sex Roles*, 15, 487–94.

Harry, J. (1975). Occupational level and the love of money. *Sociological Focus*, 8, 181–90.

Hofstede, G. (1980). *Culture's Consequences: Individual Differences in Work-related Values*. Beverly Hills, CA: Sage.

Hofstede, G. (1984). The cultural relativity of the quality of life concept. *Academy of Management Review*, 9, 389–98.

Hollenbeck, J. R., Ilgen, D. R., Ostroff, C., and Vancouver, J. B. (1987). Sex differences in occupational choice, pay, and worth: A supply-side approach to understanding the male–female wage gap. *Personnel Psychology*, 40, 715–43.

HR Focus (1994). Reengineering sick pay. 71, April, 12–14.

Jackson, L. A. (1987). Gender and distributive justice: The influence of gender-related characteristics on allocations. *Sex Roles*, 17, 73–91.

Jackson, L. A., Gardner, P. D., and Sullivan, L. A. (1992). Explaining gender differences in self-pay expectations: Social comparison standards and perceptions of fair pay. *Journal of Applied Psychology*, 77, 651–63.

Jackson, S. E., and Alvarez, E. B. (1992). Working through diversity as a strategic imperative. In S. E. Jackson and Associates (eds), *Diversity in the Workplace: Human Resource Initiatives*. (13–29) New York: Guilford Press.

Jurgensen, C. E. (1978). Job preferences (What makes a job good or bad?). *Journal of Applied Psychology*, 63, 267–76.

Kahn, A., O'Leary, V. E., Krulewitz, J. E., and Lamm, H. (1980). Equity and equality: Male and female means to a just end. *Basic and Applied Social Psychology*, 1, 173–97.

Kanter, R. M. (1987). From status to contribution: Some organizational implications of the changing basis for pay. *Personnel*, 64, January, 12–37.

Kashima, Y., Siegal, M., Tanaka, K., and Isaka, H. (1988). Universalism in lay conceptions of distributive justice: A cross-cultural examination. *International Journal of Psychology*, 23, 51–64.

Kerr, S. (1975). On the folly of rewarding A, while hoping for B. *Academy of Management Journal*, 18, 769–83.

Kerr, J., and Slocum, J. W. (1987). Managing corporate culture through reward systems. *Academy of Management Executive*, 1, 99–108.

Kohn, A. (1993). Why incentive plans cannot work. *Harvard Business Review*, 71, September–October, 54–63.

Kroesser, H. L. (1991). Selected factors affecting employees' sick leave use. *Public Personnel Management*, 20, 171–80.

Lacy, W. B., Bokemeier, J. L., and Shepard, J. M. (1983). Job attribute preferences and work commitment of men and women in the United States. *Personnel Psychology*, 36, 315–27.

Lawler, E. E. (1980). *Pay and Organization Development*. Reading, MA: Addison-Wesley.

Lefkowitz, J. (1994). Sex-related differences in job attitudes and dispositional variables: Now you see them . . . *Academy of Management Journal*, 37, 323–49.

Leung, K., and Park, H. J. (1986). Effects of interactional goal on choice of allocation rule: A cross-national study. *Organizational Behavior and Human Decision Processes*, 37, 111–20.

Lublin, J. S. (1994). Turning the tables: Underlings evaluate bosses. *Wall Street Journal*, October 5, B1, B14.

MacDonald, H. (1993). The diversity industry. *New Republic*, July 5, 22–5.

McNutt, R. P. (1990). Achievement pays off at DuPont. *Personnel*, 67, June, 5–10.

Mahoney, T. A. (1991). Job evaluation: Endangered species or anachronism? *Human Resource Management Review*, 1, 155–62.

Major, B., Bylsma, W. H., and Cozzarelli, C. (1989). Gender differences in distributive justice preferences: The impact of domain. *Sex Roles*, 21, 487–97.

Major, B., and Deaux, K. (1982). Individual differences in justice behavior. In J. Greenberg and R. L. Cohen (eds), *Equity and Justice in Social Behavior*. New York: Academic Press.

Major, B., and Konar, E. (1984). An investigation of sex differences in pay expectations and their possible causes. *Academy of Management Journal*, 27, 777–92.

Major, B., Vanderslice, V., and McFarland, D. B. (1984). Effects of pay expected on pay received: The confirmatory nature of initial expectations. *Journal of Applied Social Psychology*, 14, 399–412.

Manhardt, P. J. (1972). Job orientation of male and female college graduates in business. *Personnel Psychology*, 25, 361–8.

Meglino, B. M., Ravlin, E. C., and Adkins, C. L. (1989). A work values approach to corporate culture: A field test of the value congruence process and its relationship to individual outcomes. *Journal of Applied Psychology*, 74, 424–32.

Meindl, J. R. (1989). Managing to be fair: An exploration of values, motives, and leadership. *Administrative Science Quarterly*, 34, 252–76.

Miceli, M. P., and Lane, M. C. (1991). Antecedents of pay satisfaction: A review and extension. In K. M. Rowland and G. R. Ferris (eds), *Research in Personnel and Human Resource Management*, vol. 9 (235–309). Greenwich, CT: JAI Press.

Milkovich, G. T., and Newman, J. M. (1993). *Compensation*, 4th ed. Homewood, IL: Irwin.

Moch, M. K. (1980). Racial differences in job satisfaction: Testing four common explanations. *Journal of Applied Psychology*, 65, 299–306.

Morrison, A. M. (1992). *The New Leaders: Guidelines on Leadership Diversity in America*. San Francisco: Jossey-Bass.

Mottaz, C. (1986). Gender differences in work satisfaction, work-related rewards and values, and the determinants of work satisfaction. *Human Relation*, 39, 359–78.

Nealy, S. (1963). Pay and benefit preferences. *Industrial Relations*, 3, 17–28.

Offerman, L. R., and Gowing, M. K. (1993). Personnel selection in the future: The impact of changing demographics and the nature of work. In N. Schmitt, F. Borman, and Associates (eds), *Personnel Selection in Organizations* (385–417). San Francisco: Jossey-Bass.

O'Reilly, B. (1994). 360 feedback can change your life. *Fortune*, 130, October 17, 93–100.

Powell, G. N. (1988). *Women and Men in Management*. Beverly Hills, CA: Sage.

Rigdon, J. E. (1993). Three decades after the equal pay act, women's wages remain far from parity. *Wall Street Journal*, June 9, B1, B3.

Rogers, R. E. (1993). Patterns of absenteeism among government employees. *Public Personnel Management*, 22, 215–35.

Sampson, E. E. (1975). On justice as equality. *Journal of Social Issues*, 31, 45–64.

Schuler, R. S. (1975). Sex, organizational level, and outcome importance: Where the differences are. *Personnel Psychology*, 28, 365–75.

Schwartz, F. N. (1989). Management women and the new facts of life. *Harvard Business Review*, 67, January–February, 65–76.

Seccombe, K. (1993). Employer sponsored medical benefits: The influence of occupational characteristics and gender. *Sociological Quarterly*, 34, 557–80.

Shapiro, E. G. (1977). Racial differences in the value of job rewards. *Social Forces*, 56, 21–30.

Shellenbarger, S. (1994). Reviews from peers instruct – and sting. *Wall Street Journal*, October 5, B1, B4.

Shiflett, S. (1988). Effects of race and criterion on the predictive ability of beliefs and attitudes. *Psychological Reports*, 62, 527–35.

Sisco, R. (1992). Put your money where your teams are. *Training*, 29, July, 41–5.

Sorenson, E. (1994). The crowding hypothesis and comparable worth. *Journal of Human Resources*, 29, 55–67.

Stelluto, G. L., and Klein, D. P. (1990). Compensation trends into the 21st century. *Monthly Labor Review*, 113, February, 38–44.

Stevens, C. K., Bavetta, A., and Gist, M. E. (1993). Gender differences in the acquisition of salary negotiation skills: The role of goals, self-efficacy, and perceived control. *Journal of Applied Psychology*, 78, 723–35.

Subich, L. M., Cooper, E. A., Barrett, G. V., and Arthur, W. (1986). Occupational perceptions of males and females as a function of sex ratios, salary, and availability. *Journal of Vocational Behavior*, 28, 123–34.

Triandis, H. C., Kurowski, L. L., and Gelfand, M. J. (1994). Workplace diversity. In H. C. Triandis, M. D. Dunnette, and L. M. Hough, (eds), *Handbook of Industrial and Organizational Psychology*, 2nd ed., vol. 4 (769–827). Palo Alto, CA: Consulting Psychologists Press.

Tuch, S. A., and Martin, J. K. (1991). Race in the workplace: Black/white differences in the sources of job satisfaction. *Sociological Quarterly*, 32, 103–16.

US Department of Labor (1994). *Employment and Earnings*. Washington, DC: Department of Labor.

Wagner, J. A., III (1992). Individualism-collectivism and free-riding. A study of main and moderator effects. Presented at Annual Meeting of the Academy of Management, Las Vegas, NV.

Watts, B. L., Messe, L. A., and Vallacher, R. R. (1982). Toward understanding sex differences in pay allocation: Agency, communion, and reward distribution behavior. *Sex Roles*, 8, 1175–87.

Wayne, S. J., and Ferris, G. R. (1990). Influence tactics, affect, and exchange quality in supervisor–subordinate interactions: A laboratory experiment and field study. *Journal of Applied Psychology*, 75, 487–99.

Wayne, S. J., and Kacmar, K. M. (1991). The effects of impression management on the performance appraisal process. *Organizational Behavior and Human Decision Processes*, 48, 70–88.

Weaver, C. N. (1975). Black–White differences in attitudes toward job characteristics. *Journal of Applied Psychology*, 60, 438–41.

Wiersma, U. J. (1990). Gender differences in job attribute preferences: Work–home role conflict and job level as mediating variables. *Journal of Occupational Psychology*, 63, 231–43.

Part Three
Emerging Topics in Diversity Management

Introduction to Part Three

When designing human resource (HR) strategies for managing diversity, it is critical that organizations focus not only on how to assimilate members into a common corporate culture, but also how to meet the needs of special employee segments. This emphasis will ensure that members contribute to the fullest of their capability, since barriers impeding their productivity will be reduced. Part Three contains chapters on innovations in managing diversity to meet the unique needs of special employee groups. These topics include work/life, unions, health and safety and disability – and their relationship to diversity.

In chapter 9, we ask organizations to go beyond being "family friendly," and to think more broadly in terms of work and personal life integration. We contend that most "family friendly" policies are essentially geared toward white women in two parent families and have overlooked the work/personal life needs of other employee groups. Some of these groups include employees with elder care needs, employees with domestic partners, single employees, and employees whose ethnic values regarding work/personal life integration may not fit with the design of current HR programs. In order for work/personal life programs to be effective, we point out that there must be a focus on organizational culture change as well as particular programs. Designing cultural change efforts to respond to important issues such as workaholism, globalization, new technologies, and the growing focus on continuous quality improvement are also discussed.

In chapter 10, John Delaney and Catherine Lundy argue that because unions have long been chief protectors of individual rights and have often reached out to new workforce entrants, such as immigrants, unions can be a strong agent for managing diversity as well. At the same time, many union policies are seniority-based and seek to formalize personnel rules, which can limit flexibility in dealing with nontraditional workers. Nevertheless, on balance, unions should be viewed as key partners in developing strategies for managing diversity. Union democratic structures ensure that union preferences will grow to include the perspectives of all members in the labor force. Contracts mandating consistent treatment can also protect workers from arbitrary treatment at the whim of management.

In the groundbreaking chapter 11, Karen Brown discusses the implications of workforce diversity for health and safety. These topics are rarely seen in juxtaposition, yet she makes a convincing case for examining the linkages. She examines the direct health and safety effects of hiring new workers without modifying existing equipment, workplace design, and safety training. The chapter includes a model presenting a framework for linking diversity and safety. It traces the effects of diversity dimensions such as race, gender, and age on personal safety outcomes. She also discusses the increasing risk of potential injury and illness for co-workers due to the rise in workers who carry contagious diseases. Part of the research for the chapter is based on a series of intensive visits over several years to 25 manufacturing organizations in various parts of the US, Mexico, Korea, and Australia.

In chapter 12, Karen Roberts focuses on disability-based diversity and argues that organizations often erroneously assume that all people with disabilities have largely the same needs for support via HR initiatives. She asserts that employers tend to downplay differences in the abilities of disabled employees. She discusses how disability simultaneously can and cannot be viewed as a multicultural issue, which has important ramifications for how organizations design HR strategies. The chapter concludes with a two-tiered approach for developing policies geared at reasonable accommodation. At the organizational level, it is necessary to develop policies to eliminate discriminatory practices as well as to alter the climate to more easily assimilate individuals with disabilities into the workplace. Since under the Americans with Disabilities Act, each person requiring accommodation must be treated on a case by case basis, employers must give serious consideration to a variety of ways in which work could be done in light of the idiosyncratic nature of a person's disability and the work context in which he or she needs to function.

9

Human Resource Strategies to Support Diversity in Work and Personal Lifestyles: Beyond the "Family Friendly" Organization

Sharon A. Lobel and Ellen Ernst Kossek

In the late 1970s, as single earner, two parent families ceased to be the predominant labor force norm, a few dozen major corporations began offering family supportive policies in the US (Galinsky et al., 1991). By 1989, over 4,000 employers in the US had adopted child care support in several main forms of assistance, including dependent care pre-tax dollar spending accounts, resource and referral programs, and support of on- or near-site child care (Friedman, 1990). Elder care assistance also became more common in light of national statistics indicating that nearly a third of all primary elder caregivers are employed full time, a figure that is expected to continue to grow (Stone et al., 1987).

In recent years, HR programs to support employees and their dependents have proliferated. Support has taken the form of interventions focused on time, information, financial aid, and/or direct dependent care services. Box 9.1 gives examples for each of these categories. *Time*-based interventions, such as flextime, are designed to provide an employee with greater flexibility in the management of time-based conflicts between work and nonwork activities. *Information*-based strategies, such as stress management seminars, provide an employee with knowledge to use in making decisions regarding

The authors would like to thank Margaret Browning and Douglas T. Hall for their helpful comments on this manuscript.

> **Box 9.1** Human resource programs to support employees and their dependents
>
> *Time-based strategies* flextime, telecommuting and other work-at-home arrangements, leaves of absence, job sharing, part-time work, family leave stemming from the Family Medical Leave Act, emergency leave, and compressed work weeks.
>
> *Information-based strategies* resource and referral programs, stress management seminars, child and elder care support groups, dependent care provider fairs, relocation assistance, employee assistance programs, and pre-retirement planning.
>
> *Money-based strategies* flexible spending accounts, vouchers, flexible benefits, company discounts at local provider organizations, adoption assistance, well baby care, tuition reimbursement, college scholarships, benefits for dependents and long-term care insurance.
>
> *Direct services* on- or near-site day care centers, sick child care, company support of in-home family day care providers, Employee Assistance Programs, legal counseling, personal financial planning, emergency back-up child care centers, in-home emergency dependent care services, before and after school care programs, holiday and vacation care programs, lactation program, family day-care networks.

the management of nonwork obligations. *Financial* aid policies, such as flexible spending accounts, assist employees by providing financial resources to support dependent care and other nonwork needs. *Direct services*, such as on-site day care, are staffed by company employees or contractors.

The development of employer-sponsored programs to create a "family friendly environment" has not yet topped out. Organizations continue to offer new types of family supportive services and to extend benefits to new employee groups. For example, the latest *Working Mother* list of the top 100 employers notes such new amenities as the reservation of a room at work for nursing mothers and reimbursement of child, elder, or pet care expenses incurred while on business-related travel (Naylor, 1994). Many companies such as Apple Computer, Levi Strauss, and Lotus have also started offering benefits, traditionally reserved for spouses and family members, to same-sex domestic partners (Deck, 1993).

These benefits are likely to be valued by the workers who use them. Indeed, gratitude on the part of employees may make it difficult for them to request even more substantial efforts. None the less, we argue that these formal approaches do not go far enough unless they are accompanied by two major changes. Over the short term, we believe that interventions ought to respond to the diverse needs of employees who may differ in work and personal lifestyle, cultural background and national origin. For example, expanding the notion of what constitutes a family is consistent with this approach. Over the long term, however, we believe members of organizations must evaluate, and perhaps change, the norms and values inherent in a given organizational culture about the "appropriate" kind of interaction between work and personal life. For example, even if an organization has many formal programs in place, prevailing values, such as the belief that work should take priority over other aspects of an individual's life, may discourage people from using them. For example, data from a major survey on work/family issues indicates that many employees and employers view family supportive and career-oriented policies as mutually exclusive (Schwartz, 1994). With the exception of time-based interventions – many of which have important formal and informal cultural barriers impeding their usage (Kossek et al., 1993) – and some direct services, such as on-site day care, traditional programs do little to redesign the workplace to meet employees' personal needs. Furthermore, with the exception of organizational culture change interventions, traditional programs tend to be short-sighted, may stigmatize users, and remain unintegrated with other important organizational efforts (Kofodimos, 1995). Given these concerns, we have three main objectives for this chapter: (1) to examine the *basic assumptions* underlying family supportive initiatives; (2) to give some specific examples of the growing *diversity* in work and personal life needs in the labor force and to review HR strategies that could be adopted to meet shifting employee demands; and (3) to discuss *future directions regarding diversity and work/personal life* initiatives including integration of the two domains with each other, and with globalization, team-building, quality enhancement, and technology advances.

Basic Assumptions Behind the Design of Family Supportive Policies

According to Kofodimos (1995), family supportive policies cannot be successful in the long run if they rest on assumptions such as the following, which she believes are prevalent among senior managers in many organizations:

- Work should be the primary priority in a person's life. Therefore, programs should be designed to remove intrusions that compete for an employee's time and energy. An example of such a program is sick child care for mildly ill children.
- Programs that reduce an employee's hours at work are most appropriate for jobs that are less essential to the organization's objectives. For example, clerical workers may be considered good candidates for part-time, flextime, or job sharing options, whereas managers may not.
- Programs should be directed at individuals with the most visible kinds of work and personal life conflict. Therefore programs to assist a single mother with child care, for example, may exist; but programs to help a workaholic with a crumbling marriage probably will not.

- Programs should be designed by experts, rather than users, and their implementation should be left to supervisors, rather than teams of co-workers. For example, a supervisor may decide whether a certain job is appropriate for job sharing, without allowing the employees to develop a plan for successful implementation.

These assumptions perpetuate the existing organizational culture. In a company which relies on knowledge workers, "family friendly" programs may be seen as core to the business; but in many organizations the "family friendly" programs are seen as peripheral to the organizational purpose (Kofodimos, 1995). The programs help those who work to live; those who live to work are role models, who do not need help (Kofodimos, 1995).

Some people may resent the implication that "family friendly" programs are doing more harm than good. Indeed, employees may be grateful for employer efforts to help them with work and personal life conflicts, especially as compared to no help at all. None the less, trying to uncover the basic assumptions behind the design of "family friendly" policies in a particular organization is an important step in creating programs that will truly be responsive to the diverse needs of employees. At the same time, this process can contribute to reengineering work so as to support business needs. In contrast with the assumptions listed above, drivers such as the following can be vehicles for the long-term effectiveness of responsive programs:

- People have diverse and important commitments, outside of work, which contribute to the employee's well-being and, therefore, help the employee be more effective at work. These commitments do not merely compete for the employee's time and energy. Diverse life experiences – ranging from single parenting to an avocation in music – bring a variety of perspectives to the workplace that, when valued, can help teams to be more creative and, ultimately, find better solutions to business problems. Thus, the organization values and rewards employees who have a full life.
- Programs should be designed to meet the needs for flexibility all employees have. Furthermore, flexibility is an important skill for managers and employees to develop and exercise; it does not necessarily mean reduced commitment to work, even if it means reduced hours. Flexibility and productivity go hand in hand.
- Programs should address the diverse forms of work and personal life conflict. Policy-makers need a broad understanding of the nature of the conflicts, especially those that are more subtle.
- Employees can be empowered to suggest solutions for work and personal life conflicts. Many situations, such as having several employees on maternity leave at the same time, will appear less difficult to manage when the input of those on leave, as well as that of co-workers, is solicited in the problem-solving process.

In the next section we will describe some HR strategies which can be adopted to meet the needs of a workforce with diverse work and personal life issues. Recognition of this form of diversity is an important step in the evolution of policies that will help interventions be more far-reaching and effective.

Diversity of Work/Personal Life Interactions and Needs

The typical corporate employee of the 1950s was a male with a stay-at-home wife who cared for their children and most other household responsibilities. Today, this type of male represents fewer than 10 percent of the workforce (Rosen, 1991). The influx of women into the labor force, along with increasing rates of divorce, immigration, and aging of the population have led to a much more diverse workforce profile. Employees may be members of dual earner families or single parent families. They may be heterosexual or homosexual, living alone or with other adults to whom they are not married. The increasing ethnic and cultural heterogeneity of the workforce also creates a diversity of lifestyles, workstyles, and needs. As described below, one way to acknowledge this diversity is to expand the definition of family to include more nontraditional family types.

Definition of family

Much of the literature on the interaction between work and personal life has used the term "work/family" to describe the two domains, with work/family conflict and work/family balance defining associated issues. At the same time that interest in this area has arisen as a consequence of changing workforce demographics, it is a paradox that the term "family" in "work/family" still evokes rather traditional images. Although for many people, the "family" now also refers to a dual income, as well as a single income couple with children, and to households with single parents, less conventional kinds of families may not be included.

As noted earlier, the initial thrust of work/family initiatives during the 1970s was in the direction of dependent care, meaning child care and elder care. In recent years, flexible spending accounts, allowing reimbursement of pre-tax dollars for dependent care expenses, have become more prevalent; but they tend to be used by higher-level employees, who are more likely to be able to afford the float and are more likely to use dependent care options which are "on the books." Therefore, not only have the work/family benefits responded primarily to working parents, but also to those with the financial resources to make choices among various child care options. "Family friendly" programs have, by and large, been especially responsive to the needs of professional women.

Similarly, the research literature has tended to focus on "dual career" families, where the label "dual career" refers to professional or nontraditional jobs, held by both members of the couple. Yet, while 26.9 percent of white women are employed in managerial and professional jobs, that number drops to 18.1 percent for African-American women and 15.0 percent for Hispanic women. Over half of all African-American and Hispanic women workers are employed in clerical and service occupations (National Commission on Working Women, 1990). For married working couples, as well as for single individuals, the nature of the jobs they hold and their associated flexibility and income are important variables contributing to differences in work and personal life needs.

The legal definition of family used by the United States Census is "two or more persons related by blood, marriage, or adoption who reside together" (Ahlburg and DeVita, 1992, p. 5). The federal family-leave law includes anyone who takes the place of a parent in its definition of parent–child relationship; however it does not include gay and lesbian partners as members of a family (Shellenbarger, 1993a).

There are some signs that even the legal definition of family may be undergoing some changes. For example, the New York State Supreme Court ruled that when one member of a gay couple died, the other could not be evicted from the rent-controlled apartment. The judge wrote that protection from eviction "should not rest on fictitious legal grounds or genetic history but instead should find its foundation in the reality of family life" (Sorge, 1989).

One direction for broadening the definition of family has been to focus on the emotional bonds between individuals. For example, in a recent meeting of individuals responsible for work/family policy in several major North American corporations, this more general working definition of family was developed: "Any relationship between two or more people related by blood, legal ties, financial or emotional support" (Lobel et al., 1994). In a similar vein, a survey conducted by Massachusetts Mutual Life Insurance Company asked 1,200 adults to describe what constitutes a family. Only 22 percent picked the legal definition; 75 percent opted for "a group of people who love and care for each other" (Rosen, 1991).

The focus on emotional ties and support as a definition of family represents a significant change that would expand the numbers of families recognized by HR policies and programs. Whereas the legal definition would include single individuals who choose to have or adopt children as comprising a family, emotional ties would apply to unmarried heterosexual and homosexual couples, and the relationships of each member of these unmarried couples to any children or parents who may comprise their family. As is currently done in a few companies, under a broader definition, programs such as relocation assistance and health insurance for spouses would be extended to partners of unmarried individuals, including homosexual partners.

In many cases, the relationship of individuals to their pets also involves emotional ties and support. The positive role of caring for a pet on the mental and physical health of nursing home patients and depressed individuals has been established in the psychological and medical literature

(Boldt and Dellman-Jenkins, 1992; Hoffman, 1991; Siegel, 1990). Certainly the illness or loss of a beloved pet may affect an individual's well-being, even if only temporarily. Custody battles over pets are increasingly being fought in the courtroom (Sharpe, 1994b). Said one divorced man, "It's really easy to ridicule the situation. But if you love a dog, it becomes a member of your family" (p. A1). Another individual conceded that giving up the dog was the hardest part about ending a failed marriage. A cafeteria benefits plan with veterinary insurance might be one consequence of considering individuals and their pets as comprising families.

A cafeteria benefits plan is one means of controlling costs while at the same time offering expanded coverage to a larger group of employees by virtue of a broader definition of family. None the less, expansion of coverage, itself, may result in cost savings because of increased attraction, retention, and commitment. For an employer's investment in expanded benefits to pay off, expanded programs and policies should be part of a broader strategy to integrate work/life initiatives with business needs. For example, HR and line management should work together to identify linkages; utilization and business outcomes of work/life initiatives should be widely communicated; and research and analysis should be conducted to assess programs (Christensen, 1994).

Cross-cultural differences in meaning of family The diversity in cultural notions of family is another area which needs to be recognized. Cultures differ in the extent to which cooperation or individualism are emphasized (Mead, 1967; Hofstede, 1980). Cross-cultural differences in the perspectives of self in relation to family or group have also been well documented (Triandis et al., 1988). In collectivist cultures, such as Asian, Hispanic, and African-American, cooperation among individuals who are considered part of the "in-group," e.g. family, is high (Cox et al., 1991). Therefore, the definition of which people constitute the family, and the corresponding sense of obligation to its members, may be broader than that found in more individualist cultures, such as the Anglo-American. These cultural differences in the nature and expectations of family life may have consequences for behavior in organizations, such as an individual's desire for flexibility to be able to attend to family obligations that another person might consider unimportant. For example, a study by Triandis et al. (1982) reported on the willingness of Hispanic and non-Hispanic respondents to sacrifice for the welfare of various family members. The survey asked individuals how willing they would be to spend a substantial amount of money, e.g. travel costs, in order to be present at 19 different crisis times or celebrations involving members of their nuclear and extended families. Interestingly, Hispanics were more willing than non-Hispanics to make financial sacrifices to attend celebrations, such as birthdays, weddings, and baptisms. They were also more willing to make financial sacrifices for events involving members of the extended family, such as a nephew's baptism. Research on African-Americans has also highlighted their greater reliance on extended kin systems, both within and outside of the family, which fulfill many functions served by the nuclear family household (Hacket and Jackson, 1993).

In many collectivist cultures, individuals internalize norms about obligation to members of their in-group. Internalization of norms means that individuals behave according to inner dictates, not merely to please others or to comply in the presence of others. For example, Bontempo et al. (1990) found that in contrast to students who believed their answers would be made public, anonymity caused US students to say they would be less likely to provide assistance to someone who is seriously ill, loan money to someone, or perform other socially desirable behaviors. In other words, the US students had not internalized norms about the importance of helping others. Brazilian students responded the same way in both the anonymous and public conditions. Again, these findings suggest a strong bond to members of one's family in Latin culture, which may exceed the expectations associated with being a member of an Anglo-American family. Similar strong bonds would be expected in other collectivist cultures, such as African-American and Asian-American.

In addition to cultural differences in the nature of family and in commitment to its members, there are gender differences associated with family roles. Although fathers are showing a growing interest in child-rearing, society still sees child care as the primary responsibility of women (Couter, 1984) and women are socialized to be more directly involved in the care of children. For example, female employees assume greater responsibility for child care; and they are more likely to make child care arrangements and take care of problems when these arrangements break down, regardless of the age of the child (Galinsky, 1988; Burden and Googins, 1987). Research shows that having children is more likely to impede the career advancement of women due to career interruptions and temporary departure from the labor force, lowered job responsibilities, and supervisor beliefs of lowered job commitment (Lewis and Cooper, 1988; Schwartz, 1989; Gwartney-Gibbs, 1988).

Expanding the definition of family, as well as recognizing cultural and gender differences in its meaning and associated responsibilities, does represent a form of progress. None the less, we feel this approach is limited for several reasons. First, even with broader definitions of family, the message remains that individuals who have no obvious emotional ties with others do not need supportive corporate programs, policies or cultures to help them manage better the relationship between work and the rest of their lives.

Hall and Parker (1993, p. 9) note a second reason why expanding the domain of "family" is inadequate: "The adoption of work/family programs may reflect a shift from the prevailing belief that employees should have no major nonwork commitments to the belief that there is only one such valid commitment: family." Indeed, people may have important interests outside of family, such as volunteer and community work, continuing education, athletic or artistic hobbies, friendships and spiritual development (Kofodimos, 1993). Work/family programs, to some extent, legitimize nonwork ties and obligations; a work and personal life focus is necessary to legitimize all of these nonwork interests, as well as to address the cultural and ethnic differences in how people view issues such as "balance" and "conflict" between various domains.

In box 9.2, we indicate some examples of how an organization might respond to the diverse commitments and needs of employees with different work and personal life profiles. For example, single parents lack time, money and social support for dependent care. Therefore, they especially value sick care help, resource and referral, and vouchers for dependent care. Dual career parents, on the other hand, probably have more access to time, money, and back-up support; they may especially value the opportunity to work a part-time schedule as a means of caring for young children or elders, while remaining viable on their career track (Kossek, 1990).

To the extent that work/family issues can be addressed by work/family programs such as those listed in box 9.1, the solutions are likely to be viewed as benefits, housed in the HR department and not owned by line management. If we take a more systemic view of the relationship between work and personal life, then identification of problems, goals, and initiatives will necessarily be more complex. A program of benefits will not suffice. Indeed, as we will suggest later, the most progressive organizations are going beyond a programmatic response, for example, thinking of flexibility as "attention to the 'whole' of the employee's life" (Hall and Parker, 1993, p. 6) or as a "way of doing business" (Lobel et al., 1994), rather than as flextime or job share options. These broader perspectives can be more successful in moving the work/personal life agenda from being viewed as a marginal, soft issue to one of strategic importance.

Work/Personal Life and Diversity Initiatives: Linkages and Contrasts

In both the work/personal life and diversity arenas, researchers have developed models to describe the relative position of an organization along a continuum of progressively more broad-ranging and effective change efforts. For example, Cox (1991) describes the progression of an organization from monolithic to plural to multicultural, in the process of cultural change for diversity. The monolithic organization is one in which the presence of individuals from different cultural groups is minimal, especially when extent of integration is examined by function and level. Women, minorities, and foreign nationals are expected to adapt to existing organizational norms. The plural organization is more heterogeneous and has programs, such as training to reduce prejudice, selection and promotion efforts targeting diverse groups, and compensation audits to insure equality. As with the monolithic organization, women, minorities, and foreign nationals are expected to adapt to existing organizational norms. Finally, in the multicultural organization, diverse groups are present at all levels and in all functions, and there is a two-way socialization process in which individuals adapt to the organization's norms and, at the same time, the organization's norms

---

Box 9.2   Key work/personal life dilemmas for diverse employee groups

1   Single parent
Key dilemmas   lack of time, money, and social support for dependent care; lack of in-home back-up person to regularly help with care.
HR policy implications   single parents significantly prefer sick care help, resource and referral, voucher care; other possible services include legal aid, custody help, psychological support, reimbursement for child care.

2   Dual career parent
Key dilemmas   wanting to be involved with caregiving for young children or elders without significantly losing out on the career track; finding time to be with partner; managing relocation issues when job transfers come up.
HR policy implications   women in dual career marriages significantly prefer part-time and job sharing; other possible services include relocation assistance for spouse.

3   Individuals/families developing relationships: single persons; blended families; stepfamilies
Key dilemmas finding a partner, finding stability, taking care of significant others; balancing work with other activities.
HR policy implications   broadening eligibility for "family" benefits; educational resources; support groups.

4   Sandwiched employees: managing care for both children and elderly relatives
Key dilemmas   finding time to manage possibly conflicting care arrangements; high stress; limited dollars for care.
HR policy implications   stress management; support groups.

5   Older workers
Key dilemmas   planning for retirement and shifting to greater commitment outside work; possibly caring for sick parents or spouses.
HR policy implications   phased-in retirement plans; elder care, job sharing, work at home; contingent hiring programs.

6   Gay and lesbian employees
Key dilemmas   domestic partner equal compensation; fear of discrimination on the job.
HR policy implications   extension of benefits to domestic partners; support groups; diversity training.

7   Individuals with commitments outside of work and family life
Key dilemma   balancing work and/or family life with other activities.
HR policy implications   honoring civic leadership, community involvement, volunteer activities; encouraging flexible scheduling for all employees; work/personal life focus (rather than work/family focus).

---

change as a function of the influence of the diverse members' alternative perspectives on those norms.

In Friedman and Galinsky's (1992) work/family change model, organizations progress through three stages. In stage 1, organizations take a programmatic approach in responding to family needs. Initiatives, which do not challenge existing norms, are tried and include programs such as resource and referral services, flexible benefits plan, and parenting seminars. In stage 2, top management begins to champion some programs, a work/family manager or group may be named, and personnel policies and benefits are evaluated for their contribution to work/family issues. In Stage 3, the culture of the company changes to become truly "family-friendly." Mission statements may be changed, and managers may be evaluated as to how well they handle employees' work/personal life conflicts. Work/family issues are mainstreamed as work/life or work/personal life issues and are integrated with other efforts, such as diversity.

In both of these models, as the organization progresses further in its development, there is a greater emphasis on *changing organizational culture*, rather than merely implementing isolated programs. Norms are an important aspect of organizational culture; norms are the unstated assumptions about how people ought to behave in the organization. Friedman and Galinsky (1992) provide these examples of some traditional norms in workplaces which need to be challenged and changed in order to truly make progress with work/personal life initiatives.

- Keep your personal problems at home.
- Give them an inch and they will take a mile.
- Equity means the same for everyone.
- Presence equals performance.

Box 9.3 lists other assumptions that need to be challenged. For example, contrary to what may be believed, the same dependent care programs that work well for child care are *not* suited for elder care, because elder care responsibilities fluctuate more (Kossek, DeMarr, Backman, and Kollar, 1993). Also, adding benefits for domestic partners is *not* prohibitively expensive; rather, after the first year, offering health and other benefits to domestic partners of gay and lesbian employees is cost neutral (Deck, 1993).

Existing data provide evidence of a need for increased efforts to change organizational cultures, not merely to increase the presence of women and minorities in top positions. For example, a study by Korn/Ferry and UCLA, conducted in 1982, showed that only 49 percent of top female executives were married and only 39 percent had children. The comparable figures for top male executives in 1979 were 95 percent married and 97 percent with children. Ten years later, 69 percent of top female executives are married and 57 percent have children (Shellenbarger, 1993b). The data appear to show that in order for a woman to advance, she no longer has to make the same kind of stark choices between career and family as in the past. None the less, even the women with family obligations report that when career and family conflicts occur, they are more likely to choose in favor of their

Box 9.3   Existing basic assumptions regarding work and family: unmet expectations in the new workforce

Assumption   Dependent care is still primarily a woman's issue.
Fact   More men today are involved in parenting than ever before. Grandparents also make up an increasingly important caregiving group.

Assumption   Work/family programs should be targeted at employees with children.
Fact   Single persons and married couples without children have dependent care needs particularly in the elder care arena. They are becoming increasingly resentful of the fact that their private life needs are not being met.

Assumption   Work/family programs help individuals manage work and personal life conflicts.
Fact   Society and the employer benefit when employees' work and personal life needs are being met.

Assumption   Employees who are highly committed to their personal lives cannot be highly committed to their work.
Fact   Many employees have multiple roles to which they are highly committed.

Assumption   The same dependent care programs that work well for child care are suited for elder care.
Fact   Unlike child care, elder care tends to be more informal and more difficult to plan for than child care. Unlike child care, elder care responsibilities are more likely to fluctuate according to the health and proximity of the parent.

Assumption   The cost of adding benefits for new employee groups, such as those with domestic partners, is prohibitive, particularly in the current economic environment.
Fact   After the first year, offering health and other benefits to domestic partners of gay and lesbian employees is cost neutral.

Assumption   The home is a relatively benign haven and the workplace is the main source of stress. Programs are tailored with the view that they should buffer work from the home.
Fact   With new technology and work-at-home options, the lines between work and home are becoming more blurred.

Assumption   The one best way to work is to be in the office from 9 to 5 and to keep family matters separate from work.
Fact   More than ever before, the virtual office is providing real options for employees to integrate their work and personal lives around the clock.

career. Less than half of top female executives feel that they have enough time with their husbands and children. In other words, women who reach top executive positions may be assimilating to a widely prevalent organizational culture which requires that outside obligations cannot take precedence over work obligations.

Organizational culture change strategies provide: tools for identifying organizational norms, cultural forces, and attitudes which may hinder or facilitate individual efforts to integrate work and other roles; and training for specific skills, such as flexibility, to resolve work and personal life conflicts. Instruments to use for cultural audits specifically focused on these issues will be required. For example, Kofodimos (1993) has developed tools to measure the organizational climate regarding time and energy imbalance, that is, overinvestment in work at the expense of other aspects of life. Similarly, the Boston University Work and Family Roundtable is in the process of developing standards of excellence that can be used for self-study by corporations that want to assess how well they are doing in meeting the diverse work and personal life integration needs of employees (Center on Work and Family, 1994).

As organizations progress in development, a major objective of work/personal life initiatives will be integration with other ongoing efforts, rather than assimilation to existing practices. Galinsky et al. (1991) make a special note of *integration of diversity and work/personal life initiatives with each other* at higher levels of progress. There are several factors which need to be recognized and addressed before diversity and work/personal life initiatives can be successfully integrated. These factors include differences in historical roots, in their potential to positively affect the advancement of women, and time frame.

Diversity initiatives have their historical roots in affirmative action and EEO, while work/personal life initiatives have their roots in employer support for child care. In many cases, diversity is driven by top-level management, whereas work/personal life has been in response to bottom-up or grassroots pressures within the organization (Families and Work Institute, 1994).

Perhaps because of differing origins, diversity initiatives have been more clearly targeted towards attraction, retention, and, in more progressive companies, the advancement of women and minorities. Traditional work/family programs have been conceived to help people manage immediate conflicts between work and family life, rather than to respond to changing needs over the life cycle. In other words, traditional work/family programs take a short-term, "fire-fighting" rather than long-term, life cycle approach. A life cycle approach would be more consistent with career planning and advancement.

Indeed, according to a *Wall Street Journal* analysis of 38,000 companies that file data with the federal government, companies known for being "family friendly" have poor records for promoting women (Sharpe, 1994a). In contrast, some companies that are not particularly family friendly are doing well in terms of moving women up the ranks of management, relative to other companies in their industries.

None the less, barriers to advancement have been recognized as important issues in both arenas. These barriers are referred to as the "glass ceiling" in the diversity field and the "mommy track" in the work/personal life field.[1] There are, however, differences in the time frame associated with their specific programs, which on the surface, make it seem that diversity programs have a greater potential to help women advance. Programs such as training, recruitment, and succession planning, have a long-term focus. When a person is identified as a high-potential employee and a target for advancement in a diversity effort, then her progress in meeting her potential can be monitored over time. In contrast, programs, such as flextime and day care support, unless they are part of a wider life cycle approach, have a short-term focus. They tend to be designed to help employees cope with multiple demands, which stem from family life outside of work. Although investments in these programs may be made to further users' current productivity, there may be no clear motivation to continue monitoring impact of usage on future opportunities to advance.

Although there are differences in origin and time frame of diversity and work/personal life initiatives, we have noted that both fields face the problem of barriers to career advancement. In order to solve this problem, the managerial and co-worker biases which impede advancement need to be surfaced. In the case of diversity, prejudice and fear of loss of power are key biases underlying resistance to change (Families and Work Institute, 1994). In the case of work and personal life, using face time as an indicator of performance and commitment is an important bias. Thus, individuals who take advantage of alternative work arrangements involving fewer hours of work may be perceived as less committed. As long as dedication, commitment, and productivity are defined in terms of visible and extended presence on the job, people who choose to reduce their hours (but not their commitment) may be written off by others. This view is consistent with Grover's (1991) findings that employees without children had more negative views of those who used parental leaves. Similarly, managers may assume that when a woman leaves her job after becoming a mother, she has left to stay at home with the infant. One study suggests that the reasons women leave are more likely linked to lack of opportunities with the present employer (Deutsch, 1990; Trost, 1990). Said an HR director, "My hypothesis had been that offering a day-care center or flexible hours would solve the problem [of turnover among women]. Well, challenging job responsibilities, not family issues, were the decisive factors in why [professional] women left" (Deutsch, 1990).

Recognizing and uprooting these biases is a need common to both diversity and work/personal life management and is one argument for linkage. Both fields also face the problem of stigmatization of beneficiaries of specific programs. For example, some minorities may not want to be viewed as beneficiaries of affirmative action or managing diversity programs, because they do not want to be judged as having been recruited or promoted for reasons other than performance. Similarly, women and men may feel that if they take advantage of programs designed to help them manage work/personal life conflicts, they may be perceived as less committed employees.

The fact that designers of some family friendly and diversity programs not only fail to address the issue of advancement, but also fail to address the issue of tracking or stigmatization of users, are symptoms that they are not drivers for organizational change. Ultimately, the aim of these change efforts ought to be the well-being, broadly understood, of all employees, as well as that of the organization. Consistent objectives will help address problems common to both work/personal life and diversity initiatives, namely barriers to advancement, biases, and stigmatization of beneficiaries. The need to assess and perhaps realign fundamental individual and organizational values about definitions of successful performance in work and other aspects of life can be another common objective (Lobel, 1992). The impact of usage of work and personal life options on an individual's career over time ought to be monitored and matched with the individual's objectives. At the same time, diversity programs ought to be monitored for their impact on individuals' lifestyles and also matched with the individuals' objectives. Managers and employees need to be selected and rewarded for valuing diversity and focusing on results, not style. The director of workforce diversity at United Technologies offers an example of this kind of results focus: individuals who work especially long hours are reminded that results, not hours, are what counts (*Wall Street Journal*, 1994a).

In a survey of 25 companies done by the Families and Work Institute (1994), only six had established formal linkages between work/family and diversity. In five of the six, work/life is part of diversity; in the other organization, work/life and diversity belong to an umbrella initiative on Workplace Equality. In these companies, broad definitions that focus on full utilization exist. In half of the 25 companies, work/family programs were perceived as easier to sell than diversity, and, therefore, linkages were seen to have benefits for diversity. Some fear that dilution of efforts may occur as a result of linkages. None the less, in companies where the two functions were linked, no disadvantages to linkages were reported.

The major elements of an HR strategy that takes a comprehensive and consistent view of both diversity and work/personal life issues include the following (Christensen, 1994):

- *Policies and programs* are developed with employees to address a broad spectrum of work and personal life issues; managers receive training on policies and programs; availability, utilization and business outcomes are widely communicated; programs are assessed via research.
- *Senior management commitment* is communicated by the CEO and in the mission statement; expectations of supervisors are clear.
- *Supervisor commitment* is developed via training; supervisors know how initiatives link to their business; they talk about work/life and diversity at management meetings.

- *Rewards* are linked to employee feedback on supervisor supportiveness and climate; recognition is provided for creative solutions.
- *Communication* is two-way; information is disseminated about programs and employees provide feedback.
- *Linkages to business strategy* are developed by HR and line management; linkages between work/personal life, diversity, and business strategy are communicated to employees.
- *Individual self-management* is promoted via training to develop self-awareness of values and living in accord with them, support groups, and resources, such as time management seminars.

In summary, the integration of work/personal life and diversity initiatives, and the corresponding progress in organizational development will occur when:

- there is a focus on organizational culture change, not just program implementation; culture change supersedes membership and/or retention objectives;
- objectives of work/personal life and diversity management are consistent, especially with regard to advancement;
- programs do not stigmatize beneficiaries;
- evaluation of effects of programs takes a long-term focus.

Future Directions for Work/Personal Life and Diversity Management

New managerial skills

The kinds of skills necessary to manage a workforce, which is increasingly diverse in cultural origin and lifestyle, are different from those effective in the past when workers were more homogeneous. Organizations need to select and train individuals who value diversity, who are flexible, and who can help workers cope with work and personal life conflicts. Managers need to become aware of their own biases and how they might influence the way they react to employees who endorse different values, especially those that do not have a direct impact on work performance. Tools for developing an awareness of one's values with regard to work and personal life issues, and for setting goals if personal or organizational value change is desired, are readily available (e.g. Kofodimos, 1993).

Flexibility, which is critical to all groups of employees, has been described as a focus on getting the work done, rather than how, where and/ or when it is done (Lobel et al., 1994). Hall and Parker (1993) define flexibility as "a critical organizational ability that enables employers to help employees express, rather than suppress, the identities (such as women, Asian-Americans, etc.) and roles (such as caretakers for ill parents, community volunteers, partners, etc.) they have outside of work." This managerial style contrasts with the competitive/control approach to leadership that is typically found in organizations (Kofodimos, 1995), and which is in direct conflict with the most recent trends in "managerial best practices." Clearly, in these views, flexibility is not simply changing the work schedules of employees.

Flexibility is mutual in the sense that both employee and employer need to discuss and negotiate how to meet their needs. Thus, it is a skill needed by both employees and management. As organizations, and the people in them, become more flexible, we will need to determine the limits of flexibility, that is, under what conditions being too flexible prevents the organization from balancing customer, employer, and employee needs. For example, customers may object to being served by a part-time employee; on the other hand, a full-time, job share situation may prove to be quite satisfactory. We will also need to develop standards for evaluating how well people and organizations are performing along the dimension of balancing customer, employer, and employee needs. The issue of drawing boundaries between work and the rest of employees' lives treads on ethical and philosophical ground. It should be a matter of serious debate and consideration within organizations, involving as wide a spectrum of individuals as possible.

In addition to flexibility, managers will need to enhance their skills in promoting cross-training, improved communication and coordination, and teambuilding, so that alternative work arrangements, such as job shares, can successfully balance employee, customer, and employer needs.

It is clear that for work/personal life and diversity initiatives to be effective, there must be a focus on *organizational culture change* as well as particular programs. Thus, managers need to be skilled in the process of managing change, a skill which can have multiple applications. Part of the process involves overcoming resistance to change. For example, in the diversity arena, there has been talk of a "white male backlash" (Galen and Palmer, 1994). Left out of favoured status programs, yet threatened by the same job insecurities as everyone else in an era of downsizing, white males may feel resentful of diversity initiatives. Similarly, single individuals may be denied access to special benefits for parents, at the same time that they may have to compensate for users by traveling more or working longer hours. For example, an American Airlines single, childless, flight attendant is not entitled to free travel for her grandmother, while other employees are entitled to free travel for spouses and children. These distinctions are perceived as unfair and create resentment among childless employees (Lafayette, 1994). In such cases, a concern for these equity issues can lead to programs and policies which encompass all kinds of diversity, including that of white males, and all kinds of work and personal lifestyles. When employees believe that the change will benefit everyone, their resistance will diminish.

Joan Kofodimos (1993; 1995) has detailed the aspects of organizational culture which promote overinvestment on work at the expense of one's personal life, and which will have to be modified in the process of culture change. Over-investment in work is reinforced in cultures which reward people for behaviors like the following: having a heavy, stressful workload; working long hours; traveling to and from work destinations on weekends; putting work ahead of other commitments; and working at home after work hours. Indeed, Schor (1991) suggests that there has been a dramatic increase in the number of hours Americans work over the past two decades. Americans across all income groups are working one month longer per year now than they did in 1969. Widespread downsizing in many American corporations, along with increased global competition, are contributing factors, as those who manage to keep their jobs may be expected to do the work of those who were laid off. Interestingly, a marketing research firm reported that one in five American workers with paid vacation benefits does not take all of the time he or she is allotted (*Wall Street Journal*, 1994b). The major reason given is that they are too busy at work to get away. These data indicate that the kind of culture that encourages workers to dedicate themselves to work at the expense of other aspects of life is fairly common. Meanwhile, employees are discovering that there simply are not enough hours in the day to excel in work and home life. This idea has been wittily captured in a bumper sticker that proclaims "I'd rather be dead than excellent."

The workaholic individual may have no obvious conflict between work and other aspects of life; he or she lives to work (Kofodimos, 1995; Lobel, 1991). The individual's health and well-being may suffer, although the organization may appear to benefit from his or her dedication. Such individuals are not typically viewed as needing "family friendly" benefits, because they do not. Such benefits are generally designed to solve problems that lead to productivity loss, rather than those that lead to costs for employees' well-being and rounded development (Kofodimos, 1995). Indeed, the one-dimensional workaholic may be seen as a productive and virtuous role model, relative to the individual who, voluntarily or not, attends to concerns outside of work. None the less, even workaholics may lose their jobs in times of economic insecurity; and they may be less able to cope with such disappointments in constructive ways. When the negative personal and organizational consequences of workaholism are understood, there will be incentives to identify "heroes" of the new culture who exemplify a more balanced existence. These important ethical issues deserve attention.

Business trends and their impact on work and personal life

Planners and policy-makers need to anticipate the impact of business trends, such as the movement toward a world economy, on their organizations' competitiveness. We believe that this analysis should include consideration of the effects of major business trends on employees' work and personal life styles. We explore below the potential impacts of globalization and increased technology on work and personal life. We will also describe the links we perceive between the increasing emphasis on teamwork and quality on the one hand, and work/personal life and diversity initiatives on the other.

The changing nature of work: globalization   Globalization brings special challenges to organizations, for the management of both diversity and work/personal life issues. Globalization requires skill in effective communication with people from other countries and cultures. If an individual cannot value diversity among co-workers, it will be most challenging to value it among customers, whose satisfaction one is trying to achieve. The impact of globalization on HR practices has received attention from practitioners and scholars (e.g. Dowling and Schuler, 1990), although its impact on work/personal life issues has been largely unexplored, except in the context of expatriate relocation and the role of the spouse and family in the adaptation process (Lawson and Angle, 1994).

Globalization means an expansion of the time and space in which business is done. Business activity can go on around the clock, every day of the year, requiring that employees make themselves available to internal and external customers at all times (Dowling and Schuler, 1990). Thus, the incursion of work life into personal life is even further enhanced by the schedule demands of global activity. In addition, employees may be expected to travel more frequently and relocate to foreign settings.

On the one hand, programs can be designed to help employees cope with and adapt to these new stressors associated with globalization. Relocation of members of the employee's family, as defined by the employee, and stress management and family counseling programs to cope with increased travel and adaptation demands are examples of this approach. On the other hand, organizational practices can cause changes in the job requirements themselves so that employees do not have to continually adapt or assimilate to difficult situations. For example, more investment in the development of local workforce talent and experience can reduce dependence on relocation and travel by home country personnel (Lobel et al., 1994).

The changing nature of work: new technologies   As with globalization, advances in technology mean an expansion in the time and space when work can be performed. People can work at home, while flying from one destination to another, or at odd hours. Therefore, the incursion of work life into personal life can be enhanced by the additional flexibility in how and when work is performed, which is a byproduct of technological advances. Again, organizational practices can help the employee assimilate to the more difficult circumstances associated with advances in technology. For example, organizational resources can be liberally allocated for technology purchases and support outside of the workplace, and the impact on people's careers of taking advantage of alternate work arrangements can be monitored to make sure that they are being rewarded, rather than penalized, for using these options. Organizational practices can also spare employees from having to adapt or assimilate to increasingly blurred lines between personal and work life, brought on by advances in technology. For example, training for technology can include guidelines to prevent abuse or overuse. Individuals can be encouraged to set, and make others aware of, personal limits on incursions into nonwork life due to technology, without penalties for doing so (Lobel et al., 1994).

Linking work schedule flexibility to the Clean Air Act

The Clean Air Act requires employers in metropolitan areas with poor air quality to implement plans that reduce the use of cars during peak commuting periods. Some of the affected cities and surrounding areas include: New York/New Jersey/Connecticut, Philadelphia/Wilmington, Baltimore, Chicago, Houston, Los Angeles, and San Diego. Each affected employer must bring its "average passenger occupancy" (APO) ratio in line with the target APO ratio level determined for their state. The APO ratio is the total number of employees who are scheduled to report to work during peak commuting times divided by the total number of passenger vehicles (Kwasha Lipton, 1994). An employer's APO may be altered in some states to reflect credit for the effects of policies implemented to reduce employee commuting during peak times. Thus, the Clean Air laws provide an additional incentive to implement flexible schedules as part of a firm's overall HR strategy to increase workplace flexibility.

Although the staff that deal with work/personal life issues and those focused on responding to the Clean Air laws probably are from different parts of a firm, employers might set up a Clean Air task force, which includes participants from both staffs. The task force ought to survey employee commuting patterns. The survey would assess the extent of control employees perceive over their work hours, employees' satisfaction with their current schedules, and the level of employee willingness to participate in traffic-reducing options such as work-at-home, ride sharing, flextime, part-time work, vanpool, compressed work week, and mass transit (Kwasha Lipton, 1994).

Creating links with other business efforts: teamwork and quality

Along with globalization and technological change, fostering teamwork and quality are examples of practices that have been widely accepted as important to effective organizational functioning in today's economy. Links to these efforts need to be made by champions of work/personal life and diversity initiatives. For example, in advising how to prepare for an organizational change to self-management, Manz et al. (1990) describe several themes that are equally relevant to the organizational change for flexibility that is necessary for work/personal life and diversity management. The authors note that managers initially tend to display suspicion, uncertainty, and resistance toward the new work design. Biases regarding the ability of workers to manage themselves overlap with biases about "appropriate" work and personal lifestyles. Interestingly in the Families and Work Institute survey (1994), the major resistance to work/life issues was related to implementation – concerns about how the work will get done and how much it will cost. Clearly, linkages to teambuilding and quality can help alleviate some of these concerns. Thus, it becomes the team's business to problem-solve, not the manager's.

The change in attitude towards acceptance involves taking on new management roles, i.e acting as a facilitator of self-management, and learning the new behaviors and language to support this role. Similarly, flexibility means that more workers will be performing their jobs with less direct supervision and with less standardization of the way the work is done, thereby requiring the same process of acceptance and trust-building that is necessary for self-managed teams. Thus change efforts ought to integrate examples relevant to diversity, flexibility, and teambuilding. Quality management also requires that the manager take on the role of coach, rather than leader, and that the work process be viewed as changeable, rather than fixed. In a study examining links between work/life and quality initiatives, a Motorola manager remarked: "To get high quality, you need to be sensitive to the personal needs that employees have. There should not be a division between personal needs and what is going on at work" (Cutcher-Gershenfeld et al., 1994).

Conclusion

We have described the move towards a broader definition of family, which will better recognize the multiple types and degree of obligations to important others. At the same time, we have indicated that broader definitions of family are not enough; we need to change our focus from work/family to work/personal life. In so doing, we acknowledge that every individual needs to manage the relationship between personal life and work life. We have indicated the importance of integrating work/personal life and diversity efforts with each other, and with other organizational efforts, such as globalization, technology acquisition and change, and total quality management. We have detailed some of the concrete ways decision-makers can achieve integration, and by implication, longer-lasting, more effective interventions.

The nature of work is changing: jobs are less stable; workday hours are no longer fixed; organizations are flattening; and small companies with knowledge workers are becoming the norm. Work/life programs will need to be tailored to these dynamic conditions. The limits of corporate responsibility need to be debated. The long-term effects of recent changes in family structure, such as the increase in never-married adults over the last two decades (Kalish, 1994), have yet to be discussed. These matters present significant challenges for the future.

According to one manager:

> The optimal situation is that neither work/family nor diversity would need any designated resources. The work–family and diversity managers would integrate the two initiatives so much into the culture that they would become a way of life and those manager roles would no longer be necessary. In effect, like HR in general, if their jobs are done well, they'll eventually be out of a job. Ideally, each person in the company would automatically consider

flexibility, diversity, etc. Policy people wouldn't need to consult with a work/family or diversity manager because they'd automatically take work/family and diversity needs into account. (Families and Work Institute, 1994)

We believe that work/personal life and diversity management are not fads; rather they reflect the inevitable current and future flux in workforce demographics, attitudes, and needs and in organizational responsiveness and vitality. Although there are no easy answers for implementing work/personal life and diversity programs in a manner that promotes true culture change, we are optimistic that a growing number of organizations will achieve this vision.

NOTE

1 Interestingly, the term "mommy track" arose in the legal field and first applied to women who were considered part-time lawyers, even though they were working 35 to 40 hour weeks (Kingson, 1988).

REFERENCES

Ahlburg, D. A., and DeVita, C. J. (1992). New realities of the American family. *Population Bulletin*, 47(2): 5.

Boldt, M. A., and Dellman-Jenkins, M. (1992). The impact of companion animals in later life and considerations for practice. *Journal of Applied Gerontology*, 11(2), 228–39.

Bontempo, R., Lobel, S. A., and Triandis, H. C. (1990). Compliance and value internalization in Brazil and the U.S. *Journal of Cross-Cultural Psychology*, 21(2), 200–13.

Burden, D. S., and Googins, B. K. (1987). *Balancing Job and Homelife Study: Managing Work and Family Stress in Corporations*. Boston: Boston University School of Social Work.

Center on Work and Family (1994). *Annual Report*. Boston: Boston University, Center on Work and Family.

Christensen, P. (1994). Toward a comprehensive work–family program. Paper presented at the Drexel University Fifth Annual Stein Conference, Philadelphia, PA, November.

Couter, A. C. (1984). Spillover from family to work: The neglected side of the work–family interface. *Human Relations*, 37, 425–42.

Cox, T. (1991). The multicultural organization. *The Executive*, 5(1), 34–47.

Cox, T., Lobel, S. A., and McLeod, P. L. (1991). Ethnic diversity and cooperative behavior in small groups. *Academy of Management Journal*, 34(4), 827–47.

Cutcher-Gershenfeld, J., Kossek, E., and Sandling, H. (1994). People as a root cause. Unpublished manuscript. Michigan State University, School of Labor and Industrial Relations, East Lansing.

Deck, C. (1993). Firms begin to reach out to staffs. *Detroit Free Press*, April 19, P, 10F.

Deutsch, C. H. (1990). Why women walk out on jobs. *New York Times*, April 29.

Dowling, P. J., and Schuler, R. S. (1990). *International Dimensions of Human Resource Management*. Boston: PWS-Kent.

Families and Work Institute (1994). To link or not to link: The relationship between corporate work–family and diversity initiatives. Paper presented at the Conference on Linking Work–Family and Diversity Issues, New York.

Friedman, D. (1990). *Update on Employer-sponsored Child Care*. New York: Families and Work Institute.

Friedman, D. E., and Galinsky, E. (1992). Work and family issues: A legitimate business concern. In S. Zedeck (ed.), *Work, Families and Organizations* (168–207). San Francisco: Jossey-Bass.

Galen, M., and Palmer, A. (1994). White male and worried. *Business Week*, January 31, 50–5.

Galinsky, E. (1988). Child care and productivity. Unpublished manuscript. Child Care Action Campaign, New York.

Galinsky, E., Friedman, D., and Hernandez, C. (1991). *The Corporate Reference Guide to Work–Family Programs*. New York: Families and Work Institute.

Grover, S. (1991). Predicting the perceived fairness of parental leave policies. *Journal of Applied Psychology*, 76, 247–55.

Gwartney-Gibbs, P. (1988). Women's experience and the rusty skills hypothesis: A reconceptualization and re-evaluation of the evidence. In B. A. Gutek, A. H. Stromberg, and L. Larwood (eds), *Women and Work: An Annual Review*, vol. 3. Newbury Park, CA: Sage.

Hacket, S., and Jackson, J. (1993). African American extended kin systems. In H. McAdoo (ed.), *Family Ethnicity* (90–108). Newbury Park: Sage.

Hall, D. T., and Parker, V. A. (1993). The role of workplace flexibility in managing diversity. *Organizational Dynamics*, Summer, 5–18.

Hoffman, R. (1991). Companion animals: A therapeutic measure for elderly patients. *Journal of Gerontological Social Work*, 18(1–2), 195–205.

Hofstede, G. (1980). *Culture's Consequences*. Beverly Hills, CA: Sage.

Kalish, S. (1994). Fewer and fewer "traditional" U.S. households. *Population Today*, 22(11), 3.

Kingson, J. (1988). Women in the law say path is limited by "Mommy Track." *New York Times*, August 8, A1, A15.

Kofodimos, J. (1993). *Balancing Act: How Managers Can Integrate Successful Careers and Fulfilling Personal Lives*. San Francisco: Jossey Bass.

Kofodimos, J. (1995). *Beyond Work–Family Programs: Confronting and Resolving the Underlying Causes of Work/Personal Life Conflict*. Greensboro, NC: Center for Creative Leadership.

Kossek, E. E. (1990). Diversity in child care assistance needs: Problems, preferences, and work-related outcomes. *Personnel Psychology*, 43, 768–91.

Kossek, E. E., Barber, A., and Winters, D. (1993). An assessment of individual, work group and organizational influences on the acceptance of flexible work schedules. *Best Paper Proceedings* (116–20). Atlanta: Academy of Management.

Kossek, E. E., DeMarr, B., Backman, K., and Kollar, M. (1993). Assessing employees' emerging elder care needs and reactions to dependent care benefits. *Public Personnel Management Journal*, 22, Winter, 617–38.

Kwasha Lipton (1994). *Kwasha Lipton Executive Summary*. Fort Lee, NJ: Employee Benefits Consultants.

Lafayette, L. (1994). Fair play for the childless worker. *New York Times*, October 16, F11.

Lawson, M. B., and Angle, H. L. (1994). When organizational relocation means family relocation: An emerging issue for strategic human resource management. *Human Resource Management*, 33(1), 33–54.

Lewis, S. N., and Cooper, C. L. (1988). Stress in dual-earner couples. In B. A. Gutek, A. H. Stromberg, and L. Larwood (eds), *Women and Work: An Annual Review*, vol. 3. Newbury Park, CA: Sage.

Lobel, S. A. (1991). Allocation of investment in work and family roles: Alternative theories and implications for research. *Academy of Management Review*, 16(3), 507–21.

Lobel, S. A. (1992). A value-laden approach to integrating work and family life. Special issue on work and family. *Human Resource Management*, 31(3), 249–65.

Lobel, S. A., Googins, B., and Bankert, E. (1994). Work–family initiatives: Visioning the future. Paper presented at the Drexel University 5th Annual Stein Conference, Philadelphia, PA.

Manz, C. C., Keating, D. E., and Donnellon, A. (1990). Preparing for an organizational change to self-management: The managerial transition. *Organizational Dynamics*, 19(2), Fall, 15–26.

Mead, M. (1967). *Cooperation and Competition Among Primitive People*. Boston: Beacon. National Commission on Working Women (1990). *Women and Work*. Washington, DC: National Commission on Working Women.

Naylor, R. (1994). Mag picks working-mom friendly companies. *Lansing State Journal*, September, 21, C1.

Rosen, R. (1991). *The Healthy Company: Eight Strategies to Develop People, Productivity and Profits*. New York: Jeremy P. Tarcher/Pedigree Books.

Schor, J. (1991). *The Overworked American*. New York: Basic Books.

Schwartz, D. (1994). *An Examination of the Impact of Family-friendly Policies*. New York: Families and Work Institute.

Schwartz, F. (1989). Management women and the new facts of life. *Harvard Business Review*, 67(1), 65–76.

Sharpe, R. (1994a). Family friendly firms don't always promote females. *Wall Street Journal*, March 29, B1, B12.

Sharpe, R. (1994b). Bones of contention: When a marriage goes to the dogs. *Wall Street Journal*, August 8, A1, A4.

Shellenbarger, S. (1993a). Leave measure imposes broad notion of family. *Wall Street Journal*, February 10, B1.

Shellenbarger, S. (1993b). Executive women make major gains in pay and status. *Wall Street Journal*, June 30, A3.

Siegel, J. (1990). Stressful life events and use of physician services among the elderly: The moderating role of pet ownership. *Journal of Personality and Social Psychology*, 58, 1081–6.

Sorge, R. (1989). Gay couples defined as "family." *Gay Community News*, July 16.

Stone, R., Cafferata, G. L., and Sangl, J. (1987). Caregivers of the frail elderly: A national profile. *The Gerontologist*, 27(5), 616–26.

Triandis, H. C., Bontempo, R., Villareal, M. J., Asai, M., and Lucca, N. (1988). Individualism and collectivism: Cross-cultural perspectives on self–ingroup relationships. *Journal of Personality and Social Psychology*, 54(2), 323–38.

Triandis, H. C., Marin, G., Betancourt, H., Lisansky, J., and Chang, B. (1982). *Dimensions of Familism and Hispanic and Mainstream Navy Recruits*. Technical Report No. 14, Champaign, IL: Department of Psychology, University of Illinois.

Trost, C. (1990). Women managers quit not for family but to advance their corporate climb. *Wall Street Journal*, May 2, B1.

Wall Street Journal (1994a). Labor letter, August 23, A1.

Wall Street Journal (1994b). People patterns, September 23, B1.

10

Unions, Collective Bargaining, and the Diversity Paradox

John T. Delaney and M. Catherine Lundy

In recent years, many organizations have attempted to create work environments that foster diversity. The efforts occur because of projections indicating that women, minorities, and immigrants will comprise a large majority of new workers in coming years (Johnston and Packer, 1987). Diversity initiatives have not always been successful, however, and some have created considerable controversy (Carton, 1994). Such controversy is not surprising, given the amount of confusion across and within organizations about exactly what an emphasis on diversity entails. In some organizations, for example, the notion of diversity may be derided as a new name for affirmative action or even as political correctness run amok (see Kossek and Zonia, 1993). For diversity efforts to succeed, organization leaders must clearly define the concept of diversity and describe the purpose of diversity initiatives. As unions have important but seldom-studied incentives to address diversity, their diversity efforts may provide insight to managers contemplating the adoption of programs designed to deal with multicultural issues.

As organizational success becomes increasingly dependent on successful interactions among a more heterogeneous workforce, it is likely that diversity initiatives will be perceived as more important by organizational leaders. In fact, for diversity to matter, it must come to exist at the center of the culture that runs an organization: the relationship between men and women, whites, blacks and others, supervisors and subordinates, unions and managers. Differences must be respected if individuals are to strive for a common

We are grateful to Richard N. Block, Dale Brickner, Ellen Kossek, Sharon Lobel, and Susan Schwochau for helpful comments on an earlier version of this chapter.

organizational purpose. There must be some toleration and acceptance of employees' sexual orientation, disability status, and political views. Diversity involves broadening the definition of organizational culture so that family life is a direct concern of management policy. It means overcoming organizational hierarchies so that there is room for younger and nontraditional workers. It means providing ways for habitually confrontational managers to interact differently (Katz, 1994, p. 23). Diversity challenges traditional management thinking. Diversity is also a major challenge for unions, which have economic and political incentives for finding ways of successfully dealing with an increasingly heterogeneous labor force. More importantly, both employers and (to a greater extent) unions face the dilemma that efforts to accommodate the diversity of potential organization members may cause conflict among current members. As a result, examination of how unions address diversity may provide important information to managers.

The diversity challenge is somewhat different for unionized organizations than for nonunion ones because there is evidence that unionized workplaces are managed differently and collective bargaining encroaches on management's prerogatives (Freeman and Medoff, 1984). Paradoxically, some features of unions and bargaining promote diversity and others hinder it. For example, virtually all union contracts provide guarantees against unfair treatment at work — an outcome that should promote diversity by reducing the opportunity for favoritism. At the same time, unions often negotiate uniform contract requirements for all workers — a result that may make it difficult to deal with the unique needs of individual employees. Understanding the paradox of the nature of unions and the basis of bargaining outcomes, however, may suggest inferences about the management of diversity that would not arise from a study of business organizations.

In this chapter, after outlining specific organizational approaches relevant to diversity, we assess the extent to which unions and collective bargaining enhance or diminish those approaches. Specifically, we examine the nature of unions and aspects of unionism, such as the composition of union leadership ranks, that are relevant in a discussion of diversity. Then we examine general patterns in bargaining outcomes covering diversity-related subjects, as well as examples of provisions that occur in specific contracts. After these assessments, we discuss the implications of the findings for circumstances today and in the future. To save space, we use the term "nontraditional employee" to represent women and members of racial and ethnic minorities — individuals who were not always viewed as important organization members in the past.

Features of an Organizational Diversity Program

Although there exists no single "best method" for fostering diversity in organizations, it is possible to identify some areas of organizational policy that will influence diversity more than others. In that regard, we focus on four diversity policy areas and their implications, recognizing that these areas are not exclusive and admitting that other perspectives on the areas will exist. We also recognize that the environment faced by an organization probably magnifies or reduces the effectiveness of specific policies. Our policy areas were the product of an effort to answer the following question in a parsimonious manner: What are the principal things that any organization must do to create a working culture that is favorable to a wide variety of people?

First, it is clear that there must be equal treatment in hiring. There must be an equal probability of selecting an individual regardless of his or her individual characteristics and preferences (assuming that qualifications are held constant). An organization cannot promote diversity if it selectively screens out people who do not fit some predetermined mold.

Second, there must be equal opportunities for advancement. There must be a consistent application of whatever specific standard for organizational advancement is normally used. One aspect of this is the notion that employees need to have equal access to training, mentoring, and development activities that are requirements for advancement. In addition, information on advancement opportunities must be regularly available to all employees.

Third, employees should be permitted some latitude for expressing their individuality. Although this does not preclude organizations from adopting certain standards of dress, appearance, or demeanor, the standards should not be arbitrarily based on a singular cultural perspective. For example, policies concerning the growth of facial hair or display of religious preferences (e.g. wearing a yarmulke or a turban) need to be well thought out and consistent. Clearly, organizations can and should impose reasonable limits on expressions of individuality that impede effective operation, but overly strict, inconsistent, or arbitrary limits may create diversity problems.

Fourth, organizations need to recognize employees' responsibilities in their "nonwork" life. The increase in the number of families headed by a single person (often a woman) and the longer hours worked by employees today (Schor, 1991), indicate that nonwork issues take up a greater portion of employees' time today than they did in the past. In the late twentieth century, diversity may turn out to be nothing more than a slogan in organizations that maintain the view that employees' work always takes precedence over other activities and life events.

In turn, these four areas and their interrelation give rise to the notion that diversity must be viewed as a process rather than as an outcome or set of goals. This reflects the fact that an organization's culture will not be changed by retrofitting a series of diversity goals. In such cases, diversity programs will likely be viewed by organization members in pejorative terms – as "quota systems" or "affirmative action programs." All organizations have a political process and nontraditional employees will have limited opportunities if they are denied access to that process or receive insufficient training or mentoring in the means of developing political power and status (see Ferris et al., 1993). Thus, diversity policies, however well-meaning, will be less successful or unsuccessful in organizations that ignore the need to alter the prevailing culture and its inertia. And this notion should not be lost in an assessment of the manner in which unions and bargaining affect diversity.

Unions are complex organizations that perform internal and external functions and adopt structures to perform each function effectively. Internally, unions are political organizations that respond to the democratically-expressed wishes of members. Externally, unions are bargaining organizations that structure their activities to enhance the outcomes of negotiation. For example, unions that bargain with many local employers (such as grocery stores or school districts) adopt different bargaining structures than unions that bargain with employers at the national level (such as the auto industry). As a result, external union structures vary more than internal union structures and environmental forces (such as markets and employer reactions to bargaining) influence bargaining more than internal union activities (Wallihan, 1985). Moreover, because diversity influences and is influenced by internal and external union functions, we examine both union- and bargaining-related responses to diversity.

Union Internal Functions and the Promotion of Diversity

Unions have long relied on the fact that workers in the same employment setting have common interests. Historically, those interests have been used to build solidarity among a group of workers. But solidarity is often unattainable if the union does not recognize and respect workers' differences. A common product of this reality is the existence in many unions of specialized departments or councils for skilled workers, women, minority-group members, and members of other constituencies. As most unions have expanded their organizing jurisdictions over the past several decades (Seeber, 1984), organized labor has been compelled to develop ways of effectively addressing workers' differences.

Given that union membership as a percentage of the nonagricultural workforce has declined since the 1950s, there is room for skepticism about the effectiveness of labor's efforts to recognize diversity or the extent to which union experiences transfer to nonunion organizations. Although these concerns are legitimate, we believe that there are strong reasons why union diversity efforts may have general applications. First, like all organizations, unions face market and social forces that encourage attention to diversity. Success in organizing will suffer if unions ignore the changing composition of the labor force. As voluntary organizations, unions must understand the needs of the nontraditional workers who comprise a growing segment of the workforce. Second, the union movement historically was organized by immigrants and has dealt with diversity since its inception. "Unions in the steel, meat packing, garment, clothing, and other industries often translated union organizing literature into ten or twelve languages and had coordinating councils representing each ethnic group" (Cornell University, 1994, p. 18).

Although the immigrant population today is primarily Asian and Hispanic, organized labor's historical approach to organizing immigrants is still relevant. Third, unlike business organizations (and many others), unions operate as democracies. The politics of unions may therefore create an additional incentive to address diversity concerns. That is, union leaders must convince current union members, who vote for union leaders and affect union policies, that efforts to foster diversity are critical to future organizing success. This additional incentive may make unions more attentive than other organizations to diversity questions and it may force unions to adopt more tangible and consistent practices regarding diversity. Because it is an empirical question whether or not unions enhance employers' ability to promote diversity, we examine approaches used by unions that address workplace diversity to assess their effectiveness and transferability to the nonunion sector.

It is important to recognize that certain features and historical circumstances of unions combine to create a diversity paradox. On the one hand, as political institutions, unions gain members and strength in proportion to their ability to serve the needs of the rank and file. The experience of the Industrial Workers of the World (IWW) "demonstrated that America's growing industrial working class, its immigrants, and dispossessed could be organized despite ethnic divisions and immense corporate power. Barriers of race and nationality disappeared in IWW strikes" (Filippelli, 1984, p. 119). Similarly, the explosive growth of the Congress of Industrial Organizations (CIO) in the 1930s illustrated to union leaders that diverse workers can band together and stand united in the face of strong employer pressure. Diversity does not preclude solidarity. In essence, the broad concept of diversity that we endorsed above resembles the nature of the diversity questions facing unions: recognition of occupational as well as individual differences; concern that traditional management practices give little respect to workers on or off the job (e.g. in the 1930s, it was the drive system; see Jacoby, 1984); and desire for fair and consistent treatment. Moreover, because these questions arise from members, union leaders must pay attention to them or risk being voted out of office.

Ironically, the political nature of unions could also hamper diversity efforts. In some instances, the wishes of a majority of members may create barriers to diversity. In response to potential tyranny of the majority, a duty of fair representation was developed by labor tribunals to interpret the Railway Labor Act (RLA) and the National Labor Relations Act (NLRA). The doctrine holds that a union having exclusive recognition must represent all workers in a bargaining unit, members and nonmembers alike, in a fair and impartial manner (Repas, 1984, p. 153). That diversity issues are critically linked with the doctrine is reflected in the fact that the first duty of fair representation cases involved racial discrimination. For example, in the first case, black workers in the railroad industry charged their union with discrimination for negotiating a contract designed to eliminate all blacks from jobs as firemen (*Steele v. Louisville & Nashville R.R.* 321 U.S. 332 [1944]). Historically, groups that are different (e.g. immigrants, blacks, women, gays) have been viewed as a threat to opportunities for the politically-dominant union group. Application of duty of fair representation standards by tribunals has served as a deterrent to explicit discriminatory treatment by union leaders or majority groups within a union.

It is possible, however, that subtle forces still hinder diversity in unions. Democratic structures give union members an opportunity to elect leaders. Given that senior members are most likely to be selected as leaders and that senior members of most unions are white males, it is possible that the gap between members and leaders increases as diversity in the workplace increases through the hiring of nontraditional workers. Moreover, when faced with competing groups within the union, well-meaning leaders from the dominant group – which is often white men – may opt for policies that treat workers equally on their face but in fact discourage diversity (e.g. separate but equal). For example, seniority systems that require workers to give up their seniority when they transfer to a different plant, unit, or department can cause segregation within an organization simply because hiring opportunities existed in certain units at certain times. In combination with pressure for fair treatment coming from divergent groups, this can encourage occupational segregation. That is, because fair treatment is likely more difficult to provide if nontraditional workers are integrated across occupations (where seniority rules are disadvantageous to nontraditional workers) than if they are slotted into specific jobs (where seniority rules may be accepted as fair by all), organizations, including unions, may accept segregation as a necessary evil.

Because features of unions both promote and hinder diversity, it is necessary to focus on union action and practice. This conclusion is also suggested by an examination of research on unions and diversity. Few studies have examined unions and diversity from a general perspective (see Jones, 1993). There exists, however, an extensive literature that focuses on specific topics relevant to the concept of diversity. For example, much research has concentrated on discrimination, occupational segregation, pay equity, immigration, gender and racial issues at work, and workplace fairness (see Briskin and McDermott, 1993; Cobble, 1993; Tomaskovic-Devey, 1993; Lewin, 1991; Trebilcock, 1991; Hoyman and Stallworth, 1987; Cain, 1986). Despite the relevance of many of these studies, the sheer volume of research and conflicting conclusions preclude a concise summary here. Instead, to assess whether the theoretical forces promoting diversity in unions outweigh the forces hampering diversity, we provide evidence on the extent of diversity in the union movement and assess selected diversity issues.

The extent of diversity in unions

Membership diversity To assess the applicability of organized labor's diversity lessons, it is helpful to know just how diverse the union movement is. To that end, the Bureau of Labor Statistics (US Department of Labor, 1994) reported that there were about 16.6 million union members in the US in 1993. These individuals comprised 15.8 percent of the nonagricultural

Table 10.1 Selected characteristics of male and female union members

Selected characteristics	Women (%)	Men (%)
Occupation	100	100
Administrative support	27	9
Blue collar	18	59
Professional and technical	39	18
Sales	5	3
Service	11	11
Industry	100	100
Mining and construction	0	12
Manufacturing	17	34
Utilities	12	18
Finance and trade	8	10
Service	53	16
Public administration	9	10
Firm size	100	100
Less than 25 employees	3	6
Between 25 and 100 employees	8	10
More than 100 employees	89	84
Education level	100	100
Less than high school	12	17
High school diploma	33	44
Some college	22	24
College degree	32	15

Data are for 1987.
Source: Institute for Women's Policy Research (1994)

labor force. The data show that men are more likely than women to belong to unions: about 18 percent of men compared to 13 percent of women. Differences in membership rates also existed by ethnicity. Union membership rates were virtually equal (at about 15 percent) for white and Hispanic workers, but were considerably higher (21 percent) for black workers.

An examination of BLS time-series data indicates that membership rates for both men and women were lower in 1993 than they were in 1983.[1] Women's membership rates seemed to bottom out in 1987 and began to increase in 1992, while men's rates continued to decline. Within the unionized sector, after 1983 the percentage of white male union members fell considerably and the percentage of female members increased. By 1993, women constituted nearly 40 percent of organized labor's membership. This total represented the highest percentage of female trade unionists in the history of organized labor in the US. Over the years 1983–93, the ethnic composition of union membership remained fairly steady (the percentage of total union members who were black or Hispanic stayed relatively constant). As a result, because of the increase in unionized women, diversity among union members has increased since 1983.

Although much of the research on unions focuses on men, the face of unionism is changing. As table 10.1 shows, unionized men and women tend to be employed in different occupations and industries, and they tend to have different educational backgrounds. Female members, who have more education than their male counterparts, tend to hold white collar jobs in service industries, such as teaching, nursing, and public administration. The growth in unionization among women represents a shift from blue collar to white collar jobs, from manufacturing to service industries, and from high school to college educated members (Institute for Women's Policy Research, 1994).

In addition, general trends in the economy and society suggest that diversity in unions will grow in coming years. The Wilson Center for Public Research (1992) reported that women workers' (both unionized and non-union) union-approval ratings increased by nearly 50 percent from 1980 to 1990. Based on this evidence of growing pro-union sentiment and other information gathered in interviews with more than 95,000 workers, the Wilson Center (1992, p. 21) concluded that women were "becoming significantly more receptive to union representation." According to Eaton (1993, p. 172), "two out of every three new union members is a woman, suggesting that future union membership could be majority female." Similarly, it has been predicted that "women are likely to be heavily represented in those unions most likely to grow in the near future" (Labor Research Association, 1993, p. 38).

Although the BLS statistics show that diversity has increased in the union movement in recent years, the data do not permit identification of the cause of the increased diversity. That is, because unions often have little input into the organizational hiring process, the data may reflect any or all of three factors. First, unions have organized jobs that are becoming increasingly female and nonwhite. Second, union organizing drives now are targeting different occupations, such as service and white collar jobs — jobs that traditionally include more women and minorities. Third, the trends in the data are purely a reflection of changes in the composition of the labor force and are not the result of specific union tactics. Accordingly, it is necessary to examine other information to explain why diversity has increased in unions.

Union leadership diversity If unions have explicitly attempted to organize a diverse membership, they may also have made efforts to create a diverse leadership. Currently, however, the patterns of diversity at the highest ranks of unions are similar to patterns found in business organizations and government. Although female union membership rates have increased dramatically, as overall union membership as a percentage of the workforce has declined, women are still disproportionately underrepresented in top-level union leadership positions. For example, a 1979 survey indicated "that only 8 percent, or 1 in 12, union leaders were female" (Eaton, 1993, p. 172). By 1990, women comprised about 11 percent of leaders among all unions and about 9 percent of leaders of AFL-CIO-affiliated unions (Gray, 1993, p. 379). Although the trends suggest at best a small increase in the number of female union leaders, women have achieved top jobs in teachers' and nurses' unions – which are dominated by women – and have secured national union elective office in some public sector unions. Women have been less successful achieving leadership roles in industrial unions, and virtually unsuccessful in traditional craft unions (Eaton, 1992, p. 40). At the same time, the demographic composition of individuals holding lower-level union offices has changed. According to Shostak (1991, p. 90) the extent to which women held lower-level union offices and staff positions doubled from 1980 to 1985 (to 32 percent), raising the possibility that large future increases will occur in the proportion of top-level union leaders who are women (1991, p. 90).

Members of minority groups are also underrepresented in the top offices of unions. As Clark and Gray (1991, p. 176) noted, "almost all national union presidents are white males." Even today, only a handful of top union leaders are black or Hispanic. It is not possible to tell whether this is the product of discrimination, job segregation, or the fact that senior union members (from whose ranks leaders emerge) tend to be white men. More importantly, regardless of whether the racial composition of union leaders changes over time, the ability of those leaders to address the concerns of an increasingly diverse membership will critically affect the future of the labor movement. At the same time, the existence of democratic structures in unions will likely cause the leadership ranks to become more diverse as a more diverse group of senior members emerges. In short, although the stage may be set for an increase in union leadership diversity, such diversity does not yet exist. It cannot be ruled out that existing union diversity is simply the product of changing labor force conditions.

More importantly, rapid changes in the labor force in recent years have effectively created more diversity in the union movement than existed before and unions have found it very difficult to unify and engage their diverse memberships (Cornell University, 1994, p. 18). As a result, unions have been looking to identify more effective ways to organize and represent these workers. Some methods involve alliances with other groups, such as the women's movement or community groups. Unions have also adopted a wide variety of internal programs to ensure that diversity-related issues are addressed. A key element of these is education (Jones, 1993). Union education programs address diversity issues by stressing cultural awareness and by providing specific training to nontraditional workers to enhance their job and career opportunities.

The Auto Workers Union has one of the most developed programs on diversity; it offers educational and cultural awareness programs for women, nonwhites, and whites in order to help everyone understand the issue (UAW Women's Department, 1993). The approach reflects the philosophy that it is necessary to open the union movement up to all individuals if labor's diversity efforts are to succeed. The approach has also led to experimentation by many unions with specific diversity programs. For example, District 1199, which represents hospital and health care workers, has chosen to focus on adult education programs and teaching English to immigrant workers (*1199 News*, 1994). As District 1199 serves many nontraditional workers, these programs are designed to develop skills needed for promotion opportunities and for dealing with others. AFSCME, which represents public sector employees, has incorporated cultural diversity training into its ongoing programs for stewards, officers, and union leaders (Walker, 1994). The Machinists Union operates the IAM CARES Program, which supports initiatives aimed at women, disabled people, and minority workers. Both the Machinists and the IAM CARES Program provide diversity training (Micallef, 1994). Other diversity efforts have been undertaken by many unions, including the Office and Professional Employees; the Ladies Garment Workers; Communications Workers; Bakery, Confectionery, and Tobacco Workers; and the American Postal Workers. Although existing union diversity efforts vary greatly in size and nature, they represent one of the steps needed to institutionalize the diversity process in unions. And to understand that process better, it is necessary to examine potential union motivations for enhancing diversity and union actions (through bargaining) that directly affect diversity.

Unions, diversity, and outcomes

Before examining potential diversity outcomes achieved by unions, it is useful to identify forces that motivate unions to achieve those outcomes. We have noted that market forces affect firms and unions and that political forces in unions have potentially conflicting effects on diversity. We have not addressed the possibility that having a diverse membership influences union outcomes or requires new and different approaches to interactions with employers. Such effects could motivate unions to make more aggressive efforts to recruit a diverse membership.

Many of the arguments used to encourage organizations to appreciate diversity are predicated on the notion that organizational effectiveness is greater when organization members are more representative of the labor force. Few empirical tests of this notion exist, however, because of the difficulty in gathering appropriate data. As we have noted, the influence of diversity on union outcomes is unclear conceptually because of the contrasting potential effects of union politics. Although union leaders may recognize that diversity is critical to future success, current members may use the union's democratic political process to oppose diversity efforts. Further, although it may be more difficult to achieve solidarity in heterogeneous unions than it is in homogeneous unions, future union growth requires organizing and representing diverse workers.

Data from the National Union Survey (NUS; see Delaney, Fiorito, and Jarley, 1991) permit a crude assessment of the relationship between diversity and selected organizational outcome measures. Diversity is measured for each union in the NUS sample using a composite that accounts for female, nonwhite, and white collar membership, as well as the percentage of union members in a union's primary jurisdiction; the measure is constructed so that it increases in size as diversity in a union increases.[2] The diversity measure is positively associated with union officials' perceptions of overall union effectiveness ($r = .202$, $p < 0.10$, $n = 73$) and the extent to which a union uses innovative tactics ($r = .373$, $p < 0.01$, $n = 68$). It is possible that union effectiveness leads to a more diverse membership (perhaps through more effective organizing or bargaining) or that the extent of diversity stimulates innovations and effectiveness. Although the correlations should not be overinterpreted, they tend to support the idea that diversity in a union is an advantage. Moreover, results do not support the notion that homogeneous unions are more effective on these dimensions of effectiveness and innovation than are heterogeneous unions.

In a study focusing on women in unions, Eaton (1993) provided anecdotal evidence of factors that underlie the link between diversity and outcomes. She noted that, to show an appreciation of diversity, some unions negotiate nonsexist contract language, sponsor orientations for union staff members to help women succeed by addressing issues such as sexual harassment, male and female communication, mentoring, and family life. She concluded (p. 205) that a union's culture and diversity are critically related:

> The "culture" of a union is probably the single most powerful determinant of how people act within the organization. A union's culture is the pattern of behavior, signs, and symbols which articulate its values, what's important to its leaders, and what counts as success. Culture is evident in all the tangible and intangible elements which determine how the union "feels." It is reflected in the physical location, layout, and appearance of the office; in the language that is used daily and in public statements; and in the pictures that hang on the wall and the stories that are told to new hires, new members, or anyone who will listen. A union's culture can be open or closed, flexible or rigid, informal or formal, participatory or hierarchical, multiethnic or homogeneous, and supportive of women or "macho."

In combination, the empirical and anecdotal evidence suggests that there is a positive association between diversity and a variety of union outcomes. Although the causal order of the association is not clear, its existence indicates that successful unions must accept diversity. Moreover, as we argued earlier, the nature of an organization's culture critically affects diversity – a fact that can be illustrated by focusing on a subject such as pay equity.

Pay equity As Riccucci (1990, p. 141) noted, "wage differentials between female and male workers have not improved much within the past several decades. Today, women earn about 64 cents for every dollar earned by men." For this reason, unions and worker organizations are especially important to women and nonwhite workers, who earn lower average wages than white men. In recent decades, as women's labor force participation has increased and as a greater number of women have assumed financial responsibility for their families, concern about pay equity has also increased. In turn, women have become more willing to unionize (Wilson Center for Public Research, 1992) and unionized women have become more active in their unions (Shostak, 1991) – circumstances that have led to an increase in local leadership roles for women. Leadership positions provide women with an opportunity to shape working conditions and bargaining outcomes, as well as a chance to educate their co-workers about work and women's issues (see Roby and Uttal, 1993, p. 363).

The achievement of pay equity in or across organizations clearly promotes diversity by instituting a wage structure that is free from gender or racial bias. Concern about equal pay and comparable worth became very important in some occupations, as Alice Cook noted, because "by the late 1970s, many women's organizations realized that the long-established union demand for equal pay for equal work, in addition to its other inadequacies, did not apply to women's work in fields such as nursing, clerical occupations, child care, and much of the auxiliary health care, because there were few, if any, men in these occupations with whom women could claim equality" (Cook, 1993, p. 150). The notion of comparable worth, derived from the idea of equal pay for equally valued work, became a focal women's issue, albeit one that never received much support from business. Consequently, even landmark victories in US courts have not produced the pay equity outcomes that workers have sought (McCann, 1994).

Clearly, efforts by the women's movement, many unions, and other groups helped reduce the male–female pay gap during the 1980s (McCann, 1994). The efforts have not reduced job segregation and the potential wage disparities it creates. To the extent that a great majority of jobs are either male-dominated or female-dominated (using the criterion that a job is at least 80 percent male or 80 percent female), the idea of "comparable worth" has become important, especially in public sector occupations. Although union policies and bargaining outcomes can reduce occupational segregation and pay inequities within specific organizations, unionization cannot eliminate occupational segregation across society. Combined with business and societal resistance to comparable worth, this has ensured the continuation of gender pay disparities.

Although women's wages increased in real terms across the economy in recent years, falling real wages for men explain roughly three-fourths of the reduction in the male–female wage gap between 1979 and 1989. Moreover, from 1989 to 1991, women's median hourly wages fell faster than men's, increasing the wage gap again. In 1992, full-time median weekly earnings for women were $386, or 76 percent of the $508 median weekly earnings for men, an improvement over 1991's wage gap of 74.2 percent. During the 1989–93 period of recession and recovery, median hourly wages fell by 2.9 percent for blue collar women, and rose by 2.8 percent for white collar women. In the 1990s in the US, female college graduates earn roughly the same amount as white male *high school* graduates. Black women earn 62 percent of white male wages, and Hispanic women earn 54 percent. Women workers are paid less than men around the globe, but wage discrimination is worse in the US than in any other major industrialized country except Japan (Labor Research Association, 1993, p. 38).

There is evidence that union contracts have facilitated gains for workers who have traditionally suffered discrimination. For example, collective bargaining and union political action have been used by public sector unions to encourage pay equity. While there is evidence that the gender composition of a union and the current economic climate influence the tenacity with which pay equity is pursued, the labor movement has sought to promote equitable treatment of all workers. In 1981, the AFL-CIO adopted a resolution urging affiliated unions to: work through contract negotiations to upgrade undervalued job classifications, regardless of whether they are typically considered male or female jobs; initiate joint union-employer pay equity studies to identify and correct internal inequities between predominantly female and predominantly male classes; recognize fully their obligations to treat inequities resulting from sex discrimination like all other inequities that must be corrected; adopt the concept of equal pay for comparable work in contract negotiations (Riccucci, 1990, p. 158).

The persistence of problems such as pay inequity and discrimination indicates the difficulty of addressing societal difficulties using political and other means. Such problems also suggest that organizational attention to diversity will produce limited benefits until organizational problems disproportionately affecting nontraditional workers – such as pay inequity – are addressed in an open and fair way. Given that collective bargaining is the primary mechanism by which unions address workplace issues, including diversity issues, we turn to an examination of bargaining outcomes to assess labor's ability to deal directly with diversity issues.

Union External Functions and the Promotion of Diversity

Collective bargaining, diversity, and outcomes

It is well known that collective bargaining produces tangible benefits for workers represented by unions. Among other things, workers covered by bargaining enjoy better wages and benefits, and experience work environments that offer greater protection from inequitable managerial treatment than do similar nonunion workers (Freeman and Medoff, 1984). Unions are restrained to some extent in efforts to promote diversity, however, by the nature of bargaining. Essentially, bargaining is the product of an interaction between two parties. No matter how much one of the parties wants a particular outcome, there is no guarantee that it can be achieved over the objections of the other party. Thus, unions and employers are constrained by each other in their ability to negotiate bargaining outcomes covering diversity issues. This situation is compounded by requirements of US law. First, parties to collective bargaining must negotiate over mandatory bargaining subjects – those issues involving wages, hours, and other terms and conditions of employment. Except for a few subjects that are specifically prohibited by law (e.g. closed shop provisions, which require employers to hire only union members), all other subjects are permissive, meaning that either an employer or a union can refuse to bargain about them and an impasse is not legally permitted if such a refusal occurs. To the extent that diversity-related issues, such as recognition of responsibilities outside of work or issues concerning domestic partners, are permissive bargaining subjects, they will be included in contracts only where both parties desire them.

Second, law affects bargaining outcomes in other ways too. In situations where the legal system directly addresses diversity issues, it may not be as important for union contracts to include provisions covering those issues. For example, because the Family and Medical Leave Act provides limited protection to the job rights of covered employees who desire an unpaid leave, it may be less important to restate those rights in contracts. Instead, unions may attempt to negotiate additional family leave benefits. On the other hand, the Americans with Disabilities Act (ADA) conflicts with the National Labor Relations Act (NLRA) to some extent (Lee, 1993). The NLRA protects workers' collective activities, whereas the ADA protects the rights of individual workers who are disabled. It is illegal for employers to deal directly with individual employees under the NLRA, though the ADA requires employers to accommodate the needs of individual workers. This makes it critical for unions and employers to anticipate and address diversity conflicts, for it is possible that unions could face situations where a senior employee and a disabled employee are competing for the same job (Roberts and Lundy, forthcoming).

Because collective bargaining tends to produce contracts containing specific provisions that treat workers equally, concern has been expressed that bargaining outcomes (such as seniority systems) can perpetuate the effects of prior discriminatory treatment towards women or nonwhites. If bargaining seems only to protect a core group of white male members, then it will not promote diversity. At the same time, provisions calling for equal treatment provide an objective way of making organizational decisions that is usually acceptable to employees. Below, we discuss some ways that unions can influence diversity through bargaining and we examine contract provisions dealing with diversity to assess the nature of bargaining protection afforded to workers.

Unions' potential diversity efforts   It is possible to conduct a formal assessment of the potential diversity effects of collective bargaining using the approach outlined above. Specifically, using the four elements necessary to promote diversity in an organization as criteria, we assess the influence of unions on diversity.

First, because organizational hiring decisions are primarily reserved for management, unions typically have minimal effect on the extent to which individuals have an equal probability of selection for a job. That is, contract provisions typically cover individuals who are already employees, not potential or probationary employees. Unless an organization voluntarily opens this subject to discussion with a union, hiring remains the prerogative of management. As a result, equal treatment in hiring is affected primarily by government regulation (e.g. antidiscrimination laws), organizational culture, and management preferences. As it was noted that unions were major supporters of many of the regulations covering these issues (Delaney and Schwochau, 1993), it can be said at best that unions have indirectly affected organizational selection decisions.

Second, unions have considerable influence on employees' opportunities to advance in an organization. Unions make concerted efforts to protect employees from arbitrary treatment by management (Freeman and Medoff, 1984). For example, seniority provisions – defined as employment service credit – are found in 90 percent of union contracts (Bureau of National Affairs, 1992). Seniority, while not the only factor considered, is explicitly recognized in decisions covering promotion (72 percent of contracts), lay-offs (91 percent), and transfers (59 percent). More importantly, virtually all union contracts contain grievance procedures that address disputes arising under the agreement and 99 percent of the negotiated grievance procedures culminate in binding third-part arbitration (Bureau of National Affairs, 1992). Thus, in unionized settings, employee allegations of unfair treatment will be assessed by independent arbitrators rather than supervisors or management. This implies that typical union contracts strongly protect employees' equal opportunities for advancement and guarantee equal treatment generally.

Third, there is scattered evidence of protection of employees' individuality in contracts. In some of these instances, the negotiation of uniform rules may prohibit a willing employer from authorizing an employee's expression of individuality (e.g. by establishing different shift rules or vacation days for individuals who belong to religions celebrating the Sabbath on Saturday). In other instances, negotiated provisions covering permissible attire at work, appearance rules (e.g. covering facial hair), or family benefits for domestic partners protect the expression of individuality. In general, it is not possible to determine easily the extent to which contracts cover these issues, though it is likely that coverage varies widely.

Fourth, there appears to be attention given to nonwork responsibilities in union contracts, but once again there is no available data source that permits the calculation of precise estimates. The Bureau of National Affairs (1993, 16, 721) reported that the growth of workers with "dependent care responsibilities" had led to new contract provisions. Contractual arrangements include pre-tax spending accounts, on-site day care centers, employer pre-contracted day and elder care service arrangements with licensed facilities, explicit permission to use sick leave to deal with family matters, flextime, and job sharing arrangements (see table 10.3). Moreover, despite attention to these issues, most negotiated plans are limited in scope (Bureau of National Affairs, 1993, 16, 721).

Overall, therefore, evidence suggests that unions contribute directly and indirectly (at least to some extent) to an emphasis on diversity in organizations. The evidence is not substantial enough to indicate that unions can ensure diversity in workplaces where employers (or some union members) think otherwise or that unions always cooperate with employers desiring work changes to address diversity issues. On balance, however, because of the emphasis on formal rules and the existence of impartial grievance procedures in unionized work settings, we believe that unions generally have a positive net effect on the promotion of diversity.

Contract provisions The exact provisions included in union contracts provide another measure of the extent to which unions have followed the AFL-CIO's resolution to promote diversity. Although the classification of certain issues as diversity issues is somewhat arbitrary, table 10.2 reports data on contract provisions dealing with workers' rights, the nature of the workplace, and some women's and family issues in Canada and the US during the early 1990s. Work and family provisions, which address a wide variety of interests, can cover a broad range of subjects, including traditional (such as maternity leave), nontraditional (such as family financial planning programs), and new issues (such as elder care). As the data sources focus on "selected" contract provisions (especially "traditional" work and family clauses in contracts negotiated in the US), and the specific wording of contract provisions is not discernible from the table 10.2 categories, the data should be interpreted cautiously. For example, although the table does not report provisions in American contracts covering repetitive motion work or safety considerations for individuals working on video display terminals, it has been reported that such provisions are included in a growing number of union contracts involving office and technical employees and newspaper industry workers (Bureau of National Affairs, 1993, 95, 201). In general, the existence of data for certain provisions in Canada but not in the US is a reflection of bargaining law requirements and the Bureau of National Affairs' data collection approach, which emphasizes contract provisions that occur in many contracts.

Unreported data for US contracts in 1986 are quite similar to the 1992 US data reported in table 10.2. Although the percentage of contracts containing some provisions increases marginally over the years 1986–92, small decreases occurred for other provisions. Considering the possibility of sampling error, the results seem generally stable. Ignoring the many provisions not listed in the US contract data files, the pattern of outcomes in Canadian agreements seems somewhat different from that in US agreements. It is also striking that most of the diversity-related contract provisions are contained in less than 50 percent of the contracts in either country. Antidiscrimination and maternity leave provisions account for 6 of the 9 instances where a specific provision exists in more than 50 percent of the sample agreements.

While the pattern of results in table 10.2 may seem disappointing to some observers, an examination of approaches taken by different unions and selected union contracts suggests that the table underreports attention to diversity issues and that there is a great amount of variance across unions in attention to diversity.

In the 1990s, a variety of work and family issues have been introduced into collective bargaining agreements. Table 10.3 provides information on selected provisions addressing nontraditional bargaining issues. Because there is no baseline information on the extent to which these provisions exist in union contracts, it is not possible to estimate any trends in their growth, existence, or prevalence. But the list demonstrates that the labor movement has stressed diversity issues in some instances. For example, since the 1980s, the labor movement "has advocated federal government

Table 10.2 Selected union contract provisions in the US and Canada

	Canada 1991 (%)	US 1992 (%)
Working conditions		
Antidiscrimination	51	96
Sexual harassment	26	–
EEO pledges	–	17
Unsafe work – right to refuse	18	16
Quality of working life	13	16
Contracting out – restrictions	40	17
Flexible hours of work		
Compressed work week	15	5
Right to vary hours	9	–
Overtime – right to refuse	31	40
Technological change – protection		
Advance notice	53	17
Training or retraining	47	9
Employment guarantee	11	5
Equal rights and benefits		
Equal pay for comparable work	7	–
Bipartite participation in job evaluation	15	–
Union participation in job evaluation	31	26
Part-time workers' rights		
Health and welfare benefits	24	–
Holidays	27	–
Hours of work – limits	24	–
Part-time to full-time ratio	1	–
Pensions	5	–
Prorated benefits	9	–
Seniority	28	–
Severance pay	10	–
Sick leave	27	–
Vacation	28	–
Affirmative action programs	5	–
Family leave – paid		
Adoption leave	14	20
Illness-in-family leave	27	–
Marriage leave	20	–
Maternity leave	37	35
Parental leave (extended)	1	–
Paternity leave (extended)	1	–
Personal leave	8	76
Seniority retention during maternity leave	53	76
Child care facilities	2	–
Paid on-the-job training	27	–
Paid outside training courses	7	–
Work sharing	2	17
Job sharing	7	–

Sources: Canada (Kumar, 1993, pp. 218–19); US (Bureau of National Affairs, 1992)

Table 10.3 Negotiated nontraditional contract provisions

Provision	Selected agreements with the provision
Flexible spending accounts for child care	Los Angeles Comprehensive Program, New York Statewide Program, Massachusetts Textile Industry Program, Postal Service On-Site Center, Buffalo Hospital On-Site Center, New Chrysler-UAW Center, McDonnell-Douglas Pilot Program, Honeywell Sick Child Program, SEIU and the League of Voluntary Hospitals and Homes of New York, USWA and Inland Steel, and the Paperworkers and Procter & Gamble.
Other child care	The UAW has established a Child Care Committee that can develop a response: UAW Local 6,000 and State of Michigan, 1988; UAW and General Motors, letter of understanding, 1984, 1990; UAW and Chrysler, letter of understanding, 1985; UAW and Ford, letter of understanding, 1990. Child Care Subsidies: UAW District 65 and the Village Voice.
Elder care	UAW and Ford Motor Company pilot project, UAW Local 6,000 and State of Michigan.
Alternative work schedules	Associated Press and the Wire Service Guild (four-day work week schedule), SEIU Local 715 and Santa Clara County government (voluntary reduction in hours), UAW Local 1925 and Oakland University, 1990, UAW Local 2,071 and Wayne State University, 1990.
Benefits for part-time work	UAW Local 1925 and Oakland University.
Confidentiality of medical records	Lufkin Steel and United Steelworkers; Ethyl Petroleum and Chemical Workers.
Legal services	UAW and the Big Three Auto Makers and the IBEW and CWA and American Telephone and Telegraph Co.
Translator pay	District 1199 and some hospitals in New York.

Sources: The Labor Project (1994); Bureau of National Affairs (1993; 1992)

policies to ensure adequate income, family and medical leave, and high-quality, affordable support services, including child care, elder care, and health care" (Cowell, 1993, p. 115). Flexible spending accounts have become a popular way for employers to help address child care concerns. Two-thirds of the 1,006 respondents to a 1991 Hewitt Associates survey indicated that their firm provided some type of child care benefit, with flexible spending accounts being the most popular choice.[3]

Although there are no statistics on the extent of child care benefits in union contracts, the Service Employees International Union surveyed other unions in 1988 to gather information on union child care programs. That survey found more than 50 examples from 16 unions in 23 states. For example, AFSCME's first contract for clerical and technical workers at Harvard University included provisions for a $50,000 annual fund to provide child care subsidies and a labor-management commitment to expand the number of child care centers for children of bargaining unit employees (York, 1993, pp. 131–2). Further, York (p. 129) reported that unions "have been remarkably successful in winning parental leave contract provisions." While the Family and Medical Leave Act entitles most US employees to unpaid leave for a variety of situations, low-income employees often cannot afford to take it. In addition, workers must have worked at least 1,250 hours in a year to qualify for unpaid leave. This has led unions to focus in negotiations on modifications to leave policies that would be more valuable to part-time and lower-ranking employees. For example, the Amalgamated Clothing and Textile Workers Union has negotiated provisions that permit two months of *paid* parental leave for employees with at least one year of seniority. The Service Employees (SEIU) and Electrical Workers (IBEW) unions have also negotiated paid parental leave provisions (The Labor Project, 1994, p. 1).

As workers are increasingly caring for elderly parents, some contracts have introduced elder care provisions, as well as flexible job schedules. To address the demands of caring for elderly relatives, many unions have sought to alter contract language so that leaves are available if needed to care for dependents rather than to care for children. In some instances, contracts permit employees to use their sick leave to care for dependents who are ill (The Labor Project, 1994, pp. 1–2). Other provisions enhancing flexibility have begun to appear in contracts, including job sharing arrangements, compressed work weeks, flexible starting and quitting times built around core hours, and "V-Time," which allows a voluntary reduction of hours and pay to accommodate family needs. A 1989 survey of employers conducted by AMS indicated that 9 percent of respondents allowed job sharing arrangements – an increase of 1 percentage point since 1988. Concern about the privacy of employee medical records and access to the results of medical tests has led to provisions in a small number of contracts that ensure confidentiality of records and tests. Similarly, group legal service plans have been designed to offer affordable and extensive personal services to individual employees by using collective purchasing power to reduce costs. Employer-paid legal service plans cover about 7.3 million people, most under union contract.

At first glance, subjects such as translator pay or legal service plans may seem to be unrelated to the issue of diversity. In reality, these provisions may enhance diversity much more than cultural awareness training or the provision of certain child care benefits because they protect workers from abuse by employers. As nontraditional workers often have low skills and limited education, accessibility of legal help may be crucial at times but normally unaffordable. The provision of translator pay may ensure that other workers accept immigrants because employers are not permitted in such instances to require bilingual workers to translate orders and also complete their regular jobs. In addition, the cost of translator pay likely encourages employers to encourage employees who do not speak English to take English courses.

Some of the most aggressive and least recognized efforts to accommodate diversity have been made by unions representing nurses and teachers. Most of the members of these unions are women and many members are from ethnic minorities. The school district and health care managements with whom the unions negotiate are dominated by white men. As a result, there are some diversity issues inherent in the professional concerns that these unions attempt to secure in bargaining. In short, diversity concerns affect the bargaining issues of professional unions.

Nurses have sought contracts that cover professional issues, such as autonomy, determination of staffing ratios, and control over the quality of care (Pettengill, 1990). Similarly, teachers' unions have focused on professional issues such as student–teacher ratios, teaching assignments, teacher evaluations, and professional accountability (Bascia, 1994). Although these are not typical diversity issues, they create parameters within which many women professionals must work. If those parameters discourage women or other nontraditional workers from pursuing their profession, organizational diversity will be adversely affected.

It has been asserted that the existence of these kinds of programs and contract provisions is due to the development of more women leaders in US unions and the election of male and female union officers who are committed to work and family issues. The efforts are also the product of emphasis on internal education of union members, the development of cooperative relationships with employers, and taking a long-term perspective (York, 1993, p. 142). In short, many professional and organizational issues addressed by unions critically affect the creation of an environment supportive of diversity.

Union political action, diversity, and outcomes

Unions are political as well as economic institutions and organized labor uses political action to achieve outcomes that are not available through bargaining. In this regard, union political efforts designed to promote legislation fostering diversity affect both union and nonunion employers and employees. Historically, unions have advocated political positions that would be viewed sympathetically by individuals interested in promoting diversity – in terms of the candidates for public office supported by unions, the political expenditures made by unions, and the lobbying emphases maintained by unions (see Delaney and Masters, 1991; Delaney and Schwochau, 1993). Political efforts have provided another route for unions to use in the promotion of diversity outcomes. For example, efforts by union lobbyists on behalf of equal pay legislation have been widely hailed by pay equity groups – more than two-thirds of the activists responding to one survey indicated that unions were their single most important supporter (McCann, 1994, p. 115). More broadly, Delaney and Schwochau (1993, pp. 294–5) reported that unions regularly and actively supported legislation promoting workers' interests over the years 1977–91 (e.g. laws covering civil rights, low-income housing, the Head Start Program, and educational subsidies). Although union political efforts have not always translated into political victories, organized labor appears to be a crucial political voice of working people.

The political efforts of unions aimed at diversity outcomes have become increasingly important in recent years as more and more substantive workplace issues are debated in public forums (Weiler, 1993). For example, the public spotlight has recently been on issues such as sexual harassment, comparable worth, child care, and health care reform. Political victories in some of these debates would create diversity victories in the form of federal and state laws that cover many or all workplaces. Such victories would relieve unions of the need to negotiate basic diversity protection in contracts and allow labor to focus on other issues. At the same time, the involvement of many opposing interest groups in an increasingly mean-spirited political process has created legislative gridlock, making more important other union activities promoting diversity.

Conclusion: Managing Diversity in the Future

The union movement is frequently criticized for being resistant to change and for negotiating outcomes that hamper employers' flexibility. Some observers have suggested that this feature of unions and bargaining hampers the management of diversity. For example, as we noted earlier, mandating the use of seniority in layoffs usually means that proportionally more women and nonwhite workers lose their jobs whenever the economy contracts. Establishing work and holiday schedules using a traditional western calendar makes it difficult for some workers (for example, Muslims or Jews) to observe their religious holidays without losing pay. And requiring employers to treat everyone similarly greatly constrains management's flexibility to address the unique diversity concerns of individual workers (by, for example, treating different workers differently).

We believe that these arguments are generally overblown. Although unions are far from perfect, they have sought, on average, to negotiate uniform rules that are applied to workers consistently. In the short run, this approach could adversely affect diversity outcomes. Over time, however, it is likely to promote diversity. Unions' democratic structures ensure that union preferences will grow to include the perspectives of all members. Unions' duty of fair representation protects the rights of nontraditional members from many inequities created by majority rule. In addition, contracts mandating consistent treatment protect all workers from arbitrary management treatment, which led to unionization in many firms in the first place. Although more flexibility would allow employers to address the specific concerns of diverse workers, it would also permit inconsistent and arbitrary treatment of workers.

It is critical to note that unions often negotiated "rigid" work rules to curb management abuses and ensure uniform treatment at work. By agreeing to such work rules, management accepted limitations on its flexibility. In unionized workplaces, disputes about work rules or contract interpretation are often settled by grievance arbitration. The availability of arbitration in virtually every union contract likely benefits nontraditional employees by ensuring that neither the employer nor the union has complete discretion regarding the terms and conditions of employment. If nontraditional employees were the clear beneficiaries of total managerial discretion at work, then nonunion employers should have a better record of dealing with diversity concerns than do unionized employers, and whites and nonwhites should display equal propensities to join a union. As is noted below, however, these outcomes are currently not supported by available facts.

There is historical evidence that both craft unions and professional associations formally reserved jobs for white men (Cockburn, 1988). Cohn's (1985) analysis of clerical workers in Great Britain, however, suggested that organizational ideologies developed which supported job segregation, even in the absence of unions. Sociologists have developed social closure theory to explain why it is in the interest of the dominant members of organizations to promote job segregation. The theory suggests that the pressure to segregate any job is positively related to its desirability. "Dominants do not strive to monopolize all jobs; they reserve the best jobs for themselves" (Tomaskovic-Devey, 1993, p. 62). As we have noted above, a less conspiratorial view also suggests that segregation may occur. Specifically, it may be easier (i.e. there is less hostility and more acceptance of the fairness of the rules) to apply equal rules to unequal groups if they are segregated than if they are integrated.

There also exists substantial evidence that nonwhite workers are significantly more likely to vote for unionization than are white workers (Freeman and Medoff, 1984). Although other evidence does not show that women are more likely than men to vote for representation, the recent growth in the proportion of female union members may indicate that a shift is occurring in women's attitudes regarding unions (Bureau of Labor Statistics, 1994; Wilson Center for Public Research, 1992).

There is little systematic evidence that nonunion organizations are more supportive of diversity than unionized firms or unions. Indeed, there exists some evidence suggesting the opposite. For example, Delaney and Schwochau (1993, pp. 293–5) showed that on several issues connected with diversity (such as equal rights and family leave), business organizations actively opposed and unions strongly supported legislation that would provide additional rights to workers. Bielby and Baron (1984) concluded that creation of hierarchical management structures (i.e. a bureaucracy) in organizations contributed to the likelihood that gender and racial segregation would occur in organizational jobs. Moreover, considerable evidence suggests that unionization is associated with decreased wage dispersion both within and across firms – a finding implying greater pay equity by race and gender within the union sector (Freeman and Medoff, 1984).

One element of bureaucracy has been argued to reduce discrimination and occupational segregation – the formalization of organizational rules (Szafran, 1982). Tomaskovic-Devey (1993, p. 67) speculated that formalized workplace rules "might help reduce segregation if [they] made job-bidding processes more open to public scrutiny and insofar as more formalized employment relationships are characterized by clear job definitions and procedures for hiring and promotion that act as external logical alternatives to the sex and race of job applicants when hiring decisions are made." Whereas the formalization of workplace rules has been accomplished by many nonunion US firms, such as IBM and Frito-Lay, it is the hallmark of unionized firms. Ironically, the formalized rules characteristic of the union sector seem to promote diversity better than the managerial flexibility of the nonunion sector.

Union lessons

Several inferences on the management of diversity arise from our assessment of unions, collective bargaining, and diversity-related issues. Some of the inferences are paradoxical or counterintuitive, but receive support in the union literature. First, it is important to note that increasing heterogeneity of the union movement has not yet translated into a similarly heterogeneous top-level union leadership. Diversity in unions has been promoted in some instances by rare leaders, such as Walter Reuther of the Auto Workers and Cesar Chavez of the Farm Workers, and in most cases by agitated union members. Although the lack of top-level union leadership heterogeneity is a legitimate blemish on the face of a democratic labor movement, it indicates the difficulty of sustaining a diverse workplace. Given that businesses do not operate as democratic institutions, and given the historical occupational segregation that occurs in organizations, it is probably more difficult to nurture diversity in businesses than it is in unions. Put differently, the existence of a great amount of management discretion or flexibility does not guarantee the development of diversity. To the extent that firms do not explicitly create a nurturing environment, diversity objectives will not be attained.

Second, considerable literature suggests that the flexibility inherent in business organizations can ironically discourage diversity. That is, diversity seems to be promoted by the establishment of formalized rules that treat all employees equally (or equitably). For example, the establishment of objective criteria for promotion makes it less likely that discrimination or bias will impede nontraditional employees. This will seem counterintuitive to individuals familiar with the stereotypes of unions as outdated because they limit management discretion. With regard to diversity, an extensive, though somewhat ideological literature suggests that the hallmarks of a unionized workplace stimulate the development of diversity (see Tomaskovic-Devey, 1993; Cockburn, 1988). As a result, to the extent that organizations institute such formal procedures governing employees, the union literature suggests that diversity will be stimulated.

Third, diversity must be viewed as a process instead of an outcome if organizational prejudices are to be overcome (see Ferris et al., 1993). Organizational culture must be altered to create a climate that accepts and promotes diversity. A focus on diversity as an objective tends to promote attention to statistics on race and gender in organizations – objectifying women and nonwhites and encouraging the perspective that diversity is like affirmative action. The point is that organizations will not find a "quick fix" for diversity problems. There may be temporary changes in the composition of an organization's labor force as a result of a diversity program (especially one that sets "targets"), but nontraditional employees will not stay in an organization whose culture is unchanged. Women and nonwhite union members have emphasized that unions, union leaders, and union members must understand that race, gender, and ethnicity tend to become fundamental aspects of certain positions (for example, union president or corporate manager). "Discrimination is not something perpetuated solely by racist or sexist individuals but is fundamentally conditioned by competition for the best jobs. Inequality is not only the result of discrimination against women or minorities but also of the gendered and racial organization of production itself" (Tomaskovic-Devey, 1993, p. 6).

Many organizations striving to achieve diversity will not attain it because their leaders do not understand the underlying process that diversity requires. No organization can successfully promote diversity if its women and nonwhite members have no access to sources of political skill and information. If an organization treats diversity as the attainment of a distribution of individuals representative of the labor force, it will not address the diversity process.

Fourth, although diversity cannot effectively be proclaimed from on high, considerable top management support is needed if it is to be achieved in an organization. This is true across organizations and nations. Recognition of the legitimacy of differences and emphasis on developing a tolerant organizational climate are necessary preconditions to diversity. Moreover, these issues are magnified by trends aimed at increasing teamwork and reducing supervision in organizations because the role of majority employees in the diversity process is increased when decision-making authority is decentralized. Without clear support for diversity from executives, it is virtually impossible to achieve diversity objectives.

Future trends

Characteristics of future workers and workplaces will influence the promotion of diversity and the achievement of organizational goals. First, the transformation of organizations into leaner and less hierarchical entities increases the importance of teamwork and positive employee interactions. To remain competitive, organizations are reducing the supervisory and managerial ranks, lowering inventories, and empowering workers. These changes increase the importance of each employee's role in an organization and increase the potential stress on each employee to produce. This organizational form, however, requires more cooperation across employees and trust – in the sense that everyone must perform well for the organization to perform well – than was necessary in hierarchical organizations. If existing culture does not promote diversity, organizations taking this new form will have a difficult time surviving. To the extent that each employee has a larger role in future organizational structures, diversity will become more important.

Second, the reduction of job security that goes hand in hand with new organizational forms will increase employees' willingness to leave an organization that does not tolerate their individuality whenever alternative job opportunities arise. Failure to promote diversity, therefore, may encourage more turnover among nontraditional workers than would have occurred in the past when the promise of greater job security led workers to bear with it.

Third, there is a potential conflict between the flexibility required by organizations and the fair treatment demanded by employees. Differences in perspectives across gender, race, and other employee characteristics magnify the conflict. As a result, organizational actions must be sensitive and decisive to create a proper climate for diversity. Such decisions will not emerge from a vacuum. There must be a direct and deliberate attempt made within organizations to develop a culture of diversity. The union literature suggests that such efforts should include information sharing, provision for equitable treatment, fair opportunities for success in the organization, and consistent application of policies, as well as attention to differences among individuals.

Finally, although the changing nature of the labor force guarantees that organizations will be more diverse in the future, it does not ensure that nontraditional employees will feel an attachment to an organization or their work. We are concerned that organizational cultures will not change appreciably in the face of increased diversity. That is, although the changing composition of the labor force will cause organizations to become more diverse, it will not ensure the development of an organizational culture that is respectful of employees' differences. More importantly, if the union sector continues to decline, pressure on organizations to reform their cultures and appreciate differences may also decline. That may make workers more insecure and provide nontraditional workers with little respect and few legitimate alternatives.

NOTES

1 The BLS initiated a new survey method in the early 1980s to categorize and collect union membership data. Because comparisons to membership rates in earlier times will not be exact, we refrain from making them.

2 The heterogeneity measure is created as follows: HETEROGENEITY= $(f*(1 - f))/ s_f + (m*(1 - m))/s_m + (wc*(1 - wc)/s_{wc}) + (1 - ind)/s_i)$, where: f = proportion female, m = proportion minority, wc = proportion white collar, ind = proportion in the union's primary jurisdiction, and s = the standard deviation of the respective numerator.

3 In general, flexible spending accounts are of greatest value to high-income employees, who could afford to pay for child care anyway. These accounts often offer little assistance to low-income employees who need child care but cannot pay for it out of pocket.

REFERENCES

Bascia, N. (1994). *Unions in Teachers' Professional Lives: Social, Intellectual, and Practical Concerns.* New York: Teachers' College Press.

Bielby, W. T., and Baron, J. N. (1984). A woman's place is with other women: Sex segregation within organizations. In B. F. Reskin (ed.), *Sex Segregation in the Workplace: Trends, Explanations, Remedies* (27–55). Washington, DC: National Academy Press.

Briskin, L., and McDermott, P. (eds) (1993). *Women Challenging Unions.* Toronto: University of Toronto Press.

Bureau of National Affairs (1992). *Basic Patterns in Union Contracts,* 13th ed. Washington, DC: BNA.

Bureau of National Affairs (1993). *Current Bargaining Issues.* Washington, DC: BNA.

Cain, G. G. (1986). The economic analysis of labor market discrimination: A survey. In O. Ashenfelter and P. R. G. Layard (eds), *Handbook of Labor Economics* (693–785). Amsterdam: North Holland.

Carton, B. (1994). Muscled out? At Jenny Craig, men are ones who claim sex discrimination. *Wall Street Journal,* November 29, A1.

Clark, P. F., and Gray, L. S. (1991). Union administration. In G. Strauss, D. G. Gallagher, and J. Fiorito (eds), *The State of the Unions* (175–200). Madison, WI: IRRA.

Cobble, D. S. (ed.) (1993). *Women and Unions: Forging a Partnership.* Ithaca, NY: ILR Press.

Cockburn, C. (1988). *Machinery of Dominance: Women, Men, and Technical Know-how.* Boston: Northeastern University Press.

Cohn, S. (1985). *The Process of Occupational Sex-typing.* Philadelphia: Temple University Press.

Cook, A. H. (1993). Comments. In D. S. Cobble (ed.), *Women and Unions: Forging a Partnership,* pp. 148–56. Ithaca, NY: ILR Press.

Cornell University (1994). *Cultural Diversity: Training Materials for Labor Unions.* Supported by a grant from the Communications Workers of America–Joseph Anthony Beirne Foundation. Ithaca, NY: NYSSILR.

Cowell, S. (1993). Family policy: A union approach. In D. S. Cobble (ed.), *Women and Unions: Forging a Partnership* (115–28). Ithaca, NY: ILR Press.

Delaney, J. T., Florito, J., and Jarley, P. (1991). Union innovation and effectiveness: Results from the national union survey. Working Paper 91–01, Industrial Relations Institute, Iowa City, IA: University of Iowa.

Delaney, J. T., and Masters, M. F. (1991). Unions and political action. In G. Strauss, D. G. Gallagher, and J. Fiorito (eds), *The State of the Unions* (313–45). Madison, WI: IRRA.

Delaney, J., and Schwochau, S. (1993). Employee representation through the political process. In B. E. Kaufman and M. M. Kleiner (eds), *Employee Representation: Alternatives and Future Directions* (265–304). Madison, WI: IRRA.

Eaton, S. C. (1992). *Women Workers, Unions and Industrial Sectors in North America.* Geneva: International Labour Office.

Eaton, S. C. (1993). Women in trade union leadership: How more women can become leaders of today's and tomorrow's unions. In G. Adler and D. Suarez (eds), *Union Voices* (171–211). Albany: State University of New York Press.

Ferris, G. R., Frink, D. D., and Galang, M. C. (1993). Diversity in the workplace: The human resources management challenges. *Human Resource Planning*, 16, 41–51.

Filippelli, R. L. (1984). *Labor in the USA: A History*. New York: Knopf.

Freeman, R. B., and Medoff, J. L. (1984). *What Do Unions Do?* New York: Basic Books.

Gray, L. S. (1993). The route to the top: Female union leaders and union policy. In D. S. Cobble (ed.), *Women and Unions: Forging a Partnership* (378–93). Ithaca, NY: ILR Press.

Hoyman, M. M., and Stallworth, L. (1987). Participation in local unions: A comparison of black and white members. *Industrial and Labor Relations Review*, 40, 323–35.

Institute for Women's Policy Research (1994). What do unions do for women? *Research-in-Brief*, March. Washington, DC: IWPR.

Jacoby, S. M. (1984). *Employing Bureaucracy*. New York: Columbia University Press.

Johnston, W. B., and Packer, A. E. (1987). *Workforce 2000: Work and Workers for the 21st Century*. Indianapolis: Hudson Institute.

Jones, K. W. (1993). Cultural diversity education: What is being done? *Labor Studies Journal*, 17, 39–50.

Katz, J. (1994). Is Anna Quindlen a martyr? *New York Magazine*, 27, September 26, 22–3.

Kossek, E. E., and Zonia, S. C. (1993). Assessing diversity climate: A field study of reactions to employer efforts to promote diversity. *Journal of Organizational Behavior*, 14, 61–81.

Kumar, P. (1993). Collective bargaining and women's workplace concerns. In L. Briskin and P. McDermott (eds), *Women Challenging Unions* (207–30). Toronto: University of Toronto Press.

Labor Research Association (1993). *The American Labor Yearbook 1993*. New York: Labor Research Association.

Lawrence, E. (1994). *Gender and Trade Unions*. London: Taylor and Francis.

Lee, B. A. (1993). Individual vs. collective interests: Does the duty to accommodate supersede contractual rights? In *Proceedings of the Forty-Fifth Annual Meeting* (465–73). Madison, WI: Industrial Relations Research Association.

Lewin, D. (1991). Grievance procedures in nonunion workplaces: An empirical study of usage, dynamics, and outcomes. *Chicago-Kent Law Review*, 68, 823–44.

McCann, M. W. (1994). *Rights at Work: Pay Equity Reform and the Politics of Legal Mobilization*. Chicago: University of Chicago Press.

Micallef, C. (1994). Letter to Catherine Lundy, April 1.

Pettengill, M. M. (1990). Collective bargaining: Impact on nursing. In N. Chaska (ed.), *The Nursing Profession: Turning Points* (454–63). Indianapolis, IN: C.V. Mosby.

Repas, B. (1984). *Contract Administration*. Washington, DC: Bureau of National Affairs.

Riccucci, N. M. (1990). *Women, Minorities, and Unions in the Public Sector*. New York: Greenwood Press.

Roberts, K., and Lundy, C. (1995). The ADA and NLRB: Resolving accommodation disputes in unionized places work. *Negotiation Journal*, 11: 29–43.

Roby, P., and Uttal, L. (1993). Putting it all together: The dilemmas of rank-and-file union leaders. In D. S. Cobble (ed.), *Women and Unions: Forging a Partnership* (363–77). Ithaca, NY: ILR Press.

Schor, J. B. (1991). *The Overworked American: The Unexpected Decline of Leisure*. New York: Basic Books.

Seeber, R. (1984). The expansion of national union jurisdictions, 1955–1982. Unpublished manuscript. Cornell University.

Shostak, A. B. (1991). *Robust Unionism*. Ithaca, NY: ILR Press.

Szafran, R. F. (1982). What kind of firms hire and promote women and blacks: A review of the literature. *Sociological Quarterly*, 23, 171–90.

The Labor Project (1994). *Labor News for Working Families*, 11, 1–4.

Tomaskovic-Devey, D. (1993). *Gender and Racial Inequality at Work: The Sources and Consequences of Job Segregation*. Ithaca, NY: ILR Press.

Trebilcock, A. (1991). Strategies for strengthening women's participation in trade union leadership. *International Labour Review*, 130, 407–26.

UAW Women's Department (1993). *Women in the UAW*. Detroit, MI: UAW.

US Department of Labor, Bureau of Labor–Management Relations and Cooperative Programs (1992). *Work and Family Provisions in Major Collective Bargaining Agreements*, BLMR No. 144. Washington, DC: Government Printing Office.

US Department of Labor, Bureau of Labor Statistics. (1994). Union members in 1993. *News*, USDL 94–58, Washington, DC.

Walker, B. T. (1994). Letter to Catherine Lundy, March 16.

Wallihan, J. (1985). *Union Government and Organization*. Washington, DC: Bureau of National Affairs.

1199 News (1994). We're in this together. 12, 7–13.

Weiler, P. C. (1993). Governing the workplace: Employee representation in the eyes of the law. In B. E. Kaufman and M. M. Kleiner (eds), *Employee Representation: Alternatives and Future Directions* (81–104). Madison, WI: IRRA.

Wilson Center for Public Research (1992). Workers' views of the value of unions. Unpublished report.

York, C. (1993). Bargaining for work and family benefits. In D. S. Cobble (ed.), *Women and Unions: Forging a Partnership* (129–43). Ithaca, NY: ILR Press.

11
Workplace Health and Safety: Implications for Diversity

Karen A. Brown

This chapter addresses workplace safety issues relevant to diverse work-forces. These two topics are rarely seen in juxtaposition, but there are important linkages between them. It cannot be disputed that workforce diversity is a significant concern to organizations – the development of this book provides testimony, as do the numerous publications, news stories, and course offerings that have appeared over the past several years. We recognize that diversity will increasingly characterize our work organizations (Jackson et al., 1993; Rice, 1994) and that our once narrow definitions of diversity (i.e. race) must be expanded to include a wider range of dimensions (Loden and Rosener, 1991). Although the potential list of population subgroups is immense, this chapter will concentrate on a set for which safety and health implications are highly significant (i.e. race, gender, culture, language and literacy, age, contagious disease).[1]

In contrast to the relative currency of the diversity phenomenon, workplace safety is an issue that has been around for many years. Unfortunately, however, it has cloistered itself until recently within the closely-defined boundaries of the engineering discipline and within the occupational medicine niche of the health care field. Current recognition of workplace safety as a top-level strategic initiative, especially among manufacturing firms, has raised significantly the attention and respect given to this issue in managerial circles. Still, it is seldom mentioned in the management, operations, or HR literatures.

HR managers, in partnership with operations managers, play a central role in preventing and responding to workplace accidents, injuries, and ailments. Examples of HR responsibilities linked with safety include employee selection, work assignments, training, reporting procedures, and injury follow-up. A general thesis of this chapter is that safety-related HR systems will require redesign in light of increasing workplace diversity.

The chapter begins with an overview of workplace safety. The discussion, which addresses costs, trends, and need for change, will serve as a foundation and will convey the increasing seriousness of health and safety issues to organizations. Following that, a model is presented as a framework for linking diversity and safety. The model traces the effects of diversity dimensions such as race, gender, and age on personal safety outcomes. Summary discussions at the end of the chapter address recommendations for organizational action. These emphasize the need for cross-functional coordination between organizational units responsible for HR management and operations management.

Part of the research for the chapter included a series of intensive visits over a two-year period to 25 manufacturing organizations in various parts of the US, Mexico, Korea, and Australia — references will be made to examples from those organizations. By agreement, however, the names of these companies must be kept in confidence. The chapter will be somewhat biased toward the manufacturing sector, partly because of the focus of the field research and partly because the manufacturing sector is still a great source of workplace accidents, ailments, and deaths in the US (National Safety Council, 1994).

The Increasing Importance of Workplace Safety

Managers are becoming increasingly concerned about workplace health and safety. This is evidenced by the growing numbers of organizations in the US and other countries that have begun to include health and safety criteria in corporate performance goals. The National Safety Council (1995) estimates that the total cost of work accidents to US industry was $121 billion in 1994. To place these large numbers into a more realistic frame, let us consider the following example:

A small US manufacturing company with 20 employees earns a 10 percent annual profit on its $2 million in annual sales. An employee incurs a serious cumulative trauma injury, generating medical and compensation bills of $40,000. (Which, in the US, is the average for such claims according to Pulat, 1992.)

The cost of this injury, which could be one of several for this particular year, would be equal to nearly a quarter of the company's annual profit. If the company is self-insured, this would represent a direct out-of-pocket expense. If the company relies on state workers' compensation, it will still see a substantial rise in the insurance fees it pays to the state. Carrying this further, let us imagine that the employee feels that the company was negligent in designing the injury-causing job, and that it was not sufficiently responsive to his or her complaint. The employee might have filed a lawsuit. Moreover, let us imagine that the injured worker is a woman (most often the case in cumulative trauma injuries) and that she claims in her suit that failure to redesign the job was associated with gender discrimination (i.e. if she had been a man, would they have redesigned the job?). In one such case, a female employee was awarded $1.16 million in damages (West, 1992). Obviously, such a ruling would not only obliterate the hypothetical company's profits for several years, it might force the organization out of business entirely. Workers' compensation and legal awards are not the only sources of monetary outflow – state and federal fines for safety violations can be exceedingly high, as well. For example, the Dayton Tire Company in Oklahoma recently was fined $7.5 million over alleged safety violations (Nomani, 1994). Safety standards tend to be lowest, and the consequent risk of injury the highest, among smaller companies (Marsh, 1994) – this can result in large proportionate monetary risks for these smaller concerns. (Moreover, these small companies employ a very high percentage of racial minorities and recent immigrants.) With the Labor Department stepping up its pressure on workplace health and safety (Nomani, 1994) the potential for financially devastating fines will increase.

After a number of years of declining incidence of workplace injuries and related lost work days, the past several years have been characterized by steady increases. Figure 11.1 illustrates these trends. Some of the change in injury rates shown in figure 11.1 is apparently the result of more rigorous reporting, spurred by threats of OSHA penalties (personal communication, National Safety Council, 1994). However, trends in lost work days shown in figure 11.1 suggest that there has been a marked increase in the extent to which the workplace is causing injuries and ailments that take employees away from their jobs. Regardless of the source of any changes we may observe in incidence rates, however, the sheer numbers (e.g. $121 billion in total cost) tell us that workplace safety is something organizations cannot ignore.

HR managers can play an important role in stemming the tide of injuries and related costs, particularly if they work in partnership with their operations counterparts to remove workplace hazards and create an effective safety culture within the workforce. These two change elements, hazards and safety culture, pose special challenges in the context of a diverse workforce. Differences in physical characteristics and risk attitudes are just two examples of the factors that must be considered as we expand our perspectives on workplace demographics.

The need for a changing perspective

With some exceptions (e.g. Butler and Teagarden, 1993; Hollenbeck et al., 1992; Jermier et al., 1989; Komaki et al., 1978) the literature in HR has done little to address issues of workplace safety, leaving this topic to specialists in the areas of ergonomics, human factors engineering, industrial hygiene, or occupational medicine. Only recently have management-oriented publications begun to address the problems of workplace safety. There is a need for HR specialists to change their perspective on safety, in general, given the issue's implications for hiring, job assignments, workers' compensation, training, and reward systems. Additionally, it is imperative that operations

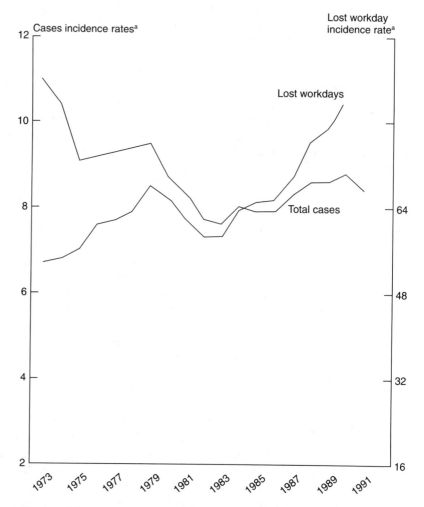

Figure 11.1 Trends in occupational injury incidence rates (National Safety Council, 1994)[2]

a Number of days or cases per 100 full-time employees per year

managers make the necessary ergonomic changes, provide the proper safety equipment, notify employees of hazards, and work to design processes in such a way that hazards are eliminated or avoided. The need for both groups to cooperate intensifies when diversity enters the equation.

Increasing complexity

Perrow (1984) provides useful insights about the increased probability of catastrophic workplace accidents in his book *Normal Accidents*. It is his thesis that as systems become more complex we increase the probability that a major accident will occur. His examples are focused on large-scale disasters such as the Three Mile Island nuclear accident, but his theoretical framework also has implications for smaller-scale systems and accidents. The generally increasing technological complexity of modern workplaces undoubtedly has contributed to the trends shown in figure 11.1. However, complexity need not be entirely technological – it can be social as well. It seems plausible to extend Perrow's thinking to social systems, and to suggest that as workplace diversity increases, the complexity of the social environment escalates along with it. A workplace that mixes races, cultures, genders, ages, languages, and illnesses is, by definition, more complex than the homogeneous work organization of the past.

One outcome of an increasingly complex social environment may be an elevation in the probability that there will be unexpected system failures such as accidents and injuries. This proposition does not stand as an entirely theoretical point of view. There is considerable evidence in the literature to suggest that the complexities associated with diversity can, indeed, lead to increases in health and safety problems. This is not intended to indicate that minority groups "cause" accidents, but, rather, that their presence often introduces safety risks and issues which have not been addressed previously by employers. For example, the increasing presence of employees who carry chronic contagious diseases is an issue that managers of the recent past did not have to consider in designing jobs and workplaces. It is often the case that awareness of the needs of minority groups leads to improvements that benefit all employees. Safety improvements designed to meet the needs of minority groups are no exception. Thus, although managers may find some distress at the safety changes they must make to accommodate a diverse workforce, all employees are likely to gain from the modifications.

Personal Health and Safety Outcomes Related to Diversity

The linkages between workforce diversity and workplace safety derive from a series of relationships, beginning with diversity dimensions and culminating in effects on employee and co-worker safety. This series is depicted in figure 11.2, and is explained in more detail below. Given that our ultimate interest is in health and safety outcomes, we will begin with the right side of the model and move to the left. This sequence of discussion allows for the establishment of definitions, which provide the foundation for the core of this chapter. The foundational discourse on outcomes, risks and responses, mediating factors, and diversity dimensions allows for the development of specific examples linking safety and diversity. These linkages are detailed following the model overview.

Personal outcomes

Diversity and safety come together via two major types of outcomes. First, there is heightened potential for *direct health and safety effects* on employees who are members of certain population groups. For example, many

Figure 11.2 Diversity and workplace safety: organizational linkages

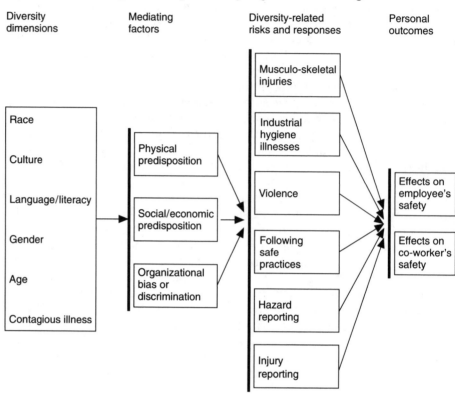

changes in workforce demographics have the effect of changing anthropo-morphic and strength profiles of a work group (Imrhan et al., 1993). Equip-ment and materials once suited to a homogeneous workforce (one composed predominantly of males of Northern European descent) may no longer be safe or comfortable for the new workforce.

The second type of outcome linking diversity and safety comes in the form of potential injury and illness *effects on co-workers*. For example, the diverse workforce increasingly includes persons who carry contagious dis-eases (Stone, 1994). Some co-workers may suffer ill health as a result of exposure, and in other cases they may inaccurately perceive themselves to be vulnerable to a non-infectious disease. Either way, organizations must adapt their operations and HR practices to cope with this new diversity issue.

Diversity-related risks and responses

Direct health effects on employees and indirect health effects on co-workers can take a variety of forms, including musculoskeletal injuries, industrial hygiene-related injuries and illnesses, violence, propensity or ability to follow safe work practices, hazard reporting, and injury reporting. For the purpose of this chapter, these are defined below. More detail about their implications for diversity will be provided in the subsequent section.

Musculo-skeletal injuries This term will be used in reference to human soft tissue or bone injuries caused by physical forces outside the body, or by harmful bodily actions. Examples include carpal tunnel syndrome, concussions, back strain, limb loss, skin abrasions, and the like. Causes may include tasks requiring repetitive motion, lifting, falling, or being struck by objects. Incidence rates for various types of musculo-skeletal injuries vary across population groups. For example, the likelihood of workplace falls increases with age.

Industrial hygiene-related accidents and illnesses This term will be used to refer to physical ailments, primarily those affecting organs such as the lungs, stomach, skin, or intestines. Within this category, we will also include risks and injuries to reproductive organs and unborn children. These types of illnesses may or may not be as readily or immediately apparent to the victim as a musculoskeletal injury might be. Causes, many of which are found increasingly in work organizations (Weiner and Brown, 1993), may include infectious agents, radiation, carcinogens, airborne toxic chemicals, air quality, or irritants such as dust and allergens. It is anticipated that these kinds of health effects will increase as a result of the astronomic growth in the introduction of toxic chemicals into the workplace: it has been estimated that a new and potentially dangerous chemical is introduced into industry every 20 minutes (Hammer, 1989). This translates to 504 new chemicals per week and 26,208 per year. Differences in exposure levels and susceptibility to industrial hygiene risk factors have been documented among various population groups. For example, predominantly Hispanic farm laborers are exposed disproportionately to toxic agricultural chemicals.

Violence This term will refer to physical harm that is inflicted intentionally by one person on another person. Although workplace violence often results in musculoskeletal injury, it is treated separately here because of its intentionality and because of its increasing incidence in the workplace (Smith, 1993). Violent acts by customers, co-workers, and personal acquaintances can lead to serious injuries and, more and more frequently, to employee deaths. Some elements of the population appear to be at greater risk of workplace violence than others. Although there is some conflicting evidence, it appears that women are most often the victims.

Following safe work practices There is currently considerable debate among members of the safety community with regard to the major sources of workplace accidents and injuries. Some individuals (and some entire organizations) have attempted to cast full blame for accidents on employees themselves. Others have taken the perspective most reminiscent of the late

Dr Deming's (e.g. Deming, 1986) philosophy[3] – that most problems are rooted in the system and not with direct labor. Regardless of the outcome of this debate, we must recognize that employees, in most situations, have *some* control over the relative safety of their work. The extent to which they properly use safety equipment and follow safety procedures can help to minimize risk, and there appear to be certain population subgroups (e.g. young men) which may be socially predisposed to take shortcuts on safety precautions.

Hazard reporting Workplace hazards can provide increasing levels of threat if they are not reported and abated. Recently, many organizations have begun to educate their employees in hazard recognition and reporting. None the less, some groups are less likely than others to report hazards to their employers or safety representatives. Causes of this hesitation may range from language difficulty to cultural factors, and its results may include a personal injury or ailment, as well as risk to co-workers.

Injury reporting There appear, also, to be variations among population groups with respect to the tendency to report injuries and other workplace health effects. Some racial groups are particularly reluctant to notify their employers when health problems occur because they feel that such reports may tend to magnify the stigmatization that they already feel. Others, by nature of factors such as literacy, are unaware of their rights to report workplace injuries and health problems.

Problem diagnosis An important component of any workplace safety program is found in an organization's approach to diagnosing the root causes of problems after an accident or injury has occurred. Unfortunately, today's highly litigious environment often leads to a finger-pointing exercise instead of a sincere effort to find problem causes and prevent future injuries. When we add culture and language diversity to this already difficult situation, it may become nearly impossible to identify the factors that have contributed to our accident or injury. The result for an organization may be that dangerous hazards and inadequate procedures will be allowed to remain intact.

Mediating factors

The extent to which the health effects described above are linked with certain population groups will depend on three mediating factors: physical predispositions, social/economic predispositions, and organizational bias or discrimination.

Physical predispositions Physical predispositions exist when one population group is found to be more susceptible than another to the physical effects of a workplace hazard. For example, workplace-related multiple chemical sensitivities have afflicted women more than men.

Social/economic predispositions Social predispositions exist when there are non-physical factors causing one group to have a disproportionate share of certain workplace health and safety effects. Social factors can influence certain racial, cultural, or gender groups to self-select themselves into specific types of jobs. (For example, women often choose jobs associated with intensive keyboard use, a prominent causative factor in repetitive motion injuries.) They also influence the extent to which some population groups engage in safe work practices or report hazards and injuries. Thus, in the absence of a physical predisposition, some groups can still be at higher risk for injury than others. Social predispositions, to a greater degree than physical predispositions, can lead to safety risks for co-workers.

Organizational bias or discrimination Finally, some organizations have, through intentional or unintentional discriminatory practices, subjected certain population groups to higher safety risks than others. Although the high concentration of some population groups in particularly unsafe jobs may be considered a self-selection bias, organizations establish and support the conditions which allow this. Rosen (1991) identifies the "ten worst" jobs in the US. These jobs, selected on the basis of risks for personal health and stress, include: data entry personnel, electronic assembly workers, garment workers, janitors and maids, food-service workers, meat packers, migrant farm workers, telephone sales people, booth sitters, and civil service workers. Several of these jobs are predominated by minority groups. (For example, many janitors and maids are racial minorities, and language skills are often limited within this group; the ranks of garment workers are predominated by female Asian immigrants; most data entry and electronic personnel are women; and migrant farm workers are generally Hispanic.)

A US example of organizational discrimination was seen in the deadly fire at the Imperial Foods Plant in Hamlet, North Carolina, in 1991. The employer, not trusting its mostly African-American workforce to stay in the building, had locked or blocked fire exits. This made it difficult for employees to escape the building, and 25 died in the fire. One must ask seriously whether the doors would have been locked if the workforce had been predominated by white males.

International examples of racial safety discrimination may be seen in the growing propensity for US companies to locate in countries such as Mexico and China (Butler and Teagarden, 1993; Kadetsky, 1994). These moves are ostensibly made because of lower wages, but another motivation is often found in the more lax safety standards that prevail in those locations (Hammer, 1989). As a consequence, Hispanic, Asian, and female population groups, all of which would be considered protected minority groups if they were working within US borders, are being subjected to health and safety risks that are unacceptable by US standards. Segregation of minority groups into unsafe jobs is not just a US phenomenon – Wokutch (1992) cites similar practices in Japan, where immigrant workers are the ones most likely to be assigned to jobs that pose safety risks.

Diversity Dimensions Relevant to Workplace Safety

In the early 1900s, manufacturing represented the major source of non-farm employment in the US and most of the employees in that sector were white males of European origin. Following the prescriptions of management scientists such as Taylor (1911), the hiring process emphasized brawn as a primary selection criterion. Taylor's ideal worker, "Schmidt the Pig Iron Handler," fit the classic description of the northern European male who was either a recent immigrant or had been enticed away from farm work in the rural US. In most factory situations, machinery, equipment, and work stations were designed to fit the anthropometrics (body dimensions) of large-statured men. Even in office settings, occupants were rarely female. The composition of the workforce has changed vastly since these early times, but our places of work have adapted very slowly, and in some cases not at all. Weiner and Brown (1993), in their book *Office Biology*, include a chapter entitled "We can't all be five-foot ten-inch males," underscoring the assumptions of standard body size that have historically typified many capital purchasing, job design, and workspace design decisions.

The workforce has become diverse in more ways than anthropometrics. Also, many of the dimensions of diversity have implications for workplace safety and health. Numerous population subgroups might be considered in this discussion, but our attention will be focused on those for which the evidence of safety–diversity linkages are most apparent and important. As shown in figure 11.2, these include: race, culture, language and level of literacy, gender, age, and affliction with a contagious illness.

Race and workplace safety

The past twenty years have seen tremendous changes in the composition of the US workforce (Johnston, 1991; Otten, 1994; Loden and Rosener, 1991). All-white and segregated workplaces have blossomed into diverse environments and many positive changes in attitudes and managerial practices have provided the support necessary for this to happen. A major contributor to the demographic change has been an influx of Asian and South American immigrants (Thomas, 1990; 1991). Another source is in the proportionately larger reproductive rates among nonwhite racial groups (Statistical Abstract of the US, 1994). It is projected that over the next 20 years, people of color will make up 18 percent of US population increases and whites will account for only 13 percent (Loden and Rosener, 1991). These new dimensions and dynamics will have a major impact on the demographics of our workplaces and will bring with them several race-related safety issues that deserve our attention.

Musculo-skeletal injuries Individuals within some racial groups (e.g. Asians) are, on average, smaller in stature than the European males who previously dominated the workforce (Pulat, 1992; Imrhan et al., 1993). Machinery, equipment, and work stations that once fit the "average" employee may no longer be appropriate. Accidents and injuries which may arise for smaller-statured racial groups include back injuries from lifting or incorrect work posture, as well as hand and wrist injuries from holding tools which are too large. Additionally, some very recent immigrants from Asia may have little experience in sitting in chairs for an entire work day. This will be particularly true for employees whose work histories involve agriculture, where a squatting posture or sitting directly on the ground or floor are standard practice. The chair is a relatively recent historical development (Grimsrud, 1990), and there is some evidence that none of us were really meant to sit in them for extended periods. Although research will be required to document this proposition, it seems possible that recent Asian immigrants may suffer disproportionately from back disorders and other problems related to sitting postures to which they are unaccustomed. (Cultural factors, discussed below, may keep these disorders hidden from view because the affected groups may be hesitant to complain.)

Industrial hygiene-related injuries and illnesses   Occupational asthma is a growing problem in the US workplace (Smith, 1993). The disease is defined as: "variable airflow obstruction caused by a specific agent found in the workplace" (1993). Agents which can lead to occupational asthma include dust particles, airborne allergens, and chemical agents which are respired or touch the skin. There is an important racial implication here: it appears that African-Americans are more likely than other population groups to die from asthma (1993). There is some debate as to whether this difference is biological or socioeconomic, but for our purposes we must address it as a racial issue. If African-Americans are more likely to die from asthma, and if occupational sources are a potential cause of asthma, then we must take special care in making sure that our workplaces limit exposure to irritating agents.

Research on lung cancer reveals that African-American smokers, even when their heavier smoking rates are accounted for, are more likely than their white counterparts to die from lung cancer (Chase, 1994a). Some researchers have proposed that black smokers are less able than white smokers to detoxify certain carcinogens found in tobacco products. Others offer a socioeconomic argument (1994a). Regardless of the cause of the black–white differences, if we carry this distinction to workplaces where smoking is allowed, we may postulate that African-Americans also may be more susceptible to cancer-related deaths from the effects of second-hand smoke. Thus, workplaces which still allow smoking may be disproportionately harmful to this racial group.

Some industrial hygiene problems unique to particular racial groups can go unrecognized or undiagnosed when managers fail to see the diversity dimension involved. For example, Weiner and Brown (1993) describe a case in which workers performing an established garment-dyeing task suddenly began to develop rashes on their upper and lower arms. The cause of this change remained a mystery until the managers realized that there had been a shift in anthropomorphics: the workforce was now predominantly composed of Asian immigrants who were smaller in stature than their workplace predecessors. When they lifted the garments out of the dye vats they had to raise their arms to such a height that the dye dripped past the elbow-length gloves, on to their upper arms, and ultimately back down into the rubber gloves. Management's failure to recognize the relationships between diversity and safety allowed the problem to continue longer than it should have. The solution was simple: raised work platforms next to the dye vats reduced the necessary lifting radius and prevented the dye from running down the employees' arms. Thus, what began as an anthropomorphic difference had evolved into an industrial hygiene problem.

Accident reporting   James et al. (1994) have demonstrated that racial minorities feel a degree of stigmatization in the workplace. This stigmatization can lead to stress, and ultimately to health problems. Stigmatized groups are likely to want to avoid feelings of segregation from their co-workers. If we carry these concepts into the health and safety arena, we may postulate that members of stigmatized groups will feel *further* stigmatized if they report accidents and injuries. Employees who report such problems may be required to perform specially designed "light duty" tasks which remove them from their co-workers. This can have the effect of singling them out and can be a potential source of stress. Thus, they may hesitate to report injuries.

Racial minorities may be among those who feel least confident in their job security. Fears that an injury claim may put their jobs in jeopardy could discourage them from reporting a safety or health problem. The difficulty is compounded when we consider what may happen in an accident investigation. It has been established that members of racial minority groups are more likely than other employees to be blamed personally for errors or mistakes on the job (Loden and Rosener, 1991). There is a tendency, in general, for supervisors to cast blame on their employees when accidents or injuries occur (De Joy, 1994). When minority status is brought into the picture, we are likely to see a further magnification of this attributional bias. As a consequence, minority employees wishing to "lay low" and avoid job loss may be reluctant to report injuries.

Organizational bias or discrimination   There is some tendency for racial groups to cluster together in certain types of jobs. If these jobs present particular kinds of safety hazards, which many of them do, there will be a disproportionate health risk exposure for that group.

US manufacturing operations that are predominated by sewing are largely staffed by recent Asian immigrants. Working conditions may meet minimum standards set by OSHA,[4] but there are new concerns about cancer caused by electromagnetic fields emitted from industrial sewing machines (Maugh, 1994). The information on this relationship is still new and is not confirmed (US Government, 1993), but there have been legitimate calls for concern among members of the scientific community (Savitz, 1993; Tenford,

1993). Thus, we may have another case of a racial group being subjected disproportionately to an industrial hygiene hazard.

Some sources of organizational discrimination are hidden from view. Specifically, Gerlin (1994) reveals the mounting problems of illegal home-sewing among Asian immigrants. Many of these people lack the language skills necessary for regular employment, or are living illegally in the US. Their working conditions, not to mention their pay, are far below accepted US standards. Moreover, they have no insurance coverage. The poor working conditions for these illegal sewers will undoubtedly lead to adverse musculoskeletal effects, but their injuries will go unreported (Gerlin, 1994). This represents a special case of workforce diversity that is often overlooked – a group of minority workers is being intentionally segregated from the workplace and subjected to higher than normal safety and health risks.

Culture and workplace safety

Culture, as a diversity issue, must be separated from race because it has more to do with a person's origin and family affiliation than it does with racial genetics. Moreover, various individuals and groups hold on to cultural identities to a greater extent than others, so it is not always possible to say that all members of a particular racial group will posses the same cultural attributes. However, as Hofstede (1984) has demonstrated through a large-scale cross-national research effort, people from different nations tend, in general, to display differences in cultural values, attitudes, and behaviors. He identifies four cultural dimensions, each measured on a continuum, which distinguish geographically-defined cultural groups from one another. These are: power distance, uncertainty avoidance, individualism, and masculinity. *Power distance* refers to the interpersonal power that subordinates view their bosses to have over them. *Uncertainty avoidance* refers to the ways in which, and the extent to which, a society uses technology, law, and religion to cope with unknowns. *Individualism* is an indicator of the relative predominance of individual focus versus collective focus within a culture. And *Masculinity* refers to the extent to which a culture takes on values which are viewed as being "masculine" or values which are viewed as being "feminine." As the diversity within any one nation increases, we would expect an infusion of individuals who are characterized by different cultural value profiles than those of the previous, and more homogeneous, workforce. These profiles can influence the way a particular cultural group is affected by safety issues in the workplace. The issues here will be related to social, rather than physical, predispositions toward accidents and injuries. Specific examples of implications for Hofstede's typology are discussed below in relation to work practices and reporting. Additionally, there also are instances of organizational bias or discrimination that lead to hazard exposures for certain cultural groups.

Following safe work practices   The US is known to have workplace safety practices which are among the most stringent in the world (Hammer, 1989).

Employees in many US organizations have adapted to an evolving "safety culture" (Pidgeon, 1991) and have bought-in to the inclusion of safety practices in work procedures. However, the assumption that this buy-in will hold for members of all cultural groups can lead to unforeseen problems, especially in overseas locations.

One Fortune 500 company which attempts to maintain uniform safety standards in all of its operations worldwide has found this commitment difficult to maintain in its Philippine operations. Filipino electricians, in particular, apparently consider the dangers associated with working bare-handed on hot wires to be a source of job satisfaction and pride. The company found it very difficult to persuade these employees to follow its US-originated safety procedures. This observation is in keeping with empirical findings by Jermier et al. (1989) who noted that perceived danger was a source of job satisfaction among some police officers. Relating this back to the electricians, it is possible that in the Philippines, which are characterized by Hofstede as being toward the upper end in terms of the masculinity dimension, we are likely to find general resistance to safety procedures. This need not be considered solely an issue for offshore manufacturers; we may also expect *employee groups* from some high masculinity cultures (e.g. Mexico, Italy) to be resistant to the practice of safety.

Two of Hofstede's other dimensions, power distance and individualism, have been hypothesized by Weiner and Russell (1993) to influence the occurrence of major accidents involving commercial airlines. They correlated the incidence rates for hull-loss accidents (i.e. total loss of plane) with ratings on these two dimensions. Their findings indicate that such accidents are 2.6 times as likely in *high* power distance/*low* individualism countries (e.g. Peru, Venezuela, Guatemala, Turkey, Greece) as they are in *low* power distance/*high* individualism countries (e.g. US, Great Britain, Canada, Denmark). It is worth noting that the *high* power distance/*low* individualism countries with higher accident rates are purchasing equipment and being trained for safety by people from *low* power distance/*high* individualism cultures. If training programs are founded on the wrong cultural assumptions, pilots may be insufficiently socialized into the "safety culture" of the international aeronautics community. Translating this finding back to offices, service environments, and factories, we may expect to find clashes between safety cultures when an organization is designed and run by Americans or Europeans, for example, and staffed by populations that have different values and norms when it comes to workplace safety practices.

Hazard and injury reporting   Although Hofstede's (1984) cultural dimensions have not been examined in relation to hazard and injury reporting, it seems that the power distance and individualism dimensions may be most important here. In cultures characterized by high power distance (e.g. Philippines, Mexico, Venezuela, India, Singapore), employees tend to accept a view of themselves as being much lower in status than their organizational superiors. A more egalitarian assumption is made by employees in low power distance countries (e.g. Sweden, Ireland, Denmark, Israel,

Australia). Resulting behaviors among employees from high power distance countries may include a reluctance to report injuries or complain about workplace safety hazards.

In Hofstede's (1984) typology, cultures characterized by high individualism include: US, Australia, Great Britain, Canada, Netherlands. Those characterized by low individualism (or collectivism) include: Taiwan, Peru, Pakistan, Colombia, Venezuela. As the category names quite aptly suggest, this dimension measures the propensity of the people within a culture to focus more on the needs and desires of themselves (individualism) or on the greater good of the community (collectivism). A real case illustrates how this cultural dimension may operate as an influence on injury reporting response:

An Anglo-American white collar employee of a US aerospace company strained his back while he was on a three-month assignment at a Japanese subsidiary. He reported the injury and was overwhelmed by the response he received from his co-workers. They were all deeply concerned about his injury, and worked intensely as a group to find ways to resolve the problem. They concluded that the injury was caused by a combination of overweight and work habits and began to badger him continuously (even at home) about resolving these problems. In the very collective Japanese society, his problem became their problem. The employee became very sensitive to the overwhelming intrusions and was so distraught that he returned to the US well short of his intended stay in Japan.

The point here is that the highly collective Japanese culture, in combination with a very serious management commitment to workplace safety (Engelman, 1993; Wokutch, 1992), leads to a markedly different approach to workplace injuries than the one we see in the US. Engelman (1993) suggests, also, that injury reporting in Japan is shamefully inadequate. As the numbers of Asian immigrants continue to expand in US workplaces, we must be conscious of cultural differences related to injury reporting and take steps to avoid underreporting.

Organizational bias or discrimination Managerial biases, supported by employee self-selection, can lead to high concentrations of certain cultural groups within jobs that pose high risks for health and safety. Agriculture represents one such arena where cultural issues and unsafe work environments collide. Agriculture has the highest annual death rate (44 per 100,000 employees) among US industries and ranks at the top with construction, mining, and manufacturing when it comes to workplace injuries (National Safety Council, 1994). This represents only those injuries which are reported; US agriculture is still predominated by a relatively large proportion of family-owned operations and Occupational Safety and Health Administration or National Safety Council reporting are likely to be relatively lax in those situations (Cordes and Foster, 1991). Risks associated with farming environments include chemical toxicity, cancer, respiratory risks, and machinery accidents. It is estimated that as many as 300,000 farm workers are poisoned by pesticides each year (Weinger and Lyons, 1992).

The agricultural workforce in the US has a very high representation of Hispanic workers. Some of this is an outgrowth of traditions which began with the Bracero program of the 1940s. Under that plan, Mexican workers were admitted into the US for agricultural work (Jessup and Jessup, 1993). The tradition continued after the program was disbanded because agricultural work offered opportunities for entry-level jobs with little requirement for English literacy. Problems are undoubtedly compounded when we bring a population with low literacy rates into a highly dangerous work environment where understanding of chemical toxicity and safety procedures is essential to health and safety. It is also worth noting that most migrant farm workers live with their families very near to the fields and orchards where they work, which provides them with continuous exposure to toxic substances associated with farming. This merger of life and work locations may be a logistic and economic necessity for farmers and farm managers, but it seems legitimate to place it in the category of discrimination or bias, given the dangers associated with proximity to farm chemicals. Here, again, then, we have a case in which a particular type of work disproportionately exposes one cultural group to dangerous workplace hazards.

Language, literacy, and workplace safety

People who struggle with basic English language reading skills are becoming a growing subpopulation in US work organizations (Szudy and Arroyo, 1994), and it is estimated that approximately 20 percent of US adults are functionally illiterate (Rabin, 1992). Recognizing their presence will be an important element of any safety program. This increase has two major sources. First, there has been a pronounced increase in the number of US residents for whom English is a second language (Barringer, 1993). Additionally, we have seen a growing incidence of illiteracy among adults for whom English is the first language (Szudy and Arroyo, 1994). One west coast Fortune 500 company, engaged in high technology precision manufacturing, recently discovered that over 10 percent of its direct labor workforce was not able to read or write above a third grade level. Most of these employees were born in the US.

A statistical analysis of federal and state safety records for 1988–92 reveals that work-related deaths and hazardous work environments are significantly more common in small businesses (20 or fewer employees) then they are in larger businesses (Marsh, 1994). When we consider that these are also the businesses most likely to hire workers who speak little English (1994), we see another instance of disproportionate exposure for a minority group.

The ability to read and understand spoken English becomes exceedingly important when we consider its potential effects on safety. Training and hazard communication are essential cornerstones of any safety program (Hollenbeck et al., 1992; Hammer, 1989) and if workers do not understand what they are being told about safety procedures, safety equipment, or hazardous material handling, they are certain to endanger themselves and their co-workers (Bruening, 1989). Even when a worker has a reasonably good grasp of standard English, US colloquialisms can restrict his or her ability to grasp the meaning of some safety terms. For example, the term "near miss," used commonly in air traffic control, is being used increasingly in organizational safety programs. If we dissect this term and consider its literal translation, it suggests a "hit" that was almost a "miss" when in fact it should suggest a "miss" that was almost a "hit." This sort of word-use can cause tremendous confusion for foreign-born workers who are attempting to understand workplace communication about safety through literal translation.

As the numbers of chemicals present in the workplace continue to escalate, hazard communication becomes increasingly critical. Yet Sattler (1992) found that the "average" worker could not understand 40 percent of the information on Material Safety Data Sheets (MSDS), a key source of information about occupational chemical hazards. In sum, then, workforce language and literacy deficiencies are increasing at the same time that the workplace is demanding greater literacy.

Safe work practices   Employees with language or literacy problems may be unable to read warning signs posted near workplace hazards, as mentioned above, or they may not be able to interpret an MSDS. As a consequence, they will be insufficiently aware of workplace hazards and may make errors that will endanger their own health and safety as well as that of their co-workers.

Employees with language problems may sit dutifully through required safety classes without really absorbing the material. For example, one west coast electronics manufacturer, with a high percentage of recent immigrants from Asia in its workforce, discovered that its employees were not gaining any information or insight from its safety training programs. Safety classes are generally offered during manufacturing production hours, so it is essential that the organization be getting its money's worth in return for lost output. If a manager is spending time and resources on signage and training, but has not accommodated the lowest language levels in the workforce, the efforts may be wasted and employees may be at high risk of injury (Szudy and Arroyo, 1994).

Let us consider an example of what might happen when an employee with a language problem does not sufficiently understand hazards and safe work practices:

Employee A has been assigned to clean a tank which normally holds toxic chemicals. He enters the tank, unaware of the need for protective safety gear and breathing apparatus (the signs on the outside of the tank make this known, but he cannot read them). He quickly succumbs to asphyxiation from the chemical residue in the tank but is able to call for help before he becomes unconscious. Employee B, who also has trouble reading, hears Employee A's call for help and quickly enters the tank to make a rescue. Before Employee B knows what is happening, she also loses consciousness. Both employees die from the toxic effects of the chemical.

289

Unfortunately, this sort of scenario is not unheard of in industry (Suruda et al., 1994). Multiple deaths in confined spaces certainly can and do occur among employees who are fully literate, but are undoubtedly more likely among persons whose ability to interpret written information leads them to incomplete understanding of the dangers involved.

Not all language-related procedural errors lead to death, of course, but there are plenty of moderate-to-serious injuries that are also worthy of our attention. Bruening (1989) cites an example in which employees were experiencing an increase in chemical burns. It became evident after some investigation that the supplier had changed bottle colors, but not labels. Employees, whose reading skills were poor, had continued to rely on bottle color as a guide for mixing, resulting in dangerous chemical combinations.

Language barriers can be especially problematic during emergencies or crises. Quick, effective communication is essential under circumstances involving fires, chemical leaks, and the like. But, if those communicating instructions speak a language that is different from that of operating-level employees, the results can be catastrophic. Examples occur in airline accidents when members of cockpit crews speak a variety of languages (Glain, 1994). As long as things are routine, the crew can work together effectively. But, when disaster strikes, language barriers overcome the group's ability to quickly solve problems. Although air disasters receive considerable media attention, similar incidents undoubtedly occur on a regular but smaller scale in diverse workplaces all over the world.

Injury reporting   Once an accident or injury has occurred, it is important that its cause be identified and that it be removed or abated. If employees who speak little or no English are involved in the accident, it may be very difficult to sort out the accident source. For example, a recent shooting incident in Seattle left two people dead and several wounded (Colon, 1994). The incident took place at a Vietnamese club. When Seattle police attempted to investigate, language barriers, combined with the self-protecting culture of the Vietnamese community, made it nearly impossible for them to identify the true perpetrators or the causes of the incident. If we carry this scenario into a workplace, with non-English-speaking employees, we can imagine a situation in which a serious accident occurs. Not only might it be difficult to communicate crisis-response instructions during the injury-causing event, it might also be very difficult to elicit employee help in diagnosing causes to prevent repeat incidents.

Gender and workplace safety

Women now represent approximately 46 percent of the workforce, and two-thirds of working-aged women are employed (Loden and Rosener, 1991). The forecast is for this trend to continue as more women enter the workforce and as women are increasingly staying on the job longer in life than men (Bennett, 1994). Several safety issues related to physical and social predispositions have emerged from these demographic changes. Some of these issues have implications which increase workplace health and safety risks to women as compared to men. Some have to do with risks to unborn children. Others affect co-workers' safety and health in both positive and negative ways.

Musculo-skeletal injuries　Not since the days of "Rosie the Riveter" have we seen so many women in the workplace, particularly in nontraditional jobs historically the domain of men. On average, women are smaller and possess less physical strength than men (Pulat, 1992). In certain types of jobs, especially in manufacturing, women may be more susceptible to musculo-skeletal injuries if they are expected to perform the same work as their larger male counterparts.

The infusion of women into the workplace has introduced styles of clothing which may be ill-suited to some work environments. High heeled shoes, once the footwear of the idle class, have become part of the accepted uniform for women in business, and can even be seen in some factory settings. High heels have been shown to cause musculo-skeletal problems for women (e.g. back pain), but there appears to be some debate in the medical literature regarding their effect on spinal curvature (de Lateur et al., 1991; Gastwirth et al., 1991). Researchers in this field do appear to support the position that high-heel-wearing can increase risk of injury (Ebbeling et al., 1994). For example, high heels can lead to a greater propensity to slip and fall. The grid work typically used as the flooring surface on walkways and catwalks in industrial settings makes high heels especially inappropriate. The more women present themselves in the workplace, the more we increase the likelihood that employees will be at risk for high-heel related accidents, injuries, and disorders. Some organizations (Boeing, for example) are responding to these risks by prohibiting the use of high heels in certain work settings. But wearing high heels is not always the choice of the employee – it can be an artefact of organizational bias. Not too long ago, United Airlines flight attendants (only the female ones, of course) successfully bargained to eliminate the requirement that they wear high heels in-flight. They successfully argued that fatigue and injury risk were intensified with heels, and also that heels could puncture an inflatable escape ramp in an emergency.[5]

Industrial hygiene-related illnesses and injuries　One element of the increasing complexity of the workplace is the introduction, in geometric growth proportions, of chemicals and other airborne hazards in work environments (Hammer, 1989). We have all undoubtedly heard of "sick building syndrome," typically found in white collar office environments (Paskal, 1993) and we frequently read about chemical sources creating health reactions among employees in manufacturing settings. Sometimes the effects of these exposures can manifest themselves in many employees, but in other cases, only a handful will raise complaints (Cullen, 1987). It does appear that some individuals are more sensitive than others to chemical exposures. For reasons unknown, women are more likely than men to suffer from a debilitating but difficult to define disease known as "multiple chemical sensitivity" (Mooser, 1987; Wilson, 1994). These sensitivities seem to be caused by the combined effects of several chemicals, the workplace levels of which may, individually, fall within accepted limits (Cullen, 1987). In combination, however, they create effects for which there is yet very little scientific understanding. Because multiple chemical sensitivity has affected women to a greater extent than it has men, there has been a tendency in some circles to blame the effect on psychological causes or "hysteria" (Wilson, 1994). It is clear, though, that different groups and individuals have different chemical tolerance levels (Mooser, 1987; Hammer, 1989) and that further research is needed.

A fundamental difference between men and women, the ability to bear children, has serious implications for workplace exposures to safety hazards (Weinstock, 1994). For example, occupational exposures to lead, mercury, pesticides, and textile dyes have been demonstrated to significantly reduce female fertility (Baird and Wilcox, 1986). Although the evidence has been contradictory,[6] it appears possible that exposure to electromagnetic fields associated with video display terminals (VDTs) and other technological devices can increase the probability of miscarriage and possibly damage a fetus (Tenford, 1993; Maugh, 1994). Women often predominate in clerical jobs (Susser, 1986) requiring intensive use of electromagnetic field-emitting equipment (e.g. VDTs, photocopiers, printers (Breysse et al., 1994)), further intensifying postulated reproductive risks. However, the highest workplace exposures (three times those of electric power line workers) to electromagnetic fields appear to come from industrial sewing machines (Maugh, 1994), again giving women a disproportionately higher exposure.

Legal developments have created new dilemmas regarding reproductive issues. A recent Supreme Court ruling precludes organizations from discrimination against women of childbearing age when it comes to hazardous work assignments (Weinstock, 1994; Wermiel, 1991). Johnson Controls Company, a battery manufacturer, had imposed a fetal protection policy on female employees of childbearing age, disallowing them from working in areas with high lead exposure. The court ruled that this was discriminatory, holding that women have the individual right to choose between having a child or having a job (Wiedis et al., 1994). Still, the ruling poses a dilemma for companies – they now face potential law suits over birth defects or miscarriages (Lublin, 1991). Given that exposures to occupational hazards such as lead, radiation, and dibromochloropropane can also present reproductive risks for men (Baird and Wilcox, 1986), the best answer seems to be in reducing hazardous exposure for *all* employees (Deitchman, 1994). It may be that the presence of women in the workplace will provide work organizations with the needed motivation to make these changes.

Some gender-specific health problems come not from the physical work environment, but from stresses associated with the social system. For example, research indicates that blue collar women have higher rates of cardiovascular disease than their white collar counterparts (Hall et al., 1993).

In a study conducted in Sweden, researchers found that women who experienced cardiovascular disease tended, among other things, to have less social support in their work environments (Hall et al., 1993). It seems reasonable to assume that social support for women will be particularly low in nontraditional industrial environments where women are unlikely to find many others of their own gender.

Workplace violence Violence in the workplace is on the rise (Rigdon, 1994; Smith, 1993) and employee homicide is becoming an extremely serious issue for organizations. It is now the third leading cause of workplace death (behind environment and machine-related (Castillo and Jenkins, 1994)). In 1992, 1,004 Americans were murdered on the job, a 32 percent increase over the annual average for the 1980s (Rigdon, 1994).

Although there are conflicting statistics (Castillo and Jenkins, 1994), some researchers report that the highest on-the-job murder rates are for women (Deitchman, 1994). Moreover, homicide is now the number one cause of workplace fatality for females (Smith, 1993). Based on analysis of violent and homicide incidents, two theories seem to emerge to explain this alarming phenomenon. First, women tend to work in low-status, low-control jobs (e.g. waitress, receptionist) where they are out on the front line (Smith, 1993) – this makes them easier targets. Second, women are more likely than men to be victimized by jilted lovers and estranged husbands (Smith, 1993). This is a safety issue that must be handled with great seriousness by employers.

Attention to safety In general, women have been shown to be more risk-averse than men (Wallach and Kogan, 1959), particularly when it comes to health and safety risks (Bromiley and Curley, 1992). Whatever the social or evolutionary roots of this gender difference, it manifests itself in the workplace through greater attention to safety precautions among women (De Joy, 1994). My interviews and observations among members of a large machinists' union have indicated that women are more likely to wear safety equipment such as eye and hearing protection, and they are less likely to remove or disable "bothersome" safety guards from machinery, when compared to their male counterparts. This greater sense of caution among women can translate into fewer injuries of all types and may serve to reduce injury statistics in areas where women are becoming represented to a greater degree than they have been in the past. This positive force may help to balance some of the heightened risks women face with regard to anthropometrics, chemical sensitivity, and job selection or assignment biases.

Hazard reporting Women appear to be less likely than men to take a "macho" stance with regard to workplace hazards, particularly in manufacturing settings. I have observed several instances in which women have lobbied to reduce maximum lifting load policies in the workplace. When the organization responded through changes in policy, lifting equipment, or maximum container sizes, their male co-workers expressed delight. They admitted that they also had been bothered by the heavy loads but had had too much pride to bring up the subject themselves. Thus, new perspectives brought by women into the male culture of manufacturing work environments (in particular) can have a positive impact on the health and safety of co-workers.

Organizational discrimination   Organizational biases have historically segregated women into particular kinds of jobs. Perhaps the most obvious example is found in the concentration of women in clerical tasks. If these clerical tasks expose women disproportionately to electromagnetic radiation from VDTs, we may have another example of increased risk for a population group.

One international issue is particularly noteworthy in discussions of organizational bias and safety for women. According to Kadetsky (1994), 70 percent of Mexican maquiladora employees are women. Although it is illegal to specify gender for jobs in the US, firms operating facilities in Mexico and elsewhere freely violate this gender-neutral doctrine. I have seen employment ads in Mexico which not only specify that workers must be women, they also specify age (17–25) and appearance (attractive). The safety connection here is that the jobs for which these companies are advertising (e.g. electronics assembly) tend to require tedious, eye-straining work which can lead to serious back and eye problems (Kadetsky, 1994). Additionally, anecdotal reports indicate that toxic materials used in some of these manufacturing plants have led to miscarriages and birth defects (Butler and Teagarden, 1993; Kadetsky, 1994). Unfortunately, the US has a history of exporting unsafe jobs to other countries (Hammer, 1991). Given the intentional selection of women, we have another example of women being disproportionately exposed to workplace hazards.

Age and workplace safety

As life expectancies have increased, and as baby-boomers mature, the average age of the workforce also has increased (American Association of Retired Persons, n.d.). The effects of aging, including deterioration of eyesight, reduction in range of motion, reduction in speed, and loss of physical strength, must be taken into account with the "graying" of the employee population (Salthouse, 1976; Garg, 1991). However, the commonly held assumption that advancing age is associated with workplace injuries has not been substantiated (Root, 1981). Moreover, a large-scale retrospective study of back injury claims by Bigos et al. (1986) demonstrated that the greatest risk occurred among workers who were in their twenties. In spite of these assurances that age is not a factor in workplace accidents and injuries, there are some good reasons for us to consider it in this discussion.

Musculo-skeletal injuries   As the workforce ages, we must be conscious of adaptations in the workplace that will be necessary to accommodate changes in physical attributes and abilities. For example, there is a shrinking in body dimensions that begins at age 40 and accelerates with advancing years (Pulat, 1992). The inflexible workplace of yesterday may or may not have caused injuries for older workers, but it certainly is likely to have caused discomfort and strain.

There is anecdotal evidence that injuries among older manufacturing workers have increased during times of downsizing. Three of the organizations that I studied experienced this phenomenon, and my interviews with managers from other companies indicate that it has come to their attention as well. The cause of this trend during layoff periods appears to be in the movement of senior workers into the jobs previously held by laid-off junior-level employees. It is well known that employees with greater seniority tend to self-select into less strenuous jobs over time. When they return to strenuous jobs during downsizing phases, they may not be in sufficient physical condition to perform the more demanding work. Additionally, they may not have received refresher training with regard to these tasks.

Along these lines, Agnew and Suruda (1993) have suggested that some of the general decrease seen in accidents and injuries among older workers may be attributed to their avoidance of the most dangerous jobs. In general, risk-taking behavior has been shown to decrease with age (Vroom and Pahl, 1971). These findings have real significance to work organizations: as corporate downsizing and reengineering efforts continue to reduce the size of company workforces, attention must be paid to increased health and safety for senior-level workers who may be moved back into riskier jobs.

Even though older workers do not have higher workplace accident rates than their younger colleagues, statistics clearly show that they *are more likely to be permanently disabled or die* when they are involved in accidents (Dillingham, 1981; Mitchell, 1988). Moreover, Root (1981) has reported that older workers suffer a disproportionately greater number of workplace falls. Agnew and Suruda (1993) confirmed these findings and also found that the height at which a fall becomes fatal decreases with increasing age. They propose that the higher incidence rates for falling are related to reduced control of postural stability, psychomotor slowing, prolongation of visual reaction time, and reduced strength. They further theorize that these factors, in combination, interfere with an older worker's ability to recover balance or regain footing. Additionally, the older fall victim is more vulnerable than the younger one to physical trauma and thus more likely than a younger worker to suffer a fatality from a fall (Agnew and Suruda, 1993). The aging issue may be compounded for older women, who are especially vulnerable to the bone-brittling effects of osteoporosis. This very serious issue for the increasingly aging workforce indicates a need for organizations to take responsibility in redesigning the workplace to minimize falling risks. Where redesign is not possible, organizations should staff falling-risk jobs with younger employees.

Violence Our discussion of age has, thus far, focused on *increased* age as a safety issue. However, we must also recognize that *younger workers* predominate some job categories which are highly susceptible to victimization by violent crime (Grossman, 1994). Teenagers make up 60 percent of the fast food workforce, and their wage-related self-selection into this industry has disproportionately increased their exposure to gun-point robbery and potentially violent death.

Contagious disease and workplace safety

We currently are witnessing an increase in the numbers of persons in the workplace who are known to carry contagious diseases. Some of this change has come about because of improvements in diagnosis and reporting, and some of it is the result of real increases in diseases such as HIV/AIDS (Stone, 1994), tuberculosis (Davisson, 1994; Bowden and McDiarmid, 1994), and hepatitis (Bovard, 1994; Chase, 1994c). One source of the increased incidence of communicable disease in the workplace is the greater global mobility that characterizes the world's population (Lemonick, 1994). Diseases once thought to have been eradicated in the US have been reintroduced by immigrants coming from countries where disease control systems are less developed than those in the US (Chase, 1994b). For example, last year in Los Angeles, 30 percent of the students in a suburban high school tested positive for tuberculosis after exposure to a new student who had carried the disease from her home country in Asia (Lemonick, 1994). Additionally, some residents of the US have become complacent about vaccination, further compounding problems caused by global mobility (Chase, 1994c).

Following an era of much "disease conquering," some infectious diseases appear to be on the rise. Estimates of the number of Americans who are infected with HIV/AIDS seem to vary, but Stone (1994) indicates that one person in every 250 is infected. Tuberculosis, once thought to be eradicated, has increased by 18 percent in the US since 1985 (Davisson, 1994). Also, according to Bovard (1994) hepatitis B infects 300,000 and kills 7,000 Americans annually. Some of the increased incidence for the latter two diseases is attributable to HIV/AIDS; victims of the human immunodeficiency virus are more susceptible than others to tuberculosis and hepatitis pathogens (Cadawallader, 1992). Advances in health care now allow AIDS victims to live longer, increasing the probability that they will continue working (Stone, 1994). Because exposure to HIV/AIDS can occur only through exchange of body fluids such as blood and semen, concerns about co-worker exposure should be minimal in settings other than the health care industry. Still, cuts and scrapes are especially common in heavy industry, increasing the chance of blood exchange. As increasing numbers of children are infected by HIV, the child care industry may also pose added risks. Diaper-changing represents one potential for exposure, but children with behavioral problems may also be prone to bite or scratch their caregivers, leading to further risk. Additionally, lifesaving procedures such as mouth-to-mouth resuscitation can entail very close contact and transfer of body fluids.

Organizations must ensure that employees understand the differences between situations that do and those that don't pose risk.

The Americans with Disabilities Act (discussed in greater detail in chapter 12) protects employees who carry contagious diseases from discrimination in the workplace. In spite of these protections, cases of discrimination and misdirected paranoia still exist (Stone, 1994; Gebbie, 1994). We must also acknowledge, however, that the presence of infected individuals in the workplace can present real health risks to them, personally, and to their co-workers.

Illness risks for the infected employee   The weakened immune systems of individuals who are victims of HIV/AIDS make them highly susceptible to hepatitis, tuberculosis, and any other pathogen that their co-workers might bring to the workplace. Thus, in spite of the flurry of concern about contagion to co-workers, employees with HIV/AIDS may be at greater risk from continuing to work than are the co-workers who are exposed to them (Cadawallader, 1992). Organizations wishing to protect *all* of their employees from contagious diseases must consider the greater vulnerability of those who are infected with HIV/AIDS.

Illness risks for co-workers   Reactions among employees who potentially could be infected by HIV/AIDS have reached hysteria in some organizations. Stone (1994) cites cases of employees who are afraid to share telephones, bathrooms, or water fountains with co-workers who are infected. In spite of clear and constant messages from the health care community that the disease is not spread through casual contact, these fears and consequent organizational discrimination have continued. George et al. (1993) found that nurses find working with HIV-infected patients to be a source of great stress. Although our focus is on co-workers who carry diseases, rather than on patients in health care settings, the nurses' reactions are worth noting because these professionals should be among the most informed and, therefore, the most comfortable, in having contact with infected persons.

Why, we may ask, is the fear of AIDS in the workplace greater than the fear of hepatitis B or tuberculosis, when the latter two diseases are actually more contagious? The answer is probably twofold. First, the history of AIDS has tied it with homosexual activity and illegal intravenous drug use, both of which are considered unacceptable by "mainstream" society (Stone, 1994). People may be more squeamish about the virus because of these connections. Second, AIDS, as we know it today, is guaranteed to end in death, and a most painful one at that. Although the death rates for tuberculosis and hepatitis B are high by modern standards, these two diseases are considered curable. Moreover, these diseases can be contracted in ways that the general populace considers to be acceptable (e.g. through the air or through water). In spite of the misdirected biases, organizations should take precautions to guard all of their employees against dangerous pathogens.

Summary

The preceding discussion has been intended to raise awareness of the workplace safety issues that may emerge in organizational settings with diverse workforces. Awareness is an important first step, but it must be followed by managerial action. The next section suggests actions which will help to create safe work environments for all organization members. The discussion, of course, will not be intended as a full treatise on organizational safety practices, but will focus on those issues most relevant to workforce diversity.

Managerial Actions

Managing diversity is a comprehensive managerial process for developing an environment that works for all employees.

This statement by Roosevelt Thomas (1991) provides a useful perspective on the recommendations to be made in this section. An environment that "works" for all employees is an environment that is safe for all employees, regardless of their race, culture, language ability, gender, age, or illness. Creating a safe work environment is the responsibility of all organizational members – nearly all failed attempts at improving workplace safety have involved the error of relegating responsibility to a single person or work unit. The two organizational functions which seem to have the greatest role to play in workplace safety are operations and HR. Because both are so critical to the process, and because their efforts must be coordinated, this chapter will depart somewhat from others in this book by including a discussion of the role of the operations function. The lines between the roles played by operations and HR are fuzzy, at best, but it is possible to specify responsibilities to some extent. A potential delineation, which will serve as the framework for this summary section of the chapter, is presented in figure 11.3.

As shown in figure 11.3, the safety responsibilities that fall into the operations camp are mostly linked with physical or procedural aspects of the work. For example, equipment selection is an operations issue because equipment (i.e. anything from a cash register to a lathe or machine tool) determines an organization's ability to achieve competitive priorities such as quality or delivery speed. Likewise, safety procedures are often closely intertwined with the way work gets done (e.g. lock-out tag-out procedures to ensure safety during equipment repair). Most safety hazards are also found within the domain of the operations function – for example, toxic chemicals used in a machine shop degreasing operation. In contrast, the HR functions related to safety have more to do with caring for the employee. For example, injury follow-up procedures are often assigned to the HR function because they will have implications for other traditional HR activities such as workers' compensation, coordination with medical caregivers, and selection of replacement personnel. On the other hand, it would be

Figure 11.3   Safety solutions for the diverse workforce

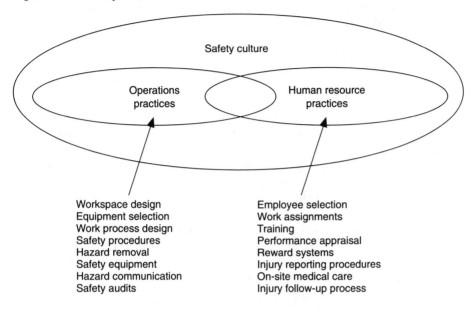

Workspace design
Equipment selection
Work process design
Safety procedures
Hazard removal
Safety equipment
Hazard communication
Safety audits

Employee selection
Work assignments
Training
Performance appraisal
Reward systems
Injury reporting procedures
On-site medical care
Injury follow-up process

Employee involvement programs
Management of change

unlikely to find an HR professional overseeing the purchase of heavy manu-facturing equipment.

The overlapping ovals in figure 11.3 symbolize the need for coordination among all of the activities listed, but particularly for those shown at the bottom of the figure (i.e. employee involvement and management of change). It has been demonstrated in many organizations that a successful safety program will involve a partnership between these two functions (Kamp, 1994). The Sara Lee bakery in New Hampton, Iowa, provides an example of an organization which made notable improvements in its safety record through a systems approach. In fact, their initial attempts at improvement failed because they did not sufficiently integrate HR and operations tactics. Inco Alloys in Huntington, West Virginia, has also made impressive gains in its safety record through changes that have combined the efforts of HR management and operations management.

Enveloping the entire operations-HR system is something we will call "safety culture" (Pidgeon, 1991). This is an intangible but real characteris-tic that distinguishes work organizations with safe from those with unsafe work environments. It involves a sincere caring about employee health and safety (at work or away from work), and it is shared by all members of the organization. A series of plant tours has provided me with the consistent impression that a positive safety culture brings far-reaching advantages to an organization. Additionally, my recent unpublished research shows that safety culture is a significant determinant of progress in implementing a total quality management program.

We must acknowledge, then, that preventive solutions will be characterized by a sociotechnical approach. Social approaches are most often found within the HR function and technical solutions are the realm of operations. The elements of safety efforts presented in figure 11.3 are discussed below in relation to workforce diversity.

Operations function

The operations function encompasses those activities which contribute to the transformation of inputs (e.g. materials, information, labor, machinery) into goods and services. Operations processes begin with strategic decisions and workplace design and continue through product or service delivery and post-delivery customer response. Several opportunities for protecting the health and safety of the workforce are found within this long sequence of activities, and many of them are worthy of special consideration in the context of a diverse workforce. Not all hazards may be *eliminated* completely; sometimes efforts must be aimed at hazard *avoidance* and in other cases we may be able to *only minimize* the effects of hazards. Many potential improvements in operations practices have been alluded to in the context of the preceding discussion of diversity. A few examples are presented in table 11.1, along with reference to the benefits that may result from each.

Table 11.1 provides a few examples of the kinds of operations practices that can improve the safety of working conditions for employees in diverse workforces. Operations practices shown in the table match those presented on the left side of figure 11.3. Application examples are drawn from previous discussions of diversity dimensions. The general theme of table 11.1 is a focus on process improvement. We often associate process improvement with quality or productivity efforts, but it is important for safety, as well. In fact, many of the tools associated with the total quality management movement may be applied to safety. For example, cause-effect diagrams, Pareto charts, run charts, and flow diagrams can be very helpful in uncovering the causes of safety problems. These analytical methods can lead us to select the appropriate corrective action, which may include one of the possibilities shown in table 11.1. The recognition of workforce diversity as a contributing factor can further ensure that the right choices are made.

The organizations which have been most successful in improving safety through operations changes have involved employees from the very beginning. For example, Inco Alloys sends line employees and maintenance personnel to vendor sites to examine and test equipment before it is purchased. The results have been positive: the safest and most effective equipment has been selected, and employee morale has been enhanced through the opportunity for involvement. At Boeing, the machinists' union played the central role in developing a computer-based self-teaching tool for hazardous materials communication. The program has been designed to meet the needs of a range of literacy and expertise levels. An important side benefit, beyond the development of a more informed workforce, has been

Table 11.1 Making the workplace safer for the diverse workforce: operations practices

Operations practice	Application example	Group(s) receiving benefit
Workplace design	Improvements in air filtering systems	Groups susceptible to occupational asthma and infectious disease
	Introduction of safe industrial personnel hoists to substitute for ladders	Groups susceptible to death and injury from falling
	Security systems to screen entry of outside intruders	Groups susceptible to violence
Equipment selection	Equipment selected based on workforce strength and size	Groups with anthropometrics and strength profiles outside the accepted "average"
Work process design	Completely redesigning processes to eliminate hazard exposure	Groups predisposed to be more sensitive to a hazard
Safety procedures	Introduce protective equipment for use in first aid (e.g. rubber gloves and personal protection for administering resuscitation)	Co-workers concerned about contracting infectious diseases
	Lower maximum lifting weight	Groups with smaller anthropometric strength profiles
Hazard removal	Test air for contaminants and toxic substances	Groups vulnerable to infection or chemical sensitivity
Safety equipment	Make certain protective clothing fits a range of body sizes	Groups with "non-standard" anthropometrics
Hazard communication	Provide simple, clear explanations – use graphics as well as words	Groups with language/literacy challenges
Safety audits	Maintain a positive tone; don't single out or reprimand individuals	Groups who may tend to feel stigmatized

an increase in the union's trust level with the company. Union members had felt previously that they were being kept in the dark about hazardous materials – their involvement in the training program provides them with full and up-to-date knowledge. At a Sara Lee bakery in New Hampton, Iowa, employees have designed and built their own equipment to meet safety needs (Rigdon, 1992). The result has been a marked decrease in carpal tunnel syndrome injuries. In all these cases, employee involvement has produced a better quality outcome and has also instilled the sort of ownership that is vital to a strong safety culture. It will be important, of course, to make certain that the employee groups involved in equipment selection are representative of the diversity of the workforce that will use the equipment. Improvements in the work environment will have benefits beyond safety and health – there is also good evidence that safety improves quality and productivity as well (Imada, 1990).

None of these improvements suggested in table 11.1 can effectively stand alone, however. Making the workplace safe is not enough – we must also find ways to change employee behaviors (Kamp, 1994). Solid safety programs, especially those geared toward diverse workforces, must have roots on the HR side, as well as on the operations side.

Human resource function

For the purpose of this discussion, the HR function will be viewed as encompassing the activities that bring employees to the workplace, provide benefits and rewards, promote safe work behaviors, and respond to accidents, injuries, and ailments. Thus, the HR function provides another set of opportunities for protecting the health and safety of employees. As with the preceding discussion of the operations function, space limitations do not allow for the full development of all of these. However, some examples are presented in table 11.2.

As with table 11.1, table 11.2 provides just a brief overview of the sorts of HR activities that will support an effective safety program within a diverse workforce. Perhaps the most important theme running through all of these examples is that of *being aware* of diversity implications in the safety arena. Several examples have been presented in the body of this paper to demonstrate the outcomes which may result from inattention to diversity. On the positive side, however, many organizations have begun to consider diversity issues in the context of safety. For example, some have effectively (and legally) used strength testing to determine job assignments. Methods of employee selection which may tend to discriminate present a sensitive issue for many organizations especially in light of the Americans with Disabilities Act. However, this should not preclude organizations from screening and placing employees based on *legitimate* job requirements and *valid* tests of employee qualifications (Lambert, 1994). Valid tests can go beyond the physical to include valid psychological measures of a job applicant's risk propensity (Kamp, 1994). In sum, then, HR practices ought to be designed to ensure that job assignments do not impose inappropriate health and safety risks, and to create a culture in which employees are well-informed, follow safe practices, and feel comfortable reporting injuries. Although minority groups within the work population will benefit from these sorts of actions, the remainder of the workforce will benefit, as well.

Just as employee involvement can create an important cornerstone for

Table 11.2 Making the workplace safer for the diverse workforce: HR practices

HR practice	Application example	Group(s) receiving benefit
Employee selection	Create valid physical selection criteria to meet specific job requirements	Groups who may not have the size or strength to handle physical job demands
Work assignments	Avoid clustering specific minority groups into unsafe "work ghettos"	All minority groups
Training	Use demonstrations of proper methods, rather than written instructions	Employees with poor reading skills. Employees for whom English is a second language
Performance appraisal	Include safe work practice as an evaluation criterion	Cultural groups in which safe work practices are not highly valued
Reward systems	Reward safe work practices	Cultural groups which may resist "non-macho" approaches to work
Injury reporting procedures	Keep them simple. Don't create barriers. Encourage reports	Employees with language problems. Employees who may fear further stigmatization
On-site medical care	Provide optional testing for communicable diseases such as tuberculosis or hepatitis	Co-workers who may be at risk for exposure
	Provide optional flu vaccinations on-site	Older employees, who are most susceptible to the effects of the flu
Injury follow-up	Use a systematic approach to problem diagnosis – avoid attributional biases that can lead to an incorrect diagnosis of "employee error"	Minority groups that may tend to receive more blame than they deserve for work-related problems
	Consider diversity-related factors in diagnosis (e.g. was the work station inappropriately designed for the body size of the employee?)	All groups

operations-related safety practices, it is also vital on the HR side. The three companies previously mentioned, Inco Alloys, Boeing, and Sara Lee, have all involved employees in safety-related training, evaluation, rewards, reporting, and follow-up. In a pluralistic workplace, the solicitation of a wide range of perspectives will be important to the establishment of an effective safety culture.

Implications for Research and Practice

Although links between diversity and safety have been addressed previously, integration of these concepts has been fragmented and has not been tied with the diversity literature. (For example, an article in the medical literature tying worker age to accident rates provides useful information on a narrow topic but does not place itself within the larger context of workforce diversity.) The efforts begun here seem worthy of further development by researchers and practitioners alike. As workforce diversity continues to grow, and as safety problems receive greater attention, we must keep in mind their interrelationships.

There are numerous opportunities for researchers who are interested in safety/diversity links. First, I would like to suggest that all of those who are engaged in diversity research consider safety issues in their investigations. For example, Jackson et al. (1993) have advanced several social propositions regarding the effects of introducing diversity to intact work teams. Their hypotheses range from issues such as cohesiveness to conflict, mentoring, and others. The discussion, and related propositions, could be extended to include safety issues. For instance, do we have more potential for violence when there is conflict between "old-timers" and "newcomers," when the two groups differ culturally? Or, do we encounter clashes over safety practices because of differences in risk aversion levels between the two groups? Might one faction tend to endanger the other? This provides one example of a discourse that could be extended to encourage research on diversity and safety. Many others exist. We might look at organizations as the unit of analysis and examine the extent to which diversity is considered in decisions about safety policies and practices. When it is considered, are safety benefits incurred? Research along these lines will not only make academic contributions but will be of value to organizations as they attempt to meet the challenges of providing a safe workplace with a heterogeneous employee population.

It is my hope that this chapter will benefit management practitioners, first, by increasing their awareness of safety issues that arise in diverse workforces. Second, the chapter is intended to focus attention on specific HR practices that may prevent safety problems for minority groups. Improvements that meet the needs of a diverse workforce *cannot* be the sole responsibility of the HR function – a partnership with operations is essential. So, for example, those who are involved with selection and staffing must draw upon assistance from their operations counterparts to inform them of equipment usage and other physical job requirements.

Conclusion

Work-related accidents, injuries, and ailments drain US businesses and public sector agencies of billions of dollars in non value-added cost. Additionally, they often represent lapses in social responsibility. Our increasingly diverse workforce presents special safety issues that may not have been considered in earlier days of workforce homogeneity. Some population groups are physically or socially more predisposed than others to injury, illnesses, and violence. Additionally, they may take views toward safe work practices, hazard reporting, or injury reporting that differ from those of the "mainstream." Organizations must respond to workforce diversity by ensuring that they provide work environments that are safe for *all* employees. Safety programs which are designed with diversity in mind are likely to benefit *all* employee groups, not just those who fall into minority categories.

NOTES

1 Physical disability might also be a logical topic to be included here, but it has been omitted from this discussion because of its more extensive coverage in chapter 12.
2 Two of the four occupational injury and illness incidence rates published by the Bureau of Labor Statistics for 1992 were the highest in 13 years. The incidence rate for total cases was 8.9 per 100 full-time workers in 1992, up 6 percent from 1991, and the highest since 9.5 was reported for 1979. The incidence rate for nonfatal cases without lost workdays was 5.0 in 1992, up 11 percent from 1991, and the highest this rate has been since it was 5.2 in 1979. The 1992 incidence rate for lost workday cases was 3.9, unchanged from 1991, and the lost workdays incidence rate was up 8 percent to 93.4.
3 Deming, who died in 1994, has often been recognized as the founder of the quality movement in Japan, and as a late-in-life quality luminary in the US.
4 However, it is my opinion and observation that many of these supposedly in-compliance factories present very substandard working conditions.
5 The airlines did partially maintain the old rules, however; female flight attendants still must wear high heels while in airport terminals.
6 Because reproductive events and attempts at pregnancy are very private concerns, the availability of data on these subjects is very limited (Baird and Wilcox, 1986).

REFERENCES

Agnew, J., and Suruda, A. J. (1993). Age and fatal work-related accidents. *Human Factors*, 35(4), 731–6.

American Association of Retired Persons brochure (n.d.) *The Aging Workforce*.

Americans with Disabilities Act of 1990, Pub. L. No. 101–336.

Baird, D. D., and Wilcox, A. J. (1986). Effects of Occupational Exposures on the Fertility of Couples. *Occupational Medicine: State of the Art Reviews*, 1(3), July–September, 361–74.

Barringer, F. (1993). When English is a foreign tongue: Census finds a sharp rise in '80s. *New York Times*, April 28, A10(4).

Bennett, A. (1994). More and more women are staying on the job later in life than men. *Wall Street Journal*, September 1, B1.

Bigos, S. J., Spengler, D. M., Martin, N. A., Zeh, J., Fisher, L., Nachemson, A., and Wong, M. H. (1986). Back injuries in industry: A retrospective study. III. Employee-related factors. *Spine*, 11(3), 252–6.

Bovard, J. (1994). Disabilities law, health hazard [Editorial]. *Wall Street Journal*, March 23.

Bowden, K. M., and McDiarmid, M. A. (1994). Occupationally acquired tuberculosis: What's known. *Journal of Occupational Medicine*, 36(3), 320–5.

Breysse, P., Lees, P. S. J., McDiarmid, M. A., and Curbow, B. (1994). ELF magnetic field exposures in an office environment. *American Journal of Industrial Medicine*, 25, 177–85.

Bromiley, P., and Curley, S. P. (1992). Individual differences in risk taking. In J. F. Yates, *Risk-Taking Behavior* (87–132). New York: Wiley.

Bruening, J. C. (1989). Workplace illiteracy: The threat to worker safety. *Occupational Hazards*, October, 118–22.

Butler, M. C., and Teagarden, M. B. (1993). Strategic management of worker health, safety, and environmental issues in Mexico's Maquiladora Industry. *Human Resource Management*, 32(4), 479–503.

Cadawallader, R. (1992). Meaningful AIDS education helps allay fears of working with infected employee. *Occupational Health and Safety*, April, 26–8.

Castillo, D. N., and Jenkins, E. L. (1994). Industries and occupations at high risk for work-related homicide. *Journal of Occupational Medicine*, 36(2), 125–32.

Chase, M. (1994a). Smoking study sparks debate on race issues. *Wall Street Journal*, April 15, B1.

Chase, M. (1994b). Pneumonic plague doesn't respect international borders. *Wall Street Journal*, October 3, B1.

Chase, M. (1994c). Roll your sleeves, close your eyes. This won't hurt a bit. *Wall Street Journal*, September 19, B1.

Colon, A. (1994). In the end, charges of murder dropped. *Seattle Times*, September 27, A1.

Cordes, D. H., and Foster, D. (1991). Farming: A hazardous occupation. *Occupational Medicine: State of the Art Reviews*, 6(3), July–September, 327–33.

Cullen, M. R. (1987). The worker with multiple chemical sensitivities: An overview. *Occupational Medicine: State of the Art Reviews*, 2(4), October–December, 655–61.

Davisson, J. F. (1994). What risk does TB pose in the workplace? *Occupational Hazards*, May, 84–7.

Deitchman, S. (1994). Occupational and environmental medicine. *Journal of the American Medical Association*, 271(21), 1691–2.

De Joy, D. M. (1994). Managing safety in the workplace: An attribution theory analysis and model. *Journal of Safety Research*, 25(1), 3–17.

de Lateur, B. J., Giaconi, R. M., Questad, K., Ko, M., and Lehmann, J. F. (1991). Footwear and posture: Compensatory strategies for heel height. *American Journal of Physical Medicine and Rehabilitation*, 70(5), 246–54.

Deming, W. E. (1986). *Out of the Crisis*. Boston: MIT Center for Advanced Manufacturing Studies.

Dillingham, A. E. (1981). Age and workplace injuries. *Aging and Work*, 4, 1–10.

Ebbeling, C. J., Hamill, J., and Crussemeyer, J. A. (1994). Lower extremity mechanics and energy cost of walking in high-heeled shoes. *Journal of Orthopedic and Sports Physical Therapy*, 19(4), 190–6.

Engelman, R. (1993). Japan leads US in safety. *Safety and Health*, April, 38–41.

Garg, A. (1991). Ergonomics and the older worker: An overview. *Experimental Aging Research*, 17(3), 143–55.

Gastwirth, B. W., O'Brien, T. D., Nelson, R. M., Manger, D. C., and Kindig, S. A. (1991). An electrodynographic study of foot function in shoes of varying heel heights. *Journal of the American Podiatric Medical Association*, 81(9), 463–72.

Gebbie, K. M. (1994). HIV, the ADA and needless hysteria. *Wall Street Journal*, April 29, A11.

George, J. M., Reed, T. R., Ballard, K. A., Colin, J., and Fielding, J. (1993). Contact with patients as a source of work-related distress: Effects of organizational and social support. *Academy of Management Journal*, 36, 157–71.

Gerlin, A. (1994). Spread of illegal home sewing is fueled by immigrants. *Wall Street Journal*, March 15, B1.

Glain, S. (1994). Language barrier proves dangerous in Korea's skies. *Wall Street Journal*, October, B1.

Grimsrud, T. M. (1990). Humans were not created to sit – and why you have to furnish your life. *Ergonomics*, 33(3), 291–5.

Grossman, L. M. (1994). Easy marks: Fast-food industry is slow to take action against growing crime. *Wall Street Journal*, September 22, A1.

Hall, E. M., Johnson, J. V., and Tsou, T.-S. (1993). Women, occupation, and risk of cardiovascular morbidity and mortality. *Occupational Medicine: State of the Art Reviews*, 8(4), 709–19.

Hammer, W. (1989). *Occupational Safety and Management*, 4th ed. Englewood Cliffs, NJ: Prentice-Hall.

Hammer, W. (1991). *Occupational Safety, Management and Engineering*. Englewood Cliffs, NJ: Prentice-Hall.

Hofstede, G. (1984). *Culture's Consequences: International Differences in Work-related Values*. Beverly Hills, CA: Sage.

Hollenbeck, J. R., Ilgen, D. R., and Crampton, S. M. (1992). Lower back disability in occupational settings: A review of the literature from a human resource management view. *Personnel Psychology*, 45(3), 247–78.

Imada, A. S. (1990). Ergonomics: Influencing management behaviour. *Ergonomics*, 33(5), 621–8.

Imrhan, S. N., Nguyen, M. T., and Nguyen, N. N. (1993). Hand anthropometry of Americans of Vietnamese origin. *International Journal of Industrial Ergonomics*, 12, 281–7.

Jackson, S. E., Stone, V. K., and Alvarez, E. B. (1993). Socialization amidst diversity: The impact of demographics on work/team old-timers and newcomers. In *Research in Organizational Behavior* (15, 45–109). Greenwich, CT: JAI Press.

James, K., Lovato, C., and Khoo, G. (1994). Social identity correlates of minority workers' health. *Academy of Management Journal*, 37, 383–96.

Jermier, J. M., Gaines, J., and McIntosh, N. J. (1989). Reactions to physically dangerous work: A conceptual and empirical analysis. *Journal of Organizational Behavior*, 10, 15–33.

Jessup, J., and Jessup, M. (1993). *Doing Business in Mexico*. Rocklin, CA: Prima Publishing.

Johnston, W. B. (1991). Global workforce 2,000: The new world labor market. *Harvard Business Review*, March–April, 115–27.

Kadetsky, E. (1994). The human side of free trade. *Ms*, January–February, 11–15.

Kamp, J. (1994). Worker psychology: Safety management's next frontier. *Professional Safety*, May, 32–6.

Komaki, J., Barwick, K. D., and Scott, L. R. (1978). A behavioral approach to occupational safety: Pinpointing and reinforcing safe performance in a food manufacturing plant. *Journal of Applied Psychology*, 63, 434–45.

Lambert, W. (1994). Have you ever? New EEOC guidelines for job interviewing baffle employers. *Wall Street Journal*, July 15, B1, B3.

Lemonick, M. D. (1994). The killers all around. *Time*, September 12, 62–9.

Loden, M., and Rosener, J. B. (1991). *Workforce America!* Homewood, IL: Business One Irwin.

Lublin, J. S. (1991). Decision poses dilemma for employers. *Wall Street Journal*, March 21, B1.

Marsh, B. (1994). Workers at risk: Chance of getting hurt is generally far higher at smaller companies. *Wall Street Journal*, February 3, A1.

Maugh, T. H. (1994). New report links Alzheimer's and electromagnetic fields. *Seattle Times*, July 31, A19.

Mitchell, O. S. (1988). Relation of age to workplace injuries. *Monthly Labor Review*, July, 8–13.

Mooser, S. B. (1987). The epidemiology of multiple chemical sensitivities. *Occupational Medicine: State of the Art Reviews*, 2(4), 663–8.

National Safety Council (1994). *Accident Facts*. Itasca, IL: National Safety Council.

Nomani, A. Q. (1994). Muffed mission: Labor Secretary's bid to push plant safety runs into skepticism. *Wall Street Journal*, August 19, A1.

Otten, A. L. (1994). The numbers bear out our diversity. *Wall Street Journal*, B1.

Paskal, S. S. (1993). New WISHA rules can open the door to trouble at work. *Pierce County Business Examiner*, February 22, 13.

Perrow, C. (1984). *Normal Accidents*. New York: Basic Books.

Pidgeon, N. F. (1991). Safety culture and risk management in organizations. *Journal of Cross-Cultural Psychology*, 22(1), March, 129–40.

Pulat, B. M. (1992). *Fundamentals of Industrial Ergonomics*. Englewood Cliffs, NJ: Prentice-Hall.

Rabin, A. T. (1992). Consequences of adult literacy reach far into the marketplace. *Occupational Health and Safety*, June, 36–40.

Rice, F. (1994). How to make diversity pay. *Fortune*, August 8, 78–86.

Rigdon, J. E. (1992). The wrist watch: How a plant handles occupational hazard with common sense. Many small changes enable Sara Lee bakery to ease carpal tunnel syndrome. *Wall Street Journal*, September 28, A1, A9.

Rigdon, J. E. (1994). Companies see more workplace violence. *Wall Street Journal*, April 12, B1.

Root, N. (1981). Injuries at work are fewer among older employees. *Monthly Labor Review*, March, 30–4.

Rosen, R. H. (1991). Sick jobs sabotage long-term investments. *The Healthy Company: Strategies to Develop People and Productivity*, pp. 209–33. New York: Jeremy P. Tarcher.

Salthouse, T. A. (1976). Speed and age: Multiple rates of age decline. *Experimental Aging Research*, 2(4), 349–59.

Sattler, B. (1992). Rights and realities: A critical review of the accessibility of information on hazardous chemicals. *Occupational Medicine: State of the Art Reviews*, April–June, 189–96.

Savitz, D. A. (1993). Commentary: Health effects of low-frequency electric and magnetic fields. *Environmental Science and Technology*, 27(1), 52–4.

Smith, S. L. (1993). Attacking asthma in the workplace. *Occupational Hazards*, August, 43–6.

Statistical Abstract of the US (1994). In *The National Data Book*, 114th ed., September. US Department of Commerce, Economics and Statistics Administration Bureau of the Census.

Stone, R. A. (1994). AIDS in the workplace: An executive update. *The Executive*, 8(3), 52–64.

Suruda, A. J., Petit, T. A., Noonan, G. P., and Ronk, R. M. (1994). Deadly rescue: The confined space hazard. *Journal of Hazardous Materials*, 36, 45–53.

Susser, I. (1986). Work and reproduction: Sociologic content. *Occupational Medicine: State of the Art Reviews*, 1(3), 517–31.

Szudy, E., and Arroyo, M. G. (1994). *The Right to Understand: Linking Literacy to Health and Safety Training*. Berkeley, CA: Labor Occupational Health Program.

Taylor, F. W. (1911). *Scientific Management*. New York: Harper and Row.

Tenford, T. S. (1993). Commentary on "health effects of low-frequency electric and magnetic fields." *Environmental Science and Technology*, 27(1), 56–8.

Thomas, R. R., Jr (1990). From affirmative action to affirming diversity. *Harvard Business Review*, March–April, 107–17.

Thomas, R. R., Jr (1991). *Beyond Race and Gender*. New York: American Management Association.

US Government Committee on Interagency Radiation Research and Policy Coordination (1993). Health effects of low-frequency electric and magnetic fields. *Environmental Science and Technology*, 27(1), 42–54.

Vroom, V. H., and Pahl, B. (1971). Relationships between age and risk taking among managers. *Journal of Applied Psychology*, 55, 399–405.

Wallach, M. A., and Kogan, N. (1959). Sex differences and judgment processes. *Journal of Personality*, 27, 555–64.

Weiner, E., and Brown, A. (1993). *Office Biology*. New York: MasterMedia.

Weiner, E. F., and Russell, P. D. (1993). Crew factor accidents: Regional perspective. Presented at the 22nd International Transport Association Technical Conference, October 6–8, Montreal, Quebec, Canada.

Weinger, M., and Lyons, M. (1992). Problem-solving in the fields: An action-oriented approach to farm worker education about pesticides. *American Journal of Industrial Medicine*, 22, 677–90.

Weinstock, M. P. (1994). How safe are women in the workplace? *Occupational Hazards*, March, 68–70.

Wermiel, S. (1991). Justices bar "fetal protection" policies. *Wall Street Journal*, March 21, B1.

West, K. (1992). Woman awarded $1.6 million: Jury finds in favor of Boeing worker. *Seattle Post-Intelligencer*, August 22, B1.

Wiedis, D., Jose, D. E., and Phoebe, T. O. (1994). The rock and the hard place: Employer liability to fertile or pregnant employees and their unborn children – what can the employer do? *Radiation Protection Management*, 11(1), January–February, 41–9.

Wilson, D. (1994). Crippling illness or just hysteria? *Seattle Times*, January 5, A1.

Wokutch, R. E. (1992). *Worker Protection, Japanese Style*. Ithaca, NY: ILR Press.

12
Managing Disability-based Diversity

Karen Roberts

Disability as a Source of Diversity

When one thinks about workplace diversity, certain dimensions of diversity spring to mind – race, gender, ethnicity. Occasionally physical abilities or characteristics are included in the list (Loden and Rosener, 1991), but not always. One reason disability may frequently be a forgotten source of diversity is that individuals with disabilities have only recently acquired legal antidiscrimination protection with the passage of the Americans with Disabilities Act of 1990 (ADA). A second reason may be that such individuals are somewhat less visible than other groups in society: often less mobile and less likely to be in the labor force (Haveman and Wolfe, 1990). A final reason is the one developed in this chapter – that while disability is clearly a dimension of diversity, it is inherently different from the other demographically based sources of diversity and as such poses some unique challenges to human resource (HR) professionals.

Most of the current models of diversity rest on a notion of group membership where individuals who are not part of the "dominant" or "majority" group belong to a "minority" group (Hahn, 1987; Wertlieb, 1985). The key concept is group membership. Good diversity management then requires understanding, respect, and valuation of the norms and qualities of the cultures of diverse minority groups (Cox, 1993; Cox and Blake, 1991). Individuals with disabilities conform to this view of diversity in that they are not members of the majority group. However, the nature of disability is such that those individuals are not members of an internally homogenous minority group. This implies that culturally-based models of diversity are inadequate for characterizing and analyzing the workplace needs of individuals with disabilities.

This chapter examines the nature of disability as a diversity issue. After a brief discussion of the ways in which the diversity debate is posed in terms of competing groups in society, there is a description of how disability fits into this debate. However, the competing group model is insufficient for the development of effective HR policy, and there follows an analysis of the ways in which disability confers a highly idiosyncratic status on individuals that must be reflected in HR policies and practices. The chapter concludes with a discussion of reasonable accommodation and how its careful implementation can form the basis of effective disability-based diversity management.

Diversity as a cultural issue

Diversity management moved to the top of the HR professional agenda initially with the recognition that the demographic characteristics of the workforce were changing (Cox and Blake, 1991). Our initial understanding of what was meant by diversity was largely formed by forecasts such as that from the Hudson Institute Report of an older, racially and ethnically diverse workforce (Johnson and Packer, 1987). One of the legacies of the Report and similar documents was that they both shaped the practitioner diversity debate and the direction of diversity scholarship in terms of demographic change and cultures that arise out of demographic diversity (Cox and Blake, 1991; Loden and Rosener, 1991; Wertlieb, 1985). By concentrating on how the composition of the US workforce was changing from one that had been traditionally male-dominated to one that included women and minorities, the discussion of diversity became one that revolved around competing group norms. Workplace conflict was conceptualized as a clash of cultures, and the challenge to HR professionals was to learn to respect and value the individual differences that emanated from these various cultures.

From a theoretical perspective, the importance of demographic group to diversity is the role that membership plays in self-definition (Ashforth and Mael, 1989). While the ultimate valuation of diversity may mean appreciating individual differences and talents, group membership influences both how individuals perceive themselves and how others perceive them. In the workplace, group membership presents often difficult behavioral choices for members of the non-dominant groups (Cox, 1993). Specifically, their choices are between assimilation, or what Cox terms adopting a monocultural identity; and biculturalism, which means maintaining strong identity with one's own group while interacting with those outside that group. Each orientation has an associated risk. Adopting a monocultural identity in order to assimilate at work jeopardizes one's connections to one's own group. On the other hand, adopting a bicultural identity often leads to isolation from co-workers and may generate hostility between different groups in the workplace.

In the context of diversity, group membership is conceptualized in juxtaposition to a dominant majority group. In the US, white males are usually the dominant group, and females and nonwhite males define their group identity in terms of minority group membership. Various definitions of minority group exist, but two common themes are that membership is based on physical or cultural characteristics; and that members of minority groups are singled out from others in society for differential and unequal treatment (Cox, 1993; Wirth, 1970). According to Wertlieb (1985), minority groups share certain defining characteristics. First, individuals are classed into the minority group because of some characteristic that is common to all members. Usually, this characteristic is viewed as a defect. Second, minority group members are kept in subordination to majority group members and are often subject to prejudice, discrimination, and exploitation. Third, minority membership is usually not a voluntary decision. Fourth, members of the minority group band together to develop a sense of group solidarity and identity. Cox (1993) extends this concept of minority grouping to include the development of cultural identity where membership in the group implies shared norms, values, and goal priorities. The discussion below shows how disability meets some of these criteria, but not all.

Why disability is a diversity issue

At first glance, disability seems a good candidate for being seen as a diversity issue. There are several ways in which individuals with disabilities constitute a group of people for whom a culturally-based diversity management paradigm can be applied. Using Wertlieb's (1985) criteria, individuals with disabilities, regardless of race or gender, are not seen as part of the dominant group in the workforce. Their exclusion from majority group membership is based on some physical or mental characteristic, often though not always visible. Like members of many other minority groups, individuals with disabilities are often targets of prejudice and misconceptions and have encountered discrimination in the workplace.

Many myths and false stereotypes pervade the workplace, perpetuating the poor labor market outcomes experienced by individuals with disabilities. Common misconceptions held by employers include the beliefs that employees with disabilities pose safety risks to themselves, other workers, and customers; that their presence increases health care costs; that they have higher rates of absenteeism; that they need more help on the job; and that they have lower productivity levels (Stone et al., 1992; Stevens, 1986). These myths survive despite empirical evidence to the contrary. According to a Harris Poll survey of 900 firms, 95 percent of surveyed managers gave employees with disabilities a "good" or "excellent" rating on job performance; 40 percent of surveyed line managers rated employees with disabilities as better on attendance and punctuality than nondisabled employees and 40 percent rated them as about the same. Seventy-five percent of the employers surveyed said that the cost of hiring an employee with a disability was no greater than that of hiring a nondisabled employee (Crow, 1993).

Despite positive employer reports, labor market statistics suggest that the workplace is inhospitable to individuals with disabilities. There are approximately 43 million individuals with disabilities in the US labor market (Schneid, 1992). They tend to work fewer hours and are occupationally segregated; thus, they are disproportionately represented in low-paying jobs (Baldwin, 1991; Burkhauser and Haveman, 1982). Approximately 19 percent of them live below the poverty line (Kirkpatrick, 1994). Approximately two-thirds of adults with disabilities are not working and about two-thirds of those want to work (Crow, 1993; Frank et al., 1989).

These figures are confounded by important labor market determinants such as skills, education, and experience, making precise measures of the impact of discrimination difficult. For example, adults with disabilities are almost four times as likely to have less than a ninth grade education compared to adults without a disability (US Department of Commerce, Bureau of Census, 1990). Nevertheless, evidence of labor market discrimination even after controlling for other determinants is fairly compelling. Research indicates that individuals with disabilities experience two types of discrimination. First, they face discriminatory hiring practices which result in higher unemployment rates and lower labor force participation rates (Baldwin and Johnson, 1992a; Hahn, 1987). Second, once they get a job, their wage rates are lower than comparable individuals without disabilities (Johnson and Lambrinos, 1985).

Labor force participation by people with disabilities Beginning with the differences in labor force participation, most studies document that the availability of benefits does reduce labor supply, but there is less consensus about why (Leonard, 1986; Weaver, 1992). Economically-based models start with the assumption that individuals prefer leisure to work and only work because they need income. According to this view, individuals assess their alternatives, including the availability of disability benefits, and the potential for income from benefits may make dropping out of the labor force a rational choice depending on one's options in the labor market (Parsons, 1980; Yelin, 1986). This argument is occasionally extended to include the idea that individuals will exaggerate their health problems in order to justify not being in the labor market, and perhaps to maintain benefit eligibility (Parsons, 1980; Stern, 1989; Stone, 1984).

An alternative explanation is that many individuals with disabilities are discouraged workers, that is, those who drop out of the labor market do so because they believe they will not find a job. According to this view, individuals want to work but because they have a disability they expect to have limited job opportunities. In other words, they feel discriminated against in the labor market and so choose to drop out.

Unfortunately, there are valid and reliable empirical studies that support both sides of this argument, leaving policy-makers and others operating in the realm of workplace disability without a definitive answer to these important questions. A good example of the importance of these unanswered questions is the difficulty in interpreting changes in the size of the Social Security Disability Insurance (SSDI) and workers' compensation disability rolls. For both types of programs, the number of claimants increases

313

when the business cycle turns down (Parsons, 1980). In addition, the number of SSDI recipients began to trend upward in the mid-1980s, reaching 5.3 million in 1993 (Stein, 1994). Two important factors behind this trend were that the number of younger males receiving benefits increased, and fewer individuals were leaving the rolls and re-entering the labor market (Haveman and Wolfe, 1990; Weaver, 1992).

Both of the business cycle swings and the upward trend can best be understood as labor market phenomena rather than the result of some objective change in the health of the population. However, there is little consensus about either the magnitude of the effects or the motivation. One can argue that sufficiently healthy individuals are using disability benefits as a source of income and using poor health as an excuse for not working. Alternatively, it may be that as labor market conditions worsen, individuals with disabilities find that they have fewer alternatives in the market, either because the range of job openings is narrower or because they face discrimination (Murphy, 1994; Yelin, 1989). In both cases, changes in the number of benefit recipients is contextually driven by changes in the labor market rather than by changes in the physical or mental health of the population. However, the policy implications are very different depending on which interpretation is correct.

One study that attempted to address the question of motivation found that knowledge of the availability of benefits appears to reduce the likelihood of dropping out of the labor force. The reason given for this anti-intuitive result was that the process for applying for SSDI benefits is fairly daunting and the likelihood of success is relatively small, so with information about the existence of benefits comes an understanding of the difficulties of obtaining them (Yelin, 1986). This suggests that response to benefit availability is not a motivator for dropping out of the labor force. Stern (1989) examined the effect of health on labor force participation using various measures of health status and found no support for the hypothesis that people describe themselves as disabled to justify dropping out of the labor force. Rather, he found that labor force participation exacerbates reported health problems: that is, working makes sick people sicker (Stern, 1989).

Earnings differences between individuals with and without disabilities Once individuals with disabilities do enter the labor market, their earnings are systematically lower than those of individuals without disabilities. After controlling for a variety of individual and labor market characteristics known to affect earnings, including industry sector, geographical region, and occupation, Baldwin et al. (1994) found that hourly earnings of males who reported some sort of physical or mental impairment ranged from 74 to 97 percent of those of unimpaired males, depending on the nature of the impairment. Comparable figures for females ranged between 85 and 101 percent (Baldwin et al., 1994). Comparison of male and female earnings suggests that about one-third of the differential can be attributed to discrimination for males and about four-fifths for females. This evidence strongly implies that women face discrimination based on both gender and disability status (Johnson and Lambrinos, 1985). One possible explanation of the gender difference for which there is some empirical support is occupational segregation, where women with disabilities are more likely than disabled males to be segregated into lower paying jobs, typically in clerical or service occupations (Baldwin, 1991; Johnson and Lambrinos, 1987).

One factor that appears to affect the labor market experience of individuals with disabilities is whether the disability is early-onset or surfaced later in life. There is evidence to support the frequently made complaint that older workers who stay in their jobs after the start of the disability are paid less because employers recognize their limited mobility within the external labor market (Baldwin and Johnson, 1992a). Further evidence that employers take advantage of the limited labor market options for individuals with disabilities is that although wages typically increase after a recession, males with disabilities are less likely to experience that cyclical increase (Haveman and Wolfe, 1990).

Two studies examine the dual effect of discrimination, that is, how it affects both labor force participation and wages. Both studies find that individuals with disabilities earn less than their counterparts without disabilities but that wage loss estimates understate the effect of discrimination because individuals with disabilities do drop out of the labor force in response to discrimination (Baldwin and Johnson, 1992a; 1992b; Mullahy and Sindelar, 1991). Just studying wage differences alone misses how discrimination leads individuals with disabilities to drop out.

Discrimination charges filed with the EEOC   Additional evidence of labor market discrimination against individuals with disabilities is the surge of discrimination charges made to the Equal Employment Opportunity Commission (EEOC) since the passage of the ADA. Within one year of the implementation of Title I of the ADA (the title governing employment discrimination), over 12,000 charges of discrimination on the basis of disability had been filed with the EEOC (Bureau of National Affairs, 1993). After fourteen months, charges of violation of the ADA constituted 17 percent of the EEOC caseload (Coil and Rice, 1994). By the end of the second year, 29,720 charges of discrimination on the basis of disability had been filed (Murphy, 1994). The mix of cases gives an indication of the nature of discrimination against individuals with disabilities: 50 percent of the cases were for wrongful termination; 23 percent for failure to provide reasonable accommodation; 13 percent for hiring discrimination; 10 percent for harassment; and the remainder were primarily over non-wage benefits (Coil and Rice, 1994).

To summarize, the discussion in this section provides support for the idea that as a group, individuals with disabilities meet Wertlieb's (1985) criteria for minority group status in that they are identified as not being part of the dominant group based on some physical or mental characteristic and that they face discrimination in the labor market that results in lower earnings and fewer job opportunities. However, as the section below describes, this characterization provides only a partial understanding of the workplace experience of individuals with disabilities and an insufficient basis for HR policy development.

Why disability does not lend itself to a cultural diversity model

At second glance, disability does not lend itself well to diversity models built on a group norm framework. Although there is strong evidence that individuals with disabilities face labor market discrimination, cultural models of diversity do not provide good bases for solutions. Disability does not confer membership into a group that is internally homogeneous or that sees itself as a group. Disability arises out of multiple pathologies that result in innumerable variations of physical and/or mental limitations with little commonality to provide a basis for group definition. For example, people with diabetes are unlikely to group themselves with people with cerebral palsy because their physical limitations and practical concerns are quite different. While it may be convenient for the purposes of devising social programs or assigning what may be socially useful labels to refer to "the disabled" as a group, individuals with disabilities do not form an internally homogenous group with respect to having common experience in the workplace or larger community; nor do they compose a group that shares traditional customs and norms (Biklen, 1987; Stone, 1984; Wertlieb, 1985). There are four primary reasons why viewing individuals with disabilities as a group is inappropriate.

Variety of reasons for an impairment First, there are multiple physical and mental sources of impairment. While an individual in excellent physical health may group an individual who is legally blind with a chair-user, those two individuals have little in common in terms of the obstacles they face navigating through life other than society's wish to stereotype them (Biklen, 1987). Two anecdotes provided to the author by an individual who is blind demonstrate the nature of this stereotyping. This individual worked in an organization that was making physical changes to the environment in preparation for ADA. He observed that while this organization was taking pride in its forward-looking approach, with the exception of braille notation on the elevator, all of the changes were to accommodate chair-users, the group that most commonly springs to mind when one hears the word "disability." Although significant alterations had been made to the doorways, bathrooms, and hallways to permit wheelchair access, not a single office number, name plate, or floor sign had been posted in braille.

The second anecdote described an experience in an airport. This individual needed to make a connection between flights that involved a gate change. The airport administration had been notified that he would need help getting from one gate to another, and sent a chair-user who wanted the blind individual to sit on his lap and ride to the next gate. The individual relating this experience described his outrage and anger at the airport administration's expectation that he would become dependent in an area in which he was fully capable – walking – in order to receive assistance in an area where he needed help – guidance to the appropriate gate. He also noted that it is common that when organizations have a disability-based problem to resolve, they frequently try to use an individual with a disability to solve it, that is, ask a chair-user to guide a blind person around a building.

He gave several explanations for these organizational tendencies. One is simple stereotyping – a belief that people with disabilities are all alike and probably prefer one another's company. Another is the prejudice that individuals with disabilities have very limited abilities and can only be given limited responsibilities. Also, this tendency reflects a societal belief that disability is the defining characteristic for the individual and thus the basis for segregating rather than integrating him or her. Another likely reason is that despite progress in general attitudes, the rights and quality of life of people with disabilities is still not a top business priority, so solutions are relegated to those the organization believes to be less capable – those with disabilities.

Disability as a matter of degree A second argument for why disability does not lend itself to a group-based model is that disability is a continuum and not a category (Stone, 1984; Wertlieb, 1985). There is an absence of commonality even with respect to the characteristic that might define one as belonging to a particular category of individuals with disabilities (Wertlieb, 1985). For example, hearing-impaired individuals vary in their ability to hear. This can range from the person who asks you to repeat what you said or who turns up the sound slightly on the TV to the person born with no capacity to hear whose language and entire ability to communicate has been affected. Further, the extent of the impairment may fluctuate. Individual health status changes can occur because a disease progresses or goes into remission or because a medication improves physical or mental health. For example, multiple sclerosis induces mobility limitations that are often temporary and psoriasis can often be controlled with topical medications. Thus the definition of who has a disability, when, and to what extent is dynamic and resists static assignment of group membership.

Disability as contextually defined The third reason that disability does not confer group membership is that, properly defined, disability depends on context (Berkowitz and Berkowitz, 1989; Sawisch, 1991). That is, individuals are disabled with respect to some task or activity. This contextual character can be seen in the four-part socio/functional definition of disability put forth in the Nagi model (World Health Organization, 1980; Sawisch, 1991). The four parts of the definition progress from pathology to disability:

1 *Pathology:* disruption of some normal bodily process or structure; damage to cells and/or tissues. Examples could include a broken leg, cancer, or multiple sclerosis.

2   *Impairment:* some loss of or aberration in mental, emotional, or physical functioning, including pain. Examples might be a dysfunctional limb, dysfunctional organ, or aberrant motor function.

3   *Functional limitation:* restricted range of some normal activity resulting from the impairment. Examples could include the inability to put weight on one leg so cannot walk unassisted; inability to digest food; or, inability to write using a pen and paper.

4   *Disability:* limitations that are defined in terms of the roles and activities associated with the job and expected in the workplace. Examples may include: inability to distribute mail to offices throughout a building; inability to sit at a desk for more than an hour without a break; or, inability to take notes at a staff meeting.

The thrust of this four-part definition is that disability is contextual, to some degree subjective, and in no way deterministic. The examples given for each step showed a progression that ended with some sort of limitation of activities in the workplace. However, the link between each step can be broken at any point. For example, an individual with multiple sclerosis may or may not exhibit some loss of motor function, depending on the state of the disease; a cancer victim may not experience any functional limitation throughout much of the disease; and someone with a broken leg may have no need to walk while on the job. While the ADA does not explicitly adopt the terminology of the Nagi definition, the spirit of the definition of disability is similar and the obligations the Act imposes on employers flow out of the assumption that disability is contextual and that it is the responsibility of employers to create a work environment that minimizes the extent of disability (Snyder, 1993).

Absence of group norms   Other indicators that individuals with disabilities do not constitute a group is the frequent absence of many of the other attributes of groups, specifically the absence of group norms, traditions, and social support systems.[1] Group norms and traditions are difficult to form and sustain because of the diversity of pathologies that lead to disability. Part of this arises from the fact that having a disability often implies some degree of "differentness" and probably some limitation on activities. Unlike other minority groups who are usually part of a minority family, individuals with disabilities do not necessarily come from a family or community with comparable disabilities (Wertlieb, 1985). As a result, the usual social support mechanisms needed to maintain a sense of community may be absent. In fact, the opposite may be true, where family and community are embarrassed by the impairment.

Why do people without disabilities want to assign group membership?

The multiplicity of ways in which individuals with disabilities clearly do not form an internally homogeneous group raises the interesting question of why they are often viewed as a minority group. One author notes the problem while describing Win, a character in *Not in the Calendar*, a novel by Margaret Kennedy: "She refuses to identify with the 'deaf,' though of course society often identifies her that way . . . [as belonging to a group] of people with whom she feels she has nothing in common, except one disability" (Biklen, 1987, pp. 518–19).

The reasons for mistakenly generalizing that individuals with disabilities constitute a group are complex. Some people, of course, are simply ignorant about what is meant by disability, the multiple forms it takes and the diverse obstacles it poses. Unless one has direct experience, it is difficult to know what is involved (Hall and Hall, 1994), and, in general, most people are taught from a young age that it is rude to ask (Biklen, 1987). Simple ignorance is not the only reason for this tendency to inappropriately group individuals with disabilities. For many without disabilities, the daily reality for those with severe disabilities is often imagined as too intolerable to seriously examine (Zola, 1987). Evidence of this view of the unthinkability of a serious impairment appears in fiction where characters with disabilities are also often given special, nearly superhuman, abilities – great upper body strength to compensate for the loss of the use of legs, remarkable hearing and memory to compensate for loss of sight, etc. (Zola, 1987).

Because illness and injury can happen unexpectedly to anyone at any time, personal fear about one's own precarious status as healthy and without disability appears to play an important role in individuals' needs to make stereotypical assumptions about disability (Stone et al., 1992; Biklen, 1987). Grouping and stereotyping help to psychologically distance oneself and solidify one's own position as superior (Stone et al., 1992; Wertlieb, 1985; Zola, 1987). Associated with this often is a need to blame the individual with the disability for their status. If people can be blamed for their situation, that implies some degree of control and ability to protect oneself from a similar fate: "that person must have done something to deserve their problems; I haven't done anything to deserve such problems so I am safe from them" sort of logic (Hahn, 1987; Stone, 1984).

Language gives a clue to the degree of our discomfort with the concept of disability and provides an indication of the attitudinal obstacles yet to be overcome. In recent years, extensive efforts have been made to find appropriate language when referring to disability. There is movement away from words like "crippled" and "retarded" which are clearly pejorative. The term "handicapped," which came into use in the 1940s was replaced with the term "disabled." This, too, was deemed to have derogatory overtones, so the currently accepted terminology is to speak of "individuals with disabilities" as in the Americans with Disabilities Act. However, there is an opinion that this, too, has negative connotations and phrases like "differently abled" or "physically (or otherwise) challenged" are more appropriate. The Cristina Foundation ran a contest and decided the phrase "people with different abilities" was best. However, another entry to the contest was "severely euphemize," indicating that efforts to find a term without negative overtones runs the risk of minimizing or trivializing the obstacles people with disabilities encounter in the work world and other places. While terminology may appear to be a small point, the difficulty of finding an acceptable phrase indicates the level of societal discomfort with the idea of disability.

Reasonable accommodation under ADA as a form of diversity management

While the ADA is not the sole reason disability is thought of as a diversity issue, it will be pivotal in developing disability-based diversity policy. There are several reasons for this assumption. First, of course, its passage has drawn attention to the rights of individuals with disabilities. Second, the ADA provides for legal restitution under the Civil Rights Act of 1991, which not only allows for back pay and reinstatement but also punitive damages, threatening employers who ignore the rights of employees and applicants with disabilities.

The basics of the ADA　The purpose of the ADA was to provide a clear, comprehensive national mandate to eliminate discrimination against individuals with disabilities (Stein, 1991). Most of the statutes that preceded it failed to sufficiently reduce discrimination because of their narrow focus. The Architectural Barriers Act of 1968 and the Voting Accessibility Act of 1984 were directed toward reducing physical barriers, the Education for All Handicapped Children Act in 1975 toward children, and the Rehabilitation Act of 1973 toward federal government and federal contractors.

Unlike its predecessors, the ADA sought to be comprehensive. It received bipartisan support in both Houses of Congress, as well as very energetic support from several public interest groups, including disability rights organizations, the Leadership Conference on Civil Rights, and the AFL-CIO. What controversy there was surrounding the Bill centered on the inclusion of AIDS as a covered source of disability, rather than on the profound implications the Act would have for employers (Schneid, 1992). The presence of bipartisan support and the fact that most of the conflict over the ADA's passage could be characterized as skirmishes rather than battles might be interpreted as an indicator of improved attitudes toward individuals with disabilities. Equally plausible is that many special interests failed to grasp the breadth of the Act and still thought in terms of improved physical access as the primary requirement it would impose.

The ADA is a landmark piece of legislation for several reasons. Its scope is broad: it expands the definition of disability and extends federal civil rights protection. Also, it puts new demands on employers: it is not enough for employers to be "disability blind;" rather, they must actively remove barriers to employment. Finally, it is far more comprehensive in its definition of the aspects of the employment relationship where discrimination may occur, going beyond the hiring and promotion decisions to include the full range of rights and privileges associated with employment.

The definition of who is covered by the ADA is straightforward. It prohibits discrimination against "qualified individuals with disabilities." It defines such an individual as: "an individual with a disability who meets the skill, experience, education, and other job-related requirements of a position held or desired, and who, with or without reasonable accommodation can perform the essential functions of the job" (EEOC, 1991b).

As the first part of this definition makes clear, employers are not required to hire or promote an unqualified or underqualified individual. The more complex part of the definition of who is covered comes with the phrases "individual with a disability," "who with or without reasonable accommodation," and "can perform the essential functions of the job." Each of these is briefly discussed below.

Who is an individual with a disability?   There is a two-prong test for determining disability. First, it must be determined whether or not an individual has a "physical or mental impairment." Second, that impairment must "substantially limit" one or more major life activities (Shaller and Dean, 1991–2). The Act deliberately does not list specific covered impairments but rather is global in its definition of major life activities, specifying caring for oneself, walking, seeing, hearing, performing manual tasks, breathing, and working. This definition is broadened to include not only the presence of a substantially limiting impairment, but can also include the record of such an impairment and/or being regarded by an employer or potential employer as having such an impairment. The important point here is that the definition of disability has a wide sweep under the ADA, adding to the difficulty of applying a culture-based diversity model to disability policy development.

The purpose of the two extensions of the definition of disability was to explicitly address two common types of labor market discrimination. The inclusion of a "record of such an impairment" was to make illegal the type of discrimination faced by individuals who had once had a disabling condition, were now recovered, but still encountered barriers to full employment because of fears of recurrence by employers and/or co-workers. The inclusion of being "regarded" as having a disability was to counter discrimination such as that based on employer fear about the limitations a disability might impose. For example, an individual with high blood pressure, a condition which can usually be controlled through medication, may encounter discrimination from an employer who fears work pressure may lead to a heart attack on the job. Although individuals with properly treated high blood pressure are no more likely to have a heart attack than other comparable people, an employer may not realize this and discriminate by not hiring or promoting that individual. Such a decision is clearly illegal under ADA.

What is reasonable accommodation?   The purpose of accommodation is to allow an individual with a disability the opportunity to perform at the same level as a comparable person without a disability. Reasonable accommodation is defined as:

any change or adjustment to a job or work environment that permits a qualified applicant or employee with a disability to participate in the job application process, perform the essential functions of a job, and/or enjoy benefits and privileges of employment equal to those enjoyed by employees without disabilities. (EEOC, 1991b, Section 3.4)

The possible forms of accommodation that firms must consider may include familiar actions such as modifying existing facilities, equipment or materials. To go back to the examples mentioned in the discussion of the Nagi definition of disability, an employer might provide a voice-activated computer to facilitate notetaking during a meeting or to rearrange office furniture to give an employee on crutches an uncluttered path.

In addition, ADA's definition of accommodation includes several potentially controversial activities, including job restructuring, changes in schedule or working hours, and/or reassignment of the individual with a disability to a vacant position. This requirement is far more extensive than under previous legislation. Accommodations like these have the potential for significantly altering how work is done, and like any large change, the capacity for generating conflict (Hall and Hall, 1994). When accommodation becomes controversial, it will require some of the tools of diversity management to be successfully implemented (Cox and Blake, 1991; Lee, 1993; Postol and Kadue, 1991; Stein, 1991). Specifically, employers will need to educate their employees about the nature of accommodation to reduce the likelihood that it be seen as bestowing special advantage. For example, giving an employee more than the usual number of scheduled breaks to accommodate a back condition may be seen as unfair by co-workers. It is incumbent on the employer to educate the workforce that such accommodations are necessary to enable that employee to perform that job and stay employed. Similarly, it is the employer's responsibility to assure that the change in break schedule does not interfere with others' ability to do their work.

What are essential job functions? The third feature of the definition of who is covered under ADA is that the accommodation required of employers must enable the covered individual to perform the "essential functions" of the job. ADA guidelines define a function as essential if: it is the reason the job exists; there are a limited number of other employees who can perform the function; and the function is highly specialized. There are several sources of possible documentation that a function is essential mentioned in the *Handbook* (EEOC, 1991a). However, because the spirit of ADA is to reduce employment barriers faced by individuals with disabilities, no single source of documentation is indisputably sufficient to establish a function as essential. This is because most existing types of documentation tend to describe how a job has been structured in the past rather than how it might be restructured so as to be performed by an individual with a disability.

One unintended consequence of ADA has been that it has heightened employer fears about the implications of employing individuals with disabilities. Employer fear about ADA is especially evident in the titles of newspaper, magazine, and practitioner journal articles on the Act. Several examples include "How to survive the new ADA litigation" (Raisner, 1992); "Management lawyer warns Disabilities Act could result in an 'explosion of litigation'" (BNAC, 1991); "The disabilities labyrinth" (McKee, 1993); "Disabling business" (Allen, 1992); and "The disabilities law: Avoid the pitfalls" (Litvan, 1994). The threat of litigation combined with the ambiguity of the Act worries employers. Many have responded by hiring attorneys to help them avoid litigation (Breuer, 1993). Others are attempting to draw up iron-clad job descriptions that will effectively screen out people with disabilities (Litvan, 1994).

Part of this concern arises our of uncertainty about exactly who, and how many, are covered by the Act. Traditional counts define the population with disabilities in terms of benefit recipient status, usually the number of people receiving SSDI (Social Security Disability Insurance) and SSI (Supplemental Security Income) benefits (Haveman and Wolfe, 1990). The ADA definition goes well beyond this to include a wide range of physical and mental impairments and also includes a history of substance abuse as a qualifying impairment. One estimate of the total population protected by ADA goes as high as 87.5 million US residents with disabilities (Allen, 1992).

In most cases, ADA imposes a reasonable standard. For example, despite initial employer fears, the Act does not require employers to hire a less well qualified individual with a disability over one who is better able to do the job. However, it does impose new obligations on employers that are more profound than previous antidiscrimination legislation. It is implied in ADA that disability is largely a function of prevailing social attitudes and the political, social, and physical climate those attitudes create (Hahn, 1987; Sawisch, 1991). Extrapolating to the organization, this means that employers must turn their attention to the organizational environment rather than just to the functionally limited individual and adapt the workplace to minimize the effects of disability.

Putting the ADA into practice   Initially, most employers concentrated their response to ADA by assuring that their hiring practices were in compliance. The thrust of these activities revolved around including references to equal employment opportunity hiring practices, adaptation of recruitment materials, improving access, revision of testing materials, and deliberate avoidance of search agencies that discriminate (Breuer, 1993). Although nondiscriminatory hiring practices are explicitly covered by ADA, hiring is only one of a wide range of employment activities covered. The Act explicitly lists promotions, training, lay-off, rates of pay, dismissal, job assignments, benefits, and leave of absence. Additionally, the phrase "any other terms, conditions or privilege of employment" is included to ensure a comprehensive definition of the work activities around which employers may not discriminate. As was evident in the mix of cases before the EEOC, discriminatory hiring practices account for only 13 percent of the charges that have been brought so far.

Emphasizing hiring not only omits a wide array of covered activities but it ignores what is unique about ADA and disability as a diversity issue. The more difficult challenge is incorporating individuals with disabilities into the full range of work activities on a sustained basis, which is at the heart of the definition of reasonable accommodation. There are some limitations on the employer obligation to accommodate. First, the employer does not have to provide the accommodation an employee requests, only one that will enable the individual to perform the essential functions of the job. Second, an employer does not have to offer similar accommodations to nondisabled employees. Third, an employer does not have to provide accommodation if it imposes "undue hardship" for himself (Wilson, 1991).

The burden of proof of undue hardship lies with the employer and must be established on a case-by-case basis (Kelly and Aalberts, 1990). Several criteria can be considered in the determination of undue hardship; however, none of these are necessarily sufficient to establish undue hardship. An accommodation may be ascertained as causing undue hardship if it is unduly costly, extensive, substantial, disruptive or fundamentally alters operations. When considering the cost to employers, factors to be considered include the nature and cost of the accommodation; the size, type, and financial resources of the specific facility where accommodation would have to be made; the size, type, and financial resources of the covered employer; the covered employer's type of operation, including composition, structure, and functions of its workforce, and geographic separation between specific facility and covered employer; the impact of accommodation on operations; and whether or not the accommodation would pose a direct threat to the health and safety of the employee and/or co-workers.

The broad definition of reasonable accommodation in ADA raises the specter of having to provide potentially very expensive and/or disruptive accommodation to remain in compliance with the law. However, current data suggest that most accommodation is relatively inexpensive. In a study of federal contractors' accommodation costs in compliance with the Rehabilitation Act of 1973, 51 percent of the accommodations cost nothing, 30 percent cost under $500, and 8 percent cost over $2,000 (US General Accounting Office, 1990). However, the definition of reasonable accommodation is broader under ADA than under previous legislation and requires that employers consider job restructuring and reassignment, the costs of which are more difficult to evaluate.

Managing disability-based diversity

Two themes emerge from the diversity management literature on how to structure effective policies that have application to disability-based diversity. The first is that when diversity is seen as somehow negative, it is the failure of the organization, not of the individual who differs from the dominant group. The second is that individual differences must be taken into consideration and respected. Management of disability-based diversity should incorporate these two requirements.

In addition to respect for individual differences and attention to organizational climate, there are two ways that disability-based diversity programs will need to distinguish themselves from programs designed to address other sorts of diversity. First, unlike demographically-based diversity, the characteristic that is the basis for diversity, that is, the disability, can fluctuate. Individuals' physical and mental heath status can change, affecting the nature or degree of functional limitation. In practice, this may mean introducing scheduling flexibility into the job to accommodate unpredictable fluctuations in health, such as the periodic loss of motor control associated with multiple sclerosis. It may also involve careful monitoring of the fit between the individual with the disability and the job, particularly if the person's health status changes.

Similarly, as new technologies are introduced in the workplace and work processes are rearranged, the context in which an individual with an impairment must operate will be altered, changing the nature of the disability. A sound policy will take this feature of disability into account. Specifically, good policy will include a readily available mechanism for revisiting and revising an accommodation, that can be triggered by the person who needs the accommodation as well as by co-workers. This is especially important when new technologies are introduced, significant personnel changes are made, or some other reorganization of work occurs.

Also, how work is done is likely to change because ADA requires employers to seriously consider job restructuring and/or reassignment as a means of successfully incorporating individuals with disabilities into the workplace. This has potentially unwelcome implications for co-workers, supervisors, managers, and subordinates. It is not enough for employers to broadly address workplace fears, prejudices, and misconceptions about disability. Rather, effective policy must extend to the specific individuals who will be affected by any accommodation that changes their jobs. In order to do a reasonable job of incorporating individuals with disabilities into the workplace with the needed micro focus, organizations have to take a two-tiered approach, developing policies at both the organizational and individual stakeholder level.

The organizational level   At the organizational level it will be necessary to develop policies to eliminate discriminatory practices as well as to alter the organizational climate to more easily assimilate individuals with disabilities into the workplace. Programmatically, efforts will include dissemination of information about the obligations and responsibilities imposed by ADA and guidelines about how specifically the organization plans to meet those. Certain features should be part of an organizational policy.

First, the organization should adopt a broad-based definition of disability and accommodation. Historically, most organizations have emphasized physical access. While that is clearly important, organizational policies will have to go further than that and incorporate the broader definition of disability inherent in ADA. The ADA definition of disability as arising from an impairment that limits a major life activity requires organizations to structure policies that address a wide range of conditions, far beyond the traditional images of people with disabilities. A few examples are cancer, asthma, and depression, which all may result in impairments of some major life activity and thus be covered under ADA. Accommodations of these types of conditions are likely to require some job restructuring and/or rescheduling – very different measures from one-time ramp installation or doorway widening. Even for some of the more familiar impairments, such as blindness, organizations are expected to go beyond conventional accommodations such as keyboards, computer screens, and elevator buttons in braille and, if necessary, provide personal readers for materials that cannot be feasibly published in braille or voice recorded (National Federation of the Blind, 1993).

Another dimension of this broad-based definition of disability is that it requires organizations to ignore the issue of potential "fault" or personal responsibility for the impairment. Most of the traditional conditions that form the basis of disability can be thought of as "no fault" – the result of disease or injury and evoke some measure of sympathy (Wertlieb, 1985). Impairments resulting from what is rightly or wrongly thought of as a behavior that is under the individual's control, such as substance abuse or obesity, also fall within the scope of the ADA definition of disability and evoke more complex responses from co-workers (Frierson, 1993). Educating the workforce about the full scope of the nature of disability will be part of good policy at the organizational level.

In addition, an effective disability-based diversity policy will require considerable flexibility and creativity. As discussed earlier, the dynamic nature of disability will require a policy that specifies a problem-solving process rather than a one-time decision or action – a dynamic problem will require a solution that can shift accordingly. This spirit of continuous adaptability will have to be incorporated into the organization-wide policy statement. A policy of regular monitoring of accommodations plus the implementation of a clear and simple mechanism for amending accommodations are key to meeting this criterion.

Also occurring at the organizational level will be programmatic efforts to dispel general misconceptions about disability and the productivity of individuals with disabilities. Diversity training that allows people with and without disabilities to interact with one another and ask frank questions can be especially valuable. One communication barrier encountered by people with disabilities is that the fear of saying or doing the wrong thing leads people without disabilities to simply avoid them rather than risk embarrassment. An opportunity to candidly ask questions about the nature of certain kinds of limitations and how those limitations are overcome reduces that fear and strengthens the ability to work effectively together.

The individual level The second level at which an effective disability program should function is at the level of the individual who requires accommodation and the relevant surrounding stakeholder group. Under

ADA, each person requiring accommodation must be treated on a case-by-case basis. This is a function of the idiosyncratic nature of disability – each person's physical/mental condition varies as does the work context in which he or she needs to function. The Act is explicit in its expectation that employers will give serious consideration to a variety of ways in which work is done in order to enable individuals with a disability to effectively do their jobs. The ADA *Handbook* (EEOC, 1991a) emphasizes the need to consult the individuals with a disability as experts – they know their capabilities and limitations and what sorts of equipment or adjustments are necessary to enable them to do the job.

Providing reasonable accommodation and incorporating individuals with disabilities into the workplace to make optimal use of their talents can be tricky. For several reasons, including workplace pressures engendered by organizational reengineering and restructuring, any group with even the *appearance* of requesting special consideration risks attracting hostility from co-workers. For that reason, effective disability policy must not only respect the rights of the individual with the disability but also those of co-workers who may be affected by the implementation of an accommodation. The key principle to producing and implementing a policy that will permit effective accommodation is that affected employees, who can be thought of as the stakeholder group, have a voice and opportunity to participate in the accommodation process.

Some accommodations will have little effect on co-workers, such as changing the height of a desk or implementing a color coding system for a hearing-impaired worker. However, those that involve job restructuring or reassignment may either adversely affect the jobs of co-workers or be perceived as conferring and unfair advantage. One example provided to the author was of an employee who was part of a pool of workers who shared the job of distributing mail throughout an office. This employee had impaired mobility that prevented her from moving from office to office with the mail. She requested that her mail duty be reassigned to others in the pool. Because mail sorting was a tedious task, that accommodation was unpopular with most of the members of the labor pool. Instead, a different accommodation was implemented, where the individual with the disability was given a motorized vehicle to move around the office. However, at the time the example was provided, the individual with a disability did not like that solution because it drew attention to her disability, and she was considering filing a discrimination charge with the EEOC.

While no processes exist that can guarantee protection from discrimination charges or other sorts of conflict, employee participation in the accommodation process can help (Fry, 1981). Important factors to consider when developing a process are first that the relevant stakeholders are identified and incorporated in the decision-making process. There is a tendency in organizations to look up the hierarchy; however, in the case of accommodation, one should look across also, because co-workers are the people most likely to be affected by a job restructuring or reassignment. Getting their perspective on the job and how it might be done is as important as getting that of the individual needing accommodation. Affected co-workers are also valid sources for creative alternatives to how work is currently structured.

A second important factor to incorporate into an accommodation process is that there is an opportunity for the stakeholders to hear one another's views and consider their perspectives. In the mail-sorting example described above, there was no such process and the situation deteriorated into a reassign/no reassign, win/lose conflict. Had the rest of the pool been able to understand the mobility limitations of the person asking for the mail to be reassigned, they might have found such a reassignment more acceptable. Or, if the individual needing the accommodation had heard the objections of the pool, she might have found the alternative more acceptable. And, finally, together, they might have generated a completely different solution that all could find satisfactory.

A third important factor is that there should be an explicit mechanism for revisiting an accommodation that is not effective or that has become obsolete. The spirit of ADA requires flexibility, innovation, and experimentation. Some experiments will not work: people will be unrealistic about their own abilities or the new workload. In addition, as people's physical or mental health status changes or as the demands of the job change, an accommodation that was previously effective may no longer be so. In addition, if personnel change, a job restructuring may not work with new co-workers. For all of these reasons, an explicit system for reexamining and revising an accommodation should be part of an effective disability-based diversity program.

There are several ways this can be put into effect. If the organization has a safety and health committee, that is a logical body to administer requests for accommodation reviews. If no such group exists, a regular review process can be implemented. In most cases, the accommodation is likely to still be effective, but a regular review gives employees a chance to surface problems they might otherwise suppress. Also, depending on the organizational climate, accommodation of disability fits well with a philosophy of continuous improvement. An accommodation, like any other aspect of work, can be subject to continuous incremental improvement. If continuous improvement is part of the organization's culture, maintaining the needed flexibility of an effective accommodation process will be relatively easy.

As a diversity issue, structuring the workplace to allow individuals with disabilities to be fully productive raises challenges for employers beyond those associated with demographically driven diversity. While appreciation of individual talents, abilities, and circumstances is at the heart of all diversity initiatives, the nature of disability is more insistent on attention to the individual and recognition of the contribution of culture and context to how a problem is defined than with most other sources of diversity. The demands on employers imposed by ADA effectively require that disability management be an ongoing process and one that requires sustained attention and maintenance.

NOTE

1 There are multiple support and advocacy groups for various subgroups of individuals with disabilities, such as the National Federation of the Blind. However, the presence of these groups does not imply a commonality of difficulties faced by all individuals with disabilities.

REFERENCES

Allen, C. (1992). Disabling business. *Insight*, 8(15), April 13, 6–13, 34–6.

Ashforth, B., and Mael, F. (1989). Social identity theory and the organization. *Academy of Management Review*, 14(1), 20–39.

Baldwin, M. (1991). Evidence on the occupational segregation of women with disabilities. *Journal of Disability Policy Studies*, 2(2), 31–47.

Baldwin, M., and Johnson, W. (1992a). Estimating the employment effects of wage discrimination. *Review of Economics and Statistics*, 74(3), August, 446–55.

Baldwin, M., and Johnson, W. (1992b). Labor market discrimination against persons with disabilities. Unpublished manuscript, November.

Baldwin, M. L., Zeager, L. A., and Flacco, P. R. (1994). Gender differences in wage losses from impairments. *Journal of Human Resources*, 29(3), Summer, 865–87.

Berkowitz, M., and Berkowitz, E. (1989). Labor force participation among disabled persons. *Investing in People*. Washington, DC: US Department of Labor.

Biklen, D. (1987). The culture of policy: Disability images and their analogues in public policy. *Policy Studies Journal*, 15(3), March, 515–35.

BNAC (1991). Management lawyer warns Disabilities Act could result in an "Explosion of litigation." *Communicator*, Spring, 8.

Breuer, N. L. (1993). Resources can relieve ADA fears. *Personnel Journal*, 72(9), September, 131–42.

Bureau of National Affairs (1993). *Daily Labor Report*, No. 141, July 26. Washington, DC.

Burkhauser, R. V., and Haveman, R. H. (1982). *Disability and Work*, Baltimore, MD: Johns Hopkins University Press.

Coil, J. H., and Rice, C. M. (1994). The tip of the iceberg: Early trends in ADA enforcement. *Employee Relations Law Journal*, 19(4), Spring, 485–506.

Cox, T. Jr (1993). *Cultural Diversity in Organizations*, San Francisco: Berrett-Koehler.

Cox, T. H., and Blake, S. (1991). Managing cultural diversity: Implications for organizational competitiveness. *Academy of Management Executive*, 5(3), 45–56.

Crow, S. M. (1993). Excessive absenteeism and the Disabilities Act. *Arbitration Journal*, March, 65–70.

Equal Employment Opportunity Commission (1991a). *Americans with Disabilities Act Handbook*. Washington. DC: Equal Employment Opportunity Commission.

Equal Employment Opportunity Commission (1991b). *Technical Assistance Manual for the Americans with Disabilities Act*. Washington, DC: Equal Employment Opportunity Commission.

Frank, K., Karst, R., and Boles, C. (1989). After graduation: The quest for employment by disabled college graduates. *Journal of Applied Rehabilitation Counseling*, 20(4), Winter, 3–7.

Frierson, J. G. (1992). An analysis of ADA provisions on denying employment because of a risk of future injury. *Employee Relations Law Journal*, 17(4), Spring, 603–22.

Frierson, J. G. (1993). Obesity as a legal disability under ADA, Rehabilitation Act, and state handicapped employment laws. *Labor Law Journal*, 44(5), May, 286–96.

Fry, R. (1981). *Getting to Yes*. New York: Penguin.

Hahn, H. (1987). Advertising the acceptably employable image: Disability and capitalism. *Policy Studies Journal*, 15(3), March, 551–70.

Hall, F. S., and Hall, E. L. (1994). The ADA: Going beyond the law. *Academy of Management Executive*, 8(1), 17–32.

Haveman, R., and Wolfe, B. (1990). The economic well-being of the disabled. *Journal of Human Resources*, 25(1), Winter, 32–54.

Johnson, W. B., and Lambrinos, J. (1985). Wage discrimination against handicapped men and women. *Journal of Human Resources*, 20(2), Spring, 264–77.

Johnson, W. B., and Lambrinos, J. (1987). The effect of prejudice on the wages of disabled workers. *Policy Studies Journal*, 15(3), March, 571–90.

Johnston, W. B., and Packer, A. H. (1987). *Workforce 2000*. Indianapolis: Hudson Institute.

Kelly, E. P., and Aalberts, R. J. (1990). Americans with disabilities: Undue hardship for private sector employers. *Labor Law Journal*, 41(10), October, 675–84.

Kirkpatrick, P. (1994). Triple jeopardy: Disability, race and poverty in America. *Poverty and Race*, 3(3), May–June, 1–8.

Lee, B. A. (1993). Reasonable Accommodation under the Americans with Disabilities Act. *Berkely Law Journal of Employment of labor law*, 14: 201–50.

Leonard, J. (1986). Labor supply incentives and disincentives for disabled persons. In M. Berkowitz and M. A. Hill (eds), *Disability and the Labor Market* (64–94). Ithaca, NY: ILR Press.

Litvan, L. (1994). The Disabilities Law: Avoid the pitfalls. *Nation's Business*, 82(1), January, 25–7.

Loden, M., and Rosener, J. B. (1991). *Workforce America: Managing Employee Diversity as a Vital Resource*. Homewood, IL: Business One Irwin.

McKee, B. (1993). The disabilities labyrinth. *Nation's Business*, 81(4), April, 18–25.

Mullahy, J., and Sindelar, J. (1991). Gender differences in labor market effects of alcholism. *American Economic Review*, 81(20), May, 161–5.

Murphy, D. J. (1994). Sorting out ADA's enforcement. *Investor's Business Daily*, 11(92), August 18, 1–2.

National Federation of the Blind (1993). Negotiation principles for reasonable accommodation. J. O. B. Employer's Bulletin No. 3, Baltimore, MD.

Parsons, D. (1980). The decline in male labor force participation. *Journal of Political Economy*, 88(1), February, 117–34.

Pope, A., and Tarlov, A. (1991). *Disability in America: Toward a National Agenda for Prevention*. Institute of Medicine, Washington, DC: National Academy Press.

Postol, L. and Kadue, D. (1991). An Employer's Guide to the Americans with Disabilities Act. *Labor Law Journal*, 42: 323–42.

Quintanilla, C. (1993). Disabilities Act helps – but not much. *Wall Street Journal*, July 19, B1, B8.

Raisner, J. (1992). How to survive the new ADA litigation. *HR Magazine*, 37(6), June, 78–83.

Robinson, J. C., and Shor, G. M. (1989). Business-cycle influences on work-related disability in construction and manufacturing. *Milbank Quarterly*, 67, Supp. 2(1), 92–113.

Sawisch, L. P. (1991). Americans with Disabilities Act: An historical overview of discrimination and legislation. Unpublished manuscript.

Schneid, T. D. (1992). *The Americans with Disabilities Act: A Practical Guide for Managers*. New York: Van Nostrand.

Shaller, E. H., and Rosen, D. A. (1991–2). A guide to the EEOC's final regulations on the Americans with Disabilities Act. *Employee Relations Law Journal*, 17(3), Winter, 405–30.

Snyder, D. A. (1993). Qualified individuals with disabilities: Defining the ADA's protected class. *Labor Law Journal*, 44(2), February, 101–9.

Stein, R. E. (1991). A new bill for millions: The Americans with Disabilities Act of 1990. *Arbitration Journal*, June, 6–15.

Stein, R. S. (1994). Does spending cripple America? *Investor's Business Daily*, 11(125), October 5, 1, 2.

Stern, S. (1989). Measuring the effect of disability on labor force participation. *Journal of Human Resources*, 24(3), Summer, 361–95.

Stevens, G. E. (1986). Exploding the myths about hiring the handicapped. *Personnel*, 63(12), December, 57–60.

Stone, D. A. (1984). *The Disabled State*. Philadelphia., PA: Temple University Press.

Stone, E., Stone D., and Dipboye, R. (1992). Stigmas in organizations: Race, handicaps, and physical attractiveness. In K. Kelley (ed.), *Issues, Theory, and Research in Industrial/Organizational Psychology*. Amsterdam, Holland: Elsevier Science Publishers.

US Bureau of Census (1990). *Labor Force Status and Other Characteristics of Persons with a Work Disability: 1981–1988*, Washington, DC: GPO.

US Department of Commerce, Bureau of Census (1990). *Labor Force Status and other Characteristics of Persons with Work Disability*. Washington DC: Government Printing Press.

US General Accounting Office (1990). *Persons with Disabilities: Reports on Costs of Accommodations*, January. Washington, DC.

Weaver, C. L. (1992). Reassessing federal disability insurance. *Public Interest*, 106, Winter, 108–21.

Wertlieb, E. C. (1985). Minority group status of the disabled. *Human Relations*, 38(11), 1047–63.

Wilson, M. D. (1991). Defense to discrimination actions filed under the Americans with Disabilities Act. *Labor Law Journal*, 42(11), November, 732–45.

Wirth, F. (1970). The problem of minority groups. In M. Kurokawa (ed.), *Minority Responses: Comparative Views of Reactions to Subordination* (34–42). New York: Random House.

World Health Organization (1980). *International Classification of Impairments, Disabilities, and Handicaps*. Geneva: WHO.

Yelin, E. (1986). The myth of malingering: Why individuals withdraw from work in the presence of illness. *Milbank Quarterly*, 64(4), 622–49.

Yelin, E. (1989). Displaced concern: The social context of the work-disability problem. *Milbank Quarterly*, 67, Supp. 2(1), 114–65.

Zola, I. K. (1987). "Any distinguishing features?" – The portrayal of disability in the crime-mystery genre. *Policy Studies Journal*, 15(3), March, 485–513.

Part Four
Linking Diversity to Organizational Strategy

Introduction to Part Four

Organizations and scholars are increasingly endorsing the belief that managing diversity can provide competitive advantage and enhanced organizational effectiveness. Yet relatively little has been written on globalization, and the widespread restructuring of organizations into team-based work systems. Gary Florkowski's chapter examines managing diversity for competitive advantage in multinational firms. He provides a framework linking an organization's labor market profile to its competitive, global environment. The chapter includes current critical topics such as managing parent country and host country dyads, international teams, and the repatriation process. Florkowski also provides suggestions for improving the effectiveness of current international HRM practices. For example, he argues that integrating the HRM function into strategic planning is likely to increase the emphasis on human resource strategies to support globalization. He also suggests conducting focused diversity audits to identify transnational managerial competencies. The altering of recruitment and career planning strategies to emphasize more heavily the utilization and integration of foreign nationals in domestic operations is another strategy recommended.

Globalization is one of many organizational strategies that can be used to gain advantage in the marketplace. Parshotam Dass and Barbara Parker provide in chapter 14 a broad view of links between diversity and organizational strategy. They present a model to help decision-makers align internal and external organizational environments, thereby enabling organizations to capitalize on diversity. For example, organizations can attract the best talent available in the labor market, better tap into the diverse demands of new markets, more rapidly adapt to shorter product life and developmental cycles, and garner multicultural resources and capabilities.

In chapter 15, Donna Thompson and Laura Gooler describe the effects of diversity on team performance and identify specific interventions to enhance the performance of diverse teams. They discuss key ways in which workteams are changing in firms today: there is greater diversity in the backgrounds of team members in general; more individuals external to the organization are involved; teams are more likely to be temporary and have changing composition over time; teams increasingly meet electronically as opposed to only face to face; and they have growing responsibility and autonomy. Thompson and Gooler point out that diversity may have either a positive or negative effect on team effectiveness, depending on how it is managed. In diverse teams, there is an increased need to manage differences in nonverbal cues and communication patterns and to handle conflict. They demonstrate the critical role that team leadership, managerial support, organizational structure and reward systems play in determining a team's effectiveness.

13

Managing Diversity within Multinational Firms for Competitive Advantage

Gary W. Florkowski

Introduction

Whether multinational enterprises (MNEs) are driven by resource, market, or efficiency objectives (see Behrman, 1984), an inevitable consequence of having operations in multiple countries is greater workforce diversity. Mobilizing an international labor force can be extremely challenging for many reasons. Conflicts may arise over basic management assumptions such as the need to minimize internal transaction costs or the extent to which firms can alter their external environment – disagreements that are not automatically reduced as a result of working for the same MNE (Adler and Jelinek, 1986; Hofstede, 1993; Laurent, 1986). There also tend to be systematic differences in work-related attitudes across countries (Hofstede, 1993; Ronen and Shenkar, 1985) that could significantly influence the acceptability of organizational and job design principles. For example, bureaucratic structures, which epitomize Schuler's (1989) human resource management (HRM) portfolio for a cost-reduction business strategy (i.e. narrowly defined jobs and career paths; hierarchical decision-making and pay; shout-term, results-oriented performance criteria; limited training), could be counterproductive in societies that have low tolerance for power distance, low needs for uncertainty avoidance, and strong "feminine" values.[1] Others have documented limited transferability of HRM practices based on the incompatibility of home-country selection, appraisal and compensation procedures and values with host-country norms (e.g. Ishida, 1986; Schneider,

1988; Von Glinow and Teagarden, 1988). Alternatively, the business and HR objectives embraced by MNE headquarters may be at odds with the HR priorities which predominate in a given host country. Appendix A shows that there is considerable variation throughout the Americas, Europe, and Asia regarding the top-rated HR goals to facilitate business success.

Given these complexities, it seems logical to assume that MNEs will devise and implement effective means of harnessing the multitude of cultures which coexist within their structures over time. Yet, available evidence indicates that multinationals often are unable to do so because of ethnocentric staffing and development policies. Adler and Bartholomew (1992) reported that senior executives in North American firms rarely come from outside the home country; often being selected with little, if any, consideration given to their cultural adaptability or foreign language skills. Their international experience, a potential mitigating factor for the lack of multiculturalism, is likely to be very limited as well. Although North American firms expatriated heavily during their early stages of globalization, high failure rates for parent-country nationals (PCNs) have resulted in a dramatic cutback in their usage in recent decades and greater reliance on third-country nationals (TCNs) and host-country nationals (HCNs) (Black et al., 1992). While Japanese MNEs are no less homogeneous at the top, they continue to expatriate much more frequently when filling senior- and middle-management positions abroad, even in host countries with advanced industrialized economies (Kujawa, 1986; Tung, 1982). These practices are in stark contrast to many European-based companies that have several nationalities represented directly on the board of directors and actively seek "Euromanagers" with extensive work histories in multiple European markets (e.g. Hagerty, 1991).

North American MNEs also tend to adopt development policies which place little value on deriving managerial synergies from cultural differences. Cultural awareness, a prerequisite for such organizational learning, is not even promoted among PCNs given the small percentage that receive any cross-cultural training before they depart overseas (American Society for Training and Development, 1994; Mendenhall et al., 1987). When culture-based training is offered, moreover, few expatriate managers report that it meets their needs (Commerce Clearing House, 1992). Rotating HCNs and TCNs through home operations for training or short-term assignments could reduce the dysfunctional aspects of these practices. However, the normal rationale for doing so among North American and European firms is to assimilate both groups into the culture which predominates at headquarters, not to evolve that culture (e.g. Copp, 1977; Desatnick and Bennett, 1978; International Labour Office, 1981). Unidirectional socialization increases the likelihood of ethnocentrism within the former set of multinationals, given their senior executive staffing patterns. One illustration of this is the fact that 75 percent of the respondents in one survey did not use multinational design or training teams for HCN and TCN development (Adler and Bartholomew, 1992). By comparison, Matsushita has instituted a program which will annually place 100 foreign managers from overseas subsidiaries into its Japanese offices and factories with the express intent of forcing home-country managers to deal with foreign colleagues and issues (*Economist*, 1991).

A growing number of management scholars are asserting that firms will be more cognizant of their market opportunities and develop more effective response capabilities if workforce diversity is increased and managed properly (e.g. Cox and Blake, 1991; Ellis and Sonnenfeld, 1994). Their core argument is that heightened multicultural sensitivities convey competitive advantage by reducing labor costs, expanding access to superior human resources, enhancing marketing expertise, improving problem-solving capabilities and creativity, and shortening response time to environmental change.[2] The strategic imperative to create a synergistic organizational culture that transcends any single national culture may be particularly acute for MNEs facing competitive environments in which there are strong, simultaneous pressures for global integration and national responsiveness. Here, competitive advantage hinges on successfully managing cultural diversity across product *and* labor markets (Adler and Ghadar, 1990; Milliman et al., 1990).

Accordingly, this chapter seeks to accomplish three fundamental objectives. First, an analytic framework is developed to assess multinationals' capacity and *need* to manage diversity effectively. Some workforce diversity proponents have charged multicultural organizations to be models of social performance, as demonstrated by their ongoing support of external institutional efforts to eliminate all forms of social oppression in the environment (Jackson et al., 1992). While laudable in theory, such mandates are less pertinent for multinationals than they might be for domestic companies. The OECD Guidelines, MNEs' current template of social responsibility in international HRM, stress respect for, and compliance with, local employment standards.[3] An inherent danger in imposing a global agenda to ameliorate social ills is that there is an inevitable bias in defining them due to cultural ethnocentrism. Furthermore, MNEs tend to encounter extensive host-country resistance when they introduce "innovative" HRM policies that challenge cultural expectations in national industrial-relations systems (see Schuler and Florkowski, 1995). Consequently, diversity will be examined solely in terms of its potential impact on internal efficiency and effectiveness.

Given the accompanying need to identify where within an MNE's operations diversity-linked challenges are most likely to arise, the second objective is to target organizational hot spots requiring careful monitoring. These include the international assignee (PCN, TCN)–host employee dyad, international teams, and the repatriation process. The third objective is to suggest how international HRM practice might be enhanced to capitalize on opportunities which do exist for competitive advantage through diversity management. The research implications of these materials will be discussed in the last section of the chapter.

Our discussion now turns to the factors that dictate how critical it is for MNEs to manage diversity well across operating units.

Global Framework for Managing Diversity

Conventional wisdom dictates that environmental and industry analyses be integral parts of any strategic planning process. In the same vein, MNEs must evaluate current labor- and product-market dynamics to determine the priority level that should be assigned to workforce diversity initiatives. As will be discussed, some multinationals experience strong pressures to deal with this issue because of the portfolio of labor markets which feed international operations. For others, it is strong because harnessing diversity is the key to being responsive to widely divergent demands from global consumers regarding products, packaging, or services. It will be argued that both dimensions must be considered to fully gauge the need for allocating resources to the management of workforce diversity. When there are weak pressures from both sets of markets, diversity programs still may be adopted based on philosophical, rather than economic, considerations.

Labor market forces

Whether the byproduct of intended or emergent strategies, multinationals inevitably draw upon multiple labor markets in the pursuit of industry market share. Economic, political, and demographic forces can impact significantly on the availability and cost of workers in a given country. For example, advanced industrialized economies (AIEs) like the United States and Germany have high investments in human capital and extensive employment regulation contributing to high earnings by world standards. Population trends indicate that there will be a substantial "graying" of the domestic workforce in AIEs over the next few decades, foreshadowing labor shortages that are projected to be most severe in Japan (Johnson, 1991; Levin, 1994). Equal employment opportunity (EEO) legislation may partially redress the problem of availability by prompting firms to stop underutilizing segments of the population that have pertinent skills and abilities. Another means of doing so would be to relax immigration policies, especially for individuals who can contribute to key sectors of the economy (e.g. Farnsworth, 1994). A third option would be to assimilate into a supranational labor market such as the one that is evolving within the European Union (EU). There, it is becoming more commonplace for professionals to migrate from countries where there is an oversupply of labor to other EU members experiencing a shortage of such talent (Rubin, 1991). However, nations are not equally predisposed to advance such public policies.

Firms also must be responsive to labor cost pressures to become and remain competitive in international business. Intercountry labor-cost differentials have changed dramatically since the early 1980s. To illustrate, Great Britain became our only major trading partner in Europe with lower hourly compensation costs in the manufacturing sector.[4] This fact at least partially explains the influx of European-based auto-makers into the Southeastern United States (e.g. Levin, 1993; *Wall Street Journal*, 1993). It also should be noted that Canadian and Japanese manufacturers now incur labor costs which meet or slightly exceed those of their American counterparts on average. The migration of Canadian production jobs to the United States in the aftermath of the North American Free Trade Agreement (NAFTA) prompted much of the opposition to NAFTA prior to its passage as the pact's opponents projected an even greater exodus of American jobs to Mexico (Fransworth, 1993). Similarly, although many US and Japanese firms flocked to Hong Kong, Singapore, Korea, and Taiwan in the past because of substantial labor savings, hourly compensation costs have doubled (or almost tripled) in these economies in little more than a decade. As might be expected, multinationals based there are shifting their production facilities to less developed nations like Indonesia, Vietnam, India and the People's Republic of China with increasing regularity. This phenomenon is consistent with the contention that countries cannot sustain long-term competitive advantage based on labor cost (Porter, 1990).

The ongoing diversification of MNE labor markets generates fundamental concerns about firms' capacity to effectively manage a global workforce. How much of a challenge this poses is expected to vary based on diversity levels *within* a multinational's home labor market and *across* its host markets. In theory, MNEs based in nations with high levels of domestic diversity should be more aware of the need to accommodate competing employee stakeholders, and possibly have engaged in more experimentation toward this end. When such learning isn't required or doesn't occur domestically, high levels of diversity across host operations may develop these competencies, although the educational process probably will be less efficient for reasons that will be addressed later.

Acknowledging the importance of diversity in international operations is far easier than specifying its determinants. In this discussion, home labor force diversity is viewed as an outgrowth of three primary factors: the population's cultural heterogeneity, prevailing labor-supply conditions in the local economy, and the extent to which there are regulatory pressures for EEO under national law. Host labor force diversity is defined similarly by the amalgam of cultures, labor supply conditions, and EEO mandates which pertain to overseas units. Each of these items is examined in more detail below.

Domestic cultural heterogeneity should intensify as the range, size, and cohesiveness of ethnic, racial, and religious groups increase. Values, norms, and customs have the potential to vary greatly across such groups. For example, it has been argued that religion may play a significant role in observed differences in the need for individual achievement across cultures (Ronen, 1986, p. 132). Other research (e.g. Adler, 1991; Randall, 1993; Smith, 1992) indicates that ethnicity/nationality may affect the perceived centrality of work, the preferred locus of control for business decision-making, the appeal of organizational rewards, and attachment to the firm, among other things. Schneider (1988) presented several anecdotes showing how MNE pay practices had to be altered to meet the expectations of individuals from different European nationalities. While the hope is that cultural pluralism in the workplace will stimulate innovations in HRM, the outcomes are not always socially progressive. There is evidence of pay differentials and staffing patterns in the US that reflect firms' willingness to reward the discriminatory preferences of co-workers and customers (e.g. Chiswick, 1973; Borjas, 1982).

Since availability *per se* does not guarantee that there will be high levels of diversity within the home labor force, other factors must be considered in tandem. During times of dramatic shortages, firms may be more willing to seek alternative sources of labor than would be evident in other periods. To illustrate, American businesses hired women *en masse* during World War II to staff production jobs that supported the war effort. The utilization and placement of female employees in that era deviated substantially from pre-war practices, but reverted quickly with their massive displacement at war's end to accommodate returning soldiers. More recently, Singapore has been battling its acute labor shortage by offering economic incentives to employ older persons, instituting child-care programs to encourage higher female labor force participation, and offering residential status to foreign workers who posses requisite skills or professional experience (Ariff, 1993).

EEO regulatory pressures may play a decisive role here as well. EEO has become a well-ingrained expectation among individuals in AIEs, reflected in the proliferation of EEO legislation in North America, Europe, and Japan over the last three decades. However, although the basic principle is embraced widely, its breadth fluctuates considerably. One survey reported that race and gender discrimination were prohibited in all ten of the nations under study, religious discrimination was barred in seven countries, ethnic-origin discrimination in six, age discrimination in five, and discrimination against the disabled in only three (Blanpain, 1985b). Consequently, the extensiveness of home labor force diversity should be strongly correlated with the set of groups qualifying for employment protection and the government's commitment to such legislation. Sasajima (1993) attributes much of the rise in labor force participation among Japanese women during the last decade to the coterminous EEO initiatives that were enacted by government.

There is conceptual overlap, but not equivalence, regarding the forces governing host labor force diversity. Within any single country, the MNE may encounter a labor market that is divided sharply along cultural lines, or culturally monolithic. Economy-wide shortages may be prevalent, typified by the labor scarcity confronting foreign and domestic firms in Hong Kong (see Chiu and Levin, 1993). This phenomenon may foster prospecting for nontraditional sources of local labor to enlarge the demographic/culture pool. Host government policies concerning discrimination may be extensive or minimal. Perhaps more importantly, these substantive requirements may be enforced selectively to benefit or disadvantage multinationals. Such variability has been characterized as the regulatory relevance of international HRM's legal environment (Florkowski and Nath, 1993). Alternatively, host law may exempt MNEs from complying with indigenous EEO legislation in certain areas of their operations. This occurs in the US by way of bilateral Friendship, Commerce and Navigation (FCN) treaties with several dozen nations. To illustrate, the FCN treaty with Japan has a freedom-of-choice clause allowing employers to discriminate based on citizenship when staffing key executive and professional positions in the other country. Mounting litigation indicates that this provision not only shields foreign parents from discrimination charges in their unincorporated US branch offices, but also authorizes otherwise discriminatory actions within wholly-owned American subsidiaries so long as the parent essentially controls such conduct and the reason for doing so is to protect the parent's business interests (Braswell and Poe, 1993). While there are no countervailing examples for American operations in Japan, US firms could utilize FCN provisions in other countries to exempt themselves from indigenous employment quotas, should any exist.

Headquarters' propensity to staff positions with nonindigenous personnel must be factored in as well. For instance, the staffing approach for lower management tends to be decidedly polycentric (i.e. high HCN usage) across nations irrespective of MNE home-country, although Japanese multinationals practice this to a lesser extent than has been observed among their Western-based counterparts (Tung, 1982). Much higher levels of expatriation were evident for middle and senior managerial slots, with systematic variations based on the location of headquarters and whether the host unit was situated in an AIE or a newly industrialized economy (NIE). Failure to maximize use of the local executive supply-pool carries some business risk, though, even when host EEO mandates are not operative. Zeira and Banai (1981) discovered that European suppliers had decidedly ethnocentric expectations for the way that multinationals filled the top executive position within their respective nations. While not explicitly addressed in their analysis, the barriers for building and sustaining local business relationships are clear.

Finally, the extent to which there is extraterritorial application of home-country EEO law may affect diversity levels in overseas units. Pursuant to federal case law, PCNs do not enjoy the same safeguards against employment discrimination in overseas assignments as do employees stateside, unless the pertinent statute *explicitly* provides for such coverage. At present, the Age Discrimination in Employment Act, Civil Rights Act of 1991, and Americans with Disabilities Act include this kind of language. These laws presumably bar American firms from withholding assignments to foreign subsidiaries under their actual or potential control based on a US citizen's age, race, gender, religion, national origin, or non-job handicaps unless required to do so by host country law (see Bauer, 1994). When home country law is silent about extraterritoriality, local labor laws may still offer resident PCNs some protection against discriminatory treatment within the host unit if fundamental public policies would be undermined (Yamakawa, 1992).

Figure 13.1 presents a classification scheme for MNEs conveying the location and magnitude of workforce diversity pressures. Quadrant I firms operate in labor-market environments where the need to manage diversity

Figure 13.1 Labor-force diversity levels within multinational firms

Home labor force diversity	Host labor force diversity	
	Low	High
Low	I	II
High	III	IV

is low at home and abroad. Many factors could account for this development. Prior research indicates that countries may be categorized into one of the following cultural clusters: Latin-American, Latin-European, Anglo, Germanic, Nordic, Near Eastern, Arab, Far Eastern, and Independent (see Ronen and Shenkar, 1985). If so, then diversity-related pressures might be low if host sites occupied the same cultural cluster as the home country or are confined to a few clusters that necessitate very limited changes in home-HRM practices. To illustrate, Japanese expatriates have reported that Southeast Asian units are further along in becoming "Japanized" than are American and German units of the same parent companies (Ishida, 1986). Instead, cultural differences within or across host nations may be high but the probability of EEO enforcement against multinationals may be low in these economies. Another possibility is that host labor surpluses abound permitting MNEs to restrict hiring to culturally compatible segments of the local populations. This is exemplified by a Japanese company in Indonesia that preferred to employ the members of one ethnic group because their characteristics were perceived to be Japanese-like (Maruyama, 1992).

Multinationals falling within quadrant II also experience weak domestic pressures to accommodate diversity, but must contend with strong needs to develop such competencies internationally. While the home population may be very homogeneous, host units are located in a set of countries where intracultural or intercultural differences run high *and* host governments demand strict observance of indigenous employment law. Several developing nations have taken concrete action to curtail the influence that MNEs have on their societies. Thailand and Kenya have adopted national development plans which explicitly incorporate commitments to cultural preservation. Others have attempted to curb the utilization of expatriates with strict residency periods or indigenous employment quotas (e.g. India, Saudi Arabia, Philippines). Still others, like Nigeria, have imposed timetables for the indigenization of foreign investments and conveyance of equity ownership to the local workforce. AIEs that serve as host countries can behave in a similar manner. For example, a majority of the Japanese firms with US operations were facing employment discrimination litigation by the late 1980s (*Wall Street Journal*, 1989).

Headquarters' interest in responding to this challenge should be moderated by MNE structure. For example, senior management arguably will be more amenable to devoting resources to this matter in structures where integrated sourcing among plants is high (i.e. components assembled in country X become critical inputs for further assembly in country Y). Here, supply disruptions or poor quality outputs from country X might seriously erode the firm's global competitive position. Similarly, home-country executives tend to have more direct contact with overseas units in national-subsidiary structures than in regional or product structures where there are intervening layers of management. Their awareness and understanding of unit-level needs are expected to be greater in the former as a result. As will be seen shortly, product-market dynamics must be filtered in as well.

Quadrants III and IV encompass settings in which there is a high need to cope with diversity in the home labor market. High intracultural diversity, aggressive EEO policies, marked shifts in population demographics, and strong full-employment pressures may jointly or severally cause domestic units to seek and hire groups with mutually incompatible expectations of the employment relationship. Reconciling these differences may be a key to acquiring and sustaining domestic competitive advantage. The larger question is whether this experience or awareness has any bearing on international competitiveness. In quadrant III, the incremental diversity encountered in and across host units is relatively small given the "wealth" of experience the MNE has acquired in coping with its home labor market. HRM practices which are sufficiently diversified for domestic needs should have broad application to foreign units as a result. For instance, home labor market diversity should increase markedly within the EU over time given legislation that promotes the free flow of workers among member nations. This cross-pollination of labor markets should lead domestic firms in any one of those countries to institute HRM practices that can be transferred to operations elsewhere in the EU with minor adjustments.

Quadrant IV multinationals, by comparison, must place more emphasis on international HRM processes to effectively manage a global workforce. Basically, the home office has only experienced a subset, albeit large, of the demographic, political, and/or economic forces that the MNE is being subjected to worldwide. This might characterize the plight of US firms seeking to expand the scope of their operations in Eastern Europe, nations of the former Soviet Union, or Africa in recent years. The value in overcoming domestic diversity lies not in program content *per se* as was the case in quadrant III, but in developing competencies for recognizing and including multiple employee stakeholders in the design process for HRM. This is akin to what has been described as the *modus operandi* for change in international HRM units (Schuler et al., 1993).

While important, labor markets are not the only engines driving the need to manage diversity. Product markets also may generate powerful stimuli, as will be explored below.

Product market forces

If nothing else, the previous section demonstrated that firms do not encounter identical challenges when they seek to transact business outside of their native land. MNEs face the prospect of not only having to differentiate their work policies, but also having to alter their products or services as they pursue customers around the world. There can be pervasive differences in consumers' needs, purchasing power, skill levels, cultural expectations, legal rights, and language requirements from one country to the next. This, in turn, might warrant considerable fluctuation in product size, use features, quality, appearance, package design and labelling, as well as servicing practices and warranty support. Market research, product design, promotion, and technical support activities become more complex as individual host markets become more idiosyncratic. Accordingly, multinationals can be viewed as facing weak or strong pressures for national responsiveness in their products. Industrial chemicals exemplify the former situation; consumer products the latter. At the same time, there will be some potential for economies-of-scale in production or managing external relationships, creating pressures for the global integration of operations. As before, these forces may be weak or strong.

Four types of competitive environments emerge from the interaction of these two dimensions: international, multinational, global, and transational. Some illustrative industries for each classification include (Ghoshal and Nohria, 1993):

- *international*: metals (except nonferrous), machinery, paper, textiles, printing/publishing;
- *multinational*: beverages, food, household appliances, tobacco;
- *global*: construction and mining equipment, nonferrous metals, industrial chemicals, scientific measuring instruments, engines; and
- *transnational*: drugs and pharmaceuticals, photographic equipment, computers, automobiles

International environments call for little in terms of responsiveness or integration, inviting MNEs to establish autonomous host units that deliver standardized products to buyers. This might occur when products originating in the home country are first exported and there is high, untapped consumer demand overseas. Global environments also demand low product differentiation, but necessitate widespread interunit collaboration to achieve the operational efficiencies essential to success in the industry. On the other hand, multinational and transnational environments both contain strong pressures for national responsiveness. The former competitive arena again tolerates independent country operations, while the latter dictates that MNEs find ways of orchestrating high integration and high responsiveness simultaneously.

Figure 13.2 seeks to link these industry forces with the labor market dynamics discussed earlier. By doing so, one better understands how compelling it is for MNEs to promote and master workforce diversity. Firms

Figure 13.2 Market forces influencing the need to manage diversity within MNEs

	Product market pressures to manage diversity effectively	
Labor market pressures to manage diversity effectively	Weak	Strong
Weak	I	II
Strong	III	IV

located in cell I appear to have little at risk if they do not strive for diversity or accommodate it when formulating international HRM practices. Pressures for national responsiveness are weak as would be the case in international or global competitive environments. Since relatively small adjustments are needed to satisfy indigenous buyers, staffing and development practices don't need to place much emphasis on the acquisition of local business expertise. Moreover the fact that these multinationals are nestled in labor markets that present few diversity challenges (quadrants I or III in figure 13.1) suggests that HRM policies and programs don't need ongoing cultural audits and modification to be more inclusive or acceptable. A hypothetical example of this might be a UK-based publisher with operating units in Australia, Canada and the US.

Although similarly situated from a product market standpoint, cell III multinationals operate in labor markets that will not readily embrace a standardized set of HRM policies anchored in home-country norms (i.e. quadrant II or IV situations in figure 13.1). This profile might describe a US-based textile manufacturer with mills in the Philippines, China, and Mexico, or a German industrial-chemicals firm with production facilities in India, the US, and Russia. Headquarters nevertheless should take a very measured approach when dealing with this problem, given the high potential costs of internal auditing and extensive environmental scanning. The level of resources committed to making HRM policies more culturally compatible should be correlated with the labor-intensiveness of host units in international competitive environments. For global competitive environments, this decision should be driven by the amount of integrated sourcing that actually exists.

National responsiveness pressures are strong in the remaining two cells, placing a much bigger premium on stockpiling and cultivating local business competencies. As noted by Cox and Blake (1991), workforce diversity has clear marketing relevance for MNEs in these circumstances. Even so, switching to less ethnocentric staffing and development patterns does not automatically bring with it the need to make sweeping changes in the firm's HRM activities on a country-by-country basis. The need to do so should not be great for MNEs occupying cell II in light of the fact that there are few cultural differences separating the home and host units. To illustrate this within a multinational competitive environment, consider a Hong Kong manufacturer of household appliances that maintains a production unit in Singapore. These two countries exhibit high levels of shared ethnicity and a common stage of industrial development, fostering domestic HRM practices that are highly similar in nature (Begin, 1992; Latham and Napier, 1989). Headquarters probably will insist on minor oversight of diversity management in transnational environments to ensure that minor HRM differentiation does not interfere unduly with integration initiatives. However, the competitiveness stakes escalate dramatically in cell IV, where companies must deal with labor markets that supply employees who generally are unwilling or unable to conform to the organizations's corporate or home country cultures. This is where the challenge of managing diversity is the largest and the returns from doing so effectively the greatest. Think of the managerial complexities confronting an automobile manufacturer that utilizes an interactive, global design network encompassing units in the UK, Germany, Italy, Japan, Australia, and the US.

Managing Diversity for Competitive Advantage

What does all of this mean in terms of practice? While promoting diversity for its own sake has an obvious moral appeal in the US, its economic value is much less certain outside of an industrial context. Unfortunately, previous descriptions of cross-national diversity initiatives have been largely anecdotal (e.g. Jackson et al., 1992; Napier et al., 1993; Rubin, 1991), conveying no insight into the strategy that headquarters should follow to maximize performance in its current set of markets. Adler and Bartholomew (1992) stressed the need for transnational HRM systems in transnational competitive environments, but did not undertake the task of specifying what kinds of diversity strategies might best serve other environments. This problem is addressed next.

Appropriate strategy

No single strategy can be equally cost-effective across countries and industries. In some situations, there are compelling reasons for MNEs to carefully monitor and control how host units respond to the subcultures which permeate their operations. Keeping a tight rein on host management may be dysfunctional in others, because headquarters lacks sufficient expertise to add value to local diversity management or will end up over-investing in a relatively insignificant area of international HRM. A more *laissez-faire* approach would be warranted in either case. Figure 13.3 is designed to assist MNEs in maximizing the return-on-investment (ROI) in diversity

Figure 13.3 Ideal approaches for managing workforce diversity

		Market needs			
		Weak		Strong	
Diversity challenges		International Responsiveness(L)-Integration(L)	Global Responsiveness(L)-Integration(H)	Multinational Responsiveness(H)-Integration(L)	Transnational Responsiveness(H)-Integration(H)
Weak	Home(L)-Host(L)	*Ad hoc* variation			
	Home(H)-Host(L)		Structural uniformity		
Strong	Home(L)-Host(H)			Differentiated fit	
	Home(H)-Host(H)				Integrated variety

(L) Low pressure to accommodate
(H) High pressure to accommodate

management by matching strategies with the product- and labor-market contingencies articulated in this chapter. Four generic diversity strategies are identified paralleling Ghoshal and Nohria's (1993) typology of organizational structures: *ad hoc* variation, structural uniformity, differentiated fit, and integrated variety. Some of these strategies have broader applications than others, but each has a particular configuration of markets for which it is best suited.

Ad hoc variation exists when there are no official or *de facto* principles guiding efforts to manage a geographically dispersed workforce. Headquarters has not created any kind of integrative mechanisms to coordinate the handling of diversity within countries, nor have explicit "grassroots" patterns materialized that interested host units could generalize from in trying to cope with their own local contexts. Ambivalence toward diversity management certainly conserves international HRM costs, but at what price? This strategy may be defensible in international competitive environments where diversity levels are low for the MNE's home and host labor force. High sociocultural and political similarities across units make it likely that a large segment of the HRM practices developed for domestic workers can be transferred overseas. Idiosyncratic HRM adjustments are likely to be small given this cultural overlap, and there is very low operational interdependence across host units, making unencumbered experimentation a minimal risk to overall MNE operations.

Structural uniformity refers to situations where multinationals institute very centralized policies about the way that diversity-related issues should be handled – policies anchored in headquarters' experiences with the demographic, cultural, and political landscapes of the home country. Little deviation from this managerial paradigm is then tolerated across units. This strategy has merit when the competitive environment is global in nature and there are weak pressures to manage host labor force diversity relative to those which prevailed in the home country. Of course, the ultimate success of this strategy hinges on being responsive to domestic HRM needs. The *ad hoc* variation strategy is much less desirable for this type of product market because host-unit interdependencies are likely to be higher in a global competitive environment, as the MNE strives for the most efficient network of production facilities worldwide. HRM practices which generate indigenous apathy or hostility may seriously impair the firm's ability to capitalize on inter-country synergies that would otherwise surface.

Differentiated fit describes a strategy which totally decentralizes the MNE's efforts to manage diversity effectively. Host managers do not merely have the latitude to tailor HRM practices to meet the unique demands of their indigenous labor markets; headquarters expects that they will engineer whatever changes are necessary to be competitive locally. Unit accountability for diversity management distinguishes this approach from *ad hoc* variation. It might be argued that such accountability also exists under structural uniformity, but the character of this obligation is decidedly different (i.e. HRM replication in the case of structural uniformity versus HRM innovation in the case of differentiated fit). Thus the performance criteria used to judge managerial success in this area could be decidedly different based on the complexity of the local market and amount of financial resources for HRM at the unit's disposal. A differentiated fit strategy should be deployed when firms are in multinational competitive environments without having the benefit of mastering extensive workforce diversity in their home-country operations (e.g. a domestic Japanese consumer-goods firm extending its operations into Central/Eastern Europe – see Maruyama, 1990). Without this experience, it is unlikely that headquarters will be sufficiently attuned to cultural "blindspots" in current staffing, development, and utilization policies. In addition, pressures for global integration are weak, as noted earlier, thus reducing the need to worry about fostering strong interunit linkages via HRM practices.

Integrated variety, the final possibility, builds upon the previous strategy to make sure that aggressive, host-specific HRM adaptations do not somehow preclude the firm from accommodating strong integration needs worldwide. There may be core corporate needs to have certain functional areas highly centralized, certain organizational subsystems highly formalized, or certain norms/values widely embraced by organizational members because one or more of these items already is contributing to competitive advantage in the industry. If left unchecked, job design, staffing, reward, development, and empowerment policy revisions could undercut these competencies at the same time as host labor-market appeal is being strengthened. Accordingly, headquarters will devise some integrative mechanisms to bound HRM variability, be that in the form of governing principles for diversity as part of its overall HRM philosophy, or review and veto power over unit requests for procedural or substantive changes in HRM programs, etc. This kind of diversity strategy is most appropriate for MNEs facing the dual challenges of transnational competitive environments, and international workforce diversity that far exceeds headquarters' competencies to manage from afar, no matter how demographically enlightened the home country forces it to be.

The framework articulated above coincides with other efforts to describe how MNEs strike an ongoing balance between fit and flexibility in international HRM policies (Milliman et al., 1991; Milliman and Von Glinow, 1990).

Situational flash points to monitor

Three aspects of international HRM should be monitored no matter which diversity strategy is chosen: the reporting relationship between international assignees and host employees, international team management, and post-assignment repatriation processes. Each area has the potential to impact significantly on strategy implementation around the globe.

International assignee–host employee dyad Technical competence is a necessary, but insufficient, factor in the successful completion of overseas assignments. The personal interface between HCNs and PCNs or TCNs can have a major effect on an MNE's ability to foster motivation and build organizational commitment within the host unit. American multinationals are not the only ones who encounter difficulty managing these relationships. A recent Towers Perrin survey revealed that Japanese firms viewed the conflict between their expatriate staff and local employees in the US and elsewhere as their primary globalization concern (Karr, 1992). This apprehension is not unfounded, as illustrated by the problems that initially plagued Mazda Motor Corporation's production plant in Flat Rock, Michigan. High mutual animosity between senior Japanese managers and the US workforce was the root cause for relatively low productivity, quality and profitability (Jackson et al., 1992). Numerous initiatives were adopted to overcome these cultural barriers including cross-cultural problem-solving teams; a joint steering committee to set priorities for managing diversity within divisions and departments; and changes in reward systems to reinforce these activities. Maruyama (1992) similarly reported that several California banks decreased markedly in profitability after being acquired by Japanese firms because the latters' management style was not adapted enough to retain key American employees.

It also should be noted that these mishaps, despite being commonplace, can have very different underlying causes. For example, the stereotypic shortcomings of US PCNs are their insensitivity, indifference or ignorance of cultural differences, while for Japanese PCNs the alleged shortcoming is oversensitivity to them, prompting a decision that indigenous workers are incapable of adapting fully to Japanese-style management practices (Maruyama, 1992; Ishida, 1986). Either mindset may lead to overseas management behavior which is diametrically opposed to more "progressive" patterns that prevail in the home country, a phenomenon labeled the "inverse practice principle" (Maruyama, 1988). Yet the implications for corrective staffing and development practices are not the same for these two scenarios.

International teams The business literature is replete with summaries of the potential advantages and managerial challenges associated with multicultural/international teams (e.g. Adler, 1991, pp. 120–42; Cox et al., 1991; Elashmawi and Harris, 1993, pp. 98–130; Phillips, 1994; Tsui et al., 1992; Watson et al., 1993). Interested readers are referred to these sources for lengthy discussions of the design and control issues that must be addressed to promote effective group process. Instead, one MNE's struggle with this area will be highlighted to show what can go awry if the situation is not tracked closely.

During the late 1980s, Becton Dickinson Corporation created worldwide teams for each of its major products, charging them to formulate global strategies and foster more intercountry integration (see Williamson and Beer, 1993). Each team was composed of the US division president, senior US staff in marketing, R & D, and manufacturing, as well as their regional counterparts within that product group. Despite some initial successes, this initiative failed to achieve its promise for a variety of reasons. To begin with, Americans with a decided US product market bias chaired virtually all of the teams, even though the European market presented the greatest opportunities for growth in certain instances. Furthermore, the chairs had no formal authority over team members, team processes were not standardized, team evaluation criteria had not been formulated, nor were there any contingency plans for corrective action in the event that US top management was not satisfied with a team's functioning. It is little wonder under these circumstances that teams often became bogged down in culture-laden debates over the appropriate agenda to follow and structuring of incentives.

Repatriation policies Home country re-entry is another area where important cultural breakdowns are likely to occur. MNEs expatriate individuals for many reasons, not the least significant of which is the desire to increase global business expertise. Yet many multinationals frustrate such organizational learning with inadequate repatriation policies. For instance, US HR managers have cited numerous deficiencies in the way that their companies are administering international assignments, including the failure to guarantee jobs to returning expatriates prior to their departure or to integrate foreign experiences into overall career planning (O'Boyle, 1989). Only one-fifth of this group felt that their firm's repatriation policies were adequate to meet the needs of returning individuals, while a *majority* indicated that foreign assignments were either immaterial or detrimental to one's organizational career. Approximately 20 percent of the expatriate respondents participating in this set of surveys reported that they were contemplating quitting their jobs as a result of re-entry stress. Even when HRM policies are not openly flawed in this regard, expatriates frequently find themselves pressured by domestic peers to suppress all "foreign" knowledge as a sign of successful reacculturation. Other research confirms that American MNEs are not alone in perpetuating these misguided practices. Foster (1994) found that most of the expatriates in his sample were very concerned about their career prospects, relationships with colleagues, current job performance, and standard-of-living changes after returning to the UK.

These illustrations underscore the need to manage reverse culture shock as a vital element of diversity management. Otherwise, it not only will become increasingly difficult for MNEs to entice their most talented human resources to take tours-of-duty abroad, but also to internalize their international business expertise to enhance strategy formulation and implementation.

International HRM practices to consider

There are no published accounts of MNEs that have a comprehensive, mutually reinforcing set of HR practices maximizing the potential gains from workforce diversity. Still, most of the commentary to this point has focused on things to avoid rather than on those to emulate. There have been scattered reports of creative diversity initiatives within particular functional areas of HRM. Some of the more interesting ones are catalogued in table 13.1 and examined briefly below.

MNEs like Baxter Healthcare (US), Grand Metropolitan (UK) and Imperical Chemical Industries (UK) acknowledge that a multicultural employee population is vital to their firm's ability to achieve and sustain industry leadership positions (Jackson et al., 1992; Hagerty, 1991). If so, then it makes a great deal of sense to award the HRM function an active role in strategy development to make sure that the requisite human capital is available to achieve global business objectives. European firms tend to be much more aggressive in incorporating the HRM function into strategic planning than are US companies. Brewster and Larsen (1992) reported that at least 40 percent of the firms surveyed directly involved HRM staff in strategy formulation in nine of the ten Western European countries studied. Such participation was the majority practice among Swedish, Norwegian, and German firms. In contrast, the HRM function is much more likely to become involved *post hoc* during strategy implementation in American multinationals (Bureau of National Affairs, 1993; Miller et al., 1986).

Given this mindset, it is not surprising that senior HRM executives in US-based firms devote no more than 10 percent of their time on average to international HRM strategy (Reynolds, 1992). Professionals desiring to break out of this mold should begin by instituting a strategic international HRM auditing process making cultural compatibility criteria a core element of

Table 13.1 Diversity-sensitive international HRM practices

Functional area	Activity	Company (home country)
HR planning	• Monitoring system to evaluate host-unit progress in improving diversity with consolidated business/country reporting; status reviewed every 6 months (under management committee review)	Grand Metropolitan (UK)
Staffing	• Recruitment program where students are offered internships outside of their home country	ICI (UK) and Hewlett-Packard (US)
	• Career planning incorporates international assignments	British Petroleum (UK)
	• Career planning done on the basis of business function rather than geographical location	Royal Dutch Shell (Netherlands)
Performance appraisal	• Improving diversity set as a performance criterion for every senior manager worldwide (under management committee review)	Grand Metropolitan (UK) and Colgate-Palmolive (US)
Development	• Multinational design team at headquarters develops training approaches and programs for localized delivery worldwide	American Express (US)
	• Regional training advisory councils/boards direct training activities	Motorola (US) and Amoco (US)
	• Management development center with staff and participants drawn from all regions; center located in "culturally neutral" country	Olivetti (Italy) and Ericsson (Sweden)
	• Multicultural seminars for international business with culturally mixed participants	Amadeus Global Travel, Mars Inc. (US), and British Petroleum (UK)
	• Domestic managers placed on project teams with colleagues abroad	3M (US) and Colgate-Palmolive (US)
Compensation	• Pay-for-performance systems for host managers based on standardized, culturally neutral business objectives	Pepsi-Cola (US)

Sources: Adler and Bartholomew (1992); Fulkerson and Schuler (1992); Greenslade (1991); Hagerty (1991); Neale and Mindel (1992); Odenwald (1993); Overman (1992); Rubin (1991)

the evaluation process (Florkowski and Schuler, 1994). For example, previous studies have shown that American-style management-by-objective (MBO) policies are transferred more readily to German enterprises than to French ones because of differences in national culture (Schneider, 1988). US MNEs seeking to coordinate and control their European units through MBO initiatives may find that they actually impede local performance unless major procedural changes or accommodations are made. Similarly, appraisal systems that emphasize explicit performance standards, individual accountability, and extrinsic rewards are much more likely to coincide with workplace norms prevailing in Thailand and Malaysia than would be the case in Indonesia (Vance et al., 1992).

When the undertaking of such audits far exceeds resource constraints, focused diversity audits might still be viable. Basic analyses could be performed regarding diversity-awareness levels among select groups within the MNE or demographic comparisons of work attitudes/behaviors like job satisfaction, commitment, productivity, or turnover (see Gardenswartz and Rowe, 1993, pp. 263–312). More comprehensive investigations would include a needs analysis regarding transnational managerial competencies – the skills needed to create synergies from cultural differences within the multinational firm (Adler and Bartholomew, 1992). Great care must be taken throughout to ensure that data collection methods meet host country norms. Table 13.1 reveals that there is at least one MNE with plans for a formal monitoring and reporting system for international diversity management. A diversity council, comprising representatives from each of the firm's business sectors, would oversee the proposed system and promote the internal diffusion of best practice.

Recruitment and career planning policies also can be modified to greatly enhance the diversity yield from external and internal labor markets. Many American firms already have experience actively recruiting foreign students in the US for technical and engineering positions in domestic operations. This practice could be extended to other kinds of professional training for host-country or regional placements, recognizing that the Civil Rights Act of 1991 may preclude undue emphasis on foreign citizenship as a recruitment or selection criterion. A growing number of MNEs (typically European) have engaged in transnational MBA recruiting in recent years (Conference Board, 1992). Some multinationals also are trying to strengthen their appeal to foreign students by offering summer internships in other nations. To illustrate, Imperial Chemical Industries (ICI) instituted a program that awards two-month internships to university students from the Continent in ICI locations outside of their home country. In a similar fashion, Hewlett-Packard Spain has swapped student interns with other regional units through that multinational's Inter-Europe Student Exchange Program. A related program extends three-month internships to the firm's US divisions.

Table 13.1 supplies examples of international career planning efforts as well. British Petroleum has commenced a planning initiative which will mandate international assignments for approximately 80 percent of the positions in targeted levels of its European operations. In Royal Dutch Shell, the function or business where one begins work is assigned the responsibility of promoting the long-term career welfare of individuals regardless of the location or nature of subsequent assignments.

At the same time, care must be exercised to prevent diversity from becoming a dual-edged sword in international performance appraisals. It is easy to envision how headquarters can proactively advance its global diversity objectives by making senior managers worldwide accountable for diversity enhancement as shown in table 13.1. However, diversity also can be an impediment to rating accuracy for international assignees. For example, PCNs, can be unfairly evaluated for overseas performance because of unacknowledged biases distorting the ratings assigned by host- or home-country evaluators. This could arise because of differences in preferred management styles or lack of awareness of host-unit contingencies. This problem will be minimal if several safeguards are built into the evaluation process including joint evaluation teams comprised of on-site and home-site managers and input from former expatriates when developing individual performance criteria (Oddou and Mendenhall, 1991). The failure to adjust for cultural differences also can be problematic when headquarters assigns unit performance goals. As illustrated by the pay-for-performance system in table 13.1, it may be necessary to articulate generic accountability statements (e.g. achieve a predetermined level of sales growth) without specifying the procedures or actions for their attainment and leave these to local management's expertise and discretion.

Two kinds of development initiatives could be utilized to facilitate improved cross-cultural interactions: awareness training and communication competency training (Tung, 1993). It is beyond the scope of this chapter to examine the logistics of devising an overarching MNE training strategy, developing individual needs analyses, finalizing program curricula, and administering a global training system. Interested readers should consult Odenwald (1993) for a detailed discussion of these matters. Black and Mendenhall (1991) also may be helpful in this regard. These authors devised an analytic framework anchored in social learning theory to guide MNEs in deciding which training modes are most suitable for a given international setting. Whatever training objectives the multinational wants to advance, the design and learning process must be inoculated against cultural ethnocentrism.

Table 13.1 displays how some companies are trying to respond through transnational teams of designers, trainers and trainees. At a minimum, MNE trainee groups should be heterogeneous culturally to challenge participants' preconceived notions about the cross-border relevance of program materials. Firms like Mars Inc. and British Petroleum already do so as a matter of HRM policy. A multicultural staff of trainers would reduce the likelihood that inefficient or inappropriate education technologies will be deployed. By analogy, Saner and Yiu (1994) discuss the difficulties that universities and consultants encounter when using Harvard-style case learning to teach management practice to students and executives in Europe and

Asia. Some MNEs have restructured their international HRM function to shield the overall design process for training and development from culture bias. American Express has created a headquarters-based, multinational design team for worldwide management development, while Motorola and Amoco rely upon regional advisory bodies to direct training initiatives in their respective areas. Olivetti and Ericsson have gone so far as to "spin off" their center for global management development, housing it outside of the home country to ensure that the national values permeating headquarters do not dominate decision-making.

Last, there is a growing awareness that MNEs' pay structures and pay mix need to be responsive to widely divergent cultural expectations across countries (e.g. Gomez-Mejia and Welbourne, 1991; Hodgetts and Luthans, 1993; Townsend et al., 1990). Depending on how much diversity actually exists within its operations, headquarters may need to adapt such fundamental aspects of compensation and benefits administration as job evaluation criteria and procedures, the number of pay grades, the width and overlap of pay ranges, pay step criteria, the practice of red-circling or green-circling jobs, the bifurcation of rewards into direct and deferred components, as well as the form of deferred compensation when it is offered. For example, it has been reported that pensions are expected to equal approximately 40 percent of salary in Southern European countries and to rise as high as 85 percent in Nordic countries (Schneider, 1988). Regrettably, there is a dearth of information on truly effective means of accomplishing these transformations on a worldwide scale.

Discussion

In summary, global diversity management, for all of its uncertainties, holds the key to competitive advantage for more and more firms that seek to enter and succeed in international markets. It is hoped that the analytic framework and illustrations discussed throughout this chapter increase MNEs' ability to master this challenge. These materials also should spur researchers to conduct more extensive investigations into the content and process associated with global diversity programs. Comprehensive surveys are needed to establish the prevalence of diversity initiatives within US multinationals and those based elsewhere. To illustrate, how many firms devote significant resources to multicultural workshops, support groups/mentoring programs, diversity advisory councils, language training and other activities targeted at individuals? How long have these efforts been in place, and what are their structural facets? Is diversity program coverage universal or restricted to select regions, business units, or job levels? How many of the individuals eligible to participate have actually done so? How are diversity policies coordinated across countries? How is program success defined and measured in-house? What attempts have been made to link appraisal, staffing, or reward systems to diversity-related performance at the individual or unit levels? What mechanisms are in place to increase organizational learning about diversity management? Who is the primary organizational sponsor of international diversity policies – senior HR executives, the chief executive officer, board members, overseas unit management, etc.?

There also is a strong need to conduct pre–post analyses of diversity initiatives to determine whether there is behavioral or economic evidence of positive organizational effects. Prior evaluations of domestic programs have relied heavily upon self-reported perceptions to judge program efficacy (e.g. Carrell and Mann, 1993). More rigorous designs should be utilized in future research to isolate the actual impact of these policies. For example, interrupted time-series analyses (e.g. autoregressive integrated moving average modelling) might clarify whether there was an abrupt or gradual change in productivity, quality, turnover, or profitability within MNE units that became more diversity-sensitive.

Until such information is forthcoming, it will remain difficult for multinationals to fully assess the ROI from greater investments in diversity management. Yet the labor market and product market forces described in this chapter make the transnational workforce a vital component of overall competitiveness for most MNEs. Firms that solve the challenges discussed here are projected to achieve great business success in the global economy in the decades ahead.

Appendix A   Top 5 HR goals necessary for business success in the year 2000

HR issue	Europe				North America		Asia Pacific		Latin America		
	Fr	Ger	Ita	UK	Can	US	Aus	Jpn	Arg	Brz	Mex
High productivity/ quality/customer satisfaction	2	1	1	1	1	1	1	1	1	1	1
Linkage of HR to business strategies	1	2	2	2	2	2	2	2	2	3	3
Attracting highly qualified employees		5	4	3	3	3			4		5*
Retaining highly competent employees	3*	4	5	4*	4	4			5		5*
Workforce flexibility	5	3	3	4*	5	5	3			4	
Strong organizational culture	3*						4*	3	3	5	2
High levels of employee satisfaction							4*	4		2	4
Management development and training								5			

* Tied for position rank.
Source: Towers Perrin (1992)

NOTES

1 *Power distance* refers to the degree of inequality in personal power that will be tolerated as normal within a given society; *uncertainty avoidance* to the preferred degree of structure in life situations; and *femininity* to a de-emphasis on assertiveness, success and competition. See Hofstede (1993) for further discussion of these terms.

2 There is not universal agreement that diversity's primary focus is increased efficiency and effectiveness. Some HR professionals have defined it as little more than a commitment to EEO/affirmative action objectives (Carrell and Mann, 1993). This narrow interpretation emphasizes the need to match the internal representation of labor-market groups with their external availability to satisfy regulatory mandates.

3 See Blanpain (1985a) and Cambell and Rowan (1983) for more details about the employment and industrial relationships implications of the OECD *Guidelines for Multinational Enterprises.*

4 These trends reflect unpublished data contained in two reports compiled by the US Bureau of Labor Statistics, Office of Productivity and Technology, entitled *Hourly Compensation Costs for Production Workers in Manufacturing in 33 (31) Countries or Areas,* November 1991 (May 1994). Hourly compensation costs are defined as the sum of direct pay (including paid non-work time and the value of in-kind benefits) and employer contributions to benefits whether they arise due to legal mandates or collective bargaining agreements. These figures are adjusted for exchange rate fluctuations.

REFERENCES

Adler, N. J. (1991). *International Dimensions of Organizational Behavior,* 2nd ed. Boston: PWS-Kent.

Adler, N. J., and Bartholomew, S. (1992). Managing globally competent people. *Academy of Management Executive,* 6(3), 52–65.

Adler, N. J., and Ghadar, F. (1990). Strategic human resource management: A global perspective. In R. Pieper (ed.), *Human Resource Management in International Comparison* (235–60). New York: de Gruyter.

Adler, N. J., and Jelinek, M. (1986). Is "organization culture" culture bound? *Human Resource Management,* 25, 73–90.

American Society for Training and Development (1994). *National HRD Executive Survey: Training for Global Competition.* Alexandria, VA: American Society for Training and Development.

Ariff, M. (1993). Singapore. In M. Rothman, D. R. Briscoe, and R. C. D. Nacamulli (eds), *Industrial Relations Around the World: Labor Relations for Multinational Corporations* (345–69). New York: de Gruyter.

Arvey, R. D., Bhagat, R. S., and Salas, E. (1991). Cross-cultural and cross-national issues in personnel and human resources management: Where do we go from here? In G. R. Ferris and K. M. Rowland (eds), *Research in Personnel and Human Resources Management,* vol. 9 (367–407). Greenwich, CT: JAI Press.

Bauer, K. T. (1994). Congress finds the key to extraterritoriality? *Labor Law Journal,* 45(7), 417–32.

Begin, J. (1992). Comparative human resource management (HRM): A systems perspective. *International Journal of Human Resource Management,* 3, 379–408.

Behrman, J. N. (1984). *Industrial Policies: International Restructuring and Transnationals*. Lexington, MA: Lexington Books.

Black, J. S., Gregersen, H. B., and Mendenhall, M. (1992). *Global Assignments*. San Francisco: Jossey-Bass.

Black, J. S., and Mendenhall, M. (1991). A practical but theory-based framework for selecting cross-cultural training methods. In M. Mendenhall and G. Oddou (eds), *Readings and Cases in International Human Resource Management* (177–204). Boston: PWS-Kent.

Blanpain, R. (1985a). Guidelines for multinational enterprises and labour relations. In R. Blanpain (ed.), *Comparative Labour Law and Industrial Relations*, 2nd ed. (129–48). New York: Kluwer Law and Taxation Publishers.

Blanpain, R. (1985b). Equality and prohibition of discrimination in employment. In R. Blanpain (ed.), *Comparative Labour Law and Industrial Relations*, 2nd ed. (451–72). New York: Kluwer Law and Taxation Publishers.

Borjas, G. J. (1982). The politics of employment discrimination in the federal bureaucracy. *Journal of Law and Economics*, 25, 251–300.

Braswell, M. K., and Poe, S. L. (1993). Employment discrimination and FCN treaties: Are foreign companies exempt from Title VII? *Labor Law Journal*, 44(12), 727–41.

Brewster, C., and Larsen, H. H. (1992). Human resources management in Europe: Evidence from ten countries. *International Journal of Human Resource Management*, 3, 409–34.

Bureau of National Affairs (1993). *Human Resources Activities, Budgets, and Staff: 1992–93*, SHRM-BNA Survey No. 58. Washington, DC: Bureau of National Affairs.

Campbell, D. C., and Rowan, R. L. (1983). *Multinational Enterprises and the OECD Industrial Relations Guidelines*. Philadelphia: University of Pennsylvania, Wharton Industrial Researdch Unit.

Carrell, M. R., and Mann, E. E. (1993). Defining workforce diversity programs and practices in organizations. *Labor Law Journal*, 44(12), 755–64.

Chiswick, B. R. (1973). Racial discrimination in the labour market: A test of alternative hypothesis. *Journal of Political Economy*, 81, 1330–52.

Chiu, S., and Levin, D. A. (1993). From a labor-surplus to a labor-scarce economy: Challenges to human resource management in Hong Kong. *International Journal of Human Resource Management*, 4, 159–90.

Commerce Clearing House (1992). International assignments require more personal and family support than what is being provided now. *In 1992 SHRM/CCH Survey*. Chicago: Commerce Clearing House.

Conference Board (1992). *Recruiting and Selecting International Managers*, Report No. 998. New York: Conference Board.

Copp, R. (1977). Locus of industrial relations decision making in multinationals. In R. F. Banks and J. Stieber (eds), *Multinationals, Unions, and Labor Relations in Industrialized Countries* (43–8). Ithaca, NY: Cornell University Press.

Cox, T. H., and Blake, S. (1991). Managing cultural diversity: implications for organizational competitiveness. *Academy of Management Executive*, 5(3), 45–55.

Cox, T. H., Lobel, S. A., and McLeod, P. L. (1991). Effects of ethnic group cultural differences on cooperative and competitive behavior on a group task. *Academy of Management Journal*, 34, 827–47.

Desatnick, R. L. and Bennett, M. L. (1978). *Human Resource Management in the Multinational Company*. New York: Nichols Publishing.

Economist (1991). The glamour of Gaijins. September 21, 78.

Elashmawi, F., and Harris, P. R. (1993). *Multicultural Management: New Skills for Global Success.* Houston: Gulf Publishing Co.

Ellis, C., and Sonnenfeld, J. A. (1994). Diverse approaches to managing diversity. *Human Resource Management*, 33, 99–109.

Farnsworth, C. H. (1993). Canada's U.S. trade experience fuels opposition to the new pact. *New York Times*, October 3, 1, 10.

Farnsworth, C. H. (1994). Canada acts to tighten immigration. *New York Times*, November 6, I 23.

Florkowski, G. W., and Nath, R. (1993). MNC responses to the legal environment of *International Journal of Human Resource Management*. *International Journal of Human Resource Management*, 4, 305–24.

Florkowski, G. W., and Schuler, R. S. (1994). Auditing human resources in the global enviroment. *International Journal of Human Resource Management*, 5, 823–47.

Forster, N. (1994). The forgotten employees? The experiences of expatriate staff returning to the UK. *International Journal of Human Resource Management*, 5, 405–25.

Fulkerson, J. R., and Schuler, R. S. (1992). Managing worldwide diversity at Pepsi-Cola International. In S. E. Jackson and Associates (eds), *Diversity in the Workplace: Human Resources Initiatives* (248–76). New York: Guilford Press.

Gardenswartz, L., and Rowe, A. (1993). *Managing Diversity: A Complete Desk Reference and Planning Guide.* Homewood, IL: Business One Irwin.

Ghoshal, S., and Nohria, N. (1993). Horses for courses: organizational forms for multinational corporations. *Sloan Management Review*, Winter, 23–35.

Gomez-Mejia, L. R., and Welbourne, T. (1991). Compensation strategies in a global context. *Human Resource Planning*, 14(1), 29–41.

Greenslade, M. (1991). Managing diversity: Lessons from the United States. *Personnel Management*, 23(12), 28–33.

Hagerty, B. (1991). Companies in Europe seeking executives who can cross borders in a single bound. *Wall Street Journal*, January 25, B1, B3.

Hodgetts, R. M., and Luthans, F. (1993). U.S. multinationals' compensation strategies for local management: Cross-cultural implications. *Compensation and Benefits Review*, 25(2), 42–8.

Hofstede, G. (1993). Cultural constraints in management theories. *Academy of Management Executive*, 7(1), 81–94.

International Labour Office (1981). *Multinationals' training practices and development.* Geneva, Switzerland: International Labour Office.

Ishida, H. (1986). Transferability of Japanese human resource management abroad. *Human Resource Management*, 25, 103–20.

Jackson, B. W., LaFasto, F., Schultz, H. G., and Kelly, D. (1992). Diversity. *Human Resource Management*, 31, 21–34.

Jain, H. C. (1990). Human resource management in selected Japanese firms, their foreign subsidiaries and locally owned counterparts. *International Labour Review*, 129, 73–89.

Johnson, W. B. (1991). Global work force 2000: The new world labor market. *Harvard Business Review*, 69(3), 115–27.

Karr, A. R. (1992). The checkoff. *Wall Street Journal*, November 24, 1.

Kujawa, D. (1986). *Japanese Multinationals in the United States: Case Studies.* New York: Praeger.

Latham, G. A., and Napier, N. K. (1989). Chinese human resource management practices in Hong Kong and Singapore: An exploratory study. In G. R. Ferris and K. M. Rowland (eds), *Research in Personnel and Human Resources Management*, Supplement 1 (173–99). Greenwich, CT: JAI Press.

Laurent, A. (1986). The cross-cultural puzzle of international human resource management. *Human Resource Management*, 25, 91–102.

Levin, D. P. (1993). What BMW sees in South Carolina. *New York Times*, April 11, F5.

Levin, D. P. (1994). The greying factory. *New York Times*, February 20, F3, F6.

Maddox, R. C. (1993). *Cross-cultural Problems in International Business: The Role of the Cultural Integration Function*. Westport, CT: Quorum Books.

Maruyama, M. (1988). The inverse practice principle in multicultural management. *Academy of Management Executive*, 2(1), 67–8.

Maruyama, M. (1990). Some management considerations in the economic reorganization of Eastern Europe. *Academy of Management Executive*, 4(2), 90–1.

Maruyama, M. (1992). Lessons from Japanese management failures in foreign countries. *Human Systems Management*, 11, 41–8.

Mendenhall, M. E., Dunbar, E., and Oddou, G. R. (1987). Expatriate selection, training and career-pathing: A review and critique. *Human Resource Management*, 26, 331–45.

Miller, E. L., Schon, B., Bhatt, B., and Nath, R. (1986). The relationship between the global strategic planning process and the human resource management function. *Human Resource Planning*, 9, 9–23.

Milliman, J. F., and Von Glinow, M. A. (1990). A life cycle approach to strategic international human resource management in MNCs. In B. B. Shaw, J. E. Beck, G. R. Ferris, and K. M. Rowland (eds), *Research in Personnel and Human Resources Management* Supplement 2 (21–35). Greenwich, CT: JAI Press.

Milliman, J. F., Von Glinow, M. A., and Nathan, M. (1991). Organizational life cycles and strategic international human resource management in multinational companies: Implications for congruence theory. *Academy of Management Review*, 16, 318–39.

Napier, N. K., Schweiger, D. M., and Kosglow, J. J. (1993). Managing organizational diversity: Observations from cross-border acquisitions. *Human Resource Management*, 32, 505–23.

Neale, R., and Mindel, R. (1992). Rigging up multicultural teamworking. *Personnel Management*, 24(1), 36–9.

O'Boyle, T. F. (1989). Little benefit to careers seen in foreign stints. *Wall Street Journal*, December 11, B1, B4.

Oddou, G., and Mendenhall, M. (1991). Expatriate performance appraisal: Problems and solutions. In M. Mendenhall and G. Oddou (eds), *Readings and Cases in International Human Resource Management* (364–74). Boston: PWS-Kent.

Odenwald, S. B. (1993). *Global Training: How to Design a Program for the Multinational Corporation*. Alexandria, VA: American Society for Training and Development.

Overman, S. (1992). A measure of success: When it comes to managing diversity, a few companies are linking pay to performance. *HR Magazine*, 37(12), 38–40.

Phillips, N. (1994). *Managing International Teams*. New York: Irwin Professional Publishing.

Porter, M. E. (1990). *Competitive Advantage of Nations*. New York: Free Press.

Randall, D. M. (1993). Cross-cultural research on organizational commitment: A review and application of Hofstede's value survey module. *Journal of Business Research*, 26, 91–110.

Reynolds, C. (1992). Are you ready to make IHR a global function? *HR News: International HR*, February, C1–C3.

Ronen, S. (1986). *Comparative and Multinational Management.* New York: Wiley and Sons.

Ronen, S., and Shenkar, O. (1985). Clustering countries on attitudinal dimensions: A review and synthesis. *Academy of Management Review*, 3, 435–54.

Rubin, B. L. (1991). Europeans value diversity. *HR Magazine*, 36(1), 38–40, 78.

Saner, R., and Yiu, L. (1994). European and Asian resistance to the use of the American case method in management training: Possible cultural and systemic incongruencies. *International Journal of Human Resource Management*, 5, 953–76.

Sasajima, Y. (1993). Changes in labour supply and their impacts on human resource management: The case of Japan. *International Journal of Human Resource Management*, 4, 29–44.

Schneider, S. C. (1988). National vs. corporate culture: Implications for human resource management. *Human Resource Management*, 27, 231–46.

Schuler, R. S. (1989). Strategic human resource management and industrial relations. *Human Relations,* 42, 157–84.

Schuler, R. S., Dowling, P. J., and De Cieri, H. (1993). An integrative framework of strategic IHRM. *International Journal of Human Resource Management*, 4, 717–64.

Schuler, R. S., and Florkowski, G. W. (1995). Research on international human resource management. In B. J. Punnett and O. Shenkar (eds), *Handbook of International Management Research*, 351–401. London: Blackwell Publishers.

Smith, P. B. (1992). Organizational behaviour and national cultures. *British Journal of Management*, 3, 39–51.

Towers Perrin (1992). *Priorities for Competitive Advantage: A Worldwide Human Resource Study.* Chicago: Towers Perrin.

Townsend, A. M., Scott, K. D., and Markham, S. E. (1990). An examination of country and culture-based differences in compensation practices. *Journal of International Business Studies*, 21, 667–78.

Tsui, A., Egan, T., and O'Reilly, C. (1992). Being different: Relational demography and organizational attachment. *Administrative Science Quarterly*, 37, 549–79.

Tung, R. L. (1982). Selection and training procedures of U.S., European, and Japanese multinationals. *California Management Review*, 25, 57–71.

Tung, R. L. (1993). Managing cross-national and intra-national diversity. *Human Resource Management*, 32, 461–77.

Vance, C. M., McClaine, S. R., Boje, D. M., and Stage, D. (1992). An examination of the transferability of traditional performance appraisal principles across cultural boundaries. *Management International Review*, 4, 313–26.

Von Glinow, M. A., and Teagarden, M. B. (1988). The transfer of human resource technology in Sino–U.S. cooperative ventures: Problems and solutions. *Human Resource Management*, 27, 201–29.

Wall Street Journal (1989). Labor Letter, August 28, A1.

Wall Street Journal (1993). Mercedes portrays new Alabama plant as key element in corporate makeover. October 1.

Watson, W. E., Kumar, K., and Michaelsen, L. K. (1993). Cultural diversity's impact on interaction process and performance: Comparing homogeneous and diverse task groups. *Academy of Management Journal*, 36, 590–602.

Williamson, A. D., and Beer, M. (1993). *Becton Dickinson (B): Global management,* Case 9–491–152. Cambridge, MA: Harvard Business School.

Yamakawa, R. (1992). The applicability of Japanese labor and employment laws to Americans working in Japan. *San Diego Law Review*, 29(2), 175–201.

Zeira, Y., and Banai, M. (1981). Attitudes of host-country organizations towards MNC's staffing policies: A cross-country and cross-industry analysis. *Management International Review*, 2, 38–47.

14
Diversity: A Strategic Issue

Parshotam Dass and Barbara Parker

Increasing diversity of people, products, and markets throughout the world are all reasons for business leaders to view diversity as a strategic tool with which to gain a competitive advantage over other businesses (Towers Perrin and Hudson Institute, 1990). The purpose of this chapter is to explore how organizations can use diversity initiatives to achieve strategic advantage – the unique and inimitable set of attributes that distinguishes an organization from all others. Issues that offer strategic advantage rarely are clearly defined, and this is true for diversity. In some cases diversity has been viewed as an issue specific to differences of gender, nationality, color, or culture (Davidson, 1991) and in other cases it has been viewed as a broad set of differences other than race or gender, including age, job status, field of specialization, educational background, (dis)abilities, ethnicity, religion, sexual orientation, national origin, lifestyle preference, and so on (Thomas, 1992). Strategic issues have an important impact on organizational performance (Ansoff, 1980; Mintzberg et al., 1976), and we believe that a key component to strategic advantage from diversity is to value differences. Accordingly, diversity as we use the term here includes more than just the broad differences such as race, nationality, and gender. Using this definition, individual organizations may achieve strategic advantage by targeting those aspects of diversity most important to organizational achievement. Through valuing differences, organizational leaders can develop unique organizational strengths, add value to organizational activities, and achieve an edge over marketplace rivals.

Although many business leaders recognize that diversity has value, survey responses from representatives of more than 300 New York-based firms illustrate that there is a gap between recognition and action because few of these organizations have moved diversity to the center of organizational strategy (Noble, 1994). Additionally, while about half of Fortune 500 firms have diversity managers (Lopez, 1992), a survey of US corporations reported that only 5 percent of personnel managers among them believe the organization is doing a "very good job" of managing their workforce diversity (Rice, 1994). At the same time, there is growing evidence that managing diversity well reduces turnover and improves productivity and profits of organizations. For example, by paying more attention to diversity Corning was able to reduce attrition among African-Americans from 15.3 to 11.3 percent and among females from 16.2 to 7.6 percent in three years (Koretz, 1991). Similarly, a 1993 comparison of Standard and Poor's 500 firms showed that those hiring and advancing women and minorities had outperformed those with poorer equal employment track records. Specifically, the 100 firms with the best equal employment histories had five-year annualized returns of 18.3 percent, while the 100 firms with the worst employment histories for women and minorities had returns of only 7.9 percent (Covenant Investment Management, 1993).

We introduce below a conceptual model of strategic behavior in organizations and a definition of strategy intended to guide the chapter. Next, we discuss various aspects of the model to illustrate how diversity can be a basis for an organization's strategic advantage. The general implications of the model are that managers need to perceive, interpret, and respond to diversity issues in ways consistent with their strategic vision, internal resources, and external opportunities. We analyze the variety of responses organizational leaders have developed in response to challenges of diversity, finding that they are likely to lead to varying levels of strategic advantage. The implications of current organizational responses to diversity are also explored.

A Model of Strategic Behavior in Organizations

Strategic management traces its roots to many academic disciplines, and this is partly why there are many different models for strategic behavior in organizations. Most of these models suggest external environment exerts considerable influence, creating opportunities and threats for any organization. At the same time, both strengths and weaknesses throughout the organization manifest themselves while opportunities are seized and threats are avoided. The model of strategic behavior appearing in figure 13.1 reflects this view of strategy by linking research on organizational external environment, including the macro environment and industry environment, to strategic responses regarding product-market diversity, resource allocations, and performance within organizations (e.g. Ginsberg, 1989; 1990; Marchington, 1990; Porter, 1980; 1985).

Figure 14.1 is intended to represent open systems where boundaries between organizations and their macro environments are fairly permeable; this is shown by the dotted-line relationships. Additionally, the figure is

Figure 14.1   A model of strategic management of diversity in organizations

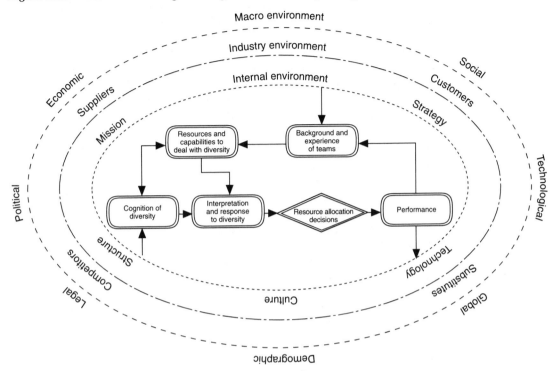

intended to show that macro environments, industry environments, and organizations are in a constant state of mutual interaction. As a consequence of this interaction, organizational leaders must focus their attention simultaneously on both internal and external concerns to add value and to achieve a long-term strategic advantage for the firm. Thus, strategic management is necessarily an ongoing and flexible process that involves specifying parameters within which organizational leaders define organizational mission, set goals and priorities at various levels, and develop and implement means to achieve them.

An organization's ability to respond to external shifts initially depends on managerial cognition – the way the external events are perceived. As shown within the internal environment represented in figure 14.1, there first must be a cognition of diversity. For example, a manager who perceives diversity as an opportunity is likely to employ resources to collect more information, before moving ahead. Additional information may lead the manager to interpret diversity as a strategic opportunity attainable through resource allocations, and affected resources could include structure, culture, and technology of the organization. Once made, these allocations are expected to improve organizational performance. Performance feeds back to signal success to internal and external constituencies and in turn generates new cognition for managers.

As drawn, the model shown in figure 14.1 assumes that a critical function for general managers is to manage both short-term and long-term goals, and address the multiple and sometimes conflicting interests of various stakeholders for organizational efficiency and effectiveness. As an example, executives might be expected to satisfy the demands of the following in the long-term interest of the organization: shareholders for return on investment, customers for maximum value, employees for fair wages and high health and safety standards, and the community for pollution control. It is usually difficult to balance among competing interests such as those represented in the example, but simultaneous focus on both internal and external sources of diversity could prove more difficult than with other strategic issues. Constituents rarely agree as to how diversity should be defined, nor is there agreement on whether resources should be employed to value diversity. Finally, few are certain that diversity provides a strategic advantage. However, we believe a balanced or dualistic view of external and internal organizational forces for diversity better prepares managers to continuously achieve "fit" or congruence of internal resources and external demands regarding diversity. The objective is to align internal structures and processes for capitalizing on the external opportunities and avoid threats that diversity creates. Combining efficiency and effectiveness to achieve strategic advantage from diversity could mean disrupting short-term efficiency in order to achieve long-term results.

Control Data's CEO asserts that diversity "brings a certain degree of chaos to an organization," but without this chaos "you risk having an environment where everybody thinks alike, acts alike, and comes to the same conclusions" (Conference Board, 1992a, p. 15). The kind of dual emphasis we describe means recognizing disagreements over goals and means to stimulate innovation and implement change capable of achieving long-term survival and success. We will describe the model in detail below to illustrate how macro environment, industry environment, and internal structures and processes in organizations can lead to strategic advantages in organizations.

Diversity as a Basis for Strategic Advantage

Organizations that seek a strategic advantage from diversity will not wait until the road is known. Instead, they will be the ones to take risks by creating mechanisms and developing a workforce sufficiently diverse to provide an advantage in a global economy. However, it is important to recognize that being diverse in terms of organizational demographics or markets served is a necessary but not a sufficient condition for making diversity a strategic advantage. This advantage comes not from the diversity itself but rather from forging a link between the external environments fostering diversity and internal organizational systems that are capable of capitalizing on it. In this context, diversity strategy involves not only a clear statement of strategic intent, but also incorporating diversity management in all functional areas and activities throughout the organization. Some argue that "unless an organization develops a culture that understands, respects and values differences, diversity is likely to result in decreased organizational effectiveness" (Conference Board, 1992b, p. 10). Decreased effectiveness may result from depressed morale throughout the organization if leaders issue statements generally understood to be public relations statements without substance. Organizational decline can also occur if leaders issue statements or introduce initiatives for which there are no implementing mechanisms. In a practical sense, leaders must be willing to articulate a vision of diversity and then acquire resources and develop mechanisms that make it possible for employees to take appropriate actions to enhance the power of diversity and differences at all levels.

Since environments are experiencing turbulence, organizational leaders prepare their organizations for rapid and unexpected changes, doing so by looking simultaneously at internal aspects of organizations and at two broad categories of environments: the macro environment and the industry environment. The macro environment is usually conceptualized as those factors external to the organization and the industry that nevertheless affect its opportunities and choices; examples include demographic, economic, social, cultural, political, legal, technological, natural, and global environments. The following exploration of several aspects of macro environment is by no means exhaustive, but is intended to demonstrate how diversity within it affects an organization.

Macro environment

Changes in the macro environment are pushing the issues of diversity into prominence and organizations are responding by altering their strategic objectives; product–market, networking, and competitive strategies; and structures and processes (Jackson and Alvarez, 1992). In this section, we discuss how diverse demands of new employees, new markets, and shorter product life cycles are leading organizations to consider diversity as a strategic weapon.

Diverse demands of new employees   Changes in the economic, social, demographic, legal, political, and global environments have brought more women, minorities, and immigrants into organizations, especially in Europe and the US (Jamieson and O'Mara, 1991). There is little that any organization can do to alter these trends. Despite traditional barriers against women and minorities in many workplaces, these new groups are finding jobs in the paid workforce and are advancing to managerial positions. For example, not only has the percentage of women in paid jobs increased worldwide, but the percentage of female managers also has increased in 39 of 41 countries studied between 1985 and 1991 (International Labour Organization, 1993). In order to contribute in new ways to the workplace, these new workers also are making increasing demands of the workplace. For example, often it is new workers who call for employment equity in job access, pay, and promotions, and often it is they who are aware of and call for diversity programs. Clearly, as women and members of minority groups become more educated and more aware of discriminatory practices through increasing access to information, the best and brightest among them may leave retrogressive organizations. For example, one-third of small business owners in the US, Germany, Canada, and France are women, and they are starting new businesses at $1\frac{1}{2}$ times the pace of men (Conference Board, 1991). This suggests that organizations that are unable to manage diversity may find themselves competing with rivals founded by former employees. For example, after conducting exit interviews with women leaving Monsanto, the chemical giant found that many of the women were leaving to start their own businesses because of perceived glass ceiling barriers to advancement with Monsanto (Fisher, 1992).

There is much an organization can do to derive strategic advantage from the above-mentioned changes. Organizations introducing diversity initiatives voluntarily are likely to be more attractive to unconventional entrants than other organizations where legal and moral mandates force a hasty response to diversity. For example, Lotus Development managers acknowledge that many serious technical people come to them because of Lotus's reputation for diversity (Stewart, 1991). Managers anticipating changes in demographics or markets may better prepare the organization for diversity initiatives by increasing awareness of and sensitivity to the varied needs new participants bring to the organization. Whereas organizations once expected employees to become part of a homogeneous entity, leaders increasingly recognize that employee diversity is a means of access to groups that have not yielded to the "melting pot." Companies like PepsiCo, Kmart, and J. C. Penney recruit minority marketing experts for help in selling to the African-Americans, Latinos, and Asians who spent $600 billion on consumer goods in 1993 (McCarroll, 1993). Additionally, increasing pride in background and ethnicity has made many unwilling to be treated as second-class citizens in organizational or national life, and they are using economic as well as legal means to retain ethnic or cultural identities. Failure to attend to a growing sense of individual identity may be costly to organizations, as Revlon discovered when its "Unforgettable" campaign used Nat King Cole's voice as background for a bevy of "unforgettable" women, all of whom were white (Bird, 1993). Conversely, organizational responsiveness to diverse groups is not only expected to attract buyers, but also to attract the types of employees the organization wants. For example, progressive organizations in the health care field have developed improved systems to retain women. Similarly, leading software companies are changing themselves to develop structures and processes to attract and retain talented programmers all over the world. For example, Microsoft's policy to offer health and other benefits to same-sex partners has led to a very positive response from on-board gay and lesbian employees (Andrews, 1993), and is likely to help Microsoft attract additional employees who view the firm as "accepting" of differences.

Diverse demands of new markets Developments in telecommunications, expectations of economic development, and emergence of free-trading blocks throughout the world have given rise to a global economy. There are more countries participating in the world economy now than ever before, and many of them are competing more aggressively than previously. These activities increase the amount of diversity to be addressed within and between domestic economies. Organizational leaders find not only more opportunity but more diversity of wants and needs among new buyers as consumers become more discriminating and more demanding of products and services. It is logical to assume that people who represent these forms of diversity can help organizations achieve a match between internal resources and external demands. Entering these markets requires firms to produce more sophisticated analyses of consumer wants and needs, and has led to a growing realization that diversity occurs on many more fronts than demographics alone. For example, capitalism has developed in different ways throughout the world (Hampden-Turner and Trompenaars, 1993), leading to differences in how markets operate. Put another way, while there are more market economies than ever before, each has developed in different ways such that firms must be flexible and responsive to each market. Until relatively recently, for example, cost accounting was not used in mainland China, and this required firms established there to devote considerable attention not only to introducing it as a practice but also to explain the assumptions behind cost accounting practices. Similarly, marketers in the former Soviet Union find that hard-sell techniques provoke a negative reaction from people all too weary of being told what to do. These examples illustrate that finding a strategic advantage in new markets opened by the global economy may include rethinking traditional modes of operation.

Shorter product life and developmental cycles An examination of product research and development worldwide suggests that products move much more quickly through their global life cycle than once was the case, requiring organizations to monitor and respond to innovation rapidly. For example, organizations such as Intel, Honda, and Proctor & Gamble are reducing developmental cycles of their products (Hof, 1992). Such technological developments increase the need for a diverse workforce capable of adapting to rapid and continual change. For example, the companies listed above are using multifunctional teams involving research and development personnel, engineers, accountants, marketers, and customers, simultaneously in the form of concurrent engineering rather than in a sequential manner. At the same time that teamwork such as this offers advantages, these teams also pose new problems of coordination, motivation, evaluation, and reward systems. Managers need to develop structures and processes to deal with quick response strategies and the stressors that come with them.

Many changes in the macro environment other than those described above are causing organizations to respond to diversity. For example, the demographics of almost all workforces are highly diverse and are expected to become more so in the years ahead. In addition, the rapid pace of change in macro environments requires full use of the intellectual potential of all organizational participants. Finally, macro environments increasingly are characterized by volatility and complexity.

Demographic change, increased need for knowledge work on the part of all employees, and a complex and volatile environment all create both opportunities and managerial challenges. In the latter category, uncertainties associated with the macro environment are likely to produce stressors, and may cause employees to look to the organization for protection and support against stress as well as for programs to mitigate its effects. Managers may become responsible not only for services and programs previously handled outside the work sphere, but also may be expected to draft policies to cover contingencies never before anticipated in the workplace. Similarly, while demographically diverse workforces may help organizations respond to many more opportunities, these employees also make new demands of organizations. Day care facilities for children and aging parents, cross-cultural training, and sensitivity awareness are only a few of these demands, and to date most organizations have limited experience in meeting them. Finally, resistance to hierarchical changes are likely to accompany efforts to elicit knowledge from all workers, and challenges to managerial authority may not be welcome. In other words, managing diversity well requires organizational changes that may be neither welcome nor easy to make.

Industry environment

A second aspect of external organizational environment is the industry environment. While most agree that industry-specific factors affect firms, there are many ways in which these effects have been explored. For example, studies that trace their roots to industrial organization economics emphasize the role industry structure (i.e. the number of companies and type of competition in an industry) plays in influencing firm conduct and performance (Scherer and Ross, 1990). Industrial economists study industry structure in terms of five competitive forces described by Porter (1980; 1985) including: (1) threat of new entrants into the industry, (2) availability of substitute products (e.g. eye glasses and contact lenses are substitute products), (3) bargaining power of buyers, (4) bargaining power of suppliers, and (5) rivalry among established competitors. Inasmuch as many industries have globalized, the buyers, suppliers, competitors, and substitutes of many industries are becoming increasingly diverse, drawing not only from domestic sources but from sources that can be located anywhere in the world. Therefore, companies are necessarily adopting diversity initiatives to cope with the changes made in their industry or related industries. As an example, the Boeing Company is in the process of developing a limited vocabulary form of English to be used worldwide when repairing Boeing aircraft, and they are achieving this and similar activities by forging tighter links with their suppliers as well as with their buyers.

Another perspective on industry environment comes from what has been called a resource-dependence model because its authors argue that an organization is dependent on its environment for its customers and resources (Pfeffer and Salancik, 1978). These resources may include capital, labor, technology, and raw materials, among others. As applied to the concept of diversity, corporations could be said to look for investors, executives, and markets from other countries in spite of the difficulties that arise from differences in language, culture, and national origins. Progressive companies such as AT&T, GTE, US West, Motorola and other transnational firms are continually looking for diversity management techniques capable of attracting and making optimal use of the best available resources in their industries. For example, Motorola's extensive and successful use of training, quality teams, and motivational rewards in Malaysian operations led them to introduce the same practices in their Florida plant. One result has been to attract and retain productive employees who recognize they are all members of the Motorola team (Engardio, 1994). Companies achieving competitive advantage through diversity initiatives also act as leaders for other companies that imitate their practices (Powell and DiMaggio, 1991). Organizations unable to match the diversity demanded from their environments are likely to lose resources to their rivals. They may fail to find a niche for themselves and accordingly be phased out much like Beta technology was edged out by VHS formats in the video-recording and playing industry.

Internal strategic choices

Macro and industry environments usually are outside organizational control, but they may be moderated by strategic choices entered into by members of the organization's dominant coalition (Child, 1972). In this context, dominant coalitions typically are defined as that group of executives who make the most of the important, non-routine strategic choices guiding the organization. These executives create some leeway for responding to external forces by generating alternative courses of action, and by trying to shape their environments via political action, e.g. lobbying activities. The responses any organization makes to its environment may depend on a wide variety of objective and subjective factors inside and outside of the organization, as depicted in figure 14.1.

Cognition of diversity Organizational actors develop their cognitions based on the subjective and objective characteristics of the macro environment, industry environment, and organizational characteristics. The collective habits of thinking among the top management teams represent the beliefs, theories, and propositions that have developed over time. These knowledge systems give rise to shared meanings in organizations called "dominant (general management) logics," creating a shared understanding within the group and eventually across the organization as to the types of thought and action that are desirable and acceptable (Prahalad and Bettis, 1986). These systems work as templates for strategic decision-making in organizations and influence organizational outcomes (Ginsberg, 1989; 1990; Glick et al., 1993). Organizational participants generally can predict the choices leaders will make once they become accustomed to the templates used in an organization.

Background and experience of teams The resources and capabilities of a team to deal with diversity are limited by the variety of their dominant logics. These logics in turn depend primarily on the composition of the management team, their experiences, and their attitude toward learning. When those teams are fairly homogeneous, their interpretations of the external environment also tend to be homogeneous. For example, whereas hindsight shows that the Organization of Petroleum Exporting Countries (OPEC) had signaled an intention to control oil supplies in the early 1970s and there was evidence that Japanese auto makers were gearing up to produce fuel-efficient cars, the cognitive mindsets for US auto makers included two misconceptions: Americans would not give up big cars, and Japanese cars could not penetrate the US market. The results tell us otherwise, and events subsequently showed that it took Detroit auto makers almost 20 years to catch up on the inroads the Japanese had made.

Top managers tend to choose new executives and board directors who are demographically similar to themselves (Westphal, 1994). For example, according to a 1994 report by Catalyst, only 4.5 percent of Fortune 500 companies have three or more women directors, and over 48 percent do not have even one female director. Applying the concept of dominant logic to diversity initiatives suggests that teams should be structured to include individuals with significantly different experience bases from the dominant coalition; this not only expands dominant logics but also serves to legitimize diversity and dissent in organizations (Prahalad and Bettis, 1986). Interestingly, organizations may have to adopt apparently conflicting practices in response to conflicting demands coming from their environments (D'Aunno et al., 1991; Oliver, 1991).

Resources and capabilities to deal with diversity Managing diversity can give rise to added value and enhanced distinctive competencies for each of the activities of the organization, according to the resource-based view of the firm. As Barney (1991) argues, the use of organizational resources can be a source of competitive parity, temporary strategic advantage, and/or sustained strategic advantage. Organizations can get sustained strategic advantages if their resources are valuable, rare, inimitable, and non-substitutable (Barney, 1992). Managing a socially complex intraorganizational phenomenon such as diversity within an organization can be such a resource. One can evaluate the characteristics of an organization's diversity resources and capabilities within its competitive context to understand their contributions to the success of the organization. Diversity resources are likely to be vitally important and valuable for an organization in enhancing its performance, as discussed below.

Interpretation and response to diversity By their nature, strategic issues are subject to different perceptions leading to multiple interpretations (Schneider and De Meyer, 1991) that then influence managements' response to these issues. For example, challenges of diversity such as demographic change inside the workplace or in an organization's buyer group could variously be interpreted as crisis, threat, or opportunity. The crisis interpretation of diversity may come from viewing it as presenting a possibility of loss under urgency and pressures of time to deal with it (Billings et al., 1980). The threat interpretation is likely to come from perceptions of diversity as negative, causing potential losses, and as an uncontrollable factor (Dutton and Jackson, 1987). Similarly, an opportunity interpretation of diversity may come from viewing it as positive, as leading to potential gains, and as a factor offering some potential for organizational control. Miles and Snow provided a typology of organizational strategies that describes "prospectors" as organizations that actively seek out opportunities, whereas "reactors" tend to wait for events to occur and then react to them. Prospectors are more likely to interpret events as opportunities (Meyer, 1982); whereas reactors may label the same events as threats or crises. In the context of diversity strategy, prospector organizations are likely to be those whose leaders immediately associate opportunities with diversity, while leaders in reactor organizations are more likely to view diversity as a threat. These opposite responses to the fact of diversity are likely to result in different resource allocation decisions that in turn determine performance outcomes for an organization.

Performance Differentiation and low-cost competitive business strategies have garnered a great deal of research attention since they were first introduced (Porter, 1980). While cost strategy relies upon economies of scale or scope that make it possible to offer the lowest price in the market, a differentiation strategy succeeds by offering a real or perceived product or service advantage that competitors cannot match. Differentiation may be achieved by high innovation, quality, and/or customization, and so employee resources and behaviors are essential for a differentiation strategy (Porter, 1980; Schuler and Jackson, 1987). Since creativity and expertise are unlikely to be the exclusive property of dominant groups, organizations practicing traditional management methods emphasizing homogeneity of thought and practice are likely to lose the cutting edge of innovation, quality, or service (Cox and Blake, 1991). In addition to enhancing the potential to achieve competitive advantage through differentiation, a low-cost strategy also can be achieved when diversity is valued. For example, managing diversity well is likely to decrease costly frictions and dysfunctional turnover, with all individuals more likely to contribute their full potential, which in turn leads to higher productivity and efficiency in organizations than when workers reserve their potential for other pursuits. In sum, managing diversity can help organizations gain a competitive edge whether they are pursuing low-cost or differentiation strategies. In the same vein, an organization following a combination of differentiation *and* low cost (Hill, 1988) can fully benefit from the diverse talents of its workforce by developing a level playing field for every one to ensure fair rewards for one's contributions. For example, by integrating many different programs that deal with child care, minority affairs, dual-career couples, sexual harassment, and related issues, the organization can simultaneously improve the effectiveness of these programs and reduce the costs (DeLuca and McDowell, 1992).

Whatever strategy organizations pursue, empirical research shows that higher levels of diversity within them result in more innovation, change and performance (Bantel and Jackson, 1989; Pearce and Zahra, 1992; Wiersema and Bantel, 1992), and other benefits for them (Kosnik, 1990). Heterogeneity in the top management team also makes it possible to obtain critical resources such as an ability to recruit key executives and board members from outside the organization (Pfeffer and Salancik, 1978). An ability to attract people from diverse backgrounds affects organizational performance because diverse groups are likely to outperform homogenous groups over time (Watson et al., 1993). Additionally, women, bilinguals, and other people from underrepresented groups are the likely sources for increasing diversity of dominant logics in organizations to reduce "groupthink" and allow greater organizational flexibility (Cox, 1993).

Diversity of composition at top organizational levels is likely to lead to higher levels of cognitive complexity and tolerance for ambiguity, which may enhance an organization's capabilities to cultivate flexibility and adaptability (Cox and Blake, 1991; Lambert, 1977; Rotter and O'Connell, 1982). However, including "non-like" members in the dominant coalition is likely to pose a perceived threat to the existing power structure and may be resisted. Thus, it is important that top management change constitutes more than tokenism. When there are diverse role models at the top of organizations, this means of managing diversity is not only likely to make organizations more responsive to their environments, but also provides a way to attract and retain additional employees from a broad range of backgrounds, experiences, and mental models. The end result is a broad base for building expertise in organizations that face a diverse market. For example, 20 years ago there were almost no clothes for US women who were not 5'7" and height/weight proportionate, despite ample evidence that most women did not fit this profile. Firms like Liz Claiborne and Donna Karan that were led by women succeeded because they were able to see additional market niches including petites, plus sizes, and others. This same principle can be applied by other organizations willing to recognize that people who are diverse are perhaps better able to assess the potential for new products and new markets than are people who are homogeneous.

In the context of understanding and managing diversity, what this is likely to mean is that those groups that are diverse are likely to see its signs or to understand what these signs mean in a practical sense. Thus, one reason to hire women, minorities, and internationals in organizations is because their background and experience cause them to acquire and rate information in different ways than would members of a management team populated by people of the same age, from the same demographic group, who share similar experiences and beliefs with one another.

In his review of research on diversity and performance, Cox (1993) concluded that there are direct and indirect positive effects of diversity on individual affective and achievement outcomes, and organizational outcomes. On the one hand, diversity is likely to enhance the problem-solving capabilities of an organization; improve the recruitment, utilization, and retention of human resources; and to serve and network with diverse populations of customers – individuals and organizations. On the other hand, ignoring the increasing need for managing diversity or the existence of diversity in organizations and their environments can have a negative impact on organizational effectiveness. Group cohesiveness may decrease and communication problems may increase, particularly with white males (Tsui et al., 1992). There may be political backlash, conflict, and chaos from the increased diversity. It may not only happen at the employee level, but also at the board level, and can lead to divergent definitions of goals and conflict (Mintzberg, 1983). The kind of conflict associated with diversity may even make organizations less likely to initiate strategic changes during critical periods of turbulence (Goodstein et al., 1994).

Approaches to the Strategic Management of Diversity

There are clearly many and varied organizational responses to increasing diversity worldwide, but we believe these responses can be organized along two dimensions: the extent to which diversity is integrated with other organizational functions, and orientation to strategic responses to diversity. The three levels of structural integration include an episodic, a programmatic, and a process approach, while orientations to strategic responses include a reactive, an accommodative, and a proactive stance.

Level of structural integration of diversity initiatives

DeLuca and McDowell (1992) suggest that diversity initiatives can be viewed as programmatic and non-programmatic, where a programmatic approach would involve developing separate but ongoing programs for each diversity concern, while a non-programmatic approach would involve creating an integrated process for dealing with diversity. This model was adapted for use here by adding a third form of structural integration called the "episodic" approach.

The episodic approach to diversity initiatives permits limited access to existing organizational structures and systems. As the name indicates, it represents an isolated, ad hoc approach for managing diversity. It can also be described as temporary or disjointed because it does not involve a link to ongoing organizational activities. For example, upon noting that a critical incident such as sexual harassment has occurred, the manager reviews the incident, takes appropriate action, and moves on. The same process is repeated when another incident arises. Managers who pursue an episodic approach to diversity maintain an arm's length distance between diversity and other organizational structures and functions, and in doing so they may not recognize, understand, or connect common threads among various incidents spanning a period of space or time. As a result, the same types of critical incidents may be resolved repeatedly without a concurrent substantive change in organizational policies and practices.

The programmatic approach to diversity involves setting up a relatively stable and ongoing program capable of addressing diversity issues. Using this approach, an organization might be expected to designate individuals to head up diversity initiatives that could range from work–family needs, immigrants' concerns, veterans' issues, minority affairs, and (dis)ability matters. Using this modular approach, an organization could easily add or subtract programs as circumstances dictated. Most organizations find it possible to add and delete programs on a regular basis. However, the existence of a plethora of programs can make their implementation quite complex and cumbersome.

The process approach represents a non-programmatic alternative that incorporates simplicity and flexibility. The example of a modern-day paint store may illustrate this approach, as suggested by DeLuca and McDowell (1992). Instead of storing gallons of hundreds of colors, the store can come up with all of these by blending varying amounts of three basic colors. Such an approach of flexible simplicity is being used by Coopers & Lybrand with a "grass-roots" strategy (DeLuca and McDowell, 1992). This method embodies the highest level of structural integration for diversity initatives. It is the process approach where rather than setting up separate programs for diversity, work–family issues, veterans' affairs, quality, learning, teams, and globalization, the organization combines them and gives responsibility to the line managers for integrating them in their own jobs.

Management's strategic response   Orientations to strategic responses found in table 14.1 represent thinking developed in the literature on strategic responses to institutional pressures (Oliver, 1991) and corporate strategic posture toward social responsiveness (Carroll, 1979; Clarkson, 1988; 1995). Oliver (1991) proposed a generic typology of the strategies organizations use for responding to institutional pressures. This typology suggested that organizations may adopt acquiescence, compromise, avoidance, defiance, or manipulation responses, depending on the level of strategic resistance in the organization. Other scholars (e.g. Carroll, 1979; Clarkson, 1988; 1995; Wartick and Cochran, 1985) categorized organizational responses in terms of reactive, defensive, accommodative, and proactive. Drawing from these two typologies, we believe organizational responses to diversity can be categorized into three broad divisions for the sake of balancing coverage and parsimony: reactive, accommodative, and proactive. Both reactive and proactive categories are commonly employed in the strategy literature and

Table 14.1   Approaches to strategic management of diversity in organizations

Strategic response (strategies) \ Level of structural integration	Episodic	Program (programmatic)	Process (non-programmatic)
Reactive (avoid, defy, manipulate)	Denial (a case of denying a woman the job of supervising men)[a]	Resistance (legal fund program)	Assimilation (come and fit in)
Accommodative (acquiesce, compromise)	Ad hoc committees (for judicial review of cases)	Affirmative action (for women and minorities)	Appraisal system (includes diversity goals for managers at different levels)
Proactive (anticipate)	Diversity workshops (for potential rewards)	Valuing differences (interpersonal relationships based on respect and trust)	Multiculturalism (structural and cultural transformation)

[a] An example of each approach is given in parentheses.

we used them earlier to describe leaders that perceive diversity as a strategic threat and take a reactive stance as opposed to those proactive leaders who view diversity as an opportunity to seize. The middle category represents various shades of compromises organizations make in accommodating the diversity pressures.

A typology

By combining dimensions of orientation to diversity strategy and level of structural integration, we get a 3 x 3 matrix as presented in table 14.1. The resulting nine cells provide means for categorizing diversity activities, and also can be used to show that diversity initiatives alone are insufficient to create a strategic advantage from diversity. Additionally, this matrix shows why some approaches to diversity can prove more harmful than helpful to organizations. In the following section, activities associated with each cell will be discussed.

Reactive strategic response   Competition for scarce resources in a world governed by rational rules has led many managers to view the world as a zero-sum game field where every gain is another's loss. Accordingly, many apply this perspective to the agenda for diversity, viewing diversity as an additional organizational cost drain in an already limited pool of resources. Arguments that affirmative action programs constitute reverse discrimination are included in this category because of their focus on individual losses rather than organizational gains. This approach is a legacy of a past when almost all US promotions went to white males, and as Fernandez (1991) indicates, white men as a group are no happier than any other group would be when asked to give up or share something conditioning had led them to believe was rightfully theirs. Charges of tokenism also are likely to lead organizations to choose a strategy of defiance by ignoring, challenging, or attacking institutional rules and values (Oliver, 1991). Alternatively, they may take a less active strategy of avoidance with tactics of concealing nonconformity, buffering from outside pressures, or escaping from outside expectations and norms. Still another alternative that organizations may follow is manipulation involving co-optation, influencing values, and controlling external environments by dominating institutional constituents and processes (Oliver, 1991). These responses may be found in organizations such as the monolithic type described by Cox (1993) where there is ubiquitous institutional cultural bias in human resources and other systems. These organizations also may be characterized by a substantial majority of white males in high-level positions with low-status jobs reserved for women and minorities. Power may be centralized and managers may be likely to follow traditional methods that value homogeneity but do not value diversity.

From the perspective of many managers, such methods are considered the time-tested ways of doing business. The management methods of an organization are the imprints of the era of its birth. Due to the predominance of the inertial forces on old and large organizations, they have difficulties unlearning their old habits. The same may be true of at least some individuals in the organizations: they tend to continue with their conventional wisdom. Due to the hardened "lenses" of experience and skewed environmental scanning processes, such organizations may not be able to register the changes in their environments (Miller, 1993; Starbuck, 1985; Weick, 1979), and this homogeneity may mean lower conflict within the organization. However, organizational policies and practices associated with apathy and reaction may lead to higher conflict with outside constituencies. This is likely to be reflected in lower innovation, productivity, and legitimacy that is likely to result in organizational death (Hannan and Freeman, 1984), unless organizational leaders recognize the cause of the problem and change accordingly. In such a case, a reactive response pattern may be indicative of an organization going through its first stage of multicultural development (Bowens et al., 1993).

(1) A reactive orientation to strategy combined with *episodic structural integration* of strategy can produce denial of an event of discrimination. An organization following such an approach is likely to treat events as isolated and rare, reaffirming its faith in its traditional practices, and taking steps on a case-by-case method to maintain the status quo. For example, managers may deny a woman a supervisory job that involves control of largely male subordinates in a construction company. Faced with the prospect of a protracted and expensive legal battle, Albertson's supermarkets agreed to pay $29.5 million to settle a suit filed by female and Latino workers who had

filed discrimination claims (*Seattle Times*, 1993). According to news services, Albertson's denied any wrongdoing and claimed to settle out of court to avoid a potentially larger penalty and higher legal bills. This type of approach may be indicative of an organization that avoids dealing with issues by denying them. Another method of denial is to attribute the behavior to another source such as the buyer or supplier. Adler (1987) provided evidence of this approach in her interviews with female expatriates in Asia, many of whom said the biggest impediment to winning an overseas assignment was North American males who believed the Japanese would not accept a female expatriate. Similarly, Gentile (1994) describes the case of a small company in which an African-American faced additional barriers for assignment to an international office in Europe, presumably on the basis of home-office fears that he would not be well received in Europe. The ill-fated "don't ask, don't tell" initiative for the Armed Forces also reflects an attempt to create a process of avoidance for a public organization.

(2)   Organizations also may practice a reactive approach to diversity (*programmatic integration*) in the form of specific programs meant to resist equal employment opportunity (EEO), e.g. an organization may rely on a legal defense fund – a separate but ongoing program – rather than follow affirmative action programs. Additionally, resistance can take individual forms that appear to be organizational. For example, CEO Robert E. Flynn of NutraSweet reported that white men had picked other white males for key positions without posting the jobs for females, minorities or others (Galen, 1994). While this form of resistance was not an organizational initiative, the fact that it involved promotions to key positions may have led some to believe the organizational entity resisted affirmative action. Efforts to undermine affirmative action and EEO following the November, 1994, US elections reflect programmatic political efforts to avoid such programs. Reviews of affirmative action programs at the national Congressional level are ongoing, while California voters face an anti-affirmative "Civil Rights Initiative" vote in 1996 elections. Resistance tactics also include selective presentation of data suggesting that affirmative action programs do not work, and editorial assertions of inequities due to reverse discrimination. These and other forms of resistance are intended to swell the tide against diversity as well as against equal protection laws at least by some groups involved in the matter.

(3)   A process approach to reactivity (*process integration*) emphasizes conformity and predictability, with individuals expected to assimilate to an already-established culture. The organization may purport to be "colorblind" and treat everybody the same as long as they fit in with existing norms and behaviors. This approach denies real differences as it attempts to eliminate them by standardizing the traditional norms for everyone. The assimilative approach may make it impossible for nontraditional workers to contribute their best, or may force them to leave the organization once differences are apparent. The latter is particularly likely to happen in the traditional

professions like law and accounting where women and men alike are expected to produce countless billable hours for promotion. While this approach appears to be equal and fair, the eventual costs may be less for men than they are for women if parenthood is postponed until it is no longer an option.

Accommodative strategic response   A majority of US organizations are now engaged in strategic responses to diversity that involve an accommodative orientation. As described earlier, environments are changing rapidly and organizations must respond quickly to these changes in order to cope with the challenges that confront them. These challenges can emerge from almost anywhere, including social, community, union, or other pressures to respond to real or potential discriminatory activities on the part of the organization. A pluralistic organization that perceives these forces as inevitable threats may find it in its own interest to tolerate diversity and respond in a favorable manner, with responses including an acquiescence strategy by way of imitation, compliance, or habit (Oliver, 1991). Alternatively, it may follow a compromise position that uses balancing, pacifying, or bargaining with external constituents, particularly under the conditions of conflicting demands (Oliver, 1991). Such organizations are likely to reflect a higher level of heterogeneity and inclusion than those subscribing to a reactive approach towards diversity, but there are varying levels of structural integration with the accommodative orientation just as there are with the reactive strategy.

(1)   An organization may conceptualize events related to diversity as isolated ones, and therefore, may respond in an isolated, disjointed fashion characterized by an *episodic* orientation to diversity. For example, instances of discrimination may take the form of judicial review when critical incidents are investigated and judgements passed. An example of this reaction is found in the Tailhook incident where a Navy Tribunal found fault with high-ranking officers. Consequently, officers were demoted, others were retired early, and the hazing behavior was subsequently banned. However, there is little evidence to suggest that the type of hazing that occurred has been phased out of other activities of the Navy or other branches of the US armed services. Thus, resolutions reached appear to bow to public opinion, but represent little or no permanent change. Decisions made in favor of diversity management by use of ad hoc committees without establishing an ongoing, stable program tend to sustain the episodic approach to diversity strategy. A more frequent occurrence of such events coupled with a better awareness of reasons to value diversity may give birth to a more permanent initiative in the form of a program.

(2)   In response to changes in institutional environments, e.g. US civil rights laws, many organizations adopted affirmative action programs to comply with the letter of the law. Interestingly, affirmative action and similar compensatory initiatives were introduced as programs because the

nation believed changing the color and gender mix of organizational participants would resolve identified problems. Thus, the government's *programmatic* initiatives encouraged organizations to introduce programs rather than ongoing processes. At the time, few recognized the problems of using a programmatic approach to solve an unprogrammatic problem. At the same time the federal mandate was for affirmative action programs, affirmative action officers were chosen, and in many organizations a cycle of acquiescence was initiated where the government dictated and the organization complied.

In many cases, diversity initiatives were captured by the programmatic stage of an accommodative response because every diversity initiative was seen as an extension of affirmative action that was rightfully allocated to the affirmative action office and program. However, this programmatic stance on diversity tends to isolate and marginalize activities associated with diversity. Moreover, this approach creates a "divide and conquer" mentality within the organization when those best served by affirmative action are encouraged to believe that diversity represents a judgement of affirmative action as a "backward-looking, strident, social-worker style" (Lynch, 1992, p. A16). While these programs have seen some successes, they have experienced backlash as well.

(3) Some organizations go further to make structural changes by integrating their accommodative stance to diversity with existing organizational processes (*process integration*). Organizations may find it helpful to develop an integrated and consistent response to the changes in various aspects of their environments. For example, coordinating the affirmative action and other programs with organizational processes is not only compliance with the letter of civil rights laws but also may be more in line with the philosophy and spirit of the laws. The use of fair work, appraisal and compensation systems to ensure equal opportunity in HR and other decisions reflects this approach. For example, Harris Bank and John Hancock Financial Services both are organizations that are using standard forms for employees who want flexible work hours (Shellenbarger, 1995). The forms encourage a systematic approach to flexible scheduling, but also ask employees to describe how their work should be evaluated. Thus, this approach not only complies with the kind of counting required for affirmative action reports, but also takes note of the fact that flexible work schedules require changes in evaluation systems.

Proactive strategic response   A small proportion of organizations approach diversity with a proactive orientation toward diversity strategy. On balance, they tend to view diversity as an opportunity. A pluralistic organization that not only has diversity, but values it, is more likely to follow this orientation, and may be an early adopter following an innovation strategy. Some organizations may be proactive in evolving a compromise among multiple and conflicting constituencies and their needs. Others may follow a total quality philosophy for continuous improvement and innovation with respect to diversity management. An innovation strategy may involve tactics of visioning, nurturing, and adoption of new programs and processes. Similar to the earlier orientations, a proactive orientation may also be at the three levels of structural integration.

(1)   An organization's approach to diversity may emerge as an opportunity in an episodic manner (*episodic structural integration*). It may be a result of the environmental scanning process or a visioning process by the top management that recognizes an unmet need, or it may emerge from grass-roots organizing from organizational members. Many organizations are adopting this approach to diversity by hiring outside trainers to teach the workforce how to be more sensitive to cultural differences or how to communicate better with one another despite differences. Other organizations follow the episodic approach to diversity strategy by helping groups to organize caucuses or interest groups as a forum for people to talk about common concerns or problems with the organization. When activities such as caucuses and training workshops occur as isolated events, they can be classified as proactive responses that are episodic in nature because they are neither permanent nor ongoing. Some diversity trainers indicate a reluctance to become involved with this type of diversity strategy, fearing that a workshop of only a few hours will create false hopes among some groups and allow other groups to conclude that there is little substance to diversity initiatives since the topics can be covered in so little time. Conversely, other trainers suggest that organizational leaders may use the episodic approach to test the waters in their own organizations. Accordingly, the latter may use an introductory workshop as a kickoff to a more intensive and prolonged involvement with diversity initiatives.

(2)   Over time, training initiatives of an episodic nature can lead to a nurturing diversity program when an organization moves further to become more aware of differing cultures, and becomes more invested in enhancing interpersonal interactions among individuals and groups. At this point, they may adopt a *programmatic* approach to valuing differences to nurture diversity and help organizational leaders and participants realize its benefits (Thomas, 1991). This approach is different from the affirmative action and EEO programs in at least two ways. First, while the former programs are federally mandated, valuing differences as a practice is an organizational choice. Second, EEO requires that organizations be blind to differences such as race or sex when making hiring decisions; whereas this approach to diversity not only recognizes differences but values them.

(3)   The highest level of diversity development – multiculturalism – recognizes managing diversity as a proactive and systemic process (*process integration*) (Cox, 1993; Bowens et al., 1993). This approach to managing diversity differs from other approaches that are accommodative or program-oriented (Thomas, 1991). First, its goal is to integrate strategic and diversity considerations for gaining long-term strategic advantage. Second, it is a

process that is integrated throughout the organization whereas affirmative action and valuing differences can be added or substracted from organizational life with equal ease. While organizations find it relatively easy to adopt and disinherit programs, organizational mission and processes are far less expendable. Finally, this approach recognizes the value of similarities as well as differences (Ofori-Dankwa and Ortega Sysak, 1994). Therefore, whereas affirmative action, EED, and valuing differences programs protect some groups and not others, multiculturalism focuses on inclusion of all individuals and all groups in the organization. It is this emphasis on inclusion that most distances multiculturalism from a zero-sum mentality. The assumption of inclusion is synergy i.e. that the parts make up more than the sum of the total; hence, diversity adds to rather than substitutes for part of an organization's capabilities. Because most of us are more familiar with the tenets of competition and zero-sum gaming that are the antithesis of multiculturalism, the latter is not readily understood nor easily adopted by many organizational participants. As a result, the challenge is not only that some white males are reluctant to dismantle the systems they painstakingly created, but that they and others express genuine social concern over how or if past inequities can be corrected without new inequities.

Organizational leaders who adopt this strategic approach of multiculturalism recognize the importance of both homogeneity and diversity in organizations. They similarly recognize the important role conflict can play in creating a common sense of vision and beliefs within an organization through debate. Honest expression of difference can lead to a synthesis of the conflicting perspectives to take advantage of the similarities as well as differences within organizations (Ofori-Dankwa and Ortega Sysak, 1994; Thomas, 1991).

The multicultural approach takes a dynamic and dualistic view, and posits that organizations can have a positive approach to developing both homogeneity and diversity that addresses core issues of race, ethnicity, and gender simultaneously with other issues of similarities and differences found within organizations. In this sense, homogeneity and diversity can be conceptualized in terms of yin and yang of the Taoist philosophy (Morgan, 1986; see figure 14.2). They represent two opposite tendencies in an organization that are interactive and changing. It makes little sense to think of one without the other. They are complementary and blend into each other such that together they make a whole. Therefore, it represents a holistic approach to dealing with the issues of similarities and differences in organizations.

Other programs such as those relating to quality, globalization, new ventures, employee empowerment, and management development may also be part of diversity initiatives. It may be noted that managing diversity goes hand in hand with many other challenging issues of the workplace. It is also complementary to a variety of management theories – of teams, globalization, culture, quality, change, learning, and reengineering – that have emerged in recent times. Further, researchers have shown that these theories, and their emphasis on doing things in new and synergistic ways have positive results for organizations. For example, a study (Parthasarthy and Sethi, 1993) found that skill diversity and team approaches interacted positively at the manufacturing level. The focus of these concepts is an integrated, ongoing, and flexible process that helps in developing an organizational culture to direct all organizational activities towards strategic goals. For example, unlike the traditional resources of capital and equipment, knowledge cannot be utilized without full cooperation from the participants who possess it. And, total quality and organizational learning emphasize the need for a systemic change to harness the full potential of knowledge of all the internal and external participants (Senge, 1990). Such a change in organizations sufficient to accommodate diversity in a variety of organizational roles could well broaden an organization's ability to gain a strategic advantage over other organizations.

There may not be one best diversity strategy for all organizations to implement a multicultural approach. Organizations need to design their own strategies, depending upon the types of diversities they face, in the context of their goals, values, and other internal and external conditions. The multicultural approach focuses on redesigning organizational systems by structural and cultural transformations that provide a level playing field for all participants, and an atmosphere where everyone can develop and contribute her/his best to the organization. In order for this to occur, organizational leaders must articulate their thinking about the appropriate balance between homogeneity and heterogeneity in the form of a diversity strategy. This is the approach adopted by leaders (at corporations such as Avon and Xerox) who view diversity initiatives as the means for removing barriers that otherwise reduce individuals' full contributions to work (Sessa, 1992; Thomas, 1991). Accordingly, activities consistent with diversity include not only the focus on targets and including all people in the workplace developed in response to EEO but also a proactive stance toward achieving competitive business advantage from diversity.

Conclusions and Implications

The foregoing discussion makes it clear that diversity represents both opportunities and threats for organizations. Among the threats shared with all other fields of management is a well-founded belief that adopting diversity as a core organizational competence represents a radical and profound change in traditional management functions. Organizations that subscribe to scientific management principles alone are most likely to be threatened by diversity initiatives, and they may avoid them despite constant evidence that diversity of people, products, and markets are increasing daily. As a group, organizations may assume postures toward diversity initiatives similar to those reflected among nation-states. That is, some may deal with diversity by means of avoidance or elimination; this example is shown in countries that for the moment are largely homogeneous as well as by those

Figure 14.2 Yin and yang: a multicultural approach to homogeneity and diversity in organizations

that are engaged in what has been called "ethnic cleansing." Given the mobility characteristic of labor today, neither avoidance nor elimination are likely to provide long-term solutions to either nations or organizations coping with diversity. Moreover, given the low birth rate in many of the more industrialized nations, many countries are faced with too few male workers and must now admit diversity in the form of either women or foreigners; Japan represents this dilemma. Other nations, and many companies, are admitting diversity under highly controlled circumstances, with tokenism as a leading indicator. Countries using easily expendable guest laborers and those shutting the doors against new immigrants may be controlling diversity to their own peril. Closing borders in Western Europe has resulted in considerable backlash, creating long-term effects as immigrants already inside these countries lobby on behalf of others and face possible retaliation from indigenous hosts. Companies pursuing this means of diversity management face similar challenges, of which tokenism is only one. Additionally, once an organization has acquired a reputation as "unfriendly" to any group, it is very difficult to change that perception.

The two most competitive nations in the world in 1993 were the US and

Singapore (*World Competitiveness Report*, 1994), both of which are characterized by ethnic and gender diversity at work. Additionally, countries like Dubai and colonies like Hong Kong continue to thrive, and a frequently cited reason for their prosperity is an ability to accommodate diversity. This suggests that countries that admit diversity, as well as those that simply make no value judgements about others are better able to function than those who take a different stance. The same may be true for organizations that are able to value both internal and external diversity. Admitting these values not only makes it possible to seize opportunities arising from a global economy, but also should help organizations to hire and retain human and other resources best prepared to act on the opportunities identified. Further research can help in developing theories on managing diversity under varying contexts, and in guiding the practice of diversity management in organizations of the future. Managing diversity demands and supports a strategic role for the HR function (Fombrun et al., 1984) in order to guide all managers in their managerial and operational roles. That is the substance of discussion in most of the other chapters of this book.

REFERENCES

Adler, N. A. (1987). Paufic basin managers: Again not a woman. *Human Resource Management*, 26: 169–91.

Andrews, P. (1993). Microsoft to offer health benefits to partners of its gay employees. *Seattle Times*, April 21, F7.

Ansoff, H. I. (1980). Strategic issue management. *Strategic Management Journal*, 1, 131–48.

Bantel, K. A., and Jackson, S. E. (1989). Top management and innovations in banking: Does the composition of the top team make a difference? *Strategic Management Journal*, 10, 107–24.

Barney, J. B. (1991). Firm resources and sustained competitive advantage. *Journal of Management*, 17, 99–120.

Barney, J. B. (1992). Integrating organizational behavior and strategy formulation research: A resource based analysis. In P. Shrivastava, A. Huff, and J. Dutton (eds), *Advances in Strategic Management*, vol. 8 (39–61). Greenwich, CT: JAI Press.

Billings, T. R., Milburn, W., and Schaalman, M. L. (1980). Crisis perception: A theoretical and empirical analysis. *Administrative Science Quarterly*, 25, 300–15.

Bird, L. (1993). Marketers miss out by alienating Blacks. *Wall Street Journal*, April 3, B3.

Bowens, H., Merenivitch, J., Johnson, L. P., James, A. R., and McFadden-Bryant, D. J. (1993). Managing cultural diversity toward true multiculturalism: Some knowledge from the black perspective. In R. R. Sims and R. F. Dennehy (eds), *Diversity and Differences in Organizations* (33–45). Westport, CN: Quorum Books.

Carroll, A. B. (1979). A three-dimensional conceptual model of corporate performance. *Academy of Management Review*, 4, 497–505.

Child, J. (1972). Organization structure, environment and performance. *Sociology*, 6, 1–22.

Clarkson, M. B. E. (1988). Corporate social performance in Canada, 1976–86. In L. E. Preston (ed.), *Research in Corporate Social Performance and Policy*, vol. 10 (241–65). Greenwich, CT: JAI Press.

Clarkson, M. B. E. (1995). A stakeholder framework for analyzing and evaluating corporate social performance. *Academy of Management Review*, 20, 92–117.

Conference Board (1991). *Europe's Glass Ceiling*. New York: Conference Board.

Conference Board (1992a). *In Diversity Is Strength*. New York: Conference Board.

Conference Board (1992b). *Workforce Diversity: Corporate Challenges, Corporate Responses*. New York: Conference Board.

Covenant Investment Management (1993). Equal opportunity, stock performance linked. Press release, April 2. Chicago, IL.

Cox, T. (1993). *Cultural Diversity in Organizations: Theory, Research, and Practice*. San Francisco: Berrett-Koehler.

Cox. T. H., and Blake, S. (1991). Managing cultural diversity: Implications for organizational competitiveness. *Academy of Management Executive*, 5, 45–56.

D'Aunno, T., Sutton, R. I., and Price, R. H. (1991). Isomorphism and external support in conflicting institutional environments: A study of drug abuse treatment units. *Academy of Management Journal*, 34, 636–61.

Davidson, E. (1991). Communicating with a diverse workforce. *Supervisory Management*, December, 1–2.

DeLuca, J. M., and McDowell, R. N. (1992). Managing diversity: A strategic "grassroots" approach. In S. E. Jackson and Associates (eds), *Diversity in the Workplace – Human Resources Initiatives* (227–47). New York: Guilford Press.

Dutton, J. E., and Jackson, S. E. (1987). The categorization of strategic issues by decision makers and its links to organizational action. *Academy of Management Review*, 12, 76–90.

Engardio, P. (1994). Importing enthusiasm. *Business Week*, special issue on 21st Century Capitalism, 122–3.

Fernandez, J. (1991). *Managing a Diverse Work Force*. Lexington, MA: Lexington Books.

Fisher, A. B. (1992). When will women get to the top? *Fortune*, September 21, 44–56.

Fombrun, C. J., Tichy, N. M., and Devanna, M. A. (1984). *Strategic Human Resource Management*. New York: John Wiley and Sons.

Galen, M. (1994). White, male, and worried. *Business Week*, January 31, 50–5.

Gentile, M. C. (1994). The case of the unequal opportunity. In M. C. Gentile (ed.), *Differences that Work – Organizational Excellence Through Diversity* (223–38). Boston: Harvard Business Review.

Ginsberg, A. (1989). Construing the business portfolio: A cognitive model of diversification. *Journal of Management Studies*, 26, 417–38.

Ginsberg, A. (1990). Connecting diversification to performance: A sociocognitive approach. *Academy of Management Review*, 15, 514–35.

Glick, W. H., Miller, C. C., and Huber, G. P. (1993). The impact of upper-echelon diversity on organizational performance. In G. P. Huber and W. H. Glick (eds), *Organizational Change and Redesign* (176–214). New York: Oxford University Press.

Goodstein, J., Gautam, K., and Boeker, W. (1994). The effects of board size and diversity on strategic change. *Strategic Management Journal*, 15, 241–50.

Hampden-Turner, C., and Trompenaars, A. (1993). *The Seven Cultures of Capitalism*. New York: Currency-Doubleday.

Hannan, M. T., and Freeman, J. (1984). Structural inertia and organizational change. *American Sociological Review*, 49, 149–64.

Hill, C. W. L. (1988). Differentiation versus low cost or differentiation and low cost: A contingency framework. *Academy of Management Review*, 13, 401–12.

Hof, R. D. (1992). Inside Intel. *Business Week*, June 1, 86–94.

International Labor Organization (1993). The unequal race to the top. *World of Work-US*, 2, 6–7.

Jackson, S. E., and Alvarez, E. B. (1992). Working through diversity as a strategic imperative. In S. E. Jackson and Associates (eds), *Diversity in the Workplace – Human Resources Initiatives* (13–35). New York: Guilford Press.

Jamieson, D., and O'Mara, J. (1991). *Managing Workforce 2000: Gaining the Diversity Advantage*. San Francisco: Jossey-Bass.

Koretz, G. (1991). An acid test of job discrimination in the real world. *Business Week*, October 21, 23.

Kosnik, R. D. (1990). Effects of board demography and directors' incentives on corporate greenmail. *Academy of Management Journal*, 33, 129–51.

Lambert, W. (1977). The effects of bi-lingualism on the individual: Cognitive and socio-cultural consequences. In P. A. Hurnbey (ed.), *Bi-lingualism: Psychological, Social, and Educational Implications*. New York: Academic Press.

Lopez, J. A. (1992). Firms elevate heads of diversity programs. *Wall Street Journal*, August 5, B1.

Lynch, F. R. (1992). Multiculturalism comes to the workplace. *Wall Street Journal*, October 26, A16.

McCarroll, T. (1993). It's a mass market no more. *Time*, Fall, 80–1.

Marchington, M. (1990). Analyzing the links between product markets and the management of employee relations. *Journal of Management Studies*, 27, 111–31.

Meyer, A. D. (1982). Adapting to environmental jolts. *Administrative Science Quarterly*, 27, 515–37.

Miles, R. H., and Snow, C. C. (1978). *Organizational Strategy, Structure, and Process*. New York: McGraw Hill.

Miller, D. (1993). The architecture of simplicity. *Academy of Management Review*, 18, 116–38.

Mintzberg, H. (1983). *Power In and Around Organizations*. Englewood Cliffs, NJ: Prentice-Hall.

Mintzberg, H., Raisinghani, D., and Theoret, A. (1976). The structure of unstructured decision processes. *Administrative Science Quarterly*, 21, 246–75.

Morgan, G. (1986). *Images of Organization*. Beverly Hills, CA: Sage.

Noble, B. P. (1994). Still in the dark on diversity. *New York Times*, November 6, F27.

Ofori-Dankwa, J., and Ortega Sysak, C. L. (1994). DiverSimilarity: The re-engineering of diversity training. In *DiverSimilarity: The Paradigm for Workforce 2000* (1–25). Conference Readings, May 12–13. Saginaw Valley State University, Saginaw, Michigan.

Oliver, C. (1991). Strategic responses to institutional processes. *Academy of Management Review*, 16, 145–79.

Parthasarthy, R., and Sethi, S. P. (1993). Relating strategy and structure to flexible automation: A test of fit and performance implications. *Strategic Management Journal*, 14, 529–49.

Pearce, J. A., and Zahra, S. A. (1992). Board composition from a strategic contingency perspective. *Journal of Management Studies*, 29, 411–38.

Pfeffer, J., and Salancik, G. R. (1978). *The External Control of Organizations*. New York: Harper and Row.

Porter, M. E. (1980). *Competitive Strategy – Techniques for Analyzing Industries and Competitors*. New York: Free Press.

Porter, M. E. (1985). *Competitive Advantage: Creating and Sustaining Superior Performance*. New York: Free Press.

Powell, W. W., and DiMaggio, P. J. (1991). *The New Institutionalism in Organizational Analysis*. Chicago: University of Chicago Press.

Prahalad, C. K., and Bettis, R. A. (1986). The dominant logic: A new linkage between diversity and performance. *Strategic Management Journal*, 7, 485–501.

Rice, F. (1994). How to make diversity pay? *Fortune*, August 8, 78–86.

Rotter, N. G., and O'Connell, A. N. (1982). The relationships among sex-role orientation, cognitive complexity, and tolerance for ambiguity. *Sex Roles*, 8, 1209–20.

Seattle Times (1993). Albertson's settles discrimination lawsuit, November 23, E14.

Scherer, F. M., and Ross, D. (1990). *Industrial Market Structure and Economic Performance*. Boston: Houghton Mifflin.

Schneider, S. C., and De Meyer, A. (1991). Interpreting and responding to strategic issues. *Strategic Management Journal*, 12, 307–20.

Schuler, R. S., and Jackson, S. E. (1987). Linking competitive strategies with human resource management practices. *Academy of Management Executive*, 1, 207–19.

Senge, P. M. (1990). *The Fifth Discipline: The Art and Practice of the Learning Organization*. New York: Doubleday/Currency.

Sessa, V. I. (1992). Managing diversity at the Xerox Corporation: Balanced workforce goals and caucus groups. In S. E. Jackson and Associates (eds), *Diversity in the Workplace – Human Resources Initiatives* (37–63). New York: Guilford Press.

Shellenbarger, S. (1995). How accommodating workers' lives can be a business liability. *Wall Street Journal*, January 4, B1.

Starbuck, W. H. (1985). Acting first and thinking later: Theory versus reality in strategic change. In J. M. Pennings and Associates (eds), *Organizational Strategy and Change* (336–72). San Francisco: Jossey-Bass.

Stewart, T. A. (1991). Gay in corporate America. *Fortune*, December 16, 42–56.

Thomas, R. R. (1991). *Beyond Race and Gender: Unleashing the Power of your Total Workforce by Managing Diversity*. New York: AMACOM.

Thomas, R. R., Jr (1992). Managing diversity: A conceptual framework. In S. E. Jackson and Associates (eds), *Diversity in the Workplace – Human Resources Initiatives* (306–18). New York: Guilford Press.

Towers Perrin and Hudson Institute (1990). *Workforce 2000: Competing in a Seller's Market*. Valhalla, NY: Towers Perrin.

Tsui, A. S., Egan, T. D., and O'Reilly, C. A. (1992). Being different: Relational demography and organizational attachment. *Administrative Science Quarterly*, 37, 549–79.

Wartick, S. L., and Cochran, P. L. (1985). The evolution of the corporate social performance model. *Academy of Management Review*, 4, 758–69.

Watson, W. E., Kumar, K., and Michaelsen, L. K. (1993). Cultural diversity's impact on interaction process and performance: Comparing homogeneous and diverse task groups. *Academy of Management Journal*, 36, 590–602.

Weick, K. E. (1979). *The Social Psychology of Organizing*. New York: Random House.

Westphal, J. D. (1994). Who shall govern? The role of demographic similarity in new director selection. Academy of Management Best Paper Proceedings, Academy of Management Meetings, Dallas.

Wiersema, M., and Bantel, K. A. (1992). Top management team demography and corporate strategic change. *Academy of Management Journal*, 35, 91–121.

World Competitiveness Report (1994). World Economic Forum (Geneva) and International Institute for Management and Development (Lausanne).

15

Capitalizing on the Benefits of Diversity through Workteams

Donna E. Thompson and Laura E. Gooler

The increasing reliance of organizations on teamwork among today's diverse workforce highlights the importance of understanding the implications of diversity for workteam functioning and effectiveness. Diversity may lead to a variety of different consequences for teams. If managed well, organizations can reap the benefits of creating an environment that enables all employees to work optimally together to achieve organizational goals. If mismanaged, organizations may suffer losses such as productivity, morale, and even staff.

The purpose of this chapter is to provide a guide for understanding and capitalizing on the benefits of diversity in and through the use of workteams. We begin by describing some key linkages between diversity and workteams. Next, we discuss the importance of optimizing team performance for organizational effectiveness. This is followed by a description of how workteams are changing. A definition of a workteam is provided along with an overview of the many types of teams that exist in organizations today. We then review theoretical and empirical work on diversity and workteams, to highlight key areas where diversity has major implications for workteam functioning and effectiveness. From this analysis, we present guidelines for managing diverse workteams. Finally, we conclude with a brief discussion of some of the implications of our analysis for research and practice.

Diversity and Workteams Go Hand in Hand

Diversity issues take on a special meaning for teams because they lie at the heart of team functioning and effectiveness. Teams, for example, often result in people working together with others who are different from them. Teams that comprise a variety of perspectives are believed to have added potential for creativity, problem-solving, and decision-making. At the same time, these differences have the potential to undermine the team's effectiveness (e.g. Cox, 1991). The differences among members of the group itself, for instance, may make communication and negotiation among team members more difficult. Moreover, some organizational diversity efforts (e.g. awareness training) may further undermine the ability of the team members to work well together. Diversity programs or interventions may sometimes promote stereotypes. They may also serve to further exacerbate the perceptions of differences among subgroups of the employee population or the perception that some groups are more privileged or better treated than others.

On the other hand, diverse workteams have the potential to enhance an organization's efforts to foster diversity. Exposing people to others who have different backgrounds can help break down stereotypic beliefs (e.g. Hewstone and Brown, 1986). Organizational practices that expose people to different others have been found to be related to success in fostering and developing diversity (e.g. Morrison, 1992). These practices include bringing together heterogeneous members from various functional areas of the company as seen in diversity councils or diversity task forces to guide an organization's diversity efforts. The diversity of perspectives expected to come from heterogeneous members on these teams is expected to lead to more successful change efforts. Such diverse teams can strengthen the quality of the decision-making process that is used to identify the organization's diversity issues. If the team is viewed as representing the diverse subgroups in the employee population, it can also lead to greater acceptance and willingness to implement changes on the part of employees. Unfortunately, diverse workteams also have the potential to thwart an organization's diversity efforts. By their very nature, they provide additional opportunities for prejudice and bias. This can, in turn, impact on the management of people's careers, and their subsequent motivation, performance, and inclination to leave the organization.

The Need to Optimize Workteam Performance

Teams are an integral part of the restructuring and redesign of work in organizations. In fact, some have argued that they represent the basic building block of organizations today and in the future (e.g. Davis, 1977; Leavitt, 1975; Peters and Waterman, 1982). As products and technology become more complex, what once could have been done by one person may now require the input and expertise of several. Many technological innovations require a high degree of task interdependence, whereby team members must rely on one another to perform their tasks effectively given the design of their jobs (e.g. Georgopolous, 1986). As demands for task interdependence increase, the requirements for coordination, communication, and cooperation also increase in order for work units to perform well. Similarly, because important decisions involve many constituencies, the use of teams increases participation in decision-making, thus increasing commitment to the decision. Clearly, the fact that more people are working together in more ways than ever before under increasing pressures to perform well underscores the importance of ensuring that such "partnerships" are successful. The potential impact of team effectiveness on the overall performance of an organization is considerable.

How Workteams Are Changing

Although teams have long been an important tool for accomplishing organizational goals, their composition, structure, and use today differ from the past. One area of difference concerns *who gets assigned to teams*. The fact is that the workteams in many of today's organizations are characterized by increasing diversity. This is due in part simply to the changing demographics of the workforce. Teams that are diverse in terms of age, sex, race, national origin, educational background, level area of expertise, and many other dimensions are increasingly common. It is also due to the frequent use of workteams, such as cross-functional teams and self-managed teams, as a tool for restructuring organizations to be more competitive (Bassin, 1988; Levine, 1987). Such teams often bring people together from different functions and geographic locations of the organization to work closely together in a highly interdependent fashion. To illustrate, the increasingly competitive domestic and global environment is calling for improved quality, innovation, and speed from our workforce. These changes are making it necessary for companies to bring together individuals from two or more separate functional areas of the company, each of whom have expertise in different areas. An example would be a new product team, comprising experts from marketing and product manufacturing. These members must combine their diverse functional expertise to create quality new products in a fast and efficient manner.

Individuals from different functional areas within a company are not the only ones being brought together. In addition, *individuals external to the organization* are increasingly being added to teams. One example is the growing trend for individuals from one company to connect with employees from two or more other organizations, such as suppliers and manufacturers, to ensure that product deadlines can be met. Furthermore, an increased emphasis on customer satisfaction is seeing a growing alliance between organizations and their customers, whereby companies are beginning to team up their marketing experts and manufacturers with their customers to ensure satisfaction. Lastly, the increasing diversity of workteams is also sometimes the result of deliberate efforts on the part of organizations to create teams (e.g. task forces, diversity councils) that balance the representation of the different groups of employees in their workforce in order to meet specific objectives.

A third area of difference concerns *how long* individuals get assigned to teams. In many cases, rather than permanently assigning individuals to teams with a fixed task or set of tasks, organizations will assign individuals to work part-time on multiple projects. Quality circles and research and design teams are examples of these types. They are usually temporary and may have membership that changes over time. In other cases, employees are expected to work closely with others for a limited, and often intense period of time, as is the case with task forces and steering committees, while simultaneously performing a prescribed set of roles and responsibilities.

A fourth difference concerns *where and how teams meet*. The increase in the number of individuals with access to computers, and the ability to connect computers, along with advances in information technology, now make it possible and common for team members to "meet" many individuals in geographically dispersed locations to hold meetings and discussions. Fax machines and email make access to essentially instant communication between team members possible. Modems and portable computers allow employees to travel away from their work site, and remain connected to their company's computer files and networking system. Such advances allow for members to remain connected even while working at home or on the road. Furthermore, local area networks allow groups of individuals to simultaneously share access to the same computer files and documents upon which they are working. Group decision support systems have also been designed to enhance the decision-making ability of groups through procedures that structure the weighting of alternative solutions.

Perhaps one of the most notable differences, however, concerns the *increased amount of autonomy, authority, and responsibility* granted to today's teams. In their attempt to become more flexible and adaptable to the accelerated pace of technological and market change, organizations are distributing more decision-making power to groups of employees lower in the organizational hierarchy.

So, What Is a Team?

Defining a team requires an understanding of when a group of individuals working together constitutes a "team" and when it does not. Part of the trouble with defining the concept of teams is that groups in organizational settings of almost all types are known as teams. Today, someone using the word team may be referring to a self-managing group of production workers, for example, who set their own goals, select their own members, and determine many of their production or service delivery functions with relatively large autonomy from top management. On the other hand, they may be referring to the accomplishment of their sales or HR team, whose joint efforts reflect individual contributions, and whose activities are closely monitored by management.

Most companies advocate teamwork because it represents a set of values that encourage listening and responding constructively to views expressed

---

Box 15.1 Types of workteams

Advisory groups	Networking groups
Board of directors	New product development teams
Coordinating committees	Policy committees
Cross-cultural groups	Project teams
Cross-functional teams	Promotion planning teams
Data processing groups	Quality circles/teams
Division operating committees	Research teams
Division task forces	Review panels
Employee involvement groups	Sales teams
Evaluation teams	Selection committees
Focus groups	Self-directed work teams
Global management teams	Self-managed teams
Internal consulting teams	Semi-autonomous work teams
Labor management committees	Senior management teams
Long-term planning teams	Steering committees
Manufacturing/assembly teams	Strategic alliances
Marketing teams	Task forces
Negotiating teams	Work crews

---

by others, providing support and assistance, and recognizing the interests and achievements of others in a group. Such values help teams perform, and they also promote individual performance as well as that of the entire company. But teamwork values by themselves are not exclusive to teams, nor are they enough to ensure team performance. Nor is a team just any group of individuals working together, and not all work is amenable to being accomplished by teams.

Types of teams

As box 15.1 shows, the types of workteams used in organizations today are numerous. They include, but are not limited to: cross-functional teams, advisory groups, self-directed teams, steering committees, research teams, marketing and sales teams, new product development teams, boards of directors, quality circles, and manufacturing and development teams, to name a few. Teams are also being used to champion diversity efforts, as seen in the establishment of diversity task forces, diversity training teams, networking groups, and senior-level diversity advisory councils.

Defining a workteam

What typically differentiates workteams from mere groups of individuals working together is a matter of performance results. A team's performance includes both individual results and collective work products that reflect the joint, real contributions of team members. Teams also require both individual and mutual accountability for performance outcomes. A key feature to teams is their common commitment to a shared purpose. Team members must have a common purpose around which they can unite and transform their efforts into achieving a specific set of performance goals. The characteristics of the set of team members, collectively, is often referred to as the team's composition. *Members in a team may be diverse with respect to any of a very large number of attributes.* The composition may be stable, or may change over time as members come and go.

Some teams, such as cross-functional teams, may be formed because they have a particular array of knowledge, skills, and abilities to accomplish a set of activities. Other teams, such as task forces, may be formed to complete certain projects. While other teams, like work crews, are established to support an ongoing technology or work system. Regardless of their mandate, for purposes of this chapter, a *team is defined as a dynamic integration of individuals who are committed to a common purpose (e.g. projects, tasks) and set of performance goals for which they hold themselves mutually accountable, and whose efforts produce something beyond individual end products.*

Are There Benefits to Using Diverse Workteams?

In his book, *Cultural Diversity in Organizations*, Cox (1993) defines managing diversity as "planning and implementing organizational systems and practices to manage people so that the potential advantages of diversity are maximized while the potential disadvantages are minimized" (p. 11). Clearly, teams represent one such system that can be used to successfully manage diversity or meet this goal. An organization's ability to successfully foster diversity has implications for its performance and effectiveness. So does its ability to handle workteams. Teams can provide the vehicle to capitalize on the wealth of resources people from different backgrounds bring to the organization. They can, however, also exacerbate or further intensify the problems that occur when people of diverse backgrounds are brought together.

When the benefits of diversity are discussed, among them are that using such diverse teams can lead to more creativity or innovation, better decision-making and more effective problem-solving (e.g. Copeland, 1988; Cox et al., 1991; Esty, 1988). The belief is that diverse teams have a broader range of knowledge, skills, abilities, and experiences that can enhance the group's ability to critically analyze problems and generate more creative solutions and ideas. In this section, we will review the findings from research which has examined the effects of diversity on team problem-solving, decision-making, creativity and innovation. As you will see, evidence exists that there are potential benefits to using diverse workteams. These benefits are not guaranteed, however – there are potential costs as well. Diverse workteams must be carefully planned and implemented to maximize the potential advantages and minimize the potential disadvantages.

Problem-solving and decision-making

Much of the support for the belief that diverse groups may be better at problem-solving and producing higher quality decisions comes from research on group composition. This research compares the performance of groups whose members share similar characteristics (homogeneous) with those whose members have dissimilar characteristics (heterogeneous). Cognitive aspects of the decision-making process have been studied, such as the generation of alternative solutions or the quality of a group's analysis of the advantages and disadvantages of potential solutions. The general findings from this body of research suggests that designing workteams that maximize member differences does appear to enhance problem-solving and decision-making (Guzzo, 1986).

The initial evidence of the positive effects of diversity (or heterogeneity) on group problem-solving came from research conducted in the 1950s and 1960s. Groups that were heterogeneous with regard to gender (Hoffman and Maier, 1961), personality (Hoffman, 1959), training background (Pelz, 1956), and attitudes (e.g. Hoffman et al., 1962; Triandis et al., 1965) produced higher-quality solutions to problems than did homogeneous groups. Subsequent research has confirmed these early findings. For example, Aamodt and Kimbrough (1982) found that groups composed of individuals with different types of behavioral styles came up with higher-quality decisions than homogeneous groups consisting of people who all had the same style. Wanous and Youtz (1986) found that groups whose members produced more diverse alternative solutions were more likely to produce higher-quality decisions. In her review of twelve studies of group problem-solving, Wood (1987) concluded that mixed-sex teams outperformed same-sex teams. For more detailed reviews of research in this area, see Guzzo, 1982; 1986; 1993; Guzzo and Salas, forthcoming; Hare et al., 1994; McGrath, 1984; Shaw, 1981.

Additional support for the link between team diversity and improved decision-making comes from research that has focused on the relationship between the composition of top management teams and their performance on indicators like strategic choices and the firm's financial performance (e.g. Eisenhardt and Schoonhoven, 1990; Finkelstein and Hambrick, 1990; Michel and Hambrick, 1992; Murray, 1989; Wiersema and Bantel, 1991). While these studies found heterogeneity in background characteristics such as education, tenure, age, and occupational function among top management teams to be associated with higher performance, the relationship was not always consistent. As an illustration, consider Murray's (1989) study of 84 Fortune 500 food and oil companies. While heterogeneity in top management teams was related to firm performance in the oil industry, it was not found to influence it in the food industry. Organizational characteristics and environmental conditions, therefore, appear to affect the relationship between the diversity of top management teams and firm performance (e.g. Jackson, 1992; Jackson et al., forthcoming).

There is another body of research that lends support to the positive link between team diversity and the group *problem-solving process*. These research studies have been concerned with examining the impact of a "minority" viewpoint in a group (i.e. presence of two or more members who share an opinion or perspective that differs from that held by the "majority" or remaining members of the team) on group effectiveness. In a series of laboratory studies conducted by Nemeth (1985) and Nemeth and Wachtler (1983), groups with minority views were more likely to consider a greater number of alternative solutions and to more carefully discuss the assumptions and implications of alternatives. The presence of a minority viewpoint improved the quality of the decision-making process the group used regardless of whether or not the minority view was adopted by the group.

Some indirect support for this relationship between team diversity and the problem-solving process can also be found in the work conducted on "groupthink," or the tendency of highly cohesive groups to exhibit ineffective decision-making behaviors (Janis, 1972; 1982). This research found that cohesive high-level government groups gathered limited information on problems and failed to critically analyze solutions, or the impact of potential solutions. Among the solutions that Janis proposed for groupthink were a set of prescriptions that encouraged team members to seek out a diversity of viewpoints from either themselves or outside experts in the organization. The presence of diverse workteams may serve to further reduce the likelihood of groupthink occurring since the phenomenon only occurs in highly cohesive groups, and heterogeneous groups tend to be less cohesive.

The findings from some of the research conducted on team decision-making and problem-solving with members who are from different race, cultural or national backgrounds have been less straightforward. In an early study, Fiedler (1966) examined the effects of leadership and cultural heterogeneity on group performance. Heterogeneous groups, consisting of Dutch and Belgian members, performed as well as homogeneous groups. However, these culturally diverse groups also experienced more communication problems. Mixed results were found in another study examining the productivity of culturally heterogeneous and culturally homogeneous workteams (Adler, 1986). While some of the heterogeneous teams were more productive than the homogeneous teams, others were less so. What accounted for the differences in productivity? The heterogeneous teams that paid attention to the impact of diversity on elements of team effectiveness (e.g. ability to handle conflict, balanced participation from the team members and cohesiveness) were more productive. In a recent study comparing culturally homogeneous and heterogeneous college students, Watson et al. (1993) found that diversity had an initial negative impact on group interaction processes and performance. Early on, diverse groups reported more difficulty agreeing on what was important and working together, and they more frequently had members who tried to be too controlling, which hindered member contributions. This coincided with observations of the students at the *beginning* of a 17-week period showing that homogeneous groups performed better than the heterogeneous groups. As time passed however, the heterogeneous groups performed *better* on the problem-solving measures than the homogeneous groups and the difference between the two groups in how well the group members worked together disappeared!

Creativity and innovation

Diverse workteams are also believed to be more creative and innovative than homogeneous teams. The rationale underlying this expectation is similar to that presented above for problem-solving and decision-making tasks. That is, members of diverse teams have a wider range of knowledge, skills, abilities, and experiences which result in a greater number of different ideas, perspectives or approaches to situations that should enhance creative thinking. In his book *Conceptual Blockbusting: A Guide To Better Ideas*, Adams (1979) notes that "groups of people can bring many diverse perceptions and intellectual specialties to bear on a problem. They can provide a supportive emotional environment and the resources necessary to develop initial concepts into believable detail in a reasonable time" (p. 131).

As in the case for the research linking diversity with enhanced problem-solving and decision-making, much of the early support for the relationship between diverse workteams and creativity and innovation is based on research conducted in laboratory settings on team composition (e.g. Hoffman, 1959; Hoffman and Maier, 1961; Triandis et al., 1965). In her review of the literature on team composition in work settings, Jackson (1991) concludes that there is support for the link between diverse workteams and enhanced creativity and innovation. Heterogeneous teams have generally been found to produce more creative and innovative solutions than homogeneous teams. Stein (1975; 1982) also found that heterogeneous groups were more creative. Later research suggests that the presence of minority viewpoints differing from the majority of members may also stimulate creative thought processes. In a series of laboratory experiments, such groups generated more alternative strategies for solving the task they were given and generated more solutions as well (Nemeth, 1985; 1986; Nemeth and Wachtler, 1983). The most recent support for the idea that culturally diverse workteams may be more innovative and creative comes from a study by McLeod et al. (1993). The performance of homogeneous groups of Anglo college students was compared with that of diverse groups of Asian, Black, Anglo and Hispanic students on a brainstorming task. The diverse groups produced ideas that were higher on both feasibility and overall effectiveness.

There is also some evidence that *real or natural diverse workteams* can also be more innovative. In her book *The Change Masters*, Kanter (1983) reported that companies high on innovation had established heterogeneous workteams because they believed that a diverse set of ideas and perspectives would result in more creative ideas that would give them the competitive edge they desired. Bantel and Jackson (1989) explored the link between the composition of 199 top management teams in the banking industry and measures of innovation. Senior management teams consisting of members with a greater diversity of educational backgrounds and functional areas of expertise were more innovative and creative in their decision-making.

In summary, empirical research exists that diverse teams can lead to enhanced problem-solving, decision-making, creativity, and innovation. This positive impact of diversity has been found for a number of different dimensions of diversity. At the present time, however, we do not actually know what types of people work best together on different types of tasks or exactly in what ways people need to be compatible with one another for a team to be most effective (e.g. Guzzo and Shea, 1992). Early research does suggest that team members may need to share some basis of similarity if they are going to be able to work together effectively (e.g. Hoffman, 1959; Lott and Lott, 1965). We do not know what the long-term effects of diversity may be on team performance, although Watson et al. (1993) suggest that the initial difficulties that members of diverse groups experience in working together disappear, and, eventually, they actually perform *better* than homogeneous groups. However, there is also some suggestion that the impact of diversity will vary over time as a function of the increased experience of individuals working together on a particular task as well as of changes that may occur in the team's composition, structure, task, technology, and the organizational context within which it operates (e.g. McGrath, 1993).

The impact of diversity is also expected to be powerfully influenced by the organizational context in which diverse teams operate. Unfortunately, this influence has not been studied. Instead, much of what we know about the potential benefits of diverse teams comes from studies that have been conducted in laboratory settings with college students. These experimental studies often use temporary groups of students who work on short-term tasks that may be of little interest and/or meaning to them. They are not influenced by organizational context variables (e.g. organizational history, demographic profile of the workforce, diversity climate of the organization, HR practices). As Jackson et al. (forthcoming) note, these types of organizational factors, as well as societal context factors, can affect relations among team members and impact on the effectiveness of diverse workteams. Models of workgroup effectiveness have also underscored the importance of organizational context in determining the effectiveness of workteams more generally (e.g. Gladstein, 1984; Hackman, 1987; Hackman and Oldham, 1980; Nieva et al., 1978; Sundstrom et al., 1990). Perhaps more importantly, we are really just beginning to conduct research on *natural or real workteams* that defines diversity along the wide range of dimensions (e.g. gender, nationality, race, ethnicity, age, work function, tenure) that are of concern to organizations. (See *Diversity in Workteams: Research Paradigms for a Changing Workplace* by Jackson and Ruderman (1996) for a more complete discussion of some of the most recent theoretical and empirical work on the topic.)

While this relative lack of research on the effects of diversity on *natural or real workteams* leaves many unanswered questions, the potential impact of diversity on team problem-solving, decision-making and creativity has been clearly established. Consistent positive findings for diversity or heterogeneity have been reported in both the research conducted in laboratory settings and that done in real world settings. A key finding from all of the research conducted thus far is that the presence of diversity in a workteam doesn't just automatically lead to positive outcomes such as enhanced productivity. Rather, as we have seen in some of the research we have just discussed, *diversity may have either positive or negative effects on team effectiveness, depending upon how it is managed.* The study cited earlier by Triandis et al. (1965) for example, found that heterogeneous teams produced more creative and better-quality decisions than homogeneous ones, if the team members were given information about the attitudinal differences of other group members. In a study that did not find diverse groups to be more creative, Thornburg (1991) suggested that the failure to find a positive effect for diversity was due to the negative impact diversity had on group process. The findings from this study and several others that we have reviewed suggest therefore, that when positive effects for diversity on problem-solving, decision-making, creativity, or innovation are *not* found, it may often be due to the negative impact that diversity has had on the interpersonal relations or interactions among team members. Cox (1991) and Jackson et al. (forthcoming) have both suggested that diverse teams may not be effective because the differences that exist among team members may impact negatively on communication processes and cohesiveness.

We will explore how diversity can affect the behavior of people in workteams in greater detail in the next section. As we shall see, reviews of basic research in the behavioral sciences also have demonstrated that the characteristics of group members can have positive or negative effects on the way they interact with one another, which in turn can impact on their performance (e.g. see Hare et al., 1994; Shaw, 1981). Consistent with this, recent work (exploring organizational demography) indicates that increasing the diversity of a workforce without developing an organizational climate that supports diversity may be associated with more negative work attitudes, higher absenteeism and turnover (e.g. Kossek et al., forthcoming; O'Reilly et al., 1989; Tsui et al., 1992). Taken together, the evidence to date suggests that it is the *successful management and leadership of diverse teams* that may be the key to capitalizing on the potential benefits of using such teams for enhanced organizational effectiveness and may provide the competitive edge organizations need in the marketplace.

How Does Diversity Impact on Team Functioning?

Since the early Hawthorne studies, we have known that the social conditions people encounter can impact on the productivity of a workgroup (e.g. Mayo, 1933; Roethlisberger and Dickson, 1939). That is, people's attitudes and the processes by which they communicate with one another can greatly influence whether or not they will fully utilize the knowledge, skills, abilities, and experiences they possess to accomplish the group's task. The

Figure 15.1 An input–process–output model of diverse workteam performance

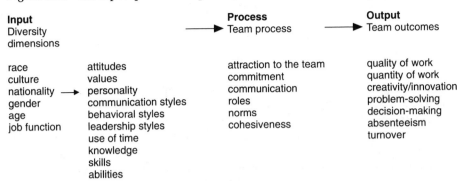

potential advantages of using diverse teams for enhancing organizational effectiveness, that we have discussed above, stem from the broader range of resources members bring to the team. As we have seen, however, in order to fully capitalize on those resources members of diverse teams must be able to work well together.

Diversity can have a tremendous impact on the social climate of a workteam. It can impact on people's perceptions of one another as well as their affective and behavioral responses to one another. A growing body of research evidence documents the effects of diversity: on attraction (e.g. Johnson and Johnson, 1982; Zebrowitz et al., 1993), perception (e.g. Carpenter, 1993; Kossek and Zonia, 1993; Wood and Karten, 1986), communication (e.g. Colarelli and Boos, 1992; Gordon et al., 1991; Kirchmeyer and Cohen, 1992; Zenger and Lawrence, 1989), interaction processes (e.g. Cohen and Zhou, 1991; Cox et al., 1991; Pinto et al., 1993), leadership (e.g. Anderson, 1983; Fiedler, 1966), influence processes (e.g. Carli, 1989; Garza et al., 1982; Mackie, 1987), cohesiveness (e.g. Colarelli and Boos, 1992; Fandt, 1991), motivation (e.g. Garza, 1989; Kossek, 1989), risk-taking (e.g. Watson and Kumar, 1992; Willems and Clark, 1971) and prosocial behavior (e.g. George, 1990). Diversity has also been linked with attitudes such as satisfaction (e.g. Colarelli and Boos, 1992; Fandt, 1991; Rubaii-Barrett and Beck, 1993) and organizational commitment (e.g. Tsui et al., 1992). In addition to its effects on team performance that we observed above, it is associated with other outcome variables such as turnover (e.g. Jackson et al., 1991; McCain et al., 1983; O'Reilly et al., 1989); and absenteeism (e.g. George, 1990).

Clearly, the scope of the potential impact of diversity on the organization, if it fails to successfully manage its diverse workteams, can be substantial. These teams must be managed successfully to capitalize on their benefits and minimize their potential short-term and long-term costs. This requires a greater understanding of how diversity can impact on team functioning. The model depicted in figure 15.1 provides a simple, but useful, starting-point to guide this learning process.

The model is an adaptation of the basic input–process–output model that

Figure 15.2 Steiner's model of workgroup productivity (Steiner, 1972)

ACTUAL PRODUCTIVITY=

Potential productivity *minus* Process losses

dominates past and current thinking about group performance (e.g. Guzzo, 1993). As you can see, it is a causal model that posits that the outcomes of diverse teams are a consequence of the nature of the interaction processes among team members, which in turn are a function of the diverse inputs they bring with them to the team. A basic assumption underlying the model is that various dimensions of diversity are associated with various types of attitudes, values, personality characteristics, communication styles, behavioral styles, leadership styles, orientations toward the use of time, knowledge, skills, and abilities. Such dimensions of diversity reflect aspects of group identities which are believed to influence people's views and perspectives and shape their expectations and behavior (e.g. Alderfer et al., 1983; Cox, 1993; Jackson, 1991; Jackson et al., forthcoming). In short, they provide the "lenses" through which people view and experience their world. People bring these various *inputs* with them to the team. These inputs affect various aspects of group *process* or group *structure*, such as: how attracted and committed members are to the team, the nature and quality of the communication among team members, the various roles played by the team members, the norms or "rules of behavior", and cohesiveness or members' sense of belonging. These processes, in turn impact on the team's effectiveness or outcomes, which include various performance indicators and absenteeism and turnover.

Consistent with this, Steiner's (1972) model of work group productivity provides a useful explanation of how the potential benefits of diverse teams may *not* be realized because of process losses.

According to this model, which is shown in figure 15.2, *potential productivity* would be determined by all of the resources members bring to the diverse work team. The *actual productivity* of the team might differ from its potential productivity because of *process losses*. Process losses reflect the failure of the work team to capitalize on all of its diverse resources. Such losses in diverse work teams might be caused by communication problems resulting from misunderstandings or an inability or unwillingness to confront and resolve conflicting points of view, or from motivational deficits, if the members are not attracted to the group or if it is less cohesive.

We believe these two models help to underscore the profound impact diversity can have on the social relationships and interactions among workteam members. However, they do not fully capture the complex set of processes through which diversity can affect a diverse workteam and its individual members. They also do not deal with the ways in which diverse teams can affect an organization's diversity efforts and vice versa. For example, absent from the models is a consideration of the impact of organizational and societal contexts in which workteams must function. The interested reader is invited to explore more complex and thorough conceptual frameworks that have most recently been proposed by Cox (1993), Jackson et al. (forthcoming) and McGrath et al. (forthcoming).

Dimensions of diversity and team process losses

Evidence does exist to support the assumption that various dimensions of diversity are associated with a number of factors that could contribute to process losses and prevent a diverse team from reaching its full potential. For example, researchers have documented that there are cultural differences in: the use of nonverbal communication (e.g. Cox, 1993; Fugita et al., 1974; Hall, 1966; Aiello and Thompson, 1980a); personal orientation, such as individualism–collectivism (e.g. Foeman and Pressley, 1987; Triandis, 1993) and cooperation versus competition (e.g. Cox et al., 1991); behaviors associated with leadership styles (e.g. Smith et al., 1989); preferred styles of conflict resolution (e.g. Ting-Toomey et al., 1991); decision-making processes (e.g. Adler, 1991; Roth, 1992); social support (e.g. Gooler and Thompson, 1994); "power distance" or the extent to which people accept the authority of more powerful others (e.g. Hofstede, 1991); and the use of time (e.g. Cote and Tansuhaj, 1989; McGrath and Rotchford, 1983). Similarly, among the gender differences that have been noted are those for nonverbal communication styles (e.g. Aiello and Aiello, 1974; Hall, 1966; Thompson and Aiello, 1988); cooperative and competitive orientations (e.g. McClintock and Allison, 1989); and leadership styles (e.g. Eagly and Johnson, 1990). Examples of age differences include those observed for values (e.g. Elder, 1975); communication patterns (e.g. Smith, 1977); and the use of space (e.g. Aiello and Thompson, 1980a; Dean et al., 1976). Each of these dimensions of diversity can potentially lead to process losses. As the following examples illustrate, they can be major contributors to miscommunications, misperceptions, errors in judgement and stereotyping. These, in turn, may lead to process losses by increasing conflict and/or avoidance, breaking down communication and making decision-making more difficult and tenuous.

Increased need to handle conflict

Consider the cultural differences in preferences for conflict-handling techniques reported by Ting-Toomey et al. (1991). In their study, people from China tended to prefer an obliging strategy, which accommodates the needs of one's opponent. Those from Taiwan expressed the strongest desire for an avoidance strategy or a preference for escaping the conflict altogether. In contrast, Americans preferred a dominating strategy that strives to defeat one's opponent. It is also of interest to note that Americans were the least likely to prefer either the obliging or avoidance strategies. In his review of cultural differences, Cox (1993) also cites research suggesting that while

Anglos, Asians, and many Hispanics may prefer more indirect ways of resolving conflict, African-Americans tend to prefer a more direct, confrontational approach. These examples show how individuals from various cultures have different rules, preferences, or expectations for living that are socially defined. These rules and expectations are driven by the values of the culture. What is appropriate and acceptable in one culture may not be appropriate and acceptable in another. Violations of "appropriate" ways to behave, in this case, for handling conflict itself, are likely to make future interactions more difficult.

Conflict is inevitable in most workteams. In part, this is due to the fact that teams represent interdependent relationships where roles and responsibilities are often either not well-defined or change frequently to meet the requirements of changing task or project requirements (e.g. Greenberg and Baron, 1995). Some might argue, as well, that conflict is even more likely to occur in diverse workteams where members have a broader range of knowledge, skills, abilities, and experiences. For example, based upon their background and experiences, different members may have totally different approaches to problem-solving and decision-making which must be reconciled in order to avoid or minimize conflict. On the other hand, conflict can contribute to workteam effectiveness and ultimately organizational effectiveness by bringing problems out in the open (e.g. Baron, 1991), and by motivating people to learn more about each other's viewpoint (e.g. Tjosvold, 1985). This in turn can lead to the generation of new ideas and approaches to solving problems, and making better decisions. These benefits only will occur, however, if the workteam adopts procedures that allow it to successfully resolve conflict situations.

In light of the research findings reported above for cultural differences in preferences for conflict resolution strategies, one might speculate that a diverse workteam composed of members from different cultural backgrounds might have more difficulty successfully resolving conflict. That is, members are less likely to be satisfied with the manner in which conflict may be handled because of their differing preferences. The short-term and long-term costs of not handling conflict effectively can be devastating. These teams are likely to provide less pleasant and comfortable environments for their members. Conflicts resulting from preferences for different resolution strategies also increase the likelihood that negative stereotyping will occur. For example, on a global workteam, Americans using a dominating strategy might be perceived by members from China and Taiwan to be hostile and unpleasant. This can, in turn, lead to process losses in a number of ways. Individuals may not fully share their ideas, knowledge, or other resources that they might otherwise contribute, and they may be reluctant to openly discuss issues or volunteer alternative approaches or solutions to a problem. Moreover, because they are apt to feel less comfortable with the team, they may be less attracted to it, become less motivated to work on its task, and as a result, engage in withdrawal behaviors, like showing up late for team meetings or being absent more frequently.

Misinterpreting nonverbal cues

Nonverbal cues are important sources of information in team interactions. In their recent discussion of social interaction processes in groups, Hare and Davies (1994) underscore the critical role nonverbal communication can play, "Nonverbal behavior has held special interest because it is often less consciously controlled and may contradict as well as amplify behavior" (p. 169). The use of space, eye contact, body orientation, head movements and other behaviors are often used to transmit messages without the use of words. Early work in the area estimated that over 65 percent, and as much as 90 percent of the social meaning of a situation is transmitted through nonverbal behaviors (e.g. Birdwhistle, 1970; Mehrabian, 1972). When people receive conflicting verbal and nonverbal messages, they often rely more heavily on the nonverbal than the verbal communication of the speaker (e.g. Bugental et al., 1970; Mehrabian, 1972). An example is when someone is asked how they are and they respond, "Fine," yet if they are crying, have a scowling facial expression, or if their voice is sharp, we tend not to believe that they indeed are "fine."

Research evidence has demonstrated that people may attribute personality traits, attitudes, and other characteristics to others on the basis of their nonverbal behavior (e.g. Ellsworth and Ludwig, 1972; Thompson et al., 1979). One consistent finding in the literature has been that people in the US generally have more positive attitudes toward individuals who display warmer nonverbal styles, which involve the use of more direct eye contact, body orientation, smiling, and a comfortable interpersonal distance (Aiello et al., 1993; Imada and Hakel, 1977; Thompson and Aiello, 1988). People who display a warm nonverbal communication style have been perceived as more qualified, more motivated and competent (e.g. Imada and Hakel, 1977). People also have expressed a greater willingness to work overtime, and to go beyond the minimum job requirements, for a manager who uses this style during interaction (e.g. Thompson and Aiello, 1988). Similar uses of various other nonverbal behaviors to form judgements about people have been documented. For example, a high degree of eye contact during social interaction is interpreted as an indication of involvement and interest (e.g. Kendon, 1967) and closer physical proximity is also frequently viewed as a sign of friendliness (e.g. Aiello, 1987; Mehrabian, 1968; Patterson and Sechrest, 1970).

Cultural patterns   Early work by Hall (1966) postulated that differences in the nonverbal communication patterns of individuals from various ethnic and cultural backgrounds were reflective of varying cultural norms governing the regulation of social interaction. He presented qualitative but detailed descriptions of Mediterranean, and Latin-American cultures as highly sensory "contact" cultures, where people were more likely to live in close physical contact and exhibit close interpersonal distances. In contrast, northern European and Anglo-American societies were described as somewhat more reserved, "noncontact" cultures, which were more likely to display larger interaction distances.

While there has been very little research systematically examining interaction between members of different groups, cultural and subcultural differences in the use of nonverbal behavior have been documented by a number of investigators. For example, African-Americans and Anglo-Americans have been found to differ with regard to their spatial behavior, such that adult African-Americans stand farther apart than Anglos and maintain more indirect body and head orientations (see Aiello, 1987; Aiello and Thompson, 1980a, for reviews of this literature). Further, differences between African- and Anglo-Americans have been found in the use of eye contact (Exline et al., 1977; Fehr and Exline, 1978; La France and Mayo, 1976) and gestures and body movements (e.g. Cook, 1972).

A considerable number of studies also have shown that men and women in the US differ with regard to their nonverbal behavior patterns. For example, women prefer to sit at closer distances and maintain more direct body orientations than men (e.g. Aiello, 1972; 1977; Aiello and Thompson, 1980b) and utilize more eye contact (e.g. Aiello, 1972; Exline, 1963; Exline et al., 1965). For a more complete discussion of research in this area, see Aiello, 1987; Harper et al., 1978; Tannen, 1990; 1994.

Communication patterns among diverse team members Hall (1966) posited that these differences in nonverbal communication patterns may result in people from different cultural and gender backgrounds "misreading" each other in social encounters. Many diverse workteams provide the opportunity for a greater number of cross-cultural, cross-race, and cross-gender interactions. Consequently, they also provide greater opportunities for miscommunication and misunderstandings. This can impact on just about every social- and task-related function of the team, thereby resulting in numerous process losses. To illustrate, once a misunderstanding occurs, less information is likely to be exchanged among team members and more negative impressions and perceptions will be formed. This in turn will have an obvious impact on subsequent interactions among team members. The incomplete sharing or withholding of task-related information can seriously affect the resources with which the group has to work, the nature of the problem-solving and decision-making strategies employed, and the team's ability to come up with innovative ideas and solutions. The negative perceptions may also lead to negative stereotyping, a less comfortable atmosphere, tendency to avoid conflict (or increase conflict), and less cohesion. Clearly, such negative outcomes will contribute to process losses which, ultimately, reduce performance capabilities.

It is also of interest to note that there is really no systematic research studying the nonverbal communication processes of diverse workteams. Based on other research, however, one might speculate that the nature of the interaction patterns might be very different from what one might observe in more homogeneous teams. For example, Fugita et al. (1974) found that the kind and amount of behavior that occurred during a cross-race interview varied as a function of the race of both the interviewer and the interviewee. The nature of the exchange of nonverbal communication in a diverse workteam is also likely to be different from that found in a homogeneous workteam.

Nonverbal communication is a reciprocal process. When someone smiles at us, we often return the smile. It is important to note that this process occurs in part because people model each other's behavior. When group members do not share common social signals, the development of group cohesiveness may be hindered and the team may have greater difficulty establishing a positive social climate.

To illustrate this, a recent study by Butler and Geis (1990) found that competent, assertive female leaders received more negative nonverbal responses from group members, and fewer positive nonverbal responses, than men offering the same suggestions and arguments. It is conceivable that diverse team members may rely even more heavily on nonverbal cues and other social behaviors than homogeneous teams to form impressions and make judgements about each other. Some support for this notion comes from research which indicates that there is a tendency to evaluate black leaders more heavily on relationship, rather than task-oriented factors (e.g. Bartol et al., 1978; Cox and Nkomo, 1986; Richards and Jaffe, 1972). Moreover, communication styles that are perceived to differ from the "norm" in organizations often have been suggested as one of the key factors impeding the successful advancement of blacks and other minorities into middle-level and upper-level management positions (e.g. Thompson and DiTomaso, 1988).

In sum, one can see that while the nonverbal behavior of its members might affect the social interaction process and effectiveness of any workteam, it is likely to have an even greater impact on the functioning of a diverse team. As the preceding discussion of research findings suggests, the nature of the communication process in diverse teams may be different from that found in homogeneous teams. Diverse workteams result in a greater number of cross-race, cross-cultural and cross-gender interactions. Research has demonstrated that the kind and amount of nonverbal behavior may vary as a function of the race, culture, and gender of the team members. These variations in behavior, in turn, may create opportunities for miscommunication because of conflicting nonverbal (as well as verbal) communication patterns. In order to prevent the potential process losses these miscommunications are likely to develop, diverse team members and leaders need to better understand the dynamics of the communication process.

More perceptual pitfalls

As seen above, differences associated with various dimensions of diversity may influence workteam members' perceptions of one another. As members of a team, individuals have many opportunities to gather, combine, integrate, and interpret information about each other. We already know from research on the use of nonverbal cues that people make inferences about what others are like from the behaviors they observe. The accuracy of these inferences gets muddled, however, by the very cognitive processing that occurs as people gather, sort, and interpret information about others.

To begin with, people tend to interpret others' behavior according to personal characteristics, yet evaluate their own behavior according to situational constraints. For example, a team member who misses a meeting might be judged as irresponsible or uncommitted to the team. In contrast, if you miss a meeting, you are likely to use situational factors (that you may see as beyond your control) to explain your behavior. Furthermore, when the behavior of others impacts us personally, we tend to assume the behavior is intentional. In the preceding example, the team member who missed the meeting might be evaluated as deliberately trying to sabotage the team.

People also have the tendency to assume that all members of specific groups share similar traits or behaviors. Known as stereotyping, this process of simplifying large amounts of data into narrower categories or dimensions is believed to provide a way to quickly make sense out of a lot of information, even though the process isn't necessarily accurate. At the same time, however, it is well known that people tend to assume that the behaviors of others can be explained according to the rules and expectations for living that we ourselves hold. Both of these types of judgements occur automatically, that is, unconsciously or unintentionally. Thus, members of diverse workteams may perceive fellow members who behave differently from themselves less positively if these observations conflict with their own values, or if they seem inappropriate or confusing, given the context within which they are working. When this happens, such evaluations may result in the negative stereotyping of other team members. These judgements, in turn, may influence the nature and frequency of interactions among team members (e.g. Stephan, 1985).

Research suggests that stereotyping is more likely to occur in diverse teams because visible dimensions of diversity (e.g. age, gender, race, nationality, disability) are more salient (e.g. Turner, 1987). Recent research findings provide confirming evidence that stereotyping is more likely to be spontaneously activated in diverse teams, even among members who believe that they are not prejudiced or biased (e.g. Devine et al., 1991). Attempts to suppress such negative feelings may leave individuals feeling uncomfortable and less positive about being a part of the team. The negative feelings may also be exacerbated if the organization has provided diversity awareness training for team members. Such training often serves to further underscore the inappropriateness and potential harmful effects stereotyping can have on organizational behavior and decision-making.

The tendency for individuals to perceive similar others more favorably than those who are dissimilar has a number of implications for the functioning of diverse workteams. Diverse team members may be less attracted initially to their teams because of this perceived dissimilarity. The extent to which members like one another impacts on the level and development of team cohesiveness. In highly cohesive teams, members are not only attracted to one another but are more likely to accept the group's goals and help work toward meeting them. In contrast, members often work at cross-purposes in teams that are not cohesive. Research on group composition has found that heterogeneous groups tend to be less cohesive than homogeneous ones (e.g. Hare et al., 1994).

Generally speaking, most people find it easier to communicate with others whom they perceive to be similar. Thus, diverse workteams are more likely to experience more communication difficulties (e.g. Fiedler, 1966; Mathews, 1982; Steiner, 1972). As research has shown, effective communication processes contribute to all major aspects of effective team functioning. For instance, the judgements we make about people have to do not only with what others are actually like, but our own characteristics as well (e.g. Greenberg and Baron, 1995). In a diverse team, members are likely to perceive the same behavior in others differently, based on their own personal characteristics, backgrounds, and experiences. There may be less agreement on the meaning of the messages being sent among members and as a result, it may take a diverse team longer to reach consensus. People also are more likely to interact with team members that they perceive as similar to themselves. This may lead to the formation of coalitions or subgroups within diverse teams. Hoffman (1965) reported that formal and informal meetings among peers and with immediate subordinates are lower in racially diverse groups.

The link between perceived similarity and positive attitudes has implications for the supportiveness of the climate a diverse workteam can establish for its members. George (1990) reported that negative affect in a group was found to be negatively associated with prosocial behavior initiated by group members. The climate can impact on other affective reactions, including the extent to which members perceive they "fit" with, or belong to, the team. Team members' motivation, performance, and inclination to stay may be affected as a result. Indirect support for this possibility can be found in more general research concerned with employee motivation, which has linked individuals' work attitudes to both withdrawal behaviors (e.g. lateness, absenteeism, turnover) and various aspects of performance (e.g. Katzell and Thompson, 1990; Thompson and Katzell, 1995). Additional indirect support can be found in Schneider's (1987) attraction–selection–attrition model and research on relational demography (e.g. Jackson et al., 1991; McCain et al., 1983; O'Reilly et al., 1989; Tsui and O'Reilly, 1989; Tsui et al., 1992), described earlier, which links diversity with less positive job attitudes and higher rates of absenteeism and turnover.

How Can We Enhance the Performance of Diverse Workteams?

As we have made clear, there are benefits to be gained from using diverse workteams. These benefits aren't a given, however. That is, they are *not* likely to occur unless the team is successfully managed. Diversity can have a tremendous impact on team members' perceptions, attitudes, and the processes with which they communicate with one another. This in turn, can have a tremendous impact on whether or not the team can capitalize on the wide range of knowledge, skills, abilities, and experiences it possesses.

So, how exactly does one successfully manage a diverse workteam? Unfortunately, there is currently no well-tested and accepted body of research or theory to guide practitioners in designing and using diverse teams to ensure that the advantages that can be gained by using them will be achieved. We do believe, however, that much of what we have learned about effective performance in workteams more generally, can be used to enhance the effectiveness of diverse teams. In this section, we will first briefly identify the fundamental characteristics of effective workteams. We will then highlight the importance of conducting a systematic assessment before launching any efforts to enhance the performance of a diverse team. Such an assessment will identify the specific needs and unique diversity issues which a particular team has to ensure that the interventions most relevant for improving the functioning of that specific team are implemented. We will then present a brief overview of organizational interventions that have been developed to improve the performance of workteams more generally. This will be followed by a more detailed discussion of techniques that may be particularly useful for addressing some issues that are more likely to arise in diverse teams. We strongly expect that these techniques will frequently enhance the effectiveness of diverse teams.

Characteristics of Effective Workteams

A useful starting-point for understanding how to best structure and develop diverse workteams is to examine factors known to be related to effective team functioning. Before doing so, it might be helpful to define what is typically meant by the term, team effectiveness. Common criteria for evaluating a team's effectiveness include both organizational outcomes (e.g. productivity, profits, increased creativity, innovation) and individual team-related outcomes (e.g. job satisfaction, cohesiveness, as well as motivation and commitment to remain on the team). While the actual criteria of effectiveness can be expected to vary according to the mandate of any given team, the characteristics of effective teams outlined in box 15.2 represent the structural design factors and team processes known to be critical for effective performance. These characteristics are based upon current models of workgroup effectiveness, which have their roots in earlier input–process–output models (similar to Steiner's model presented in figure 15.2). Unlike earlier models, they place a much greater emphasis on contextual influences of team performance, rather than on just intragroup factors (e.g. for more comprehensive reviews, see Gladstein, 1984; Goodman et al., 1988; Guzzo and Shea, 1992; Hackman, 1987; Hackman and Oldham, 1980).

The characteristics of effective work teams shown in box 15.2 are believed to be applicable to all different types of effectively performing teams.

Box 15.2 Characteristics of effective workteams

- Organizational context

  1 Supportive organizational climate The organization provides the team the requisite autonomy, informational and material resources, support, feedback and rewards that reinforce the team's work.

- Workteam structure and design factors

  2 Team mission The team has a clear understanding of its mission or purposes.

  3 Clearly defined objectives The team members all agree on the team's objectives which are clear, specific, and measurable.

  4 Role differentiation The responsibilities of each member of the team have been clearly defined.

  5 Team boundaries The team's roles, responsibilities, and outcomes are well differentiated from other teams of individuals in the organization's work units.

  6 Team composition The team members have the appropriate knowledge, skills, abilities, and motivation for the tasks they are assigned.

  7 Leadership One or more internal or external member serves to direct the team, keep it focused and provide needed coaching, informational and material resources.

- Team process issues

  8 Systematic planning The team has a well-formulated plan of how they will proceed before they begin any implementation. The team avoids a "bias for action."

  9 Effective team communication Members share information freely with all other members and use effective communication skills such as active listening techniques so that tensions, defensiveness and distortions in the communication process are minimized.

  10 Use of team resources The strengths, expertise, and ideas of each of the members are utilized throughout the lifespan of the work team.

  11 Accountability Each member of the team feels responsible and is held accountable for the team's performance. All members participate in discussions and decision-making.

  12 Supportive workteam climate A climate of shared norms and values is established in the team that includes: commitment to the task, openness to learning, candor, conviction to stand up for views, trust, encouragement of conflict (e.g. people are encouraged not to smooth over differences), freedom to experiment, and interest in one another as people.

13 Team synergy The team uses appropriate performance strategies (e.g. problem-solving, decision-making, and goal-setting skills) that optimize the achievement of work outcomes.

14 Evaluation The team takes the time to periodically evaluate its progress against the task-oriented goals as well as assess how that progress is being achieved (e.g. group processes). The team also monitors how it uses time to ensure that time is scheduled for each of the preceding factors.

As you can see, they include the organizational context as well as team structure and process factors. Each of them contributes both uniquely and jointly toward team effectiveness. All of these factors are important; they are also dependent upon one another. A deficiency in any one of them can impact on the overall effectiveness of the team. Design factors associated with effective teams include the team's mission, objectives, role differentiation, boundaries, composition, and leadership. On the other hand, team process issues associated with effective work teams include the extent to which members engage in interaction processes that result in the establishment of such things as systematic planning, accountability, effective communication, a supportive work climate, the full utilization of the team's resources and evaluation systems.

Conducting a Systematic Assessment of a Diverse Workteam

We believe the characteristics of effective workteams provide a useful framework for helping organizations assess the impact of diversity on team functioning. Using the set of effective team characteristics as a guideline for conducting an assessment, one might then begin to ask questions such as, is the team appropriately structured to foster effective performance? Does it, for example, have a clearly defined mission? Does it have the right mix of talents and expertise to get the job done? Are its boundaries clearly differentiated from other teams and groups in the organization? Do members know what roles they are to perform and do they have the appropriate leadership to guide them? Furthermore, does the team work well together, or are there deficits in team processes that inhibit optimum performance? Which, if any, processes are negatively impacted by diversity issues?

Any attempt to make a diverse team more effective must therefore begin with a careful assessment of what it is trying to accomplish and what it needs in terms of material, social, and technological resources to achieve its desired outcome(s). More importantly, it must include a systematic examination of how the organizational context, within which the diverse team has to operate, may be impinging on the team's performance. *The critical role that a team's work environment can play in determining its effectiveness must be underscored.* Both the manner in which members interact with one another and the team's performance effectiveness are likely to be a consequence of the way a team is set up and managed (Hackman, 1987). Groups that are well designed and well supported have a better chance of achieving excellence in process and in performance than do groups with poor designs or unsupportive organizational contexts.

Factors in the work environment that have been linked with team effectiveness include leadership (e.g. Kolodny and Kissundu, 1980); managerial support (Pearce and Ravlin, 1987); organizational structure (e.g. Gladstein, 1984); and reward systems (Shea and Guzzo, 1987). At the present time, we do not know exactly how, or in what unique ways, contextual factors may influence diverse workteams. While it is also beyond the scope of this chapter to speculate on all the possible ways the organizational environment may impact on a diverse team, we would like to suggest, however, that it may play an even more vital role in determining the effectiveness of a diverse team than other types of teams. Designing the team according to the set of characteristics just described may help ameliorate many of the ways in which diversity can potentially impact negatively on it (described in the preceding section). It may also be the case that an additional context variable that has not been examined for its impact on team performance, an organization's diversity climate, may impinge on a diverse team's effectiveness. The extent to which the organization has a history of fostering diversity or valuing differences may determine the ease with which a diverse workteam can establish a positive, supportive team climate which will in turn, enable it to function more effectively. It may prove useful, therefore, to conduct a systematic assessment of how well the organization is doing in providing a work environment that allows for the development of all employees. It would also be important to focus on which barriers, if any, may exist for certain subgroups of the employee population. This type of approach would provide important information about the kinds of work experiences and resources diverse team members bring to the group. We have recently developed a diagnostic tool, *VIEWS*, in order to provide such an assessment (Thompson et al., 1994).

Additional factors are also important to include in any systematic assessment of a workteam. These include determining what developmental stage the team is in (e.g. the forming, storming, norming, or adjourning stages identified by Tuckman, 1965) and the temporal dimension of the team's project (i.e. its awareness of time and deadlines, Gersick, 1988). Both of these factors have been shown to be relevant for understanding the needs of a team at any given stage of its lifespan. Given the advances in technology and the fact that team effectiveness is dependent upon how well its structure fits its technology and environment (e.g. Goodman et al., 1987), assessments must also include the technological aspects of team functioning and the fit between team structure and technology. These include the equipment, materials, physical environment, and programs, involved in acting on and/or changing an object from one state to another, that constrain and pattern group activity. Each of these factors must be evaluated with respect to how they impact on team effectiveness.

The strengths and weaknesses in team functioning identified by assessment can be used to design appropriate interventions to enhance the performance of a workteam. Without proper assessment of the multiplicity of factors affecting team functioning, *organizations may easily misread the cause of their team's troubles, and attempt to fix the wrong problem*. The reality is that such a systematic assessment is rarely done and, as is the case with other types of organizational interventions, pre-packaged or pre-developed programs are usually used in attempts to improve team functioning. Because of the complexity associated with diverse teams, such programs may not only fail to produce their desired effects, but may further contribute to the deterioration of team functioning. Tailoring an intervention to meet the specific needs of the diverse workteam identified by an assessment is more likely to result in the desired enhancement of the team's performance.

Interventions to Enhance Team Performance

The primary ways in which companies attempt to optimize on the talents and skills of their workteams are through team development or team building interventions. The objectives of these programs are to remove barriers to effective group functioning and to develop within a group the ability to manage group process in order to more effectively solve future problems. Team development often follows an action research model, which incorporates the processes of collecting information about the team, feeding that information back to the team, and developing action plans based on this information (e.g. Woodman and Sherwood, 1980). There are many types of team development interventions and, like any organizational development effort, they can be classified in terms of the organizational issues they are intended to resolve. The four main types of interventions include interpersonal process, goal-setting, role definition and problem-solving interventions (e.g. Beer, 1976; Sundstrom et al., 1990). A brief description of each of these can be found in box 15.3.

Reviews of research designed to evaluate the effectiveness of team development interventions indicate that while such efforts do tend to have consistently positive effects on members' perceptions and attitudes toward one another and the team, they do not necessarily enhance team performance (e.g. Buller and Bell, 1986; Shea and Guzzo, 1987; Sundstrom et al., 1990; Woodman and Sherwood, 1980). This is particularly true for team development programs that only focus on the social interaction among members. Those that incorporate an emphasis on task-related interactions (e.g. clarification of goals, delineation of roles and responsibilities) are somewhat more likely to be related to improved task performance. Several criticisms have been offered as to why researchers' attempts to develop teams or

> **Box 15.3** Main types of team building interventions
>
> 1 *Interpersonal process interventions* assume that teams operate best with mutual trust and open communication. Attempt to build cohesion by facilitating candid discussions of relationships and conflicts among members, often directed toward resolving "hidden agendas."
>
> 2 *Goal-setting interventions* involve clarifying the team's general goals and specific objectives, sometimes by defining subtasks and establishing timetables. Often combined with performance measurement and feedback.
>
> 3 *Role definition interventions* entail clarifying individual role expectations, group norms, and shared responsibility of members.
>
> 4 *Problem-solving interventions* clarify task-related processes within the group, such as identifying problems, causes, and solutions, and developing and implementing action plans.

successfully intervene have failed to have a positive impact on performance. Among them are: researchers' failure to consider all of the relevant factors affecting team functioning, such as the physical, temporal, and social contexts in which groups exist; their failure to implement change programs that actually impact on the factors that most directly affect performance; and their failure to use evaluation criteria that adequately reflect aspects of team functioning (e.g. see McGrath, 1991; Ancona, 1987).

In spite of this failure to link team development and performance, these interventions have already provided organizations with a number of tools (e.g. team building, goal-setting, brainstorming, decision-making techniques) and technologies (e.g. computer networks, email, teleconferencing) that may be used in their efforts to extract the benefits of diversity among their workteams. However, as noted above, the appropriateness and use of these tools or technologies depend on the degree to which organizations can successfully identify (and in some cases, manipulate or gain control over) the variety of diversity-related factors that impact upon team functioning and those which may contribute to process losses. We will next explore how some of these techniques can be used to enhance the performance of diverse workteams.

Some Techniques for Improving the Effectiveness of Diverse Workteams

As we noted earlier, evidence does exist that various dimensions of diversity are associated with a number of factors that can contribute to process losses and prevent the team from reaching its full potential. The number and types of diversity-related problems that can affect the functioning of a diverse team are potentially great, and can be expected to vary according to the design and mandate of any given team. In our review, we highlighted several dimensions related to team conflict. We also explored how differences among diverse members' verbal and nonverbal communication styles can lead to various negative outcomes and process losses, including negative stereotyping and unwillingness to work closely with others who are different. We also showed how people's natural perceptual processes can contribute to process losses in terms of the nature and frequency of interaction. The following review describes team development interventions for these and other issues most commonly attributed to diversity among team members.

Resolving team conflict

Research suggests that conflict among team members tends to be beneficial up to a point, and beyond that level, it becomes detrimental (e.g. Wall and Nolan, 1986). Conflict is believed to facilitate processes such as decision-making, as long as it serves to encourage the airing of different ideas and an examination of alternative solutions that otherwise might be too quickly accepted or rejected. The presence of conflict may also cause members to become more involved in the decision-making process. In contrast, conflict is viewed as destructive to team processes when it escalates beyond the initial causes, takes on a life of its own, drains the team of needed energy, or motivates any of the involved parties to try to destroy the others (e.g. Wall et al., 1987).

Several major team design and composition factors have been identified as contributors to team conflict. As shown in box 15.4, these range from the personality characteristics of the individuals involved in the conflict to the sharing of common resources by the team members (for more detailed reviews, see Knutson, 1985; Thomas, 1976; Walton and Dutton, 1969). Different theories posit how these factors are believed to lead to conflict among team members through: the degree of similarity between members; perceived inequity by individuals within the team (e.g. Wall and Nolan, 1987); the quality and amount of contact occurring between members (e.g. Nelson, 1989); and the nature of the team's communication patterns (Bales and Cohen, 1979).

To illustrate, both verbal and nonverbal communication messages express, create, or resolve conflict in different ways. These messages are often believed to depend upon members' personalities or team norms that have developed regarding how members should communicate or behave with one another (e.g. Bales and Cohen, 1979). For example, members may recognize and resolve problems by communicating their views in an assertive and procedural way. Or, they may challenge the group to express their inner emotions. Others may tend to display uncooperative or self-serving behaviors which may result in frequent disagreements within the group as well as estrangement from other members. In contrast, they may act in a

---

Box 15.4   Team design and team composition factors contributing to team conflict

1   Personality characteristics of the conflicting parties.

2   The style of interaction that gets set at the initial formation of the team, which is subsequently reinforced and sustained by individuals either internal or external to the team.

3   Whether competition or cooperation is rewarded.

4   Rules and procedures governing decision-making when conflict arises.

5   The cultural context through which different groups interact.

6   Communication obstacles.

7   Mutual dependencies whereby two or more individuals or groups depend upon each other for assistance, information, and coordination.

8   Role dissatisfaction.

9   Ambiguous goals, roles, and responsibilities.

10   Dependence on common resources.

---

very friendly manner by engaging in active listening and involvement. Some individuals may seek to dominate the team's discussions and opinions, while others may display submissive behaviors. Such inclinations must be explored in teams in order to resolve conflict effectively. For instance, a dominant member can easily lead the team astray if she or he is providing the team with erroneous information. This type of individual prevents the team from exploring ideas that contradict her/his own. At the same time, a submissive person may withhold information from the team that is necessary for successful completion of the task. This type of member is limiting the team's resources.

In trying to understand the sources of team conflict, it is also useful to pay attention to the communication dimensions the team employs at each phase of the decision-making process, before it arrives at a solution. Examining the different communication dimensions and communication styles used by members can help a team diagnose sources of conflict and can lead to the selection of an appropriate solution. Depending upon the root of the intragroup conflict, interventions can be behaviorally oriented, and attempt to change members' behaviors, attitudes, values, norms, or beliefs. They can also be structurally oriented, and focus on changing the team's structural design characteristics. For example, if the conflict stems from miscommunication and misunderstandings between members, one effective behavioral strategy is for individuals to engage in active listening and an improvement of their observational skills. Active listening involves paraphrasing other members' verbal and nonverbal messages (Penn and Bolding, 1974) and can help members identify the emotional messages that are often hidden in communication. Active listeners have been found to be more accepting of other ideas and often do not ignore ideas that contradict their own (e.g. Penn and Bolding, 1974). For a more comprehensive discussion of these and other strategies for dealing with group conflict, see the review by Rahim (1985).

Perceptions: how to see what's really there

We often are told that first impressions are very important. And while we are advised never to "judge a book by its cover," there is considerable evidence that people often do just that – make judgements on the basis of appearance alone. Such judgements involve a set of inferences as to what the person we see is like "underneath." However, we do not respond to others simply on the basis of their external characteristics. Rather, our experiences also provide a strong role in shaping our knowledge of and expectations about others. This was illustrated most recently in a study by Thomas and Ravlin (1995), examining responses of American subordinates (who had experience with Japanese managers through their employment with Japanese-owned firms in the US) to a Japanese manager who displayed American behavior patterns. Interestingly, the responses of the participants to the manager were not uniformly positive or negative. Rather, they were related in part to the fact that the participants had different expectations or stereotypes about managerial behavior based on the nationality (American or Japanese) of the manager. Culturally adaptive behavior had the anticipated positive effect on subordinates' perceptions to the extent that it matched these expectations and induced perceptions of similarity between the manager and the subordinate.

Clarifying team members' perceptions about others who are different from them requires them to gain an understanding of their own perceptual organizing processes. That is, they need to learn more about how they take in information about others, store and retrieve it from their memories, and how they use that information to explain the behaviors they observe. Moreover, they need to learn that because people often have limited experience with others who are different from them, they are prone to errors in judgement that cause them to quickly and unconsciously judge and categorize the behavior of others. The challenge for organizations, therefore, is to teach the members of their diverse workteams how their backgrounds and experiences provide the framework through which they perceive the world. They need to learn how to stop and reconsider the assumptions and conclusions they make about their teammates, who are different from them. This will require raising their awareness of cultural differences and interaction processes, as well as their own cognitions.

Raising awareness of cultural differences In one of the earliest studies examining interaction between members of different cultural groups, Collett (1971) investigated the feasibility of training English students in "Arab-like" nonverbal behaviors, so that they could communicate more effectively with Arab students. Results indicated that the Arab students preferred the Englishmen who had been trained to exhibit "Arab-like" behavior. Initial training efforts in cultural differences largely focused on improving the effectiveness of individuals working in foreign countries and counselors with their patients. Examples of early multicultural training programs include the Culture Assimilator developed by Fiedler et al. (1970), the Contrast American Method developed by Stewart et al. (1969) and the Minnesota Multiethnic Counselor Education Curriculum by Johnson (1982). For a more thorough comparison of these programs, interested readers are invited to read the review by Johnson (1987).

Diversity training is the primary tool used in most organizations today to raise employee awareness and understanding of the impact of diversity. A recent study by the Conference Board (1994) found that more than 60 percent of the companies they surveyed had diversity training programs and even more were planning to implement one. The content of most of these programs places a very strong emphasis on race, gender, and compliance topics, such as sexual harassment and affirmative action. Other topics include: stereotypes, ethnicity, business objectives, age, and sexual orientation. This study also found that among the variety of educational tools used to teach about diversity, participative exercises, followed by videos, were rated most effective.

Most diversity training programs do appear to raise awareness about differences and some of the impact that behavior can have on others. Unfortunately, there appear to be several factors that inhibit the successful attitude change required for valuing diversity. To begin with, stereotypes are powerful and people have a tendency to discount information that contradicts stereotypic beliefs and thoughts. That is, stereotypes tend to remain intact even in the presence of disconfirming information (e.g. Rothbart and John, 1985). An example is that when I meet a black, female nuclear physicist, I am likely to think that person is not a typical African-American, or typical female. In addition, most information provided to break down the stereotypes or to falsify the myths attached to various groups of individuals is provided in absence of the requisite skills or new behaviors that are needed in the workplace to effectively deal with diversity issues.

Faulty training program design factors also contribute to the relative ineffectiveness of diversity training programs. For example, these training efforts are usually not tailored to the specific needs of an organization. Often, they are short (e.g. 3 or 4 hours) and are a mandatory requirement for all employees. One critical factor behind their ineffectiveness may be the failure of organizations to identify criteria for what constitutes "cultural expertise," (.e.g. Johnson, 1987), which represents the knowledge, skills, and abilities required for multicultural interaction. This is commonly associated with a lack of clear objectives for the overall training program. It is also of interest to note that diversity training is rarely conducted with intact diverse workteams, which could help members to understand the diversity issues that are unique to their team or to their organization. In addition, most corporate cultures do not promote an atmosphere of confrontation and discussion of these issues. Avoidance is a more typical response. So, when individuals return from their diversity training programs, the dominant culture is not likely to be open to discussions on how diversity impacts on team interactions. In many cases, the diversity training itself may exacerbate the perceptions of differences among subgroups of the employee population. Group polarization may result, along with the perception that some groups are treated more fairly than others in the organization.

Nevertheless, we believe that if done correctly, diversity awareness training can be a useful tool for helping diverse team members to gain an understanding of how diversity is currently impacting, and potentially could impact on the functioning of their team. Further, we suggest that it may be critical to the long-term effectiveness of a diverse team to spend a considerable amount of time when the team is initially formed on such an educational effort because of the numerous ways diversity can affect both team design and team process factors related to high-performing teams.

Overcoming stereotypes and prejudice All people have the tendency to make assumptions about others and to classify them into categories that make them easier to comprehend. As indicated earlier, a stereotype is a set of traits or characteristics ascribed to all members of a social group. Stereo-types influence how we process information about others. Since they are often inaccurate, they can lead to negative or unfair evaluation and treatment of others who are different from ourselves (e.g. Schaller and Maass, 1989). This is due, in part, to ethnocentrism and an overall lack of understanding about other cultures and their values and practices.

There are several strategies that organizations might use to combat the use of stereotypes among diverse workteam members. Although stereotypes are resistant to change, we do know that they can be altered when people encounter enough contradictory information. Sometimes, organizations use diversity awareness training to provide this type of information, so that employees gain a better understanding of what stereotypes are and how they might impact negatively on team interactions. Another strategy might involve increasing the amount of contact members have with "different" others (e.g. Hewstone and Brown, 1986). This is based on the contact hypothesis, which states that, in general, the more interpersonal contact we have with different others, the less likely we are to misinterpret their behavior and to hold stereotyped notions about them (Allport, 1954; Brewer and Miller, 1984; Hewstone and Brown, 1986; Pettigrew, 1986; Rothbart and John, 1985; Stephan, 1985; 1987; Stephan and Stephan, 1985).

By their very nature, diverse teams may provide an opportunity for people to have contact with diverse others. Contact is assumed to lead to greater perceptions of similarity and, subsequently, higher levels of mutual attraction. As people spend more time together and get to know one another, it is likely that they will be exposed to information that is inconsistent with their stereotypic beliefs. However, evidence exists that simply increasing contact may not result in the reduction of stereotypes and prejudice. Rather, certain conditions must be met for contact to be effective (e.g. Aronson et al., 1978; Cook, 1985; Riordan, 1978; Wilder, 1984). For example, the people interacting must be approximately equal in status (e.g. social, economic, or task-related) and must be cooperatively working together to achieve shared goals. To some extent, the contact must also be informal, so that they get to know one another on a one-to-one basis. They must communicate in a way that disconfirms negative stereotypes which they may have about one another. Lastly, the contact should take place in a setting that fosters equality.

If care is taken to design and ensure that a diverse workteam has the characteristics of effective teams described earlier, then it is likely that these conditions will be met. As a result, the use of stereotypes will decrease among members. Research also suggests that friendly, cooperative contact among diverse others can result in increased liking and respect (Cook, 1984). In light of these findings, diverse teams may serve as a vehicle for fostering the organization's overall diversity efforts.

Other interventions to combat the use of stereotypes and prejudice might focus on teaching diverse team members to pay close attention to fellow teammates' personal attributes, rather than the groups to which they belong (e.g. race, ethnic background, or gender). A series of studies by Fiske and her colleagues (e.g. Erber and Fiske, 1984; Fiske, 1989; Fiske and Neuberg, 1990) suggests that telling people that it is important to form an accurate impression of another person or that their own fate is dependent on that person's performance can motivate them to form accurate impressions of the individual and reduce their tendency to rely on stereotypes.

Additional ways to achieve an understanding and acceptance of differences involve active efforts to bring these issues out in the open to discuss them, along with teaching diverse members to be more open-minded. Discarding stereotypes requires people to actively work at not assuming they know the rules or intentions behind someone's behavior. This can be achieved, in part, by teaching members to practice "shifting perceptions." When evaluating each other's behavior, they need to consider how they are viewing their teammate and the situation, as well as how their teammate may be viewing them and the situation. Lastly, teaching members not to tolerate racist, sexist, or other biased behaviors is critical. This holds true whether or not the behavior is directed at fellow members or at someone else outside of the diverse work team.

Overcoming other errors in judgement   Many of the difficulties incurred by diverse individuals working together involve the degree to which they can accurately understand the motives and intentions behind others' behavior. Training in how we process information and make judgements about our own behavior and others can help meet this goal. Several theories have been developed that describe how individuals use information to arrive at causal explanations for events. These include: Heider's theory of naive psychology (1944; 1958), Jones and Davis's correspondent inference theory (1965), Kelley's theory of causal attribution (1967; 1972), and Weiner's attribution model (1979; 1980). According to Fiske and Taylor (1991), these theories can be classified as normative (i.e. they outline the appropriate norms or guidelines for how a cognitive process should proceed) or as spontaneous (i.e. the social perceiver appears to seize upon a sufficient causal explanation without performing the additional cognitive work to determine if it is accurate or the best causal explanation).

Understanding the motives and intentions behind others' behavior also requires an understanding of how we may "misperceive" the information and facts we take in about diverse others. As noted earlier, we all have the tendency, to some extent, to infer that someone's behavior that affects us personally is intentional. In addition, we have a tendency to judge other people's behavior based on personal characteristics, but to judge our own in terms of situational constraints. Also, we tend to assume that the behaviors of others can be judged according to the rules and values of our own culture. While there really are not any specific interventions designed to overcome perceptual errors in workteams, educating diverse members about how people process information, and make judgements about others, can help avoid some of the perceptual pitfalls that may lead to potential process losses.

Improving communication

As we have shown, communication is likely to be more difficult among diverse team members. A number of techniques have been developed to improve team decision-making more generally which also may be useful for addressing some of the communication issues that often arise in diverse teams. These techniques (e.g. the Delphi technique, the nominal group technique) are used to structure the team discussion to keep it focused with balanced participation among members, so that everyone's ideas are heard and are relevant to the task (e.g. Dalkey, 1969; Van de Ven and Delbecq, 1971).

Decision-making techniques can affect the quality of the team's decision, the amount of time it takes to reach a decision and the commitment that members may have to their decision (e.g. Stumpf et al., 1979). These tradeoffs must be considered when decisions are made to employ one of these techniques. Research suggests, for example, that the Delphi and nominal group techniques may result in better decisions than simply having team members interact with one another because they require less face-to-face contact (e.g. Gustafson et al., 1973). Diverse teams might benefit from using these techniques in the *early* stages of their development, since they provide the opportunity for more balanced participation among members. This would allow members to see the value of the different resources and perspectives each of them brings to the team and control the potential negative impact of stereotyping, prejudice and other perceptual biases. However, since these techniques may result in groups being less likely to accept and become committed to their decisions, eventually teams should also engage in face-to-face decision-making.

A study by Schweiger et al. (1989) compared the effectiveness of dialectical inquiry, devil's advocacy, and consensus approaches to group strategic decision-making. Both dialectical inquiry and devil's advocacy approaches encouraged conflict among group members through formalized debate. No differences were found between the two approaches on group members' reactions, critical reevaluation, meeting duration and performance. However, compared with the consensus approach, both of them lead to better assumptions and recommendations, as well as to a higher level of critical reevaluation among members. These results suggest that debate itself, through its presence, rather than its format, improves group performance by formalizing and legitimizing conflict and encouraging critical evaluation. With all three approaches, experience improved performance. On the cost side, both dialectic and devil's advocacy approaches initially consumed more meeting time than the consensus approach. However, these differences disappeared, suggesting that groups gain procedural efficiency with modest experience in the two conflict approaches. It may be fruitful to use debate-encouraging approaches, such as these, with diverse workteams facing strategic decisions. Formally requiring conflict among the team members by using these techniques may enhance the likelihood that all of the diverse perspectives of the members will be considered in the decision-making process. It may also help members value and encourage debate over their different views, opinions and perspectives, which can result in more creative and better-quality decisions.

The decision-making effectiveness of diverse teams may also be enhanced if members receive some individual training in effective problem-solving and decision-making techniques. The skills of individual members can have a significant impact on how well the team performs. Some support for this can be found in a study by Bottger and Yetton (1987), which found that the number of mistakes made by groups attempting to solve a creative problem was significantly reduced by training the individual members to avoid several types of common errors. However, in a culturally diverse team, additional training may be necessary since people from various cultures may differ in how they approach decision-making even when using the same basic steps (e.g. Adler, 1991; Roth, 1992). Thus, it may greatly enhance the decision-making capabilities of the team, if members understand their cultural differences in decision-making processes (e.g. determining: if a problem exists, the nature of the decision-making process, the time required to make a decision, or the appropriate implementation of a decision) that the members bring to the team.

Using technology to enhance team functioning

Advances in computing and communication capabilities are becoming widely available to teams to help them work more effectively and efficiently.

425

It is now possible, for example, to design integrated computing and information technology into a cohesive network, providing corporate-wide information for decision-making. Computer systems are now extended outward to link companies with their suppliers, distribution channels, consumers, and business partners. This "extended reach" enables the recasting of relationships with external organizations and with employees in geographically dispersed locations. In fact, information technology can enable an organization to have high-performing teams by allowing geographically dispersed individuals to function as integrated teams.

The most recent trend of potential value to diverse teams is the development of group support systems (GSS). These systems are "information aids" designed to support communication among group members (e.g. Pinsonneault and Kraemer, 1989). GSS are defined as contextual variables that affect outcomes indirectly through their effects on task and communication processes (McLeod, 1992). Examples include teleconferencing and email. These can be contrasted with group decision support systems (GDSS), which provide a structured approach for the group to use when working on a decision-making task. Examples of GDSS include decision room software, or an automated Nominal Group Technique. In a recent experiment, Gallupe et al. (1992) found that groups that brainstormed electronically (using computer terminals) generated more high-quality decisions than groups using the traditional face-to-face method.

In a review of experimental studies published between 1980 and 1990 focusing on the relationship between the use of electronic GSS and group process and outcomes, McLeod (1992) found that GSS leads to increased task focus, increased equality of participation, higher decision quality, longer time to reach a decision, lower consensus, and lower satisfaction. Although McLeod's findings suggest that GSS improves decision quality, she argues that the use of these systems may not improve overall group performance. She further cautions that the generalizability of these research findings to intact work groups in organizations may be limited because of the research designs that were employed. For example, groups in experimental conditions tended to use an electronic communication channel exclusively, whereas groups in control conditions met face-to-face. Computer supported groups also had software that mediated their task work, whereas groups without computer support did not. In some cases, the software actually presented a specific structure or strategy for working on the task. In all cases however, the software at least facilitated task communication.

Summary

Diverse workteams are here to stay. Teams in many of today's organizations are characterized by increasing diversity and will continue to be so in the future. As we have seen, while evidence exists that there are potential benefits to using diverse teams, there are potential costs as well. Diversity can have a tremendous impact on the functioning of a team. The key finding from our review is clearly that effective diverse teams don't just happen. Rather, they must be designed, implemented, and managed in order to maximize the potential advantages and minimize the potential disadvantages. It may be particularly important to pay attention to the organizational context within which they must operate. As we have noted, the extent to which an organization has a history of fostering diversity or valuing differences may impact on the functioning and effectiveness of diverse teams. These, in turn, have the potential to either enhance or thwart an organization's efforts to foster diversity.

When we look back over our chapter, we are struck by the number of times we noted the lack of research that has actually been done to examine the effects of diversity on real or natural teams. There is a tremendous need for more research that defines diversity along the wide range of dimensions of concern to organizations. This research needs to explore such questions as: how diversity impacts on team functioning over time, what leadership skills are required for leading diverse teams, and how contextual factors in the organization impact on diverse teams.

Consistent with this, we reported a lack of intervention techniques designed to specifically address some of the special issues that are more likely to arise in diverse teams. We would like to encourage the writing of case studies of both successful and unsuccessful organizational experiences with such teams so that we can begin to build our knowledge base of which techniques work and which don't. Evaluation or assessment tools that organizations can use to diagnose team problems to determine if they are caused by diversity issues or structural factors are needed so that appropriate interventions can be designed to ensure team effectiveness. Other measurement systems that would allow organizations to track the development of diverse teams or measure their effectiveness would also be of considerable value.

In sum, the potential benefits of using diverse workteams for fostering an organization's diversity efforts, enhancing organizational effectiveness and providing the competitive edge in the marketplace are great. Future research and practice is expected to play an important role in ensuring the effectiveness of diverse workteams.

REFERENCES

Aamodt, M. G., and Kimbrough, W. (1982). Effect of group heterogeneity on quality of task solutions. *Psychological Reports*, 50, 171–4.

Adams, J. L. (1979). *Conceptual Blockbusting! A Guide to Better Ideas*, 2nd ed. New York: W. W. Norton.

Adler, N. (1986). *International Dimensions of Organizational Behavior*. Boston: Kent Publishing.

Adler, N. J. (1991). *International Dimensions of Organizational Behavior*, 2nd ed. Boston: Plus-Kent.

Aiello, J. R. (1972). A test of equilibrium theory: Visual interaction in relation to alienation, distance, and sex of interactants. *Psychonomic Science*, 27, 335–6.

Aiello, J. R. (1977). A further look at equilibrium theory: Visual interaction as a function of interpersonal distance. *Environmental Psychology and Nonverbal Behavior*, 1: 120–40.

Aiello, J. R. (1987). Human spatial behavior. In D. Stokols and I. Altman (eds), *Handbook of Environmental Psychology*. New York: John Wiley and Sons.

Aiello, J. R., and Aiello, T. D. (1974). The development of personal space: Proxemic behavior of children 6 through 16. *Human Ecology*, 2, 177–89.

Aiello, J. R., Kirkhoff, K. L., and Jussim, L. (1993). Effects of manager feedback and nonverbal behavior on employee attitudes, motivation, and behavior. Unpublished manuscript. Rutgers University.

Aiello, J. R., and Thompson, D. E. (1980a). Personal space, crowding, and spatial behavior in a cultural context. In I. Altman, J. F. Wohlwill, and A. Rapaport (eds), *Human Behavior and Environment*, Volume 4: *Environment and Culture*. New York: Plenum Press.

Aiello, J. R., and Thompson, D. E. (1980b). When compensation fails: Mediating effects of sex and locus of control at extended interaction distances. *Basic and Applied Social Psychology*, 1, 65–81.

Alderfer, C. P., Tucker, R. C., Morgan, D. R., and Drasgow, F. (1983). Black and white cognitions of changing race relations. *Journal of Occupational Behavior*, 4, 105–36.

Allport, G. W. (1954). *The Nature of Prejudice*. Reading, MA: Addison-Wesley.

Ancona, D. G. (1987). Group in organizations: Extending laboratory models. In C. Hendrick (ed.), *Groups Processes and Intergroup Relations* (207–30). Newbury Park, CA: Sage.

Anderson, L. R. (1983). Management of the mixed-cultural work group. *Organizational Behavior and Human Performance*, 31, 303–30.

Aronson, E., Bridgeman, P. L., and Geffner, R. (1978). Interdependent interactions and prosocial behavior. *Journal of Research and Development in Education*, 12(1), 16–27.

Bales, R. F., and Cohen, S. P. (1979). *SYMLOG: A System for the Multiple Level Observation of Groups*. New York: Free Press.

Bantel, K. A., and Jackson, S. E. (1989). Top management and innovations in banking: Does the composition of the top team make a difference? *Strategic Management Journal*, 10, 108–24.

Baron, R. A. (1991). Positive effects of conflict: A cognitive perspective. Special issue: Positive Conflict. *Employee Responsibilities and Rights Journal*, 4(1), 25–36.

Bartol, K. M., Evans, C. L., and Stith, M. T. (1978). Black vs. white leaders: A comparative review of the literature. *Academy of Management Review*, 3, 393–404.

Bassin, M. (1988). Teamwork at General Foods: New and improved. *Personnel Journal*, 67, 62–70.

Beer, M. (1976). The technology of organizational development. In M. D. Dunnette (ed.), *Handbook of Industrial Organizational Psychology*. Chicago: Rand McNally.

Birdwhistle, R. L. (1970). *Kinesics and Context*. Philadelphia: University of Pennsylvania Press.

Bottger, P. C., and Yetton, P. W. (1987). An integration of process and decision scheme explanations of group problem-solving performance. *Organizational Behavior and Human Decision Processes*, 42, 234–42.

Brewer, M. B., and Miller, N. (1984). Beyond the contact hypothesis: Theoretical perspectives on desegregation. In N. Miller and M. B. Brewer (eds), *Groups in Contact: The Psychology of Desegregation* (287–302). San Diego, CA: Academic Press.

Bugental, D. E., Kaswan, J. E., and Love, L. R. (1970). Perception of contradictory meanings conveyed by verbal and nonverbal channels. *Journal of Personality and Social Psychology*, 16, 647–55.

Buller, P. F., and Bell, C. H. (1986). Effects of team building and goal setting on productivity: A field experiment. *Academy of Management Journal*, 29(2), 305–28.

Butler, P., and Geis, F. L. (1990). Nonverbal affect responses to male and female leaders: Implications for leadership evaluations. *IPSP*, 58(1), 48–59.

Carli, L. L. (1989). Gender differences in interaction style and influence. *Journal of Personality and Social Psychology*, 56, 565–76.

Carpenter, S. (1993). Organization of in-group and out-group information: The influence of gender-role orientation. *Social Cognition*, 11(1), 70–91.

Cohen, B. P., and Zhou, X. (1991). Status processes in enduring work groups. *American Sociological Review*, 56(2), 179–88.

Colarelli, S. M., and Boos, A. L. (1992). Sociometric and ability-based assignment to work groups: Some implications for personnel selection. *Journal of Organizational Behavior*, 13(2), 187–96.

Collett, D. (1971). Training Englishmen in the nonverbal behavior of Arabs. *International Journal of Psychology*, 6, 209–15.

Cook, B. G. (1972). Nonverbal communication among Afro-Americans: An initial classification. In T. Kochman (ed.), *Rappin' and Stylin' Out! Communication in Urban Black America*. Urbana: University of Illinois Press.

Cook, S. W. (1984). Cooperative interaction in multiethnic contexts. In N. Miller and M. B. Brewer (eds), *Groups in Contact: The Psychology of Desegregation* (281–302). San Diego, CA: Academic Press.

Cook, S. W. (1985). Experimenting on social issues: The case of school desegregation. *American Psychologist*, 40, 452–60.

Copeland, L. (1988). Valuing diversity: Making the most of cultural differences at the workplace. *Personnel*, 65(6), 52–60.

Cote, J. A., and Tansuhaj, P. S. (1989). Culture-bound assumptions in behavior intention models. *Advances in Consumer Research*, 16, 105–9.

Cox, T. (1991). The multicultural organization. *Academy of Management Executive*, 5, 34–47.

Cox, T. H. (1993). *Cultural Diversity in Organizations*. San Francisco: Berrett-Koehler.

Cox, T. H., Lobel, S. A., and McLeod, P. L. (1991). Effects of ethnic group cultural differences on cooperative and competitive behavior on a group task. *Academy of Management Journal*, 34(4), 827–47.

Cox, T. H., and Nkomo, S. M. (1986). Differential appraisal criteria based on race of the ratee. *Group and Organizational Studies*, 11, 109–19.

Dalkey, N. (1969). *The Delphi Method: An Experimental Study of Group Decisions*. Santa Monica, CA: Rand Corporation.

Davis, L. E. (1977). Job design: Future directions. In L. E. Davis and J. C. Taylor (eds), *Design of Jobs*, 2nd ed. Santa Monica, CA: Goodyear.

Dean, L. M., Willis, F., and LaRocco, J. M. (1976). Invasion of personal space as a function of age, sex, and race. *Psychological Reports*, 38, 959–65.

Devine, P. G., Monteith, M. J., Zuwerink, J. R., and Elliot, A. J. (1991). Prejudice with and without compunction. *Journal of Personality and Social Psychology*, 60, 817–30.

Eagly, A. H., and Johnson, B. T. (1990). Gender and leadership style: A meta-analysis. *Psychological Bulletin*, 108, 233–56.

Eisenhardt, K. M., and Schoonhoven, C. B. (1990). Organizational growth: Linking founding team, strategy, environment, and growth among US semi-conductor ventures, 1978–1988. *Administrative Science Quarterly*, 35, 504–29.

Elder, G. H., Jr (1975). Age differentiation and the life course. *Annual Review of Sociology*, 1, 165–90.

Ellsworth, P. C., and Ludwig, L. M. (1972). Visual behavior in social interaction. *Journal of Communication*, 22, 375–403.

Erber, R., and Fiske, S. T. (1984). Outcome dependency and attention to inconsistent information. *Journal of Personality and Social Psychology*, 47, 709–26.

Esty, K. (1988). Diversity is good for business. *Executive Excellence*, 5(1), 5–6.

Exline, R. V. (1963). Explorations in the process of person perception. Visual interaction in relation to competition, sex, and need for affiliation. *Journal of Personality*, 31, 1–20.

Exline, R. V., Gray, P., and Schuette, D. (1965). Visual behavior in a dyad as affected by interview context and sex of respondent. *Journal of Personality and Social Psychology*, 1, 201–9.

Exline, R. V., Jones, P., and Macrorowski, K. (1977). Race affiliation, conflict theory, and mutual visual attention during conversation. Paper presented at the meeting of the American Psychological Association, San Francisco.

Fandt, P. M. (1991). The relationship of accountability and interdependent behavior to enhancing team consequences. *Group and Organization Studies*, 16(3), 300–12.

Fehr, B. J., and Exline, R. V. (1978). Visual interaction in same- and interracial dyads. Paper presented at the meeting of the Eastern Psychological Association, Washington, D.C.

Fiedler, F. E. (1966). The effect of leadership and cultural heterogeneity on group performance: A test of the contingency model. *Journal of Experimental and Social Psychology*, 2, 237–64.

Fiedler, F. E., Mitchell, T., and Triandis, H. C. (1970). The culture assimilator: An approach to cross-cultural training. *Journal of Applied Psychology*, 55(2), 95–102.

Finkelstein, S., and Hambrick, D. C. (1990). Top management team tenure and organization outcomes: The moderating role of managerial discretion. *Administrative Science Quarterly*, 35: 484–503.

Fiske, S. T. (1989). Interdependence and stereotyping: From the laboratory to the Supreme Court (and back). Invited address at the meeting of the American Psychological Association, New Orleans.

Fiske, S. T., and Neuberg, S. L. (1990). A continuum of impression formation, from category-based to individuating processes: Influence of information and motivation on attention and interpretation. In M. P. Zanna (ed.), *Advances in Experimental Social Psychology*, 23, 1–74. San Diego, CA: Academic Press.

Fiske, S. T., and Taylor, S. E. (1991). *Social Cognition*, 2nd ed. Reading, MA: Addison-Wesley.

Foeman, A., and Pressley, G. (1987). Ethnic culture and corporate culture: Using Black styles in organizations. *Communication Quarterly*, 35, 293–307.

Fugita, S., Wexley, K., and Hillery, J. (1974). Black–white differences in nonverbal behavior in an interview setting. *Journal of Applied Social Psychology*, 4, 343–50.

Gallupe, R. B., Dennis, A. R., Cooper, W. H., Valacich, J. S., Bastianutti, L. M., and Nunamaker, J. F. (1992). Electronic brainstorming and group size. *Academy of Management Journal*, 35, 350–60.

Garza, R. T. (1989). Group ethnic composition, leader ethnicity, and task performance: An application of social identity theory. *Genetic Social and General Psychology Monographs*, 115(3), 295–314.

Garza, R. T., Romero, L. G., Cox, B., and Ramirez, M. (1982). Biculturism, locus of control, and leader behavior in ethnically mixed small groups. *Journal of Applied Social Psychology*, 12, 237–53.

George, J. M. (1990). Personality, affect and behavior in groups. *Journal of Applied Psychology*, 75, 107–16.

Georgeopolous, B. S. (1986). *Organizational Structure, Problem Solving, and Effectiveness*. San Francisco: Jossey-Bass.

Gersick, C. J. G. (1988). Time and transition in work teams: Toward a new model of group development. *Academy of Management Journal*, 31, 9–41.

Gladstein, D. (1984). Groups in context: A model of task group effectiveness. *Administrative Science Quarterly*, 29, 499–517.

Goodman, P. S., Devadas, R., and Hughson, T. L. (1988). Groups and productivity: Analyzing the effectiveness of self-managing teams. In J. P. Campbell and R. J. Campbell (eds), *Productivity in Organizations*. San Francisco: Jossey-Bass.

Goodman, P. S., Ravlin, E., and Schminke, M. (1987). Understanding groups in organizations. *Research in Organizational Behavior*, 9, 121–73.

Gooler, L. E., and Thompson, D. E. (1994). How support impacts on motivation: A longitudinal analysis. Paper presented at the 6th annual American Psychological Society conference, Washington, DC, June.

Gordon, G. G., DiTomaso, N., and Farris, G. F. (1991). Managing diversity in R&D groups. *Research Technology Management*, 34, 18–23.

Greenberg, J., and Baron, R. (1995). *Behavior in Organizations*, 4th ed. Boston: Allyn and Bacon.

Gustafson, D. H., Shulka, R. K., Delbecq, A., and Walster, W. G. (1973). A comparative study of differences in subjective likelihood estimates made by individuals, interacting in groups, Delphi groups, and nominal groups. *Organizational Behavior and Human Performance*, 9, 280–91.

Guzzo, R. A. (1982). *Improving Group Decision Making in Organizations*. New York: Academic Press.

Guzzo, R. A. (1986). Financial incentives and their varying effects on productivity. In P. Whitney and R. B. Ochsman (eds), *Psychology and Productivity* (81–92). New York: Plenum.

Guzzo, R. A. (1993). Potency in groups: Articulating a construct. Special Issue: Social issues in small groups: I. Theoretical perspectives. *British Journal of Social Psychology*, 32(1), 87–106.

Guzzo, R. A., and Salas, E. (eds) (1995). *Team Effectiveness and Decision Making in Organizations*. San Francisco: Jossey-Bass.

Guzzo, R. A., and Shea, G. P. (1992). Group performance and intergroup relations in organizations. In M. D. Dunnette and L. M. Hough (eds), *Handbook of Industrial and Organizational Psychology*, 2nd ed., vol. 3. Palo Alto, CA: Consulting Psychologists Press.

Hackman, J. R. (1987). The design of work teams. In J. Lorsch (ed.), *Handbook of Organizational Behavior* (315–42). Englewood Cliff's NJ: Prentice-Hall.

Hackman, J. R., and Oldham, G. R. (1980). *Work Redesign*. Reading, MA: Addison Wesley.

Hall, E. T. (1966). *The Hidden Dimension*. Garden City, NY: Doubleday.

Hare, A. P., Blumberg, H. H., Davies, M. F., and Kent, M. V. (1994). *Small Group Research: A Handbook*. Norwood, NJ: Ablex Publishing.

Hare, A. P., and Davies, M. F. (1994). Social interaction. In A. P. Hare, H. H. Blumberg, M. F. Davies, and M. V. Kent (eds), *Small Group Research: A Handbook*. Norwood, NJ: Ablex Publishing.

Harper, R. G., Wiens, A. N., and Matarazzo, J. (1978). *Nonverbal Communication: The State of the Art*. New York: Wiley.

Heider, F. (1944). Social perception and phenomenal causality. *Psychological Review*, 51, 358–74.

Heider, F. (1958). *The Psychology of Intergroup Relations*. New York: Wiley.

Hewstone, M., and Brown, R. (1986). Contact is not enough: An intergroup perspective on the "contact hypothesis." In M. Hewstone and R. Brown (eds), *Contact and Conflict in Intergroup Encounters* (1–44). Cambridge, MA: Blackwell.

Hoffman, L. R. (1959). Homogeneity of member personality and its effect on group problem-solving. *Journal of Abnormal and Social Psychology*, 58, 27–32.

Hoffman, L. R. (1965). Group problem solving. In L. Berkowitz (ed.), *Advances in Experimental Social Psychology*, vol. 2 (99–132). New York: Academic Press.

Hoffman, L. R., Harburg, E., and Maier, N. R. F. (1962). Differences and disagreement as factors in creative problem solving. *Journal of Abnormal and Social Psychology*, 64, 206–14.

Hoffman, L. R., and Maier, N. R. F. (1961). Quality and acceptance of problem solving by members of homogeneous and heterogeneous groups. *Journal of Abnormal and Social Psychology*, 62, 401–7.

Hofstede, G. (1991). *Culture and Organizations*. New York: McGraw-Hill.

Imada, A. S., and Hakel, M. D. (1977). Influence of nonverbal communication and rater proximity on impressions and decisions in simulated employment interviews. *Journal of Applied Psychology*, 62, 295–300.

Jackson, S. E. (1991). Team composition in organizational settings: Issues in managing an increasingly diverse work force. In S. Worchel, W. Wood, and J. A. Simpson (eds), *Group Process and Productivity* (138–73). Newbury Park, CA: Sage.

Jackson, S. E. (1992). Consequences of group composition for the interpersonal dynamics of strategic issue processing. *Advances in Strategic Management*, 8, 345–82.

Jackson, S. E., Brett, J. F., Sessa, V. I., Cooper, D. M., Julin, J. A., and Peyronnin, K. (1991). Some differences make a difference: Individual dissimilarity and group heterogeneity as correlates of recruitment, promotions, and turnover. *Journal of Applied Psychology*, 75(5), 675–89.

Jackson, S. E., May, K. E., and Whitney, K. (1995). Understanding the dynamics of diversity in decision-making teams. In R. A. Guzzo and E. Salas (eds), *Team Effectiveness and Decision Making in Organizations*, pp. 204–61. San Francisco: Jossey-Bass.

Jackson, S. E., and Ruderman, M. (1996). *Work Team Dynamics and Productivity in the Context of Diversity*. Washington, DC: American Psychological Association.

Janis, I. L. (1972). *Groupthink: Psychological Studies of Policy Decisions and Fiascoes*. Boston: Houghton-Mifflin.

Janis, I. L. (1982). *Groupthink: Psychological Studies of Policy Fiascoes*, 2nd ed. Boston: Houghton-Mifflin.

Johnson, D. W., and Johnson, R. T. (1982). Effects of cooperative, competitive, and individualistic learning experiences on cross-ethnic interaction and friendships. *Journal of Social Psychology*, 118, 47–58.

Johnson, S. D. (1982). The Minnesota Multiethnic Counselor Education Curriculum: The design and evaluation of an intervention for cross-cultural counselor education. Unpublished doctoral dissertation. University of Minnesota, Minneapolis.

Johnson, S. D., Jr (1987). Knowing that versus knowing how: Toward achieving expertise through multicultural training for counseling. *The Counseling Psychologist*, 15(2), 320–31.

Jones, E. E., and Davis, K. E. (1965). From acts to dispositions: The attribution process in person perception. In L. Berkowitz (ed.), *Advances in Experimental Social Psychology*, vol. 2. New York: Academic Press.

Kanter, R. M. (1983). *The Change Masters: Innovation for Productivity in the American Corporation*. New York: Simon and Schuster.

Katzell, R. A., and Thompson, D. E. (1990). An integrated model of work attitudes, motivation, and performance. *Human Performance*, 3(2), 63–85.

Kelley, H. H. (1967). Attribution theory in social psychology. In D. Levine (ed.), *Nebraska Symposium on Motivation*, vol. 15. Lincoln: University of Nebraska Press.

Kelley, H. H. (1972). Causal schemata and the attribution process. In E. E. Jones, D. Kanouse, H. H. Kelley, R. E. Nisbett, S. Valins, and B. Weiner (eds), *Attribution: Perceiving the Causes of Behavior*. Morristown, NJ: General Learning Press.

Kendon, A. (1967). Some functions of gaze-direction in social interaction. *Acta Psychologica*, 26, 22–63.

Kirchmeyer, C., and Cohen, A. (1992). Multicultural groups: Their performance and reactions with constructive conflict. *Group and Organization Management*, 17(2), 153–70.

Knutson, T. J. (1985). Communication in decision-making groups: In search of excellence. *Journal for Specialists in Group Work*, 10(1), 28–37.

Kolodny, H. F., and Kissundu, M. N. (1980). Towards the development of a sociotechnical systems model in Woodlands Mechanical Harvesting. *Human Relations*, 33(9), 623–45.

Kossek, E. E. (1989). The acceptance of human resource innovation by multiple constituencies. *Personnel Psychology*, 42, 263–81.

Kossek, E. E., and Zonia, S. C. (1993). Assessing diversity climate: A field study of reactions to employer efforts to promote diversity. *Journal of Organizational Behavior*, 14(1), 61–81.

Kossek, E. E., Zonia, S. C., and Young, W. (forthcoming). The limitations of organizational demography: Can diversity climate be enhanced in the absence of teamwork? In S. E. Jackson and M. Ruderman (eds), *Diversity in Workteams: Research Paradigms for a Changing Workplace*. Washington, DC: American Psychological Association.

LaFrance, M., and Mayo, C. (1976). Racial differences in gaze behavior during conversations: Two systematic observational studies. *Journal of Personality and Social Psychology*, 33, 547–52.

Leavitt, H. H. (1975). Suppose we took group seriously. In E. L. Cass and F. G. Zimmer (eds), *Man and Work in Society* (67–77). New York: Van Nostrand Reinhold.

Levine, M. (1987). Making group collaboration work. *Production and Inventory Management*, 28, 31–3.

Lott, A. J., and Lott, B. F. (1965). Group cohesiveness as interpersonal attraction: A review of relationships with antecedent and consequent variables. *Psychological Bulletin*, 64, 259–309.

Mackie, D. M. (1987). Systematic and nonsystematic processing of majority and minority persuasive communications. *Journal of Personality and Social Psychology*, 53, 41–52.

Mathews, R. C. (1982). Toward designing optimal problem-solving procedures: Comparisons of male and female interacting groups. *Group and Organization Studies*, 7, 497–507.

Mayo, E. (1933). *The Human Problems of an Industrial Civilization*. London: Macmillan.

McCain, B. E., O'Reilly, C., and Pfeffer, J. (1983). The effects of departmental demography on turnover: The case of a university. *Academy of Management Journal*, 26, 626–41.

McClintock, C. G., and Allison, S. T. (1989). Social value orientation and helping behavior. *Journal of Applied Social Psychology*, 19(4), 353–62.

McGrath, J. E. (1984). *Groups: Interaction and Performance*. Englewood Cliffs, NJ: Prentice-Hall.

McGrath, J. E. (1991). Time interaction, and performance (TIP): A theory of groups. *Small Group Research*, 22, 147–74.

McGrath, J. E. (1993). The JEMCO workshop: Description of a longitudinal study. Special issue: Time, Task, and Technology in Work Groups: The JEMCO Workshop Study. *Small Group Research*, 24(3), 285–306.

McGrath, J. E., Berdahl, J. L., and Arrow, H. (forthcoming). Traits, expectations, culture and clout: The dynamics of diversity in work groups. In S. E. Jackson and M. N. Ruderman (eds), *Work Team Diversity: Research Paradigms for a Changing Workplace*. Washington, DC: American Psychological Association.

McGrath, J. E., and Rotchford, N. L. (1983). Time and behavior in organizations. *Research in Organizational Behavior*, 5, 57–101.

McLeod, P. L. (1992). An assessment of the experimental literature on electronic support of group work: Results of a meta-analysis. Special Issue: Computer-supported cooperative work. *Human Computer Interaction*, 7(3), 257–80.

McLeod, P. L., Lobel, S. A., and Cox, T. H. (1993). Cultural diversity and creativity in small groups: A test of the value-in-diversity hypothesis. Unpublished working paper. University of Michigan.

Mehrabian, A. (1968). Relationship of attitude to seated posture, orientation, and distance. *Journal of Personality and Social Psychology*, 10, 26–30.

Mehrabian, A. (1972). *Nonverbal Communication*. Chicago: Aldine-Atherton.

Michel, J. G., and Hambrick, D. C. (1992). Diversification posture and top management team characteristics. *Academy of Management Journal*, 35, 9–37.

Morrison, A. (1992). *The New Leaders*. San Francisco. Jossey-Bass.

Murray, A. I. (1989). Top management group heterogeneity and firm performance. *Strategic Management Journal*, 10, 125–41.

Nelson, R. E. (1989). The strength of strong ties: Social networks and intergroup conflict in organizations. *Academy of Management Journal*, 32(2), 377–401.

Nemeth, C. (1985). Dissent, group process, and creativity: The contribution of minority influence. In E. Lawler (ed.), *Advances in Group Processes*. Greenwich, CT: JAI Press.

Nemeth, C. (1986). Differential contributions of majority and minority influence. *Psychological Review*, 93, 23–32.

Nemeth, C. J., and Wachter, J. (1983). Creative problem solving as a result of majority and minority influence. *European Journal of Social Psychology*, 13, 45–55.

Nieva, V. F., Fleishman, E. A., and Reick, A. (1978). *Team Dimensions: Their Identity, Their Measurement, and Their Relationships* (Final Tech Report for Contract No. DAHC 19-78-C-0001). Washington, DC: Advanced Research Resources Organization.

O'Reilly, C. A., Caldwell, D. F., and Barnett, W. P. (1989). Work group demography, social integration, and turnover. *Administrative Science Quarterly*, 34, 21–37.

Patterson, M. L., and Sechrest, L. B. (1970). Interpersonal distance and impression formation. *Journal of Personality*, 38, 161–6.

Pearce, I. A., and Ravlin, E. C. (1987). The design and activation of self-regulating work groups. *Human Relations*, 40, 751–82.

Pelz, D. C. (1956). Some social factors related to performance in a research organization. *Administrative Science Quarterly*, 1, 310–25.

Penn, L., and Bolding, I. (1974). Helping talks for helping children. *Elementary School Guidance and Counseling*, 9(2), 132–7.

Peters, T. J., and Waterman, R. H., Jr (1982). *In Search of Excellence: Lessons from America's Best Run Companies*. New York: Warner.

Pettigrew, T. F. (1986). The intergroup contact hypothesis reconsidered. In M. Hewstone and R. Brown (eds), *Contact and Conflict in Intergroup Encounters* (169–95). Cambridge, MA: Blackwell.

Pinsonneault, A., and Kraemer, K. L. (1989). The impact of technological support on groups: An assessment of the empirical research. *Decision Support Systems*, 5, 187–216.

Pinto, M. B., Pinto, J. K., and Prescott, J. E. (1993). Antecedents and consequences of project team cross-functional cooperation. *Management Science*, 39(10), 1281–97.

Rahim, M. A. (1985). A strategy for organizing conflict in complex organizations. *Human Relations*, 38(1), 81–9.

Richards, A. S., and Jaffe, C. L. (1972). Blacks supervising whites: A study of interracial difficulties in working together in a simulated organization. *Journal of Applied Psychology*, 56, 234–40.

Riordan, C. (1978). Equal-status interracial contact: A review and revision of the concept. *International Journal of Intercultural Relations*, 2(2), 161–85.

Roethlisberger, E. J., and Dickson, W. J. (1939). *Management and the Worker*. Cambridge, MA: Harvard University Press.

Roth, K. (1992). Implementing international strategy at the business unit level: The role of managerial decision-making characteristics. *Journal of Management*, 18(4), 769–89.

Rothbart, M., and John, O. P. (1985). Social categorization and behavioral episodes: A cognitive analysis of the effects of intergroup contact. *Journal of Social Issues*, 41, 81–104.

Rubaii-Barett, N., and Beck, A. C. (1993). Minorities in the majority: Implications for managing cultural diversity. *Public Personnel Management*, 22(4), 503–21.

Schaller, M., and Maass, A. (1989). Illusory correlation and social categorization: Toward an integration of motivational and cognitive factors in stereotype formation. *IPSP*, 56(5), 709–21.

Schneider, B. (1987). The people make the place. *Personnel Psychology*, 40(3), 437–53.

Schweiger, D. M., Sandberg, W. R., and Rechner, P. L. (1989). Experiential effects of dialectical inquiry, devil's advocacy, and consensus approaches to strategic decision making. *Academy of Management Journal*, 32, 745–62.

Shaw, M. E. (1981). *Group Dynamics*, 3rd ed. New York: McGraw-Hill.

Shea, G. P., and Guzzo, R. A. (1987). Group effectiveness: What really matters? *Sloan Management Review*, 28, 25–31.

Smith, K. K. (1977). An intergroup perspective on individual behavior. In J. R. Hackman, E. E. Lawler, and L. W. Porter (eds), *Perspectives on Behavior in Organizations*, 2nd ed. (397–407). New York: McGraw-Hill.

Smith, P. B., Misumi, J., Tayeb, M., Peterson, M., and Bond, M. (1989). On the generality of leadership style measures across cultures. *Journal of Occupational Psychology*, 62, 97–109.

Stein, M. I. (1975). *Stimulating Creativity*, Volume 2: *Group Procedures*. New York: Academic Press.

Stein, M. I. (1982). Creativity, groups, and management. In R. A. Guzzo (ed.), *Improving Group Decision Making in Organizations*. New York: Academic Press.

Steiner, I. D. (1972). *Group Processes and Productivity*. New York: Academic Press.

Stephan, W. G. (1985). Intergroup relations. In G. Lanzey and E. Aronson (eds), *Handbook of Social Psychology*, 3rd ed., vol. 2. New York: Random House.

Stephan, W. G. (1987). The contact hypothesis in intergroup relations. In C. Hendrick (ed.), *Review of Personality and Social Psychology*, vol. 9. Newbury Park, CA: Sage.

Stephan, W. G., and Stephan, C. W. (1985). Intergroup anxiety. *Journal of Social Issues*, 41(3), 157–75.

Stewart, E. C., Danielian, J., and Foster, R. J. (1969). *Simulating Intercultural Interaction through Role Playing*. Washington, DC: George Washington University, Human Resources Research Office.

Stumpf, S. A., Zand, D. A., and Freedman, R. D. (1979). Designing groups for judgmental decisions. *Academy of Management Review*, 4, 589–600.

Sundstrom, E., DeMeuse, K. P., and Futrell, D. (1990). Work teams: Applications and effectiveness. Special Issue: Organizational psychology. *American Psychologist*, 45(2), 120–33.

Tannen, D. (1990). *You Just Don't Understand. Women and Men in Conversation*. New York: Ballantine.

Tannen, D. (1994). *Talking from Nine to Five*. New York: Ballantine.

Thomas, D. C., and Ravlin, E. C. (1995). Responses of employees to cultural adaptation by a foreign manager. *Journal of Applied Psychology*, 80, 133–46.

Thomas, K. (1976). Conflict and conflict management. In M. J. Dunnette (ed.), *Handbook of Organizational Psychology* (889–935). New York: Rand McNally.

Thompson, D. E., and Aiello, J. R. (1988). Male and female managers: Effects of nonverbal communication style. Presented at the meetings of the Academy of Management, Anaheim, California, August 1.

Thompson, D. E., Aiello, J. R., and Epstein, Y. M. (1979). Interpersonal distance preferences. *Journal of Nonverbal Behavior*, 4, 113–18.

Thompson, D. E., and DiTomaso, N. (1988). *Ensuring Minority Success in Corporate Management*. New York: Plenum.

Thompson, D. E., and Katzell, R. A. (1995). How human resource practices affect inclination to stay: A causal correlational analysis. Unpublished manuscript. Baruch College, City University of New York.

Thompson, D. E., Morrison, A. M., and Iwata, K. (1994). *VIEWS*. Copyrighted instrument.

Thornburg, T. H. (1991). Group size and member diversity influence on creative performance. *Journal of Creative Behavior*, 25(4), 324–33.

Ting-Toomey, S., Gao, G., Trubisky, P., Yang, Z., Kim, H. S., Lin, S. L., and Nishids, T. (1991). Culture, face maintenance, and styles of handling interpersonal conflict: A study of five cultures. *International Journal of Conflict Management*, 2, 275–96.

Tjosvold, D. (1985). Implications of controversy research for management. *Journal of Management*, 11(3), 21–37.

Triandis, H. C. (1993). Theoretical and methodological approaches in the study of collectivism and individualism. In U. Kim, H. C. Triandis, and G. Yoon (eds), *Individualism and Collectivism: Theoretical and Methodological Issues*. Newbury Park, CA: Sage.

Triandis, H. C., Hall, E. R., and Ewen, R. B. (1965). Member homogeneity and dyadic creativity. *Human Relations*, 18, 33–54.

Tsui, A. S., Egan, T. D., and O'Reilly, C. A. (1992). Being different: Relational demography and organizational attachment. *Administrative Science Quarterly*, 37(4), 549–79.

Tsui, A. S., and O'Reilly, C. A., III (1989). Beyond simple demographic effects: The importance of relational demography in superior–subordinate dyads. *Academy of Management Journal*, 32, 401–23.

Tuckman, B. W. (1965). Developmental sequences in small groups. *Psychological Bulletin*, 63, 384–93.

Turner, J. C. (1987). *Rediscovering the Social Group: A Self-categorization Theory.* Oxford: Blackwell.

Van de Ven, A. H., and Delbecq, A. L. (1971). Nominal versus interacting group processes for committee decision-making effectiveness. *Academy of Management Journal*, 14, 203–12.

Wall, V. D., Jr, Galanes, G. J., and Love, S. B. (1987). Small, task-oriented groups: Conflict, conflict management, satisfaction, and decision quality. *Small Group Behavior*, 18(1), 31–55.

Wall, V. D., and Nolan, L. L. (1986). Perceptions of inequity, satisfaction, and conflict in task-oriented groups. *Human Relations*, 39(11), 1033–52.

Wall, V. D., and Nolan, L. L. (1987). Small group conflict: A look at equity, satisfaction, and styles of conflict management. *Small Group Behavior*, 18(2), 188–211.

Walton, R. E., and Dutton, J. M. (1969). The management of interdepartmental conflict: A model and review. *Administrative Science Quarterly*, 4, 73–84.

Wanous, J. P., and Youtz, M. A. (1986). Solution diversity and the quality of group decision. *Academy of Management Journal*, 29(1), 149–59.

Watson, W. E., and Kumar, K. (1992). Differences in decision making regarding risk taking: A comparison of culturally diverse and culturally homogeneous task groups. *International Journal of Intercultural Relations*, 16(1), 53–65.

Watson, W. E., Kumar, K., and Michaelsen, L. K. (1993). Cultural diversity's impact on interaction process and performance: Comparing homogeneous and diverse task groups. *Academy of Management Journal*, 36(3), 590–602.

Weiner, B. (1979). A theory of motivation for some classroom experiences. *Journal of Educational Psychology*, 71(1), 3–25.

Weiner, B. (1980). A cognitive (attribution) emotion–action model of motivated behavior: An analysis of judgments of helping. *Journal of Personality and Social Psychology*, 52, 316–24.

Wheeler, M. L. (1994). *Diversity Training: A Research Report.* New York: The Conference Board.

Wiersema, M. F., and Bantel, F. A. (1991). Top management team demography and corporate strategic change. *Academy of Management Journal*, 35, 91–121.

Wilder, D. A. (1984). Predictions of belief homogeneity and similarity following social categorization. *British Journal of Social Psychology*, 23, 323–33.

Willems, E. P., and Clark, R. D., III (1971). Shift toward risk and heterogeneity of groups. *Journal of Experimental and Social Psychology*, 7, 302–12.

Wood, W. (1987). Meta-analytic review of sex differences in group performance. *Psychological Bulletin*, 102, 53–71.

Wood, W., and Karten, S. J. (1986). Sex differences in interaction style as a product of perceived sex differences in competence. *Journal of Personality and Social Psychology*, 50, 341–7.

Woodman, R. W., and Sherwood, J. J. (1980). The role of team development in organizational effectiveness: A critical review. *Psychological Bulletin*, 88, 166–86.

Zebrowitz, L. A., Montepare, J. M., and Lee, H. K. (1993). They don't all look alike: Individual impressions of other racial groups. *Journal of Personality and Social Psychology*, 65(1), 85–101.

Zenger, T. R., and Lawrence, B. S. (1989). Organizational demography: The differential effects of age and tenure distributions on technical communications. *Academy of Management Journal*, 2, 353–76.

About the Contributors

ELLEN ERNST KOSSEK (editor and contributor)

Ellen Ernst Kossek is an associate professor of human resource management and organizational behavior at the School of Labor and Industrial Relations at Michigan State University. She was a visiting scholar at the University of Michigan for a recent sabbatical. She has a PhD from Yale University in organizational behavior, an MBA from the University of Michigan, and an AB cum laude in psychology from Mount Holyoke College. She has consulted to many organizations on human resource issues and is a member of the Wharton/Merck Work/Life Roundtable. Her articles on human resource innovation, work/family initiatives, and workforce diversity have appeared in *Personnel Psychology, Journal of Organizational Behavior, Journal of Applied Behavioral Science, Human Relations, Human Resource Planning Journal, Human Resource Management Journal, Center for Creative Leadership* publication, and elsewhere. Her article on reactions to employer efforts to promote diversity won a best award from the *Journal of Organizational Behavior.* Her published books include *Child Care Challenges for Employers* and *The Acceptance of Human Resource Innovation: Lessons for Managers.*

SHARON A. LOBEL (editor and contributor)

Sharon A. Lobel (PhD, Harvard University) is an associate professor of management at Seattle University. Previously, she taught at the University of Michigan and at Universidade Gama Filho in Rio de Janeiro, Brazil. She is a research fellow at the Boston University Work and Family Roundtable, a business partnership dedicated to playing a leadership role in shaping corporate and public responses in the work/life arena. Her research, examining links between work and personal life and effects of ethnic diversity on performance, has appeared in *Academy of Management Journal, Academy of Management Review, Journal of Cross-Cultural Psychology, Organizational Dynamics*, and elsewhere. As a member of the Wharton/Merck Work/Life Roundtable, she has been active in efforts to develop curriculum for business schools on work/life concerns. She is an associate editor of *Human Resource Management* and is on the editorial board of *Academy of Management Journal*.

RICHARD D. ARVEY

Richard D. Arvey is a professor of industrial relations, University of Minnesota. He received his PhD from the University of Minnesota in psychology in 1971 and has taught at the University of Tennessee and the University of Houston. Professor Arvey teaches and conducts research in the areas of staffing, training, and development, as well as organizational behavior and human resource management.

ROSS E. AZEVEDO

Ross E. Azevedo is an associate professor in the Industrial Relations Center, University of Minnesota. He holds a MA and PhD in Industrial and Labor Relations from Cornell University. Professor Azevedo currently teaches human resource planning at the University of Minnesota and has consulted with a variety of private and public organizations in the area of workforce planning. He has taught industrial relations, collective bargaining, compensation, systems of conflict resolution, and labor market analysis at UCLA and the University of Minnesota.

ALISON E. BARBER

Alison E. Barber (PhD, University of Wisconsin, 1990) is associate professor of management at the Eli Broad Graduate School of Management, Michigan State University. She has published articles on the topics of compensation and recruitment in *Journal of Applied Psychology, Personnel Psychology*, and *Academy of Management Review*.

KAREN A. BROWN

Professor Karen A. Brown is professor of operations management and director of operations programs in the Albers School of Business and Economics at Seattle University where she teaches courses in operations and leads an annual study tour of Mexican factories. She holds BS, MBA, and PhD degrees from the University of Washington and has served as a faculty member at Northern Arizona University and as a visiting faculty member at the University of Washington. Prior to her graduate studies, she held positions in health care administration. Professor Brown's research interests are centered around the interactions between social and technical factors in manufacturing and service environments. She has published articles in several journals, including the *Academy of Management Journal, Academy of Management Review, Journal of Operations Management, International Journal of Production Research, Human Relations, International Journal of Production Economics, Personnel Psychology and IEEE Transactions on Engineering Management*, and *The Puget Sound Business Journal*. Dr Brown is an associate editor of the *Journal of Operations Management*, and a member of the editorial board of the *Operations Management Review*.

CHAO C. CHEN

Chao C. Chen is an assistant professor of the faculty of management, Rutgers University. Professor Chen received his PhD on organizational behavior and human resources from SUNY Buffalo, 1992. His primary research interests include national, ethnic, and organizational cultures, individual values and attitudes, rewards and compensation, management of diversity, and communication. He has published in top journals of management and industrial psychology including *Academy of Management Journal, Journal of Applied Psychology* and *Administrative Science Quarterly*. He teaches in areas of organization behavior, management of diversity, and culture. Professor Chen has also been conducting seminars to international business managers on cross-cultural management and consulting US companies on rewards, culture, and diversity.

MICHELE CUSHNIE

Michele Cushnie is a doctoral student in the Human Resources Development Program at the Ohio State University. Her research interests are in the areas of managing and valuing diversity in the workplace, and organizational development.

CHRISTINA L. DALY

Christina L. Daly is a doctoral candidate in the Department of Management, Eli Broad Graduate School of Management, Michigan State University.

PARSHOTAM DASS

Parshotam Dass earned his PhD degree at Michigan State University and is an assistant professor of management at the College of Business Administration, University of Arkansas. Earlier, he taught at a university in India for five years. He teaches in the areas of strategic management and organization theory. His current research interests are strategic changes in product, international geographic and cultural diversities of organizations. He is a member of the Academy of Management and the Strategic Management Society, and has presented papers at the regional, national, and international meetings of the Academy of Management. He co-edited *Readings in Strategic Management* and has published in *Human Relations* and *Applied Psychology: An International Review*.

JOHN T. DELANEY

John T. Delaney is a professor of management and organizations at the University of Iowa College of Business Administration. Before coming to Iowa in 1989 he was an assistant and associate professor at the Columbia University Graduate School of Business. He received his BS degree from LeMoyne College, and his MA and PhD degrees from the University of Illinois at Urbana-Champaign. He has written extensively about employee relations, negotiations, and ethical issues in the private and public sectors. He regularly teaches courses on negotiation, ethics in business, and employee relations. He has done consulting for large and small businesses, as well as government agencies and local economic development organizations. He has provided expert testimony in Washington, DC, to the National Labor Relations Board and the Subcommittee on Labor of the US Senate Committee on Labor and Human Resources.

NANCY DiTOMASO

Nancy DiTomaso is professor and chair of organization management on the Faculty of Management at Rutgers, the State University of New Jersey. Her research specialties include the management of diversity and change, the management of scientists and engineers, and organizational culture. Her PhD is from the University of Wisconsin–Madison, and she previously taught at New York University and Northwestern University. She also has a Certificate in Business Administration from the Wharton School of the University of Pennsylvania and attended Proyecto Linguistico in Quetzeltenango, Guatemala.

She has co-authored and co-edited four books and many articles, including *Ensuring Minority Success in Corporate Management* (Plenum Publishing Corporation, 1988) and has had recent articles published in *Leadership Quarterly*, the *Journal of Engineering-Technology Management, Research-Technology Management, Journal of Management Studies*, and *IEEE Spectrum*. Her current research includes two major projects: (1) a survey of 3,200 scientists and engineers from 25 major companies on managing diversity in R&D, and (2) analysis of a database on 100+ companies on the causes and consequences of corporate culture.

She has been active in a number of professional associations including, among others, the Academy of Management and the American Sociological Association.

SANDRA FISHER

Sandra Fisher is a doctoral graduate student in the Industrial and Organizational Psychology Program at Michigan State University. Her research interests are in the areas of career development, skill acquisition, and cross-cultural influences in international joint ventures. She is a student affiliate of the Society of Industrial and Organizational Psychology and the American Psychological Association. She holds a BS in psychology from Valparaiso University.

GARY W. FLORKOWSKI

Dr Gary W. Florkowski is an associate professor of Business Administration at the Katz Graduate School of Business, University of Pittsburgh. He received his PhD and law degrees from Syracuse University, and was a member of the New York Bar prior to joining the University of Pittsburgh business faculty. Dr Florkowski teaches international business and human resource management courses in the MBA and executive programs of that institution. He has consulted for several private-sector organizations in the US regarding the design, implementation and evaluation of group-based incentive programs. Dr Florkowski's primary research and consulting interests focus on the use of human resource management practices for international competitive advantage. Dr Florkowski has published numerous articles in professional journals such as the *International Journal of Human Resource Management, Academy of Management Review, Industrial Relations, British Journal of Industrial Relations*, and *Human Relations*. He also is a member of the editorial board for the UK-based *International Journal of Human Resource Management*.

J. KEVIN FORD

J. Kevin Ford is a professor of industrial and organizational psychology at Michigan State University. Professor Ford's research interests include issues of workplace training design, evaluation, and transfer as well as organizational-level issues of continuous learning and adaptability. Dr Ford has published over thirty articles and chapters, is on three editorial boards – *Academy of Management Journal, Personnel Psychology*, and the *Training Research Journal* – and is a fellow of the American Psychological Association. In addition, Dr Ford has consulted on a variety of training and organizational change projects for several corporations, governmental agencies, and small businesses. He holds a PhD in psychology from the Ohio State University and a BS in psychology from the University of Maryland.

LAURA E. GOOLER

Laura Gooler is a PhD candidate at the Graduate School and University Center's Industrial and Organizational Psychology program at Baruch College, the City University of New York (CUNY). She received her BA in psychology from the University of the Pacific and her MS in I/O psychology at Baruch College, CUNY. Laura has previously taught as an adjunct professor on the faculties in the Department of Psychology at Baruch College and Hunter College, CUNY. She has served as a research consultant to the City University of New York Academic Affairs Consortium for Disability Studies, where she served to identify ways to establish a more stable minority workforce in the MR/DD field in the New York metropolitan area. Her research has spanned the areas of personality differences in performance and motivation. For her dissertation, Laura is studying the impact of organizational resources and support for helping employees cope with balancing the demands of their work and personal lives. Laura currently manages the Workforce Diversity/EEO Unit in the Corporate Human Resources Division at Chemical Banking Corporation.

DOUGLAS T. (TIM) HALL

Douglas T. (Tim) Hall is a professor of organizational behavior and director of the Executive Development Roundtable in the School of Management at Boston University. He previously served as acting dean, associate dean for faculty development, and faculty director for masters programs. He has held faculty positions at Northwestern University, the US Military Academy at West Point, and Yale, York, and Michigan State.

Tim is the author of *Careers in Organizations*, and the co-author of *Organizational Climates and Careers, The Two-Career Couple, Experiences in Management and Organizational Behavior, Human Resource Management, Career Development in Organizations, Turbulence in the American Workplace*, and co-editor of *The Handbook of Career Theory*. He is a recipient of the American Psychological Association's James McKeen Cattell Award (now called the Ghiselli Award) for research design. He is a fellow of the Academy of Management and the American Psychological Association and is currently serving on the board of Governors of the Center for Creative Leadership. His research interests include work/life balance, career planning and development, executive succession, and managing diversity.

ROBERT L. HENEMAN

Robert L. Heneman is an associate professor in the Max M. Fisher College of Business at the Ohio State University. His research interests are in the areas of performance management, compensation, and staffing.

KATHY E. KRAM

Kathy E. Kram, PhD, is an associate professor in the Department of Organizational Behavior at the Boston University School of Management. Her primary interests are in the areas of adult development and career dynamics, values and ethics in corporate decision-making, organizational change processes, gender dynamics in organizations, and workforce diversity.

In addition to her book *Mentoring at Work*, she has published in journals including *Organizational Dynamics, Academy of Management Journal, Academy of Management Review, Organizational Behavior and Human Performance, Business Horizons, Qualitative Sociology, Mentoring International*, and *Psychology of Women Quarterly*. Her work has been widely cited in business and trade publications such as *Industry Week, Training and Development, Working Woman, Psychology Today, Business Week, Fortune*, and the *Wall Street Journal*.

Professor Kram teaches courses in human behavior in organizations, leadership and team dynamics, career management, organizational development, and global management. She is currently investigating the individual, interpersonal, and organizational conditions that enable women and people of color to successfully move into executive roles. Professor Kram regularly consults with private and public sector organizations on a variety of human resource management concerns.

She received her BS and MS degrees from the MIT Sloan School of Management, and a PhD from Yale University. Prior to her academic career, she was an internal organizational development consultant in a large insurance company.

M. CATHERINE LUNDY

Ms Lundy is an associate professor in the Labor Education Program at the School of Labor and Industrial Relations at Michigan State University. She specializes in the areas of arbitration, collective bargaining, employment law and labor relations in the health care industry with special emphasis on registered nurses and women's employment issues including sexual harassment, diversity, women in unions, and mentoring.

She administers and teaches in joint-management programs that include clientele such as GM/UAW and PEL Program; State of Michigan/Department of Social Services and UAW; Mead Paper Company, and IUPU, IBT and IBEW; Consumers Power Company and Utility Workers. Other Labor Education Program clientele include such organizations as AFL-CIO locals and independent labor unions.

Before coming to MSU she worked as a labor relations representative for the Michigan Nurses Association and is a registered nurse.

DANIEL J. OSTGAARD

Daniel J. Ostgaard is a PhD graduate student in the Industrial Relations Center, University of Minnesota. His research interests include such areas as staffing and selection, diversity issues, training and development, and organizational behavior.

BARBARA PARKER

Barbara Parker earned her PhD degree from the University of Colorado, and is an associate professor of management at the Albers School of Business and Economics, Seattle University. In addition to consulting on strategy and diversity, she pursues research on international strategy, managing decline, gender, and diversity. She has presented papers and has participated in various capacities at the national meetings of the Academy of Management. Her publications have appeared in *Sex Roles, Human Relations, Management International Review, Journal of Business Research*, and the *International Journal of Intercultural Relations*. She has consulted with Fortune 500 companies and with a number of US schools of business on diversity strategy issues, and she conducts diversity workshops for the American Assembly of Collegiate School of Business programs in the USA.

SUMITA RAGHURAM

Sumita received her PhD in human resource management from the University of Minnesota in 1992. Currently she is a faculty member at Fordham University in New York City. Her research interests include telework issues, workforce diversity, and strategic human resource management. She has made conference presentations and published papers in research journals on these topics.

KAREN ROBERTS

Karen Roberts is an associate professor in the School of Labor and Industrial Relations at Michigan State University. Her disability-related research interests include the Americans with Disabilities Act, workers' compensation and workplace disability, medical cost containment, and dispute resolution. Her published work on disability has appeared in journals such as *Industrial Relations, Journal of Risk and Insurance, Journal of Labor Research*, and *Negotiation Journal*. She regularly teaches on the ADA, disability management, workers' compensation, and the challenges of disability to collectively bargained workplaces.

She received her PhD from the Department of Urban Studies at MIT. She received an MSW from West Virginia University and a BA in English literature from Wells College.

DONNA E. THOMPSON

Donna E. Thompson is an associate professor in the Industrial and Organizational Psychology program at Baruch College, City University of New York. She was previously on the faculties in the Department of Psychology at New York University and the Graduate School of Management, Rutgers University. An active researcher, Donna's current research on diversity includes projects on: organizational socialization experiences of African-American managers, cross-race and cross-gender issues in mentoring, career experiences of women in senior-level management positions, assessing and evaluating the impact of work–life issues and initiatives on employee motivation and productivity, and exploring the relationship among racial/

ethnic identity, work experiences and motivational processes. The research underlying Donna's book (with Nancy DiTomaso), *Ensuring Minority Success in Corporate Management*, was among the first to focus on organizational policies and practices related to successful diversity efforts.

She has served as a consultant on a wide range of diversity issues for a number of Fortune 500 companies. Her consulting assignments have ranged through serving as an advisor to diversity task forces or councils, developing strategic plans for fostering diversity, conducting organizational assessments, training and other educational efforts. An expert on organizational change and development, Donna has most recently developed (with Ann M. Morrison and Kay I. Iwata) an Organizational Diversity Assessment system for identifying areas in which improvement is needed and areas in which progress has already been achieved in fostering diversity. Donna received her doctorate in social and personality psychology from Vanderbilt University and did post-doctoral work in industrial/organizational psychology at New York University.

NANCY E. WALDECK

Nancy E. Waldeck is a doctoral student in the Labor and Human Resource Program at the Ohio State University. Her research interests include diversity issues in the workplace and the training of the long-term unemployed.

ELAINE K. YAKURA

Elaine K. Yakura is an assistant professor at the School of Labor and Industrial Relations at Michigan State University. She received her PhD in organization studies at MIT's Sloan School of Management, a JD from Boalt Hall School of Law at UC Berkeley, and a BA in economics from Yale University. Elaine has taught at UCLA's Anderson Graduate School of Management, and also worked as an attorney in California for several years before beginning her doctoral studies. Her research interests include the study of power and difference in organizations, and her field work includes studies of consultants, nuclear power plants in Japan and the US, and high-technology organizations.

Index